PSYCHOTHERAPY
THEORY AND RESEARCH

Contributors

JOSEPH M. BOBBITT, Ph.D., National Institute of Mental Health

JOHN A. CLAUSEN, Ph.D., National Institute of Mental Health

LEE J. CRONBACH, Ph.D., University of Illinois

JOHN DOLLARD, Ph.D., Yale University

STANLEY G. ESTES, Ph.D., Harvard University

FRED E. FIEDLER, Ph.D., University of Illinois

J. McVICKER HUNT, Ph. D., University of Illinois

LEONARD S. KOGAN, Ph.D., Community Service Society of New York

BERNARD H. LIGHT, Ph.D., West Virginia University

LESTER LUBORSKY, Ph.D., Menninger Foundation

ZELLA H. LURIA, Ph.D., University of Illinois

ROLLO MAY, Ph.D., Practicing Psychotherapist, New York

LOUIS L. McQUITTY, Ph. D., University of Illinois

LAWRENCE I. O'KELLY, Ph.D., University of Illinois

WILLIAM G. PERRY, Jr., M.A., Harvard University

NATHANIEL J. RASKIN, Ph.D., American Foundation for the Blind

CARL R. ROGERS, Ph.D., University of Chicago

JULIUS SEEMAN, Ph.D., University of Chicago

EDWARD J. SHOBEN, Jr., Ph.D., Teachers College, Columbia University

MILTON WEXLER, Ph.D., Menninger Foundation

MARJORIE A. ZELENY, M.S., University of Illinois

PSYCHOTHERAPY
THEORY AND RESEARCH

By

O. HOBART MOWRER, Ph.D.

RESEARCH PROFESSOR OF PSYCHOLOGY
UNIVERSITY OF ILLINOIS

and

TWENTY-ONE CONTRIBUTORS

THE RONALD PRESS COMPANY · NEW YORK

2

Library of Congress Catalog Card Number: 53-5714

PRINTED IN THE UNITED STATES OF AMERICA

PREFACE

Mental disorder and the challenge of its more effective understanding, treatment, and prevention constitute one of the major preoccupations of our contemporary civilization. Somewhat paradoxically, psychologists, in the more restricted sense of that term, have been slow to take cognizance of and respond to this challenge. Other, older professions—religion, medicine, and the law—have all manifested interest in the problem; but in each instance it has continued to have something of the status of a stepchild. Who other than psychologists might be properly expected to concern themselves centrally with *psycho*pathology and *psycho*therapy! Yet it is only since World War II that this has been in any pervasive sense the case.

Today psychologists are active on a wide variety of fronts in attempting to advance knowledge and improve practice in this important field. The present volume is a tangible expression and exhibit of some of the many ways in which this effort is being made. Contributors to the volume, with but few exceptions, represent psychologists who not only possess special research interests and skills but who also are themselves active, experienced therapists. Fortunately our society is able to provide a considerable number of psychologists with the opportunity to combine research and practice to a degree which would be quite impossible if they were not protected in some measure from the burden of service and administrative duties which others bear. This book, then, is a partial report on the progress which has been made possible by these favorable circumstances.

With two exceptions, all of the chapters have been written expressly for inclusion in this book. Acknowledgment for permission to reprint is made to the *Journal of Abnormal and Social Psychology,* the original publishers of Chapter 10, somewhat revised here, and to the *International Journal of Psychoanalysis* for Chapter 7, here published in expanded form.

It is anticipated that this book will be of greatest value to practitioners, researchers, teachers, and advanced students in the field of personality disorder and its treatment. Broader implications of the work will interest psychologists generally, other social scientists, and persons in related professions.

Grateful acknowledgment is made to Rita Lovell Moss for skillful services in the preparation of typescript, proofreading, indexing, and other tasks involved in the making of this book, and to Austin C. Hershberger for special assistance with the indexing.

O. H. MOWRER

Urbana, Illinois
March, 1953

iii

CONTENTS

PART I

THEORY, CONCEPTS, AND APPLICATIONS

PART II

RESEARCH METHODS AND RESULTS

ILLUSTRATIONS

TABLES

PSYCHOTHERAPY
THEORY AND RESEARCH

INTRODUCTION

PSYCHOTHERAPY AS SERVICE AND RESEARCH

Research on psychotherapy poses an important problem. The need for more thoroughly validated knowledge and for more effective technical skills in this field is everywhere admitted, but the question of precisely how to secure this greater knowledge and therapeutic efficiency has not been an easy one to answer. A common, and somewhat superficial, response has been to say: More research! But research in its most familiar form implies *experimentation;* and for reasons which need no elaboration, persons who seek professional help for personality disorders are likely to be alarmed if they feel that the expert to whom they have appealed is going to regard them as mere "subjects" rather than as *patients.* These people are in deep trouble, and they are understandably more concerned in finding answers to their immediate personal difficulties than in "advancing science," especially if the latter goal presupposes a sacrifice of the former one.

Sometimes, in the field of physical medicine, human beings have volunteered either to receive an unproved, doubtful form of treatment or to forego a promising one; and drugs and biological remedies are constantly being "tried out" by physicians in an informal way. But the greatest boon to strictly medical research has been the availability and practicality of *animal experimentation.* Because man is physiologically only slightly removed from various other members of the animal kingdom, these creatures have been able to take the brunt of his scientific attempts to comprehend and fight disease in his own species.

But in the realm of psychotherapy the picture is very different. Physiologically, man is truly brother to the beast; but from the standpoint of mentation and culture, there stands between them, in the words of Susan Langer, "a whole day of Creation." Neurosis is a product of man's attempt to be uniquely human, and no other living organism comes close enough to his accomplishments in this respect to provide more than a vague intimation thereof. While the study of animal psychology has provided highly useful leads for understanding the more rudimentary aspects of human nature, it can never perform a service with respect to psychopathology in any way comparable to that of animal research in the medical setting.

For the reasons just indicated—the dignity and value of human beings and the noncomparability of animals—it is manifestly impossible to make a frontal experimental attack upon the problem of human personality

3

disorders and their treatment. A most natural next question is whether the attack can be oblique, and the answer seems definitely to be in the affirmative. With modern electronic devices it is now entirely feasible, at relatively small cost and trouble, to obtain a complete record of the verbal behavior of both patient and therapist during the course of treatment; and since psychotherapy is pre-eminently a matter of conversation, a relatively complete replica of therapy is thus obtained. Under these circumstances the patient can be given whatever type of treatment the therapist believes is in the patient's best interests; and then, when the treatment is concluded, the recordings can be subjected to the most minute and searching kinds of scientific analysis, with no sacrifice whatever of therapeutic considerations. And since, in the ordinary course of events, different therapists will employ different types of approach, comparisons become possible which are only a little less interesting and significant than would be the results of formal experimentation. In this way every patient receives the best professional attention which the therapist of his choice can provide, while at the same time psychotherapy produces valuable scientific data. This strategy is now aptly known as *process research* and holds many promising possibilities.

A step removed from process research but still closely related to it is *outcome research*. Here the emphasis is upon measuring significant aspects of personality before and after treatment and noting the nature and extent of the resulting changes. Many patients are no less willing to submit to pre- and posttherapy tests in reasonable number than they are to permit recordings to be made of their verbal interactions with the therapist; and when test results and complete recordings are available for a large number of patients, of varied diagnosis, who have been treated by therapists of differing persuasion, the opportunities thus afforded for checking hypotheses and making new scientific inferences will be by no means unimpressive. (Parenthetically, it should be added that by "therapy" is meant mainly *individualized adult* treatment. While child and group therapy are recognized as promising from the research as well as practical standpoint, it is felt that psychopathology, in both its neurotic and psychotic guises, can be studied to best advantage in individual adults.)

But the recording, and the subsequent (and more expensive!) transcription, of interview material and the collecting of test results are only beginnings from the standpoint of systematic research on psychotherapy. One next faces what is in many ways the greater task: that of determining the scientifically meaningful dimensions and implications of the enormous mass of data thus accumulated and of inventing units of measurement whereby the powerful quantitative methods of science may become more fully applicable. In this volume will be found, along with many references to process research, discussion of a number of personality assessment methods which involve the newer thinking with respect to "statistics of the individual," as opposed to the more conventional type of group-centered, normative statistics. Here, it seems, are developments which will be important, not alone for research in psychotherapy, but for the advancement of psychological and social science in general. Statistics in its purely *descriptive* or representational phase is much needed as a means of condensing into curves and similar graphic devices information which can otherwise be communicated only by endless hours of record playing or transcription reading. And *inferential* statistics, which tells us how much confidence to attach to a given finding, will be no less useful in interpreting and evaluating the extensive and enormously complex data which accrue in therapy.

At the same time, it should not be supposed that the conception of what is legitimate and fruitful inquiry in psychotherapy is here restricted to purely quantitative methods. Important and, in many instances, truly exciting as these methods are, there is no lack of appreciation of the continuing contributions of the gifted intuitive observer and the brilliant and original conceptualizer: hence the equal emphasis upon research *and* theory. While the various chapters can be roughly classified under one or the other of these headings, the two functions are intertwined throughout. Part I consists of those chapters having a preponderant emphasis upon theoretical considerations, while Part II contains chapters in which the accent falls more upon research techniques and findings. The last chapter in Part I is intended to suggest (rather than demonstrate in an all-inclusive way) the extent to which efforts are now being made to "plow back" into the culture at large, as rapidly (yet prudently) as possible, the implications of psychotherapeutic research for mental hygiene, more stable family life, industrial relations, social ethics, and education in its broadest sense. While it must be admitted that many of the "discoveries" which have been announced in this field have represented little more than half-truths (and sometimes no truth at all!), there can be no turning back: the scientific study and interpretation of man's peculiar nature, destiny, and psychic dis-eases must go forward until as sound a body of fact, theory, and technique is available here as in the physical and biological sciences. The present volume is predicated on this conviction.

One thing is already sufficiently clear: personality disorders, in the great majority of cases, have no demonstrable physical basis and no proved physical treatment. The problem, from the standpoint of both causation and correction, is basically psychological or psychosocial and revolves around the phenomenon of *learning*. Within the last half-century "learning theory" has become perhaps the most vigorous branch of laboratory psychology, and there has been much talk of the advantages of cross-fertilization between it and the body of theory and practice derived from psychotherapy. While the more rigorous methods and sharper postulates of learning theory can unquestionably contribute potently to the development of a sounder and more comprehensive conception of neurosis and its treatment, the stimulation and other benefits will not all be in one direction. Learning theory, as we have known it in the past, is decidedly limited and far from being a psychology of the "total personality." At a symposium on learning theory and psychotherapy, a wag recently observed that a "marriage" of these two disciplines would probably be a fine thing, indeed. "It might," he said, "make a *man* out of learning theory and an honest woman out of psychotherapy!"

One of the objectives of this volume is to encourage such a union. Whatever else therapy may be, it is a teaching-learning relationship; and no conception of this process seems likely to be ultimately satisfactory which does not give a prominent place to learning principles. Likewise, no psychology of learning which aspires to comprehensiveness can afford to aim at anything short of a full account of neurosis, its genesis, and its possible liquidation.

While psychologists are as mindful as most scientists of their ultimate social responsibilities, they are generally agreed today that they can make their greatest contribution in the realm of psychotherapy, not by yielding to the growing demand for them to do more and more therapy, but by a conjoint research attack upon basic issues of theory and technique. They are, however, well aware that there cannot be a complete division of labor here, between "practitioners" on the one hand and "researchers" on the other. Poets have likened eyes to "windows of the soul." With more literal justification one might use the same metaphor to describe psychotherapy; and there is a growing feeling that the would-be researcher ought to be present, in the person of the therapist, in order to understand the therapeutic process in all its complexity and deep significance. Psychotherapy is a broader enterprise than the treatment of troubled individuals, important as that service obviously is. It provides, perhaps better than any other known procedure, an opportunity to see how the traditions, values, and institutions of a society are functioning, or malfunctioning, and to study the innermost workings of the human personality. The practitioner of this remedial art is therefore not only a purveyor of clinical skills; he is a strategically placed observer and reporter, with obligations which exceed the treatment of particular persons and their problems. No other area of inquiry offers such rewarding possibilities for the study of emotion, perception, thought, language, learning, and interpersonal relations. Human personality has defied our attempts to capture its deepest secrets by ordinary experimental or observational means, whereas in therapy patients surrender up these prizes as if they were more burdensome than valuable. Indeed, the problem is not how to procure such materials, but rather how to process, systematize, and turn them to full scientific and social account. The chapters that follow indicate some of the ways in which contemporary investigators are attempting to answer this question.

PART I
THEORY, CONCEPTS, AND APPLICATIONS

CHAPTER 1

HISTORICAL AND PHILOSOPHICAL PRESUPPOSITIONS FOR UNDERSTANDING THERAPY

By Rollo May, Ph.D.

Every alert practicing therapist must have asked himself countless times the naïve question, Why do people come for psychotherapeutic help? The symptoms which are their *occasions* for coming and the reasons why they *say* they come are simple enough : they are caught in marital conflicts, they cannot love or accept love, they are always quitting jobs, they feel perpetually unhappy, or they experience anxiety attacks and sudden fits of hostility, depression, or despair. But the incidence of this or that symptom changes from decade to decade. Most people came for therapy in Freud's day because of some conflict related to the repression of sexual impulses. While this is no longer the case, no one would hold that the degree or extent of psychological illness is less in our day than in Freud's. So the therapist cannot answer his question by citing symptoms; the naïve question leads to the most profound problems : What is the nature of the human mammal that it should be peculiarly prey to psychological conflict, anxiety, and despair? What goes wrong in a given culture, such as ours, that so many people should need to come to therapists for help? And, assuming the nature of the human being was much the same throughout recorded history, did such psychological problems occur in other historical periods, possibly more in certain periods than in others? And to whom did people go for help before Freud and the development of modern psychotherapy?

Every alert therapist has likewise asked himself countless times why Mr. Jones overcame his psychological problems in therapy and attained a great deal of release of creative potentiality, while Mrs. Smith made only partial gains and we could not help Mr. Brown at all? Many of us have endeavored, over a period of months and years, to determine what factors are at work in our therapy with the subjects who make excellent progress, and what factors are present in the cases which turn out to be psychotherapeutic failures. But to arrive at any communicable understanding of the conditions for therapeutic success or failure, we need first to arrive at some sound presuppositions as to what the nature of therapy is.

These questions are broad, to be sure, and they point toward the various areas of therapy which the succeeding chapters of this book will

9

seek to explore. But investigations are effective, in therapy or any other human endeavor, roughly to the extent that the investigators have clarified their assumptions and thus know what they are seeking.

The task in this chapter, therefore, is to clarify the presuppositions underlying the above questions. *We seek to discover so far as we can the historical and logical position of psychotherapy in the human situation, and thus to provide for researches and hypotheses on therapy a sound orientation.* We shall first inquire what people in some other historical periods did about their psychological problems. Second, we shall try to discover the underlying nature of emotional difficulties which lead people in our age, or any other, to seek help. And in the third section we shall consider the implications of this analysis for the conceptualization and methods of research in therapy.

A Historical and Cultural Perspective on Therapy

A historical perspective should help the therapist to achieve a more dynamic attitude toward the problems of the persons who come to him. With this perspective, he can more easily see, in the form of a trajectory, how certain cultural forces and events have shaped and formed the attitudes and behavior patterns which underlie contemporaneous psychological conflicts. Furthermore, a historical perspective can help the therapist to free himself from the danger of absolutizing a theory or method which is really relative to a given point in history. Freud's universalizing of certain sexual patterns is a clear case in point: the specific sexual problems which Freud in his Victorian culture thought were universal would not have occurred in the same way in ancient Greece or in the Middle Ages, and indeed they do not emerge in exactly the same way in the middle of our twentieth century. Lastly, a historical perspective can help us to see the common sources of human behavior problems as well as common goals through our observing how people in different ages have struggled through their conflicts with authority, anxiety, and responsibility, and how they have sought in their literature, science, philosophy, and religion to bring their wisdom—or lack of it—to bear on their common problems.

But as soon as one endeavors to explore history, one confronts the almost insuperable hurdle of limitations of time and space. In this paper we shall limit ourselves to certain significant aspects of the culture of ancient Greece which bear on psychological illness and therapy and then trace certain motifs in the modern period since the Renaissance.

In classic Greece one discovers immediately a kind of "normal" psychotherapy operating spontaneously through certain commonly accepted symbols and practices in the Greek religion, philosophy, art, and drama. This is to be seen most clearly in the Greek myths. The stories of Oedipus' conflict with his father, of Prometheus' struggle with forbidden creative urges, and of Orestes' slaying of his mother obviously had powerful psychological meaning for the Greek people. Aristotle spoke of the "cathartic," purging effect of these dramas upon the observers. And it is not difficult to imagine how profound and clarifying a psychological effect the presentation of Sophocles' Oedipus trilogy might create in some young man who was struggling with an authoritarian father. Or imagine some person who was burdened with guilt feelings because of hostility toward an exploitative mother observing the drama of Orestes killing the mother who had assassinated his father, then being pursued to the ends of the earth by the fierce Erinyes,[1] and finally achieving peace when he was forgiven by Zeus. How abreactive must have been the emotional impact!

We do not mean to imply that these psychotherapeutic experiences would be consciously articulated by the citizen of Greece in the fifth century B.C. Indeed, it seems that just the opposite was true—that "therapy" in that period was part of the normal, unarticulated functions of the drama, religion, and other forms of communication of the day. These Greek myths—born back in unknown sources in the archaic days of the culture, related by the early poets like Homer, shaped, reshaped, and passed on by later dramatists in the classical period, discussed by the philosophers, presented in religious ceremonies in which the whole citizenry participated, and used as a basis for education of the young—these myths in their very existence must indicate how therapeutic processes and experiences are developed and operate in a society by spontaneous, natural means. The fact, also, that these myths have become classics demonstrates that they speak out of profound human conflicts and struggles which were and are felt by human beings in other periods and other parts of the world as well as by the ancient Greeks. Despite Freud's predilection for interpreting the myths too narrowly, it was part of his genius that he sensed the deep, classical meaning of the Greek myths and borrowed from them for the central concepts in modern psychoanalysis.

If a citizen of Greece in the fifth century B.C. had a psychosomatic illness and if he were sophisticated and at least of medium wealth, he would go to the town of Epidaurus. Here, centering around the shrine dedicated to Aesculapius, the god of healing, medical and religious practices had developed and dramatic, social, and vocational "therapy" took place. The health activities at Epidaurus are an original example of the endeavor to cure a human being not by isolating him from the community but by aiding him to participate with others in activities which minister to the many different sides of his personality.

Or, if the citizen were not symptomatically ill but were sensitive enough to want to achieve greater self-knowledge and inner integration, he might go, as Socrates did, to the shrine of the god Apollo at Delphi. Socrates sought help in his endeavors to unmask hypocrisy, false piety, and self-deceit in himself and in others, faults which he believed were due to the fact that men did not honestly examine their inner motives. As

[1] Avenging spirits who pursue evil-doers and inflict madness; hence undoubtedly mythological symbols of guilt and remorse.

a method for achieving this examination of motives he developed the "Socratic dialogue," which chiefly consisted (how like good therapy of any period!) of asking the right questions. The Socratic method of unmasking self-deceit and rationalization had at least three evidences of efficacy as a therapy: it enabled Socrates himself to become a model of probity and courage; it was of great help to Socrates' friends in their quest for inner integration; and it called forth the rabid anger and opposition of the conventional members of the populace of Athens. On his trip to Delphi, Socrates followed the custom of breathing the fumes which emerge from the fissure in the rocks at the shrine of Apollo (fumes which perhaps had a hypnotic effect). In the succeeding ceremony he was told by the god—so he relates in the *Apologia*—that he was the wisest man then living in the world, and he was given the famous injunction "Know thyself." The former encomium Socrates explained as being related to the fact that he publicly admitted his ignorance. What the god meant, then, was that the person who had broken through his need to pretend, the need to absolutize his beliefs, and had arrived at a humble, seeking attitude toward truth is the wise man. (This is, of course, parallel to one tenet of modern psychotherapy—a tenet often used for the unjustified criticism that therapy causes one to be "too introspective"—namely, that the wise and mature man is he who realizes that his motives never are entirely pure but always involve some rationalization, who tries to admit and work through this rationalization, but who nevertheless acts as best he can on his insights at the time.)

The dictum given currency by Socrates, "Know thyself," is one of those seminal phrases which psychologically avid people all through the ages have tried to interpret and reinterpret. For one example, Nietzsche in the nineteenth century wrote, "What did the God mean who gave the advice 'Know thyself!' to Socrates? Did it perhaps imply: 'Cease to be concerned about thyself! become objective!'?" Thus Nietzsche, with his customary psychological acuteness, suggests that objectivity is to be achieved as the end result of knowledge of one's self, that objectivity (as we shall point out later in this chapter) is arrived at, not by *suppressing* one's subjective interests, but only by knowing one's self so well that one can transcend the boundaries of subjectivity in favor of objective interest in the problem at hand. How self-knowledge, religion, and ethics are united in Socrates' attitude is shown in Kierkegaard's* comment (1946):

In the Socratic view each individual is his own center, and the entire world centers in him, because his self-knowledge is a knowledge of God. It was thus Socrates understood himself, and thus he thought that everyone must understand himself, in the light of this understanding interpreting his relationship to each individual, with equal humility and with equal pride. He had the courage and self-possession to be sufficient unto himself, but also in his relations to his fellowmen to be merely an occasion even when dealing with the meanest capacity. How rare is such magnanimity! (p. 7).

* References are to the bibliography at the back of the book.

The "knowing" in the Socratic dictum cannot be taken in an intellectualistic or rationalistic sense, for it means an endeavor to know one's self on the various levels within one's personality which in modern parlance would be termed unconscious levels. Socrates' idea (and later Plato's) was that every person, through intuition or dreams or fantasies, remembers truths which he learned in a previous existence. This is the doctrine of "reminiscence." [2] Shorn of its mythological character, this concept is simply a way of describing something which becomes clear in every psychoanalysis, that a person knows much more than he is consciously aware that he knows, that what Freud called the unconscious depths of personality contain not only impulses and desires but observations, previous learning, and past experience which have for various reasons been blocked off from the individual's conscious awareness. Furthermore, this "store of learning" is not to be thought of as the result solely of one's own past experience; there is in it much that is the residue of the teachings of the culture which the individual is unaware that he has learned.[3] As a person progresses in psychotherapy and gradually overcomes the anxiety which forced him to repress his awareness of certain things, it is not at all uncommon for him to arrive at a startling discovery and then say, "Well, I knew this all the time, but I never admitted it to myself."

Knowing one's self meant to Socrates a continuous, rigorous, and relentless, though joyful and immensely gratifying, endeavor to penetrate to deeper levels within one's self, and then to act on the basis of a unity of these levels with the conscious self. As he phrased it in his prayer at the conclusion of the *Phaedrus,* "May the outward and the inward man be at one." [4] He believed that ethics and value judgments must be based on this deeper self-knowledge; his picturesque term was that he had a *daimon* (conscience) within him which always told him what he should not do.

Indeed, the pilgrimage to Delphi and the ceremony there were religious practices designed to facilitate this arriving at his own deepest insights. It would obviously be a complete mistake to be misled by Socrates' terms (e.g., *daimon*) into assuming that his approach was authoritarian. Actually his attitudes, his manner of teaching, and his

[2] The term "reminiscence," which is the usual English translation of the term in Plato's dialogues, is actually too passive a word to do full justice to the active uncovering of truth within one's self which Socrates was talking about. Kierkegaard's term when discussing this point in Socrates—"recollection"—is much better in that it suggests an active re-collecting of one's knowledge

[3] It is not necessary to accept Jung's hypothesis of the existence of archetypes in the collective unconscious (incidentally, a direct adaptation of Plato's theory) to agree that every individual has picked up considerable stores of experience and judgment which are the residue of his historical culture.

[4] The whole prayer is so beautiful, and so revealing of Socrates' emphasis on sound value judgments as intimately intertwined with psychological clarification, that we quote it *in toto:* "Beloved Pan, and all ye other gods who haunt this place, give me beauty in the inward soul; and may the outward and inward man be at one. May I reckon the wise to be the wealthy, and may I have such a quantity of gold as none but the temperate can carry."

emphasis on the individual's arriving at truth through penetrating into himself are exactly the opposite to the authoritarian approach in religion or psychotherapy. His central point is that the individual, by rigorous honesty and by symbolic processes that go far beyond mere intellectualizing, is able to arrive at truth within himself, that this is the closest he can get to objective knowledge, and that his happiness depends upon his finding and following this inner truth. In Socrates self-knowledge and ethics are given a common base. A parallel in contemporary writing is Fromm's idea of conscience as "man's recall to himself" (1947).

The culture out of which the Greek dramatists and Socrates spoke was moving toward unity in its basic symbols in art, philosophy, science, and religion—a unity discernible particularly in the art of the Golden Age and the works of Plato and culminating in the thought system of Aristotle in the fourth century B.C. But in the decline of Hellenic society which began shortly thereafter, following the conquest of Greece by Alexander and later by the Romans and the dispersion of Greek culture to Asia Minor and to Rome, this unity was progressively lost.

The citizens of Hellenistic society, particularly in the second and first centuries B.C., no longer supported by an integrated culture, were thrown on their own, as it were; and psychological insecurity and anxiety, together with attitudes of cynicism and hopelessness, are much more discernible than in the earlier periods. Gilbert Murray speaks of this period of the second and first centuries B.C. as the time of the "failure of nerve," a phrase which might well characterize the condition of citizens of any social period which is in the process of disintegration and basic change. A number of philosophical schools flourished during that period— the Stoics, Epicureans, Cynics, Cyrenaics, and Hedonists, together with the traditional Platonists and Aristotelians. What is significant about these diverse schools is that they take the form of psychological and ethical systems designed to help the individual find some source of strength and integrity to enable him to stand securely and gain some happiness in a changing society which no longer lent him that security. In this period, thus, the philosophical systems assume very much the character of methods of *overt* psychotherapy, good or bad as they may be.

The Stoics developed the doctrine of *apatheia,* meaning a passionless calm attained by the exercise of strong will. One should assert one's mastery over outward events, or if one could not do that, one should at least be unaffected by them.[5] Great individual strength was often produced by the beliefs and practices of Stoicism, but it was a strength gained at the price of suppression of all emotions, negative and positive alike. The Epicureans, on the other hand, sought to achieve tranquillity of mind by rationally balancing their pleasures—a doctrine called *ataraxia* —with special value placed on intellectual pleasures. But again, as in the case of the Stoics, this in practice entailed an emasculation of dynamic

[5] The writings of Epictetus, though he was Roman and lived in the first century A.D., are excellent examples of Stoicism attempting to perform services for the individual like those of some modern forms of psychotherapy.

urges; one writer of the period even refers to the Epicureans as eunuchs. The Hedonist tradition emphasized finding pleasure in sensual satisfaction. But one teacher, Hegesias, despairing of ever attaining happiness, became the philosopher of pessimism; and his lectures in Alexandria had to be prohibited by Ptolemy because they resulted in so many suicides.

These ancient methods of trying to avoid anxiety and attain happiness by repression of parts of one's experience are not at all foreign to us in the twentieth century, for they have their parallels (as we shall see) in the compartmentalization of emotion, will, and intellect in the nineteenth century which preceded the development of psychoanalysis.

From this brief glance at the parallels to modern psychotherapy in two phases of the ancient Greek period, it seems clear that the state of the culture, its relative unity or disunity,[6] is closely related to the character of the "therapeutic" activities in the society. In comparing the time of Socrates with the later period, we noted that in the former the therapeutic activities were much more intimately a function of the normal practice and expression of philosophy, religion, and drama in the society. One gets the impression in the earlier classic period of *education* more than r*e-education,* of normal development of the individual toward integration rather than desperate endeavor to overcome neurosis and attain reintegration. In Socrates there is the assumption that, if one develops in unity with his own deeper self, the problems which we normally call "neurotic" will be largely obviated. This kind of normal development is relatively more possible for the individual when his culture is moving toward, or has achieved, some unity. But in the later period of social change (the "failure of nerve" period), the individual was anxious and insecure, and his problems seem to be much more like those we would today term "neurotic."[7] Then the function of the systems of "therapy" (as we have noted in Stoicism and Epicureanism) is to help the person back to some unity, to help him *overcome* some unfavorable pattern, to give him *re-education* and *reintegration,* in contrast to education and integration.[8]

[6] We are not speaking chiefly of political unity and peace; the Hellenistic period, after the Roman conquest, had peace, and Greece, in the Golden Age in Athens, did not. Rather, we are speaking of the unity of a culture in terms of those symbols which give meaning to it: its artistic, philosophical, scientific, ethical, economic, and religious symbols. I realize the difficulty in defining specifically what one means by cultural unity without going into a wealth of historical data. But I assume the unity of the classic period in Greece and the disunity of the later centuries are so well accepted that they do not need to be proved here.

[7] It is difficult to find discussions of anxiety (as distinguished from fear) in the Socratic period or in Plato or, for that matter, in Aristotle. It is as though they did not experience anxiety in the pervasive way we do in the twentieth century (see also Spinoza and the seventeenth century in this respect). But in the first centuries B.C. and A.D., one finds plenty of descriptions of anxiety: Plutarch paints a very vivid picture of an anxious man, and Epictetus describes anxiety-like states in detail. It is very clear that they knew in the Hellenistic period what anxiety was.

[8] Though we shall make no endeavor here to explore the Hebrew or the Roman culture, it can be remarked in passing that these are both exceedingly important areas for research for the student who wishes to understand how human beings dealt with psychological problems in previous ages. The ancient Hebrew psycho-

We now turn to the modern period. Psychological analyses of this period, which began in western Europe with the Renaissance and Reformation and of which we are direct heirs, have been given elsewhere.[9] Hence we shall here only summarize some of the main points in the development of the modern period which bear on the present state of psychotherapy.

The distintegrating phase of medievalism, out of which the modern period was born, was marked by rampant anxiety, despair, and pessimism. It was a time similar in psychological mood to the "failure of nerve" period in the disintegrating phase of Greek culture. Anxiety about death and fears of the devil, sorcerers and witches were prevalent, particularly in the fourteenth and fifteenth centuries. During the previous centuries in the Middle Ages, an individual would have sought security, relief from anxiety, and answers to his psychological and ethical problems in the collective structure of the church and the feudalistic hierarchy. But in the phase of the "waning of the Middle Ages," multitudes of people believed in sorcery and witchcraft and apparently resorted to the sorcerer and witch to find answers to their problems. The religious practices likewise tended to become magical. The distinction between the spiritual meaning of a religious sacrament and objective fact was increasingly lost. Not only was the use of symbols rampant, but the symbols either became empty and without emotional meaning for people at large or on the other hand were identified with objective reality. In the sacrament of the mass, for example, the tendency was to consider the bread the real body of Christ. The practice of indulgences grew apace, not only because it was a good way for the papacy to raise money, but because people were so anxious about their sins that they were always willing to try to buy off some future punishment. The need of many persons to go to confession more and more frequently tended to become obsessional. These religious practices illustrate the deteriorated, disunified state of the culture at that time, with the church seen as one aspect of the culture (an ecclesiastical deterioration which Catholic scholars readily admit, and which was followed by a partial reformation within the Roman church).[10]

---

logical approach avoided the dualism which became increasingly prominent in Greek thought; and in its emphasis on psychophysical interrelations, the Hebrew psychology was in many ways close to the modern emphasis. See Mowrer's discussion (1950) of the Hebrew psalms with reference to anxiety. One especially important period is the fifth century A.D., when Rome began to disintegrate and later fell. This also was a period of widespread psychological upheaval, as would be expected; and it produced, in Augustine, some of the most astute depth-psychological writing to be found before the modern period. Augustine, for example, held that it is possible for the individual to arrive at a level within himself in which objectivity and subjectivity are not opposite but are united.

[9] See May (1950b), chaps. ii and vi; also "The Historical Roots of Modern Anxiety Theories," chap. i in Hoch and Zubin (1950). For a similar sociopsychological analysis to which I am indebted, see Fromm (1941). Abram Kardiner has written a brief description of the cultural history from a psychodynamic viewpoint (1945).

[10] Cyril Richardson, to whose historical studies I am indebted for part of the above material, proposes the thesis that one can discover the chief anxiety-allaying

A radical change occurred with the Renaissance and Reformation in the form of belief in the power of the individual, together with a new concrete and empirical concern with physical nature. These changes had as one of their obvious psychological results the increase of the individual's confidence that problems could be overcome by his own courage, by knowledge that he could obtain by his own study and travel, and by following the guidance of his own conscience in religious and ethical matters. The method which became the tool of the new devotion to knowledge and individual reason was mathematics, Arabic mathematics having been introduced into western Europe after the crusades in the thirteenth century. The understanding and control of physical nature became Western man's dominant concern, an enterprise greatly expedited by Descartes' dichotomy between mind and body, with its corollary that the body and physical nature could be understood by mathematical, mechanical laws.

In the late Renaissance (the sixteenth century) there are several writers who, though unfortunately rarely studied in connection with modern psychological developments, presented germinal ideas for the modern period. One is Giordano Bruno (later to be burned at the stake by the Inquisition) whose idea of Creation as concentric circles with the self at the center gave the original philosophical orientation for modernism. Another is Jacob Boehme, a German mystic and precursor of Protestant thought, who wrote with amazing insight about the relation between anxiety and individual creative effort. And a third is Paracelsus, a physician in the Renaissance who emphasized the influence of the patient's own will (decision) in the achievement of health. It is with Paracelsus, according to Tillich, that the physician began to take over in modern culture the role which the priest had played in medievalism.

The systematization of the philosophical viewpoints which were to dominate most of the modern period occurred in the seventeenth century. This century—the time of that group of seminal thinkers of modernity including Spinoza, Descartes, Leibnitz, Locke, Galileo, Newton, and others—is the classical phase of the modern period as the fifth century B.C. was of the Greek period. An excellent example of the use of the

---

methods of a historical period by noting what the reformers in the subsequent period attacked. This interesting hypothesis strikes me as being exceedingly fruitful for further study. Thus, Luther and the other leaders of the Protestant Reformation attacked the reliance on external sacramentalism of late medieval Catholicism, and the leaders of the Renaissance attacked the scholastic symbolism and corporate authority of medievalism as opposed to their new individualism and naturalism. Thus, the reformers following the disintegrating phase of Hellenistic culture (for example, the early Christians) attacked the vapid and arid rationalistic philosophies of the Hellenistic time. I should only add to Richardson's hypothesis that it seems to me that the central "motif," the particular "genius" or "charter" (in Malinowski's sense) of a given historical period, will be what, in deteriorated form, is obsessively clung to at the time of disintegration of the period. With regard to the present period, we shall indicate below that the dependence on science as a form of magic is what many persons in our day cling to as a method of allaying anxiety and may well be what the next age will attack. These propositions are suggested not as answers but as hypotheses for future psychocultural investigations.

dominant concepts of the day in the service of overcoming problems of fear and hatred is seen in Spinoza, who used mathematical reason as a basis for a theory of the emotions and the ethical life. "Reason" in that day did not at all mean arid intellectualism coupled with the repression of emotion, which the term often connotes in both academic and popular circles now. For Spinoza, reason was an "ecstatic" term;[11] it meant a general attitude toward life which penetrated below the customary distinction between subjectivity and objectivity and included emotions and decision for action as well as thinking.[12]

We have elsewhere pointed out that Spinoza does not discuss anxiety as the term is used in modern psychotherapy.[13] Given the cultural milieu in which he lived, it seems that his confidence in individual reason served him satisfactorily. That was a time, again parallel to the fifth century in ancient Greece, when the culture was moving toward unity in its basic symbols. Thus the citizens found in their society more psychological support. One has the impression that the problems which we in the twentieth century describe as calling for therapy were met more by the natural, spontaneous processes of education and religion in the society of the seventeenth and eighteenth centuries.

The disunity which became apparent in the middle and second half of the nineteenth century and became much more extensive in the twentieth century has also been described elsewhere.[14] We wish here only to emphasize that this disunity went hand in hand with the great progress which had been made in the application of mathematical reason and mechanical laws to physical nature. The far-reaching achievement of the physical sciences, with the promise of making Nature man's servant, together with the vast progress of industrialism and its promise of meeting human physical needs, gave ample support for the great confidence which had been placed in the endeavor to understand and control Nature by mechanical laws. By the nineteenth century the earlier confidence in individual reason as related to all aspects of life had changed to an emphasis on techniques and the application of reason more and more exclusively to technical problems. There was no common view of man except those of the various sciences, and these different sciences had no basis of unity with each other. Cassirer points out that this disunity with respect to views of man was a grave "threat to the whole extent of our ethical and cultural life."[15]

The psychological aspect of this disunity lay in the compartmentalization of the personality, the tendency to see man as consisting of different "faculties"—e.g., reason, emotion, and will power. The nineteenth cen-

---

[11] The term "ecstatic" in this use is a technical one, coming from the Greek *ecstasis* (a standing out from). It implies the kind of activity in which a person is wholly caught up or absorbed.

[12] A close parallel in this use of "reason" as involving ethical and emotional factors is seen in our day in the writings of Fromm (1947).

[13] May (1950*b* and 1950*c*).

[14] May (1950*b*).

[15] See his excellent discussion in chap. i of *An essay on man* (1944).

tury man was supposed, like a successful businessman or industrialist, to make decisions by practical reason and then to enforce these decisions by his strong will power. It was as though the citizen of the nineteenth century were trying to solve his personal psychological problems by the same methods which had been so effective in mastering physical nature and so successful in the industrial world. This process meant in practice a repression of the emotions and the irrational aspects of experience. In the nineteenth century, penetrating thinkers like Kierkegaard, Nietzsche, and Dostoievski saw the psychological havoc that was to result from this compartmentalization. They tried to find a new basis for individual action which would involve a unity of reason and emotion and would include the dynamic aspects of experience which had previously been repressed. These thinkers were centrally concerned with ethics, and ethics not consisting of repression of emotion to fit bourgeois mores but rather of actions proceeding from an individual who had inner unity and integrity.[16]

The psychological disunity and conflict resulting from nineteenth century compartmentalization underlay in general the symptoms for which people came to Freud. His genius was that he took the central emphases of our period, the methods of science, and made them applicable to the areas which previously had been excluded, namely the dynamic, so-called irrational, unconscious aspects of human experience. The radical distinction between our age and previous ages, with respect to therapy for people's problems, is that for the first time in history we have methods for dealing with emotional problems which are partially objective (in the scientific sense) and thereby communicable.

In this brief historical survey we have noted several points, which we suggest here as tentative conclusions.[17] Whereas people in different historical ages and presumably in all ages have the problems which in our own day bring them to the therapist, the degree of these problems, both in the extension of psychological difficulties throughout the society and in the "overtness" and articulateness of the problems, varies at different phases of a given historical period. We observed that, when the culture is moving toward unity and integration, as in Greece in the fifth century B.C. or in the seventeenth century in the modern period, anxiety and psychological disunity are less discernible and the functions of "therapy" seem more to be taken care of by the normal functions of education, art, religion, philosophy, and the like in the society. But in the phases of the period when the culture is involved in basic change and disunity or disintegration, as for example in the later centuries of the Greek period, the last of the Middle Ages, and the later nineteenth and in the twentieth

[16] See Nietzsche's concept of the "transmoral" conscience, in *Beyond good and evil*.

[17] We well realize the necessity of keeping conclusions on such complex matters as cultural history tentative. There are, however, many more data supporting these tentative conclusions than could be given here. In any case, our task here is to get compass readings for help in further explorations rather than to arrive at dogmatic finalities.

centuries in our own period, *anxiety, isolation, pessimism, and despair are much more in evidence.* The individual is driven within himself to find security and integration. The problems which we would term "neurotic" and the specific functions of therapy in the society become more overt and articulate, more to be described as re-education and reintegration than as education and integration.

We also noted that in all ages, with the partial exception of our own period from Freud to the present, people went for help on their problems to the ethical and religious leaders in their society. That is to say, psychotherapy historically has been until the modern period a function of philosophy, ethics, and religion.

As indicated earlier, the chief values of a historical perspective are that it frees us from being blindly determined by our given historical position, it enables us to avoid universalizing a viewpoint which is actually relative to and a product of our own particular stage in history, and it enables us to correct the particular biases and errors of our culture in the light of the wisdom and learning of previous periods in history.[18] The perplexing difficulty is that the chief constructive contribution of any period and the particular biases of that period will be intertwined, since they both arise from the dominant motif of the culture.

The great contribution of our period has been the applying of science to psychological and personal problems. But that also involves our greatest danger of error unless we can free ourselves from two tendencies. One is the widespread tendency in our society to place a magical faith in the powers of science. The fact that "Dianetics" swept the country is a staggering and sobering testimony to this tendency. It seems to me that "Dianetics" bears a relation to modern science similar to the relation of witchcraft and sorcery to the religion of late medievalism. "Dianetics" illustrates how the faith of large numbers of persons in our age of science tends, in a time of anxiety, to cling to a practice which has all the external markings and all the claims to power of science but none of its inner meaning, and that is as good a definition as any of what constitutes magic.

Another danger from which we must free ourselves arises from a particular conception of science which has dominated our society since Descartes introduced his dichotomy between body and mind in the seventeenth century. We must find new methods which will not involve the disunity arising from that dichotomy. Medicine, for example, has

---

[18] In my judgment, Kardiner illustrates the error of universalizing a viewpoint which is actually historically relative when he states that he takes "modern science as an absolute base" (1945) from which to study and criticize other periods. Kardiner uses this base particularly to criticize the absolutism of the Middle Ages, but actually his own method is parallel to that absolutism. The difference is one of symbols—he uses for his absolute base the symbol of "science," instead of which the medieval scholar would use "the Church" or "God." But both are used as absolutes. The fact that the term is "science" rather than the medieval "God" doesn't make either symbol the less relative to a point in history. The sound scientific approach, I submit, is to see all our presuppositions as relative to our position in history and as our approximations to truth. The only tenable absolute from the scientific viewpoint is that the quest for truth is worth making.

made great and laudable progress in the past century, chiefly because its methods have fitted the traditional emphasis in our historical culture. But the tendency to try to stretch the methods of medicine to fit all problems of health, emotional and psychological as well as physical, is to fall into the error of universalizing a method which actually is relative and specific. The methods which have been traditionally dominant in academic psychology have in general been taken over from the methods of the physical sciences; and, like medicine, they are a product of the traditional dichotomy between subjective and objective phenomena. Hence they cannot serve as a basis for a new unity. Though Freud so clearly saw these points, it is fairly widely recognized that his chief error also was in uncritically taking over some of the dominant concepts of the Newtonian mechanics and physics of the nineteenth century, as particularly illustrated in his physiochemical libido theory.

It is our task, as therapists and investigators in psychotherapy in the middle of the twentieth century, to appropriate the gains and insights not only of our own period but of previous ages as well, that we may correct the particular errors to which our period is heir, and that we may find a new basis for therapy which will as effectively as possible fit the particular needs of persons in our day.

The Nature of Neurotic Problems

Let us now look specifically at the citizen of the middle of the twentieth century who comes into an office for psychotherapy. He is the heir and the product of the long historical tradition of Western culture, and he carries within himself the particular conflicts which have prevailed in our society; he is probably a relatively sophisticated person who has heard that science now has techniques for helping people in emotional conflicts and difficulties. Again, the symptoms which are the occasion for his coming will vary all the way up and down the gamut, but can we discern some common patterns in our day which will give us a basis for understanding the conditions for adequate therapy?

First, there are some dimensions of this person's problems which he assumedly holds in common with persons of all other literate cultures. He was born into a world in which it was of paramount importance for his survival as well as for his pleasure and security (and later his self-esteem and his feeling of power) that there be workable relations between himself and the other significant persons in his environment. These important others are typically the mother and father, who feed him, take care of him, and provide an interpersonal world of love or hostility. Very early in his life career he senses, by empathetic means long before he is consciously aware of it, that certain behavior will be approved of and will gain him love and further care and that other behavior will be disapproved of and will result in punishment. This latter behavior, therefore, becomes anxiety-creating. In this social milieu there may begin the process of blocking off from awareness the thoughts and experiences related to the anxiety-creating situations, and then there eventually occur the well-known neurotic processes of repression, inhibition of action, and symptom-formation. As Liddell (1950) puts it, consciousness and unconsciousness are originally functions of ease of communication with parents; what can be communicated becomes conscious, and what will be disapproved of or punished cannot be communicated, and it is repressed and thus becomes unconscious.

These processes are closely related to language development in the child. Kubie (1950) phrases this well:

We know that the neurotic process arises with the development of language in infancy and early childhood, that is with the development of the capacity to act and think and ultimately to speak in symbols. The symbols of neurosis parallel the symbols of language and depend upon many of the same fundamental human capacities; and the neurotic distortion of these symbolic functions occurs as a result of a dichotomy between conscious and unconscious processes which starts early in the development of each human infant (p. xiii).

Though these learning processes begin very soon after birth and are to proceed throughout life as functions of maturation and learning, a radical change occurs sometime between the first and third years. This is the emergence of the capacity of the individual for self-consciousness or self-awareness (referred to often, though somewhat inadequately, as the emergence of the ego). This self-awareness is *the capacity of the individual to treat himself as subject and object at the same time.* While man is the *object* of natural forces, physical and other needs, social influences, and conditioning, he can at the same time see himself as the *subject.* He can ask, "Why did I do that yesterday?" In anticipation of some important event to happen on the morrow or next month, he can project himself in imagination as an actor in that event and observe himself in fantasy, and thus he can plan how most effectively to gain his goals when the real event occurs.

The ability to treat himself both as subject and object is, so far as we can tell, the unique difference between the human being and other mammals. This capacity underlies the human being's capacity to reason, to think in past and future time dimensions (that is, his ability to abstract himself from the immediate situation). This is, also, the capacity which makes man a historical creature—one able to have awareness of and to some extent the ability to influence and correct the historical processes in which he finds himself. The capacity to see one's self as subject and object at the same time is furthermore the basis for the ability to use language and to communicate in symbols.[19] This capacity is not only the source of the creative potentialities of the human being: it likewise makes the human being uniquely heir to neurotic anxiety and other neurotic processes. For, granted the capacity for self-awareness, the individual must

[19] The reader who is interested in further discussion of these highly important points is referred to Goldstein (1939), Mowrer and Ullman (1945), and Cassirer (1944), as well as my own more detailed discussion (1950a).

not only adapt himself to his surrounding world (as any animal must), but he must also do it by making *self-conscious, responsible* choices.

In this structure of psychological problems, the citizen of the twentieth century would not differ radically from human beings in any other period. So we now come to the second point: the *content* of the problem or emotional difficulty the person brings to the psychotherapist will be directly interrelated with the particular conflicts in his historical period. This content is the *area* in which that particular human being, living in a particular society at a particular point in its historical development, finds it impossible successfully to deal with himself as subject and object simultaneously. In Freud's Victorian culture, conflicts and consequent repression, inhibition, and symptom-formation occurred mainly in relation to the repression of sexual and like impulses in that society. Rank in the 1920's held that the common denominator of the neurotic type of his day, as Bailey (1935) relates it, was "feelings of inferiority and inadequacy, fear of responsibility and guilt feelings, in addition to hyper-self-consciousness." And in the 1930's, Horney described the neurotic personality of that time as arising from mutually contradictory goals within the personality and involving chiefly repression of hostile rather than sexual impulses.[20] The general trend among psychoanalysts during the last three decades has been to see neurotic problems less as matters of particular symptoms and more as matters of "character neurosis," that is, neurosis arising from a faulty pattern of behavior which the individual has been forced to develop as an infant in order to survive psychologically in his interpersonal milieu.

This trend in the theoretical way neurotic problems are conceived has gone hand in hand with greater emphasis, from the 1920's to the present time, on what is called "ego analysis." The term "ego analysis" is as infelicitous and as misleading as "analysis of the unconscious." All such terms imply some compartmentalization of the personality, which is understandable because the terms emerged in a time when the breaking of the personality into parts was the accepted method of objective understanding. I believe the trend summarized above can more adequately be described as a trend *away from* defining neurotic problems as particular, localized conflicts (which generally are symptomatic) and *toward* seeing the problems as based in the character structure of the individual, his whole set of attitudes and behavior patterns by which he attempts to relate to himself and the other persons in his world. This trend is caused on one hand by the progress of psychoanalysis and the other forms of understanding human emotional ills, but it is also a result of cultural and social changes by which the underlying psychological problems of our

[20] We do not mean, of course, that these were the only psychotherapists who tried to arrive at a formulation of the common denominator of neurotic problems of their day; practically every seminal thinker in the field has stated his formulation in various ways. We believe, however, that the summary above correctly reflects the general trend since the time of Freud in what were considered the basic aspects of neurotic problems.

day are coming closer and closer to the surface and are less covered by the various symptoms.

We wish here to propose a hypothesis which will serve as a description of the common bases of psychological problems in our period. *The common objective aspect of these neurotic problems is that the individual cannot act as an independent entity, and the common subjective side is that he cannot experience himself as a self in his own right.* This description of neurotic problems, it is hoped, will give us a common ground for understanding the problems of our day below the various symptomatic conflicts. This formulation is not contradictory, for example, to Freud's early formulation, but rather pushes it to a level below the symptom: in Freud's description of sexual repression and inhibition, the problem can really be described as the inability of the individual to experience himself as a sexual being (the subjective side) and to act as a sexual being (the objective side). Our description also accords with the phenomena which appear in contemporaneous consulting offices all the time: in our day persons come very rarely because of hysterical symptoms, for example, but rather because they cannot work, cannot make marriage decisions, cannot love or accept love; or if they do make vocational or marital decisions, they find themselves compelled to revoke the decisions and shift to a new job or new marriage partner (which simply indicates that they never have really made the decisions.) Or the persons complain of anxiety, depression, weakness, and powerlessness. All these complaints, broadly speaking, are symptomatic of the damming up of capacities and potentialities which occurs when the individual is unable to use his powers in action.

Further evidence for this hypothesis is the great frequency with which the Rorschachs of persons who are in emotional difficulty in our society indicate that the individual has no sense of being a person in his own right, but rather experiences himself as a set of mirrors reflecting what is around him or a vague switchboard whose function it is to relay what is channeled into it. Though he talks about "wanting" things, he really means what others say he should want; and when he uses the term "ought," he means what he thinks others require of him. My observations as a therapist suggest that the most common condition of persons in our society who come for psychotherapeutic help is that they have no sense of autonomous power as a self but feel themselves—to the extent their defenses have broken down—as powerless, empty, and isolated. It is, of course, not at all surprising that such persons should have great conflict with authority and responsibility. Since they lack experience of themselves as of worth or possessing power in their own right, their decisions would always be made at the command of other powers, and then they would tend always to welsh or renege on the decisions.[21]

[21] The formulation offered here of neurotic problems has something in common with those offered by Erich Fromm (who describes lack of mental health as lack of "the sense of I-ness"), Kurt Goldstein, and Harry Stack Sullivan.

This description of the common denominator of neurotic problems of our time accords also with the wider cultural phenomena in our day. Vivid portrayals of this point are given in Kafka's writings, to cite only one example. He describes the individual who cannot, no matter how hard he tries, become a person in his own right in modern bourgeois society and hence is isolated and anxious (*The castle*); the less fortunate person who does not even try to achieve selfhood and hence feels pervasive guilt (*The trial*); and—as if in logical conclusion—the individual who is no longer a human being but a cockroach (*Metamorphosis*). The parallel to our description can be found in almost every other phase of modern literature, as well as in the writhing emptiness of so much modern art. It is shown vividly also on the socioeconomic level in the development of fascism and other forms of authoritarian collectivism. Fascism, for example, is the binding together of large numbers of people who have lost their experience of power and worth as individuals, who cannot bear the anxiety and emptiness of this state, and who therefore try to grasp substitute symbols of power and prestige by subordinating themselves to the authoritarian hierarchy.[22]

It will immediately be seen that this common denominator of neurotic problems—the incapacity of the person to experience himself as a being in his own right and the inability to act as an autonomous self—is closely related to the cultural and historical situation of modern Western man in the twentieth century as we have discussed it in the previous section. The preoccupation with mechanical ways of interpreting experience and nature, the great emphasis on methods which analyze the body, physical nature, and other "objects," the tendency to rule out personal and subjective factors so far as possible in the interests both of the control of physical nature and the progress of industrialism, the great emphasis on wealth and value as defined by industrial progress and the criteria of the market place, with human beings valued as commodities which could be bought and sold—all these tendencies in the latter nineteenth century and in the twentieth century have aided in producing human beings who feel empty, passive, and powerless as selves.

These tendencies likewise show themselves in the general attitudes in our culture toward health and therapy. There is a clear tendency in our society for people to think of physical sickness and health in "passive" terms, as though the flu or tuberculosis were an external infection that you "caught" accidentally and over which you had no more control than you have over the stock market. The value of the traditional medical view of sickness as something which occurs *to* the organism is that it overcame the morbid view inherited from older periods that sickness was "punishment from God" and that one should hide his disease in shame rather than deal with it as objectively as he would with other difficulties in the natural world. But this "objective" attitude toward disease and health, along with its helpful influences, has had the harmful tendency

[22] Cf. Fromm (1941).

of leaving individual responsibility out—a tendency that is not healthy in the long run even in physical medicine (as psychosomatic studies have clearly indicated) and works directly contrary to the best interests of health in the psychological sphere.

The tendencies we have been discussing partially explain why people in our culture would prefer to have a physical rather than a psychological ailment or to get medical rather than psychological treatment; and why they prefer to speak of their emotional difficulties as "medical" problems. They can then view the illness as something objective to themselves, something for which they are not responsible. This is a great boon to persons who feel, as they often do when caught in psychological conflicts, that they are powerless to do anything about the problem. And when they do come for psychotherapy, these tendencies condition their attitudes toward the therapy itself. They wish to be "treated," as though their responsibility was to be passive and to let the therapist work on them, or at best as though all that could be expected from them was cooperation in coming to the sessions, communicating as best they can, and paying their bills. When at the outset the therapist explains to a person with this typical attitude that he can only help the person to help himself, that he cannot predict the outcome of the therapy as one could predict the probable outcome of a given case of typhoid fever, and that it depends chiefly on what goes on within the person himself—that is, when the therapist keeps the central responsibility on the person who comes for help, the person often has the feeling of being "gypped." Unless the therapist has some great and magical power (magic here meaning the "magic of science"), therapy may not be worth much. And when the therapist raises the question of whether it is not a much greater service to the person that he be helped in the therapy to discover and to learn to use his own powers and potentialities than for the therapist to deliver masterful *ex cathedra* statements of wisdom, the person often has had so little experience of his own inner powers and their value that he does not know what the therapist is talking about.[23]

One of the immediate problems in psychotherapy arises from the fact that almost the whole vocabulary in the science and art has been taken over from the field of medicine. This is partially because of the historical accident that Freud was a physician; and partially because physicians in daily contact with ill people have had to face immediate human problems, whereas other disciplines, like psychology, have tended to close themselves

---

[23] It is a very significant commentary on how people view themselves in our society to note how they value learning a skill as compared to learning to overcome their emotional problems. If one went to a piano teacher to take lessons and the piano teacher consumed all the time playing with his expertness rather than teaching the pupil to take the first inexpert steps, the person would rightly feel the pianist was a conceited authoritarian and not a useful teacher. But when people come for psychological help, they often see no value whatever in their learning to live their own lives effectively but seem to place a value only on the therapist's making their decisions, which means living their lives for them. The fact that they have this passive attitude toward themselves is, of course, one of the central reasons they need therapy.

off in the laboratory. But more importantly it is because the whole central emphasis in our historical period has been on attitudes which, on the level of sickness and health, fitted the medical attitudes. The person who comes for therapy is generally referred to as a "patient," a term which comes directly out of the traditional viewpoint that the sick person is acted upon by an outside force and that cure consists of his being patient while the doctor and other more powerful forces act against the disease. This term directly hinders the therapeutic process in that it places a premium on the person's being "passive." The Rogerian term "client," used also in social work, has the advantage of emphasizing the other person's activity in coming in, but it has the disadvantage of its association with commercial activities. Rogers has assiduously emphasized that therapy be centered on the needs of the client, and the viewpoint here is in accord with his on the point of a nonauthoritarian process in therapy concerned centrally with the other person's autonomy and indigenous potentialities. But Rogers' term "nondirective" is a negative term, and furthermore it leaves unsolved the real problems involved in the fact that every relationship is to some extent and in various ways directive.[24] Hiltner's term for the process of therapy, "eductive," has much to recommend it. "Analysand" is often used as a substitute term for patient, but it implies an exclusive connection with psychoanalysis, and furthermore is a foreign term to most people. The present writer, as the reader has no doubt discovered in many ambiguous contexts in the above pages, capitulates and simply uses the term "person" for the patient. In any case, we need to work out a new vocabulary for psychotherapy which will more adequately reflect the nature of the problems dealt with and the nature of therapy.

[24] It seems to me clarifying and healthy that the directive implications of any relationship be admitted openly. These directive influences, for example, inhere in the reputation and position of the therapist (which certainly influence the person's choice of him as a therapist); they exist in the unspoken attitude of the therapist in the session itself, and in countless subtle ways in addition to the outright beliefs and value judgments of the therapist. I believe it essential that the therapist frankly admit these directive influences to himself, and sometimes (though not necessarily always) to the other person. This not only may have a clarifying effect, but it also gives the only basis for moving beyond the actually directive elements in the situation to a greater objectivity. I do not mean at all that it is the therapist's function to impose himself upon the relationship; I do mean that the autonomy of the person is best protected by a frank realization on both sides that no human relationship is entirely nondirective. Likewise I do not mean to imply that Rogers himself may not be aware of these problems; but it is my experience that the term "nondirective" as often used in academic circles does not take these points into consideration. Rogers has performed an invaluable service in his indefatigable attacks on the kinds of psychology and psychiatry which in effect try to make over the client into the image of the therapist's particular school. But such a philosophy of therapy is shared by therapists using different techniques. All good therapy, whether employing the psychoanalytic technique on which this chapter is based or otherwise, is nondirective in the sense that the primary concern is the needs, values, and potentialities of the person who comes for help. Fromm's writings are classical analyses and criticisms of the authoritarian approach. See also Fromm-Reichman's recently published book (1950), which I was able to read only after this chapter was complete. This is a superb exposition of psychoanalytic technique based on a profound concern with the potentialities and autonomy of the patient.

If we are correct in our analysis that the central neurotic problem of our time is the inability of the individual subjectively to experience himself as a person in his own right, and his inability objectively to act as a unified, autonomous individual, the efficacy of our therapy will depend on how well we understand what it means for a human being in a given cultural situation to experience himself and to act as a person in his own right. Let us now explore on a more profound level what it means for a human being to act as subject and object at once.

It is important to see at the outset that every real life situation for a human being is one in which the person is deciding something, taking some stand in relation to his environment. For a human being to be living means that he is engaged continually in forming and reforming himself in relation to his environment (including other selves) and his environment in relation to himself.[25] He is engaged in adapting himself to his environment and vice versa—the word "adapt" here being used not in its mechanical sense that the person is "adjusting to" something but in its dynamic sense that the person is changing his environment as best he can in order to achieve his goals.[26] This is true not just in actions as such but also in contemplative thinking or reverie: the individual is assuming some attitude in imagination; he is molding himself in relation to his world. And it is likewise true in dreams. Dreams are never static photographs; rather, the dream is the person's endeavor to work out some situation in symbolic or in dramatic form. In clinical work, thus, the *verbs* in dreams generally are more significant than the nouns: that is, what the figures or objects in the dream are *doing*, how the dreamer is trying to mold and remold his interpersonal world, are what is most important.

It is difficult to find the right term for this characteristic of the human being—that he is continually forming and reforming himself in relation to his environment. We do not at all mean *activism,* the compulsion to plunge into activities that is characteristic of our industrial and commercial society, a form of behavior which in most cases is an endeavor to escape from facing one's self. What we are describing may be shown as much when a person is in repose or taking a vacation. Indeed, since these latter activities generally involve standing *against* the momentum and regular routine of one's existence, they may represent for many persons a more definite attitude of decision and choice than would continuing at work, just as for many persons in our society going to a party involves less decision than staying quietly home and listening to one's

[25] Cf. Goldstein's statement that an organism has only one need, namely to make itself adequate to its environment and its environment adequate to itself (1939).

[26] To my mind the term "adjustment," as it has so often in past decades been used in clinical psychology, is an excellent example of the carry-over of the traditional mechanical approach. "Adjustment" of one thing to another—making them fit—has a thoroughly sound meaning when one is speaking of the carburetor of a car or turning dials on a machine to produce a slightly different chemical mixture. See Mowrer (1950) for a discussion on the basis of learning theory of the deficiencies of that term and the superiority of the term "integration."

music. In our day the contemplative person and the mystic often represent more clearly this capacity to form and reform one's environment in relation to one's self (and vice versa) because they are not simply going along with the common current of the environment. The capacity we are describing is implied in Dewey's emphasis on the point that all thinking is problem solving. But the phrase "problem solving" is not entirely felicitous because of its negative quality. We prefer to emphasize the positive, creative aspect of this capacity to reform the world in relation to one's self, as it is shown in the random playing of a child with blocks, of a poet with words, or of a painter with colors, simply because one gets joy from finding things which fit harmoniously or in being able to *make* them fit harmoniously.

This indicates what it means to be "alive" or "dead" psychologically. The fact of someone's being alive or dead physically can be ascertained by simple tests, such as heartbeat and breathing. And even the degree of being alive or near death physically can be measured by a physician by testing blood pressure, elasticity of tissues, reflexes, and so forth. It is proposed here that "aliveness" psychologically consists of the individual's capacity to form and reform himself in relation to his environment and his environment in relation to himself; and that, furthermore, the *degree* of his being alive psychologically is the degree to which he can do this. The importance of this criterion is that it will help us to see that though two persons are apparently equally alive physically, one can be much more alive than the other psychologically. This definition has more to recommend it than simply its speculative promise. We know clinically, for one thing, that neurosis consists of a constriction of awareness and an inhibition of the power to act and that it results in relative rigidity and incapacity for new learning. Neurosis thus can be described as a partial death psychologically for the organism. The final form of this constriction of awareness and power for creative activity would be psychological death, and though this coincides at one point in everyone's career with physical death, the two are not to be identified through the life history of the organism. Our definition brings into place many obvious observations, such as that psychological aliveness is the degree of one's capacity to grow, to experience new learning, and so forth.

Another significant implication arising from seeing the human being as the acting subject is that we are saved from a rigid dichotomy between the person and his external world. One of the traditional errors in psychological thinking (a logical result of the historical dichotomy of subject and object since Descartes) has been the assumption that the objective environment was in itself the "reality." Thus the tendency was to set the human being over against the environment and to assume that his job was to size up the environmental situation and then act appropriately. But if we free ourselves from traditional grooves of thinking, we shall discover that the reality of any situation cannot be known apart from our intent, or someone's intent, in relating to it. That is to say, an individual's subjective readiness for activity (his plan or attitude) in viewing a certain situation *partially determines the reality of that situation.* This fact is well known to psychotherapists through the phenomenon of selective awareness: people are aware of certain things in some situation they observe and are unaware of other things—not at all solely because they did not "see" the latter things, but because they must for very good reasons repress their awareness of them. I wish to go a step further and point out that it is an illusion to assume that if one ideally had no neurotic problems, he would see the situation without any subjective element entering the picture.[27] Actually we cannot know the reality of any situation apart from our intent, or someone's intent, in relating to it. That is to say, the reality of a given situation cannot be ascertained by divorcing subjectivity and objectivity, or by the traditional means of suppressing the former and overemphasizing the latter, but only by seeing reality as an interaction of the living, acting human being *and* the other persons or objects which constitute the environment. This point has profound and crucial bearings on the methodology to be used in psychotherapeutic research, a topic to be considered in the next section; but here we return to the practical implications for therapy.

One central practical implication arising from this discussion is that the criterion of progress in therapy is how well the individual can choose and act as an autonomous being. The great contribution of Freud was to uncover the conflicts and blockages which kept persons from acting, and his emphasis on the innumerable deterministic factors in unconsciousness was a historical gain of incalculable importance. His discoveries successfully defeated the hypocritical and delusive nineteenth century concept of voluntarism, namely that all one needed to do was to decide on the right course of action by his reason and then force himself, via "will power," to act on the decision. In this discussion, therefore, we do not wish in the slightest to underestimate the significance of Freud's emphasis on the deterministic power of motives of which the individual is unaware and all the other deterministic aspects involved in his concept of the "unconscious." But there has been a danger that the baby would

---

[27] A well-known illustration will make this point clear. Three different persons stand on a ridge overlooking a woods in the valley. One of them is an artist considering painting the scene; another is a farmer who is planning to chop down some of the trees for firewood; the third is looking at the woods against the possibility of making love to his fiancée there on the morrow. Each of these persons would see a quite different picture; and if we had a photograph of the "reflection" in the mind of each, it is very doubtful whether we could conclude they were looking at the same scene. Now suppose I, as a psychologist, come along, resolved to have nothing to do with this subjectivity and determined to arrive at a completely objective description of the scene before me. I then note that I am looking at a wood of such-and-such size, of such-and-such color—and the more consistent I am in trying to rule out the subjective element, the more will I reduce the scene before me to quantitative figures. Finally, I arrive at a series of mathematical formulae as my description of the wood—and lo and behold, what I have is a completely symbolic, completely subjective description of the scene! The endeavor to rule out the subjective factor has resulted in my picture of the woods being divorced entirely from the objective reality, and it is "less real" than the pictures in the minds of the farmer, the artist, or the lover.

be thrown out with the bath water in psychoanalytic development and that the individual would become passive in the face of his "unconscious" tendencies, as he had been, for example, passive in the face of the economic forces of his day. This is shown often by naïve persons when they say, "My unconscious wouldn't let me do—or kept me from doing—something." And it is present in more subtle forms in any psychoanalysis in the tendency of the person to rationalize his avoiding some responsibility by the fact that he "has a neurosis" and is getting analyzed. A chief reason the emphasis on the "analysis of the ego" arose in the 1920's (which we have mentioned before) is that great numbers of analyses were arriving at standstills, with the analysand apparently having worked through all "repressed childhood memories and other unconscious material" and having arrived at good intellectualized formulations of the causes of his neurosis—but still he kept the neurosis. Rank and Wilhelm Reich most clearly observed—with Freud and others in the traditional analytic development also partially agreeing—that the essential dynamic aspect of human psychological behavior was being omitted. Rank then developed his "will therapy," and Reich his techniques of character analysis. While each tended, Reich most flagrantly so, to go to extremes after cutting himself off from the central tradition, each has made a lasting contribution to the development of therapy with respect to the problem of decision.[28]

No matter how many deterministic factors are involved in any individual's problems—and they will be legion, arising from childhood, conditioning, physical needs, external events, *ad infinitum*—the individual himself, simply by virtue of the fact that he is living, is always taking a stand with regard to something. Even in his being aware of things (or refusing to be aware), he is making some decision. The person's first decision to come for therapy is, of course, an exceedingly important act or sign of intent. But once he has embarked on therapy, it often is a slow process for him to begin to take his intentions seriously and to act on them. His deciding to remember dreams and taking responsibility for bringing in significant material, for example, are emerging indications of his capacity to deal with himself as an autonomous, responsible entity who has some say in the molding of his environment and himself in relation to it. While in therapy, he still exists in a real life situation—not only outside the consulting room but likewise in the immediate relation with the therapist. If he uses talking about his problems as a substitute for action, a stalling of the therapy sooner or later occurs. Freud's caution against the analysand's making radical, irrevocable decisions, such as changes in marital or vocational status, in the course of therapy is sound in the respect that transference factors very often operate and an analysand may tend to act on only a partial insight. But this caution

---

[28] Reich's *Character analysis* (New York: Orgone Institute Press, 1945; German edition, 1935) is to be recommended to students of therapy; but practically all of Reich's later concepts and theories are considered by most analysts of other schools to be among the most dubious and unsound in the whole field.

can easily be used as an excuse for the passive renouncing of personal autonomy. As Alexander and French succinctly point out (1946), the patient comes for psychoanalysis not because he wants to learn a body of analytic data but because he is blocked in his day-to-day activities. "Serious delay of therapeutic progress," they remark, "may result from adherence to the rule of 'no important, irreversible changes during treatment!'" The aim is not that the analysand not make basic decisions, but rather that his motives for the decisions be so well clarified in the therapy that he will make the decisions soundly.

It is my observation in therapeutic work that a person often cannot get new insight until he affirms and acts on the insight he already has—which is a way of saying, in the context of this discussion of seeing the individual as a thinking-feeling-acting entity, that this entity cannot take a future step until the one at hand has been taken. It is a curious and interesting phenomenon that willing, or decisions, can influence what one dreams. A person has been having dreams on both the constructive and negative side of a conflict of leaving home, let us say, and getting an independent job. He finally makes a practical decision to move out on his own, and then he has dreams firmly on the constructive side of the issue and dreams which point toward further steps ahead.[29] We are well aware, of course, that the decision could not be made unless there had been long and patient work on clearing up the unconscious aspects of the conflict. No decision is made *de novo;* actually therapeutic progress is a constant series of minor decisions, a continuous chain of putting one's intents into practice.

We certainly do not mean in this discussion to underestimate in the slightest the importance of unconscious, deterministic factors or to imply any semblance of the old idea of "will power." But we do mean that traditional phrases like Groddeck's "We are lived by our unconscious," or Jung's "the autonomy of the unconscious" actually leave out the most important fact, namely that our unconscious is not a separate power, or something which, when liberated, will automatically carry us toward health. The concept of the unconscious formulated by Freud, to counteract the compartmentalizing of personality in the Victorian period, runs the risk of serving as a new dichotomy unless it is continually emphasized that the unconscious is still part of the living human being, even though he is not aware of its contents at a particular time. The goal is that the person learn to act so far as possible as a unity, with awareness of previously unconscious factors and tendencies at deeper levels not cut off from the influence of his decisions, but amenable to them. Most therapists would agree, no doubt, that the most significant signs of progress in therapy—that is, progress defined as psychological growth—are the little decisions the person is able to make here and there. This emerging

[29] Of course, he may well have reaction dreams also; some reaction after a crucial decision is to be expected, but generally the reaction is not too great, or too prolonged, if the preliminary steps toward the decision have been patiently and steadily worked through.

capacity may be the surest sign that sooner or later he will be able to make crucial and basic decisions independently.

Conceptualization and Methods of Testing Therapy

Therapy as a Relearning Process.—The historical and logical analysis in the preceding pages indicates that psychological therapy is a learning, or more accurately a relearning, process. It is a process by which an individual overcomes his previous unfortunate learning experiences which have resulted in blocking off of awareness (repression), curtailing of actions (inhibitions), and development of the complicated processes of substitutive gratification on less mature levels (symptom formation). The goal of clarified relatedness to one's self and to the other persons in one's interpersonal world, so that one can give and accept mature love and utilize one's powers in mature, responsible decisions, is generally achieved only through long-time, profound learning and relearning processes.

It was observed in an earlier section of this chapter that historical periods vary with respect to how much therapy is learning and how much it is relearning. In the phases of a given historical period in which the culture is moving toward unity in its cultural symbols the individual receives psychological support and relatively consistent education in the society. We proposed that "therapy" in those historical phases was more a part of the spontaneous function of the acculturation process; the individual generally received what therapy he needed without its being defined or articulated as such. But in periods of profound social change, when the culture is marked by relative disunity (such as in the Hellenistic period, the last centuries of the Middle Ages, and the twentieth century), the individual receives less psychological support, anxiety and feelings of isolation are more prevalent, and unconstructive patterns and substitute gratifications are more inclined to develop. Hence in these periods the process of gaining emotional integration is more a *relearning* process, and therapy becomes an articulate, specific concern in the society. In therapy as relearning, it is generally necessary that the neurotic defenses be broken down before the individual can relinquish unsatisfactory behavior patterns, to replace them by more satisfactory ones. Hence, in a period like our own, the chief practical difference between therapy as conducted by trained psychotherapists on one hand and education via the social institutions like school and church on the other, is that the former is specifically concerned with the difficult technical procedure of breaking down defenses that new learning may proceed.[30]

Alexander and French have so pertinently stated the fact that therapy is a learning process that we wish here to quote them at some length.

[30] It is, incidentally, this breaking of defenses, together with the transference and resistance processes which accompany it, which makes deep therapy a difficult, exacting, and sometimes hazardous procedure. Hence the long and specialized training required for its practice.

They indicate that psychoanalysis is a "procedure aimed at achieving permanent changes in the ego's functional capacity by a slowly progressing emotional training—more an educational process than a therapy in the original sense" (1946). In their volume they speak continually of psychoanalysis as a "kind of emotional training," and Dr. French concludes one chapter with an excellent description of psychotherapy which is in many ways parallel to the concepts in this paper:

The more we keep our attention focused upon the patient's immediate problem in life, the more clearly do we come to realize that the patient's neurosis is an unsuccessful attempt to solve a problem in the present by means of behavior patterns that failed to solve it in the past. We are interested in the past as the source of these stereotyped behavior patterns, but our primary interest is in helping the patient find a solution for his present problems by correcting these unsuccessful patterns, helping him take account of the differences between present and past, and giving him repeated opportunity for actual efforts at readjustment within the transference situation. Then, when the patient attempts to put his new attitudes into practice in outside life, he will find they have become second-nature. Thus does psychotherapy indeed become a process of emotional re-education (p. 95).

The fact that therapy is a learning process is the chief reason it takes so long. Regardless of the fact that in many instances insight may emerge as a sudden experience (and one only realizes later how long a building-up process was required to arrive at the point where a sudden insight was possible), and despite the fact that real therapeutic help may be given in rare cases in one or a few sessions, the important process is still one of changing reactions, attitudes, and habit patterns that are complex and have infinite ramifications. This can be done overnight only when there has been a long process of building up of intention, conscious or unconscious, along with maturation within the personality. When the basic change in attitude and behavior does occur, it is not at all a matter of a chance motive or a lucky accident. Clara Thompson makes the point that since therapy is a relearning process, basic change takes a long period, the length of which is not centrally dependent on whether the person comes three times or five times a week. The person "seems to require the passage of time in order to consolidate his new insights and incorporate them as a part of his daily living. The repeated testing out and seeing over and over again what is going on seems to be the prerequisite for the process of growth and change. This is what makes treatment so long no matter what method is used" (1950).

We believe that the term "social learning" has more promise as a description of psychotherapy than any other yet discovered. But it should be stated clearly that the term "social" does not refer to the popular superficial concept of "social adjustment," or simple adaptation to the mores or social manners of one's group. "Social," rather, refers here to the process of *relationship to one's own self* as a person as well as to other selves. It is as much in operation in Socrates' struggle with himself in deciding to drink the hemlock, or in the scientist's solitary work in the laboratory, as it is in the market place or in a family discussion. The term "interpersonal" is a good synonym to keep in mind for this use of the term "social."

Likewise it will of course be obvious that the learning theory we referred to is not the oversimplified and nondynamic theories of learning that stress simply the overt application to the subject matter, but rather is a dynamic theory based especially on the study of motivation. We would also emphasize that a relevant learning theory must include the element of the maturation of the capacities within the individual. Thus curiosity and the gratifications which an individual experiences in the development and use of his own powers are sound and important motivations in therapy.[31] Horney writes (1950):

Whatever the conditions under which a child grows up, he will, if not mentally defective, learn to cope with others in one way or another, and he will probably acquire some skills. But there are also forces in him which he cannot acquire, or even develop by learning. You need not and in fact cannot teach an acorn to grow into an oak tree, but when given a chance, its intrinsic potentialities will develop. Similarly, the human individual, given a chance, tends to develop his particular human potentialities. He will develop then the unique alive forces of his real self: the clarity and depth of his own feelings, thoughts, wishes, interests; the ability to tap his own resources, the strength of his will power; the special capacities or gifts he may have; the faculty to express himself, and to relate himself to others with his spontaneous feelings. All this will in time enable him to find his set of values and his aims in life. In short, he will grow, substantially undiverted, toward *self-realization*. And that is why I speak now and throughout this book of the real self as that central inner force, common to all human beings and yet unique in each, which is the deep source of growth (p. 17).*

The Need for a New Methodology.—It is clear from the foregoing historical discussion that methodology in studying therapy cannot be taken over from traditional medicine or traditional academic psychology. Freud himself made these points very emphatically, despite the fact that, inconsistently, he himself erred by taking over some of the methods of traditional physiochemical science.[32] Both of these disciplines arise out of the historical dichotomy which is intrinsically bound up with the very problems therapy seeks to solve. The dominant method until a few years ago in academic psychology, following Wundt and Titchener (who, in turn, were representatives of the central nineteenth

---

[31] No attempt to define these aspects of learning theory more accurately will be made here; other chapters in this book deal with that area. I wish only to emphasize that these aspects must be taken into consideration if learning theory is to be relevant to a great part of what goes on in psychotherapy. This is a point made in various ways by Horney, Goldstein, Sullivan, and Fromm. See May (1950b), p. 106, and elsewhere in that volume. See also the writings of Mowrer (1950).

* By permission from Karen Horney, *Neurosis and human growth.* Copyright, 1950, W. W. Norton & Co., Inc.

[32] For a discussion in greater detail of these points, see Freud's *The problem of lay-analysis* (1927); Mowrer (1950); May (1950a).

century trend inherited from Newton in the seventeenth), was to separate behavior and experience into events which could be dealt with experimentally and quantitatively. As pointed out by Hadley Cantril (1950) in an excellent brief summary of the main trends in the development of psychology from 1900 to 1950, the traditional method at the turn of the century was to "fractionate experience, taking the pieces apart, examining them and then fitting them together again." We do not need here to go into the fact that many psychologists, especially the clinicians and therapists, found that this traditional method did not yield the central data which they sought.[33] What is needed is a method of testing and analyzing therapy which will retain the conscientious and careful aspects of the older mathematical methods, but will at the same time be applicable to human beings in crisis situations.

On the basis of the analysis in this paper, the crucial prerequisite for a new method is that the *irreducible unit for study be taken as the individual human being in a real-life situation.* The term "real" here means a situation in which the given human being is confronted with some decision (in the particular sense this term is used previously in this paper) which involves in greater or lesser degree his own happiness and welfare and for which, therefore, he has some inescapable responsibility. The unit is not a person plus a vocational or marital decision, for example. The existence of the particular decision is inextricably bound up with what the person has been and is, and thus it cannot be subtracted or added without the reality of the situation being destroyed. This is why confronting an individual with a conflict situation for experimental purposes in a laboratory does not produce a "real" situation. The person's "real" situation is not that of a human being facing the situation of, let us say, having to turn on the light at one signal and off on another, and then being confronted with the conflict situation of both signals at once, but rather that of a person cooperating with a friend or teacher in an experiment. His actually "real" state of mind may well not be the conflict —from which, he knows, he will be entirely free when he leaves the laboratory in an hour—but rather that of curiosity or boredom or mild frustration and resentment that he is subjected to the experiment. We do not mean at all to imply that many illuminating studies and researches on various aspects of psychotherapy may not be engaged in experimentally, but we do mean that the cogency and value of these experiments will depend on how clearly the experimenter discerns the way in which the particular segment being isolated for the experiment fits into the total situation of the human beings involved.

A chief reason, of course, why the unit of the living person in a situation of responsibility cannot be reduced to its component parts is that the person is at every moment influencing the situation by his willing, intent, and decisions. In an analytic session, for example, an analysand cannot tell the therapist about his wife or mother or father without an intention to take some stand toward these other persons being formed

[33] See Symonds (1946) and Mowrer (1950).

and molded even as he talks. He may be thinking that he needs to be more independent from his father, more considerate of his wife or what not. His intention even structures the relationship between him and the therapist (and is in turn conditioned by this relationship), for the stand he is considering taking toward these other persons will to some degree determine what he tells the therapist about them. It often seems to me doubtful whether the real motives and dynamics of a subject's behavior can be uncovered unless the relationship between the subject and the "listener" has the purpose of helping the subject. Without this proof that the "listener" affirms the good of the other person, the great degree of trust, intimacy, and honesty required for the revealing of underlying motives possibly could never be achieved.

The "real situation," furthermore, for the given human being involves dynamic temporal qualities: the "now" includes the past events which have influenced him as well as his future plans.[34]

The term "irreducible" in our previous statement means that a unit cannot be fractionated without losing its reality. For example, in mathematics, the figure 20 can be reduced to 10 and 10 or to many other parts, all of which still equal 20. But if we describe the situation of the human being as an individual *plus* his past *plus* his environment *plus* the decisions he needs to make, we do not have the reality situation. The unit of the living human being is much more analogous to the pattern in a

---

[34] It is no easy task, of course, to determine what the "real situation" is at any given moment with a given person. In actual therapy, we generally make it a point to let the person talk "where he is," that is, about what is on his mind at that time. When he comes in and asks at the beginning of a session, "What shall I talk about today?" it is often very important that the therapist not give him a topic. His asking the therapist may well be a way of trying to get someone else to "take over," which tendency may be the problem underlying the particular symptom for which he came for therapy. If the therapist had suggested he talk about his "job problem," the real problem at that moment (e.g., evading responsibility) would have been covered by what was at that moment a pseudo-real topic. This oversimplified illustration also indicates the great importance of keeping the relationship between the subject and the therapist clear. This relationship is always to some degree a "real-life situation." (We are not forgetting the transference elements, but they cannot be seen clearly unless the real relationship is seen clearly also.) Often, for obvious reasons, the "real-life situation" involved in the way the subject relates to the other person in the room at that moment—the therapist—may be the best clue to his underlying problems. As a practical measure, I often remark, when the subject asks where he should begin, "All roads lead to Rome when one is discussing his problems—start with whatever is uppermost in your feelings now." It is demonstrably true that all roads do lead to Rome—i.e., the center of his particular "real situation" at that moment, and this is what we chiefly want to discover. These remarks are not meant to imply that the therapist never asks the subject questions or confronts him with issues: the old idea that the therapist was a lifeless mirror is as untrue in fact as it is unhealthy in practice. But when the therapist does confront with crucial issues, the important point to be observed is how the subject reacts. If the confrontation seems theoretical, academic, something to be "discussed" by the subject rather than tackled with affect, then the therapist did not pick the right time or else he made the confrontation inadequately. Furthermore, in letting the person talk at the point where he is, we do not mean to overlook the fact that some persons will talk as a defense against getting at real issues; and hence it is important to be able to tell whether the other person's talking is a real communication or something else—such as a method of exhibitionism, or a means of filling up time, etc.

painting or a musical composition than it is to the laws of Newtonian physics. A painting has meaning and beauty not because it is a tree plus a mountain plus some clouds, but because the objects and masses of color and forms have a significant relationship to each other. One cannot change the color tone of one item in the picture, strictly speaking, without all the others looking different; the significance is in the relationship, and to add or subtract an item changes not just that particular part but every other part of the picture as well. This point can likewise be illustrated in the use of mathematics in the Rorschach technique. Quantities have a given meaning because of their relationship to each other, that is, they have significance because of their existence in the total configuration. Two *CF*'s in one record may mean something quite different from the two *CF*'s in another record, or they may carry more weight than six or eight *CF*'s in another record. The meaning of the Rorschach is to be understood as a set of relationships which—if one has arrived at the correct interpretation—comprise a whole which has internal, logical consistency.[35]

Objectivity and the Personal Element.—In the approach to theory and research here recommended, how are we to attain *objectivity?* That is, how can we achieve the capacity to discover some truth which is not a product of our own prejudices and wishful thinking? Often the expression "rigorous theory" is used to refer to the traditional scientific approach, as though other methods were "loose" and the last resort of investigators who did not wish to make too much effort. True, the traditional mathematical scientific method, particularly in previous decades, was a great help in attaining objectivity. Tests of the quantity of tuberculosis bacilli in the patient's sputum, for example, were sound checks against the physician's wishful thinking with respect to whether the patient was getting better. But we wish here to propose that, with respect to the scientific understanding of human psychological problems, the traditional approach does not really lead to objectivity; and that the

---

[35] The point we are making is, as many readers will have seen, parallel to the mathematical field theories and the theories of relativity (i.e., one cannot define one variable except in constant reference to another) which characterize modern physical theory as contrasted with Newtonian physics. We do not make this analogy to modern physics in order to "sell" our emphasis above. There is no reason that psychology should take over a method because physics has found it useful—and, indeed, part of the trouble is that psychology has traditionally tried to take over its methods from other sciences. But we cite the above analogy to physics as refutation of those who still argue for a Newtonian method as the only "scientific" one in psychology. There is, however, one significant psychological point in the development of modern physics. Cantril (1950) points out that one element in the new physics is the realization that the subjective, personal element inevitably permeates all research. The physicist Percy Bridgman "argues that scientific research is an individual matter, that there is a 'private component' involved in all creative science" (*op. cit.,* p. 80). The physicist naturally turns to the psychologist to explain this subjective component, but finds all too often, unfortunately, that the psychologist is still modeling his concerns and research on the older concepts in physics which were based on the mistaken assumption that one could attain a pure objectivity.

approach proposed in this chapter, contrary to what one might expect, does make an objectivity possible.

The assumption in scientific research has been that if the personal element in the equation could be eliminated, if we could rule out all subjective factors or reduce them to figures which did not admit of diverse interpretations, then we would be "objective." Thus objectivity was thought to be the absence of subjectivity. This assumption underlies the convention in scientific writing that the personality of the author should so far as possible be excluded, that one should use the passive voice, as in such phrases as "it is said"; or, if the author must refer to himself, he should do it as if he were some abstract stranger with whom he has only a speaking acquaintance, and write "the present author believes...." It is as though the author's judgments or beliefs had nothing whatever to do with what he is writing—as though, indeed, the ideal scientist were like a superelectronic calculating machine. Of course the laudable motive behind these conventions was humility and a conviction that the truth is what is important, and therefore the experimenter and writer should be as much in the background as possible and should guard at every point against forcing their subjective concerns on the data. Actually, however, in the sciences of human nature, such an approach, if carried to any logical conclusion, results either in aridity or hypocrisy: aridity if the writer *does* succeed in ruling out all the living qualities of what he is trying to say, and hypocrisy if he does not rule them out but *pretends* that what he is saying is universal truth rather than his own modest endeavor to approximate the truth. It can be aggressively stated, against the dichotomy of our day, that for logical as well as practical reasons we can never arrive at pure objectivity if we divorce it from subjectivity. For, as illustrated earlier, we then tend to arrive more and more at a purely symbolic description of the problem, and at that point we end in pure subjectivity.[36]

The sound criteria for objectivity, in dealing with therapy, must be arrived at on another basis. We must get below the split between objectivity and subjectivity, which split is the real source of error. To that end, we propose this definition: *Objectivity is the capacity to affirm the growth and development of the other person (if one is doing therapy) or scientific truth (if one is doing research) as more important than one's own prejudices or needs or wishes.* It thus is not the opposite to subjectivity, but an attitude and way of behaving that arises from a level within one's experience which undercuts the dichotomy between objectivity and subjectivity. Objectivity in the last analysis is an ethical as well as a psychological quality—it is a characteristic of maturity of personality in the therapist (or experimenter) by which he becomes able, or as able as any human being can become, to transcend wishful thinking and *see* the situation he is confronting, be it the problems of someone else or a problem of scientific research, without distortion. On the psychological side, such objectivity presupposes a clarification of the therapist's

[36] Cf. footnote 27, page 30.

own neurotic tendencies to distort reality and his unconscious need to enforce his own will on the situation before him; and on the ethical side objectivity presupposes an overcoming of egocentricity and an honesty and humility in the sense we observed in Socrates.

To be objective, thus, means not to be *less* of a person in the sense of being *im*personal, or *dis*interested with respect to truth or human happiness and welfare (and to be disinterested at these points would indicate a highly dubious morality in the scientist); one cannot arrive at meaningful truth about persons by a method which in itself involves ruling out all personal elements. Objectivity consists rather of precisely becoming *more* of a person. It is parallel in science to what Albert Schweitzer (1911) finds in art, as he discusses Bach's music, "The art of the objective artist is not *impersonal* but *superpersonal.*" Objectivity is a quality of personality enlargement rather than personal truncation; it means taking the approach not of the question, "How can I *rule out* my own interests in dealing with this person's problems or this piece of research?" (which is a self-deluding aim anyway); but rather, "How can I sufficiently value the truth in the research problem or the potentialities in this other person that I can affirm them as much as my own interests?" Arriving at that kind of objectivity is obviously neither easy nor simple. As a matter of fact, it would be much easier to let our objectivity rest on methods of quantification, for it is not difficult to change one's opinion when the mathematical equation changes. But in dealing with human beings we cannot allow our mathematical equations to serve as a substitute for the difficult process of the development of personal integrity in the therapist that will make *him,* rather than his technique, objective.

The Ethical Aspect of Therapy.—A final practical implication is that value judgments and ethical standards are inextricably interwoven with the process and the goals of therapy. By "value judgments" we simply mean the conviction, for example, that it is better for the human being to expand in his capacities, to be free, to love, and to be happy than not to be and do these things. And we define ethics for the present purpose as the application of such value judgments to one's interpersonal relations—ethical behavior thus being ways of acting which affirm the growth, freedom, and happiness of others in the community as well as one's self.

The progress of psychoanalysis in the last decade could be judged, on one side, by the increasing recognition that it is an illusion for the analyst to suppose that he can avoid value judgments. This recognition is explicit, to mention only a few examples, in the writings of Fromm and Horney, and implicit in the work of Fromm-Reichmann, Kubie, Alexander, and French. Among the psychologists who are concerned with practicing or testing therapy, the same conclusion is being reached. In a very pertinent article on this point, Hunt (1949b) notes that it has been generally "claimed that values do not belong to the subject matter of science." He remarks that he endeavored to devise instruments for the measuring of therapeutic results which would not involve value judgments, and then he writes these significant words:

. . . but after over four years of work . . . I have reluctantly come to the conclusion that the scientist cannot avoid the value assumptions merely by deciding to do so. Precisely because casework and psychotherapy are directed toward helping people with their problems of adjustment and adaptation which involve value concepts, the instruments designed to measure the results in behavioral or situational change must inevitably take human values into account. I contend, therefore, that the theory of measuring instruments in this frontier area should be explicit not only about the fact that values are involved, but about *whose* values are taken into account in each instrument (p. 125).

The only question we would raise about Hunt's excellent statement is his curious use of the word "reluctantly" in the first sentence quoted above. It is as though those of us in the field of social science in the modern day still assume that it would be "better" if we did not have to make value assumptions, and as though the necessity to take "human values into account" is a kind of concession we have to make to the imperfections of knowledge and human nature. But is not our "reluctance" clearly a product of the Cartesian dichotomy of which we are heirs, and the particular compartmentalization of human experience which occurred in the nineteenth century as a final outworking of this dichotomy?[37] The long historical perspective is at this point a most persuasive corrective to our contemporary distortions: all through history until about the last seventy-five years it has been recognized that value judgments are a central aspect of an individual's interpersonal clarification. From Socrates and Isaiah down to Spinoza and Kierkegaard, it has been repeatedly stated that the problems of how a human being is to overcome hate, anxiety, and guilt and to achieve some psychological freedom and capacity to love and to use his power in creative productivity involve ethical attitudes and decisions. Our contemporary problem, therefore, is not merely that we must "bring back" value judgments into consideration, but rather to ask why we ever in the first place attempted to separate elements which are in reality inseparable. For, as is pointed out in the second section of this chapter, if therapists or social scientists endeavor to deal with a human being—who is of necessity continuously engaged in making decisions which affect his welfare as well as that of others—without taking into consideration the value judgments on which these decisions are based, they are dealing not with a living human being but an abstraction which has reality only in the subjective categories in the mind of the therapist or scientist.

The upshot of this discussion is not at all that there should be less emphasis on the specifically scientific techniques in therapy, but rather

[37] See discussion, page 38. One chief aspect, of course, of the compartmentalization in the nineteenth century was the endeavor to separate ethics from work and other aspects of daily life. Cf. May (1950*b*).

that these techniques can and should go hand in hand with a clarification of the value judgments and the ethical aspects of therapy. One of the most insidious illusions in much of the therapy of two and three decades ago was the supposed "neutrality" of the process of therapy on ethical questions, with the implication that it doesn't matter very much what value judgments the analysand or therapist makes. It was not seen that this attitude is actually not at all neutral but is based on a particular ethical viewpoint, namely that of a fairly complete relativism. Ethical and value judgments are inescapably present whenever one deals with living human beings. To try to suppress these judgments only tends to confuse the goals of the therapy or results inadvertently in the therapist's value judgments being impressed rigidly on the patient or produces a vapid and undynamic form of therapy.

The practical problem, therefore, is to be openly aware of the presence and significance of ethical aspects in therapy. By this open awareness, several pitfalls can be best avoided. First, the person in therapy can then find a sound basis for distinguishing neurotic guilt feelings from real guilt feelings, and he can thus avoid being blocked in his development by the former.[38] Secondly, the client or analysand need not fall into the pit of unconsciously taking over the superficial mores of his culture, which may not be productive of his best development. And third, the therapist is helped to realize that his particular value judgments and ethical standards are not absolute, and do not *ipso facto* constitute the universal goals of mankind's development. Just as the therapist can avoid projecting his own resentments, for example, into his relation with the subject by being aware of these resentments, so he can avoid projecting his particular ethical judgments on the patient only by being consciously aware of what his judgments are. Particular and specific forms of value judgment will, of course, vary with the diverse problems and configurations of different clients and analysands. Certain sexual actions may represent genuine and constructive values for one person and not for another; or, to learn to apply himself persistently in work may represent an important value for the passive individual, but for the compulsive person the capacity to say "no" to the demands of his work may be equally important as a specific value. We shall not endeavor here to go into the problem of the relation between immediate value judgments in a given culture and the long-term, underlying ethical meaning in human relations. Suffice it to say that the customary ethical relativism or authoritarian absolutism are not the only alternatives; there are the classical ethical traditions in Western history as well as in the history of other cultures, and there are the common needs of man in his human relations upon which we have much more light since the development of depth-psychological techniques. We suggest the problem of the relation of the various ethical approaches to psychotherapy as one of

[38] For discussions of the distinctions between neurotic and real (objective, constructive) guilt feelings, see Fromm (1947) and May (1950*b*).

great fruitfulness for future students of the field who can utilize the contemporary understanding of unconscious motivations.

It should be obvious in this discussion that we are not suggesting that explicit—and certainly not theoretical—discussions of ethics as such will come up in the therapeutic hour. After the initial agreement on the goals of therapy, it may well be that not much specific reference will be made to value judgments as such. We mean, rather, to emphasize that ethical aspects will always be part of the *presuppositions*, part of the context, of therapy, not only with respect to the goals of therapy but also with respect to the relation between the therapist and the other person. The therapist's aim, with regard to ethical standards, is to help the other person to remove distortions and the various forms of neurotic contradictions within himself that he may arrive at and choose freely the value judgments and ethical standards which are most constructive for him. This ability to be a "midwife," to use Socrates' word, is not easy of attainment, and it can well be a goal toward which a therapist works in his own development year in and year out. As Kierkegaard remarked about Socrates, "how rare the magnanimity" of a helper who can be sufficiently concerned with the other person's self-realization and sufficiently free of his own need to dominate that he is willing to be merely an "occasion" for the other's achievement of his own values.

CHAPTER 2

SOME DIRECTIONS AND END POINTS IN THERAPY

By CARL R. ROGERS, Ph.D.

The process of psychotherapy, as we have come to know it from a client-centered orientation, is a unique and dynamic experience, different for each individual, yet exhibiting a lawfulness and order which are astonishing in their generality. As I have become increasingly impressed by the inevitability of many aspects of this process, I have lost interest in the type of questions which are so commonly raised in regard to it: "Will it cure a compulsion neurosis?" "Do you claim that it will erase a basic psychotic condition?" "Is it suitable for dealing with marital problems?" "Does it apply to stutterers or homosexuals?" "Are the cures permanent?" These questions, and others like them, are understandable and legitimate. They are, however, it seems to me, the wrong questions to ask if we are trying to further a deep knowledge of what psychotherapy is or what it may accomplish. In this chapter I should like to ask what appears to me a sounder question in regard to this fascinating and lawful process we term therapy and to attempt a partial answer.

Let me introduce my question in this way. Whether by chance, by insight into personality, by scientific knowledge, by artistry in human relationships, or by a combination of all these elements, we have learned how to initiate a describable process, which appears to have a core of sequential, orderly events and which tends to be similar from one client to another. We know at least something of the attitudinal conditions for getting this process under way. We know that if the therapist holds within himself attitudes of deep respect and full acceptance for this client as he is, and similar attitudes toward the client's potentialities for dealing with himself and his situations; if these attitudes are suffused with a sufficient warmth, which transforms them into the most profound type of liking or affection for the core of the person; and if a level of communication is reached so that the client can begin to perceive that the therapist understands the feelings he is experiencing and accepts him at the full depth of that understanding, then we may be sure that the process is already initiated. Then, instead of trying to insist that this process serve the ends we have in mind (no matter how laudable those goals may be), let us ask the only question by which science can genuinely be advanced. This question is: "What is the nature of this process, what seem to be its inherent characteristics, what direction or

44

directions does it take, and what, if any, are the natural end points of the process?" When Benjamin Franklin observed the spark coming from the key on his kite-string, he did not, fortunately, fall under the spell of its immediate and practical uses. Instead he began to inquire into the basic process which made such a phenomenon possible. Though many of the answers which were put forward were full of specific errors, the search was fruitful, because the right question was being asked. Thus I am making a plea that we ask the same question of psychotherapy, and ask it with open mind—that we endeavor to describe, study, and understand the basic process which underlies therapy, rather than attempt to warp that process to fit our clinical needs or our preconceived dogma or the evidence from some other field. Let us patiently examine it for what it *is*, in *itself*.

I have recently made an attempt to begin such a description of client-centered therapy.[1] I will not repeat this description here, except to say that from the clinical and research evidence there seem to emerge certain persistent characteristics in the process: the increase in insightful statements, in maturity of reported behavior, in positive attitudes, as therapy progresses; the changes in perception of, and acceptance of, the self; the incorporation of previously denied experience into the self-structure; the shift in the locus of evaluation from outside to inside the self; the changes in the therapeutic relationship; and characteristic changes in personality structure, in behavior, and in physiological condition. Faulty as some of these descriptions may prove to be, they are an attempt to understand the process of client-centered therapy in its own terms, as revealed in clinical experience, in electrically recorded verbatim cases, and in the forty or more research studies which have been completed in this area.

My purpose in this chapter is to push out beyond this material and to formulate certain trends in therapy which have received less emphasis. I should like to describe some of the directions and end points which appear to be inherent in the therapeutic process. We have only recently begun to discern these phenomena with any clarity, but they appear to us to be significant learnings, despite the fact that research on them is, as yet, nonexistent. In an attempt to convey meanings more adequately, I shall use illustrative material from recorded interviews, largely from one case. I shall also limit my discussion to the process of client-centered therapy, since I have reluctantly come to concede the possibility that the process, directions, and end points of therapy may differ in different therapeutic orientations.

[1] See chap. IV, "The Process of Therapy," in my book, *Client-centered therapy* (Rogers,* 1951b).

* References are to the bibliography at the back of the book.

The Experiencing of the Self (or Potential Self)

One aspect of the process of therapy which is evident in all cases might be termed the awareness of experience, or even "the experiencing of experience." I have here labeled it as the experiencing of the self, though this also falls short of being an accurate term. In the security of the relationship with a client-centered therapist, in the absence of any actual or implied threat to self, the client can let himself examine various aspects of his experience as they actually feel to him, as they are apprehended through his sensory and visceral equipment, without distorting them to fit the existing concept of self. Many of these prove to be in extreme contradiction to the concept of self, and they could not ordinarily be experienced in their fullness, but in this safe relationship they can be permitted to seep through into awareness without distortion. Thus they often follow this schematic pattern: "I am thus and so, but I experience this feeling which is very inconsistent with what I am." "I love my parents, but I experience some surprising bitterness toward them at times." "I am really no good, but sometimes I seem to feel that I'm better than everyone else." Thus at first the expression is, "I am a self which is different from a part of my experience." Later this changes to the tentative pattern, "Perhaps I am several very different selves, or perhaps my self contains more contradictions than I had dreamed." Still later the pattern changes to some such pattern as this, "I was sure that I could not be my experience—it was too contradictory—but now I am beginning to believe that I can be *all* of my experience."

Perhaps something of the nature of this aspect of therapy may be conveyed from two excerpts from the case of Mrs. O. Mrs. O. was a housewife in her late thirties, who was having difficulties in marital and family relationships when she came in for therapy. Unlike many clients, she had a keen and spontaneous interest in the processes which she felt going on within herself, and her recorded interviews contain much material, from her own frame of reference, as to her perception of what was occurring. She thus tends to put into words what seems to be implicit, but unverbalized, in many clients. For this reason, most of the excerpts in this chapter will be taken from this one case.

From an early portion of the fifth interview comes material which describes the awareness of experience which we have been discussing.

C.:[2] It all comes pretty vague. But you know I keep, keep having the thought occur to me that this whole process for me is kind of like examining pieces of a jigsaw puzzle. It seems to me I, I'm in the process now of examining the individual pieces which really don't have too much meaning. Probably handling them, not even beginning to think of a pattern. That keeps coming to me. And it's interesting to me because I, I really don't like jigsaw puzzles. They've always irritated me. But that's my feeling. And I mean I pick up little

[2] In these excerpts, C. stands for client, T. for therapist.

pieces [she gestures throughout this conversation to illustrate her statements] with absolutely no meaning except I mean the, the feeling that you get from simply handling them without seeing them as a pattern, but just from the touch, I probably feel, well it is going to fit some place here.

T.: And that at the moment that, that's the process, just getting the feel and the shape and the configuration of the different pieces with a little bit of background feeling of, yeah they'll probably fit somewhere, but most of the attention's focused right on, "What does this feel like? And what's its texture?"

C.: That's right. There's almost something physical in it. A, a—

T.: You can't quite describe it without using your hands. A real, almost a sensuous sense in—

C.: That's right. Again it's, it's a feeling of being very objective, and yet I've never been quite so close to myself.

T.: Almost at one and the same time standing off and looking at yourself and yet somehow being closer to yourself that way than—

C.: M-hm. And yet for the first time in months I am not thinking about my problems. I'm not actually, I'm not working on them.

T.: I get the impression you don't sort of sit down to work on "my problems." It isn't that feeling at all.

C.: That's right. That's right. I suppose what I, I mean actually is that I'm not sitting down to put this puzzle together as, as something, I've got to see the picture. It, it may be that, it may be that I am actually enjoying this feeling process. Or I'm certainly learning something.

T.: At least there's a sense of the immediate goal of getting that feel as being the thing, not that you're doing this in order to see a picture, but that it's a, a satisfaction of really getting acquainted with each piece. Is that—

C.: That's it. That's it. And it still becomes that sort of sensuousness, that touching. It's quite interesting. Sometimes not entirely pleasant, I'm sure, but—

T.: A rather different sort of experience.

C.: Yes. Quite.

This excerpt indicates very clearly the letting of material come into awareness, without any attempt to own it as part of the self or to relate it to other material held in consciousness. It is, to put it as accurately as possible, an awareness of a wide range of experiences, with, at the moment, no thought of their relation to self. Later it may be recognized that what was being experienced may all become a part of self.

The fact that this is a new and unusual form of experience is expressed in a verbally confused but emotionally clear portion of the sixth interview.

C.: Uh, I caught myself thinking that during these sessions, uh, I've been sort of singing a song. Now that sounds vague and uh—not actually singing—sort of a song without any music. Probably a kind of poem coming out. And I like the idea, I mean it's just sort of come to me without anything built out of, of anything. And in—following that, it came, it came this other kind of feeling. Well, I found myself sort of asking myself, is that the shape that cases take? Is it possible that I am just verbalizing and, and at times kind of become intoxicated with my own verbalizations? And then uh, following this, came, well, am I just taking up your time? And then a doubt, a doubt. Then something else occurred to me. Uh, from whence it came, I don't know, no actual logical kind of sequence to the thinking. The thought struck me: We're doing bits, uh, we're not overwhelmed or doubtful, or we can show concern or, or any great interest when, when blind people learn to read with their fingers, Braille. I don't know—it may be just sort of, it's all mixed up. It may be that's something that I'm experiencing now.

T.: Let's see if I can get some of that, that sequence of feelings. First, sort of as though you're, and I gather that first one is a fairly positive feeling, as though maybe you're kind of creating a poem here—a song without music somehow but something that might be quite creative, and then the, the feeling of a lot of skepticism about that. "Maybe I'm just saying words, just being carried off by words that I, that I speak, and maybe it's all a lot of baloney, really." And then a feeling that perhaps you're almost learning a new type of experiencing which would be just as radically new as for a blind person to try to make sense out of what he feels with his fingertips.

C.: M-hm. M-hm. [Pause.] . . . And I sometimes think to myself, well, maybe we could go into this particular incident or that particular incident. And then somehow when I come here, there is, that doesn't hold true, it's, it seems false. And then there just seems to be this flow of words which somehow aren't forced, and then occasionally this doubt creeps in. Well, it sort of takes form of a, maybe you're just making music. . . . Perhaps that's why I'm doubtful today of, of this whole thing, because it's something that's not forced. And really I'm feeling that what I should do is, is sort of systematize the thing. Oughta work harder and—

T.: Sort of a deep questioning as to what am I doing with a self that isn't, isn't pushing to get things *done, solved?* [Pause.]

C.: And yet the fact that I, I really like this other kind of thing, this, I don't know, call it a poignant feeling, I mean—I felt things that I never felt before. I *like* that, too. Maybe that's the way to do it. I just don't know today.

Here is the shift which seems almost invariably to occur in therapy which has any depth. It may be represented schematically as the client's feeling that, "I came here to solve problems, and now I find myself just experiencing myself." And as with this client this shift is usually accompanied by the intellectual formulation that it is wrong, and by an emotional appreciation of the fact that it "feels good."

We may conclude this section by saying that one of the fundamental directions taken by the process of therapy is the free experiencing of the actual sensory and visceral reactions of the organism without too much of an attempt to relate these experiences to the self. This is usually accompanied by the conviction that this material does not belong to, and cannot be organized into, the self. The end point of this process is that the client discovers that he can *be* his experience, with all of its variety and surface contradiction; that he can formulate himself out of his experience, instead of trying to impose a formulation of self upon his experience, denying to awareness those elements which do not fit.

The Full Experiencing of an Affectional Relationship

One of the elements in therapy of which we have more recently become aware is the extent to which therapy is a learning, on the part of the client, to accept fully and freely and without fear the positive feelings of another. This is not a phenomenon which clearly occurs in every case. It seems particularly true of our longer cases, but it does not occur uniformly in these. Yet it is such a deep experience that we have begun to question whether it is not a highly significant direction in the therapeutic process, perhaps occurring at an unverbalized level to some degree in all successful cases. Before discussing this phenomenon, let us give it some body by citing the experience of Mrs. O. The experience struck her rather suddenly, between the twenty-ninth and thirtieth interview, and she spent most of the latter interview discussing it. She opens the thirtieth hour in this way:

C.: Well, I made a very remarkable discovery. I know it's—[laughs] I found out that you actually *care* how this thing goes. [Both laugh.] It gave me the feeling, it's sort of well—"maybe I'll let you get in the act," sort of thing. It's—again you see, on an examination sheet, I would have had the correct answer, I mean—but it suddenly dawned on me that in the—client-counselor kind of thing, you *actually care* what happens to this thing. And it was a revelation, a—not that. That doesn't describe it. It was a—well, the closest I can come to it is a kind of relaxation, a—not a letting down, but a— [pause] more of a straightening out without tension if that means anything. I don't know.

T.: Sounds as though it isn't as though this was a new idea, but it was a new *experience* of really *feeling* that I did care and if I get the rest of that, sort of a willingness on your part to let me care.

C.: Yes.

This letting the counselor and his warm interest into her life was undoubtedly one of the deepest features of therapy in this case. In an interview following the conclusion of therapy, she spontaneously mentioned this experience as being the outstanding one. What does it mean?

The phenomenon is most certainly not one of transference and countertransference. Some experienced psychologists who had undergone psychoanalysis had the opportunity of observing the development of the relationship in a case other than the one cited. They were the first to object to the use of the terms "transference" and "countertransference" to describe the phenomenon. The gist of their remarks was that this is something which is mutual and appropriate, while transference and countertransference are phenomena which are characteristically one-way and inappropriate to the realities of the situation.

Certainly one reason why this phenomenon is occurring more frequently in our experience is that as therapists we have become less afraid of our positive (or negative) feelings toward the client. As therapy goes on, the therapist's feeling of acceptance and respect for the client tends to change to something approaching awe as he sees the valiant and deep struggle of the person to be himself. There is, I think, within the therapist, a profound experience of the underlying commonality— should we say brotherhood—of man. As a result he feels toward the client a warm, positive, affectional reaction. This poses a problem for the client, who often, as in this case, finds it difficult to accept the positive feeling of another. Yet, once accepted, the inevitable reaction on the part of the client is to relax, to let the warmth of liking by another person reduce the tension and fear involved in facing life.

But we are getting ahead of our client. Let us examine some of the other aspects of this experience as it occurred to her. In earlier interviews she had talked of the fact that she did *not* love humanity, and that in some vague and stubborn way she felt she was right, even though others would regard her as wrong. She mentions this again as she discusses the way this experience has clarified her attitudes toward others.

C.: The next thing that occurred to me that I found myself thinking and still thinking, is somehow—and I'm not clear why—the same kind of a caring that I get when I say "I don't love humanity." Which has always sort of—I mean I was always convinced of it. So I mean, it doesn't—I knew that it was a good thing, see. And I think I clarified it within myself—what it has to do with this situation, I don't know. But I found out, no, I don't love. but I do *care* terribly.

T.: M-hm. M-hm. I see. . . .

C.: . . . It might be expressed better in saying I care terribly what happens. But the caring is a—takes form—its structure is in understanding and not wanting to be taken in, or to contribute to those things which I feel are false and—It seems to me that in—in loving, there's a kind of *final* factor. If you do that, you've sort of done *enough*. It's a—

T.: That's *it,* sort of.

C.: Yeah. It seems to me this other thing, this caring, which isn't a good term—I mean, probably we need something else to describe this kind of thing. To say it's an impersonal thing doesn't mean anything because it isn't impersonal. I mean I feel it's very much a part of a whole. But it's something that somehow doesn't stop. . . . It seems to me you could have this feeling of loving humanity, loving people, and at the same time—go on contributing to the factors that make people neurotic, make them ill—where, what I feel is a resistance to those things.

T.: You care enough to want to understand and to want to avoid contributing to anything that would make for more neuroticism, or more of that aspect in human life.

C.: Yes. And it's—[pause]. Yes, it's something along those lines. . . . Well, again, I have to go back to how I feel about this other thing. It's—I'm not really called upon to give of myself in a—sort of on the auction block. There's nothing final. . . . It sometimes bothered me when I—I would have to say to myself, "I don't love humanity," and yet, I always knew that there was something positive. That I was probably right. And—I may be all off the beam now, but it seems to me that, that is somehow tied up in the—this feeling that I—I have now, into how the therapeutic value can carry through. Now, I couldn't tie it up, I couldn't tie it in, but it's as close as I can come to explaining to myself, my—well, shall I say the learning process, the follow-through on my realization that— yes, you *do care* in a given situation. It's just that simple. And I hadn't been aware of it before. I might have closed this door and walked out, and in discussing therapy, said, yes, the counselor must feel thus and so, but, I mean, I hadn't had the dynamic experience.

In this portion, though she is struggling to describe her own feeling, it would seem that what she is saying would be characteristic of the therapist's attitude toward the client as well. His attitude, at its best, is devoid of the *quid pro quo* aspect of most of the experiences we call love. It is the simple outgoing human feeling of one individual for another, a feeling, it seems to me, which is even more basic than sexual or parental feeling. It is a caring enough about the person that you do not wish to interfere with his development, nor to use him for any self-aggrandizing goals of your own. Your satisfaction comes in having set him free to grow in his own fashion.

Our client goes on to discuss how hard it has been for her in the past to accept any help or positive feeling from others, **and how** this attitude is changing:

C.: I have a feeling . . . that you have to do it pretty much yourself, but that somehow you ought to be able to do that with other people. [She mentions that there have been "countless" times when she

might have accepted personal warmth and kindliness from others.]
I get the feeling that I just was afraid I would be devastated. [She
returns to talking about the counseling itself and her feeling toward
it.] I mean there's been this tearing through the thing myself.
Almost to—I mean, I felt it—I mean I tried to verbalize it on occasion—a kind of—at times almost not wanting you to restate, not
wanting you to reflect, the thing is *mine*. Course, all right, I can say
it's resistance. But that doesn't mean a damn thing to me now. . . .
The—I think in—in relationship to this particular thing, I mean, the
—probably at times, the strongest feeling was, it's mine, it's *mine*.
I've got to cut it down myself. See?

T.: It's an experience that's awfully hard to put down accurately into
words, and yet I get a sense of difference here in this relationship,
that from the feeling that "this is mine," "I've got to do it," "I am
doing it" and so on, to a somewhat different feeling that—"I could let
you in."

C.: Yeah. Now. I mean, that's—that it's—well, it's sort of, shall we
say, volume two. It's—it's a—well, sort of, well, I'm still in the
thing alone, but I'm *not*—see—I'm—

T.: M-hm. Yes, that paradox sort of sums it up, doesn't it?

C.: Yeah.

T.: In all of this, there is a feeling, it's still—every aspect of my experience is mine and that's kind of inevitable and necessary and so
on. And yet that isn't the whole picture either. Somehow it can be
shared or another's interest can come in and in some ways it is new.

C.: Yeah. And it's—it is though, that's how it should be. I mean,
that's how it—has to be. There's a—there's a feeling, "and this is
good." I mean, it expresses, it clarifies it for me. There's a feeling—
in this caring, as though—you were sort of standing back—standing
off, and if I want to sort of cut through to the thing, it's a—a slash-
ing of—oh, tall weeds, that I can do it, and you can—I mean, you're
not going to be disturbed by having to walk through it too. I don't
know. And it doesn't make sense. I mean—

T.: Except there's a very real sense of rightness about this feeling that
you have, hm?

C.: M-hm.

May it not be that this excerpt portrays the heart of the process of
socialization? To discover that it is *not* devastating to accept the positive
feeling from another, that it does not necessarily end in hurt, that it
actually "feels good" to have another person with you in your struggles
to meet life—this may be one of the most profound learnings encountered
by the individual, whether in therapy or not.

Something of the newness, the nonverbal level of this experience is
described by Mrs. O. in the closing moments of this thirtieth interview:

C.: I'm experiencing a new type, a—probably the only worth-while kind of learning, a—I know I've—I've often said what I know doesn't help me here. What I meant is, my acquired knowledge doesn't help me. But it seems to me that the learning process here has been—so dynamic, I mean, so much a part of the—of everything, I mean, of me, that if I just get that out of it, it's something, which, I mean—I'm wondering if I'll ever be able to straighten out into a sort of acquired knowledge what I have experienced here.

T.: In other words, the kind of learning that has gone on here has been something of quite a different sort and quite a different depth; very vital, very real. And quite worth while to you in and of itself, but the question you're asking is: Will I ever have a clear intellectual picture of what has gone on at this somehow deeper kind of learning level?

C.: M-hm. Something like that.

Those who would apply to therapy the so-called laws of learning derived from the memorization of nonsense syllables would do well to study this excerpt with care. Learning as it takes place in therapy is a total, organismic, frequently nonverbal type of thing which may or may not follow the same principles as the intellectual learning of trivial material which has little relevance to the self. This, however, is a digression.

Let us conclude this section by rephrasing its essence. It appears possible that one of the characteristics of deep or significant therapy is that the client discovers that it is not devastating to admit fully into his own experience the positive feeling which another, the therapist, holds toward him. Perhaps one of the reasons why this is so difficult is that essentially it involves the feeling that "I am worthy of being liked." This we shall consider in the following section. For the present it may be pointed out that this aspect of therapy is a free and full experiencing of an affectional relationship which may be put in generalized terms as follows: "I can permit someone to care about me, and can fully accept that caring within myself. This permits me to recognize that I care, and care deeply, for and about others."

The Liking of One's Self

In various writings and researches that have been published regarding client-centered therapy, there has been a stress upon the acceptance of self as one of the directions and outcomes of therapy. We have established the fact that in successful psychotherapy negative attitudes toward the self decrease and positive attitudes increase. We have measured the gradual increase in self-acceptance and have studied the correlated increase in acceptance of others. But as I examine these statements and compare them with our more recent cases, I feel they fall short of the truth. The client not only accepts himself—a phrase which may carry

the connotation of a grudging and reluctant acceptance of the inevitable—
he actually comes to *like* himself. This is not a bragging or self-assertive
liking; it is rather a quiet pleasure in being one's self.

Mrs. O. illustrates this trend rather nicely in her thirty-third interview.
Is it significant that this follows by ten days the interview where she
could for the first time admit to herself that the therapist cared? Whatever our speculations on this point, this fragment indicates very well the
quiet joy in being one's self, together with the apologetic attitude which,
in our culture, one feels it is necessary to take toward such an experience. In the last few minutes of the interview, knowing her time is
nearly up she says:

C.: One thing worries me—and I'll hurry because I can always go back
to it—a feeling that occasionally I can't turn out. Feeling of being
quite pleased with myself. Again the Q technique.[3] I walked out
of here one time, and impulsively I threw my first card, "I am an
attractive personality"; looked at it sort of aghast but left it there, I
mean, because honestly, I mean, that is exactly how it felt—a—well,
that bothered me and I catch that now. Every once in a while a sort
of pleased feeling, nothing superior, but just—I don't know, sort of
pleased. A neatly turned way. And it bothered me. And yet—I
wonder—I rarely remember things I say here, I mean I wondered
why it was that I was convinced, and something about what I've felt
about being hurt that I suspected in—my feelings when I would hear
someone say to a child, "Don't cry." I mean, I always felt, but it
isn't right; I mean, if he's hurt, let him cry. Well, then, now this
pleased feeling that I have. I've recently come to feel it's—there's
something almost the same there. It's—We don't object when *children* feel pleased with themselves. It's—I mean, there really isn't
anything vain. It's—maybe that's how people *should* feel.

T.: You've been inclined almost to look askance at yourself for this
feeling, and yet as you think about it more, maybe it comes close to
the two sides of the picture, that if a child wants to cry, why shouldn't
he cry? and if he wants to feel pleased with himself, doesn't he have a
perfect right to feel pleased with himself? And that sort of ties in
with this, what I would see as an appreciation of yourself that you've
experienced every now and again.

C.: Yes. Yes.

T.: "I'm really a pretty rich and interesting person."

C.: Something like that. And then I say to myself, "Our society pushes
us around and we've lost it." And I keep going back to my feelings

[3] This portion needs explanation. As part of a research study by another staff
member, this client had been asked several times during therapy to sort a large
group of cards, each containing a self-descriptive phrase, in such a way as to portray
her own self. At one end of the sorting she was to place the card or cards most
like herself, and at the other end, those most unlike herself. Thus when she says
that she put as the first card "I am an attractive personality," it means that she
regarded this as the item most characteristic of herself.

about children. Well, maybe they're richer than we are. Maybe we
—it's something we've lost in the process of growing up.

T.: Could be that they have a wisdom about that that we've lost.

C.: That's right. My time's up.

Here she arrives, as do so many other clients, at the tentative, slightly
apologetic realization that she has come to like, enjoy, appreciate herself.
One gets the feeling of a spontaneous relaxed enjoyment, a primitive
joie de vivre, perhaps analogous to that of the lamb frisking about the
meadow or the porpoise gracefully leaping in and out of the waves.
Mrs. O. feels that it is something native to the organism, to the infant,
something we have lost in the warping process of development.

Earlier in this case one sees something of a forerunner of this feeling,
an incident which perhaps makes more clear its fundamental nature. In
the ninth interview Mrs. O. in a somewhat embarrassed fashion reveals
something she has always kept to herself. That she brought it forth at
some cost is indicated by the fact that it was preceded by a very long
pause, of several minutes' duration. Then she spoke.

C.: You know this is kind of goofy, but I've never told anyone this
     [nervous laugh] and it'll probably do me good. For years, oh, prob-
     ably from early youth, from seventeen probably on, I, I have had
     what I have come to call to myself, told myself were "flashes of
     sanity." I've never told anyone this [another embarrassed laugh]
     wherein, in, really I feel sane. And, and pretty much aware of life.
     And always with a terrific kind of concern and sadness of how far
     away, how far astray that we have actually gone. It's just a feeling
     once in a while of finding myself a whole kind of person in a terribly
     chaotic kind of world.

T.: It's been fleeting and it's been infrequent, but there have been times
     when it seems the whole you is functioning and feeling in the world, a
     very chaotic world to be sure—

C.: That's right. And I mean, and knowing actually how far astray
     we, we've gone from, from being whole healthy people. And of
     course one doesn't talk in those terms.

T.: A feeling that it wouldn't be *safe* to talk about the singing you [4]—

C.: Where does that person live?

T.: Almost as if there was no place for such a person to, to exist.

C.: Of course, you know, that, that makes me—now wait a minute—
     that probably explains why I'm primarily concerned with feelings
     here. That's probably it.

T.: Because that whole you does exist with all your feelings. Is that
     it, you're more aware of feelings?

[4] The therapist's reference is to her statement in a previous interview that in
therapy she was singing a song.

C.: That's right. It's not, it doesn't reject feelings and—that's *it*.

T.: That whole you somehow lives feelings instead of somehow pushing them to one side.

C.: That's right. [Pause.] I suppose from the practical point of view it could be said that what I ought to be doing is solving some problems, day-to-day problems. And yet, I, I—what I'm trying to do is solve, solve something else that's a great, that is a great deal more important than little day-to-day problems. Maybe that sums up the whole thing.

T.: I wonder if this will distort your meaning, that from a hard-headed point of view you ought to be spending time thinking through specific problems. But you wonder if perhaps maybe you aren't on a quest for this whole you and perhaps that's more important than a solution to the day-to-day problems.

C.: I think that's it. I think that's it. That's probably what I mean.

If we may legitimately put together these two experiences, and if we are justified in regarding them as typical, then we may say that both in therapy and in some fleeting experiences throughout her previous life, she has experienced a healthy satisfying enjoyable appreciation of herself as a whole and functioning creature; and that this experience occurs when she does not reject her feelings but lives them.

Here it seems to me is an important and often overlooked truth about the therapeutic process. It works in the direction of permitting the person to experience fully, and in awareness, all his reactions, including his feelings and emotions. As this occurs, the individual feels a positive liking for himself, a genuine appreciation of himself as a total functioning unit, which is one of the important end points of therapy.

The Discovery That the Core of Personality Is Positive

One of the most revolutionary concepts to grow out of our clinical experience is the growing recognition that the innermost core of man's nature, the deepest layers of his personality, the base of his "animal nature," is positive in character—is basically socialized, forward-moving, rational, and realistic.

This point of view is so foreign to our present culture that I do not expect it to be accepted, and it is indeed so revolutionary in its implications that it should not be accepted without thoroughgoing inquiry. But even if it should stand these tests, it will be difficult to accept. Religion, especially the Christian religion, has permeated our culture with the concept that man is basically sinful and that only by something approaching a miracle can his sinful nature be negated. In psychology, Freud and his followers have presented convincing arguments that the id, man's basic and unconscious nature, is primarily made up of instincts which would, if permitted expression, result in incest, murder, and other crimes. The whole problem of therapy, as seen by this group, is how to hold these untamed forces in check in a wholesome and constructive manner, rather than in the costly fashion of the neurotic. But the fact that at heart man is irrational, unsocialized, and destructive of others and self—this is a concept accepted almost without question. To be sure there are occasional voices of protest. Maslow (1949) puts up a vigorous case for man's animal nature, pointing out that the antisocial emotions—hostility, jealousy, etc.,—result from frustration of more basic impulses for love and security and belonging, which are in themselves desirable. And Ashley-Montagu (1950) likewise develops the thesis that cooperation, rather than struggle, is the basic law of human life. But these solitary voices are little heard. On the whole the viewpoint of the professional worker as well as the layman is that man as he *is*, in his basic nature, had best be kept under control or under cover or both.

As I look back over my years of clinical experience and research, it seems to me that I have been very slow to recognize the falseness of this popular and professional concept. The reason, I believe, lies in the fact that in therapy there are continually being uncovered hostile and anti-social feelings, so that it is easy to assume that this indicates the basic nature of man. Only slowly has it become evident that these untamed and unsocial feelings are neither the deepest nor the strongest, and that the inner core of man's personality is the organism itself, which is essen-tially both self-preserving and social.

To give more specific meaning to this argument, let me turn again to the case of Mrs. O. Since the point is an important one, I shall quote at some length from the recorded case to illustrate the type of ex-perience on which I have based the foregoing statements. Perhaps the excerpts can illustrate the opening-up of layer after layer of personality until we come to the deepest elements.

It is in the eighth interview that Mrs. O. rolls back the first layer of defense, and discovers a bitterness and desire for revenge underneath.

C.: You know over in this area of, of sexual disturbance, I have a feel-ing that I'm beginning to discover that it's pretty bad, pretty bad. I'm finding out that, that I'm bitter, really. Damn bitter. I—and I'm not turning it back in, into myself. . . . I think what I probably feel is a certain element of "I've been cheated." [Her voice is very tight and her throat chokes up.] And I've covered up very nicely, to the point of consciously not caring. But I'm, I'm sort of amazed to find that in this practice of, what shall I call it, a kind of sublimation that right under it again words—there's a, a kind of passive force that's, it's pas—it's very passive, but at the same time it's just kind of *murderous*.

T.: So there's the feeling, "I've really been cheated. I've covered that up and seem not to care and yet underneath that there's a kind of a, a latent but very much present *bitterness* that is very, very strong."

C.: It's very strong. I—that I know. It's terribly powerful.

T.: Almost a dominating kind of force.

C.: Of which I am rarely conscious. Almost never. . . . Well, the only way I can describe it, it's a kind of murderous thing, but without violence. . . . It's more like a feeling of wanting to get even. . . . And of course I won't pay back, but I'd like to. I really would like to.

Up to this point the usual explanation seems to fit perfectly. Mrs. O. has been able to look beneath the socially controlled surface of her behavior, and she finds underneath a murderous feeling of hatred and a desire to get even. This is as far as she goes in exploring this particular feeling until considerably later in therapy. She picks up the theme in the thirty-first interview. She has had a hard time getting under way, feels emotionally blocked, and cannot get at the feeling which is welling up in her.

C.: I have the feeling it isn't guilt. [Pause. She weeps.] Of course I mean, I can't verbalize it yet. [Then with a rush of emotion.] It's just being *terribly hurt!*

T.: M-hm. It isn't guilt except in the sense of being very much wounded somehow.

C.: [Weeping.] It's—you know, often I've been guilty of it myself, but in later years when I've heard parents say to their children, "stop crying," I've had a feeling, a hurt as though, well, why should they tell them to stop crying? They feel sorry for themselves, and who can feel more adequately sorry for himself than the child. Well, that is sort of what—I mean, as though I mean, I thought that they should let him cry. And—feel sorry for him too, maybe. In a rather objective kind of way. Well, that's—that's something of the kind of thing I've been experiencing. I mean, now—just right now. And in—in—

T.: That catches a little more the flavor of the feeling that it's almost as if you're really weeping for yourself.

C.: Yeah. And again you see there's conflict. Our culture is such that —I mean, one doesn't indulge in self-pity. But this isn't—I mean, I feel it doesn't quite have that connotation. It may have.

T.: Sort of think that there is a cultural objection to feeling sorry about yourself. And yet you feel the feeling you're experiencing isn't quite what the culture objected to either.

C.: And then of course, I've come to—to see and to feel that over this— see, I've covered it up. [Weeps.] But I've covered it up with so much *bitterness*, which in turn I had to cover up. [Weeping.] *That's* what I want to get rid of! I almost don't *care* if I hurt.

T.: [Softly, and with an empathic tenderness toward the hurt she is experiencing.] You feel that here, at the basis of it as you experience it, is a feeling of real tears for yourself. But *that* you can't show, mustn't show, so that's been covered by bitterness that you don't like, that you'd like to be rid of. You almost feel you'd rather absorb the hurt than to—than to feel the bitterness. [Pause.] And what you seem to be saying quite strongly is, I do *hurt*, and I've tried to cover it up.

C.: I didn't *know* it.

T.: M-hm. Like a new discovery really.

C.: [Speaking at the same time.] I never really did know. But it's—you know, it's almost a physical thing. It's—it's sort of as though I were looking within myself at all kinds of—nerve endings and bits of things that have been sort of mashed. [Weeping.]

T.: As though some of the most delicate aspects of you physically almost have been crushed or hurt.

C.: Yes. And you know, I do get the feeling, "Oh, you poor thing." [Pause.]

T.: Just can't help but feel very deeply sorry for the person that is you.

C.: I don't think I feel sorry for the whole person; it's a certain aspect of the thing.

T.: Sorry to see that hurt.

C.: Yeah.

T.: M-hm. M-hm.

C.: And then of course there's this damn bitterness that I want to get rid of. It's—it gets me into trouble. It's because it's a tricky thing. It tricks me. [Pause.]

T.: Feel as though that bitterness is something you'd like to be rid of because it doesn't do right by you.

C.: [Weeps. Long pause.] I don't know. It seems to me that I'm right in feeling, what in the world good would it do to term this thing guilt. To chase down things that would give me an interesting case history, shall we say. What *good* would it do? It seems to me that the—that the key, the real thing is in this feeling that I have.

T.: You could track down some tag or other and could make quite a pursuit of that, but you feel as though the core of the whole thing is the kind of experience that you're just having right here.

C.: That's right. I mean if—I don't know what'll happen to the feeling. Maybe nothing. I don't know, but it seems to me that whatever understanding I'm to have is a part of this feeling of hurt, of—it doesn't matter much what it's called. [Pause.] Then I—one can't go—around with a hurt so openly exposed. I mean this seems to me that somehow the next process has to be a kind of healing.

T.: Seems as though you couldn't possibly expose yourself if part of yourself is so hurt, so you wonder if somehow the hurt mustn't be healed first. [Pause.]

C.: And yet, you know, it's—it's a funny thing. [Pause.] It sounds like a statement of complete confusion or the old saw that the neurotic doesn't want to give up their symptoms. But that isn't true. I mean, that isn't true here, but it's—I can just hope that this will impart what I feel. I somehow don't mind being hurt. I mean, it's just occurred to me that I don't mind terribly. It's a—I mind more the—the feeling of bitterness which is, I know, the cause of this frustration, I mean the—I somehow mind that more.

T.: Would this get it? That, though you don't like the hurt, yet you feel you can accept that. That's bearable. Somehow it's the things that have covered up that hurt, like the bitterness, that you just—at this moment, can't stand.

C.: Yeah. That's just about it. It's sort as though, well, the first, I mean, as though, it's—well, it's something I can cope with. Now, the feeling of, well, I can still have a hell of a lot of fun, see. But that this other, I mean, this frustration—I mean, it comes out in so many ways, I'm beginning to realize, you see. I mean, just this sort of, this kind of thing.

T.: And a hurt you can accept. It's a part of life within a lot of other parts of life too. You can have lots of fun. But to have all of your life suffused by frustration and bitterness, that you don't like, you don't want, and are now more aware of.

C.: Yeah. And there's somehow no dodging it now. You see, I'm much more aware of it. [Pause.] I don't know. Right now, I don't know just what the next step is. I really don't know. [Pause.] Fortunately this is a kind of development, so that it—doesn't carry over too acutely into—I mean, I—what I'm trying to say, I think, is that I'm still functioning. I'm still enjoying myself and—

T.: Just sort of want me to know that in lots of ways you carry on just as you always have.

C.: That's it. [Pause.] Oh, I think I've got to stop and go.

In this lengthy excerpt we get a clear picture of the fact that underlying the bitterness and hatred and the desire to get back at the world which has cheated her is a much less antisocial feeling, a deep experience of having been hurt. And it is equally clear that at this deeper level she has no desire to put her murderous feelings into action. She dislikes them and would like to be rid of them.

The next excerpt comes from the thirty-fourth interview. It is very incoherent material, as verbalizations often are when the individual is trying to express something deeply emotional. Here she is endeavoring to reach far down into herself. She states that it will be difficult to formulate.

C.: I don't know whether I'll be able to talk about it yet or not. Might give it a try. Something—I mean, it's a feeling—that—sort of an urge to really get it out. I know it isn't going to make sense. I think

that maybe if I can get it out and get it a little—well, in a little more
matter-of-fact way, that it'll be something that's more useful to me.
And I don't know how to—I mean, it seems as though I want to say,
I want to talk about my *self*. And that is of course as I see, what
I've been doing for all these hours. But, no, this—it's my *self*. I've
quite recently become aware of rejecting certain statements, because
to me they sounded—not quite what I meant, I mean, a little bit too
idealized. And I mean, I can remember always saying it's more
selfish than that, more selfish than that. Until I—it sort of occurs
to me, it dawns, yeah, that's exactly what I mean, but the selfishness
I mean, has an entirely different connotation. I've been using a word
"selfish." Then I have this feeling of—I—that I've never expressed
it before, of *selfish*—which means nothing. A—I'm still going to
talk about it. A kind of pulsation. And it's [words lost]. But I
mean, I want to put it into—words because it's something aware all
the time. And still it's there. And I'd like to be able to utilize it, to
—as a kind of descending into this thing. You know, it's as though—
I don't know, damn! I'd sort of acquired some place, and picked up
a kind of acquaintance with the structure. Almost as though I knew
it brick-for-brick kind of thing. It's something that—an awareness.
I mean, that—of a feeling of not being fooled, of not being drawn into
the thing. And a critical sense, of knowingness. But in a way—the
reason it's hidden and—I mean, it almost is a part of—it's a part of
me, but it somehow can't be a part of everyday life. And there's
something of—at times I feel almost a little bit terrible in the thing,
but again terrible not as terrible. And why? I think I know. And
it's—it also explains a lot to me. It's—it's something that is *totally*
without hate. I mean, just *totally*. Not with love, but *totally without hate*. But it's—it's an exciting thing too. . . . I guess maybe I
am the kind of person that likes to, I mean, probably even torment
myself, or to chase things down, to try to find the whole. And I've
told myself, now look, this is a pretty strong kind of feeling which
you have. It isn't constant. But you feel it sometimes, and as you
let yourself feel it, you feel it yourself. You know, there are words
for that kind of thing that one could find in abnormal psychology.
Might almost be like the feeling that is occasionally, is attributed to
things that you read about. I mean, there are some elements there—
I mean, this pulsation, this excitement, this knowing. And I've said
—I tracked down one thing, I mean, I was very, very brave, what
shall we say—a sublimated sex drive. And I thought, well, *there* I've
got it. I've really solved the thing. And that there is nothing more
to it than that. And for a while, I mean, I was quite pleased with
myself. That was it. And then I had to admit, no, that wasn't it.
'Cause that's something that had been with me long before I became,
so terribly frustrated sexually. I mean, that wasn't—and, but in the
thing, then I began to see a little, within this very core is an acceptance of sexual relationship, I mean, the only kind that *I* would think

would be possible. It was in this thing. It's not something that's been—I mean, sex hasn't been sublimated or substituted there. No. Within this, within what I know there—I mean, it's a different kind of sexual feeling to be sure. I mean, it's one that is stripped of all the things that have happened to sex, if you know what I mean. There's no chase, no pursuit, no battle, no—well, no kind of hate, which I think, seems to me, has crept into such things. And yet, I mean, this feeling has been, oh, a little bit disturbing.

T.: I'd like to see if I can capture a little of what that means to you. It is as you've gotten very deeply acquainted with yourself on kind of a brick-by-brick experiencing basis, and in that sense have become more *self*-ish, and the notion of really,—in the discovering of what is the core of you as separate from all the other aspects, you come across the realization, which is a very deep and pretty thrilling realization, that the core of that self is not only without hate, but is really something more resembling a saint, something really very pure, is the word I would use. And that you can try to depreciate that. You can say, maybe it's a sublimation, maybe it's an abnormal manifestation, screwball and so on. But inside of yourself, you know that it isn't. This contains the feelings which could contain rich sexual expression, but it sounds bigger than, and really deeper than that. And yet fully able to include all that could be a part of sex expression.

C.: It's probably something like that.... It's kind of—I mean, it's a kind of descent. It's a going down where you might almost think it should be going up, but no, it's—I'm sure of it; it's kind of going down.

T.: This is a going down and immersing yourself in your self almost.

C.: Yeah. And I—I can't just throw it aside. I mean, it just seems, oh, it just *is*. I mean, it seems an awfully important thing that I just had to say.

T.: I'd like to pick up one of those things too, to see if I understand it. That it sounds as though this sort of idea you're expressing is something you must be going up to capture, something that *isn't* quite. Actually though, the feeling is, this is a going down to capture something that's more deeply there.

C.: It is. It really—there's something to that which is—I mean, this— I have a way, and of course sometime we're going to have to go into that, of rejecting almost violently, that which is righteous, that which is good. I would suppose though that there's a kind of rejection of the ideal, the—as— and that expressed it; I mean, that's sort of what I mean. One is a going up into I don't know. I mean, I just have a feeling, I can't follow. I mean, it's pretty thin stuff if you ever start knocking it down. This one went—I wondered why—I mean, has this awfully definite feeling of descending.

T.: That this isn't a going up into the thin ideal. This is a going down into the astonishingly solid reality that—

C.: Yeah.

T.: —is really more surprising than—

C.: Yeah. I mean, a something that you don't knock down. That's there—I don't know—seems to me after you've abstracted the whole thing. That lasts . . . .

Since this is presented in such confused fashion, it might be worth while to draw from it the consecutive themes which the client has expressed.

1. I'm going to talk about myself as *self*-ish, but with a new connotation to the word.
2. I've acquired an acquaintance with the structure of myself, know myself deeply.
3. As I descend into myself, I discover something exciting, a core that is totally without hate.
4. It can't be a part of everyday life—it may even be abnormal.
5. I thought first it was just a sublimated sex drive.
6. But no, this is more inclusive, deeper than sex.
7. One would expect this to be the kind of thing one would discover by going up into the thin realm of ideals.
8. But actually, I found it by going deep within myself.
9. It seems to be something that is the essence, that lasts.

Is this a mystic experience she is describing? It would seem that the counselor felt so, from the flavor of his responses. Can we attach any significance to such a Gertrude Stein kind of expression? The writer would simply point out that many clients have come to a somewhat similar conclusion about themselves, though not always expressed in such an emotional way. Even Mrs. O., in the following interview, the thirty-fifth, gives a clearer and more concise statement of her feeling, in a more down-to-earth way. She also explains why it was a difficult experience to face:

C.: I think I'm awfully glad I found myself or brought myself or wanted to talk about self. I mean, it's a very personal, private kind of thing that you just don't talk about. I mean, I can understand my feeling of, oh, probably slight apprehension now. It's—well, sort of as though I was just rejecting, I mean, all of the things that Western civilization stands for, you see. And wondering whether I was right, I mean, whether it was quite the right path, and still of course, feeling how right the thing was, you see. And so there's bound to be a conflict. And then this, and I mean, now I'm feeling, well, of course that's how I feel. I mean there's a—this thing that I term a kind of lack of hate, I mean, is very real. It carried over into the things I do, I believe in. . . . I think it's all right. It's sort of maybe my saying to myself, well, you've been bashing me all over the head, I mean, sort of from the beginning, with superstitions and taboos and

misinterpreted doctrines and laws and your science, your refriger-
ators, your atomic bombs. But I'm just not buying; you see, I'm
just, you just haven't quite succeeded. I think what I'm saying is
that, well, I mean, just not conforming, and it's—well, it's just that
way.

T.: Your feeling at the present time is that you have been very much
aware of all the cultural pressures—not always very much aware,
but "there have been so many of those in my life—and now I'm going
down more deeply into myself to find out what I really feel," and it
seems very much at the present time as though that somehow separates you a long ways from your culture, and that's a little frightening, but feels basically good. Is that—

C.: Yeah. Well, I have the feeling now that it's okay, really. . . .
Then there's something else—a feeling that's starting to grow; well,
to be almost formed, as I say. This kind of conclusion, that I'm
going to stop looking for something terribly wrong. Now I don't
know why. But I mean, just—it's this kind of thing. I'm sort of
saying to myself now, well, in view of what I know, what I've
found—I'm pretty sure I've ruled out fear, and I'm positive I'm not
afraid of shock—I mean, I sort of would have welcomed it. But—
in view of the places I've been, what I learned there, then also kind
of, well, taking into consideration what I don't know, sort of, maybe
this is one of the things that I'll have to date, and say, well, now, I've
just—I just can't find it. See? And now without any—without, I
should say, any sense of apology or covering up, just sort of simple
statement that I can't find what at this time, appears to be bad.

T.: Does this catch it? That as you've gone more and more deeply
into yourself, and as you think about the kind of things that you've
discovered and learned and so on, the conviction grows very, very
strong that no matter how far you go, the things that you're going
to find are not dire and awful. They have a very different character.

C.: Yes, something like that.

Here, even as she recognizes that her feeling goes against the grain
of her culture, she feels bound to say that the core of herself is not bad,
nor terribly wrong, but something positive. Underneath the layer of
controlled surface behavior, underneath the bitterness, underneath the
hurt, is a self that is positive and that is without hate. This, I believe,
is the lesson which our clients have been facing us with for a long time
and which we have been slow to learn.

If hatelessness seems like a rather neutral or negative concept, perhaps
we should let Mrs. O. explain its meaning. In her thirty-ninth interview, as she feels her therapy drawing to a close, she returns to this
topic:

C.: I wonder if I ought to clarify—it's clear to me, and perhaps that's
all that matters really, here, my strong feeling about a hate-free kind

of approach. Now that we have brought it up on a rational kind of a plane, I know—it sounds negative. And yet in my thinking, my— not really my thinking but my feeling, it—*and* my thinking, yes, my thinking too—it's a far more positive thing than this—than a love— and it seems to me a far easier kind of a—it's less confining. But it—I realize that it must sort of sound and almost seem like a complete rejection of so many things, of so many creeds and maybe it is. I don't know. But it just to me seems more positive.

T.: You can see how it might sound more negative to someone, but as far as the meaning that it has for you is concerned, it doesn't seem as binding, as possessive I take it, as love. It seems as though it actually is more—more expandable, more usable, than —

C.: Yeah.

T.: —any of these narrower terms.

C.: Really does to me. It's easier. Well, anyway it's easier for me to feel that way. And I don't know. It seems to me to really be a way of—of not—of finding yourself in a place where you aren't forced to make rewards and you aren't forced to punish. It is— it means so much. It just seems to me to make for a kind of freedom.

T. M-hm. M-hm. Where one is rid of the need of either rewarding or punishing, then it just seems to you there is so much more freedom for all concerned.

C.: That's right. [Pause.] I'm prepared for some breakdowns along the way.

T.: You don't expect it will be smooth sailing.

C.: No.

This section is the story—greatly abbreviated—of one client's discovery that the deeper she dug within herself, the less she had to fear; that instead of finding something terribly wrong within herself, she gradually uncovered a core of self which wanted neither to reward nor punish others, a self without hate, a self which was deeply socialized. Do we dare to generalize from this type of experience that if we cut through deeply enough to our organismic nature, that we find that man is a positive and social animal? This is the suggestion from our clinical experience.

Being One's Organism, One's Experience

The thread which runs through much of the foregoing material of this chapter is that psychotherapy (at least client-centered therapy) is a process whereby man becomes his organism—without self-deception, without distortion. What does this mean?

We are talking here about something at an experiential level—a phenomenon which is not easily put into words, and which, if apprehended only at the verbal level, is by that very fact already distorted. Perhaps if we use several sorts of descriptive formulation, it may ring some bell, however faint, in the reader's experience, and cause him to feel "Oh, now I know, from my own experience, something of what you are talking about."

Therapy seems to mean a getting back to basic sensory and visceral experience. Prior to therapy the person is prone to ask himself, often unwittingly,"What do others think I should do in this situation?" "What would my parents or my culture want me to do?" "What do I think *ought* to be done?" He is thus continually acting in terms of the form which should be imposed upon his behavior. This does not necessarily mean that he always acts in *accord* with the opinions of others. He may indeed endeavor to act so as to contradict the expectations of others. He is nevertheless acting *in terms of* the expectations (often introjected expectations) of others. During the process of therapy the individual comes to ask himself, in regard to ever-widening areas of his life-space, "How do *I* experience this?" "What does it mean to me?" "If I behave in a certain way, how do I symbolize the meaning which it *will* have for me?" He comes to act on a basis of what may be termed realism—a realistic balancing of the satisfactions and dissatisfactions which any action will bring to himself.

Perhaps it will assist those who, like myself, tend to think in concrete and clinical terms, if I put some of these ideas into schematized formulations of the process through which various clients go. For one client this may mean: "I have thought I must feel only love for my parents, but I find that I experience both love and bitter resentment. Perhaps I can be that person who freely experiences both love *and* resentment." For another client the learning may be: "I have thought I was only bad and worthless. Now I experience myself at times as one of much worth, at other times as one of little worth or usefulness. Perhaps I can be a person who experiences varying degrees of worth." For another: "I have held the conception that no one could really love me for myself. Now I experience the affectional warmth of another for me. Perhaps I can be a person who is lovable by others—perhaps I *am* such a person." For still another: "I have been brought up to feel that I must not appreciate myself—but I do. I can cry for myself, but I can enjoy myself too. Perhaps I am a richly varied person whom I can enjoy and for whom I can feel sorrow." Or, to take the last example from Mrs. O., "I have thought that in some deep way I was bad, that the most basic elements in me must be dire and awful. I don't experience that badness, but rather a positive desire to live and let live. Perhaps I can be that person who is, at heart, positive."

What is it that makes possible anything but the first sentence of each of these formulations? It is the addition of awareness. In therapy the person adds to ordinary experience the full and undistorted awareness of his experiencing—of his sensory and visceral reactions. He ceases, or at least decreases, the distortions of experience in awareness. He can be aware of what he is actually experiencing, not simply what he can permit himself to experience after a thorough screening through a conceptual filter. In this sense the person becomes for the first time the full potential of the human organism, with the enriching element of awareness freely added to the basic aspect of sensory and visceral reaction. The person comes to *be* what he *is,* as clients so frequently say in therapy. What this seems to mean is that the individual comes to *be*— in awareness—what he *is*—in experience. He is, in other words, a complete and fully functioning human organism.

Already I can sense the reactions of some of my readers. "Do you mean that as a result of therapy man becomes nothing but a human *organism,* a human *animal?* Who will control him? Who will socialize him? Will he then throw over all inhibitions? Have you merely released the beast, the id, in man?" To which the most adequate reply seems to be, "In therapy the individual has actually *become* a human organism, with all the richness which that implies. He is realistically able to control himself, and he is incorrigibly socialized in his desires. There is no beast in man. There is only man in man, and this we have been able to release."

So the basic discovery of psychotherapy seems to be, if our observations have any validity, that we do not need to be afraid of being "merely" *Homo sapiens.* It is the discovery that if we can add to the sensory and visceral experiencing which is characteristic of the whole animal kingdom the gift of a free and undistorted awareness of which only the human animal seems fully capable, we have an organism which is beautifully and constructively realistic. We have then an organism which is as aware of the demands of the culture as it is of its own physiological demands for food or sex—which is just as aware of its desire for friendly relationships as it is of its desire to aggrandize itself—which is just as aware of its delicate and sensitive tenderness toward others, as it is of its hostilities toward others. When man's unique capacity of awareness is thus functioning freely and fully, we find that we have, not an animal whom we must fear, not a beast who must be controlled, but an organism able to achieve, through the remarkable integrative capacity of its central nervous system, a balanced, realistic, self-enhancing, other-enhancing behavior as a resultant of all these elements of awareness. To put it another way, when man is less than fully man—when he denies to awareness various aspects of his experience—then indeed we have all too often reason to fear him and his behavior, as the present world situation testifies. But when he is most fully man, when he is his complete organism, when awareness of experience, a peculiarly human attribute, is most fully operating, then he is to be trusted, then his behavior is constructive. It is not always conventional. It will not always be conforming. It will be individualized. But it will also be socialized.

A Concluding Comment

I have stated the preceding section as strongly as I am able because it represents a deep conviction growing out of many years of experience. I am quite aware, however, of the difference between conviction and truth. I do not ask anyone to agree with my experience, but only to consider whether the formulation given here agrees with his own experience.

Nor do I apologize for the speculative character of this chapter. There is a time for speculation, and a time for the sifting of evidence. It is to be hoped that gradually some of the speculations and opinions and clinical hunches of this paper may be put to operational and definitive test.

CHAPTER 3

NEUROSIS AND PSYCHOTHERAPY AS INTER-PERSONAL PROCESSES: A SYNOPSIS

By O. HOBART MOWRER, Ph.D.

In this chapter an attempt will be made to give as comprehensive and precise a statement as possible of one conception of neurosis and its treatment. Many details both of theory and of technique must necessarily be omitted; but by thus trying to see the field whole, issues may be sharpened, similarities and differences highlighted, and new problems set for further inquiry.

For the sake of simplicity and economy of exposition, the chapter will consist of a series of numbered sections, each of which may be thought of as a link in the chain of argument. While it would be too much to call the result a formal "scientific system," the effort is in that direction and may be regarded as a first crude approximation thereof.

The sections are titled and numbered as follows:

1. The Presenting Picture of Neurosis
2. Necessity for Theory and Method
3. Assumptions Regarding Normal Development: Developmental Identification
4. Defensive Identification
5. Identification and Sex Typing
6. The Nature of Normal Anxiety
7. Intractable Anxiety and Dissociation
8. Anxiety, Interpersonal and Endopsychic
9. Puberty, a Common Occasion for Dissociation
10. The Reinforcement of Dissociation
11. Neurotic Anxiety: the Aftermath of Dissociation
12. Symptom-Formation
13. Interpretation as Association
14. Resistance and Repression
15. Resistance and Negative Transference
16. Management of Transference and Countertransference
17. The "Direction" of Repression: a Controversial Issue
18. Repression and Transference
19. Transference and Identification
20. The Role of Cross-Identification in Neurosis
21. The Problem of Diagnostic Types

1. THE PRESENTING PICTURE OF NEUROSIS. Many vivid and valid descriptions have been given of the types of "difficulties of living" (Sullivan,* 1947; Fromm-Reichmann, 1950) which bring human beings into psychotherapy. In the first chapter of this book, May has given one such description, and others might be cited. Such descriptions vary in detail, but in one central respect they agree: the patient always feels that there is something unintelligible, unfathomable, and *mysterious* about his problems (Mowrer, 1950, chaps. xix, xxii). Other persons may have problems, perhaps extremely serious and seemingly insoluble problems; but if these problems are fully comprehensible, such persons are not neurotic and not proper candidates for psychotherapy. Such persons will often be benefited by realistic information, advice, and personal or financial assistance; but this is not true of the neurotic.[1] It is as if he has a sealed compartment within himself in which the explanation of his difficulties has been hidden, with the *key* also locked up therein. As experience has repeatedly shown, the therapist can never give the neurotic patient "the answers"; they must always, in some manner, be found *within the patient himself.*[2]

2. NECESSITY FOR THEORY AND METHOD. The aid which the neurotic needs is thus of a special kind, and it is evident that the person who is expert in rendering such aid must have a general understanding of how such mysterious internal states arise and *a theory* as to how they can be resolved, even though the specific circumstances surrounding any given neurosis are in the beginning always unknown. Freud made the first concerted attempt in modern times to elaborate such a theory and to develop *a method* which could be used to implement the theory in treatment and, as a research tool, to modify or refine the theory. While the method has undergone many modifications in the hands of different investigators (see Section 23), the essential feature of the method, which has been very generally retained by contemporary psychotherapists, is that it solicits the patient's *active participation* in the treatment process. As Dollard and Miller (1950) have recently observed, this approach to "mental disease" contrasts strikingly with conventional medical treatment, wherein the patient briefly reports his complaints and the physician then assumes the responsibility both for further diagnosis and for treatment. These writers remark:

* References are to the bibliography at the back of the book.
[1] In another paper (Mowrer, 1951), this distinction between conscious and "unconscious" problems has been proposed as a basis for differentiating between counseling and psychotherapy.
[2] For a different point of view, see Fisher (1950) and Thorne (1950). These writers express greater confidence in the ability of the therapist to find solutions to the patient's problems and present them to him.

The patient expects from the psychiatrist the same behavior that he has learned to expect from other doctors. This was exemplified in the case of Mrs. A. She came to the therapeutic situation with hope for a quick, magic cure. This expectation was almost certainly generalized from her previous experience with physicians. She had learned that you tell a doctor what your symptoms are—where it hurts—and then he tells you what to do. She therefore quickly recited all her symptoms—her concern about her heart, her nausea and loss of weight, her fear of going out alone. Then she said, "That's all; I have told you everything," and sat back waiting for the doctor to provide a simple cure. The therapist had to explain to Mrs. A. that psychotherapy is different from medical treatments. He pointed out that in order to help her he would need to know a great deal more about her. Her job was to talk, to do the patient's work. However, the discrimination between this and other types of treatment was not easily set up. Mrs. A. kept pleading for advice throughout the first several hours of the therapy. She expected the usual prescriptions, rules, and instructions (p. 267).

In Chapter 4, Perry and Estes properly note that the psychotherapeutic relationship is one of *collaboration* (see Fromm-Reichman, 1950), with the therapist in certain respects playing the less active role. Indeed it may be said that one of the principal responsibilities and actions of the good therapist is to encourage the patient to become more responsible and more active and, in the end, to take over as self-functions such activities as must in the beginning be performed by the therapist (see Sections 13, 15, and 19).

3. Assumptions Regarding Normal Development: Developmental Identification. The particular conception of neurosis and its treatment which will be outlined here starts with the assumption that personality development in children is determined, in part, by the direct, self-conscious attempts which parents make to teach and train their offspring but also, perhaps even more importantly, by indirect, often nonconscious influences; (cf. the theory of "concomitant learning" advanced by Kilpatrick, 1925). Although mothers rarely think of the loving care and attention which they give to their infants as "training," evidence which has been reviewed elsewhere (Mowrer, 1950, chaps. xxi, xxiv), indicates that in this way the basis is laid for many of the child's most important later learnings. The "positive cathexis" or "secondary reinforcement value" which the good mother thus acquires for her infant (by the principle of conditioning or sign learning) makes the sounds she utters and the things she does seem good, interesting, comforting, important, and when the infant discovers that he, too, can make some of these sounds and do some of these things, they will have immediately satisfying qualities for him (solution learning). It is apparently through this mechanism of *developmental identification,* more than perhaps any other, that the infant learns to *talk,* to *walk,* and to perform other rudimentary *ego functions.*

4. DEFENSIVE IDENTIFICATION. But soon, between the ages of two and four years in our society, both parents begin to *discipline* the child. Now less attention is paid to what he *wants* and more to what he *does*. Parents who have previously been wholly "good" in the eyes of the child now become also partly "bad," and this admixture of attitudes on the part of the child produces a developmental crisis. If a child has never known a normal degree of parental love during the infantile period, parental discipline produces comparatively little conflict: since the child has but weak "positive cathexis" for the parents, he simply retreats when they become more actively punitive toward him, withdraws, breaks away from them, and begins to "go his own way." It is these children of neglect and rejection who recruit the army of juvenile delinquency and adult criminality; and such persons, because they lack the internal structure necessary for neurotic suffering, do not ordinarily respond favorably to (nor do they ordinarily seek) psychotherapy. Our knowledge of them is therefore more theoretical than intimately clinical.

But the case of the normally loved child is different: the disciplinary demands of his parents cause him first of all to attack his parents (since their discipline frustrates him and he is too dependent to retreat from them), and when this behavior meets with still further punishment, he is likely to be thrown into *intolerable anxiety*.

At this point a most remarkable thing normally occurs. At the height of his conflict, the child discovers that he can satisfy his parents and at the same time still his own inner turmoil if he will do one thing: accept the standards of conduct and social values which his parents are holding up to him and make them *his* standards, *his* values. Now when he deviates, or even starts to deviate, from parental and from social standards generally, the child *punishes himself* and thus learns to refrain from such behavior even when parents or others are not present, and even when they have no certain way of knowing about the behavior. In common parlance, we say that the child now has a *conscience* or that, in the language of psychoanalysis, his *superego* has begun to function. Sometimes the development of such an agency within the total personality seems to occur suddenly, as the resolution to some particularly turbulent conflict; at other times conscience develops more gradually, as the product of a succession of smaller crises. But in any case the induction stands that character, conscience, or superego (the term is not important) is forged as a solution to the unbearable conflict generated during the period of intensive "socialization" by the great love for and equally great fear (and/or hatred) of the parents.

5. IDENTIFICATION AND SEX TYPING. The human organism is born with, or maturation later provides, the biological impulses which Freud (1935a) has collectively termed the *id*. Through developmental identification and related experiences, the *ego* emerges; and by means of defensive identification parental (and through it social) authority become internalized as *conscience* or *superego*. These three agencies, then—id,

ego, and superego—together constitute what we ordinarily refer to as *a personality* or the "total person." But in the interest of clarity of statement, one important aspect of personality development has thus far been omitted. It is not enough that children be socialized, trained, educated in such a way that they will feel and act *like human beings;* they must also learn to feel and act *like men* or *like women.* Depending, that is to say, upon their biologically given sex type, human beings must specialize in such a way that their personalities will further distinguish them from members of the opposite sex. "Sex" is therefore not merely a matter of anatomy and physiology; it is also importantly related to *character.*

All too little is yet understood concerning the conditions under which that particular aspect of character development which is related to psychosexual differentiation normally comes about; but we know that certain forms of familial pathology (typically the "broken" or disharmonious home) may produce adults with the anatomy and physiology of one gender and the character structure and interests and attitudes of the other. When this "inversion" is relatively complete and without great internal conflict, the individual will be a *pervert* and, like the criminal, relatively inaccessible to psychotherapy. When, on the other hand, bodily structure and character are highly congruent in this respect, the individual is not likely to need therapy; he will tend to be normal. For reasons which will be developed later, it now appears that *confusion* in terms of sex type and identification may be associated with acute pathology (Mowrer, 1950, chaps. xxi, xxii).

6. THE NATURE OF NORMAL ANXIETY. The self or total person consists, as we have seen, of id, ego, and superego, i.e., of the biologically given *impulses,* the intellectual and motor *skills* of the individual, and the socially instilled *emotions* of fear, love, and loyalty (see Chapter 6). In the secure, psychologically adequate individual, all these parts or aspects of the personality work together harmoniously, integratively. Such a person may be under considerable objective or physical stress, e.g., he may be hungry, fatigued, in danger, or in pain, but so long as the various parts of the personality are functioning in an organized, unitary way, the individual will experience no great *psychic* stress or discomfort. If, however, circumstances are such that parts of the personality are thrown into severe conflict, if, that is to say, the harmonious, integrated functioning of the self is threatened, then the individual will have that unique form of distress or psychic pain known as *anxiety;* and since in the beginning of such conflict the individual can ordinarily identify the origin of his distress and the nature of his conflict, the resulting experience can be properly termed *normal,* or *situational,* anxiety. It is, in other words, anxiety which is intelligible, appropriate to the psychological situation, "normal." Recognition of the existence of this type of anxiety is essential to understanding the genesis of neurosis and the resistances which patients offer to treatment (May, 1950c; Snygg and Combs, 1949).

7. INTRACTABLE ANXIETY AND DISSOCIATION. Normal anxiety is usually of tolerable proportions and is reacted to constructively, that is to say, it leads to decisions and actions which will bring the part, or part*ed,* selves back into harmonious and mutually reinforcing interaction. Indeed it may even be said that normal anxiety is the force which keeps driving the personality toward wholeness, toward unity, and toward maximal effectiveness. It is the force which helps the personality achieve ever higher levels of synthesis, new integrations, and a more stable and durable organization (cf. Rogers, 1951*b*).

But some conflicts are so severe and their solution so difficult that *the constructive use of anxiety is abandoned.* When anxiety proves intractable to all ordinary modes of response, the ego may institute, half deliberately, half automatically, the fateful strategy of *dissociation* or, as Freud (1934*b*) preferred to say, *repression.* The essence of this strategy is that the conflict is resolved, not realistically and integratively, but by a more definite *separation* of the elements of the conflict. It is an old saying that it takes two persons to make a quarrel; in like manner it takes two forces within a personality to make a conflict, and if one of these forces can be banned, excluded from the arena of consciousness, locked up, then peace can be restored, even though it be achieved at the cost of partial self-repudiation, partial self-destruction. In short, then, otherwise unmanageable anxiety may activate the strategy of dissociation and in so doing introduce the first (latent) phase of neurosis.[3]

8. ANXIETY, INTERPERSONAL AND ENDOPSYCHIC. In principle, serious and seemingly irreconcilable conflicts may arise at any period after early childhood and under a variety of circumstances. During the first years of life the personality seems not to be sufficiently differentiated or structured for powerful struggles of a purely internal nature to occur. Prior to the occurrence of defensive identification and the establishment of conscience, the small child may experience anxiety, but it is an *interpersonal anxiety,* born of the child's great dependence upon and love for the parents.[4] But when the parents' values and authority have been internalized as superego, the possibility exists that powerful internal conflicts can occur, and we may then speak of *endopsychic anxiety.* In a

---

[3] In order to anticipate possible misunderstanding, it should be stated that the present discussion presupposes that anxiety, as such, is neither "constructive" nor "destructive": these adjectives are applicable only to the ways in which the individual (in the sense of ego) *responds* to his anxiety. As will become evident later, it is here assumed that an individual may react to normal anxiety either constructively (integratively) or destructively (dissociatively or by means of drugs and distractions) and that in the event that the management (or, more precisely, the *mis*management) of normal anxiety leads to neurotic anxiety, the individual may likewise react to it, again either constructively (by trying to reverse the dissociative trend, as in therapy) or destructively (by means of continued repression, symptom-formation, etc.).

[4] This statement is consistent with the empirical clinical observation that an "infantile neurosis" is always an expression of a disturbance in the parent-child relationship and that the child can, under these circumstances, rarely be successfully dealt with therapeutically in social isolation.

sense, this type of anxiety is also "interpersonal" since it commonly involves a struggle between the ego, or infantile self, and the superego, which is the internal delegate or representative of the parents and of society at large. But such anxiety is nevertheless usefully distinguished from clearly interpersonal anxiety in that it may arise without any immediate reference to the behavior of others; it is related instead to the behavior and feelings of the individual himself. However, we may still characterize endopsychic anxiety, along with interpersonal anxiety, as "normal" so long as the individual can identify and describe the nature of the underlying conflict; but when such anxiety has had to be dealt with by dissociation rather than by more constructive measures, the first step has been taken toward psychopathology.

9. Puberty, a Common Occasion for Dissociation. The interpersonal anxiety of early childhood tends to be resolved by the mechanism of defensive identification and the establishment of conscience. Ordinarily the grade school years mark a period of relative tranquillity. This is not to say that minor conflicts do not arise during this period, or that there may not be some children who display severe personality and behavior disorders at this time.[5] But for most children this is a comparatively peaceful time; and with the aid of superego, reinforced by continued parental vigilance and protection, the average child avoids during this period both delinquency on the one hand and serious psychological difficulty on the other. However, with the advent of puberty, a new and to many children unmanageable burden descends upon them. They now have a sex drive of unprecedented intensity, with the result that in many instances they experience conflicts and anxieties which activate for the first time, in any major way, the strategy of dissociation with attendant personality changes of various kinds. This statement could be illustrated many times over from the recorded interviews of adult neurotics undergoing psychotherapy, but the following excerpts from the sixth interview with a young salesman will suffice:

P.:[6] I think one of the things that troubles me most today is the fact, uh, the fact that I don't have enough intelligence, enough IQ, as they say, to do all the things I want to do: make a million dollars, what not. It worries me quite a little bit. I, I don't know quite, uh, why, but everything seemed to change tremendously somewhere along between the seventh and eighth grades for me. Before that time I seemed to be fairly bright. For one thing, maybe it's when I was in either fifth or sixth grade—and I don't remember which; I wish I did, I think the fifth grade—they gave us these, uh, uh, reading tests. I don't know what kind of tests they were; I didn't know anything at all about such things in those days, but I do remember that

---

[5] Such children reflect identification dilemmas of such a serious nature that, in later life, they are disposed less to neurosis than to psychosis and criminality.

[6] In case reports in this chapter, P. stands for "Patient" and T. for "Therapist."

I had a reading comprehension of about a sophomore in high school at that time. I read an awful lot.

. . . This continued through the seventh grade. I got good, good grades except for two subjects, manual training and gym, neither of which I liked—gym as I've already explained why—but, uh, the rest of my grades were good. I got quite a number of A's. And that continued in the seventh grade.

But, uh, that seemed to stop the next year, and I don't know why. Uh, that was when I started reading the books in science class, which just about ruined my background in science. And, uh, I didn't get along with the kids too well; some of them I did, yes—that's true enough—yes, I did; that hadn't begun to show its effect yet, but I wasn't just as aggressive, didn't want to fight all the time like I had earlier. I began to be more afraid again; and it might be interesting to note at this time that when I was in the seventh grade I was in the choir, which was quite prominent o-, over there, and sang soprano. When I was in eighth grade I sang bass—quite a little change!

Chronic neurotics often date the onset of their difficulties from the years of twelve to fifteen; but, as in the above instance, they usually do not at first connect them with specifically sexual conflicts. Adolescence is a period of stress and challenge to everyone, but most persons come through it successfully and look back upon it as a period of highly useful, albeit sometimes painful, personal growth. But the individual who succumbs to his conflicts and anxieties during this period and resorts to the strategy of repression pays a high price for the relief thus attained. In order to maintain repression, it is necessary, as we have already seen, for the ego to exercise a devitalizing kind of vigilance; and the fact that repression, as such, is self-destructive further depletes and dissipates the individual's energies. It is no accident, therefore, that an individual so afflicted commonly complains of feeling stupid, inadequate, inferior, little, worthless, weak, fatigued.

When patients date their difficulties from later decades, one usually discovers that these difficulties are largely situational or that they have roots which extend back to adolescent conflicts which were never completely resolved in a mature way and are later activated by developments such as marriage, parenthood, or the like. And the unresolved adolescent problems can, in turn, often be traced still further back into childhood and related to difficulties in child-parent and parent-parent relationships.

10. THE REINFORCEMENT OF DISSOCIATION. Every normal person has experienced the relief and satisfaction which occur as the result of having effected an integrative solution of some conflict that has been the occasion for anxiety and worry. Relief and satisfaction are similarly experienced when a realistically unsolved conflict yields to the strategy of dissociation; and, following well-known principles of learning, we may

infer that each time this strategy is used successfully, the stronger will be the tendency to use it again and again under similar circumstances. Dissociation, as a solution to the drive of normal anxiety, will thus become a "habit" and, as such, will tend to function automatically.

The onset of dissociation may be dramatic or relatively gradual; it may, in other words, occur first on a grand scale, as a kind of over-all solution to a conflict or it may be instituted piecemeal; but in any event dissociation is a strategy which, once commenced, must be continually practiced and extended (Chapter 6). It is a truly malignant process, a process whereby the self, paradoxically but quite literally, tries to *preserve itself by destroying itself*. Like other forms of persistent non-integrative behavior (Mowrer and Ullman, 1945), dissociation achieves its rewarding consequences immediately and the punishing, self-defeating consequences are delayed. One of the functions of therapy is to help the patient consider his neurotic feelings and symptoms in the context of, and indeed as a consequence of, his habit of dissociation.

11. Neurotic Anxiety: the Aftermath of Dissociation. Although dissociation is likely, for reasons just considered, to be powerfully reinforced and thus perpetuated and extended as a way of dissipating conflict and the attendant anxiety, there are also factors which tend to limit and counteract the process. Although it is in one sense correct to speak of dissociation as involving successive acts of partial self-destruction, it must be noted that the parts of the total personality which are thus fissioned off in order to reduce anxiety are not destroyed in what Freud has called the "economic" sense; that is to say, they are excluded from consciousness, but they retain much of their *energy* and as the combined force of the dissociated elements begins to approximate that of the remaining parts of the personality, there is growing danger of a *counterattack* by the banished elements. In warfare generally, surprise and disguise are two master tactics; and it is therefore understandable that the dissociated or "outlawed" elements of personality are most likely to try to regain lost ground and re-enter consciousness when the defending forces are off guard and to hit in ways which involve minimal risk of identification and exposure. This is an admittedly loose way of speaking, but it nevertheless bears a considerable resemblance to what one observes clinically. Depression, inferiority feeling, obsessive doubting, loss of sexual responsiveness, psychosomatic disturbances, and related experiences are the ways in which the dissociated forces attack, punish, harry, and try to contact and communicate with the conscious self; and when these forces strike with special fury, the individual experiences *neurotic anxiety,* i.e., anxiety which, because it occurs *out of context,* without warning or explanation, is perceived as meaningless, mysterious, and malevolent. Nothing is so well calculated as such an attack to make a person feel that he is "going crazy" or "losing his mind," for there is indeed a compelling sense of "the mind" being disorganized and overwhelmed.

12. SYMPTOM FORMATION. The word "symptom" is often used in clinical psychology and psychiatry in two ways: (*a*) to refer to anxiety, depression, inferiority feeling, and the other *distressing affects* which are a regular feature of neurosis; and (*b*) to refer to those responses which are developed by the patient as *defense mechanisms* or "security operations" (Fromm-Reichmann, 1950), as means of diminishing or forestalling the painful experiences just cited. In the one case we are referring to neurotic *motives* and in the other case to neurotic *habits*. In the present chapter we shall use the term "symptom" to cover only the second of these usages. In this sense the term includes compulsions, addictions, phobic (avoidance) reactions, protective distortions of perception and thought, and so on.

The total sequence, then, is as follows: intractable (but "normal") anxiety; reduction of conflict and anxiety by means of dissociation; attempted return to consciousness by repressed, dissociated elements of the personality with attendant (now "neurotic") anxiety; and the development of habits, or symptoms, which help reduce or avert this type of anxiety. We may say, therefore, that dissociation bears the same relation to normal anxiety that "symptoms" bear to neurotic anxiety: both are self-protective and defensive, both serve to diminish or avert anxiety, but they accomplish this end in what, in the long run, are self-defeating, destructive ways.

There is some question as to just what point in the sequence here described marks the beginning of "neurosis." The following definitions seem useful: (*a*) since dissociation, at least in the beginning, is prompted by normal anxiety and is instituted in at least a partly conscious manner, it is most appropriately referred to as the *primal pathogenic act,* but not as neurosis proper; (*b*) the period of internal peace achieved by dissociation, which may be free of neurotic affects and of symptoms, is appropriately described as *latent neurosis;* and (*c*) the phase in which the patient experiences neurotic motives and tries to deal with them symptomatically—this is *manifest neurosis.*

13. INTERPRETATION AS ASSOCIATION. Therapists rarely see as patients persons who are in the latent stage of neurosis; during this period dissociation is working effectively and there is little or no therapeutic motive. Prior to the onset of dissociation, while conflicts are still fully conscious and there is "normal" anxiety, persons may seek advice, assistance, or "counseling" and may in this way be so aided that dissociation is averted. Counseling thus renders one of its most useful services as a prophylactic measure which enables the troubled but still *normal* person to work out a more realistic and more constructive solution to his problems than would be provided by dissociation.

It is, then, the individual with a *manifest* neurosis (Section 1) who most often becomes a candidate for psychotherapy, and here the distinction is in order between acute and chronic cases. Still more refined distinctions of a diagnostic nature can, of course, be made and are often of great practical importance; but once a patient is accepted for therapy, the procedure is, in principle, essentially the same in all cases. The person is invited to *talk*—about symptoms, feelings, interpersonal difficulties, past experiences, dreams, fantasies, anything that comes to mind, relevantly or irrelevantly. It makes little difference whether or not the therapist explicitly enjoins the patient to observe the rule of "free association," for the patient, in any event, will not and cannot observe it. It is the very fact that the patient's associations are *un*free, blocked, overcontrolled that has brought him to therapy; and it will hardly be expected that the situation will be suddenly altered on command. The patient will in the beginning necessarily speak *selectively,* but there is no great disadvantage in this, for as long as he speaks at all—and sometimes even where and when he does *not* speak—the therapist will soon begin to "see connections" between the seemingly unrelated, heterogeneous mass of things that constitute the patient's productions. With an appropriate degree of tentativeness and timeliness, the therapist then begins to report *his* associations to the patient; and it is these which constitute the essence of "interpretation" and which set in motion forces which are designed to arrest and reverse the dissociative trends within the patient (cf. Chapter 18).

14. RESISTANCE AND REPRESSION. As the therapist thus begins to bring *back together* things which the patient has *put apart,* it is understandable that he will encounter *resistance;* and it was one of Freud's (1922) epochal insights that this resistance involves the same forces as those which have been responsible for the antecedent act of repression, or dissociation. The associations of the therapist serve to reinstate the conflicts which the repression resolved (at least on a short-term basis); and since the "return of the repressed" to consciousness is likely to be painful, the patient, however reasonable and cooperative he tries to be, will automatically feel, and in some degree show, resentment and opposition. All this can be illustrated in the following clinical material. A gifted young physicist, in his twenty-sixth interview, produced material which prompted the therapist to point out an inconsistency between his professed attitudes and some of his daily-life practices. This occurred at the very end of the hour. After the patient had made an appointment for the next interview, he remarked that maybe it would be a good thing if he *stopped therapy* in order, as he said, "to try to assimilate some of these things you have been saying to me." However, by the next hour this suggestion had been abandoned and the patient reported the following experience:

P.. It was interesting to me that this morning, in—oh, this was in the middle of the morning; I was tossing around in my sleep last night—and I started working through a problem; and then I hit a certain embarrassing point in it; and in a kind of typical seizure of anxiety I kinda stiffened and put my head back, just like I was in bodily pain, anda, for a little bit, and then just relaxed.

And then I tried to think what it was that brought this on, and it was an entire blank; just immediately, that thing had completely left me. It seemed to me that this was one of the clearest examples I had been able to experience within myself, or been aware of, of repression. This is what I, you probably understand, this is what I understand to be repression. And the only way I could get that again was to start way back with what I'd been thinking and follow it through; and somehow or other I finally got up to the thing that made me flinch. I started back with the thing I was thinking, just about my work anda, about a certain period; and I got to thinking then about, uh, working last spring, translating this big French article, highly mathematical; at the same time working out my troubles with Betty. And much of the time that I spent working out this article I spent actually with her, over in the Art Institute where she was doing her work—we'd work independently, of course, but we would be together. But the net result of that work was very inferior, and yet, it was a big thing to me....

T.: Is it implicit in what you were saying that you felt that you would have done better on this if you hadn't been quite so preoccupied with your love affair?

P.: Oh yes.

T.: I see. Well, then, does this further follow, that you, that there was some feeling here that you had sort of lived off the company, gone through the motions of doing your job and accepting money therefor, without really doing it, and as a means of subsidizing you in a kind of personal venture? Does that hit it at all?

P.: Yes, it is. And it's not only that, but I was putting on the act of having gone through the motions. I, of course, I can't bring myself to get up before a group like that and just humbly say: "Well, I'm sorry; I've been busy with a lot of other things. I don't really understand what this means, but here, here are formulas." Uh, I got up and put on a good show.

The extent to which the struggle with dissociation was tied up in this case with negative feelings toward therapy and the therapist is indicated by the fact that the patient missed his next appointment, later reporting by telephone that he had come an hour later than the appointment was made for and found the therapist had another patient. Since the therapist is necessarily associated in the patient's mind with the painful "return of the repressed," it is almost axiomatic that during the period when the dissociated material is being readmitted to consciousness and assimilated, the patient will have a highly brittle and ambivalent attitude toward the therapist.

15. RESISTANCE AND NEGATIVE TRANSFERENCE. The concept of resistance gives the therapist an opportunity, if he cares to use it, to hide behind a cloak of infallibility; for if the patient, however justifiably, differs or takes issue with him, the therapist can dismiss the patient's behavior

as "resistance" (cf. Dollard and Miller, 1950, on the subject of "earned" resistance). For this reason it would appear that interpretations should always be made in a tentative, exploratory vein; sometimes seeming inconsistencies or contradictions turn out not to be, and it is a good thing if the therapist can set a personal example which is as reasonable and undefensive as he hopes the patient will become.

Yet there can be no doubt of the reality of resistance, in the neurotic sense of the term, and at times it takes the form of behavior which is so blatantly irresponsible, immature, and regressive that we are justified in applying to it Freud's term, "transference." Though subtle, the suggestion of the patient, mentioned in the preceding section, that it might be well for him to stop therapy carried overtones which sounded as if they came out of the past: "Be careful how you talk to me. Don't criticize me, or I won't like you and won't come to see you any more." Or equally, "If you aren't nice to me, I won't love you and be your boy. I will *leave* you." And in still other instances it seems equally unmistakable that the oppositional tactics which the patient, under the prompting of resistance, uses with the therapist are revivals of strategies which in bygone times he used with his parents and other would-be socializers. This phenomenon, which Freud clearly described, raises important issues, which cannot, however, be easily handled within the scope of conventional psychoanalytic theory. These will be returned to shortly, but let us proceed a step further in describing the observed clinical facts.

16. MANAGEMENT OF TRANSFERENCE AND COUNTERTRANSFERENCE. Here it is not necessary to indicate the full range and variety of strategies which patients mobilize under the promptings of resistance. Since these strategies are usually *acted out* rather than explicitly announced by the patient, it often taxes the therapist's ingenuity to understand them and his forbearance to tolerate their personal reference and implications. However, once understood by the therapist, these strategies lose much of their emotional force and when interpreted to the patient they usually disappear. If, on the other hand, the therapist does not see the meaning of such behavior, he will almost certainly personalize it and, consciously or unconsciously, begin to show similar antagonisms with respect to the patient. When this occurs, the therapist is said to have fallen into the error of *countertransference,* to be *countering* the transference rather than understanding, interpreting, and resolving it.

Since so much of the transference reaction of patients is unspoken, implicit, acted out, the therapist is often hard put to "get" what it is that the patient is communicating to him. All the therapist is likely to know immediately is that the patient's behavior has made him anxious, angry, disgusted, impatient, sexually alerted, guilty, or emotional in some other respect. If the therapist tries to be wholly "objective," "rational," unemotional, he is likely never to "hear" (cf. Reik's aptly titled book, *Listening with the third ear,* 1948) what the patient is "saying," and therapeutic collaboration is likely to stop at this point, even though interviews con-

tinue for months or even years thereafter. If, however, the therapist
notices that the patient's productions have made him emotional and if,
after careful thought and self-examination, he is reasonably certain that
his reaction is one which the patient in some sense "intended" to elicit, it
is a simple matter to indicate to the patient that his communication has
been "received"; and together therapist and patient may then proceed
with the all-important task of translating the message from *affective* to
explicit *verbal* terms. Since the patient is unable or unwilling to tell the
therapist directly what his feelings are and must instead communicate
them through a kind of pantomime (or "dumb acting," to use Dollard and
Miller's colorful phrase), it is essential that the therapist not "pantomime
back" at the patient. *He,* at least, must *speak about* emotions and not
"act them out." In this way the patient is encouraged likewise to speak
about his emotions and to "work through" (i.e., become consciously aware
of and abandon) his transference reactions—and the therapist is likewise
enabled to tolerate the patient's attacks and tricks without either with-
drawing or becoming punitive in his relationship with the patient. By the
correct management of transference and countertransference, therapy is
potently forwarded. Indeed, in combination with associative interpretation, it is the very essence of therapy!

17. The "Direction" of Repression: a Controversial Issue.
With what has been said up to this point, most Freudian analysts and
"analytically oriented" psychotherapists are probably in basic agreement.
But neurosis and its treatment have thus far been described only in general terms, and there are more specific issues which must be considered
even though they carry us into areas of uncertainty and disagreement.
A scientific frontier, like a geographic one, is likely to be characterized
by conflict, danger, and excitement, but it is here that the "advances"
must be made. However much the Freudian system of thought has contributed to our understanding of these matters, it is by no means either
a complete or perfect system, as anyone who has immersed himself in
therapeutic endeavor can attest. And one of the greatest difficulties
which this system has presented is the assumption that repression, or
dissociation, which is the acknowledged forerunner of neurosis, takes the
form of a campaign by ego and superego *against* the forces of the id. More
specifically it has been assumed that the forces which are particularly
likely to be so condemned, repudiated, and repressed are those of *sex* and
aggression. For reasons which have been developed at length elsewhere
(Mowrer, 1950, chaps. xviii-xxii), it would appear that often, perhaps
always, pathogenic dissociation is in the reverse direction to what Freud
supposed, i.e., consists of an attempt on the part of an *id-dominated ego*
to "wall off" and "still the voice of conscience." This modification of
Freudian theory has a number of implications, but an especially important
one for present purposes will be considered in the following section.

18. Repression and Transference. As intimated on an earlier
page, the established fact of negative transference does not find a natural

and logical place in traditional Freudian theory. If the typical neurotic is a person in whom an "excessively severe superego" has overwhelmed the ego and forcibly barred important id forces from access to consciousness and motor expression, it is not easy to understand what happens in transference. Many analysts take the position that it is their duty, in therapy, to align themselves with the supposedly repressed id forces and to try to provide the ego with enough support, or "ego strength," to be able to hold off the "tyrannical" pressures of the superego sufficiently to allow for the re-establishment of id expression and at least modest gratification. But this is not the role into which the patient tries to cast the therapist! As the facts of transference indicate, the patient soon invests the therapist with the mantle of parental and social authority and begins to re-enact with him an interpersonal struggle, or debate, which has its roots in childhood and which has been represented in neurotic form by the conflict between id-ego (pleasure-self) and superego (moral authority). And the fact that it is the qualities of the superego which the patient quickly attributes to the therapist (thus freeing himself of them and the inner distress they produce) suggests that it is this part of the personality which has been "in the minority" and is now "thrown back" at the therapist at the first opportunity. The transference thus provides the occasion for a kind of "therapeutic regression" (Mowrer, 1950, chap. xxi) wherein the patient is able to replace his internal conflicts by interpersonal ones, and it is this circumstance which provides the chance for the *new learning* which makes radical ("deep") therapy possible. To use a homely example, it is as if the patient has "swallowed" something which he found "indigestible" and therapy provides an opportunity for him to regurgitate it and "chew it over," *ruminate upon it,* and, in the fortunate instance, later reswallow and fully assimilate it. So long as one accepts the special dynamics of repression posited by Freud, one does not clearly perceive the nature of the transference and is unlikely to turn it to maximal therapeutic account. So long as the therapist takes the position that the patient is "too good" and needs to "express" himself more fully, just so long will he be aligned with the personal attitudes and immaturities of the patient which have brought the neurosis into existence, and the fully therapeutic potentialities of the transference will remain unexploited (see Wexler, Chapter 7).

19. TRANSFERENCE AND IDENTIFICATION. If the transference involves a type of therapeutic regression, a return to the "unfinished business" of growing up, it is not surprising that patients tend to identify with the therapist from time to time. If identification is one of the principal ways in which a child finds himself (or his *self*) in the course of normal development, it is not surprising that the neurotic will try to make similar use of the therapist in his search for personal security and selfhood.

Identification with the therapist has as yet been studied comparatively little, but tendencies of this kind are common. A verbatim account of this sort of thing has already been published in another connection (Mowrer,

1950, chap. xxi), and many other examples could be given. This phenomenon often takes two different forms. One of these may be called "defensive identification," but it is not exactly like the defensive identification involved in normal childhood. In therapy there is sometimes an "identification with the aggressor" in the sense that it represents an attempt to hold the "aggressor" (therapist-parent) at arm's length by the trick of *appearing* to accept him completely (see Section 17). This often takes the form of the patient's indicating that he, too, is thinking of becoming a therapist, a clinical psychologist. The following excerpts from the thirtieth interview with the young physicist mentioned earlier will illustrate this tendency.

T.: I was interested in the fact that you went back today and touched on the matter of identification again. All right, I'd like to talk about this a little more, too, because I've had some afterthoughts on our earlier work on that.

P.: M-hm.

T.: It seems to me entirely possible that the period when you were reading the book and thinking about the possibility of becoming a clinical psychologist, that this was a kind of pseudo-identification, or defense strategy, that might have gone something like this: "Look, I think you're pretty good. You've written a great book. I've been reading it, spending my time on that in preference to physics; think it's, think it's pretty good stuff. As a matter of fact, I'm *even* thinking of becoming a clinical psychologist myself *just like you*." Now notice how that could have been intended to operate, intended unconsciously or only quasi-consciously. It could have been designed to do this, to say to me in effect: "Look, what more could you ask of me? I acknowledge that you're just okay; what's more, I've indicated that I'd like to be just like you. Now what more could you ask for in the way of change? Surely no man in authority could ask any more of anybody else."

Now I'm sure that there's something very sincere and something very constructive about that. But I think there may have been a kind of overtone of protective coloration in it, a kind of, a device for holding the line, a form of resistance.

Now we didn't, if there was anything of that there, we didn't get it at the time; but perhaps we can be wise in retrospect and conjecture that what you were doing, without really knowing it of course, was saying to me: "For God's sake, don't make me face this business of my hostility toward you, my hostility toward my boss, my roommate, toward my former research director, my hostility toward mankind in general. This—I—must—not—do! This will be too much. I will go through any kind of disgraceful self-abasement, licking your boots, anything, just so long as I don't have to do this."

P.: Well, I don't know if it's important; I mean, the idea is probably the main thing; a little detail that I think, I think may operate there and, but it may come out at the same point, and that is this, that I only told you once that I'd be a clinical psychologist and that was really interjected, uh, rather, rather quickly. I, I didn't dwell on that at all. But, before doing that I only, I went up to Philadelphia; this was just after I, I was so hot on this subject, right after I got the book, and I really got interested in that, and uh, I was very glowing in my praise of it. And then, I went on up to New York. I told one of my brothers that, in my unsettled state, I was even considering a couple of other things, going to medical school possibly, or even a further break with physics and going into clinical psychology. So, oh, this, this idea of becoming a clinical psychologist is one that I'd developed at *great length,* apart from, from you, in which I mentioned only, just. I wouldn't say casually, but just, I think I said I'd dreamed of going into medicine, I'd even thought of going into clinical psychology.

Well, the reason I say it might come out to the same place is that I feel that, uh, that by fully identifying myself with the theory of being good and being happy, this type of psychology, that now I'd be able to go on, *right as of now;* and it was all part of, of what I, uh, what I believed; I now had it, I really had the spirit, so to speak. And, I think it was the great hope that I thought I had enough now, so since I didn't have to go any further, which, I think, probably comes out at the same place, but puts the emphasis on a different point.

When the possibility has been thoroughly explored that the patient's interest in adopting the same profession as the therapist is a form of resistance to continued therapy, the patient very commonly drops the idea of becoming like the therapist in the professional sense and settles down to "identifying" with him in the more basic ("developmental") sense of using association rather than dissociation as a means of dealing with one's conflicts and of "introjecting" other attitudes and skills of the therapist. The patient, in doing this, is identifying with the therapist in the sense of trying to be simply a *normal person,* and as this end is approximated the practical considerations which usually militate against his taking up the therapist's profession are evaluated more realistically and lead to a continuation of the patient's present vocation or a change to another vocation which is a more ideally suitable one.[7]

20. THE RULE OF CROSS-IDENTIFICATION IN NEUROSIS. It has been a basic assumption of this chapter that dissociation is a crucial determinant of neurosis: without it neurosis cannot occur and with it neurosis, at least in latent form, exists. At the same time, in Section 5, considerable importance has been attached to the pathogenic implications of identification with the cross-sex parent. It is an empirical fact that psycho-

[7] The reader may miss in this discussion any reference to what has been called "positive transference." It is the author's impression that many of the phenomena which have been subsumed under this term are actually just subtle manifestations of resistance! What is most "positive" in the patient-therapist relationship is usually *new, earned* (learned), therefore *not* "transferred."

neurotic patients commonly display evidence of divided affiliations with respect to masculinity and femininity. But the precise nature of the causal connection is uncertain. However, this much may be tentatively suggested, that mixed-sex identification and cross-sex identification, per se, are not pathogenic. We are familiar with the overt homosexual whose principal concern is with the social difficulties which his inversion causes and who is comparatively free from inner conflicts (thus giving his character more of a criminal than neurotic cast). There are also men and women in whom masculinity and femininity are fairly evenly divided and who, aside from some eccentricity in respect to the kinds of persons they can marry, often appear to be relatively "normal." The issue seems to hinge, therefore, upon whether the person has *accepted* his inversion, in whatever degree it exists, and taken the consequences or has been severely conflicted, ashamed, and covert with respect to it. In the latter type of person there is the possibility that the conflict thus engendered has at some time been resolved by dissociation; if this has happened, the individual is "neurotic," and his tendency toward inversion may be said to have been "the cause." But it apparently is not a *necessary* cause. The critical question is whether the individual has accepted ("associated") his deviant tendencies with respect to masculinity and femininity or has reacted dissociatively with respect to them.

On the assumption that conflict between cross-sex identification and common social (superego) values (which stress like-sex identification) may lead to neurotic resolutions, the next problem is to determine exactly *what* it is that gets repressed or dissociated under these circumstances. There is a widespread belief that it is the individual's "homosexuality" or "cross-identification" which gets repressed and that when this happens the individual is particularly disposed to paranoia or paranoid trends. This assumption is illustrated in the following passage from Fisher (1950)*:

Paranoic trends or reactions are strictly of endogenous origin. No type of maladjustive reaction is less dependent on existing situational factors. And, although much remains to be learned about the genesis of paranoia, the development of a typical case can be roughly sketched. Early in life the individual acquires a homosexual and, often, an inverted sexual orientation. Subsequent to this but still during the pre-teen age, he strongly represses his homosexual tendencies and interests. . . . Since his libidinal drives are partly or wholly directed to his own sex, he is incapable of making a workable and satisfying adjustment to persons of the opposite sex. . . . Since his repressed tendencies would be utterly obnoxious to his conscious and accepted system of personal values, he stolidly refuses to perceive or recognize their existence. Holding an antithetical relationship to his conscious ideals, they generate feelings of guilt and moral depravity; and because they comprise a constant threat to his self-esteem and moral integrity, and being thoroughly unaware of their subjec-

* By permission from V. E. Fisher, *The meaning and practice of psychotherapy.* Copyright, 1950, The Macmillan Company.

tive origin, he projects them onto others. He then feels that other persons, particularly members of his own sex, are suspicious of him, unfriendly toward him, or persecuting him. In some cases wherein the patient has tried particularly hard to make a normal psychosocial adjustment, the homosexual tendencies become projected onto some person of like sex. He then thinks that this person has improper sexual designs on him.

The writer has never become well acquainted with a case of manifest paranoic reactions in whom evidence of repressed homosexual inclinations could not be discerned. Once a diagnosis of paranoic reaction is fairly certain, a subconscious homosexual orientation should be taken for granted (pp. 90-91).

In keeping with the foregoing hypothesis, the suggested logic of treatment takes the following form:

Inasmuch as the patient is utterly intolerant of his repressed desires, and since he usually lacks psychic flexibility to a normal degree, the first step in therapy is *preparatory*. The patient's perspective on personal relationships must be broadened and his psychic rigidity (affective intolerance) softened.

The second objective, of course, is the complete exposure and examination of the patient's homosexual propensities. But in doing this the therapist must persistently endeavor *to lead the patient into making a discovery of these propensities by himself*. In no instance should their existence be *forced* on the patient's awareness (p. 91).[8]

In this brief illustration [omitted] the point of therapeutic significance was not so much the patient's recalling the incident as it was his reliving it. By doing that he discovered quite by himself that he had once been fond of his father, a fact which he theretofore had strongly denied. And the return to his integration of *conscious* interests and attitudes of this long repressed affectionate capacity toward a member of his own sex tended to increase his tolerance for friendliness toward men and to temper his psychic rigidity (p. 93.).[9]

The therapist should substantiate his diagnosis of repressed cross-identifications in terms of the information secured from the analysis of the patient's past history. This should be done as convincingly as possible, for it is of the greatest importance that the patient accept the diagnosis and interpretations which are made at this point. Otherwise the therapist may find that he is unable to lead the patient to a discovery of the repressed homosexual tendencies later (pp. 95-96).

[8] The danger which the author presumably has in mind here is one which is commonly referred to as "homosexual panic," i.e., a panic which supposedly occurs when the individual realizes, without proper "preparation," that he has homosexual tendencies. An alternative interpretation of the clinical facts will be suggested shortly.

[9] For reasons given elsewhere (Mowrer, 1950, chaps. xxi, xxii), one may reasonably doubt that any little boy ever became a homosexual because he "had once been fond of his father." In fact, a strong affectional bond between son and father appears to be the best possible insurance of like-sex identification and normal heterosexuality. In the example given, one may conjecture that it was the *disruption* or *loss* of the once good relationship with the father that caused the trouble, not the affection or fondness for him. Indeed one can go further and conjecture that it was the repression of these positive feelings for the father that had made a cross-identification and homosexual trends possible.

No particular effort should be made to keep the patient whose transference feelings become markedly suspicious and unfriendly, unless the therapist would invite possibly serious trouble for himself (p. 97).

There is an alternative possibility that, when there is acute conflict occasioned by homosexual trends, it is, again, the critical, condemning part of the personality that gets repressed rather than the sexually aberrant part. It seems likely that in every instance of paranoid personality there will be found, not simply a history of perverse wishes, but a history of actual practices of a forbidden and secretive nature and that these have been preserved and protected by dissociation of the self-criticisms and social disapproval which would otherwise accompany them. Here the assumption is that the dissociation (or neurosis) is in the service of the individual's immaturity and quest for pleasure, not that it occurs because of the triumph of his attempt to be "good."

In general, Freud has thrown his weight toward the view that paranoia involves repressed homosexuality (see the case of "Dr. Schreber," Freud, 1933a), but in a generally neglected passage he has provided the basis for a different line of thought. In the *New introductory lectures on psychoanalysis* (1933c), Freud says:

They [the insane] have turned away from external reality, but for that very reason they know more of internal psychic reality and can tell us much that would otherwise be inaccessible to us. One group of them suffer what we call delusions of observation. They complain to us that they suffer continually, and in their most intimate actions, from the observation of unknown powers or persons, and they have hallucinations in which they hear these persons announcing the results of their observations: "now he is going to say this, now he is dressing himself to go out," and so on. Such observation is not the same thing as persecution, but it is not far removed from it. It implies that these persons distrust the patient, and expect to catch him doing something that is forbidden and for which he will be punished. How would it be if these mad people were right, if we all of us had an observing function in our egos threatening us with punishment, which, in their case, had merely become sharply separated from the ego and had been mistakenly projected into external reality? (p. 85).[10]

Freud wrote the foregoing passage in an effort to make more graphic and tangible his concept of the superego, but the same facts and argument can be equally used to support the notion that delusions of observation and persecution spring from an attempt on the part of repressed superego functions to return from repression and reassert themselves. It would appear that they have "merely become sharply separated from the ego and . . . mistakenly projected into external reality."

It would seem more natural, certainly more parsimonious, to interpret paranoid delusions as projections of dissociated conscience than as pro-

[10] Essentially the same line of thought is briefly adumbrated by Freud in his *General introduction to psychoanalysis* (1935a).

jections of "repressed homosexuality." Indeed, such an interpretation of paranoid projection makes it seem not so very different from the extremely familiar and clinically commonplace "projection" that occurs in every instance of negative transference. Moreover, this point of view provides a possible key to the riddle which psychoneurotic states associated with homosexual trends have long presented. It suggests that the therapeutic approach to these states should not be in the area of psychosexual differentiation at all, but instead at the level of values which are shared equally by men and women: panhuman values which have to be accepted for the attainment of full femininity no less than full masculinity. Honesty, at least with one's self, is such a value, and dissociation is its antithesis. Thus, in dealing with a person whose central conflicts have to do with tendencies toward inversion, it would follow that the basic difficulty is the same as that found in any other neurosis: a tendency to deal with conflicts dissociatively rather than associatively. Perhaps we also have here an intimation of why it is that the gender of the therapist makes less difference in dealing with persons of the same and of the opposite sex than one might expect. Despite the great emphasis which has often been put upon the attainment of fuller masculinity or fuller femininity (as the case may be) in therapy, perhaps the therapist's most basic job is to help the patient achieve a *fuller humanity*. And once the patient has begun to move forward toward this objective, there will be the same opportunity for new learnings in the psychosexual sphere as in other specific areas of experience and conduct.

But these are admittedly obscure and complex matters which suggest continued study and inquiry rather than certainty.

21. THE PROBLEM OF DIAGNOSTIC TYPES. The foregoing discussion raises the question of the relationship between the psychodynamics of neurosis and diagnostic classifications or types. One example has just been given of the way in which the central thesis of this chapter—that neurosis involves a fission between id-ego and superego rather than between ego-superego and id—can be made to accommodate the paranoid syndrome. In order to indicate the way in which other clinical types fit into the same frame of reference, it will be useful to note three or four tendencies which are likely to be present, in some degree, in even relatively mild neuroses. One of these is the tendency toward *"sensitivity."* Patients commonly report that they "overreact" to criticism or rejection from others. Dynamically, the explanation for this tendency seems to run as follows. Since the neurotic, per hypothesis, is always an individual in whom there is feuding, not to say open warfare, between an id-dominated ego and the superego, it is understandable that whenever there is an ego insult or affront, however slight, it provides an occasion for the superego to attack with renewed vigor and evident justification. Thus the neurotic becomes excessively fearful of real rejection for the reason that to every ounce of objective punishment received is added a pound of internal punishment. Although other trends are likely to be present, too,

this trend toward sensitivity and *social withdrawal* is one of the most distinguishing features of *schizophrenia*.

Related to the trend just considered is that toward *emotional instability*. Neurotic patients very commonly report *mood swings*. The depressed and elated phases may be *reactive*, i.e., precipitated by objectively identifiable events, or they may be *endogenous*, i.e., apparently spontaneous in origin. But in either case the depressed phase is one in which there is superego ascendancy, with attendant retreat, defeat, and suffering on the part of the ego. And in the elated phase the ego has gained the ascendancy and is boastfully expansive, unchecked for the time being by superego forces. That depression is the fundamental phenomenon in the *manic-depressive* syndrome has been suggested by many writers, with euphoria or elation representing the relief experienced in escaping from the dread ache of depression. Or, viewed more behaviorally, the manic phase of the disturbance is perhaps not so much an expression of the pure joy of relief from depression as it is a systematized denial of and defense against depression.

Another trend commonly noted in almost every neurosis is *indecisiveness*. The dynamics appear to be these. Let us suppose that one of the two warring factions within the personality makes a decision. Decisions nearly always have some attendant disadvantages, often unanticipated consequences, and sometimes they are nearly calamitous. If there is, therefore, within the personality an opposing part (somewhat analogous to a rival political party) which is ready to pounce upon the other part for its mistakes (but, because of dissociation, without giving explicit reasons for its attacks), rather than giving it support and comfort in time of adversity, the decision-making process will become increasingly hazardous and will tend to be exercised less and less. In extreme cases, this trend gives the syndrome of *abulia*. In less extreme form it may be perceived and reported by the patient as "poor will power."

In so-called *neurasthenia*, two common complaints are *fatigue* and *poor concentration*. Patients so afflicted readily understand if an analogy is drawn between the contending forces within their personality and two equally powerful electric motors which, connected by a common shaft, are being driven in opposite directions. If the two motors are receiving about the same amount of current, neither will turn or they will turn very slowly and will develop very little momentum. If, on the other hand, the two motors are reconnected ("learn") in such a way that they work *together* rather than against each other, they will mutually support and strengthen rather than cancel each other. In like manner, the erstwhile neurotic whose personality has undergone a reorganization along constructive lines finds new interests, strength, and staying power.

In what has been said there is no intention to exclude constitutional or organic factors as partial determinants of the syndromes referred to. Such influences deserve particular notice in connection with *involutional melancholia*. But, here again, we can see the same type of dynamic processes operating. The involutional syndrome typically appears, both in men and in women (though somewhat more commonly in the latter), when there is a decline in physical attractiveness and/or a decline in personal importance and usefulness. It is as if some persons contrive during the early and middle decades of their lives to wrest from the environment enough ego support to enable this part of the personality to hold at bay the hounds of conscience. But when this precarious source of ego strength is lost or its decline is clearly foreshadowed, submerged self-condemnations often rush forward with overwhelming ferocity.

Other illustrations of the way in which a single, basic pattern of psychopathology may operate to produce various clinical syndromes could be given—for example, see Mowrer (1950, chap. xxii), for a discussion of alcoholism—but the principle has already been sufficiently indicated. This discussion has not, of course, attempted to account for the "choice" of symptomatology made by different classes of patients. Constitutional, experiential, and perhaps adventitious factors may be relevant here; but in all cases there appears to be a psychodynamic element, which means that there is a place, large or small, for psychotherapy.

22. Implications for Psychotherapeutic Technique. The question may legitimately be asked: What are the distinctive implications for therapeutic technique of the particular theoretical point of view presented in this chapter? Most important, perhaps, is the bearing it has upon the management of transference. Instead of seeking to advance the patient's psychological welfare by dissolving ("analyzing") a supposedly too severe superego, a therapist operating within the present frame of reference *accepts* the patient's high standards as evidence of good character and works toward the goal of making these standards more understandable and helpful, so that they may ultimately be harmoniously integrated with the rest of the personality. Consistent with this point of view, the therapist also takes the attitude that depression, inferiority feeling, anxiety, and the other painful affects which the neurotic experiences are *signs of strength* within the personality. It is true that if there were not something "wrong" with the individual, these affects would not be experienced, or at least not in anything like the same intensity. But an individual with internal disharmony who is experiencing these distressing emotions is not nearly so badly off as he would be if, under the same circumstances, he were bland, unconcerned, unmotivated. The patient's distress holds the key to his salvation, and he must come to see its true meaning and potential usefulness.

It will also be obvious that a therapist's interpretations will be different according to whether he believes that repression typically goes in the direction of the id or in the direction of the superego. Other variations in technique follow from the conception of neurosis here described, but they cannot relevantly be discussed at this time.

23. Interpretive and Reflective Technique Compared. As others have suggested, the distinctive feature of the psychotherapeutic

technique which is associated with the name of Carl R. Rogers is perhaps neither its "nondirectiveness" nor its "client-centeredness"; rather is it the emphasis which is placed upon *clarification* of the client's thoughts and feelings by the technique of *reflection*. At first the rationale of this approach seems to be almost the antithesis of that involved in any form of interpretation; but further analysis of the two methods reveals a surprising similarity. The interpretive therapist may be no less nondirective, client-centered, and *accepting* of the patient than is the reflective therapist; only in one respect does there appear to be a difference. The interpretive therapist *does not accept* the dissociative trends within the patient; he opposes them with all the energy and resourcefulness at his command. Superficially, the reflective therapist goes a step further than the interpretive therapist and "accepts" even the dissociative trends. But in recent writings Rogers (1951) and some of his students have increasingly used the phrase "denial of feeling" to characterize the neurotic personality; and at least tacitly this is something which these therapists themselves do not accept. By their repetitive example, if not by explicit command, they insistently focus attention upon the client's *feelings:* "You *feel* thus and so. . . . You somehow *feel* that . . . ," etc.

Now "denial of feeling" and the concept of dissociation are perhaps less different than they would appear; and if a therapist replaces the patient's "selective inattention" (Sullivan, 1947) with respect to certain feelings by a thorough and intent examination of them, the effect, at least up to a point, should not be very different from that produced by interpretation, which commonly takes the form of the therapist's positing that "this *may* go with this." "Denial of feeling" is surely not so very different from "repression," and any technique which successfully remedies one might be expected to influence the other. These, however, are only conjectures and need to be followed up by empirical research.

24. SOME OBJECTIONS AND REJOINDERS. The position taken in this chapter with respect to neurosis and its treatment has sometimes been said to imply that the principal task of psychotherapy is to "increase the strength of the superego." This is not at all the case. Elsewhere in this book (Chapters 6 and 17) the author has said what he would repeat here, that in his judgment superego functions or values can be influenced very little, if at all, by psychotherapy. From the lack of success of psychotherapy in the treatment of delinquents and adult criminals, one must conclude that this technique does not readily lend itself to a strengthening of the superego; and it appears that an attempt to *reduce* the "severity" of the superego in a neurotic is not only strategically wrong but futile. As repeatedly indicated, the emphasis is instead upon reestablishing normal *communication* between ego and superego and upon changing *ego functions* rather than superego values or standards.

It may also be objected that any system of therapy which accepts the patient's ethical and social values as they are, and makes no attempt to modify them, must be *politically reactionary*. It may seem to imply that the *status quo* is necessarily right and to be opposed to social reform or progress. This does not follow. A psychotherapist, as such, is neither politically reactionary nor politically radical; he is neutral. As an individual citizen, he may have any of a wide range of political sympathies; but as a professional man or woman practicing the art and science of psychotherapy, he works with the personality which the patient brings to him and does not try to impose his own values upon the patient—save in one respect: he will oppose the patient's dissociative trends by associative ones!

The now commonly accepted Freudian view that the neurotic's difficulties arise because of overrestraint, unrealistically high moral standards, or a too severe superego gains a certain superficial plausibility from the fact that neurotics often exhibit what seems to be clear evidence of abnormal conscientiousness. Neurotics are often excessively cleanly, punctual, industrious, thrifty, or "honest." But in every instance, such behavior, under clinical scrutiny, turns out to be bogus: it is a way of drawing attention away from the areas of real immaturity, inadequacy, and inconsistency within the personality. It will not be possible here to reproduce the clinical evidence on which these impressions are founded, but they are very similar to conclusions independently arrived at by the theologian-psychologist, Dr. John W. Stafford. In a paper entitled, "Psychology and Moral Problems," Stafford (1950) asks this question: "Is scrupulosity a mark of insincerity?" His answer is as follows:

The scrupulous person is often popularly confused with a person of delicate conscience, who is always careful to avoid any moral taint. It is, of course, well known that this is not true. We all have respect for the person of delicate conscience: the conscientious person who does his duty, who is kind and helpful to his fellow-men, who is careful to keep always close to his God. But that is *not* scrupulosity. I suggest the following analysis of a scrupulous person: he wants to eat his cake and have it; he wants to do wrong but have no guilt for having done wrong. This looks like an improper way to characterize the scrupulous: they seem to be the opposite. On the surface they are: they always seem afraid to do anything for fear it is wrong; they always seem to have guilt for past faults and fear of future ones. Here I propose to unmask the scrupulous! He sets up, perhaps always unconsciously, impossible conditions for morality. The most harmless act or thought he pretends is sinful. . . . [The scrupulous] are insincere people, even though on the conscious, surface level they often appear loudly and vociferously sincere.

A psychologist or psychiatrist, dealing with a scrupulous person, must somehow help him to unmask himself, to develop insight into his perverted conscience. Perhaps the most effective treatment is to bring the scrupulous to see that he is really no different from the rest of men; that he has the same drives, and is governed by the same moral law. The scrupulous always tells you: "But my case is different." The case may be different, but it is only by getting the person back into the family of the human race that the case can be cured (pp. 122-23).

Instead of speaking of the overly scrupulous person as having a "perverted conscience," it is perhaps more accurate to characterize such a person as a *perverter of* conscience. He presents to the world a false conscientiousness as a means of protecting himself against self-criticisms which are socially valid but which he carefully protects from social scrutiny. Here, as in neurosis generally, the problem is immature and defective ego functioning, not an excessive or perverse superego as such.

CHAPTER 4

THE COLLABORATION OF CLIENT AND COUNSELOR [1]

By William G. Perry, Jr., M.A., *and* Stanley G. Estes, Ph.D.

. . . the modern educator is aware that his role is not only that
of conveying knowledge . . . but that of a strategist leading those
entrusted to him . . . to a deeper realization of their own inherent
qualities. This paradoxical task is given to us as educators because
human beings are what they are.[2]

R. Ulich

Two Philosophies of Education and Psychotherapy

The reader is doubtless alerted by our title to the probability that
we shall become involved in the issue between the "directive" and "nondirective" aspects of interviewing. This will, indeed, be our major concern. It seems unfortunate that the discussion of these terms remained
forensic for so long that it became dreary before it became productive.
Even the recent substitution of the word "client-centered" seems to have
soothed no one's nerves, for its suggestion of moral complacency has
obscured its psychological referents and produced only the retort, "But
that's what all *good* therapists have *always* been." In the interests of
calm sense, many thoughtful clinicians have therefore attempted to shelve
the debate by placing it "on a continuum" (Bordin,* 1948; Collier, 1950;
Stone, 1950) where boundaries melt and contrasts fade. Others are
simply turning away, weary of presumptuous partisanship among the
contestants. We believe that this evasiveness, whether by denying the
problem or ignoring it, results in a serious loss of brain-work on a vital
and promising inquiry. The controversy seems to have been one in which
semantic and forensic confusion has created what has looked like a big
fight about nothing, and so has obscured the importance of the real issue.
The issue is central to all education, that is, to all learning which is
intentionally mediated, guided, or facilitated by another person.

The psychotherapeutic role is not historically an offspring of pedagogy,
but whether the psychotherapist calls his goal of change within the client

[1] This paper presents the conceptual framework of a study in progress in the
Harvard Bureau of Study Counsel. The study is facilitated by the Laboratory of
Social Relations, Harvard University.

[2] R. Ulich, *Fundamentals of democratic education* (New York: American Book
Co., 1940).

* References are to the bibliography at the back of the book.

95

"cure," "symptom-remission," "adjustment," "integration," "normality," "emotional maturity," or "growth," his sole medium must be his client's learning processes. Since the therapist or psychological counselor acts as a mediator or facilitator of this learning, his profession is properly considered a special and recent form of educational practice. It is therefore in the thinking of teachers, in their centuries-old and fervent debate about the learner's spontaneous, self-directing rediscoveries as against the pedagogue's authoritative preformulations, that clinicians may find a suggestive discussion of the directive-nondirective issue as they themselves face it.

The pertinence of this educational discussion to the present clinical one may be judged from the similarity of its wording. The basic postulate of nondirective theory is that the individual possesses "an inherent tendency toward growth and self-actualization," a spontaneous "drive toward maturity even in the face of present pain" and the "capacity to solve his own problems" given a proper environment (Rogers, 1942, 1951b). Its main theorem is that growth takes place when the tendency toward growth is freed, rather than when preconceived knowledge is imposed. Seeds of this thought may be found in the educational ideas of Aristotle, but its first full modern statement was made by Comenius in 1668: "It is the nature of man without ceasing to discover the infinity of his own desires and of his capacity; . . . he finds no resting place for himself in the finite world but has within his own heart inducements and indeed relentless spurs, which make him climb and struggle, panting onwards . . ." (p. 2). Comenius' plea was that this disposition be given major consideration in educational practice so that the individual might get his education through those activities "to which his nature impels him." Elsewhere he emphasized the importance of skill in perceptual discrimination for the fostering of this process, a matter we shall treat later in this paper. These principles, in their battle against "traditional" authoritarian and directive pedagogy, worked out their development under the generalship of such varied men as Rousseau, Pestalozzi ("a helping hand to the instinctive efforts after self-development"), Herbart, Fichte (who introduced the "self-concept"), Froebel, and others (Mossman, 1938), to find their most unequivocal statement in the earlier works of John Dewey.

Dewey (1920) spoke of the positive force of the *"power* to grow," stating that growth "is not something done to [students] ; it is something they do." He attacked those who by their activities or philosophy denied "the power of common life to develop its own regulative methods and to furnish from within itself adequate goals, ideals, and criteria" (Dewey, 1926, p. 38). The extreme statement that the process of evaluation is the proper affair of the growth alone, a formulation which Dewey later seems to have retracted (Ulich, 1945), appeared in 1920 in the words "there is nothing to which growth is relative save more growth" (p. 60).

In the subsequent revolution and counterrevolution of the progressive education movement, the theory received its practical test. The apparently simple antithesis of the notions "teacher knows best" and "students know best" was revealed as extraordinarily complex. Before this complexity could become apparent, partisanship had to run its course. In an interesting forecast of the preferences of modern clinicians, the progressivists turned eagerly for scientific respectability to analogies in the new schools of organismic biology and Gestalt psychology. They even had recourse to the word "child-centered" (traditional teachers, like traditional therapists, angrily: "But that's what all *good* teachers have always been!"). The feelings engendered became so strong that the words "progressive" and "child-centered" are now avoided in favor of the equivocal "modern" by educators who sponsor programs which involve elements of the original movement (Burton, 1944). We cannot trace here the many efforts at resolution of this educational conflict, but it is important to observe that the best of these resolutions have taken the form not of simple compromise between extremes but of a skilful interrelating of complementary processes.

Yet this is not to say that the processes are not in some respects antagonistic. Perhaps the most important product of the educational battle has been the discovery that under any but the best conditions the issue is a real one, rather than the artificial product of a merely verbal dichotomy. It is, of course, easy to point out the semantic and logical difficulties surrounding the "growth" concept as it is usually worded. The phrase "self-actualization" is bare-faced in its teleology, and "the will to grow," as an explanatory postulate, suffers from all the logical weaknesses commonly attributed to it (Howie, 1950). The analogy drawn from organismic biology has apparently been applied too abruptly and oversimply to human behavior. Perhaps the instinctive (self-actualizing?) behavior of organisms less at the mercy of their capacity to learn any variations has offered a tempting stepping-stone to this oversimple thinking. But the vulnerability of the verbal formulation should not detract from an appreciation of the behavioral tendency it purports to explain. On a purely descriptive level, human beings must be accorded the attribute of self-direction as a salient tendency.

The particular direction this tendency takes at a given moment may reflect some life line built into the chromosomes, or more probably it is the resultant of such a line and innumerable vectors built from cultural experience. But what is crucial is that this self-determination is characteristic of man not only in his expression of immediate needs but also in the direction in which he attempts to extend his mastery through learning (i.e., "growth"). The individual determines the direction of this extension of mastery through the manner in which his values and dispositions of the moment influence his selection, whether deliberate or unconscious, of the stimuli to which he will attend. These values and dispositions, sensed by the person as his individuality, show sufficient continuity through time to produce an expanding directional behavior describable, nonteleologically, as "self-actualization."

Observers of this tendency in its fullest operation have always found its productivity impressive. They have usually spoken of the "power" or "will" to grow, or posited a basic "drive" (Rogers, 1942). Descriptively, the individual, free from reactive need for independence (negativism) and reactive need for dependence (overconformity), free from fear and from the passivity of discouragement, does indeed appear to undertake hopefully, and often effectively, such expanding activities as he finds congenial and possible (Angyal, 1941). A "respect for" (single-minded attention to?) this tendency appears to lead logically to the most extreme position taken by progressivists and nondirectivists. Growth fortunately appears to be normally in the general direction of maturity, culturally defined; but, individual differences being what they are, who can search out his particular fulfilment but the individual? The "locus of evaluation" resides properly in the person himself (Rogers, 1948), never in the dogma of teacher or therapist. And since the conditions of growth are commonly described negatively, the main duty of teacher and psychologist must be to create a social environment which releases growth by the "absence" of threat. The sole positive function permitted them by such a view as Rogers' is that of "understanding." That the respect for the individual's integrity explicit in this position is a necessary basis for the democratic ethos seems undeniable.

If we now go on to observe that it is the essence of civilization that culture—with its customs, accumulated skills, and problem solutions—be passed from generation to generation through education, the conflict with the view we have been describing is perhaps not immediately apparent. But even when we leave aside the problem of discipline which may arise in training the young in the customs of even the most benign society and consider only the communication of the culture's skills and knowledge, we are faced at once with violating the individual's integrity, which we have described as residing in his right to protect and develop his individuality by choosing for himself what he will learn.

This dilemma does not arise artificially from a false assumption of antagonism between the individual and society as such (Benedict, 1934). It springs from the structural properties of the learning situation. In "growth," learning is strongly inductive; and even the more deductive or reorganizational learning, called "insight," is mediated almost entirely by the individual's own self-determined activity. In education, sheer limit of time demands that learning of solutions constructed by previous generations be often largely deductive and analytical. On the assumption that the learner can learn something faster through the directions of someone who has previously learned it, even the best teacher demands of the learner frequent periods of relative passivity in which there is no question but that the "lead" and "locus of evaluation" rest in the authority. The authority selects what is "important" for the learner.[3]

This act of selection by the teacher or psychological counselor precludes any resolution of the dilemma by such evasions as: "The giving of

[3] The two types of structure are represented in their extremes in psychological literature by Rogers on the one hand and Skinner on the other (see his *Walden two*, 1951).

information, as distinct from advice, is not incompatible with the client- (or child-) centered point of view." "Information" quite acceptably refers to "how" to solve mathematical problems or "how" to run a machine. Such items as "how" to solve personal problems or "how" to handle a personal relationship are of the same order. Of course, by being more personal they look perilously close to advice, but surely we cannot withhold from students and patients certain areas of the wisdom of the race simply on the grounds that the materials might be of personal importance to them. The critical point we would emphasize about the giving of information is that it is the teacher or therapist who selects the information. It is therefore the representative of the culture who is exerting active control over the stimuli to which the individual is to respond.

Nor is the clinician to avoid the issue by drawing an arbitrary distinction between education and psychotherapy. Differences of degree in factors that interfere with learning and differences in structure of subject matter should influence emphasis in practice; but, at the level of principle in the issue between self-selection and teacher-selection, no distinction appears warranted. Rogers himself makes no such distinction,[4] and yet he countenances, in classroom practice, lectures by the teacher "at the request of the class," as well as information about resources "they would probably have been unaware of if the instructor had not mentioned them" (1951b, p. 398). In giving such lectures and information, the instructor must obviously respond not only in the light of his understanding of the students' requests, but as well in the light of his knowledge as a representative of the culture, as a specialist. Any such activity, however, Rogers denies to the counselor *in principle,* regardless of the nature or quality of a client's request or need. Rogers appears to believe that for clients, in contrast to students, there are no useful matters or resources of which they would be unaware unless the counselor provided them.[5] If on the other hand we attempt to separate therapy from education by reversing this distinction and say that therapist-direction is appropriate for the more disturbed persons who are less able to direct themselves, and unnecessary for "normal" students, we are in an equally untenable position. As learning situations, education and psychotherapy appear to be continuous in principle; along the whole scale the issue remains: is the teacher-therapist or the student-client to take the lead in selecting the attitudes, understandings, and skills which it will be "good" for the client to learn, and the manner in which he may the better learn them?

That this act of selection is crucial to the argument is evident in recent findings on preference and defense in perception. The influence of the values of the perceiver upon his perceptual thresholds has been reported by Postman, Bruner, and McGinnies (1948) : "As frequently as possible

[4] That is, he shows that effective learning of any subject matter involves growth of a necessarily personal nature.

[5] "We have come to recognize that if we can provide an understanding of the way the client seems to himself at this moment, he can do the rest" (Rogers, 1951b, p. 30).

and as long as possible, perceptual guesses are made in conformity with prevailing value orientation" (p. 153). These directional tendencies are evident in the responses of the subject whose strong preference for scholarly and humane pursuits and carelessness of economic values led him to offer the following *prerecognition* guesses to a tachistoscopic presentation of the word "income": "learning, knowledge, literature, learning, loving, income," his threshold rising to three times its average height. Here the subject's directional tendency toward certain kinds of "learning" make it reasonably certain that he would not at this moment learn much about income unless it was forcibly brought to his attention. The cause here is apparently another incompatible motive. That reactive *resistance* may also have a part is evident in patterns of hostile or derogatory prerecognition responses.

Selective learning, then, appears as the major process through which self-direction enhances individuality. However freely it may operate in vertebrate species where social discipline is not pronounced, it meets the particular conflict we have been discussing in the emergence of culture in man. Here the society, through the active selection inherent in education, forces upon the individual's attention stimuli which, in the pursuit of his self-directing tendency, he might have avoided through a high perceptual threshold, through unconscious or voluntary shifting of attention, or other selective devices. It is, of course, true that by this overriding of immediate preferences, the individual is brought to learn many exceedingly useful skills which he later espouses as an integral part of the very individuality he will defend to the death, and it is a consolation to observe with Benedict (1934) that others of these cultural learnings supply the individual with the very material through which he may express his individuality. But at the moment when the individual is being introduced to these materials, the conflict may be sharp between the process called teaching and the selective and resistive tendencies of self-direction. Sometimes the conflict is so sharp as to defeat both the individual and the culture. This is why the central technical problem of education, and re-education, is the problem of *resistance* [6] (Barzun, 1946; Mowrer, 1948; Perry, 1948 and 1950).

It may now be clear that the dilemma is real and that the processes of direction and nondirection are best conceived as belonging not to a continuum but to two distinct realms. Direction pertains to the reflexive bearing of man's accumulated experience upon man, the active selection and arrangement of stimuli by a teacher so that the learner may the better learn something known to the teacher. Nondirection refers to the strengthening and fostering of the individual's own selective tendencies through a social acceptance and sharing of his exploratory experience.

[6] Resistance is also noticeable when a learner is moving too rapidly under his own power. It is attributable to the fact that he is exposing himself to involvement with ego-relevant stimuli faster than he can assess their safety (i.e., the nature of the integrations they will demand). It is also attributable to the resistance to change inherent in the self-system per se. This latter is generally considered an integral force in opposition to even self-directed growth (Lecky, 1945).

This separation of directive and nondirective processes into two realms exposes the false compromise offered by the "middle ground" of a uni-dimensional continuum. But it offers more positive hopes. The two concepts no longer refer to simple polar opposites. Rather they refer to complex constellations of processses (Bordin, 1948), some polar antago-nists, others not, with rich possibilities both of conflict *and of coordination.* In this complexity, also, a given act, instead of occupying a single position on a continuum, may be perceived and experienced by the learner as directive in one set of conditions and as nondirective in another. Perhaps before the advent of monistic theories it would have been only obvious to remark that it is the interweaving of these processes of learner-direction with learnéd-direction which sets for the teacher and the psychotherapist the critical test of skill. In this paper we examine the relation of this woof and warp in the pattern of a particular counseling form.

Counseling in the College Setting

It is our belief that those who would theorize about counseling would do well at present to limit their attentions to a particular setting and to a narrow range of clientele. We wish to theorize about short-term coun-seling with college students, above average in intelligence, who are not performing academically up to their own or someone else's expectations. The clinical phenomena involved have been roughly described as disturb-ances of a "nonimbedded, nonincapacitating, nonorganic" type (Pepin-sky, 1947). The therapeutic focus proper to dealing with such disturb-ances in later adolescence is commonly accepted as the building of "ego adequacy" rather than the analysis of infantile conflict (Blos, 1946; Gitel-son, 1948).[7] The age is one of emergence from the peculiar inconstancy of adolescence proper into a period of crystallization of adult character. In this period, when the individual can neither escape from an under-taking through inconstancy of purpose nor feel through experience a confidence in his capacity to tolerate defeat, threat in a vulnerable area tends with special frequency to produce intense disorganizing emotions or rigid, self-defeating behavior designed to ward off such emotion. These reactive neurotic defenses, instead of evaporating as they more usually do in the volatile shifts of adolescence proper, too often crystallize, in this later period, into lasting aspects of character. In persons of this age, experiencing what may be their first prolonged self-defeat, brief integra-tional counseling can precipitate enduring reversals of neurotic trends which might otherwise become habitual.

[7] What is meant, presumably, is that with near-normals of this age there is no reason to assume that an effective, resilient character cannot be developed without analysis of infantile conflicts. The very obviousness and surface quality of these conflicts at the time may be itself an aspect of adolescent "working through." In the last decade and a half, psychoanalysts themselves have emphasized the ego-integrative aspect of their work, regardless of setting and age groups (Alexander, 1935; Nunberg, 1931; Perls, 1948).

Up until this period the child-adolescent has cherished the fantasy that once clear of the tyranny of parental (educational) authority he will be "free." Now, at the threshold of adulthood, he faces the realization that he is actually exchanging the tyranny of authority for the tyranny of fact. In college, where the overt symbols of this step are postponed (Blos, 1946) and educational authority is still manifest, there is a strong tendency to dodge an acceptance of fact by perpetuating, as rigid maladaptive character traits, the revolt, negativism, and superficial conformity "normal" to American adolescents. By continuing to ascribe all frustration to the restraints imposed by authority, the individual can postpone at a fatal moment the formation of an adult character.

What internal act comprises the shift of the sense of identity from the childish "me" of wish and impulse (antithetic to the "they" of ought and must) to the mature "self" of choosing and doing (Perry, 1950) is not yet known. But the special character of the therapy we wish to describe springs from the fact that the shift is normally made in one area of life at a time, seldom all at once. Usually, for example, boys attain a factually oriented selfhood first in extracurricular activities and summer jobs, last in home and studies, where the infantile role tends to perpetuate itself. This means that the typical client of the college clinic *has already learned* in some (perhaps minor) aspect of life most of the skills and attitudes which are necessary for an integrated, nonneurotic handling of his situation, be it to remedy it or to bear with it. That is, where a client is not the atypical victim of a long-standing and pervasive character disorder, he has discovered at least once, somewhere, that self-esteem need not always be dependent upon having one's way, that disappointment and frustration can be lived through without loss of personal worth, and that the limitations imposed by fact can be accepted without shame as applying even to one's self (MacPherson, 1949). At one time or another he has at least tasted the satisfaction of self-esteem and assertive competence in dealing directly and "on his own" with a reality unbuffered and undistorted by authoritarian mediation. As a part of this experience he has also at some time or other communicated intimately and freely about his feelings, perhaps with a childhood chum (Sullivan, 1947).

The learning through which a client with such a history appears to free himself from an acute reactive maladjustment is distinguished by its swift, reorganizational character. The therapy of a chronic neurosis, on the other hand, must depend to a large extent upon modifying the client's reactions inductively, through an extended relationship with the therapist, into learnings which have been previously excluded from experience. The process must be slow also because the client is identified with his defenses; they are so extensive a part of the only "me" he knows that he cannot relinquish them until he has built some other self to be.[8] In contrast, integrational counseling focuses on the client's transfer of learnings already

[8] The existence side by side of the old and the new "me" is a commonplace of extended therapy in its mid-stages. The processes are commented upon by Alexander (1941).

established and imbued with positive selfness. It is a process of sentient *problem solving*.

The "problem" to be solved is not, of course, the merely external academic or personal difficulty; for integrational counseling, as for any therapy, it is the internal defensive structure which has distorted, perpetuated, or aggravated the external situation. In the clientele we have described, the solving of such problems, affect-laden as it must be to be productive, nevertheless resembles strikingly its analogue in more purely intellectual areas.[9] The resemblance is revealed both in the character of heuristic activity and in the apparent nature of cognitive reorganization. In broadest terms, these clients solve their problems by applying to the disturbed area of defensive reaction (i.e., relationships to parental and educational authority and their surrogates in the ideal) those more integrative modes of perception, cognition, and feeling which have been experienced in some other area in the past. When such a reorganization or insight is rewarded by a sharp reduction in anxiety, the client may be counted upon to "rehearse" it and thereby achieve by himself the necessary stabilization of the "new" adjustment over a period of time (Alexander, 1941).

As in any therapy, when it is successful, what the client should achieve is not only a particular step toward maturity, but also a changed self-expectancy, an increased confidence in the power of his own problem-solving capacity, and as well a sense for how this capacity may be enhanced by collaboration with the agency of the culture. In the next section we shall rough out a description of the general nature and condition of this collaboration.

Two Stages in Counseling: A Reconciliation

The manner of counseling which we shall describe in this section consists of two phases in which the counselor participates in somewhat different ways. In the first phase the counselor attempts to behave consistently within the Rogerian, nondirective framework. In the second he is free to perform certain additional, more "active" roles as a collaborator in problem solving. The turning point between the two phases is indicated by certain cues in the client's behavior from which the counselor infers that the client has come to perceive the counseling situation from what we shall call the "heuristic set."[10] We shall spell these matters out in more detail.

[9] "The essential features of problem solving are independent of the specific thought material" (Duncker, 1945, p. v). There are two prominent *learning* aspects of problem solving in this form of counseling: first, the client learns the new organization and the concomitant alteration of "feelings" in regard to its parts, and second, the client appears to learn a "learning set" (Harlow, 1949) or generalized notion of how to solve similar problems by searching fruitful areas, asking himself productive questions, etc.

[10] A similar division into phases has been suggested in the literature of vocational counseling (Bixler, 1948; Bordin and Bixler, 1946; Butler, 1948; Kilby,

Like, we suppose, all other clients, students who apply or are referred for this type of counseling almost invariably preconceive the situation as a problem-solving relationship in which the counselor is to be an authority or expert who is to take the lead (and presumably the concomitant responsibility for the outcome). Their own role they perceive at most as that of "assistant" in the process. If they are passive (and resistant), they will either wait for questions or announce, "I'd be glad to tell you anything you want to know." If they look on themselves as cooperative, they say, "Well now, I have to give you something to work on, don't I ?" Even if they have "studied" Rogerian theory in psychology class and have been warned that the counselor has nondirective leanings, they appear simply to encapsulate this information in the larger frame of conventional expectations about authority: "Now I know *you want me* to start talking." All this is a predictable function of "complementary projection," "parataxis," "transference," "wishful distortion," and suchlike processes. It is a structuring of the field which must sooner or later be altered in any therapy worthy of the name. In this form of counseling it is attacked at once, the risk of wrecking rapport or of precipitating anxiety being, with these clients, a tolerable one.

We used the verb "attack," above, deliberately. In view of the very deviance of Rogerian nondirective behavior from our clients' preconceptions, it is in its impact far from "passive" or "accepting"; it is the most violent attack that can be made upon these preconceptions. In its unrelieved *contrast,* it cuts the ground from under the client's expectations by offering these no sensory support whatever (Hebb, 1949). The counselor offers instead the elements of a role unassimilable to the client's prototypes of authority. Only such *consistent* behavior can force the client rapidly to reorganize the field, and only great compensating warmth from the counselor can keep him from leaving it before he does.

The extraordinary rigidity of the client's expectations of the counselor's role is evident in the ingenuity employed in exploiting any available circumstances which may make his nondirective behavior assimilable to them—e.g., of a young counselor, "Oh, he behaved that way because he just didn't know the answers" (Seeman, 1949) ; of a nondirective dean, "It was just another form of inquisition—he was trying to draw me out."

The requirement that the counselor behave in consistent contrast to the client's initial expectations raises serious problems for rapport which we shall mention in the last section. Where these are overcome, the clients we have been speaking of typically reverse their notions of role

---

1949; Seeman, 1948). But the rationale has not been explored, and the shift is usually related to steps in the process (i.e., test selection, interpretation, etc.) rather than to the client's perceptual set. The most suggestive parallel of this presentation appears in the brief quotation by Rogers (1951b, p. 399) from an unpublished article by Shedlin. The excerpt describes the shifting role of the teacher toward more active participation once the permissive "mood" has been established. We use the word "heuristic" here in its pedagogical meaning, to refer to conditions "which lead a person to find out for himself" (*Webster's New International Dictionary,* 1947).

within the first forty minutes of interview.[11] It is as if they say to themselves, "We're here to solve problems; he's not taking the lead; someone
has to; I guess I'm elected." They then perceive themselves as carrying
the initiative and the counselor as their assistant. In this set, the counselor can be perceived as a sustainer of self, and the active assistance
which he subsequently offers will not per se be perceived as threatening,
or as lacking in "respect" (Estes, 1948).

We shall call this new perception of the counseling situation the
"heuristic set." Its essence consists of the client's feeling that he is
ultimately responsible for two functions in the problem-solving process:
initiative and *evaluation*. We mean to give these terms special referents.

Verbs of general process, like the Greek εὑρίσκειν, "to find," commonly include the sense of both beginning and end processes, in this case
"to search" and "to discover." We wish the word "initiative" to refer
to an aspect of searching, that is to the sense: "I am he who must undertake the exploration and determine its broad direction." Its opposite
appears clinically in the question, "Have you any questions you'd like to
ask me?" or, after a set speech, "Is there anything else I can tell you?"
Its positive assumption appears in: "Well, I don't know if this is related
or not, but I may as well take the plunge and see what happens."

The phrase "and see what happens" connotes the client's sense of
responsibility for *evaluation* of the outcome of the search, the determination of the relevance of discoveries to his concept of his self, to his "feelings," and to his behavior. Its opposite may be inferred from, "Do you
think *that's* my trouble?" and its effective function from, "I don't like
that, but it's *so.*" It is equally inferrable when the client assumes responsibility for rejecting his findings or applies the brakes to his assimilation
of them: "Gee, I'm going to have to let that one set a bit."[12]

We say, then, that when a client perceives these two functions as his
own rather than the counselor's, he has assumed the "heuristic set." Such
a frame of mind makes a critical difference in the way the client will perceive active participation by the counselor. We postulate that *any coun-
selor-participation which is assimilated by the client to a set in which he
perceives himself as ultimately responsible for initiative and evaluation
is properly describable as client-centered.*

We shall return in a moment to the important adverb "ultimately."
First, it is necessary to take what may be the crucial step in our argument. This step is contained in the observation that once the client has
reorganized his conception of his and the counselor's roles, his new conception is subject to the same laws of stability as governed his original
preconception concerning these roles. The new structure may not be so
strongly supported at first by generalizations from other experience, but
it will possess its own stability. It will, in fact, assimilate, without threat

---

[11] The normal range for our sample seems to be from ten minutes to the end of
the second hour.

[12] A remark from a follow-up interview reveals this same operational frame:
"I knew that that was the solution, whether or not I was ready for it."

to its integrity, many activities of the counselor which are conventionally excluded from the nondirective repertoire. These activities will then be "client-centered" in function even though, when judged in isolation by an external observer, some might be assigned positions well toward the "active" end of the conventional directive-nondirective continuum. It is through these activities, perceived by the client in the context of his heuristic set, that the counselor may put at the client's service the knowledge and skills of that part of the culture in which the counselor is a specialist.

That these activities do not destroy the heuristic set, but assimilate to it, is ascribable to their failure to group consistently enough to develop a role in *contrast* to the counselor's new conceived role. Or better, the counselor does not appear to behave in a consistent manner which is *incompatible* with the client's new notion that the responsibility for initiative and evaluation is ultimately his own.

Here we are with the word "ultimately." What we mean is best revealed by the manner in which clients appear to fit the counselors' active participation into their new conception of roles. The methods used may be inferred from protocols of follow-up interviews designed to reveal the client's perception of the counseling experience.[13] The protocols reveal two broad methods of assimilation.

The first is utterly simple. The client appears merely to absorb the counselor's active participation into so strong a conviction of his own responsibility that he either fails entirely to notice the "real" extent of the counselor's activity, or in any case fails to recall it. A client who early shifted his perception of roles reports of two interviews in which counselor participation might reasonably be called "bold": "I didn't realize that I would have to do almost *all* the talking."

The second method of assimilation is more complex and suggestive. Many clients appear to maintain their own sense of responsibility while from time to time they *delegate* [14] a segment of problem-solving activity to the counselor as a temporary expedient useful to themselves. They then appear to look upon the counselor's activity as something they have authorized, a potentially enlightening realignment of problem elements, the outcome of which they alone can assess. "He helped to put things out there where I could look at them." Here the perception of active counselor participation is clearly assimilated to the notion of the client's ultimate responsibility for evaluation. Most commonly this temporary delegation concerns initiative in search, the counselor's participation consisting of various procedures designed to facilitate exploration. These

---

[13] These interviews are carried out by the coauthor, who is not a member of the clinic's staff. The technique employed is Merton and Kendall's "focused interview" (1946). The quotations in the remainder of this section are statements elicited by stimuli offering a maximal freedom of response.

[14] Compare Rogers (1951b) on teacher activity "at the request of the class" mentioned earlier. Here "delegation" need be neither explicit nor even an action taken in advance of the counselor's response; the word refers to the attitude taken toward the response.

procedures will be illustrated in the section on "Collaborative Searching-and-Finding." Very rarely, as we shall specify, the counselor may effectively share in evaluation of findings.

A client who employs this second, more complex method of assimilating counselor participation to his perception of himself as responsible for his own self-direction may go on to differentiate more subtly his own and the counselor's roles. Where in the first case the client experiences a rather gross sense of being on his own, of having to "figure things out for myself," in this latter differentiation of roles he appears to feel a general equality of status with the counselor as a person: "We were both up there working on the problem." But within this equality he perceives a sharp division of expertness and function: *"I was the one who had the key. I knew what was on the inside; he knew how these things could work."*

Here the client is secure in his possession of "the key"; the responsibility is his as to what he will do with it. The sharp distinction he draws between his expertness and the counselor's means that he will feel no loss of self-esteem or "respect" if the counselor offers assistance which he could not readily provide for himself. He himself is the professed expert as to "what is on the inside," the special, particular, idiosyncratic problems which are his. The counselor he sees as an expert in something else—in problems in general, and in procedures—in "how these things *could* work." [15]

This client's statement, then, portrays the web of which we have been speaking, the collaboration of the client as a self-directing learner and of the counselor as his "learnéd" consultant.

The Dynamics of Nondirectiveness

Strictly nondirective procedures form such a necessary background for the counselor's consultative activities that we shall pause to analyze in this section the ways in which these procedures seem of themselves to aid the client's problem solving. That their consistent use at the outset tends to structure the relationship in the way we have just described is, of course, enough to make them indispensable to this type of counseling, for until a client accepts initiative and evaluation as ultimately his responsibility, he will find no solution to his particular problems. But nondirective procedures promote problem solving in other ways, not only in the initial phases of interview, but subsequently.

A client comes or is sent to the counselor because he has been unable to meet his own demands or the demands of others, or because he is involved in conflicting demands, internal, external, or both. His state of

[15] Or from a client's dream: "I was driving the car; you helped me learn to shift the gears." This distinction is precisely that drawn by Howie (1950) in his discussion of insight into affairs-in-general and into affairs in their personal significance (p. 238). One wonders how Rogers can trust the client's capacity to solve his problems, yet appear to distrust his capacity to draw this distinction between his own and the counselor's field of special knowledge.

disorganizing emotion, or his anxious anticipation of it, produces an intense goal-centeredness (Wertheimer, 1945), a narrowness of thinking and a defensiveness which are well-known inhibitors of problem-solving activity (Beier, 1949). As long as the client assimilates the counselor to prototypes of authority which in the past have been productive only of further demands, this inhibiting condition will continue. Nondirective procedures appear to reduce this condition through catharsis, through the supportiveness of an accepting and understanding social context, and through an absence of new demands. The absence or presence of new demands is, however, relative to the degree to which the particular client inclines toward considering his *feelings* with the counselor. For clients not so inclined at the moment, the counselor's implication that he will consider nothing else can create a demand provocative of thoroughly disruptive anger and fear (English, 1948; Robinson, 1950). This factor presents special problems whenever a client is not yet ready to acknowledge any relationship between his "presenting problem" and his feelings.

An examination of the whole concept of "reflection of feelings" will lead us to the ways in which nondirective procedures aid problem-solving proper. The term "feelings" in this phrase appears usually to refer to those often unconceptualized, personally relevant expectancies about objects by which our behavior toward the objects is largely determined. In this sense, the interrelations of feelings parallels the structure of character itself (compare MacLeod, 1949). The counselor's "reflection of feelings" tends to produce a resonance of this particular mode of experience so that the client's associations enlarge the problem field in its special, self-relevant bearing.

As the client enlarges on his problem, the emphasis of the counselor's response on the active verbs—"you resent . . . you distrust . . . you want . . ."—tends to bring these feelings out of background and to present them as salient figures where they become symbolized and available for manipulation as problem elements. Another way of putting this process is to say that the client gradually abstracts values from their imbeddedness in objects and relates them to his perception of objects (Duncker, 1945; Rogers, 1951b). The generic verb, "you *feel* that . . . ," emphasizes the perceptual act itself. Initially, values (e.g., usefulness, unkindness) have a way of seeming to be properties of objects or of persons, rather than of perception. They appear to reside in the origins to which we attribute them. Hence a client's statement, "My professor is down on me," means one thing; and the counselor's response, "You feel your professor is down on you," means quite another. That clients are sometimes aware of what is happening to them under this kind of tutelage is evident in the occasional retort: "No, I *don't feel* my professor is down on me; he *is* down on me." For the most part, however, the training is too subtle to excite resistance, and clients simply start looking within themselves as perceivers and start manipulating as attitudes within their control many values which previously seemed inseparable from objects.

That the client's feelings then change in nature, in part because of their association to the counselor's accepting tone as he reflects them, is clearly one of the most important effects of nondirective counseling (Rogers, 1951b; Shaw, 1949; Shoben, 1948). Not only do the feelings alter in quality or intensity, but more important the client changes his feelings toward his feelings.

Nondirective procedures also further exploratory activities in a special way. Searching normally progresses from one "solution area" to another as new hypotheses come to mind. Duncker has shown that the move to a new hypothesis is a function of the "saturation" of an old one (Duncker, 1945). Clinically, where an unproductive area has been chosen by a client (e.g., "if they'd only change the rules, I'd be all right"), the client has reasons for preferring to find a solution in that area. These reasons imbue it with what Duncker called "functional fixedness" and make it improbable that new hypotheses or areas will occur to the client, or that he will be ready to consider any, until he is himself completely convinced of the fruitlessness of the first. As we hope to show later, the counselor may assist in the original exploration of such an area, but the conventional nondirective response is probably the only sensible and respectful noise the counselor can make while a vain hope is being tenaciously researched (Schaeffer-Simmern, 1948). What is involved at such a time is the act of judgment as to when an area is to be abandoned. Since the original choice of an area represented in itself a partial "solution phase," or "finding" (Duncker, 1945), the ultimate judgment of its fruitlessness falls under the heading of *evaluation* as we have defined it. Except for a special case to be mentioned below, the counselor's intrusion into this act can be expected to retard movement rather than to promote it.

In addition to helping the client with these aspects of problem solving, nondirective procedures provide the counselor with the understanding and materials which he needs for taking part effectively as a consultant. The freedom which the nondirective procedure offers the client, within its demand that he shall attend to his feelings, allows him to produce materials as unbiased as interviewing can reveal. From these materials the counselor, who in our theory is explicitly aware that he responds from his own frame of reference as well as from the client's, must derive his judgment of how and when he may serve the client within the frame of the latter's heuristic act. That is, these materials provide the counselor with the vocabulary, concepts, symbols, and analogies which he will need for effective communication, and they are his indispensable guides to the only things about which he may be helpful—those immediately related to the feelings the client is at the moment contemplating.

Collaborative Searching-and-Finding

The ways we have just described in which nondirective procedures play a part in the client's searching-and-finding point, of themselves, to those more "active" contributions of the counselor which are conventionally excluded from the "client-centered" repertoire and which seem to us both productive and also readily assimilable by the client to the client-centered, heuristic set. At the mention of "active" or "directive" counseling, one usually thinks first of "interpretation." We shall not use this term, for it has been too frequently accused of referring to the flat presentation by the counselor of "solutions" of the class: "You act this way because. . . ." When "interpretation" refers to a skilful and productive act, that act seems usually to be a special case of enlarging the problem field in the facilitation of search. We shall therefore illustrate in this section special techniques through which the counselor can serve the client effectively by furthering the processes of searching-and-finding.

The client's sensation that the counselor's activities are directed not toward him but toward the processes of problem solving gives the heuristic set its collaborative structure. A clearer picture of this structure will help to reveal the nature of the counselor's consultative functions which we intend to exemplify. Let us consider first the spatial properties of "directive counseling" in its worst connotation. In Figure 1, the client senses that the counselor is "seeing through" him at his problem and has a generalized image of it at the back of his head. He perceives the counselor as interpreting his problem to him in a form distorted by his own personality and training:

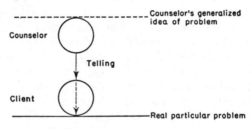

FIG. 1.—Directive counseling.

In strictly nondirective interviewing, the counselor attempts to "divest himself of his own individuality" (Rogers, 1951b) and acts as a "mirroring" *alter ego* in which the client sees his problem objectively:

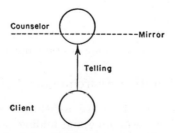

FIG. 2.—Nondirective counseling.

In this case, it is obvious that the counselor cannot "move" without distorting the image. He must indeed divest himself of his individuality and of the frame of reference that goes with it. However, many of the "best" nondirective protocols and the reports of successful clients (Rogers, 1951b) reveal that as the relationship matures a change often comes over it in the sense of a "we-ness," a perceiving-together of an objectified problem. This change is perhaps mediated by such counselor expressions as: "As I see it, you feel that . . . ." The structure is triangular in form and explicit in the statement of a client who, in a follow-up interview, was discussing the mirror effect as he had experienced it: "And so [the counselor] was the mirror, or else we were *both* standing in front of the mirror." It is this latter structure that we believe the Rogerians have failed to exploit. As is evident in Figure 3, the counselor is now free to move, to be *himself,* without shattering either the mirror or his relationship to the client. This personal relationship has now been separated, in a sense, from the problem-solving activity proper:

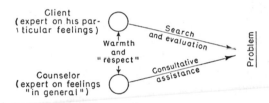

FIG. 3.—Joint perception of the counseling problem.

Here it is clear that the client will feel much less *pressure* from the counselor than in the "directive" structure (Figure 1) because the counselor's activities are directed toward the perceptual aspects of the problem, not toward the client himself. The client will in consequence feel free to reject contributions which seem to him unhelpful without fearing that he is rejecting the counselor, and to accept, without wasteful interpersonal resistance, the useful consultative assistance for which he came. In turn, the counselor's contributions of special skills and understandings may be taken as no reflection whatever upon his respect for the client.

Analogous here is the comparison between the teacher who stands between blackboard and students, talking at them, with the teacher who stands to one side of the direct line between students and subject, assisting in their interpretation of it. Many therapists deliberately or unconsciously introduce this structure by frequently looking to one side as they speak, and by other gestures suggestive of the "out there" objectification of the problem. In our work we think of the mirror as a "screen" upon which the client's perceptions are projected, and use a hand gesture to suggest its presence. As one client reported:

At the beginning of the hour it was . . . I was all wrapped up in the problem, and [the counselor] was over in that chair trying to get at it. . . . I had the feeling I was going to sit here and he was going to work on me. . . . After that first interview, I felt that I was up there alongside [the counselor] and the problem was over here . . . and we were *both* working on the problem. . . . He used his hands over here somewhere. . . . He made it so real I really thought that these things were out there, and it just drew me out of myself so that I looked *at* these things in myself, which I could see, out *here.*

Neurotic patterns have at their foundation a number of interlocking erroneous "beliefs," often primitive and archaic identities, assimilations, or equations constructed in childhood (e.g., disaster will follow if I even accidentally hurt someone; all assertiveness = hostility, etc.). These beliefs will appear behind a client's perceptions as a groundwork of inarticulate major premises. They are often highly affect-laden and subtly interdependent: "I'm a good boy—I'd die without a mummy or a daddy to take care of me." In our clients, they frequently appear more as reawakened residuals which tend to disintegrate rapidly when they become explicit.

Actions helping to make these archaic beliefs explicit are, in our mind, perhaps the principal expression of the counselor's role. An illustration (from notes) follows:

CLIENT [who "has no interest in a college education," has been unable to study, feels anxious and "trapped," and has repeated the same circular thinking in two interviews]: This brings me back to the feeling that if it was just me I'd leave college; but this would break my parents' hearts, and I can't bear the thought of hurting them. I simply can't do it, that's all.

COUNSELOR [looking and gesturing slightly toward "screen"]: As I see it, you feel, for yourself, it would make sense to leave, but you could not forgive yourself for hurting your parents so.

CLIENT: Yeah, I can't seem to get around it. I *always* come back to this.

COUNSELOR: Would you like to say how you think it would feel, out there now, if you were to suppose that you weren't responsible for your parents' feelings?

Obviously there is "a lot going on here," as there is at any moment in counseling. We shall limit our discussion to one function of the counselor's question. This question could be asked only after the heuristic set had been firmly established—previously it would have been perceived as a flat recommendation for irresponsibility, a relief from guilt on covert demand. In this context its intent was to introduce upon the screen a contrast to the apparent "ground" or fixed "given," i.e., the inarticulate major premise upon which the counselor felt the client had been operating, namely, the child's wish-belief: "I am in control of my parents' feelings (toward me); I am hence wholly responsible for them." Should the counselor be wrong, or the issue too hot, the client could easily insist on his conviction about the matter without feeling that he was rejecting the counselor. The way such a contrast sometimes acts to bring a fixed assumption from ground to figure, "loosening" it and making it available for problem solving, is evident in this client's reply:

CLIENT [startled]: Well, I *am* . . . I mean maybe I'm *not* . . . Well, I guess only *partly.*

The critical position which such a belief system can occupy in the dynamics of this age group, together with the reorganizations resulting from its modification, may be inferred from this client's subsequent behavior. He reported in his next interview that, free from a sense that he *had* to stay in college, he had come to feel that he preferred to "for my own purposes" and was now able to get to work. He added that he felt he would visit his parents over the vacation, as he had not previously planned. "It'll give them a break. [Then smiling.] Besides, I might get a chance to find out what they're really like."

The word "really" can be a powerful tool in the counselor's helping to bring to light the implied antithesis of fantasy or unrealistic assumption. In place of the question reported above, for example, the counselor might have substituted, should previous cues have suggested it, the proposition: "Suppose we were to put out there the question: If you *were* to leave college, what do you feel would *really* happen?" The question is not asked directly of the client, but is put "out there" for his consideration. If he explores its answer, he will discover any discrepancy between probable fact and fantastic apprehensions residual from infantile hostilities. As another client reports of a similar instance: [16]

There were other things he would put out there. "Now suppose this problem out here, ah . . . suppose your aunt wasn't pleased . . . suppose your parent wasn't pleased . . . *then* what?" I mean, he would pick up my little fears, ah, doubts, something like that, and make me think of what the *real* consequences would be.

I don't know if it was that I was always afraid of what the consequences would be or if I just never questioned about them but . . . I realized there'd be *no* serious consequences . . . although I was really afraid of them before.

The counselor, therefore, puts his training at the service of the client primarily through this kind of "loosening" of fixed, unsymbolized equations and beliefs. He is thus an active agent in helping to bring them into salient awareness, where their elements may become available for the reorganization called "growth." Other techniques for bringing these rigid assumptions into awareness include the sharpening of implied conflict, the use of analogy (Duncker, 1945), and the tentative introduction of a general hypothesis ("interpretation").

Another use of contrast—aimed this time at revealing a feeling tone which is unverbalized but inferrable from voice, posture, or emphasis—is the "reflection" of the content of a statement in a *different* feeling tone from that in which it was expressed. This technique is difficult to reproduce in print, but its tenor may be apparent in the following example:

[16] From a recorded follow-up interview.

STUDENT: I don't know why I got stuck on that paper. Everything was going fine, . . . I mean, I was really turning the phrases. [Voice rising.] I felt this was sure going to be a whiz of a paper.

COUNSELOR [objectively]: You felt the paper would convey clearly the ideas you had in mind.

STUDENT [pause]: Well . . . no, that's *not* what I felt; I suppose I felt "Gee, am I going to look good" . . . *uh,* oh . . . maybe I know now why I cramped up.

These illustrations have each concerned the facilitation of the client's search. In each, as in many other familiar techniques, like pairing things the client has said (e.g., "Are there two kinds of feelings here—sometimes . . . other times . . . ?"), the re-emphasis of certain words (Deutsch, 1949), or even the statement of a generality ("Sometimes these things work this way . . ."), the counselor attends not only to the client's perceptual field, as best he can understand it, but to his own external one as well. His effort in each case is aimed at helping the client to broaden and to explore the general problem area into which his own initiative has taken him.

Much more rarely can the counselor participate in the client's evaluation of his findings, and then only indirectly. A special case, however, illustrates the usefulness of two frames of reference, as compared to the client's alone. The solution of a problem of any complexity involves several steps or "solution phases" (Duncker, 1945). Not infrequently the finding of a new solution phase produces such a release of tension that the client feels that the final solution has been found. Usually a counselor will accept this state of affairs as a part of the wavelike character of this kind of learning; it often expresses those complex internal conditions implied by the expression "the rate at which the client wants to go." But occasionally the client's "sitting down" on such a solution phase may appear as a superficial perceptual phenomenon such as occurs often enough even in mathematical problem solving, and it may at such times result in a serious waste of time or even in action with irreversible consequences. At this time the counselor does well, we believe, to bring up for his client's consideration those problem aspects of his "solution" that he has failed to observe. He may easily do so in question form, "out there," where the results will be appropriate to the relevance of the matter rather than a function of the pressure of his opinions.

We wish we could illustrate here the use of humor both in bringing problem elements into sharper awareness and in cushioning the pain of their evaluation. We lack the gift of writing dramatic dialogue with a twinkle in its eye, and a protocol wrenched from its context of gesture and expression would only awaken the reader's worst fears. Perhaps many persons are leery of all "active" counselor techniques through a justifiable apprehension that they will be misused in the service of the counselor's sadistic or narcissistic impulses. We believe this possibility to be a serious problem, but a separate one. We picture, in our theory, a hypothetical counselor neither omnipotently free of exploiting impulses nor impotently enslaved by them.

In any case, we hope to have illustrated ways in which we believe the counselor can serve his client through a collaborative role while still freeing and supporting the client's selective powers of initiative in search and while according him the dignity of the final responsibility for accepting or rejecting those findings which apply to his self.

Some Objective Confirmation and Conclusions

Evidently, a major problem in this kind of interviewing is to identify those cues in the client's behavior from which a heuristic set may be inferred. It would be helpful to find that some objective measure would coincide with the judgment of the counselor-in-action. We have made only a beginning in this matter. Figures 4 and 5 below show the course of certain categories of counselor and client activity in a series of four interviews in a brief case of this type of counseling. The first interview was "preliminary."

This analysis was made by Bales with his Interaction Process Analysis technique, which he designed for the study of small groups. As scored, the category we have labeled A in Figure 4 (Bales's $6c$) covered most of the "nondirective" repertoire, while B and C (Bales's $5c$ and 8) were felt to include roughly the activities proper to the second or collaborative phase of this type of counseling. If the category graphed in Figure 5 (Bales's 11) may be taken to refer to cues in the client's behavior (tension, asking for help, withdrawal, etc.) from which may be inferred the opposite of the heuristic set, the reduction of this category to near zero at period 4 should be followed by the first change in counselor behavior as reflected in Figure 4. This is seen to be the case.

The graphs therefore appear to reflect some of the processes we have been describing. It is a great day in the life of a clinician when he finds quantitative evidence that suggests he is indeed doing some of the things he thinks he is doing. It is with great reluctance, therefore, that we confess some qualification of confidence in these charts. Bales's measure must be considered a refined tool for the purpose for which it was designed, but we have at this point in our research no good right to assume that its categories are satisfactory correlates of our particular clinical constructs. For example, "tension" in the student's category is not incompatible with self-direction, nor even is "asking for help," in some senses. Similar problems arise in respect to the counselor categories. However, the coincidences revealed by these measures appear to be more than fortuitous, and we present the charts as a picture of what this interviewing seems like to the counselor.

What it seems like to the client we hope to learn more about when we have accumulated more follow-up interviews. Here again we shall be faced with serious methodological problems should we hope to go beyond the kind of clinical persuasion conveyed by the excerpts we have quoted.

At present we can hope only to expand the same kind of "evidence" in respect to the nature and sources of the heuristic set, the course of the problem-solving process, and the way in which these are functions of the interpersonal relationship itself.

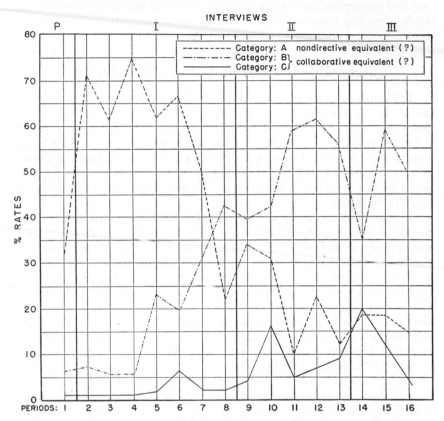

Fig. 4.[17]—Counselor rates of activity in three noninclusive categories by ten-minute periods through four interviews (case of "Mr. Strand").

We should like this further evidence to give us some idea of the fate of the heuristic set when in our more extended cases it is successively strengthened by confidence and buffeted by despair. We hope to learn from the longer cases, too, how the set is best supported through those phases of narrowly classical "transference" which are not uncommon even in counseling of this sort.

But the problems we feel most intensely in present practice are those of the interpersonal relationship leading up to the client's changed perception of roles. It has been reported (Seeman, 1949; Snyder, 1947) that

[17] Figures 4 and 5 are reprinted from Robert F. Bales, *Interaction process analysis* (Cambridge, Mass.: Addison-Wesley Press, Inc., 1950), by permission of the publisher. Categories have been relabeled for pertinence to this article.

client resentment of the nondirective structure is often highest where no explicit statements about it are made by the counselor and lowest where the counselor describes the relationship as cooperative. In our experience, clients often disregard structuring statements or distort them to fit preconceptions. This distortion is particularly easy with statements de-

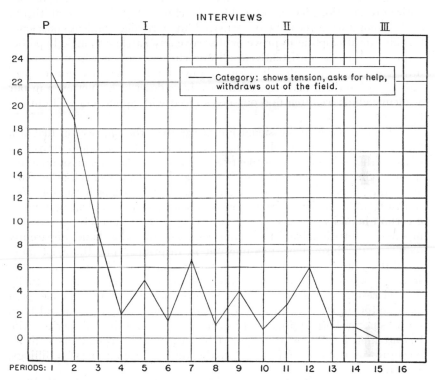

INTERVIEWS

—— Category: shows tension, asks for help, withdraws out of the field.

Fig. 5.[17]—Student's rate of activity in one noninclusive category (case of "Mr. Strand").

scribing a collaborative structure. Statements like "Well now, why don't we work on this *together?*" seem to present inadequate contrast to expectations in that their *form* is that of a suggestion, or direction. They too frequently elicit only the reply, "Fine, where shall we begin?" In view of our present limitations of knowledge and skill, there seems to be nothing to do but suffer with the client as he struggles to make sense out of the counselor's actual failure to support his expectations. The counselor's warm, attentive understanding offers compensation in most cases but not in all.

Perhaps the problem of "cases" has been uppermost in the reader's mind. Has the range in our clientele been so limited that our theorizing is of no general use? Or are our clients so well within the limits (now discarded) once set for nondirective counseling proper (Rogers, 1942,

1951*b*) that they could be expected to find their own answers just as rapidly and to more effect without all this superfluous exercise of the counselor's training and talents? These questions are at present answerable only at the level of clinical opinion.

That our implied opinions on these fundamental matters are largely generalizations from clinical observation reveals the character of our entire presentation: it is a rationale at the clinical level rather than theory at the laboratory level (Mayo, 1945). Our particular clinical conscience forbids our attempting to prove or disprove any single, monistic hypothesis by applying it consistently to all our clients, each of whom seems so different. Our rationale, therefore, allows for a wide variation of procedure within the range of problems we have described. Yet even in our academic clinic we often find ourselves faced with applicants well outside this range.

Somehow recent professional literature gives the impression that if a therapist is to follow a school, be it psychoanalytic or nondirective, he must faithfully apply the same procedure to all comers, assuming his theory to be all-embracing. If he is to be an eclectic, it seems that he must apply the "appropriate" procedure to all comers, perhaps assuming *himself* to be all-embracing. Members of a school, it is true, can pretend to a certain humility, because it is to a theory, not to themselves, that omnipotence is attributable. To be an eclectic, on the other hand, apparently requires utter insouciance; as one put it, in print: "The therapist must be all things to all men"; and another: "We have no hesitancy in shifting from one approach to another if the first does not produce the mutually desired results." Somehow the word "eclectic" has come to be accepted as an antonym for "systematic" (Bixler, 1948), a kind of technical term for a "smorgasbord approach" (Snyder, 1947); and the only writer who has attempted to flavor this approach with humility complains with an engaging wistfulness of feeling "in the thick of thin things" (Billings, 1949).

It is our notion, on the other hand, that a clinician's proper task is to construct a small-scale system as a rationale for what he sees. At the present state of knowledge, it has seemed to us that the clinician does well to make use of various concepts, principles, and laws, however unrelated they have been claimed to be, provided only that he make a reasonably coherent synthesis. But if his rationale is to be clinically useful, he should neither claim it to be applicable to all clients nor limit it as uniquely "appropriate" to an individual. It is his responsibility to do thinking which is to a degree *ad hoc,* but the *hoc* must be both general enough to include a range of cases and also specific enough to provide coherent data; it must offer a mean between the normative and the idiosyncratic. Within this range, the clinician may then go on to observe differences among individuals and to speculate, on the basis of his rationale, upon the relations among variables.

Within our own clinical range we have attempted to describe a frame wherein self-direction and consultative assistance can act as complementary rather than antagonistic processes. We have selected our different materials from the schools in clinical and experimental psychology in which they have been further developed, but we trust them to fit closely enough around a central process to make a workable context for the study of variables. As for our procedures themselves, although we cannot recommend them at large, we can find some confirmation for them in what seem to be the most productive syntheses of teaching and learning in other education forms.

Perhaps we draw some of our own conviction from the observation that progress toward democratic maturity itself seems to consist of the development, in broadening sectors of life, of a point of view analogous to the heuristic set. It is a point of view not of an absolute but of a *related* autonomy which enables the individual to assimilate life's necessities by choice rather than bowing to them in resentment. Just as a client may learn to include among events of his own volition first the counselor's mild, then his more rigorous, assistance, so outside the clinic he learns to collaborate with fact and necessity. Possibly, therefore, it is through such a general educational principle that the young may learn the earlier to seek their self-realization through the cultural materials at their disposal. Where they sense the culture broadly as inimical and restricting, they can find safety only in passive submission, and dignity only in wasteful resistance; where they sense it as their own, even in its conflicts and frequent immutability, they may grow to express themselves more productively through it, and so to participate more creatively in the molding of its destiny.

CHAPTER 5

SOME OBSERVATIONS ON PSYCHOTHERAPY AND THE LEARNING PROCESS

By Edward Joseph Shoben, Jr., Ph.D.

The place of psychotherapy among human activities is admittedly nebulous, but it can perhaps be most fruitfully understood as one of the applied social sciences, those types of inquiry into human relations aimed at solving some formulated "practical" problem. As Merton * (1949) has pointed out, one of the chief characteristics of the applied social sciences is that the levels of knowledge upon which practice is based range from sheer empiricism to systematic theory guided by intensive research. Generally, the effectiveness of practice in achieving its goals tends to increase with advancements in the sophistication of the knowledge from which it is derived.

Following Merton, the point can be exemplified by an analogy from medicine. A herbalist finds that cinchona bark, for no known reason, is a specific antidote for a particular symptom complex and proceeds to use it and to recommend its use; this illustrates the level of *empiricism* in applied science. When the identification of malaria as a disease entity and of quinine and atabrine as chemical specifics is accomplished, the level of *cumulative research* is achieved, and practice is enriched through the possibility of standardized treatments. *Systematic knowledge* is reflected in specific researches oriented toward new problems such as the investigation of areas with high malaria rates to determine causative agents; investigation of identified causative agents, making possible improved control and prophylaxis and pointing the way toward more effective methods of treatment; and investigation of the biochemistry, constitutional background, and medical histories of those who do and those who do not succumb to the disease in epidemic areas, also leading to new insights with regard to preventive and remedial practice. At this level, that of systematic knowledge, the role of theory tends to be vitally important. Through such researches, general principles come to be formulated which act as time-saving guides to the discovery of new facts and, ultimately, to modifications of practice.

A point of tremendous consequence must be noted in this connection. The general principles or theoretical statements formulated need not bear an immediate relationship to the "practical" problem at hand and may

* References are to the bibliography at the back of the book.

seem to have no implications for practice. The implications may not emerge until some "applied" worker has made a synthesis of available research findings and general ideas, often borrowing from "pure" science, i.e., scientific inquiries not begun under the press of a practical problem, for his enlarged understanding of the job he must do. In the engaging language of the Liebers (1944) :

> Take the radio for example . . . this could not have happened had it not been for Marconi . . . who sent the first crude radio messages. And even his work would have been impossible had it not been for another man, named Hertz . . . who proved that the very idea of sending a wireless message was actually possible, since he demonstrated the existence of electromagnetic waves. But where did he get the idea of even looking for these waves? Why, from . . . Clerk Maxwell, who first conceived the idea of waves in an "electromagnetic field" and applied the calculus to it, obtaining a set of differential equations from which he declared the consequence followed that there MUST be electromagnetic waves. . . . And, obviously, Maxwell could not have done his job had not Newton invented the calculus.

And Newton might not have invented the calculus had it not been for pressing seventeenth century needs for more adequate artillery and timepieces (Hogben, 1940) !

Thus, scientific advance in both the building up of fundamental knowledge and the sharpening of applications seems to involve a reciprocal relationship: practical problems may supply motivation for work in pure science; and the findings and ideas of pure science, whether or not developed under such a motivation, may supply new insights into the solutions of practical problems. In any event, the efficiency of applications seems to grow as a function of the kind of knowledge it has to draw on.

Psychotherapy: Art or Science?

In the light of all this, it seems accurate to say that the knowledge upon which psychotherapy has been able to levy has been essentially empirical or, at best, at the level of cumulative research. One of the richest sources of observations and ideas in the development of psychotherapy is that provided by Freud and the proponents of the various splinter schools of psychoanalysis. Another is the work of Rogers and his followers. While the debt to these investigators on the part of all who are genuinely interested in psychological treatment is tremendous, their insights and general ideas have been founded on clinical observation, with all its sources of error, of special populations, with all the difficulties introduced by such biased sampling. And for all their important contributions, the various types of psychoanalysts and the client-centered group have, in the main, worked apart from their experimental confreres. What this means is that the "applied" science of psychotherapy has been essentially divorced from the "pure" science that presumably should most

nourishingly feed it, general psychology. While the point may legitimately be regarded as moot, this seems most unfortunate. Certainly
medicine would not have made the striking advances it has were it not
for underlying developments in physiology and biochemistry, nor would
engineering be capable of its dramatic accomplishments were it not for
the growth of physics.

Though unfortunate, the divorce between psychotherapy and general
psychology is understandable. In the first place, psychotherapy has historically been closely associated with medicine and religion. The organi-
cist tradition of the one and the dogma of the other have both been
inimical to intensive research into behavior. In medicine it was implicitly
assumed that the answer to behavioral difficulties lay in an exploration of
tissues; in the church it was explicitly assumed that the answer lay in
man's relationship to God and/or the acceptance of given moral canons.
In neither case was behavior conceived of as a proper domain of inquiry,
obedient to its own laws.

Second, one consequence of this limiting of psychotherapy to the
doctor's office or the pastor's study has been to place it almost wholly in
a service, rather than a research, context. This is a descriptive and not
a pejorative statement and takes due account of the realities of the ethical
restrictions on research with human subjects and the fact that demands
for service leave therapists little time for research. Yet this is not a
situation that leads to the enlargement of relevant knowledge and the
improvement of therapeutic techniques. It has prompted Shaffer (1947)
to say, "The need to improve our psychotherapy is so great that ultimate
gain probably would accrue if all psychologists stopped the practice of
therapeutic counseling for the next few years and devoted their entire
energies to research designed to increase the value of the process" (pp.
461-62).

Third, the psychotherapeutic process is obviously complex, one that is
extremely difficult to break down into units that are manageable from the
standpoint of the research worker. Involving the complicated interactions
of the personalities of both therapist and patient, psychotherapy is in many
respects so difficult a field of inquiry as to be uninviting to the investigator. Considering the lack of work on possibly less subtle and intricate
forms of interrelationship at the human level, it is not surprising that
therapy as an object of study has been bypassed in favor of matters that
lend themselves more readily to the methodological techniques psychology
currently has ready to hand.

Finally, in the face of traditions that are to a degree incompatible with
rigorous investigation—demands for service that leave little room for
research, and a complexity that understandably checks impulses toward
inquiry—clinicians themselves have tended to confuse the problem still
further. Working on the basis of necessity and with little help from their
experimentally inclined colleagues, they have built up a body of "intuitive" techniques which have been reinforced by a sense of inner certitude
and quasi success. That such attitudes are unwarranted is borne out by

such studies as those by Wilder (1945) and Knight (1941) on the efficacy of psychotherapy, but that they exist to a troublesome degree and are incompatible with research seems to be generally true. Where certainty exists, no matter how tenuously based, there is little motive for investigation.[1]

All this means that clinical psychology, especially in its therapeutic aspects, has become widely conceived of as an art, something not amenable to scientific investigation. Thus, one finds Alexander and French (1946) saying, "It is admitted that psychotherapy is . . . more an art, requiring a constant intuitive response to the patient, than it is an exact science." Westburgh (1937) and Louttit (1936) give categorical expression in their textbooks to the idea that clinical work, both diagnostically and therapeutically, is an art rather than a science.

This notion implies that the clinician, through some kind of nebulous gift, adds something to assessments made by measurement or facilitates behavioral change through processes qualitatively different from those which can be employed in a laboratory. Indeed, credence is given—at least by implication—to such an idea by conversations with practicing therapists. It is not unusual to hear them say (or, it must be ruefully admitted, to say to one's self), "I'm not quite sure why I said what I did, but I felt certain it was right." It is more than probable that the response in question often *is* "right," but inner certitude is both a dubious criterion of validation and a deterrent to discovering *why* it was right and *how* it may be more generally formulated in the interest of greater clinical utility.

As Sarbin (1941) has pointed out, however, diagnosis and therapy both imply prediction, the *sine qua non* of science. Clinical diagnosis, for example, is a description of a present state of affairs but with a future reference; it is a statement of the conditions from which a prediction is made about a subject's behavior, assuming the described conditions are not altered. Here is where psychotherapy enters the picture. Each time a therapist responds to a patient, *he implicitly predicts that his response will produce or contribute to some kind of behavioral change in that patient,* either immediately or in some longer-range sense. True, the predictions tend to have large margins of error at this phase of psychotherapy's development, but the point that they are made is important for three reasons.

The first is that it eliminates art, in the sense of some supra-empirical form of knowledge, in favor of experience, controlled observation, and logical inference as the techniques for improving both the understanding and the practice of psychotherapy. This certainly does not simplify the problem in any dramatic way. The personality of the therapist, for instance, may be, and probably is, one of the most important variables by

[1] It is, of course, a moot question as to whether this position is any less conducive to increasing knowledge about the therapeutic process and sharpening therapeutic tools than is the attitude which holds that psychotherapy cannot be investigated because of its difficulties and complexities. Necessary knowledge may be slow in coming unless clinicians and experimentalists can begin to work together on problems of real human importance without a sacrifice of scientific rigor.

which what happens in therapy may be explained. But if this is so, it should be potentially possible to stipulate the characteristics of effective therapist personalities, to indicate how they work in achieving therapeutic results, and to estimate the degree to which this factor contributes to the total therapeutic process. Further, such a position leads to inquiries regarding what cues successful clinicians are responding to (especially when they cannot themselves state them) and what experiences enable clinicians to perceive such cues whether or not they can verbalize them. It is hard to see how the therapeutic "culture" is to be advanced unless some such line of research is undertaken.

Second, if psychotherapy intimately involves the task of predicting alterations in a patient's behavior as a function of the therapeutic situation as it is structured by the therapist, it may be that this permits a conceptualizing of therapy in ways that allow more relevant and helpful borrowing *from* general psychology and greater trenchancy in forming problems to put *to* general psychology.[2] Changes in behavior (including symbolic and "emotional" as well as nonsymbolic instrumental acts) as a function of experience is essentially McGeoch's (1942) widely accepted definition of learning. With psychotherapy tentatively formulated as a learning situation,[3] it should be able to levy more profitably upon the psychology of learning, motivation, and perception in sharpening both understanding and technique.

Third, attempting to conceptualize the kinds of predictions made in psychotherapy in terms of the psychology of learning may permit the formulation of a much more adequate theory of psychotherapy than any of those that have yet been devised. That there is a great diversity of *conditions*—techniques, devices, adjuvants, and general settings—by which therapy proceeds does not necessarily mean that there are different *principles* involved in the different kinds of therapy practiced. It is important to note that all schools of psychological treatment, from Christian Science to Freudian analysis, with some justification claim cures (Rosenzweig, 1936), but an adequate theory should explain *all* instances of successful therapeutic endeavor. A practical outcome of the development of such a theory might well be the isolating of the useful factors common to the many schools and a defining of differences among them in ways that would be testable in clinically relevant terms. If this would lead to greater emphasis on study and less on polemics, to more light and less heat, it might do much toward advancing the efficiency of psychotherapy in meeting the tremendous social demands put upon it.

[2] It should be pointed out that one of the values of clinical work lies in its fruitfulness as a hypothesis-forming experience. There are few kinds of extra-laboratory contacts so productive as this of potentially formulatable problems to put to psychological science. One may indeed legitimately wonder if the clinic and the laboratory might not each live more richly if their relationship were closer and more deliberately symbiotic.

[3] There is, of course, nothing particularly new about the suggestion that psychotherapy can be profitably conceptualized as a learning process. See the papers by Darley (1943), French (1933), Kubie (1934), Magaret (1950), Shaffer (1947), Shaw (1946), and Shoben (1949).

A Definition of Psychotherapy

To suggest that all psychotherapy may be fruitfully understood as a learning process is to imply the question: How do psychotherapists, regardless of the theoretical banners they fly, facilitate desired changes in a patient's behavior? What do therapists do to help a client feel more self-confident, to get on more effectively with his wife, to be less irritated by his family and work associates, to be less troubled by hostile impulses toward figures of authority, to overcome stage fright, to be less demandingly dependent in his social relationships, or to be free of irrational fears?

Upon examination of the activities of therapists who call themselves analysts (either orthodox or modified), individual psychologists, Meyerians, nondirectivists, eclectics, or whatever, a kind of operational definition of psychotherapy emerges rather quickly. Psychotherapy is a certain kind of social relationship between two persons who hold periodic conversations in pursuit of certain goals: namely, the lessening of emotional discomfort and the alteration of various other aspects of client behavior. True, the conversations may be tricked out in all kinds of special trappings. There may be a free associational method, Herzbergian (1948) directions as to tasks to be performed by the patient, deliberate emphases on current events in the patient's life (Rogers, 1942; Rank, 1945) or on his historical circumstances (Freud, 1935a), psychodramatic play as an accompaniment to the conversation (Moreno, 1945), or adjuvants such as drugs or hypnosis. But all cases seem primarily to involve interpersonal situations and a heavy reliance on talk. Therapy proceeds by virtue of communication and the therapist-patient relationship, toward the goal of alleviating symptoms and increasing the patient's affective comfort and social utility. Can these two basic aspects of the therapeutic process, elsewhere styled "relationship" and "conversational content" (Shoben, 1949), be more specifically delineated?

Fiedler (1950a, 1950b; see also Chapter 9) has shown experimentally that experience and "expertness" are more important than theoretical persuasion as determiners of the way in which therapists conceive of effective therapeutic relationships. Both in describing an ideal therapeutic relationship and in creating a working relationship within the therapeutic process, there is greater agreement among therapists of comparable experience and professional reputation than there is among therapists adhering to the same theory but having different degrees of competence. Thus, it seems quite possible to describe "the" therapeutic relationship without regard to the various schools of psychotherapy.

The attributes of the relationship are, first, friendliness, warmth, and a comfortable emotional closeness. The therapist is genuinely interested in his patient as a person, not as an object to be dissected and coldly studied. This implies a second characteristic, permissiveness. The therapist gives the patient full freedom to discuss any topic he chooses, including his reaction to the therapist and the therapeutic situation. But this does not mean only that the therapist follows a mechanical rule of allowing the patient to engage in whatever kinds of verbal behavior he chooses. It also has an affective side: regardless of what his client talks about, the therapist maintains an attitude of calmness and understanding. He remains unshocked and unruffled even in the face of attack, but he evidences a genuine concern for what each item discussed means in terms of the patient's comfort and welfare.

Warmth and permissiveness, so described, shade into a third aspect of the therapeutic relationship, its "safety." The therapist is nonjudgmental and noncondemnatory in his reactions; he never rejects his patient because of the behavior he reports or the attitudes and affects he verbalizes. This is sometimes spoken of as "acceptance," a term which is a little troublesome because it has connotations of approval. While the therapist may approve the patient's efforts to alter his behavior, he certainly does not approve the behavior, both overt and covert, which the patient finds disturbing. It is plain that the client does not approve of these things himself, else he would not be in therapy. Safety, in the sense of freedom from rejection and punitive action, seems to cover more exactly what is meant.

Fourth, the therapist seems to be constantly attempting to clarify his own understanding of the patient and to communicate that understanding within the therapeutic context. It is as if the therapist constantly kept before himself the question, "What is this person trying to tell me and how can I make it clear to him that I understand, not only intellectually, but in an empathic sense?" The important proposition here is that therapists not only make attempts to formulate coherently the data of therapeutic interviews—i.e., the client's expressions of affect and reports of behavior—but also try to make clear to the patient that they are fully cognizant of and sympathetic toward the degree of discomfort he experiences.[4]

If warmth, permissiveness, safety, and understanding seem to be prerequisites of any desirable human relationship rather than being peculiar properties of psychotherapeutic interaction, this is precisely the case. Fiedler (1950b) found that therapists and laymen tended to be in substantial agreement in describing ideal therapeutic relationships and the degree to which these were approximated in actual clinical interviews. His conclusion that the therapeutic relationship is, in many respects, the same as any psychologically sound human relationship seems eminently acceptable.

---

[4] It is possible (although by no means inevitable) that some proponents of the nondirective school might argue that the therapeutic function consists only in the relationship. That this is an incomplete view of the process of psychotherapy is attested to by the fact that client-centered therapists study their patients, hold case conferences about them, and are quite healthily self-critical in their examinations of the kinds of *content* material they choose to respond to. Too, Rogers has stressed the importance of psychological knowledge in counselors, presumably as something valuable in dealing with the conversational content side of psychotherapy.

But there is an important difference. Psychotherapists generally make every attempt to keep themselves as anonymous as possible in their dealings with their clients. They tend to restrict their contacts with patients to clinic hours. They do not share their own troubles or pleasures with patients, and they prevent their own affairs and values from intruding into the content of the interviews. By the same token, they do not ordinarily accept gifts from patients during the course of therapy nor do they generally try to intercede for them in their dealings with family, friends, work associates, or others. In short, there are limits placed on the therapeutic relationship which are somewhat atypical of other interactions that might be regarded as psychologically healthy.

As for the conversational content, it can be typified very briefly as primarily concerned with the client's affects, his reactions to them, and the situations, both contemporaneous and historical, which evoke them. Put in different language, talk in psychotherapy involves mainly the patient's affective motivations, the mechanisms by which he reduces them, and the social stimulus situations that elicit the emotional instigators to further behavior. It should be made explicit that the therapeutic process itself may be a very important item included under the last category.

From the standpoint of what the psychotherapist does, then, psychotherapy may be defined as a warm, permissive, safe, understanding, but limited social relationship within which therapist and patient discuss the affective behavior of the latter, including his ways of dealing with his emotionally toned needs and the situations that give rise to them. The goal is that of helping the patient to learn more comfortable affective responses and more rewarding ways of coping with his motivations.

On the Nature of Neurosis

Turning now from the therapist to the patient, one finds generally a person [5] who has failed to acquire the interpersonal skills, including affective responses as well as centrally mediated ones, necessary to performing successfully the role activities his social contexts require of him [6] (Rohrer, 1949). In other words, neurotics (or maladjusted individuals) show defects in their social learning; they are persons whose socialization experiences have ill prepared them to live comfortably in society, to relate themselves effectively to the various groups in which they hold membership, or to other individuals in ways that are mutually satisfying.

[5] Nothing said here is intended to apply to psychotics, psychopaths, or cases of organic pathology. This paper is concerned only with the category of "neurotic" or "maladjusted" persons.

[6] This idea of a learning defect is somewhat different from Mowrer's (1948) concept of a learning "deficit." The position represented here is that neurotics have learned as much—possibly more—than their "normal" brethren; they have learned the "wrong" things, however, in the sense that they have acquired (a) high degrees of anxiety and (b) nonintegrative anxiety-reducing mechanisms that militate against their being well received in most social groups.

Space hardly permits the development here of a well-documented theory of neurosis; but this notion of interpersonal incompetence is one on which there seems to be increasing agreement among psychopathologists (Coutu, 1949; Cameron, 1947; May, 1950b; Ruesch, 1948, 1949;. Sullivan, 1947), and it is necessary to pursue it further to clarify the functioning of psychotherapy. The basic question has to do with the nature of the defective learning which produces interpersonal inefficiency. How does one learn to act in ways inimical to his position as a person-in-society? It is suggested that the answer [7] lies in experiences which begin rather early but which are relatively ongoing in the life history of the individual, especially those involving relationships within the family.

As Singh and Zingg (1942) dramatically point out, children of the genus *Homo sapiens* become human only through exposure to a society of persons who have already become human. Further, the process of becoming human involves a long period during which the child is dependent on others for the satisfaction of virtually all his primary drives. This sets the stage for the development of a number of affective reactions to persons which become, in turn, important determiners of subsequent social behavior. Chief among these affective responses is anxiety.

Basic to anxiety is fear, an acquired response derived from pain. Miller (1948) and May (1948) have provided excellent experimental paradigms of the learning of fear. Stimuli paired with the experience of pain take on the capacity to elicit the affective components [8] of the pain reaction. Labeled fear, this new response acts as an instigator to further behavior until the stimuli evoking it are somehow eliminated or escaped from. Thus, rats which have learned to escape from shock received in a *white* compartment by running through an open door into a *black* compartment can readily learn a new habit, rotating a little wheel to open the door between the two compartments, *with no shock whatsoever* when they are placed in the white box on later occasions. The drive of pain is absent; motivation is provided by the new reaction made to the white walls, the tactual stimulus of the grid floor, and whatever other cues discriminate the white "place of danger" from the black "place of safety." Likewise, a child learns to avoid a hot radiator through the same process. He either burns himself on the object or it is labeled "hot" (and therefore, through previous learning, dangerous) for him. Through association with this direct or vicarious experience of pain, the cues characteristic of the radiator tend to arouse fear, which in turn instigates behavior which keeps the child and radiator safely out of contact. Fear, then, may be

---

[7] For the sake of brevity, a series of hypotheses is offered here in language more doctrinaire and assured than present knowledge really permits. It is hoped that this specific disclaimer of dogmatism will free the writer from charges of expressing his views with an illegitimate finality that he does not feel.

[8] Physiologically, these affective components of the pain reaction may involve viscero-vascular activity of a specific sort. For present purposes, however, it is not necessary to give fear or other "emotional" responses a somatic locus. It is sufficient to define them functionally in accordance with the idea that behavior constitutes its own domain and obeys its own laws.

characterized as a response acquired through punishment, anticipatory in character, and having definite drive value. Subjectively, it is unpleasant and uncomfortable.[9]

With anxiety, it is suggested that the fear paradigm holds without alteration except that the principal cues eliciting the reaction are impulses to act in forbidden ways that have met with punishment. Thus, anxiety differs from fear primarily in that it is a response to internal rather than external stimuli, it does not involve an objective danger, and the punishment which mediates its acquisition is socially administered, chiefly by parents or parent surrogates.

To elaborate on all this in the interests of clarity, it must first be pointed out that acts involving sexuality, aggression, dependency, and affection-seeking are required, in the Western world at least, to take only certain culturally approved forms. Since these are relatively high in the early hierarchy of responses (Hull, 1934) for any individual, they come in for rather protracted and intensive socialization. A general practice exercised by parents is to punish such responses when they occur in other than the culturally sanctioned ways. Thus, for example, the relatively strong and recurrent impulses to act sexually or aggressively become associated with parentally imposed punishment and therefore become stimuli for anxiety.

Second, in terms of this associative theory of anxiety formation, it follows that parents, through their being associated or paired with punishment in the child's experience, also become cues for fear. This lays the groundwork for the well-nigh inevitable ambivalence that occurs in most civilized cultures. Since parents both punish and reward, since they are associated both with the reduction of the child's drives through their care of him and the arousal of his drives through punishment, they almost inescapably become loved and desired, on the one hand, and feared and disliked, on the other. To the degree that they punish and therefore become feared and disliked, they increase the probability of the child's reacting to them with resentment and hatred (Dollard et al., 1939). But hatred of the parents is perhaps one of the most severely punished of all forms of aggression, and the whole process of anxiety acquisition is set in motion again.

Third, the whole picture is enormously complicated by the occurrence of repression. Since anxiety has drive properties, it initiates variable behavior, which is likely to continue until the uncomfortable stimulation is reduced. The number of possible types of response, however, is severely limited by the fact that the stimulus is an impulse, not an external cue. Freud (1934b) describes three techniques that may be used: (a) flight from the stimuli arousing the impulse; (b) condemnation, i.e., voluntary

---

[9] Obviously, this subjective side of fear is something that can be directly investigated only at the human level where subjects can report the hedonic aspect of frightening experiences. It is assumed, however, that the situation is in no way different for infrahuman animals except that their lack of speech makes it absurd to talk about their experience of pleasantness and unpleasantness.

suppression of the impulse; or (c) repression. Of these, flight is virtually impossible; it is not very probable that one can with any consistency avoid situations that call into play tendencies toward, for example, sexuality, aggression, or the seeking of affection and still remain a social being. Condemnation or voluntary rejection of the impulse on the basis of judgment requires a degree of maturity and discrimination that most children have had no opportunity to acquire during the formative years (extending into late adolescence in Western cultures) when anxiety is being developed. This means that there is a high probability that repression will occur as a means of reducing anxiety.

Freud's statement that "the essence of repression lies simply in the function of rejecting and keeping something out of consciousness" seems quite acceptable as a definition needed here, provided a useful definition of consciousness can be provided and an indication given of what is kept out of it. Here Freud (1934a) provides his own answers; he says, ". . . repression denies . . . translation of the idea into words which are to remain attached to the object." Thus, the unconscious may be thought of as the unverbalized, and the process of repression consists in excluding from verbalization the impulse activating the painful anxiety. As a function of repression, one is unable to say, either overtly or in the implicit speech called "thought," such things as, "I would like to perform sexual acts contrary to my parents' taboos" or "I hate my mother." Since consciousness consists in symbolization, the individual is essentially unaware of the forbidden impulses, the interdicted acts do not occur, and punishment is avoided. The reinforcement (Hull, 1943) of the repression is of large magnitude.

If repression were complete and permanent, it would be of little interest to the psychopathologist and psychotherapist. Occurring automatically, without effort, it would be an almost ideal way of coping with anxiety. But it seems fair to say that repression is probably never complete. Various cues escape the bonds of repression, and anxiety is experienced, though its source remains obscure. This is what frequently gives anxiety its peculiar character of "dread" or "fear of nothing." This explains the frequent statements of neurotics that their fears are irrational, i.e., attached to objects that they "know" to be irrelevant, but uncontrollably strong; and this explains the occurrence of free-floating anxiety, the reported intense uneasiness of neurotics without discernible cause. How does this happen?

In the first place, there seems to be a flaw in the all-or-none conception of unconscious processes as *unverbalized* processes. Rather, it seems more fruitful to think of unconsciousness in relative terms and as involving a lack of *symbolization,* a much broader concept than that of words alone. Thus, an individual may not be able to verbalize his sexual impulses, but he may have anxiety-evoking dreams with more or less masked sexual connotations. He may not be able to give voice to his aggressive urges, but he is unaccountably either fascinated by or unable to observe comfortably a boxing match or a mild quarrel between his associates.

Objects may take on symbolic values and trouble him in puzzling ways. While the forbidden impulse may be denied representation in language, it may well enter consciousness through a diversity of nonverbal symbols.

Second, the impulse may involve nonverbal cues that do not undergo repression. Incipient motor responses and proprioceptive stimuli associated with the beginning of tabooed acts may touch off anxiety even though the urge itself cannot be labeled. If this happens, the discomfort of the anxiety is likely to be compounded by the individual's inability to identify its source.

But in the face of these possibilities, the question arises as to why the repression is kept in force. The answer seems to lie in the fact that repression does reduce anxiety and reduce it immediately. This probably occurs through a reduction in stimulus intensity (Hull, 1949) ; elimination of the ability to verbalize a punished impulse, making it unnecessary for one to admit to a forbidden desire, very likely robs the urge of some of its force, and the anxiety it elicits is therefore less strong. This method of cutting down the strength of disapproved instigations to act costs much, however, because the experience of anxiety without "reason" is in itself troublesome, and the inability to identify the source of the discomfort makes most difficult any attempts to remedy its causes. This leads to a discussion of the consequences of anxiety.

The first major characteristic of anxious persons seems to be a kind of social uneasiness. Neurotics generally report themselves as being unable, in varying degrees, to feel comfortable with different kinds of individuals —authority figures, those with certain kinds of physical attributes, members of the opposite sex, etc. Often they are able to indicate that their uneasiness has no objective foundation, but it is nevertheless "real" and strong. In other cases, they may attempt to rationalize their feeling by attributing traits to others which justify mistrust, suspicion, and fearfulness. This seems to be readily explicable in terms of two factors. First is the strong possibility that the persons who evoke the uneasiness serve as stimuli for the punished impulses that have undergone repression. A clinical example is the bachelor executive in his mid-thirties who refused to hire a particularly competent and attractive secretary because she made him feel uncomfortable, i.e., she aroused sexual urges which in his history had been sharply dealt with by his ambitious but puritanical parents and which had been denied verbalization. Second, fear of punitive parents,[10] by the principle of generalization (Dollard and Miller, 1950; Hull, 1943) may spread to others in terms of their similarity in appearance and/or behavior to the parents. This is what is meant by the oft repeated state ment that one's family relationships are prototypical of his later ones.

Second, anxious persons tend to develop symptoms, behavior modes which are generally regarded as inappropriate to the situations in which they are exercised. These may involve the various mechanisms, such as

---

[10] The term "parents" here, of course, must be stretched to cover any agent of the socialization process who has been important in the child's psychological development.

rationalization, projection, regression, and displacement or broader, more pervasive ways of dealing with the social environment. This again is a product of the fact that anxiety has drive properties. Persons under the pressure of anxiety must cope with it by techniques which allay their discomfort, and according to the gradient of reinforcement (Hull, 1943), the techniques most likely to be built up to an effective level of habit strength are those which work most quickly (Mowrer and Ullman, 1945). As Dollard and Miller (1950) point out, anxiety tends to inhibit foresight, planfulness, and judgment and to facilitate behavior that is unconsidered and "stupid." Likewise, Horney (1950) says that the anxious person:

. . . may try to cling to the most powerful person around him; he may try to rebel and fight; he may try to shut others out of his inner life and withdraw emotionally from them. In principle, this means that he can move toward, against, or away from others . . . these moves become extreme and rigid. Affection . . . becomes clinging; compliance becomes appeasement. Similarly, he is driven to rebel or keep aloof, without reference to his real feelings and regardless of the inappropriateness of his attitude in a particular situation. The degree of blindness and rigidity in his attitudes is in proportion to the intensity of the basic anxiety lurking within him (pp. 18-19).

The central point is that symptoms [11] of tremendous scope and widespread implications for one's social relationships develop according to the principle of reinforcement as what might be called shortsighted anxiety-reducing mechanisms. This is what Freud (1933c) meant when he spoke of the "interchangeability of symptom and anxiety." Growing out of anxiety, the socially self-defeating habit patterns of the neurotic are kept in force because they afford some immediate relief from the discomfort of this acquired drive state. Without his symptoms, the neurotic is the helpless victim of an overpowering affect. With them, he can at least minimize his emotional discomfort.

In sum, then, the neurotic is a person who, driven by anxiety, acquires responses which are ultimately more punishing or drive-arousing than they are rewarding or drive-reducing (Mowrer and Ullman, 1945). Kept in effect through the immediacy of its relief from anxiety, neurotic behavior elicits punishment in two ways. First, it fails to prevent the experience of affective discomfort; the anxiety tends to escape its bonds

[11] A concomitant of the development of symptoms is the development of conflict, simultaneous instigations to act in incompatible ways. Thus, if a small child's dessert is taken away by his mother for misconduct at the dinner table, he may be strongly motivated to strike her. Previous attempts to attack the mother have been met with punishment, however, and the impulse to behave aggressively elicits anxiety, which motivates him to inhibit his incipient blow. Caught between these powerful instigations to perform incompatible responses—hitting and not hitting—the youngster is said to be in a state of conflict, which is accompanied by its own acute affective discomforts. Dollard and Miller (1950) use conflict as the central concept in their useful and stimulating theory of personality and psychotherapy. The point of view here represented is that anxiety is the concept basic to an adequate understanding of neurosis and psychotherapeutic procedure and that the essential notions about conflict can be derived from an effective conceptualization of anxiety.

and manifest itself in social uneasiness. Second, since neurotic responses are inappropriate to one's social circumstances—taking the form of demandingness, withdrawal from affectionate relationships, aggression, isolation, avoidance of responsibilities toward others, etc.—they militate against competent interpersonal performance. But man is pre-eminently a social organism by virtue of his prolonged infantile dependence and continued exposure to the socialization process. Virtually all his rewards are socially mediated, his values are socially inculcated, and his very existence as well as his humanity is intimately bound up with society. If he is unfitted by anxiety and its consequences to live effectively in social groups, he must inevitably suffer from rejection, loneliness, and the frustration of those very needs established in the course of his growing up. That these are precisely the reported feelings of neurotics is well attested to by multitudes of clinical instances.

Thus, what has been attempted here is a formulation of neurosis that first stresses both its social origins within the family (and other primary groups to which the child is early exposed) and, its social consequences as they affect later interpersonal behavior. Second, the principles by which these experiences produce neurotic patterns of behavior have been drawn from laboratory studies of conditioning and instrumental learning.[12] This involves the same assumption of continuity between man and other animals that is characteristic of biological science and, conversely, does not require the setting up of uneconomical new assumptions on the ground that human data are somehow discontinuous with those obtained from other phylogenetic sources. It offers the further advantage of freeing the theorist (and the practitioner using the theory) from the necessity of falling back on such difficult-to-define concepts as "id," "ego," "superego," "psychic energy," and the like. Certain objections that might be raised, however, desire special consideration and will be briefly treated in the following section.

Three Objections

The first criticism that might be raised against this view of neurosis is that it does violence to the uniqueness of the individual case (Allport, 1943; Snygg and Combs, 1949). This position is difficult to understand. The concept of the "unique case" is itself logically meaningless; if a case is truly unique, there is no way of knowing what it is a case of, and it is

[12] The theory of learning from which these ideas derive is of the two-factor variety most recently given articulateness by Mowrer (1947) and his students. This point of view holds that there are two separate learning processes, each obeying its own laws. Specifically, the acquisition of motives and affects (probably autonomically mediated and viscero-vascular in their physiology) proceeds through conditioning by contiguity. The acquisition of instrumental responses (probably centrally mediated and involving the striate musculature in *their* physiology), on the other hand, proceeds through "problem-solving" or reinforcement (Hull, 1943). It is possible that a monistic reinforcement theory may prove to be the more useful when the crucial evidence is in. Should this happen, no alteration of what is said here would be necessary. While this paper is *consistent* with the two-factor theory, which the present writer believes to have the greater utility, it does not *demand* it.

not subject to understanding by any but supra-rational and supra-empirical techniques. This would make it pointless to study the phenomena of neurosis, an inference which few therapists and psychopathologists would accept. If the notion of uniqueness merely involves the fact of individual differences, there is no argument. Certainly all organisms are different from one another. These differences are exactly the reason why neurosis requires an understanding of the social conditions under which it is produced as well as of the laws of learning. It does not mean, however, that the conditions cannot be meaningfully or usefully categorized, and it has no bearing whatsoever on the assertion that the laws of learning are universal.

The second objection that may be anticipated is that the theory here proposed is inadequate because it omits the phenomena of guilt and the self-reference that guilt implies. Hilgard (1949) has pointed out that such self-reference is frequent among neurotics, and certainly many clinical cases report themselves as feeling guilty in various ways. The omission here has been quite deliberate on the ground that guilt is not functionally different from anxiety. Both are anticipatory, both have drive properties, both are acquired on the basis of punishment, and both are cued off primarily by impulses to act in tabooed ways. Is it not possible that the only discernible difference lies in the verbalizations of the neurotics classified as "guilty" and "anxious"? In guilt, the individual speaks of himself as having transgressed some parental edict either in his overt activity or in his desire and ascribes to the transgression the cause of his affective discomfort. In anxiety, the individual, unable because of repression to identify the true origins of his emotional turmoil, either says that he does not know why he feels as he does or tends to connect the affects verbally with irrelevant "causes." It seems plausible to think that the verbalized connection between the experience of anxiety and the commission of or desire to commit an interdicted act may be just as unexplanatory as the phobiac's connecting the experience of anxiety with the experience of being in the dark.[13]

The last objection has to do with another sin of omission, this time of the concept of conscience or the superego. In the light of the heavy social emphasis in the approximation to a theory of neurosis offered here,

[13] The reported experience of guilt is often spoken of in connection with the development of the "self-concept" (Snygg and Combs, 1949). Thus, an individual who seeks punishment is said to do so because he conceives of himself as having "sinned." A relevant question seems to be this: Is one's self-concept really anything more than one's implicit speech about himself or his "as if" behavior? In answering such a question, two points may be tentatively made. First, if this is the case, there is little doubt that it constitutes an important and potentially fruitful type of data to investigate, but it implies no new principles; presumably, language behavior follows the same general laws as any other kind of behavior and "as if" acts certainly follow them. Second, it is hard to see why the fact that something called "the self" as here involved should be particularly puzzling psychologically. There is no obvious reason why making statements about one's self should be more remarkable than making statements about others. More experimentation and theoretical analysis are required, however, before one can afford the luxury of feeling well settled in his views on this point.

this may seem especially peculiar. The reason for doing without it essentially involves (a) the assumption that it is undesirable to multiply concepts needlessly and (b) an inability to understand how the usual phenomena of conscience can be defendably conceptualized apart from affective reactions conditioned to situations involving social approval or disapproval (Klein, 1944). When "temptation" occurs, an individual may experience anxiety which he has learned to reduce by obedience to social norms; he conforms, and his superego is said to be "strong" or "severe." On the other hand, an individual may be faced with the same "tempting" kind of situation, but let us assume he has built up through reinforcement a set of responses to such situations which are in keeping with social norms. *He* conforms, but the only affect he experiences is one of pleasure in carrying out acts essentially similar to those of the first example. *His* superego, it is said, is "highly socialized." Yet the only difference involves the *affective* reactions made to stimulus situations involving social or moral judgments. There seems to be legitimate room to doubt the necessity of the concept, although this idea is admittedly heterodox and requires both research not yet done and a careful theoretical analysis not possible here to give it substance.

Psychotherapy as Social Learning

Both the picture here drawn of psychotherapy and the general statements put forward regarding the nature of neurosis emphasize social factors. Psychotherapy is a special kind of social situation. The phenomena of neurosis are social in their origins and important because of their social consequences. How can the two be joined, through a levying on the learning process as it has become clarified through laboratory research, to account for the neurotic's learning to act in more integrative ways, to acquire a greater degree of interpersonal competence?

The chief hypothesis here advanced is that psychotherapy provides a kind of microcosm in which the patient has the opportunity to learn new patterns of response which better enable him to function as a social being. This is the same as saying that therapy affords the patient a safe world within which the process of socialization may be reconstructed and from which he can generalize his new learning. Magaret (1950) has made a similar point in speaking of psychotherapy as a place where new "learning sets" (Harlow, 1949) are formed which are then generalized to the client's extra-clinical relationships.

This central assertion involves a kind of conceptualization by analogy. The individual tends to become neurotic (or "normal") through the influence of the rewards and punishments administered by his family. The chief function of the rewards is to establish instrumental responses and, on the affective side, needs, i.e., emotionally toned choices of goal objects, through the pairing of these objects with the experience of drive reduction. The punishments, on the other hand, serve primarily to establish secondary drives, affective states which instigate variable behavior and the reduction of which reinforces certain instrumental act sequences. This total process of response acquisition, administered by societal agents in the persons of parents, parent figures, teachers, the clergy, and many others, constitutes socialization. If a neurotic develops his pathology on the basis of exposure to certain social experiences, is it not tenable to reason that he overcomes it through exposure to certain other social experiences, through a *resocialization* experience?

The central necessity in this resocialization process, as neurosis has been here formulated, is the elimination of anxiety, the chief instigator of the social uneasiness and nonintegrative behavior that characterizes the maladjusted person. Anxiety is a product of punishment, cruelty, rejection, and loss of love. It is suggested that anxiety is overcome through a process of counterconditioning through the agency of the nonpunitive social situation structured for the patient by the therapist (Shoben, 1949). What is meant may be clarified by a schematic outline of events as they occur in psychotherapy.

The primary thing that the patient does overtly in the course of therapy is to talk, and the primary content of his talk is concerned with the anxiety he experiences and, in so far as he can delineate them, the cues that touch it off. The therapist responds to client talk in various ways. He may ask questions which serve as stimuli to further symbolic explorations of the client's response tendencies and formative experiences. He may simply demonstrate his friendly acceptance of what the patient is saying by nodding or the use of the Rogerian "uh-huh." Such responses, it is submitted, are extremely important as reinforcements of the patient's verbal self-revelatory behavior. They constitute the therapist's approval not of the content of the client's speech but of the speech itself, the symbolic reinstatement of his feelings and of stimulus situations that he would prefer to avoid. As such, they are useful in keeping the patient's instigation to continue therapy stronger than his instigation to stop it. Psychotherapy is almost inevitably a painful business; but if it provides a place where social approval can be won at the same time a hope of relief from psychological pain is held out, it acquires a positive goal value, and the patient is more likely to keep his appointments and work actively with the therapist.

But the therapist also *clarifies* affects and connections between affects and stimulus situations. This is accomplished through interpretation or the client-centered categories of reflection and clarification (Rogers, 1942). These are often spoken of as facilitating insight, defined as the client's ability to verbalize the connections between his stimulus experiences, the affects they have produced, and his use of anxiety-reducing nonintegrative mechanisms. Whether insight, so conceived, is in itself therapeutic is doubtful. That being able to verbalize correctly the cues for anxiety promotes a lessening in anxiety seems to be a highly intellectualistic notion, contravened by the reported experience of therapists for the past half-century. Certainly, there are many examples available of patients who can talk at great length and with probably a high degree of accuracy about their own dynamics but who still suffer greatly from anxiety and interpersonal incompetence. Likewise, there are many examples available of patients who have been successfully treated who are quite unable to explain how they acquired a greater measure of affective comfort and social adaptability. This is not to say that insight does not occur or that it is unnecessary for the achieving of therapeutic goals. It merely means that the equating of insight with cure seems fallacious.

Nonetheless, the clarifying responses of the therapist—his interpretations or reflections—do seem aimed at the lifting of repression or the development of insight. The central question has to do with the importance of insight in the total therapeutic process. Actually, if insight alone occurs, if the patient is merely brought to the point where he can label the cues for his anxiety responses, it seems legitimate to predict that he would be rendered more anxious rather than less because of the enhancement of the stimulus (Hull, 1949) through its verbalization. Something else seems necessary to explain the new learning that takes place in successful therapy.

That "something else" is afforded by the nature of the therapeutic relationship. As a warm, permissive, safe, and understanding kind of human interaction, free from condemnation and punishment, it acts as a stimulus for affective responses that are "pleasant" or "comfortable." There seems to be a strong probability that the pairing of this relationship, eliciting nonanxious affective reactions, with the symbolic reinstatement of the cues for anxiety gives rise to a new connection, according to the conditioning paradigm, between the verbalized anxiety stimuli and the comfort reaction made to the therapeutic relationship.

Evidence for this point of view can be cited from a wide variety of sources: Pavlov's (1927) reports of the "unlearning" of fear by dogs through the pairing of food stimuli with the previously established cues for fear, Mary Cover Jones's (1924) classical work by a conditioning method with the boy Peter, and Razran's (1938) alteration of attitudes toward various forms of art by what he calls "the luncheon technique." It is also nicely illustrated by Farber's (1948) experiment on fixation and its extinction in laboratory rats.

The latter investigator trained two groups of rats in a single-unit T-maze with food reward in the goal box on the preferred side. During the last sixty of the one hundred training runs, the animals were shocked immediately after the choice point in the maze. At the completion of training, one group was fed at the locus of shock for two ten-minute periods. The next day the food reward was shifted to the nonpreferred side with no shock to the maze, and the animals were run until their original turning response was extinguished. When the number of trials to extinction in each group was compared, it was found that the shocked animals showed much greater resistance to extinction than the shocked-fed animals. In clinical language, the responses of the shocked animals were pathologically fixated, whereas those of the shocked-fed animals were much more integrative.

The rationale here is that in the training trials the animal's response of approaching the choice point had built up considerable habit strength by virtue of the forty food-rewarded nonshock runs. When shock was introduced, the habit of turning to the preferred side was further reinforced by the escape from pain. At the same time, the point of shock became a stimulus for fear. Thus, the sequence of stimulus-approach-pain (fear)-escape was powerfully reinforced. In short, the response of turning to the preferred side was fixated owing to the effect of fear-reduction. In the shocked-fed animals, the procedure of feeding at the point of shock served to replace the fear reaction by a "comfort" reaction conditioned from the food. Unhampered by fear, the animals could learn to behave appropriately in the changed situation of the test trials. That the feeding at the locus of shock did not affect the original responses directly but through the process of fear-elimination was demonstrated by proper control experiments.

Here the various stimuli provided by the maze evoke fear. The fixated response is the nonintegrative mechanism by which the animals dealt with this acquired drive. Food, on the other hand, evokes nonfearful affects. The fear is dissipated by the development, according to conditioning theory, of a new connection between the choice-point cues and the comfort reaction to the food, leaving the organism free to act more integratively.

In psychotherapy, it may well be that a very similar process occurs. The lifting of repression through the clarifying responses of the therapist results in the symbolic reinstatement within the therapeutic situation of the repressed impulses which, because of the patient's social experience, touch off anxiety. The social relationship of therapist and patient replaces the food in the experiment. A new bond between the impulse (and the stimuli associated with it) and the nonanxious reaction to the relationship is formed by conditioning, and the patient is free to develop more integrative modes of response to replace his pretherapeutic defense mechanisms.

All this squares with the time that effective psychotherapy seems to require. Repressions cannot be lifted and therapeutic goals attained until the relationship has reached a sufficient degree of strength to elicit comfort reactions which are stronger than the anxiety released by the verbalization of the repressed cues. This means that the process of interpretation must proceed slowly; otherwise the patient develops a kind of intellectualized glibness about himself or discontinues therapy.

But how is this new affective learning brought into play outside the therapist's office? The argument here is that this occurs through the mechanism of generalization. Herein lies the reason for the personal anonymity upon which most therapists insist. The therapeutic relation is a prototype for human relationships generally, not a highly differentiated interaction between the patient and the therapist as an individual. Magaret (1950), in making a similar point, says that through therapy the patient:

. . . learns to know many persons, none of whom is actually the therapist, but each of whom is an organization of behavior—a role or a person—projected upon the therapist. What the patient learns, then, is not to know one person, the therapist. Nor does he learn a repertory of specific reactions which he then employs outside the therapeutic hour . . . (p. 67).

Departing a little from Magaret's viewpoint, it is here asserted that what the patient learns is to react nonanxiously to that vast range of human interactions which involve impulses that have historically become associated with punishment. Freed from the peculiar distorting effects of anxiety, he can then go ahead to develop a wide variety of instrumental social responses on the basis of how they are reinforced in the groups in which he gains or holds membership. Thus, social competence develops.

This implies an answer to the objection that might be made on the ground that anxiety is an important element of social control. Is there not a danger of society's disintegration should the individuals composing it not have their impulses checked by anxiety? The point is that one does not learn to act in socially useful ways through having all responses in a given category—sex, aggression, dependency, affection-seeking, etc.—punished; one learns desirable social responses by having desirable social responses reinforced. This means that sexual, aggressive, and affection-seeking responses must be rewarded differentially in terms of the situations in which they are and are not appropriate. For child-care practice, this means that discriminations must not be forced upon a child before he is able to make them; for psychotherapy it means that the discriminations cannot proceed until the effects of anxiety have been dissipated through the patient's learning a more comfortable affective reaction to his tendencies to act in ways that are often appropriate but are distorted through the fact that his impulses, regardless of whether or not they are elicited in proper contexts, evoke anxiety and the symptoms by which he reduces it. Thus, "responsibility" and "self-control" grow out of nonanxious conditions of learning, not out of blanket inhibitions on certain forms of behavior that occur as a function of anxiety.

To sum up briefly, then, psychotherapy is conceived as a resocialization process by which the patient learns a new comfort reaction to replace his anxiety reaction to his own impulses. Because of the deliberately prototypical nature of the therapeutic social situation, these comfort reactions generalize to extraclinical situations. Free of anxiety, the patient is then able, both in society itself and with the continued help of symbolic explorations in the safety of the therapeutic microcosm, to develop new instrumental social acts according to their appropriateness to the groups to which he belongs. Through the reinforcements provided in his social experience, in therapy and out, he builds up ways of behaving that are socially useful and acceptable without necessarily involving a strict conformity that would deny the individuality of the person and militate against healthy change in society.

CHAPTER 6

NEUROSIS, PSYCHOTHERAPY, AND TWO-FACTOR LEARNING THEORY

By O. Hobart Mowrer, Ph.D.

In the present uncertain state of our knowledge regarding neurosis and its most effective treatment, it is useful to continue to scrutinize the phenomena in question from as many different vantage points as possible. In this way we can check one approach against another and discover, perhaps, the common elements and the eccentricities in the varying points of view. With this procedure in mind, the present chapter will be devoted to a consideration of neurosis and psychotherapy from the standpoint of two-factor learning theory.

Two-Factor Theory Delineated

There have been, and are, numerous multiprocess conceptions of learning. However, the one here denoted by the term "two-factor learning theory" holds that there are two and only two different learning processes: *solution learning* and *sign learning*.[1] Solution learning involves the central nervous system and the skeletal musculature and results in those voluntary, instrumental response patterns which we call "acts" or "habits." Sign learning, by contrast, involves the autonomic nervous system and visceral-vascular tissue and results in those involuntary reactions which we call "attitudes," "feelings," or "meanings." The first of these exemplifies the law of effect as formulated by Thorndike and elaborated by Hull; the second exemplifies associative learning or conditioning as defined by Pavlov.

One of the basic assumptions involved in two-factor theory is that we not only learn solutions to problems but that we also *learn problems*. Early animal work on learning was largely concerned with trial-and-error learning or problem solving in situations wherein the problem was an organically given drive, such as hunger, thirst, or some other type of recurrent discomfort. More recent work has shown that both animals and human beings are importantly motivated, not only by these primary

[1] These two processes are both *inductive* and are to be distinguished from insight or reasoning, which is *deductive*. Although reasoning makes use of the results of prior learning, it is here assumed not to be a form of learning (see Mowrer,* 1950, chaps. ix-xi).
* References are to the bibliography at the back of the book.

drives, but also by *secondary drives,* and that the latter are acquired on the basis of a different principle, namely, the mere paired presentation of two stimuli—an old, potent one and a new, neutral one. The organism's total experience thus involves two kinds of learning: (*a*) sign learning, or conditioning, which makes an organism have fears, aversions, appetites, and other secondary drives in the presence of stimuli which formerly did not elicit such reactions; and (*b*) solution learning, whereby the organism tries to find ways of reducing or perhaps avoiding drives, both those which are organically given and those which are acquired in the manner just indicated.

Provision is thus made for a two-way relationship between organisms and their environment; they are able both to *modify* and to be *modified* by their environment. Normally, there is a give-and-take between living organisms and the outside world; they are constantly changing and being changed by their surroundings. And while both of the forms of learning which mediate these reciprocal processes are similar in the sense that they make for increased chances of survival on the part of organisms, they are quite dissimilar, though complementary, in the ways in which they work.

In a seminar conducted jointly with the author, I. A. Richards once conjectured that learning would turn out to be related, perhaps rather precisely, to the phenomenon of causality. We see some realization of this prediction in the fact that sign learning enables living organisms to take account of the fact that event A, which is perhaps quite unrelated to the organism, is followed by ("causes") event B. By learning to react to A as a sign of B, i.e., being "problemed" or driven by A *as if* it were B, living organisms are able to manifest the rudiments of anticipation and foresight. And we see a further confirmation of Richards' remark in this, that living organisms, through solution learning, are able to profit from the fact that some of their own response events produce beneficial results and others do not. Sometimes called *selective learning,* solution learning enables an organism to pick out those responses which, from the organism's point of view, are *effective,* or causal, from those which are not.[2]

This dichotomy, which has been more fully developed elsewhere (Mowrer, 1950, 1951*b*; and see also Mowrer, 1952*a* and 1952*d*; Mowrer and Aiken, 1953; Mowrer, Aiken, and Solomon, 1953; and Mowrer and Solomon, 1953), is suggested by a variety of other considerations; but it becomes particularly pertinent when one attempts to deal with clinical phenomena. A special advantage which it has over monistic conceptions is that it provides a possible basis for understanding the

---

[2] At the risk of anticipating later parts of the discussion, it is instructive to extend this line of reasoning one step further. If, as suggested above, learning is importantly related to causation, it is easy to see that disturbances in this process would result in "irrationality," i.e., in distortions and misestimations of "reality" and in incorrect attribution of cause-effect relationships. It is therefore of the utmost importance to understand precisely the learning anomalies involved in neurosis, their genesis, and the gains which perpetuate them.

dynamic opposition of forces or conflict which constitutes a central feature of every functional personality disorder. At the same time it lacks the overspecificity of those conceptions of learning which posit almost as many learning processes as there are types of learning situations.

Neurosis: a Problem in Sign Learning or Solution Learning?

Whatever else the psychoneurotic complains of when he presents himself for diagnosis or therapy, he is sure to give a prominent place to the fact that he is having emotional reactions which he dislikes, does not understand, and feels unable to control. Patients express this differently, but one has recently put it well when she said, after complaining of various emotional and psychosomatic reactions: "The thing about them that is strange and interesting to me—and inexplicable—is that they seem to go on almost entirely independently of me. It is kind of as if I were living two lives, one I know about and one I do not, except for these symptoms." Here and in similar statements it is apparent that the patient is saying that he or she is suffering, feels helpless, trapped, and perhaps panicky, and that the nature of the suffering is *emotional*.

Taking these facts as a starting point, it might be inferred that the treatment of neurosis is, as has sometimes been suggested, simply a matter of modifying attitudes, of changing the individual's emotions and feelings. Since most adults both have had and have been parents and since attitude modification and emotional conditioning are prominent among the special responsibilities of parenthood, it is easy to make the assumption that when *adults* need attitudinal or emotional change the proper treatment is much the same as that accorded to children in the name of discipline and character training. This is presumably what some clinicians have in mind when they speak of "becoming authoritative" with patients, alternatingly scolding and lavishly approving them, as circumstances seem to warrant. Or a clinician, while abstaining from the attempt to change the patient *directly,* may seek to do it *directively;* that is, he may urge the patient to enter into various new activities and to desist from others, in the hope that in this way the patient will undergo a pattern of experience which will bring about the desired emotional modifications.

Common to both Freudian psychoanalysis and Rogerian psychotherapy is a different point of view: the view that treatment is not a simple matter of either directly or directively reconditioning the patient. Instead the inner dynamics and autonomy of the patient are taken into more active account, the premise being that a neurosis is a function not only of what has been *done to* the patient but also, perhaps more importantly, of what the patient has done and is still doing *to himself* and *for himself.* Repression, dissociation, denial of feeling, rejection of self—these are operations in which the patient plays an *active* role; and it is believed no less by Rogerians than by Freudians that a neurosis is never liquidated until *the patient* substitutes self-scrutiny for repression, association and synthesis for dissociation, examination of feeling for denial of feeling, self-acceptance for self-rejection. In other words, we may say that for both Freud and Rogers neurosis is not simply a matter of under-, mis-, or malconditioning but represents instead *inadequate and inappropriate habits of dealing with one's feelings.* While neither Freudians nor Rogerians would presumably exclude the role of aberrant conditioning in the genesis of neurosis, neither would they give it a central emphasis; and in therapy the accent is upon the formation of new habits, new solutions—be they called "gain in ego strength," "self-actualization," or something else.

Neurotic Problem Solving

Granting that neurosis is not simply a result of mis- or malconditioning and that therapy is not merely a matter of re- or deconditioning— granting, that is to say, that problem solving is also importantly involved here—we must look more closely at the interaction of these two types of learning.

While it will be obvious that solution learning is in keeping with what has been variously called the pleasure principle, hedonism, or the law of least effort, sign learning goes against the pleasure principle in that it is *problem making* rather than problem solving. Under "normal" circumstances, an organism in the course of pursuing solutions to its problems, is "willing" to expose itself to the risk of new conditioning, whereby new problems, new secondary drives will come into existence. But for reasons which we shall explore presently, problem-solving learning is sometimes *turned against* sign learning—and here lies the crux of psychopathology. That is to say, when an organism begins using its problem-solving capacities defensively, begins to engage in actions that protect the organism against new conditioning and attitude change which, in the long run, would be useful to the organism, then and there, psychological dysfunction or abnormality has begun.

But instead of speaking in terms of these abstractions, let us attempt to make the analysis more specifically relevant to the problem of human psychoneurosis. All theorists—save, I suppose, extreme constitutionalists—today hold that neurosis in some way has its inception in the clash between the child and his would-be socializers. The child has problems, needs, drives; he engages in variable, exploratory behavior, and he finds satisfying solutions. However, some of the solutions hit upon by the child will not be acceptable, or will be only temporarily acceptable, to his elders; and if the child persists in his "immaturities," "naughtiness," and "perversity," he will be *punished.* The tacit intent of this punishment is to establish new drives—notably fears—which are specifically associated with, or conditioned to, the objectionable problem-solving behavior and are thus made to compete with the underlying motivation for such behavior. Or, said more precisely, the punishment is designed to produce drives that will elicit responses which will be incompatible with the responses instigated by the original impulses or motives.

In one type of situation, punishment may be designed merely to block certain types of solutions and to encourage the learning of other, socially more acceptable ones. This is likely to be true, for example, of habits of eating and elimination. In other areas, however, the punishment may be designed to block solutions to drives more or less completely, as in the case of sexuality and aggression.

Now in Freudian circles and in many related groups, the assumption is that the predisposition to neurosis is laid down whenever parents punish their children so severely that they abandon all overt behavior in response to certain drives and, further than this, use their problem-solving abilities (symbolic and otherwise) to avoid being reminded of or thinking about these drives. Such an individual is said to have *repressed* the tabooed impulses. Where parental punishments are strong enough to produce repressions and dissociations which last through the so-called latency period but are abrogated at puberty, essentially normal adolescent and adult development are predicted for the individual. But in instances where the punishment or disciplinary conditioning of a child has been so severe that it persists well into adolescence, it is assumed that the now intensified drives of sex and aggression, while not able to gain full expression and gratification, will periodically intrude into consciousness far enough to activate old fears and thus produce neurotic anxiety and symptom formation.[3]

This approach makes neurosis an active, problem-solving phenomenon as far as the patient is concerned in that the patient is said to continue to repress impulses which he might better acknowledge and work toward gratifying. But it makes the patient passive in that it assumes that his social conditioning or sign learning ("sex means punishment," "aggression means punishment") has been so severe that he is helpless to do anything but continue, out of fear, to repress those impulses covered by the taboos of childhood. According to this conception of neurosis, therapy should consist of a combination of fear deconditioning or extinction and reinforcement of the habit of being "realistic," "facing reality," and, especially, facing the drives which have been dissociated and denied expression (Dollard and Miller, 1951).

Now this is not a wholly bad theory; it has coherence and some factual support. But neither is it entirely satisfactory, since it leaves much to be desired both conceptually and in terms of therapeutic efficacy. Let us, therefore, make somewhat different assumptions and see what the outcome is.

A Revision of Freudian Assumptions in Terms of Two-Factor Learning Theory

Before attempting to advance an alternative to the Freudian conception of neurosis, it will be helpful to recast it in terms of two-factor learning theory. It is evident, first of all, that what Freud referred to as id

[3] For a discussion of anxiety theory see May (1950) and Mowrer (1950).

corresponds roughly to the *primary drives* as defined by learning theorists. It is likewise clear that what Freud called superego is a product of social conditioning or sign learning. And it is equally evident that the *ego* is that part or agency of the personality which mediates *solution learning*.

Having established these equivalences, however approximate they may be, we can now restate the Freudian theory of neurosis in terms of two-factor learning theory. The development of a neurosis may be said to proceed in two stages, the first covert, the second manifest. As a result of unduly severe social conditioning (parental discipline), the child's secondary drives (particularly fears) come into conflict with the child's primary drives; and the only successful solution to this conflict which the child can find, in his particular life situation and stage of development, is one which consists of walling off (repressing) the offending primary drives (id forces) and thereby denying them access to the problem-solving (ego) mechanisms. In this way the conflict is ended and the individual is left free, for a time, to direct his attention and problem-solving, instrumental behavior toward the secondary, socially acquired (superego) drives, i.e., toward being "good."

The second stage in the development of a neurosis materializes when the habits (repressions) which have been devised as solutions to the earlier conflict between certain primary and secondary drives become weakened and there is a threatened recrudescence of the conflict. Now new, more elaborate habits, or "symptoms" (Frieda Fromm-Reichmann, 1949, has used the colorful expression "security operations") have to be instituted, and these give the picture of a full-blown, clinically manifest *neurosis*.

As indicated on other occasions (Mowrer, 1950, chaps. xviii-xxii), my own clinical experience leads me to believe that neurosis follows a different course. In Freudian terms, this alternative view is that neurosis arises, not when an excessively severe superego develops and overpowers the ego, thus forcing a repudiation or repression of id forces, but rather when the ego, which is initially under the *complete* sway of the id, remains essentially id-dominated and directs repressive action *against the superego*. In terms of two-factor learning theory, this alternative view holds that the neurotic individual is one in whom the primary drives not only have had but still have major control over the problem-solving processes and cause these to be directed toward the blocking, inhibition, or nullification of the secondary, acquired drives of guilt, obligation, and fear. The problem-solving activity which is usually referred to clinically as self-protectiveness or defensiveness thus functions in the interest of the primary drives or id, rather than, as Freud posited, in the services of the socially derived forces of the superego.[4]

---

[4] For evidence that Freud, in his later years, was moving toward a point of view similar to the one just expressed, see Mowrer (1950). The publications of Freud which are most pertinent in this connection are "Splitting of the ego in the defensive process" (1950) and the posthumous volume, *An outline of psychoanalysis* (1949).

From the standpoint of the Freudian interpretation of neurosis, it is a contradiction in terms to refer to a neurotic as "immature." Since the Freudian interpretation is based upon the premise that socialization has not only done its necessary work but done it all too well, the neurotic is a kind of supermature person—and therapy is supposed to consist of helping him become a little less so. Clinical experience and research confirm the impression that there is a sense in which the neurotic is genuinely and historically immature, and the view that seems to take best account of this is that the neurotic remains id-dominated to an extent that is normal for very small children but not for adults (cf. Wexler, Chapter 7).

The Genesis and Direction of Repression: Learning Not to Learn

The Freudian conception of repression holds that this process is the intrapsychic equivalent of earlier interpersonal events. The parent apprehends the child gratifying tabooed impulses and punishes the child. The parent, being more powerful than the child, is thus able to inhibit disapproved behavior. But the process does not stop here. Since the child has in some measure identified with the parent, i.e., has incorporated ("introjected") many parental values into the superego, there is an internal repetition of this drama: the tabooed impulses appear in consciousness, are disapproved by the superego, and the ego (being poorly developed and inferior to the powerful superego) is compelled to reject these impulses and deny them further access to consciousness. Social intimidation is thus assumed to be the forerunner of psychic repression, which, in turn, sets the stage for subsequent neurotic developments.

Little attention has been given to another possibility, one which is equally logical and indeed clinically better supported. It, too, starts with the observation that parents punish their children for displaying certain forms of behavior. But there is an immediate divergence. Instead of assuming that parental discipline always has the intended effect of blocking the behavior toward which it is directed, the alternative possibility is that very commonly—perhaps uniformly in situations which are to lead to neurosis—parental discipline has the effect of merely teaching the child to be *evasive and deceitful!* Gratification of the forbidden impulses may in this way be restricted but not entirely stopped, and each surreptitious indulgence will now be followed, not only by fear of discovery, but also by the knowledge that to the first act of disobedience and defiance has been added a second one of duplicity. Most children are taught that they must be truthful and overt with their parents; and if they thus compound their disobedience with dishonesty they are likely to have guilt that is all but intolerable. Conscience becomes a constant tormenter in such situations, and one of two consequences is likely to ensue: the child will either bring his suffering to an end by confessing and taking whatever chastisement may be in store for him, or he may further extend the strategy of duplicity and social isolation by an attempt to deceive the internal representative of parental authority. This takes the form either of rationalization or repression [5]—but repression that is turned toward the conscience, in the interest of preserving the possibility of continued impulse gratification, rather than toward the id, as Freudian theory would hold.

Let us examine this point of view in the light of two-factor learning theory. We see at once that problem-solving activity which takes the form of social duplicity and conscious deception and repression amounts to an attack upon the sign-learning functions. Parents are the source of much social conditioning, and conscience is the reservoir of that conditioning. Self-protective strategies of the kind just described are thus designed to neutralize the second form of learning in large and important areas of the individual's life. To put the matter somewhat enigmatically: the neurotic is an individual who has *learned how not to learn*. What such a statement means is that the neurotic is a person in whom solution learning is directed *against* sign learning, instead of these two forms of learning functioning harmoniously and complementing each other. E. B. Holt once remarked that conditioning, or associative learning, "brought mind into being." It is hardly surprising, therefore, that the individual who systematically attempts to keep this mechanism from operating commonly complains of "poor memory" and of the feeling that he is *losing* his mind. Perhaps a more apt formulation is that he is *destroying* his mind, or at least an essential part of it!

Personality disturbances, especially the more severe forms, are often referred to as "mental disease." Much misunderstanding has resulted from the use of this phrase, but in a limited sense it is apposite: neurosis represents a kind of *malignancy,* which bears more than a superficial similarity to that which attacks the body. As good a theory of cancer as any is that it starts as a response to and *solution of* some minor irritation of bodily tissue. Cells begin proliferating and in this way eliminate the irritation, but the process which provides the solution becomes self-perpetuating and is soon, in its own right, a *problem*—one which is far more serious than the one which initially set the "protective" process in motion.

In like manner, neurosis seems to start as an attempt on the part of a person to control by means of rationalization or repression a limited source of psychological irritation or conflict, but the success of this

[5] In rationalization, it is as if the ego or primary self says to conscience ("parents"): "I agree with you that acts of a given class are bad, but the action I have just performed does not really fall into this category"; or, "This action belongs to a class of actions which, generally speaking, are wrong; but in the present instance there were extenuating circumstances." The other strategy, of repression, is a more directly defiant one. In it, it is as if the ego says to the superego, "I will have none of you. I am my own boss. Say what you will, I shall not listen to you. As far as I am concerned, you do not exist; you are dead; and I do not hear you speak." Cf. "The Life and Work of Edgar Allan Poe—a Study in Conscience-Killing" (Mowrer, 1950, chap. xxii). The same type of drama is symbolized in Lorenzeni's *Pinocchio*.

strategy requires that it be constantly expanded in its scope, until a point is reached where the "solution" has itself become a "problem." Medical pathologists have pointed out that a cancer involves a normal process, namely *growth;* in like manner, neurosis involves the same adjustive powers of the individual as those which, when turned in other directions, make for effective, successful living. More specifically, when an individual directs his abilities toward finding solutions both to biologically given (id) impulses and to the socially derived (superego) drives, he may be, on occasion, frustrated, conflicted, and unhappy, but he is essentially "normal." But when an individual begins to use his problem-solving abilities either to avoid new emotional learning or to paralyze existing emotional reactions, he is embarked upon a career of abnormality.[6]

Two-Factor Theory and Psychotherapy

Psychotherapy is a complex procedure, and there are many valid and suggestive ways of describing it. In the concluding section of this chapter, no attempt will be made to describe this procedure comprehensively; attention will be limited to those of its features which are highlighted by two-factor learning theory.

One of the major inferences to be made from the foregoing discussion is that, although the neurotic's principal complaint is that of emotional suffering, the most effective therapeutic attack is made in the area of problem-solving behavior. Attempts to deal with the neurotic's problems either directly or directively have not brought very satisfactory results, and we can now see that in some ways these approaches probably perpetuate the strategies which constitute the very essence of neurosis.

Rogers (1951) has announced that preliminary results obtained by use of the S sort technique show that in the course of (client-centered) therapy the greatest changes occur within the perceived self (ego?) rather than in the ideal self (superego?). Translated into two-factor terms, this finding would seem to support the view that in psychotherapy the greatest changes occur in the area of solution learning rather than in the area of sign learning.

Somewhat parenthetically, it may be noted here that much has been made of the so-called disproportionality and inappropriateness of emotions in the neurotic. We can now see that the neurotic's emotions only *appear* to be disproportionate, for the reason that they are dissociated, and that when the patient takes a realistic problem-solving approach and

[6] By thus shifting the accent in the theory of neurosis from overconditioning to a *perversion of the problem-solving process,* an old dilemma is resolved: namely, why it is that, if neurosis represents overconditioning during childhood, the excessively severe emotions (fears) thus acquired do not extinguish as the years pass and external realities alter. If, however, as now seems probable, neurosis involves a set of "bad habits" which are constantly being reinforced, the dilemma disappears. The only thing that will eliminate these habits (of dissociation) is integrative, associative thinking, and this is precisely what such habits prevent. This is why neurosis is often susceptible to being reversed only through the intervention of the associative trends supplied by another person.

allows his experiences to come back together, we find that his emotions, now in proper context, are both proportionate and appropriate. To repeat, the fundamental task of psychotherapy is not that of emotionally re-educating the patient but of helping establish problem-solving habits which will enable emotions to operate as they are normally intended to.[7]

It is the writer's belief that Freudian analysts have made a major error in assuming that neurosis arises because of repression of id forces, notably those of sex and aggression.[8] But it is noteworthy that the Freudians have been pioneers in stressing repression as such and in fostering, in therapy, the recovery and resynthesis of all facets of the patient's past and present experience. While they seem to have erred in their assumptions regarding the direction and content of repression, the Freudians have been on firm ground in opposing repression in general and in working for conscious recognition and assimilation of all the forces within the entire personality. They have, in other words, stood for a policy of realistic problem solving through compromise, integration, and synthesis, as opposed to dissociation; and if we are now correct in revising the Freudian view with respect to the direction and content of repression, the way should be cleared for a new level of therapeutic accomplishment—and, hopefully, for a more effective philosophy of mental hygiene and prophylaxis.[9]

[7] As therapy proceeds and the patient begins to experience relief from his anxiety and symptoms, he commonly develops a very positive, kindly feeling toward his therapist which plays an important role in the consolidation of treatment (Mowrer, 1950, chap. xxi). However, this type of emotional change is more of a by-product of therapy than its immediate and major objective.

[8] This is not to say that such repression, if it occurred, would not be pathogenic. All that is assumed here is that, in point of fact, this is not the way repression usually operates. Nor is there any negation here of the view that neurotics commonly present a picture of serious inhibitions in the area of sex and self-assertiveness. However, as indicated elsewhere (Mowrer, 1950, chaps. xviii, xix, xx), it would appear that these impairments are derived rather than primary in the etiology of neurosis.

[9] For further discussion of the relationship between two-factor learning theory, neurosis, and therapy, see Mowrer (1952b, 1952c, 1953a, and 1953b).

CHAPTER 7

THE STRUCTURAL PROBLEM IN SCHIZOPHRENIA: THERAPEUTIC IMPLICATIONS

By MILTON WEXLER, Ph.D.

Love in all its myriad forms still stands as the principal prescription for the treatment of schizophrenia. Affection and sympathy, tenderness and approval; these are the medicines of choice. Dosage, of course, depends only on the capacity of the therapist to give, and he is the best therapist who has the greatest libidinal resources. To all of which one might ask: How can it be that such a commodity so lavishly expended can be so potent? Or, how can it be that so potent a commodity is so lavishly and incautiously prescribed?

I believe that Eissler * (1943) is right when he indicates that the love and patience we would shower upon the psychotic is connected developmentally with earlier phases of contempt and enmity. Few things are so calculated to terrorize at least some schizophrenics as untimely affection, however real and unambivalent. Indeed, the same is true of some skittish children who can be won only by disinterest. If the veriest show of encouragement can be translated by a neurotic in the analytic situation as a seduction, its counterpart with the schizophrenic may be perceived as a rape. Love is no doubt an effective medicine but, as Freud indicated, many effective medicines are poisonous in nature. We must have caution how we use it.

I have a special interest in this problem for I have been through two years of hell-fire and heaven with a schizophrenic patient [1] who could, on occasion, speak the violent language of a jungle tigress. One gets introspective in the face of such assaults (afterward of course) and begins to think about the attitudes which call them forth. If some more helpful attitude can be discovered and made explicit, the temptation exists to cast about for theoretical explanations. This is the temptation to which I have succumbed.

At some future time I will present the treatment of this case in some detail. For the moment a few historical facts and some brief abstracts from the electrically recorded treatment sessions will provide sufficient

* References are to the bibliography at the back of the book.

[1] My research on the problem of the psychoanalytic therapy of schizophrenia has been conducted with the support of the Menninger Foundation, supplemented by grants from the Lester H. Hofheimer Estate and the Pepsodent Company. [For circumstances under which this study was first reported, see Acknowledgments.]

basis for my present speculations and a discussion of the pertinent literature.

Nedda is now forty years old. She was hospitalized early in 1943 and had been continuously in an institution from that time until treatment began in June of 1948. The diagnosis of hebephrenia seemed substantially applicable to her condition in 1948, although paranoid ideas were certainly plentiful. The diagnostic problem is not of prime relevance here, except to convey that the patient was regarded as a chronic schizophrenic and had not proved amenable to a variety of treatment programs, including electric and insulin shock and a number of kindly and even fairly persistent attempts at psychotherapy.

During my first ten months of working with Nedda I was not markedly impressed by the effectiveness of the therapeutic measures I employed. To my kindliness and what I felt to be an affectionate interest in her welfare, she responded mainly with crude sexual overtures or violent rage and overt attack. Parallel to and intermingled with such raw instinctual gestures was a puritanical saintliness which had its own peculiar quality of violence.

To my persistent pointing out what was real and unreal in her productions, she responded either with queer symbolic expressions or rigid and stereotyped paranoid ideas. Deep interpretations, which were on occasion offered with all the rapidity of my own free associations, brought from her, most frequently, blank denial, anger, or indifference. The main positive result of this tumultuous period seemed to be in the growing interest the patient manifested in being with me, demonstrated not only in her behavior but in delusional formations in which I occupied a central position.

In March of 1949, ten months after the intensive psychotherapeutic treatment began, I took up a position with respect to the patient's productions which I had not previously attempted in any consistent, self-conscious way. This new position was taken up partly on an intuitive basis, partly because of some theoretical considerations which had been growing on me for some time. The theoretical basis will be presented to you shortly. For the moment I would like to set out the events of a single session during this month, as well as some later observations with similar implications.

Early in this session, Nedda complained of priests and nuns who refused to get up and dress and just wanted to sit there and play with themselves. She said, "If I had my life to live over again I'd never be a Catholic." She then referred to the hospital and spoke angrily of the patients on the ward as whores, suggesting that she never would have come to this hospital if she had known they would be around. She "thought sure it would be different when I got here." Then with intense feeling she spoke of masturbation. "I hate it, I just hate it, I absolutely despise it. That's why I hate myself. Every time it enters my mind, I just hate—that's why I can't enjoy life, because I hate myself." It was at this point that I decided to agree with the patient and when she referred again to masturbation as a sin I injected the comment, "a terrible, terrible sin."

Nedda's immediate response to this statement was to say, "It's serious to abuse your own body, let alone abuse somebody else's body. And you know I can't do that. I'd rather have a fight. Just a common fight. I just hate. I just hate the wrong kind of sex. I just despise it." Adding piety to piety, I avowed, "Sex is bad anyway." Now Nedda said, "I know it. Well, I was cured."

The patient was so quiet, agreeable, and relaxed at this point that I ventured further on the same course. I knew she was very disturbed by the open sexual activity on her ward, and said to her, "But it must be terrible to see those people around here who do it." To this she responded thoughtfully, "I don't know if they do it or not. I examine my conscience and I know they do. They say it's responsible for all insanity." Having abandoned interpretation in the usual sense, I continued to agree with her conscientious scruples concerning sexual behavior and felt almost immediately that she responded by becoming more communicative and in many respects more reasonable.

Almost for the first time in the therapy she became somewhat introspective about what had happened to her. Statements such as the following were new in her treatment and seemed to represent a struggle to reach some realistic appraisal of her situation. "Well, something's happened to me because I always, pretty nearly always when I was outside, I would pray, say prayers that I'd get immediate relief. Something's happened, and I don't know what it is." A few moments later she added, "I used to have the nicest temper and best disposition. And every time I think about that, I—I know I can't kill myself because that would be another sin." And again, "I don't know what to do. I set over there and think a lot of something going to happen, something, uh, something will happen." I thereupon enjoined her against the sin of thinking about me or some other soul in a sexual way. Having bad thoughts about us would make her no longer sure of getting relief from prayer. I told her I wanted to help her get well, that we had to stop the bad thoughts, and even suggested that if it would help her any I would pray for her that the bad thoughts would stop.

With this suggestion, Nedda agreed heartily and *laughingly said that all of this should have happened right from the beginning!*

We were smoking, and in a burst of moral enthusiasm I suggested it might even be a temptation and a sin to continue with cigarettes. At the moment she agreed, and then became doubtful, making the statement that she would hate it for a man to lose his business since, if people stopped smoking, the business of people who sold tobacco would be injured.

I had here cynically overstepped the mark, but it nevertheless brought a statement from Nedda which had in it a new and strange quality. She said, "Maybe I try to be too good. I don't know." Feeling that Nedda was becoming more courageous in assessing her situation, I pressed forward on the same tack. I insisted that we ourselves should avoid all temptations and thoughts about sex. Together we entered a period of agreeable moralizing and condemnation of evil, into which, from time to time and to my delight, the patient injected a note of rather realistic skepticism. For example, when we discussed the forgiving of one's body for sexual temptations and I spoke of the need for forgiving my own body for its evil enjoyment of sex, she corrected me mildly, saying, "Well, it (sex) may be right, I don't know."

A bit later she went beyond this and said, "I don't know whether somebody made those rules that I'm going by, if they're fanatic, or whether that's right. I'm at a loss as to which is correct." Immediately afterwards she said, "I know it's nature to be passionate." I entered a cautious agreement and she added, "To have sex, I know that's natural. But to use it—I don't know if—what about that?—I believe that—I know right now I'm not in a condition to use it." Then she offered her reason: "I have a hurt feeling in here (pointing to the region of her heart). I'm sorry, but I have a hurt feeling in here."

What followed in this session frequently approached the same introspective note. She spoke of herself as having been angry and impatient with her sexual thoughts and feelings. She indicated that I could not depend on her judgment, that she was kind of guessing at things. She really didn't know if a man would like her as well if she had had sexual intercourse before marriage as if she were a virgin. She didn't have nerve enough to indulge in sexual behavior. It made her nervous and she felt like getting up and walking off.

This kind of talk from the patient, even though interspersed with schizophrenic productions, represented a very marked change from previous communications. I had not previously encountered such a reasonable attitude, such an ability to communicate personal thoughts and feelings. I was intrigued with the notion that something in my moralizing, something in this agreeable condemnation of frightening impulses, was responsible for the change. Nedda was verbalizing better, took a more sensible attitude toward her own impulses, and seemed to be dealing with reality situations far more effectively than in any previous session.

In subsequent sessions I went much further. Having reached the point where I verbally agreed with the patient that sexual and aggressive manifestations were sinful and therefore to be eliminated, having even offered myself as an agency for prayer that such sins be stopped, it was no great leap to offering myself as a more active agent in the prevention or suppression of their occurrence. From this point on in the treatment, I took a very active part in forbidding any sexual or aggressive provocations which threatened to disturb the therapeutic relationship. If Nedda threatened to use force against me, I made it clear I would employ an equivalent amount of force against her. When, with rapidly diminishing frequency, I was actually assaulted by her, I did what I could to immobilize her. When the physical provocation was severe enough to arouse in me strong resentment and a wish to put a quick end to her assaultive behavior, I did more than inhibit her movements. I fulfilled my promise to meet force with force. I can say this about our struggles together: With but one exception, never did any of our vehement verbal and physical battles end without peace-making and affectionate exchanges of devotion; rarely did she omit to thank me for putting an end to the threatening and overwhelming forces which had seized control of her and driven her to violence.

I would summarize the course of events in the following way: Almost every struggle with the patient led to clinical improvement as this can be judged by increased reality testing and diminished anxiety and guilt. Every such clinical improvement was followed up by me with a relaxation of demands upon the patient and with increased dosages of affection, interpretation, and education. Until much later, every such relaxation of the relatively strict, demanding, sometimes punitive, sometimes moralistic atmosphere tended to bring on some disturbance of the patient's equilibrium and necessitated the reinstitution to some degree of the former psychological position. The main line of progress was forward, and, like the frog who jumped up three feet and fell back two in getting out of the well, we began to observe a considerable amount of daylight immediately ahead. It seems enough to say that this chronic, hospitalized patient whose weird dress, bizarre manner, and assaultive behavior presented such an impossible problem on her ward, has lived in a foster home for nine months, travels alone to daily therapeutic appointments, does rather complex work in ceramics, helps very efficiently in the home, and above all seems in the process of surmounting the severe thought disorder with a rapidly increasing differentiation between objective reality and her subjective thoughts.

I have several grave concerns about presenting and elaborating on these clinical observations. The first relates to the fact that I am concentrating on only one aspect of the treatment and it may be lost sight of that many other elements in the treatment are necessarily omitted. I would not wish it to be understood that these few observations constitute the key to the improvement of this patient or that broad generalizations can now be drawn concerning the treatment of schizophrenia in all its variegated aspects. Furthermore, my concern extends to the possible misuses of the theoretical considerations I wish to present. Whatever the provocation or the theoretical necessity, it is not easy to acknowledge, outside the context of the total treatment situation, isolated incidents involving the use of physical force in the management of the patient. And, as you are already aware, there is much in what I have to say which will easily lend itself to interpretation as an endorsement of acting out on the part of the therapist in his relationship to schizophrenic patients. However, as Winnicott (1949) has pointed out, there is always the problem of hate in the countertransference, most especially in the treatment of psychotics. I can only hope with him that such hatred becomes less of a countertransference problem and more of a sorted-out, conscious, and objective experience. Only then will we be able to use our hatred, our fears, and our urges to dominate and master as instruments of our love and therapeutic zeal.

What I have indicated so far is really nothing so new in the psychoanalytic literature. It is merely undigested and without adequate placement in the theoretical frame of reference. I would like to illustrate how easily we overlook this aspect of our work by citing a recent case report offered by Hayward (1949).

We are told that one day Hayward's schizophrenic female patient stripped naked and began making forceful sexual advances. Having previously been impressed by reports of Rosen's work, Hayward now met the sexual attack with a barrage of interpretations. Following these interpretations the patient quieted down, dressed, and discussed the interpretations with the therapist in some detail. Immediately afterward a marked clinical improvement was noticeable.

Hayward makes the following comments concerning his interpretations:

> Hindsight shows an outstanding and very injurious error in the management of this case—namely the handling of the transference relationship at the time of the sexual attack. The reader can see that the therapist changed abruptly from a clarifier into a forbidding moralist, saying in effect: "Get away from me, I am married." Instead of this he should have continued to clarify the situation by asking, "Why do you like me so much?" And, "How will intercourse help you?" (Pp. 733-34.)

How strange it is that Hayward should apologize so strenuously for an approach which apparently resulted in the patient's improvement! He seems uncomfortable with his moralizing and rather convinced that he needs to explain himself to the profession for failing to behave in some preconceived "psychoanalytic" manner. I would prefer to think that whether we are "psychoanalytic" or not depends neither on the clinical outcome nor on professionally stereotyped attitudes. For me it depends solely on the conscious utilization of metapsychological principles to guide and explain the therapeutic endeavor.

This brings me back to a statement I made earlier. I said that some theoretical considerations had prompted my taking up a position with respect to the patient which might easily be characterized as oscillating between superego and ego-ideal representative. I would emphasize again that this position was only occasionally maintained and much more than this went on with the patient. But I speak with great certainty when I say that clinical improvement followed hard on either kindly or sharp condemnation and rejection of the patient's crudest instinctual impulses, especially when these threatened to come to motor expression. How can we see such harsh and punitive treatment within the framework of psychoanalytic technique and psychoanalytic metapsychology?

Fenichel (1941) provides us with a metaphor for the treatment strategy which I consider to be applicable only to the psychoanalytic therapy of neurotics. He writes:

The unconscious impulse which pushes towards consciousness and motility is our ally, the defensive ego our enemy. But we are in the situation of a commander whose troops are separated from his allies by the enemies' front. In order to unite our forces with those of our allies, the warded-off instinct, we must first break through to him, and for that we need another ally acceptable to us, the reasonable ego, which must first be detached from the defensive ego. To remain in the metaphor, we must first disintegrate the enemies' ranks with propaganda and win over large portions of his forces (p. 37).

In psychosis, it seems to me, the situation is rather reversed. What we need to resurrect and bring from hiding is an ego which has become separated from a world of reality and for which, to varying degrees and in varying ways, cathexis of external objects has become impossible. If we ask ourselves what it is that separates us in our therapeutic endeavors from access to an adequately functioning ego, then I think clinical observation suggests the following answer in many instances of schizophrenic psychosis. *Between us and the ego which has abdicated its legitimate function of reality testing lies a turbulent and chaotic battleground where instinctual impulses of many varieties threaten constant eruption even in the face of unremitting superego pressures which threaten annihilation as the measure to be paid for the least gratification of such impulses.* In the face of such a devastating conflict, with death as the seemingly inevitable outcome, it is the ego which has abandoned the struggle for control, lost its interest in the external world, and given itself over to fascinated and horrified subjugation to the life-and-death struggle between psychic instances which have proved more powerful.

If in a general way, and at least for certain phases of the illness, psychological forces are deployed in this new fashion, we are confronted with a therapeutic task which is very different from that in the treatment of neurosis. In the latter instance we need first to break through to the warded-off instinct and for this purpose we seek to ally ourselves with the remnants of a reasonable and critical ego. In schizophrenia, on the other hand, our need is ordinarily to break through to and resurrect remnants of a reasonable ego, and our ally will necessarily be something lying nearest to the surface, closer to our reach, more accessible to our propaganda, seductions, or injunctions. In short, it is our task to shift the balance of forces by throwing in our weight either on the side of id or on the side of superego. Neutrality would be as futile as if we were to maintain a controlled impartiality between the executioner's axe and his block in the hope thereby to save a head from rolling.

For purposes of simplification I have chosen to ignore a number of important considerations. I am well aware that even in the psychotic we are always working in and through the ego, an ego which is now largely given over to an incessant and horrified watch of the id-superego conflict and to efforts at restitution. (The complexity of that ego organization and the variability of its functioning is such that I will do no more at present than to describe it with such a loose and no doubt faulty anthropomorphism.) I am also well aware that a schizophrenic psychosis represents no static internal or external conflict and that the answer to the question of when and to what extent and to what side in the id-super-ego struggle we lend our strength depends largely on economic issues which I am not now prepared to discuss. I have also chosen to neglect such problems as the strong masochistic trends, regression of the superego to primitive and archaic forms, and issues concerning constitutional pre-disposition. At this time it is impossible to do more than acknowledge some of these problems. Perhaps additional clarification will come if we turn our attention to the rich clinical and theoretical material to be found in the literature.

Erickson and Kubie (1941) have provided us with a report of the treatment under hypnosis of an acute hysterical depression which comes very close to being a model for the aspect of technique I am discussing. In three hypnotic sessions a most remarkable change was effected in a patient. I would like to focus on one aspect of their approach in which, as the authors noted, "treatment proceeded along lines which are the reverse of the usual psychoanalytic technique."

The following passage will make this evident:

Although it was clear, almost from the start, that the patient's passive and submissive dependence upon the mother's commands would have to be broken, it was equally evident that the image of the dead mother played a role in her life which overshadowed that of any living person and that this idolized super-ego figure could not be dislodged from its position by any direct frontal attack. For this reason, the hypnotist's stratagem was to adopt a point of view as nearly identical with the mother's as he could. He had first to identify himself entirely with this mother image. Only at the end did he dare to introduce a hint of any qualifying reservations. Therefore he began by giving the patient immediate and emphatic assurance: "Of course you always will be a good girl." Then in a manner which was in harmony with the mother's stern, rigid, moralistic, and forbidding attitudes (as judged from the patient's manner and words), each idea attributed to the mother was carefully reviewed in the same terms, and each was earnestly approved (pp. 594-95).

So went the first phase of the hypnotic treatment. In the second phase, the therapist made the point that the patient's mother had died when the patient was thirteen years old. Had the mother lived, she would then have told the girl differently, would then have allowed more and freer expression of her sexual purposes. The attack on the superego began, then, with complete support of its most repressive features. Only later were the rigidity and archaic punitiveness of this structure under-mined. In this case the clinical outcome was excellent.

I am reminded of a spontaneous statement made by my patient, Nedda. In discussing the sinfulness of sex, she said, "I think they tell you it's a sin until you're a certain age, I imagine." We shall all be reminded, no doubt, of the resemblance the treatment bears to a common child-rearing problem in which the effective atmosphere for proper ego functioning is the creation of clearly definable boundaries and restrictions which may subsequently be relaxed following the growth of ego strength. More specific, though still relevant, are the views of Anna Freud (1949) that an excessively permissive form of upbringing does not differ in result from dictatorial, prohibiting forms, since the expectation of sexual partnership by the child is not realized. The most complete tolerance toward infantile masturbation may then not have the anticipated effect. This is particularly true when the child experiences the adult's failure to participate in its sexual activity as an actual rejection.

Knight (1946) gives most pertinent advice in his report of the treatment of a catatonic schizophrenic. To my mind it is advice steeped in the same clinical acumen which permeates the Erickson-Kubie report.

Therapy in such a state must, therefore, be a vigorous and persistent intrusion of the therapist into the patient's trance, forcing him to make contact again with an object. Affection, interest, sympathy—all the good attitudes of the good therapist may not be enough to pierce the daze, and must be supplemented by physical contact, an insistent voice, and a forcing of the patient to focus his attention on the therapist (p. 338).

And again:

Some comments have already been made about the necessity, in such a case as this, of active firmness on the part of the therapist in breaking through the barriers of the trance and defiance. Firmness has further values. It makes the patient feel more secure from his own "bad" impulses if he can count on the therapist adding his considerable strength in the struggle against the "bad" impulses. Thus a too permissive or indulgent attitude on the part of the therapist may lead the patient to feel that he is without an ally, helpless against his own overwhelming hates, defiant feelings, and primitive erotic wishes, and a prey to the intolerable anxiety they cause him. The protective strength of the therapist may thus be experienced by the patient as reinforcement of his own enfeebled ego, making it possible for him to contemplate eventual success in his struggle if this good ally will stay in the fight (p. 339).

These therapeutic recommendations are at odds with a number of ideas on technique advanced by Federn and Fromm-Reichmann. For the moment I would prefer to consider a theoretical issue which Knight does not touch upon except by implication. I refer to the topographical problem. Freud (1933b) differentiated neurosis and psychosis by indicating that in psychosis the conflict between ego and id is solved by severing the relation to reality and by yielding to the instinctual unconscious, the id; in neurosis the conflict is solved by severing relations with the instinctual unconscious and by saving the reality relationship. Does this statement imply that schizophrenia is essentially an inundation of the ego by rampant id forces with a corresponding dilution or disappearance of superego functioning? Knight, of course, lays principal emphasis on the need to contain and control the instinctual impulses, and mainly in the reference to schizophrenic anxiety is the possibility of a structural conflict hinted at. But then Knight's superbly clear report is primarily clinical, with technical recommendations for treatment. Theoretical issues of this nature were not central to his purpose.

Alexander (1931), on the other hand, deals with the problem more directly. He states:

One may define the chief difference between a psychosis and a psychoneurosis by stating that whereas the psychoneurosis is chiefly a conflict between the different structural parts of the mental apparatus, in psychosis the relation of the mental apparatus to the external world is disturbed in a pronounced manner (p. 819).

Later he says:

Hallucinations and illusions, in general, do not presume such an inner conflict between superego and ego tendencies; they simply are solutions of a conflict of the ego with external reality. Therefore, I called this mechanism more infantile because it corresponds to an early stage of development, in which the conflict between subjective demands and reality is not yet internalized as a conflict between subjective demands and superego (p. 820).

Alexander then makes some exceptions for paranoid delusions and paranoid hallucinations, in which the threats of the superego are projected into external reality. However, with respect to such hallucinations the concept of regression is introduced to explain that it is not really an internalized superego structure which is in conflict with other dynamic tendencies but rather that there is a return to a childhood period in which the ego was controlled by external persons, forbidding and punishing parents. Alexander finds it unjustifiable to regard the impulsive self-mutilations of schizophrenics as self-punishing reactions induced by a harsh superego. He asks how it is possible for the same schizophrenic person who has lost such fundamental functions of the superego as pity and disgust, who indulges in coprophilic satisfactions, to retain the exquisitely moral reaction of the need for self-punishment.

I have no doubt that self-mutilation in schizophrenics has little in common with the "exquisite morality" of the ascetic. I would also accept the explanation that such self-mutilations are partially determined, at times, by passive feminine wishes. But to explain them wholly as expressions of "disorganized instinctual demands that have lost their interconnections" is a travesty on the clinical picture of schizophrenia, which often reflects some of the most brutal morality I have ever encountered. Certainly we are not dealing with a superego intact in all its functions, but a primitive, archaic structure in which the primal identification (incorporated) figure of the mother holds forth only the promise of condemnation, abandonment, and consequent death. Though this structure may only be the forerunner of the superego which emerges with complete resolution of the Oedipus situation, its outline and dynamic force may be felt in both young children and schizophrenic patients. In this primitive and defective structure, there may be little or no vestige of love, little or no remnant of the ideals which characterize a later stage of superego development. Nevertheless, a savage, self-destructive morality, either internally directed or projected to the outer world, is rarely missing. And if we do not see it, I suspect it is because we have not yet learned to recognize the most archaic aspects of its development.

I used the term "defective" superego a moment ago with the purpose of calling attention to the brilliant theoretical argument advanced by Pious (1949), to whom I am greatly indebted for help in every area of my research. Pious refers to the view that the superego serves to restrain pent-up aggressivity (or *mortido*). It functions as an elastic container, so that increases in its tension affect the ego organization, producing a pressure toward activity which would tend to bring about a reduction in superego tension.

Pious then asks, what if the superego is defective?

It would no longer act to contain the *mortido,* but instead, the *mortido* would flood the psychic apparatus. . . . There would be no pressure on the ego organization to undertake aggressive or adaptive behavior. Instead, just as in an organic illness, the libido would be drawn away from its attachments in the ego organization in order to neutralize the *mortido* (p. 157).

There is some difference between what I have been saying about the savage, archaic superego of the schizophrenic and the defective superego postulated by Pious. I am not yet able to resolve that difference or to provide adequate clinical data upon which to make a choice. On a number of occasions I have heard schizophrenic patients report experiences which duplicate the clinical data upon which Pious based his formulation of the pathogenic process in schizophrenia. Nevertheless, whether one accepts the version of a superego which is aggressive toward the ego or a defective superego which fails to contain the *mortido,* the basic emphasis is the same. Moreover the clinical implications are the same.

What are these clinical implications? In the first place the reduced, fragmented, and defective ego functions are seen as a product of an internal structural conflict among all psychic instances and not simply as a disturbance in the relation of the mental apparatus to the external world. Our task is, on the one side, to deal with the poorly controlled id-impulses which threaten always to seize the channels of motility. On the other side, it is our task to foster those primitive identifications which are nuclear to superego development. In this latter effort we may sometimes behave like the hypnotist of the Erickson-Kubie case, preliminarily agreeing with the rigidities of the archaic superego figures. At other times we may offer ourselves as a superego figure (perhaps more properly, ego ideal) which, as Brill (1929) mentions, is a precipitate of "the consoling, loving mother." At all times we would do well to bear in mind the value of Knight's advice to compel "the patient to focus his attention on the therapist." We should see this advice in relation to the conception of Pious that the "mental image" of the analyst functions as a superego, tending to seal off the pathogenic process in the psychosis. And, finally, we should recognize that the observations of Freud (1921), Rado (1925), and Strachey (1934), identifying the superego as the fulcrum of psychotherapy, hold true for schizophrenia as well as for neurosis.

Federn (1943b) recognized the importance of the superego in schizophrenia, but mainly he emphasized the masochistic guilt feelings and needs for self-punishment which are psychotically satisfied in paranoid and catatonic states. He also understood the danger of passivity (1943a) and cited the case of the analyst who neither encouraged nor discouraged the patient's free associations but listened quietly to a growing stream of erotic, delusionary ideas. "He was allowing the patient free outlet and was taking the case history while the psychosis developed."

In other respects Federn reached conclusions concerning the treatment about which I have considerable doubt. He emphasized the establishment of positive transference and indicated treatment was to be interrupted when transference became negative. In this he went so far as to suggest that the schizophrenic patient must be allowed to go to another analyst when he did not wish to continue with the one who was treating him. A proviso was made here that some motherly nurse, whom Federn characteristically employed in the treatment, might attempt to make the patient understand his inconsistency and change his mind. But she, too, was under the injunction not to suggest continuation lest this destroy the patient's transference to her as well.

Can you picture what it would mean to treat an angry, rebellious, and helpless child in this fashion? He threatens to run away from home and, if mother cannot make him understand the inconsistency of such behavior, father quietly sanctions his leaving. Not for me and not for my children! I would not grant them such a terrifying power over their environment at the moment when their most frightening and uncontrollable impulses threaten expression. We may be justified in our reality fears of some psychotics. We are not justified in permitting such fears to invade the whole of our relationship so that we are never able to face squarely and deal firmly with the negative transference.

Forgive me for a personal anecdote. Some time ago my mother objected to the fact that I wished to make a certain recommendation to a physician who was treating a schizophrenic patient in whom my mother had a strong personal interest. The recommendation was simply that the physician should actively put some brakes on the negative, hostile, tempestuous acting out which characterized the patient's behavior at the time. My mother's feeling was that such behavior could only be dealt with by sincerity, kindness, love, understanding, and a host of other verbal shibboleths which, though valuable as abstractions, say not a thing about the kinds of behavior which will communicate such sentiments.

"Mother," I said, "how would you feel if you were suddenly made the governor of New York State?" "Why, I'd die of fright," she said. "And that," I said, "is what it is like for an unprepared and weak child to be made governor of the household with unprecedented power to gratify its wishes. It isn't love but fear, and sometimes hatred, which makes us abandon the child (and the patient) to his own emotional devices. You must sometimes hold the baby, and hold it tight, or it will be too much frightened by the rage and lust inside."

I suppose there are some who will appreciate the thesis I am developing only as a circuitous and rationalized return to medieval treatment methods. Perhaps they will be tempted to link the sometimes forceful control of instinctual expressions with the brutal exorcising of devils in primitive psychiatry, with the whipping post and the dungeon. Deep down there may be some relationship. There is, however, also a relationship between the blood-letting barber of several centuries ago and the modern surgeon. We should not be embarrassed by the relationship, but rather inquire what unconscious insights led to such approaches and what fears led our predecessors to place their remedies in such a brutal cast. The dynamic unconscious operated even in prepsychoanalytic psychiatrists. It was merely discovered by Freud, not created by him. And we should not be so ready totally to discard our history with contempt and horror, however justified these feelings may be. After all, what we know about medieval treatment for psychosis is mainly the savagery of some of its methods and very little of its clinical experience.

We might even look a little closer home and wonder about the scientific objectivity of some of our own procedures. I have in mind the use of such a debatable technique as vasectomy in the treatment of schizophrenia. Wagner-Jauregg and Federn had some disagreement as to why vasectomy had some curative effect with young schizophrenics. Federn put principal emphasis on the increased libido supply through the Steinach effect. Wagner-Jauregg saw the explanation in the diminished masturbation. I feel relatively sure the effects are due to more complex phenomena than are inherent in either explanation, but I would certainly see the curtailed sexuality of such (unnecessarily) sterilized patients as one avenue along which the ego has ventured forth from hiding. Federn himself saw the necessity for giving deliberate and direct advice concerning the sexual life, and urged the "control of autoerotism" (1947).

Aside from what effect this will have in terms of libido supply, I believe we should not lose sight of the relationship between our behavior as educators and the creation of an auxiliary superego, a partly externalized, perhaps later totally internalized "mental image" which will act to contain or at least to diminish the threatening instinctual eruptions. The same could be said for many of our educational procedures. Too often we conceive of the persistent explanations of reality we give to the schizophrenic as if our words appealed directly to and increased the cathexis of some reasonable ego. We sometimes overlook the fact that educative procedures are, in childhood, designed to act as curbs on free instinctual expressions, to postpone the gratification of pleasure, and to build the structure we refer to analytically as the superego. It is not strange, therefore, that persistent educational procedures followed with schizophrenic patients sometimes prove quite effective. The reason, however, does not lie in the acquisition of rational attitudes and knowledge through rote learning. I would suggest rather that it lies largely in the employment of an attitude which is genetically significant for superego development and reinforcement.

Eissler (1943) remarked on the Babylonic confusion which exists concerning the diagnosis of schizophrenia. This is largely a derivative of our chaotic understanding of the disease process itself. As a corollary, the technical recommendations for treatment have all the orderliness of a Donnybrook fair. I will address myself to a narrow aspect of the problem simply to indicate the luxuriant contradictions which lie at hand for harvesting. Schilder (1939) speaks of extensive changes in the superego of schizophrenics, with the development of primitive tendencies to cruelty and self-punishment. Menninger (1940) refers to the behavioral symptoms in psychosis as "self-destructive techniques, in which a part is sacrificed to save the whole." Federn (1943b) refers to the schizophrenic's guilt and the unreasonably distorted influence of the superego. Eissler (1943) remarks on the dangers of increasing the guilt reaction in schizophrenics. Nunberg (1948) says that the ego of the schizophrenic suffers in a manner similar to that of the melancholic, from self-reproaches of his conscience, although here he undoubtedly refers only to certain phases of the psychosis.

On the other hand, Eissler (1943) sees the superego as regressing to such a friendly level that it permits the patient to employ neologisms as if they were a universal language. In certain passages of Nunberg's truly classic papers (1948), the dissolution of the superego in schizophrenia is postulated. This is seen as a concomitant of the schizophrenic withdrawal of libido during which the objects which entered into the erection of the superego are more or less lost. Alexander (1931), as I previously mentioned, denies a place to the superego as a functioning part of the mental apparatus of the schizophrenic and places principal emphasis on the conflict with reality and on the contradictory instinctual impulses.

So much for the theoretical differences in this narrow area. If we consider treatment recommendations, much less reconcilable statements appear. Fromm-Reichmann (1948), long an advocate of gentle, friendly permissiveness, objects to Kurt Eissler's alleged remarks that the therapy of schizophrenia is effective solely by virtue of the love offered the patient. Kurt Eissler, as I read his remarks, actually made a rather opposite statement. He pointed to love and patience as the two prevailing emotions in Fromm-Reichmann's technique and said that he doubted whether it was right to build the psychotherapy of schizophrenia on these two emotions. He indicated that love may drive the schizophrenic into deeper withdrawal if it increases guilt feelings and patience may hurt the schizophrenic who senses in it the quality of a defense against impatience. Eissler advocated a matter-of-fact, objective attitude but realistically acknowledged that the schizophrenic's treatment requires an emotional language and must be conducted in an emotional medium.

Federn (1943a), as we have seen, went to considerable lengths to foster positive and avoid negative transference. Fisher (1944) employs "psychic shock treatments" in which he interprets ruthlessly, often being disparaging and overwhelming, sparing the patient's feelings not at all. Fromm-Reichmann (1939, 1948) has, if anything, been even more cautious than Federn. When, several years ago, she wished to qualify the generalized prescription of permissiveness and acceptance, she merely added "respect and understanding according to the patient's chronological age." Rosen's (1947) method of direct analytic therapy [2] certainly offers a challenge to such an approach, shows no special concern about developing negative transference, and focuses largely on direct and immediate interpretation. Hoch (1947), in so far as he trusts in the efficacy of psychotherapy for schizophrenia, advocates a "continuous drip method containing affection and protection." Winnicott (1949) believes that hate is actively sought by some patients, especially psychotics, and what then must be supplied is hate that is objective. Schwing (1940) leaves no doubt that she considers love as the main highway to reach the schizophrenic, while Alexander (1931) simply advocates fostering the positive transference.

Such is the state of affairs in our theory and practice. Of course some of these differences are more apparent than real and are matters of terminology. Some are referable to the varying times at which authors presented their thinking. There is no doubt, too, that some of these conflicts derive their conspicuous character from the extreme condensation I have made of the authors' views. Nevertheless, sharp differences in theory and practice do actually exist, and it is of the utmost importance to clarify our thinking on these issues.

At the moment I cannot carry the discussion beyond the presentation of my own views and a statement of the questions as I see them. It is my belief that these views have very practical consequences both for the individual psychotherapy of schizophrenic patients and for their hospital management. It is also my conviction that a considerable body of clinical data already exists in the literature which, when abstracted from the theoretical interpretations in which they are imbedded, will lend credence to these views. Such problems I hope to take up in a subsequent report. My present purpose is served if I have stated the issues clearly enough to invite a new examination of the clinical data in the light of the structural conflict in schizophrenia.

[2] I have purposely avoided extensive reference to the work of Rosen, whose methods deserve the most careful attention. I have been privileged to observe his treatment of patients on many occasions and have received a large share of my initial interest in the therapy of schizophrenia from my contacts with him. His extensive and earnest research is in the process of development. Until he is further along in conceptualizing his methods and his views on schizophrenia, my own impressions had best be reserved for those personal exchanges between us which have been such a source of pleasure to me.

Postscript [3]

I have had occasion to offer further support for the views expressed above and to extend the theoretical conceptions somewhat (1952). In summary fashion I would like to call attention to some confirmatory clinical data reported in the literature, as well as to a significant omission in the theoretical presentation to this point.

The thesis has been advanced that it is sometimes helpful for a therapist to behave in relation to a schizophrenic patient as an external superego, controlling the flood of instinctual expressions. Adequate ego functioning in the patient may depend on the degree to which such reinforcement is obtained in the struggle against unacceptable impulses. On this issue, Bleuler (1950) makes an interesting observation:

. . . a great deal can be accomplished by issuing precise commands which render resistance useless. At the Rheinau Hospital, I once encountered a number of patients who appeared to be unmanageable. The nursing staff insisted that it was impossible, for instance, to comb or to wash them. Firm and unconditional adherence to the hospital rules in this respect resulted within a few days in obtaining the desired result in all cases; the patients gave up their resistance *and the majority of them became, also in other respects, a good deal more accessible* (italics added) (p. 477).

Nunberg (1948) describes an occasion, some years ago, when he extracted the tooth of a schizophrenic woman. This patient had been most hostile to him, but she permitted the minor operation when the pain became insufferable. Immediately afterward, she knelt before him, extolling his strength and confiding in him as a friend. The following day, however, she showed great terror, crying out against her doctor, "Go away, your hands, your hands are snakes."

This observation is employed by Nunberg as an illustration of the danger which attends even entirely incidental erotic stimulation of the oral zone. What is omitted from consideration, however, is the patient's immediate admiration for the doctor's strength, her sudden attachment to him, and her communication of confidences. It is as if some relatively strengthened ego had briefly come closer to judging the reality of the therapist-patient relationship than had been possible prior to that time. And all this seems to come in some close connection with the patient's submission to and appreciation of the doctor's power. If we scotomize the need of the patient that at times we should play God and the father, we may cancel out some important leverage in the therapeutic task.

Another observation by Nunberg (1948), given in his remarkable report on the treatment of a catatonic male patient, has similar implications. He writes:

[3] Condensed from Wexler's "The structural problem in schizophrenia: the role of the internal object." In *Psychotherapy of schizophrenia*, International Universities Press, 1952.

He ceded to me his own omnipotence and as he had thought in the beginning to win me through words, so he now hoped I would cure him through the magic of words. And it should be noted that from then on, with slight oscillations, he steadily improved. He became interested in the outside world, in political events, he read a great deal, learned other languages, and busied himself in the ward. However, a striking feature was that he wished to work under the direction of a superior, to take orders from him and execute them dutifully. "I will carry out all orders and submit to them completely," he protested. He submitted to my authority, felt helpless and dependent on me, asked for orders and commands from me on how he ought to behave. "You must teach me how to do everything," he told me (p. 50).

It is impressive here, too, that the patient's submission to the doctor's authority, to his magical power through words, was followed directly by a steady improvement.

Winnicott (1949) has given an extraordinary description of his relationship to a boy of nine he took into his home during the war. Quite frankly he says of this lad, "He was the most lovable and most maddening of children, often stark, staring mad." Reminiscent of my first approach to the patient, Nedda, is Winnicott's early experience with this truant, rebellious boy. "We dealt with the first phase by giving him complete freedom and a shilling whenever he went out. He had only to ring up and we fetched him from whatever police station had taken charge of him."

Apparently "hell broke loose" around the home as an aftermath of such kindly treatment, and as the author indicated, "It was really a whole-time job for the two of us together, and when I was out the worst episodes took place." Winnicott then describes how he gradually developed a hatred for this boy and what he did about it. At crises, he would take the boy by bodily strength and, without anger or blame, put him outside the front door. Each time he was put out, he was told that what had happened "had made me hate him." There was a special bell the boy could ring, and he knew that if he rang it he would be readmitted and no word would be said about the past. He used this bell when he had recovered from his maniacal attack.

Winnicott observes that the verbal expressions of his hatred for the boy were of some importance in connection with the considerable progress made in treatment. However, principal emphasis is placed on the importance of these expressions "in enabling me to tolerate the situation without letting out, without losing my temper and every now and again murdering him." True enough, but there is here some tendency to overvalue the magical power of words and verbal communications. The impelling, forceful, physical management in the presence of maniacal rage is also a vital communication to the patient. It may prove crucial to the resurrection of an ego adequate to deal with the therapeutic task.

Instances and technical recommendations with similar implications can be multiplied. Betz (1950) makes the strength of the therapist fairly central to the treatment program. Rosen's (1946, 1947) reports often indicate his role as a powerful, omnipotent, and controlling figure. Leuba (1949, 1950) has commented on a type of patient whose emotionally impoverished ego structure leans heavily upon moralistic taboos and other obsessive defenses. The strict superego alone creates the impression of a balanced personality.

The patients would stumble and fall whenever their ego was deprived of its superego support by the sudden impact of a rising, though still unconscious, sexual or aggressive demand (p. 14).

On the other hand, Gertrud Schwing (1940), whose work with schizophrenics has been highly praised by Federn, approached her patients mainly with a warm and tender devotion. Eissler (1943) makes the astute remark, in this connection, that Schwing worked in a hospital where patients were exposed to mistreatment and severe mishandling. Relieved by this of feelings of guilt as a consequence of the punishing attitudes of nurses and physicians, they were prepared for love "as the gesture of the savior."

Going beyond this, Eissler remarks on his experiences in the use of hypnosis in a hospital setting. His success decreased when a new chief assistant, far gentler to the patients than his predecessor, was installed. Eissler then compares this change with the situation in Schwing's therapy where success was achieved against the backdrop of harshness and punitiveness.

The introduction of the problem of hypnosis in relation to the treatment of schizophrenia has some special interest for me. Despite the obvious negativism of many schizophrenics, I have often been struck by the strange, fascinated attention which some schizophrenic patients give to the therapist at certain times. I have frequently had the impression that there is something trancelike in this attention. It is certainly not a state of being hypnotized in the usual sense, but some qualities which may be observed are very similar. Often there is a fixed, attentive stare, but not in the sense of being absent; rather in the sense of being unable or unwilling to change the focus. There is often a painful struggle to comprehend communications and to respond to them acceptably, as if obedience was essential and desirable. There is sometimes difficulty in dismissing the patient. I have observed patients walking backward to the door, hesitating, stopping, needing to be urged along. Suddenly, as they cross the threshold, they may emerge from that sticky, dependent, fascinated relationship to the therapist and move again as if magically freed from some strong attachment.

I have introduced this observation here, even though without very extensive documentation, because of its possible relevance to the problem of the therapist acting in the role of auxiliary superego. According to Rado's (1925) formulation, in hypnosis the hypnotist becomes "the parasitic double of the superego." I have hypothesized that the therapist who treats schizophrenics will often encounter situations in which he must consciously endeavor to make an ally of the superego, to act with injunctions, moral strictures, even force in order to combat the patient's frightening impulses. It seems to me of utmost interest, and a strong reinforcement of Rado's formulation, that such an approach may produce hypnotic phenomena in schizophrenic patients by methods quite opposite from the soothing suggestiveness of the customary hypnotic induction.

To this point, however, I have merely documented my observations concerning the clinical effects of behavior by the therapist which resembles his functioning as an external superego. The reader would be thoroughly justified now in raising the question as to whether the whole theoretical issue revolves around control of the patient's urgent and overwhelming impulses. There are more than adequate clinical data to indicate that patients experience relief from anxiety on this basis, and even some increased adequacy of ego functioning. But this can hardly be the whole story, for if it were there could scarcely be any hope for the eventual emancipation of the patient. The crutch or the whip, however you care to characterize what I offered the patient, would become a lifetime addiction. The patient could live only on borrowed strength, collapsing when this is withdrawn.

I am indebted to Dr. Merton Gill (personal communication) for suggesting a first step in the expansion of the theoretical framework. He writes: "Accepting the patient's moralistic point of view is analogous to accepting a delusion, and I think has, as one of its major results, the fact that communication is established." To go beyond this point, we must ask ourselves to what end such communication needs to be established.

Psychoanalytic theory has generally considered the pathogenic process in schizophrenia to relate to some regression to primary narcissism with an attendant loss of objects (Fenichel, 1941). It is easily observable, however, that most schizophrenic patients display rather intense interest in external objects, and tender, sensual, or hostile transference reactions may be exhibited in a highly erratic fashion. Such flighty and unreliable cathecting of objects is ordinarily considered as a restitutional phenomenon issuing out of, and as a return from, the regression to an objectless primary narcissism.

In my experience, it is easily observable that most schizophrenic patients have a similar, perhaps even more intense relationship to their internal objects. This idea is implicit in the conception of an archaic superego which functions during the psychotic state, for this superego is nothing but an internalized parental figure dressed in the variable garb of one's childhood mythology. The patient, Nedda, provides a graphic description of the struggle with these inner figures:

I think about different ones having such a horrified life, all inside of them, afraid to tell anybody, don't have nobody to talk to. Oh, what on earth am I going to do. I feel like I'm going to commit suicide, I feel like I'm going to kill myself if I don't get to do so and so, if I don't get somebody to speak to, to talk to that will agree with me that I'm wrong. . . . If it didn't look so silly, I'd just take the brush and just slap my own behind. . . . And maybe all the time those old thoughts are going on, I'm washing the dishes and I'm sweeping the kitchen, I'm doing my chores and I'm trying to do what's right and when I get tired I sit down and rest. . . . See, it takes a long time to learn new things. Just like me, I'd never been anywhere, I'd always been right at home—go wash the dishes—that's about all I did. That's all I know, just go wash the dishes and stuff like that. And I was scared not to.

These statements by a patient fairly advanced in treatment are more comprehensible if it is known that, at an early age after abandonment by the father and something tantamount to abandonment by the mother, she was required to do household chores by a cold and threatening older sister who used a razor strop on the patient with any sign of laziness or recalcitrance. Now, within herself, she re-enacts for us the brutal charade of her rebellion and her punishment. The ghosts of the past are certainly not laid to rest nor generally immersed in some retreat into an objectless, oceanic narcissism.

The specific importance of this description lies in the fact that these internal objects in the schizophrenic are generally paradigms of the cold, unloving, hostile mother. Until, as therapists, we have succeeded in behaving in such a way as to make it possible for the patient to build within herself a clear and steady image of another kind of person, no consistently effective ego functioning is possible. This, to me, is the final importance of the struggle against overwhelming instinctual expressions. This is the basic reason for establishing communication with the patient either via the route of interpretation or via the route of participating in the psychotic delusions as Dr. Gill suggested. We have, by these methods, the possibility of fixing ourselves in the patient's psychic structure, perhaps at first as a counterpart and ally of the "archaic superego," [4] and perhaps later as a more differentiated image involving many more thoughts, feelings, and values.

It is my growing conviction that the major function of participating in the patient's delusional system, of communication in accord with the "archaic superego," and of lending support in the struggle against primitive impulses is to facilitate the development of a constant "mental image" of the therapist. We must begin with the patient at the place where he is and communicate with him in his own conflict ridden language, taking sides whether we like it or not. This is the source of the patient's immediate contact with objects in the outer world. Later, as an internalized constant figure, we will be able to lend further support and strength, love, and even punishment, and come to represent thereby that continuity of relationship to a significant object without which a conception of reality is impossible.

---

[4] This term is used very loosely and needs more precise definition. It is probably more accurate in a terminological sense to speak of the antecedents or forerunners of the superego. I prefer, however, not to attempt a greater precision in language than exists at present in my understanding.

This sequence of events can be seen in relation to my patient, Nedda, who in the earliest phases of treatment sought to take me in, to incorporate me in the most literal way, by trying to bite my hands and face. Later she merely expressed the angry wish to chop me up and eat me. Still later she referred to a photographic film which she felt unwinding from her head with my image upon it. At a much later stage in treatment, she referred to spirits coming inside of her saying:

I think they come in there to save me, that—to get over that horrible, terrible, murderous thought, although I know I'll never do anything like that. I know I'll never do it.

Asked who she was thinking about as a spirit inside her, she said, "You."

In these expressions we get not only the sense of the gradual development of the internal image but some hint of its most primitive function in stemming the tide of uncontrollable impulse. Here is at least one point of leverage in the therapeutic effort, one channel of communication, one prescription given us by our patients. It is my conviction we should exploit it actively and decisively, being ever careful to explore within ourselves not only the irrationality of our rational approaches but also the rationale for our irrationality.

CHAPTER 8

PSYCHOTHERAPY AND ITS PUBLIC HEALTH IMPLICATIONS

By Joseph M. Bobbitt, Ph.D., *and* John A. Clausen, Ph.D.

During the last ten years, and particularly since the end of the last war, there has been a tremendous increase in the interest directed toward the mental health field. There are many reasons why the problem of mental health has become a major concern, not only in the United States, but also in many other countries. As frequently occurs, the clinical aspect of the health problem has served as the chief stimulating source of this interest. Wartime experience showed the importance of mental illness as a cause both for rejecting young people for military service and for the early release of many of those who were accepted. Since the war, the Veterans Administration has found it necessary to develop a tremendously large-scale treatment program for the psychiatric disorders of veterans and has thereby highlighted the great deficit in professional personnel needed to do the job. Concomitantly, the problem of overcrowding in our mental hospitals and the lack of adequate professional staff for them have also been brought forcefully to the attention of the country. In other words, the problem of mental health, in terms of clinical end products, has become a matter of justifiable and real concern both to professional health workers and to responsible lay citizens.

The difficulty of dealing with any health problem adequately on a purely clinical basis has long been realized; and since the end of the last war, the mental health problem has become a public health concern as well as a clinical one. It is not accurate to say that there is any uniform public-health approach to various kinds of health problems, but there are some fairly uniform requirements that must be met regardless of the field involved. Essentially, a public health approach calls for (*a*) measurement of the magnitude and distribution of the problem, (*b*) reliable, valid, and inexpensive case-finding methods, (*c*) the development of rapid and economical methods of treatment, (*d*) effective preventive measures, and (*e*) efforts actually to improve the general health of the population above the present norm. It should be noted that while the public health approach goes beyond clinical measures as such, it also includes treatment. The public health interest in treatment is not, however, a clinical interest in the individual case. The interest is twofold. Frequently, treatment of individual cases is preventive in that it prevents the spread of the disease. Venereal disease and tuberculosis represent good examples of this relationship. Also, it is true that the methods of treatment and clinical care may give the cues necessary for the development of generalized preventive and health improvement measures that represent the essence of public health work.

An assessment of the present status of knowledge necessary for an adequate public health approach to mental health problems reveals that substantial efforts have been expended in all the categories mentioned above but that progress has been slow and often uncertain. With respect to the measurement of the magnitude and distribution of mental health problems in the population, for example, data are fragmentary and the methods of investigation have not been sufficiently uniform to make available data additive. Faris and Dunham * (1939), as well as others, have studied the distribution by place of residence of psychiatric patients at the time of their first admission to mental hospitals. Whether or not these studies reflect the actual distribution of psychotics at the time of the onset of their illness is open to serious question. Moreover, except for the studies involving delinquency and criminal behavior, almost no systematic efforts have been made to study the distribution of individuals showing neurosis and the behavior disorders.

Studies which have attempted to ascertain prevalence or incidence of a range of mental illnesses have been confined to relatively small areas, such as the work of Lemkau, Tietze, and Cooper (1941-43) in the Eastern Health District of Baltimore and the investigation of Roth and Luton (1943) in Williamson County, Tennessee. Variations in nomenclature, in sources of data used as a basis for classification, and in the temporal phase of data collection make any over-all estimate a sheer guess. The only other type of data of any importance in this field is that afforded by studies of mental health problems in specific population segments or social settings, such as surveys of the prevalence of neuroses among industrial workers, surveys of emotional problems among school children, and the systematic examination of small children in local child health projects. However, even if it is not possible to estimate accurately either incidence or prevalence of the wide range of mental illnesses and disorders for the total population, the fragmentary data available do provide some basis for planning special services aimed at treatment or prevention.

More adequate case-finding methods than those now available are prerequisite to better estimates of the magnitude and distribution of mental health problems and to providing treatment in the early stages of illness. Two major approaches to case-finding may be noted: (a) the assessment and classification by professional personnel of reports made by others concerning the behavior of individuals regarded as deviant and (b) the systematic screening or examination of a population by properly qualified diagnosticians. The former method has many defects, such as errors of observation and interpretation, and the distortions resulting

---

* References are to the bibliography at the back of the book.

from the unwitting intrusion of bias. However, such studies can be conducted without the necessity of securing the actual cooperation and participation of all the individuals in the population studied. The second approach, systematic diagnostic screening, has to date been used most frequently and most effectively in the military situation. The fact that military personnel may be required to accept direct personal evaluation makes the utilization of this superior method possible and feasible for military purposes. Ultimately, it is, of course, only by systematic, direct assessment of all individuals in a population that truly effective screening can take place.

It may further be noted that several of the major efforts in case-finding at the present time are to be found in community mental health projects which combine research and service objectives—Lindemann's Wellesley (Massachusetts) Human Relations Service, the Phoenix (Arizona) Mental Health Center of the National Institute of Mental Health, the Stirling County (Nova Scotia) project of Alexander Leighton, and Ernest Gruenberg's Syracuse epidemiological project of the New York State Mental Hygiene Commission. These projects involve both systematic efforts to exploit all local resources for reporting deviant or problematic behavior and routine screening of some population segments. These projects, which are largely unreported in the literature, represent a concerted effort surpassing any previously made in this field. Also unreported in the literature is the large-scale investigation of McQuitty (see Chapter 16), based at the University of Illinois. McQuitty is attempting to develop methods capable of discriminating, in the population studied, between those who need full psychiatric examination and those who do not need such consideration. This distinction is the same one that is made in chest X-ray surveys, blood test studies, and other firmly established case-finding methods. Perhaps these various developments will result in case-finding methods that have practical, large-scale utility, but no timetable can be given at the moment.

The development of rapid and inexpensive treatment procedures has not shown a great deal of progress to date. In addition to the various forms of shock therapy currently in use, there are some possibly encouraging developments, such as group psychotherapy, psychotherapy with limited objectives, and the brief analytic psychotherapy to which Alexander and French have given attention (1946). Perhaps it is not realistic to hope for quick and rapid treatment methods for the psychoses in the near future. However, many persons with minor problems may obtain some help through short-term and relatively inexpensive therapeutic experiences. Certainly the facilities for treatment have expanded in the last few years. The states have established many new clinics, and they have expanded old ones. Treatment is still not as available as is desirable, but it is more available than it has been at any time in the past. The value of these resources will be magnified when case-finding methods make it possible to assure early treatment for many incipient psychiatric disorders.

The prevention of mental illness, especially the psychoses, and the general improvement of mental health are formidable tasks. It must be candidly admitted that relatively little is known about these problems. It is important to make it clear that this problem is not a simple one. There are many factors that contribute to the variance of mental health, and probably there are several continua involved rather than only one. These factors include hereditary, physiological, biochemical, and other organic ones. However, interpersonal relations are also of great importance. Without the intention of indicating any rank order of importance, the present discussion will devote itself to the problem of interpersonal relationships as an area in which work can be done with the objective of preventing psychological or personality difficulties.

Specifically, the major concern in this discussion will be with what can be learned from the psychotherapeutic process that can be useful in helping individuals to achieve desirable or improved interpersonal relationships without resort to individual or even group psychotherapy. Moreover, the effort here is not primarily that of solving problems in this connection. Rather, the objective is that of indicating some of the kinds of questions that should be asked and the research problems that need solution.

Mental Health and Interpersonal Relationships

Disturbed interpersonal relationships must be considered in terms of their origin or development and of their course and perseverance. It is widely accepted that important aspects of one's interpersonal patterns are developed early in life and in response to one's early experiences. No particular difficulty is encountered up to this point. The child develops behavior which is, understandably, learned behavior. That a child, reacting to hostility, rejection, or other unfortunate parental treatment, does not learn the most effective way possible of handling the situation offers no difficulty of understanding. Learning does not always result in the best possible behavioral outcome. It does result in a way of reacting that has value for the person involved in the situation. Therefore, there can be no argument with the contention that early experiences may produce what is considered undesirable behavior from the point of view of facilitating smooth interpersonal relations later.

The real difficulty lies in the fact that early interpersonal habits survive beyond the kind of situations that originally produced them. It can be safely assumed that nobody meets, in every situation, in and out of the home, the same interpersonal threat to his personal integrity that he may have experienced in the home. Some of the persons that a child meets are not the potential danger that he has learned his parents and possibly his siblings to be. Since the learning of interpersonal relationships is a continuous process, experiences with nonthreatening persons outside the family could undo some of the effects of early home experiences. However, what actually occurs, in many cases at least, is a tendency to treat all persons with the same interpersonal habits that have been developed in the original learning situation. The individual is, of course, not conscious of this tendency to generalize the way he treats people; but he gives the appearance of having developed an interpersonal hypothesis that influences all or most of his reactions to other people. It is as if he assumes that all persons are dangerous persons; and his behavior, based upon this assumption, makes it appear to be a correct one. It is true that most persons meeting hostility, for example, will react with hostility. The whole sequence seems to support the rather loose generalization that interpersonal behavior tends to beget similar interpersonal reactions or at least responses that reinforce the person's way of dealing with others. This formulation is, of course, entirely too simple to explain the facts adequately, but there is at least superficial observational support for it.

It appears that inadequate interpersonal reactions tend to persist either in their original form or in equivalent forms appropriate to successive age levels of the individual. The literature is replete with studies showing complicated adult behavior that is the equivalent of early reactions to frustration or psychological trauma. If such developments occur, even in some instances, it is of considerable interest and importance. It is necessary to explain not only the origin of difficulties but also their perseverance, possibly through various equivalent expressions, in the face of experiences that could produce new learnings in the interpersonal sphere or revision or even unlearning of the original patterns. To summarize what has been said, important characteristics of one's interpersonal relationships are learned early in life, usually as a consequence of parental relationships. These patterns tend to persist in their original or equivalent forms as a consequence of their generalization and indiscriminate use, which elicits reinforcing experiences.

It is widely accepted, however, that psychotherapy has potentialities for changing the way that one deals with other persons. In other words, this kind of interpersonal experience appears to be more effective in altering interpersonal patterns than do other kinds of social interaction, even very intimate ones. Therefore it appears necessary to look carefully at psychotherapy with the hope of determining some of its essential aspects. An understanding of the factors that make psychotherapy effective with clinically ill persons may give clues to nonclinical methods of preventing mental illness or of improving mental health.

Some Essential Aspects of Psychotherapy

Limiting the consideration at the moment to individual psychotherapy, it is important to ask why psychotherapy appears to be more efficient in producing changes in one's interpersonal behavior than are other kinds of experience. First, the psychotherapeutic situation is designed to be as nonthreatening as possible to the person receiving treatment. The psychotherapist, initially at least, is a noncritical person. The patient has the experience of finding an acceptance of his behavior as reported and of his actual behavior in the therapeutic situation. Perhaps this experience is not a unique one for him; but perhaps the consistency with which the psychotherapist avoids any expression of criticism or hostility is usually a new experience for the patient. It is certainly true that nearly every individual entering psychotherapy is tentative with respect to his attitude toward the therapist. The mere intellectual appreciation that the therapist is motivated to be helpful does not destroy the patient's hypothesis that any person is potentially dangerous. An adult, seeking or accepting therapy, is showing a willingness to explore the possibility that this interpersonal hypothesis is wrong. He is not showing that he has finally decided that it is wrong. A child who is introduced into a psychotherapeutic situation usually cannot even formulate an intellectual acceptance of it. He merely faces it. In either event, the experience of dealing with a person who fails and who even refuses to verify the individual's interpersonal hypothesis appears to be one salient aspect of the value of psychotherapy.

Also, the psychotherapist facilitates learning of new patterns by serving as a person who can validate new formulations or new behaviors developed by the patient. This statement does not mean that the therapist says that this or that is "right" or "wrong." However, he has the opportunity to guide the explorations and to continue them until the patient achieves understandings or ways of behaving that appear adequate and realistic to him. The fact that there is a resource of this kind is one reason that the patient can afford to re-examine his problems. To put the matter simply and even naïvely, the therapist, no matter how indirect his methods, represents the law-of-effect factor in the situation. He is effective in this role, of course, only after the patient has in fact perceived him as a dependable, nondangerous, wise person—after the phenomenon of transference has occurred. As long as the patient lacks a person who represents this validating resource, he finds it difficult to effect behavioral changes that can be accepted by him as better or more satisfactory than his previous ones.

The psychotherapist, as a consequence of his training, also has some basis for discriminating between the crucial and the incidental or noncrucial aspects of the patient's history. In terms of his own theoretical position, he evaluates the adequacy of the data the patient presents for explaining his behavioral problems. Essentially, therefore, the patient is protected from and even prevented from accepting in a final manner explanations of his difficulties or beliefs concerning them that are superficial and spurious, no matter how plausible they may appear. This ability on the part of the psychotherapist is of great value in that it not only protects the patient from final reliance upon spurious understandings but also assures that he will ultimately deal with and understand the really important and crucial aspects of his history.

During the last ten years, group psychotherapy has been increasingly used for the treatment of a wide variety of personality disorders, and much material concerning it is now in the literature. However, there is relatively little information available concerning what actually occurs in the group psychotherapeutic situation. In general, journal articles by those who have used the technique describe a setting in which group work or group therapy has been found helpful. They mention some of the high spots of the group's development, cite a case history or two to show how individual members of the group have benefited, and offer a few statements on possible pitfalls or potentialities in the use of the technique. Of the few more systematic attempts to analyze in some detail what happens, that of Coffey and his associates (1950) will be briefly examined here.

The subjects with whom these investigators worked were self-selected, college-level members of a church, individuals who felt themselves to be maladjusted and unable to form satisfying social relationships. After twenty-four weeks of meeting with a trained leader, a majority of the members felt that they had benefited from the group experience, and this assessment was generally agreed to by the others.

Of interest here is the answer to the question: What happens in such a group experience? Coffey *et al.* report that, in their experience, three stages or phases in the course of group development could be distinguished:

(1) The period of defensiveness and resistance which answers the questions, "Who are you?" and "What are your problems?" (2) the period of confiding which aims at the production of genetic material, dreams, and memories and which answers the question, "Why are you this way?" (3) the integrative period in which the total therapeutic force of the group is aimed at integrating the material of the period and generalizing to the future. The questions discussed in this stage are "Where are you going?" "What will you become?" (p. 30).

In the first of these periods individuals tended to display the same self-defeating, isolating defenses that they had previously used in crucial life situations. The first meetings of the group were filled with anxiety for members and for the therapist alike. This phase of group therapy was utilized to bring out the response tendencies of the members, and the therapist's task was to allow the defensive roles to develop while at the same time preventing any member from completely traumatizing, monopolizing, or boring the group. At the end of seven or eight meetings, the therapist announced that the next session would be devoted to a summary in which each patient would contribute his impressions of his own roles and his problems and those of the other members. The interpretation of social roles came first from the patient himself, next from the other group members, and finally was summarized by the therapist. The problems of each member were made clearly explicit.

In the second stage, the period of confiding, the leader pointed out that certain problems had now been recognized but that their understanding could be achieved only by examining not alone immediate emotional responses but the meaning of dreams, fantasies, early memories, parental relations, and other mental content. The confiding period served to unify the group in that the members were enabled to see beyond defensive roles and to acquire sympathy with the inner needs of other individuals.

In phase three, the activities of the group were directed toward carrying over the new understanding to settings outside the therapy group.

The individual, now aware of his rigid social techniques and the inner conceptions of "self" and "other" on which they are based, has new views of himself and the world which move him toward change. He understands the interpersonal techniques with which he handles anxiety. He understands the effect his social role has on others. He understands better the dilemmas and defenses of others. He has some insight into the unconscious self-conceptions which motivate his defensive behavior. He glimpses the root of his derogatory self-conception in the traumata of the past. He becomes aware of the irrational expectations he projects on to "significant others" and the genetic causes for his current misperceptions of others. He realizes that he has changed his role and dropped his social defenses in the group, and he is encouraged to do so in his life outside the group (Coffey et al., 1950, p. 35).

Coffey and his co-workers report that therapeutic failures occurred in the case of those individuals who could not accept their role in phase one and who continued the defensiveness through the later sessions—usually increasing their isolation from the other members.

Ackerman (1945), describing group psychotherapy with veterans, listed as his objectives (a) emotional support through group relationships, (b) emotional release in the area of conflicts, (c) reduction of guilt and anxiety, (d) reality testing, (e) increase in self-esteem and recognition of constructive capacities, and (f) development of insight arising from an actual living-out of emotional drives in the context of the multiple interpersonal relationships within the group. He has not analyzed his experience in terms of phases as have Coffey et al., but the same general pattern seems apparent from the description. Like Coffey, Ackerman emphasizes the value of letting the patients themselves interpret to one another the real meaning of their behavior. The greater possibility of testing the nature of social reality in the group as contrasted with individual therapy is stressed by Ackerman and also by Slavson (1950) in his more detailed description of group methods. The latter therapist notes the special importance of this element of reality testing for the younger child under treatment, pointing out that the child "can accept direct impediment of his behavior whereas he may not understand the reasons for it. Controls are particularly telling when they come from his peer culture; there is less resentment than when controls are imposed by adults" (p. 91).

There seems to be general agreement among those who have practiced group therapy that it is not an adequate means of dealing with serious intrapsychic distortion and the more deep-lying defenses. This feeling stems partly from the difficulty of producing enough significant genetic material for exploration of unconscious mechanisms and partly from the relative lack of control by the therapist with respect to the influences impinging on any one patient. The seriously disturbed individual may not be able to cope with the pressures upon him in the early stages of group development and may react with so much anxiety that effective communication is prevented.

It is of particular interest to note that in group therapy the patient is not met with the complete acceptance that characterizes individual therapy. True, the therapist himself may strive to be accepting and permissive; but the interaction of the patients involves many displays of hostility, and their effects can often be only partly mitigated by the therapist. It is only when empathy and understanding begin to replace defensive reactions that the group offers the kind of support to the individual members that a therapist offers from the start of treatment.

If the principles which operate in group therapy are to be utilized in other settings, the task would seem to involve: (a) facilitating accurate perception of one's own social roles and defenses, (b) providing emotional support in order to reduce guilt and anxiety and to permit the individual to accept the task of seeking new ways of behaving, (c) producing understanding of the circumstances under which inadequate defenses are used and the reasons underlying their use, and (d) providing opportunities for testing new understandings and consolidating new behaviors. The provision of opportunities for emotional release might be added as a separate principle, but it seems more properly to be an aspect of several of the others.

There are other factors that contribute to the effectiveness of both individual and group psychotherapy, but the ones that have been mentioned are probably the major ones. The objective in describing these factors has not been merely an expository one. Rather, the purpose has been to make it meaningful to ask now what lessons can be learned from psychotherapy that are valuable from the point of view of the prevention of mental illness and the general improvement of mental health. The question is not that of how psychotherapy can be accomplished outside the clinical setting but how some of the values of the psychotherapeutic approach can be utilized elsewhere with persons who are not clinically ill.

Necessary Conditions for a Preventive Approach

It is necessary first to state clearly the major assumptions that underlie the effort to influence interpersonal patterns through methods other than individual or group psychotherapy. There are three such important assumptions. First, it is assumed that most persons desire, at least consciously, to establish interpersonal relationships that are favorable ones in terms of the clinician's frame of reference. This statement does not refute the claim that many persons need to establish hostile or other patterns of relationship of the kind that are the concern of the clinician. It is merely a statement that most persons would accept as desirable a pattern of interpersonal relationships similar to one the psychotherapist would evaluate as consistent with mental health.

Second, it is assumed that all persons have some potentiality for changing the ways in which they deal with others without recourse to psychotherapy. Many persons have a wide latitude for change; some persons have very little. It is the latter group, of course, for whom psychotherapy is indicated. Regardless of this difference, though, all persons have common needs (such as those for acceptance, a feeling of worthiness, and the like), and these needs are met or satisfied through their interpersonal habits—habits which most persons can modify to some extent if they perceive a good reason for doing so. Many persons, for example, in demonstrating their own worthiness to others (and to themselves) may utilize sarcasm which causes them to lose the acceptance of many of their associates. Such behavior by these individuals is incompatible with multiple-need satisfaction, and it may be called inefficient or inadequate. These persons can, with varying degrees of ease, abandon such an interpersonal technique when they perceive that it has liabilities that outweigh its benefits. They are able to seek new ways of demonstrating their worthiness—ways that do not conflict with their other interpersonal goals. It is this flexibility and latitude for change that educational efforts to improve interpersonal behavior must exploit. Mental health can be promoted by educational methods only in so far as there are large numbers of persons with a reasonably large latitude for changing their interpersonal habits as the result of experiences that are different from those of psychotherapy. The results, however, should be cumulative with time and particularly from generation to generation. At any one time, though, the efforts to change attitudes and behaviors will depend not only upon the effectiveness of techniques but also upon the psychological ability of people to change.

Finally, it is safe to assume that enough is known about interpersonal behavior and about the conditions that promote harmonious relationships to make it possible to supply information that is useful to most individuals. Not all the answers are known, but enough of them are known to justify the effort to make present knowledge available and understandable to all persons. As research continues, this information will increase. To summarize, any effort to improve the interpersonal habits of individuals must assume (a) that most persons want to change their ways of dealing with others in a direction which clinicians would approve, (b) that for most persons the psychological barriers to change in this respect are not so great that they make modification impossible, and (c) that valid and usable knowledge is available and that it will increase as research continues in the sciences that deal with behavior, personality, and interpersonal habits.

It should also be indicated that public education in the interpersonal sphere is not dealing with a neutral area. Health education in other

areas has been most effective when it has been clearly recognized that
the task is not only the giving of valid and defensible information but
that much of the effort must be directed toward misconceptions and
beliefs that have great tenacity. In dealing with interpersonal problems
this difficulty is particularly acute. Individuals treat others as they
do, not merely because they have learned a particular set of interpersonal
habits, but also because they have developed role functions and attitudes
that satisfy their personal and cultural value systems. Everyone derives
from his parental home and from the various groups to which he belongs a number of expectations as to how given situations are to be
met. Whether one meets aggression with physical violence or with
neatly turned phrases, whether a husband and father insists upon making
all final decisions for the family—these and innumerable other ways
of behaving are not merely a matter of individual choice. They are also
supported in part by the sanctions of one's social class, by one's ethnic
group, and by one's family group. To attempt to change the interpersonal habits of individuals is therefore to attempt also to change their
value systems or at least to demonstrate that no violence is being done
to these patterns of belief. Much of what happens in individual psychotherapy can be described as a revaluation and reordering of value systems.
It is on the basis of this change in fundamental beliefs that behavior
changes can be effected. The fact that a different set of methods is
used to attempt to change interpersonal habits does not make these
fundamental attitudes and beliefs any less important than they are for
the individual psychotherapist. These value systems have their roots
in personal experiences, particularly in the childhood home, in religious
experience, in the subcultural group with which the individual identifies,
and in other comparable sources. In short, parents behave as they do
not only as a result of their actual experience in dealing with their
children but also as a result of their efforts, consciously or not, to fulfil
their own conception of the proper role function of the parent. Any
attempt to change parental behaviors that does violence to the role concept already held will be resisted and will be relatively unsuccessful:
Recognition of this fact will not only prevent wasted effort but can serve
as a basis for determining methodological techniques and substantive
content of educational material.

The actual job of influencing mental health resolves itself into that
of changing the daily behavior of the individual. These changes have the
purpose of benefiting those whose behavior is changed and those (such
as children) with whom they deal and for whom they have responsibility.
For practical reasons, major reliance cannot be placed upon the method
of individual psychotherapy, although it is the most trustworthy method
available for the individual case. It is true, of course, that a public
health or preventive function is served when successful psychotherapy
is accomplished with a person who has responsibility for children or who
figures significantly in the lives of a large number of people. However,
even this secondary effect of psychotherapy cannot be expected to reach

a number of persons large enough to meet the needs of the public mental health approach.

Whether they are aimed at modifying the individual's tendencies or habitual ways of behaving or whether they are aimed at restructuring systems of relationships in significant social situations (so as to reduce the stress impinging upon individuals), the remaining methods for influencing patterns of interpersonal behavior rest essentially on educational techniques. These methods all require the communication of information and skills which can be utilized by the individual, and this communication can take place in any one of a number of ways. To utilize educational devices successfully it is necessary to define (a) general and specific objectives, (b) the relevant available and necessary substantive materials and content to be utilized, and (c) the methods that are available and needed.

Some Positive Mental Health Goals

There are several general objectives that may be described. First, in any educational program aimed directly at modifying significant behaviors, it is necessary to develop upon the part of individuals an interest in the possibility of improving interpersonal relationships and a belief in the importance of this goal. It has already been stated as a necessary assumption that a desire for good interpersonal relations is a prerequisite to modification of habitual inadequate behaviors by means other than formal psychotherapy. Indeed, most therapists would probably agree that such a desire is a prerequisite to successful therapy. There is no intention to imply that reaching this objective will in itself actually improve the way that individuals deal with one another. However, the creation or strengthening of such attitudes is a first step in gaining acceptance and utilization of specific mental health information. If good interpersonal relationships can be made a more positive value in our culture and its subcultures, the effectiveness of mental health education will be increased. It is certainly true that the success of educational efforts in the field of physical health is in large part due to the fact that health is an accepted positive value. Mental health (or rather, the avoidance of severe mental illness) is also a positive value in our culture. However, the concept of optimal mental health and its identification with the problem of interpersonal relationships is not well understood. Consequently, not many persons think clearly (or probably very often) about the need for improving their interpersonal relationships. Here, then, is a first step that must be taken. Some efforts in this direction have already been made; but they have not been extensive, and they certainly have not been systematic.

Second, it is necessary, too, for all persons to accept the fact that personality and behavior are understandable and naturalistic phenomena. They must realize that the way the individual behaves and deals with other persons is comprehensible even though it is extremely complex.

This is not to suggest that an effort be made to provide all persons with a theoretical understanding of personality development, but merely to say that educational programs must establish a general realization that personality development is a naturalistic phenomenon. In the field of physical health education, no effort is made to present detailed knowledge of physiology, biochemistry, and bacteriology. However, to a remarkable extent people have been taught to view physical health problems from a naturalistic point of view. On the other hand, personality development, problems of interpersonal relationship, and mental health are frequently regarded as inevitable consequences of heredity, "temperament," "badness," etc. Beliefs about causation of mental illness and about its treatment are very inadequate and inaccurate. Similarly, beliefs and knowledge about personality development are naïve and inadequate. These facts are of importance. Such inaccurate and inadequate conceptions may lead to attitudes of defeatism with respect to the possibilities of change and improvement, to resistance to treatment and other forms of professional assistance, and to susceptibility to spurious and indefensible offerings of such varieties as the faith cure. If a naturalistic point of view concerning behavior, personality development, and interpersonal habits can be achieved by all or most of the people, another basic step will have been taken that will permit specific mental health education.

Specific mental health education must be developed with respect to the groups toward which it is directed, such as parents, teachers, work supervisors, and the like. These groups are not, of course, homogeneous. Cultural and socioeconomic differences among each of these groups call for specialized treatment of the material. It is possible, however, to describe some of the kinds of learning that can be promoted through a variety of methods.

One of the important objectives of education in the field of interpersonal relationships is that of enabling most persons, particularly parents and teachers, to make discriminations and judgments concerning behavior and development that are compatible with those of the professionally trained individual. The disparity of the value judgments of trained and untrained persons has long been recognized. Wickman's (1928) early study has frequently been cited to show the difference in the seriousness of various behaviors of children as rated by teachers and by clinical psychologists. The training and orientation of teachers with respect to the evaluation of children's behavior has certainly improved in the years since this study, but further progress of this kind is clearly needed.

To be sure, parents, of all social and economic groups, cannot be expected to view behavior characteristics in the same way that clinicians do. As a matter of fact, the goal is not necessarily that of having parents and teachers accept exactly the same set of values as clinicians. They are dealing with children in different contexts. Parents and teachers are evaluating behavior from a point of view that has to encompass criteria different from those of the clinician. They must concern themselves with producing cultural conformity and educational achievement as well as desirable personality patterns. On the other hand, the parents and teachers should recognize what is serious and what is not serious from the clinician's point of view. The behaviors that are clinically serious have prognostic value, and sophistication in this respect has value in enabling parents and teachers to seek assistance for significant problems at an early date. Also, the development of behavior symptomatic of interpersonal disturbance, even when the actual manifestations are mild, can serve as danger signals indicating that the relationships of significant persons with the child are not optimal. The recognition of this fact will, of course, do nothing except produce anxiety unless the parents and teachers have additional information that will enable them to formulate hypotheses concerning the source of the difficulty and unless they have some knowledge of behavior variations upon their own part that might be effective in developing a solution. It should also be clear that knowledge of what is clinically serious may reduce anxiety that would otherwise be generated by parents and teachers concerning what is not clinically serious. At any rate it appears to be a reasonable task to help teachers and parents become sensitive to behavior manifestations that are clinically significant as contrasted with those that are merely troublesome and inconvenient.

Another goal that mental health education can attempt to reach involves developing an awareness upon the part of individuals that their own psychological needs structure the pattern of their interpersonal relationships. It also has to be made clear that the way in which these needs are interpersonally reflected is not obviously related to the nature of the needs involved. As a start toward developing such awareness, it would be valuable even if all persons could simply be brought to realize that they frequently do not know and understand their own motivations. The suggestion is not that people be taught self-diagnosis or self-analysis. It is possibly true, though, that a recognition of the fact that interpersonal behavior is motivated in ways not always understood by the individual himself may increase his ability to develop flexibility and to accept behaviors in others of which he would otherwise be critical. Perhaps this hope or hypothesis doesn't have much justification. However, it is worth trying to determine whether or not it is correct.

A closely related objective involves an effort to help people secure some insight into their values, and thereby some idea of the basis of the demands they make upon others. It has been noted above that each person incorporates within himself values and expectations derived from his culture and from his unique social experience within that culture. Many parents use these expectations as standards against which to measure the child's performance, without ever being aware of the fact that they are doing so. The mother who wants her daughter to be a perfect little lady or the father who wants his son to be a star athlete may assume that these are natural goals that any child would accept. An important task for mental health education, then, involves bringing to such parents a realization that their own needs and expectations are often not the same as the child's needs and expectations, and it also involves leading them to examine the demands they make upon their children. Methods for accomplishing this objective (which sounds a great deal like what happens in psychotherapy) certainly are not easily available. It is, therefore, just at such a point that resourcefulness is needed. The present writers do not have a set of answers. Later, however, one example of a possible method that might be used to reach this objective will be described in connection with comments concerning group discussion and decision.

Publications as Mental Health Media

Consideration will not be given to the various channels and methods that can be used to accomplish the educational tasks described above. Some of the things that are being done have already been mentioned, but it is necessary to indicate the values and utilities of the various approaches. The ways of proceeding may be classified in general terms into (a) utilization of the mass media, (b) use of group activities, and (c) use of consultants to encourage measures that will result in decreasing the pressures and demands upon children and adults in the school, the home, and the work situation. The matter can also be viewed as involving efforts to present actual information, principles, and concepts concerning mental health and interpersonal relationships to the ultimate consumer and the effort to change the way large-scale activities are actually conducted. That is, parent education programs are aimed at presenting concepts and information about mental health and interpersonal problems to parents in a form that they can utilize in dealing with their children and the entire home situation. On the other hand, programs may be aimed at key personnel in industry for the purpose of inducing them to revise the organization's personnel practices in accordance with what is known about the way people react to demands made upon them and to the authority exercised over them. Such programs ease interpersonal tensions upon the part of both the supervisor and those supervised.

The mass media include, of course, books, magazines, newspapers, pamphlets, pamphlet series, motion pictures, the radio, television, and any other resources for reaching large numbers of people on a more or less impersonal basis. Each of these media has been utilized to some extent for mental health education, but the medium of the printed word has been by far the most widely used. A number of magazines with readership in the millions carry regular features or departments in the field of child-rearing practices. Books like those of Spock (1945), Gesell and Ilg (1943), and the Aldriches (1947) have likewise been widely read and in some segments of the population have undoubtedly had great influence.

Anthropologists and others who have sought to characterize the American culture have noted the lack of consistent patterning of child-rearing practices, especially among the members of the urban middle class. In most other cultures there exist much more clearly defined standards as to the proper ways of rearing a child. Such matters as time of weaning and cleanliness training, degree of freedom of locomotion, disciplinary measures to be used, etc., are matters of folk knowledge which by and large simply are not open to question. Every mother knows the correct ways of rearing children, and any marked deviation from these ways is likely to evoke negative responses from other members of the society. In middle-class America, however, mothers are likely to be searching for "the right way" to raise their children and to lack the easy assurance of the mother who can simply accept the traditional ways. The reasons for this development seem at least in part to be related to the repudiation of Old World values and customs on the part of the children of immigrants, as well as to the diversity of cultures and values which were brought into interaction and partially merged, particularly in urban centers, in the New World. In rural areas, because there was greater homogeneity of population and less violent cultural conflict, there seems to have been not so much a repudiation of traditional patterns as an evolving of somewhat modified patterns which incorporated some of the values of the New World with those derived from the Old.

In any event, the departure from traditional practices of child-rearing in urban America has its correlates in our striving for technological excellence and efficiency. Expert opinion has supplanted folk wisdom. Unfortunately, the competence of the professed expert has often been difficult to assess, and variations in expert opinion have left a large measure of uncertainty for many mothers. The consequences of this have in some instances been reflected in overanxiousness or in overly rigid adherence to formulae based on spurious generalizations. Where uncertainty prevails, there is always the danger that someone with a few pat answers will appear and set a new fad in motion.

Whether or not the fact of reliance upon experts rather than upon tradition is a salutary state of affairs in the long run, this seems to be the prevailing condition. It is not possible to summarize all the values and influences of child care books. However, it is important to note that books like those mentioned above can possibly reduce the anxiety of parents about the adequacy with which they are handling their responsibilities by describing the complexities and stresses inherent in child development, by indicating what are considered good and desirable parental behaviors, or by leading parents to realize that they have considerable latitude to determine their own methods without danger of doing harm to the child. Where emphasis is given to meeting the needs of parents and children with special reference to individual differences, these books can do much to develop a belief upon the part of parents that behavior and personality development are naturalistic and understandable phenomena. It has already been indicated that this is an important objective in the field of mental health education.

Magazine offerings, pamphlets, and pamphlet series have about the same relationship to the problem of mental health education as do books. For a more detailed consideration of the kind of materials being utilized by health educators to modify child-rearing practices or parental attitudes and some of the problems involved, the "Pierre the Pelican" newsletters may be cited. They consist of a series of twelve four-page leaflets written by Loyd W. Rowland for distribution to parents of first-born children.[1] A letter is mailed each month, beginning one month after birth, or as soon thereafter as possible, using the resources of the local or state offices of vital statistics for prompt compiling of the list of names and addresses of parents.

The series is written in an informal conversational style which should be understood by most parents possessed of at least a fifth grade education. Essentially it suggests that babies can be fun, that they don't have to be raised by the book or by the clock, that they should be given lots of affection without fear of spoiling them, and that a generally permissive attitude will make life more pleasant to parents and child. The first few messages discuss security needs, sociability needs, food habits, sleeping habits, and other matters primarily pertinent to early development. The discussion of these needs necessarily suggests that personality development is a naturalistic phenomenon.

Beyond the first six months, the Pierre messages deal with matters pertinent to the entire preschool age range and not merely with aspects of infancy. In general, emphasis is on parental understanding of what is natural or normal for a child, and common "problems" are discussed with a light touch. For example, behavior which a parent might label "lying" or "stealing" is examined from the standpoint of the child's world. Again, punishment is considered from the standpoint of parental motivation as well as direct effect upon the child.

The educational effectiveness of such materials may be considered at several levels:

1. How many persons read the series with sufficient thoroughness to be able to verbalize the preferred information and attitudes?
2. To what extent is the information offered accepted as a basis of guidance by the parents?
3. To what extent are parental behavior and feelings toward the child modified by virtue of the material read? Conversely, are any feelings or actions modified negatively through creating resistances?

[1] The first letter explicitly states that the series is interested in the child's mental health. The letters were checked over for accuracy and agreement by several prominent mental health specialists, including Dr. C. Anderson Aldrich, Dr. Milton Senn, Dr. Dorothy Seago, and Dr. Robert Sutherland.

4. To what extent will modification of parental attitudes and behaviors in the direction advocated by Pierre lead to a mentally
healthier child?

Most clinicians and social scientists probably would not anticipate any
very great effects from such a series of brief pamphlets received through
the mail or from other similar materials. Even though most parents may
be sufficiently motivated to read them, parental roles toward the infant
may be too closely tied to deep-rooted emotions and long-existent response tendencies to be markedly affected by casual reading. There are
clearly great differences between individual parents in the extent to which
their attitudes, feelings, and practices are subject to change either by
psychotherapy or by other educational techniques. Parents whose lack of
display of affection and approval of a child stems from rejection of the
child or from patterns of hostility which pervade all their interpersonal
relations are not likely to be able to modify behavior toward the child
without intensive psychotherapy. On the other hand, parents who withhold approval or the display of affection because they have been led to
believe that a child will be "spoiled" if it does not receive firm undemon-
strative treatment may be able to change their habitual practices as a
result of exposure to a provocative educational program. It is recognized
that misconceptions and other types of ignorance may simply be a cover-
up for underlying rejection and hostility. It seems unlikely, however,
that this is always or even usually the case. The point is that new knowledge may sometimes serve as an entering wedge to get parents to take
stock of their relations to the child and to each other. Ideally, of course,
the new knowledge should be communicated early enough to prevent the
development of a patterning of hostile response tendencies within the
family.

In the case of the Pierre pamphlets, there may be some parents who
gain confidence or simply feel somewhat less anxious about the child by
virtue of the point of view expressed. Also, some may gain in understanding and sensitivity with respect to certain critical areas in which the child
may very easily be traumatized. For example, they may restrain tendencies to invoke the "bogey man" against an obstreperous child. In such
instances, a little learning on the part of the parents can profoundly
modify the child's learning situation. The importance of such modification is certainly suggested by much current theory and by descriptive
accounts of psychotherapy, even if not rigorously proved. Future research on psychotherapy can put such assumptions on much firmer
ground to the extent that anxieties, in appropriate roles, and other behavioral tendencies reflecting erroneous generalizations by the patient
can be related systematically to specific elements in the learning situations
—i.e., to the extent that it can be demonstrated how erroneous generalizations were derived. From such research in psychotherapy and from
direct evaluation research on the health education materials, it should be
possible to narrow down (or broaden) the approach used so as to incor-

porate a maximum of effective material and a minimum of ineffective material.

Movies, Radio, and Television as Mental Health Media

In recent years motion pictures have been increasingly used for the purpose of mental health education. A fairly large number of films has been produced since the end of the second World War. Many have dealt with behavior problems and psychiatric disorders as such. However, films have also been produced that deal with sociological considerations, child and family life, marriage, the physiology of human reproduction, and teacher education.

While it is not a completely clear distinction, it can be said that there are two general orientations apparent in the production of mental health films. Some of them deal with particular symptom patterns in a semi-technical manner and attempt to show their origin and development and methods of treating them. The films produced in the series titled "Mental Mechanisms" by the National Film Board of Canada are good examples of this approach in mental health film-making. Some of the titles are *The feeling of hostility, The feeling of rejection,* and *Overdependency.* The titles are descriptive of the kind of problem involved. Each film is essentially a case history woven into a supporting story.

The other general approach in the development of mental health films involves the presentation of a general or particular mental health problem in a provocative and informative manner. These films do deal with symptomatic behavior and some of the reasons behind it. However, they are less didactic and are not characterized as much by the introduction of specific psychiatric concepts as are films in the other group. In some of the films in this grouping, treatment problems receive little attention, if any. Some of them do not use any psychiatric terminology and do not introduce any professional personnel into the story. The objectives of these productions are (*a*) to create awareness of the nature and pervasiveness of mental health problems, (*b*) to encourage a naturalistic interpretation of personality and its development, and (*c*) to promote constructive interest in and consideration of the problems with which the films deal.

Preface to a life, produced for the National Institute of Mental Health, is one example of this type of film. It shows the influences that parents have on the development of the child and the ways in which the hopes and aspirations of parents for the child determine their way of behaving toward him. Another film that can be mentioned in this connection is *Angry boy,* produced under the auspices of the Mental Health Film Board for the State of Michigan. It deals with hostility shown by a young boy in the school situation. It does portray treatment in a child guidance clinic, but the real emphasis is upon the roles played by the members of the household and upon the way in which they change as the mother and boy develop some new understandings of each other. Parents who see this film should learn a great deal about the importance of their ways of dealing with their children and the effects upon the child of unfavorable relationships between the parents themselves and between them and others in the household. Other good films of the kind under discussion here include *The quiet one, Palmour Street,* and *The steps of age.*

The mental health films now available are best used as a method for stimulating discussion in the group that sees them. It is particularly important that there be a discussion leader who can help the members of the group to clarify their reactions and to resolve any anxiety the films may have produced. Many of the films are accompanied by study guides. It is hoped that these materials will make it possible for persons other than psychiatrists, clinical psychologists, and other highly specialized personnel to serve as discussion leaders. One of the problems in the use of films is that of determining the kinds of experience and background the discussion leader must have. Certainly interpersonal sensitivity and the possession of group skills are two requirements for the discussion leader, regardless of the specific area of his professional competence. Some well-informed laymen who recognize their own limitations of knowledge and who can be objective in dealing with the problems covered in these films may be able to do an adequate job as discussion leaders, if not an excellent one. The discriminating use of such persons would greatly increase the effective use of mental health films. The general problem of the utilization of mental health films has been well handled by Middlewood (1951) who deals with the dangers of their unwise use as well as the values derived from their proper use; and Prados (1951) has described his experience in utilizing films in group psychotherapy.

There is not space to discuss in detail the contributions already made or potentially to be achieved through the use of other mass media. The radio, in programs like CBS's "Doorway to Life" series and in occasional documentary broadcasts, has demonstrated the possibility of using case materials for positive effect without being either dogmatic or superficial. Radio and television offer at least one very important potentiality not possessed by any of the other media: they make it possible for a whole family unit to share simultaneously a given presentation. Parents who have become sufficiently aware of the desirability of trying to understand the child's point of view may learn much through informal family discussion of the broadcast, noting the identifications made by each family member and the justifications or rationalizations for various types of behavior.

There is a need for at least a modicum of observational data as to what happens in various types of families which tune in such broadcasts. Indeed, it would be of great value merely to know something of the characteristics, in terms of family structure and interpersonal patterns, of the audiences that listen to broadcasts which seek to explore problems of personality development and interpersonal relations. In many instances, probably in most cases, families do not listen as a unit. Even if only a small segment of the vast potential audience is really involved, however, the effect may be more widespread than that achieved by a great many local meetings.

The possibility of using television for demonstrations of skilful handling of children or of other persons in group situations is another unexplored area. Such skills cannot, of course, be divorced from the personality of the person possessing them, but much more successful communication is possible when the audience is not merely told the principles and the need for sensitivity but can actually see the results that may be achieved.

To sum up the implications of what has been said about the use of mass media for producing significant learning in the field of interpersonal relations, they can stress the value of good interpersonal relations; they can strengthen the trend toward a more naturalistic view of personality development; and they can offer an entering wedge for producing awareness of areas where improvement is possible. The dramatic media can facilitate accurate perception of the individual's own social roles and defenses through the process of identification, and they may produce some understanding of the circumstances under which inadequate defenses are used. The printed word can impart much more theory than can radio and television concerning the reasons underlying one's use of defenses, but there is reason to doubt that theory alone will be effective in changing behavior. One major shortcoming of the mass media when used alone is the fact that they cannot provide the individual with emotional support in order to reduce the guilt and anxiety they may arouse. It is possible that these feelings will sometimes be increased. Another shortcoming of the mass media lies in the fact that they afford the individual no possibility for testing the effectiveness of newly achieved understandings he feels he has acquired. Little is known on the effect of the various media in terms of emotional release through subsequent activity, although the occasional heightening of guilt and anxiety suggest that such release often is not achieved.

Group Discussion and Decision

It has been suggested at several points that group discussions may greatly increase the value of the printed word, movies, or other means of mass communication aimed at influencing interpersonal behavior. The use of small, informal discussion groups does not make it easy to reach large numbers of persons. However, the value of systematic exploration of this approach is indicated because there is some evidence that it has good possibilities for producing change in parental behavior and feelings. Lewin (1947) has shown the potency of group decision in effecting habit changes in the field of nutrition—including such things as getting mothers to give cod-liver oil and orange juice to their infants. In one experiment using this approach, a nutritionist devoted twenty-five minutes of individual attention to each of several mothers in a maternity ward and the same amount of time to six other mothers in a group situation. In the latter case, the mothers discussed the desirability of the proposed program (that of giving a specified amount of cod-liver oil to the infant) and agreed to try it. In a checkup after four weeks, the mothers who had decided as a group were all following the proposed routine, while only half of the mothers dealt with individually were doing so. These results were duplicated in a number of other experiments. The modification of group values and standards thus proved a basis for changing individual performance. Moreover, the act of decision, and the formulation that it entailed, seemed to provide a link between motivation and action which was lacking when only the nutritionist and the individual mother were involved.

To be of any real value in the area of child-rearing practices relating to emotional development, one may surmise that the kind of group decision to be attempted would not relate to any specified do's or don't's but rather to a generalized approach to the child and his problems. It might, for example, prove feasible to have groups of mothers and fathers decide to make a fairly systematic assessment of their own responses toward each other and toward their children in the course of a single day. The results might then be used as a basis for asking what might be done differently in order to handle the simple tasks of everyday life a little more effectively—that is, with less stress and effort. One area of particular interest to the writers would be the possibility of reducing unnecessary restraints upon the child. Thus, parents might agree to determine how many times a day they said "No!" simply because it seemed expedient and not because the child was attempting or proposing a dangerous or seriously improper action. A group of parents might even be brought to decide to try to avoid saying "no" for a period of days or weeks unless the "no" did seem to be necessary. Our own experience suggests that the consequences might be extremely gratifying to the parents as well as beneficial to the child in terms of healthy interpersonal relations.

One of the positive mental health goals mentioned above is that of helping people to secure some insight into their values and thereby some idea of the bases of the demands that they make upon others. An approach that has possible value for reaching this objective has been described recently to the writers by Tamara Dembo in personal conversations and in unpublished communications. Dr. Dembo's interest in this connection lies in the direction of studying the value structure of parents. She proposes to ask the prospective mother (or father) how she or he would use seven wishes for the child at the time of his birth. After expressing these positive wishes, the parent is given an opportunity to express seven guardian wishes—things from which the child is to be protected during his lifetime. Finally, the parent is given a large number of additional wishes, presumably to prevent the development of anxiety as a consequence of the parent's feeling that the first fourteen wishes were inadequate or incomplete. This method does appear to be capable of securing some ideas about the basic values of prospective parents. A little additional questioning could indicate the meaning of such frequently appearing wishes as those for "health," "a good education," "success," "happiness," and the like.

The general method just described could possibly be utilized effectively in prenatal education. This service usually involves discussion between a public health nurse and the mother. Increasingly an effort is being made to hold group discussions with the mothers either at the time of visits to the clinic or in classes and meetings at other times. There is also an increasing tendency to encourage the participation also of prospective fathers in these group discussions. It would be interesting to experiment with Dembo's wishes-technique in a prenatal discussion group, particularly one comprised of both prospective mothers and fathers. Several things could conceivably occur. First, the parents could be shown that they do have wishes for their children. Second, it could be demonstrated that they also, consequently, have expectations of them. Third, it would become obvious that the wishes and expectations of parents from different families and of the spouses of any one family differ. Even where the generic wishes are the same (such as those for health, educational achievement, etc.), the discussion should indicate the wide range of individual differences in the definition of these values. Fourth, it should be possible to show parents in this way that not only are they desirous of doing good things for their child but also that they expect the child to give them satisfactions by growing, developing, and achieving in conformity with their wishes for the child. The present writers feel that participation by prospective parents in discussions leading to the kind of understandings just mentioned could do much to make them more flexible, more self-critical, and less rigid in the acceptance of their pre-existing concepts of parenthood. If these results could be achieved only in a small degree, it would be a very great advance in parent education. And there are several additional possibilities in the situation that has been described. A skilful leader could, after feeling that the above understandings had been in some part achieved, ask the group how they as parents would or could react if the child fails to meet the parental expectations. Specifically, what is the problem of a parent who defines a good education as college graduation if the child is intellectually capable of only grammar-school graduation? It is rather exciting to think about the possibilities of such a discussion by parents who have not yet seen their child and who have not changed their conscious wishes on a reality basis. It might produce concern and anxiety for parents to be brought squarely face to face with these possible disparities between their hopes and possible reality. Could the leader suggest the possibility of parental rejection growing out of frustrations the parents may experience as a consequence of these possibilities? Would parents, thus forewarned, be able to accept the development of their child as it actually occurs rather than accept it only if it occurs in the way they hope it will happen? Would this group discussion be a good place to develop some meaningful definitions of many of the clinician's terms such as permissiveness, acceptance, and rejection? The

method just described does appear to have some possibilities of creating
attitudes, beliefs, and awarenesses that can affect the way parents perceive
their children and deal with them. To explore these potentialities at all
fully, of course, would require highly skilled leadership and a substantial
series of meetings. It might also be desirable to provide access to individual therapy in the case of persons who were made anxious by being
confronted with value conflicts of which they had been unaware.

The well-baby conference or clinic is another setting in which public
health personnel have been attempting to combine attention to mental
health principles along with services designed to maintain and improve
physical health. As described by Lemkau and Cooper (1947), the task
is essentially one of sizing up the problems and needs of a mother who
comes to the clinic and of developing a course of cooperative action in
which the mother receives supportive guidance without any attempt at
the complicated and time-consuming task of deep personality analysis.
Discussion groups using Dembo's wishes-technique might be used in this
setting as well as in the prenatal clinic.

Approaching Mental Health Through Responsible Group Leadership

Turning now to a brief consideration of other settings in which significant work aimed at prevention of mental health problems or the development of positive mental health has been done, consideration will be
given to methods that aim at influencing leaders or key figures in a given
setting to modify the structure of relationships in the direction of decreasing stress and increasing understanding and attention to individual personality needs. Three settings will be briefly examined: (a) human
relations institutes or workshops for personnel in health, welfare, and
educational agencies (people whose work brings them into frequent contact with individuals in trouble and who, therefore, receive considerable
displaced aggression), (b) the classroom, and (c) business and industry.

The mushrooming of human relations laboratories or workshops,
focusing upon group dynamics and interpersonal relations, is a recent
development of considerable interest. One type of workshop has stemmed
less from psychiatric or mental health sources than from the activities of
social scientists interested in applying their knowledge to social action
programs. The group experiences involved in several days or several
weeks of intensive meetings with the same individuals, taking as subject
matter the group's own process, tend to be difficult to communicate but
compelling for the individuals involved. They frequently provide the
individual with a completely new perception of the role or roles he tends
to play. Through role-playing and observations, the group member acquires sensitivities and skills which can be carried over outside the laboratory setting.

Groups operating within such workshops differ in several important
respects from the therapy groups that have been described. For one

thing, the motivations of the members are not so much to discover the reasons for disturbed relationships as they are to gain additional skills and knowledge for professional use; hence, there is relatively little probing of deep-seated needs and tendencies. Also, the leaders do not make a strong effort to supply ego support for group members. This practice may be partly due to the fact that the leaders are seldom clinically oriented. Leaders may occasionally traumatize group members by passing judgments in terms of their own value systems. They may label as "resistance" adherence to a value system different from their own. From the standpoint of producing social action workers, this way of handling groups may be generally defensible and effective; but it may leave some participants far more anxious than they had been previously. On the positive side, however, such workshops usually have as a major objective the broadening of participation in community programs and the lessening of intergroup stresses in the community. Their net effect is probably to increase measurably the valuing of good human relations.

A somewhat parallel approach, but with a different orientation, has been confined almost exclusively to public health personnel. A series of "institutes" has been held recently for state and local public health officers. These sessions have considered the human relations aspects of public health work. The first of these institutes, staffed by psychiatrists and by public health specialists, and held under the auspices of the California State Department of Public Health and the Commonwealth Fund in July, 1948, has been described in publications by Smith (1949) and Ginsburg (1950). Subsequently, similar institutes have been held for public health personnel in a number of regions, under grants from either the Commonwealth Fund or the National Institute of Mental Health. Institutes have also been held for medical personnel within the armed forces.

A typical institute combines formal presentation of knowledge derived from psychiatry and social science with clinical practice, observation, and discussion. In the latter phase, a variety of public health clinics may be utilized. Individually, or in small groups, each with a psychiatrically trained leader, the students interview patients in order to comprehend the meaning of the clinic experience to the patient. Thus, they get at first hand the feel of interpersonal relationships within the health department or involved in its services to the public. Sensitivities to critical areas of interaction and awareness of some of the problems of adequate communication seem to be fostered by such direct experiences and their subsequent exploration through group discussion. The majority of participants in such institutes, when subsequently interviewed, have reported not only an increase in the amount of attention given to human relations aspects of public health but also dividends in terms of greater ease and effectiveness in their own interpersonal relations.

The potentialities of the classroom setting are illustrated by a description of one teacher's efforts to help her pupils better understand their own problems and emotions. This experience is reported in a recent study by Taba and Elkins (1950), titled *With focus on human relations*. This

teacher's school was a cooperating unit in a national program of intergroup education, and the achievement described undoubtedly resulted
from combination of the teacher's skill and understanding with the suggestions of the highly trained specialists who were her consultants. The
whole orientation of the program in this eighth grade group was toward
diagnosing the social and emotional needs of the students and toward
making the classroom a place where, at least partially, those needs could
be met or understood by the child. By studying the sociometric choices
of the children and the reasons given for those choices, by talking with
parents in their homes, and by the use of themes and discussions as
projective materials, the teacher secured some clues to children's human
relations problems and anxieties and also some identification of the situations that had produced these problems and anxieties. She then varied
the content of her class periods in social studies and literature to provide
a basis for very free discussion in critical areas—family living, peer relations, sibling relations, and intergroup relations in the community, with
encouraging results.

In reading this account, one is struck by the high proportion of children whose interpersonal relations are marred by conflict and worry in
the home situation and by displaced aggression, coupled with fear of
rejection, in the peer group. The family settings have a close resemblance to those cited in descriptions of serious delinquents or mentally ill
patients—often presented with the implicit assumption that such a background of conflict, rejection, and lack of guidance can only lead to a court
or to an institution for mental patients.

One feels that these parents and children deeply needed a respite from
environmental pressures and a chance to get to know themselves and
others. Psychotherapy would seem to have been indicated in a number
of instances, but these were working-class families, to whom expensive
forms of professional treatment were not available. Even with psychotherapy, in the face of the social pressures upon them, progress for the
more seriously disturbed children probably would have been meager.
For some of the children, though, one feels that the probability of the
need for psychotherapy in the future was lessened by what the teacher
managed to accomplish by her own accepting behavior, by working toward acceptance of the children by one another, and by guiding the
children in a sympathetic exploration of some of the areas of stress and
hostility that they had encountered.

The area of industrial mental health is almost virgin territory, although
research at its boundaries indicates that thorough exploration and ex-
ploitation are overdue. It may safely be assumed that the personality
has acquired its basic shape and content long before the individual enters
the field of employment, yet the kinds of experiences that one has on the
job tremendously influence and are influenced by his interpersonal relationships in other spheres. Further, in a culture where occupational
success is a major criterion for upward social mobility and where upward
social mobility is a major goal, the way in which occupational experiences

are squared with one's self-concept may be critical with respect to mental health.

A study by Fraser (1947) among industrial workers in postwar Britain revealed that from one fourth to one third of all absences were definitely attributable to neurotic disturbances and that 10 per cent of all workers suffered from disabling neurosis. Again, the studies of Mayo (1945), Roethlisberger (1943), and their associates at the Western Electric Company and other industrial plants have revealed, on the one hand, the extent to which on-the-job performance is hampered by worries and anxieties and, on the other hand, the extent to which the closely knit organization of the work group and its relationship to management practices can improve worker morale and performance and decrease absenteeism. To be maximally effective, it appears that industrial mental health programs must go beyond the provision of clinical and counseling services to include the analysis and possible modification of organizational structure and supervisory practices. Indeed, the role of the worker in the community at large may be considered a legitimate problem for industrial mental health programs that seek to achieve maximum on-the-job effectiveness for a total work force, especially as older workers are increasingly utilized and as conservation of human resources becomes necessary.

Research Needs

Finally a brief look at research needs is called for. In order to obtain knowledge necessary for a really effective public health approach to mental health, two major types of research using data derived from therapy should be undertaken. First, there is need for research into the social and cultural correlates of specific disorders and also into the correlates of particularly effective functioning in the area of interpersonal relations. We have mentioned above that a number of studies have shown differential distribution of hospitalized psychotics with respect to residential area at the time of first admission to the hospital. Studies conducted in the United States and abroad have likewise found that certain psychoses (schizophrenia, for example) are much more prevalent in certain occupational groups than in others. At the same time, clinical studies have stressed psychogenic factors in the early life of schizophrenic patients which seem to have led to withdrawal and disruption of communication with others. Unfortunately, the several types of data which are available from clinical and statistical studies cannot be put together to yield a well-knit theory, even though they may suggest compatible elements which will eventually go into such a theory.

It is our belief that crucial data for the development of a coherent theory pertaining to the role of interpersonal relationships in severe mental illness can only be obtained by subjecting clinical data, secured through therapy, to the same kind of analysis to which the crude data on hospital admissions have been subjected. To be sure, the problem of classification—whether according to diagnostic labels, to observed behavioral groupings, or to dynamic categories and interpretive labels derived from theory—is enormous and will require a great deal of research and pooling of experience by numerous investigators. The task of conceptualizing and recording the most relevant materials yielded by psychotherapy will require reorientation of many therapists. It may require the kind of training, not now generally available, which will seek to produce a measure of research competence as well as skills in clinical practice.

It is probable that longitudinal studies of personality development will in time establish the relative importance of various experiences and relationships in early childhood for personality structure and dynamics in later life. Ideally, one would like to secure for those individuals who had been included in intensive longitudinal studies the kinds of data that a therapist would obtain in attempting to ascertain the reason for a neurotic disturbance. There is a need for data which will reflect not only what happens to the child, but also how the child incorporates his experiences into his self-image. This need is one reason why it is so important to study individuals whose interpersonal performance and general mental health are scored on the positive end of the scale in addition to studying those on the negative end of the scale.

The other major area of research relates to the evaluation of various approaches which seek to prevent mental illness or to build positive mental health. The evaluation of therapy itself is perhaps the most difficult of all tasks in the evaluation field. Some of the problems involved in the objective evaluation of psychotherapy have been stated and explored in the report of a round table on this subject, chaired by Bronner (1949), at the 1948 American Orthopsychiatric Association meetings. The writers wish merely to raise a few general questions with respect to the evaluation of approaches that do not employ psychotherapy but that seek to modify attitudes and practices which are not interwoven with strong and deepseated internal conflicts.

For any specific program to be evaluated, the first requisite is a careful definition of the objectives of the program. In some instances a program may be designed simply to lead members of the population to reconsider their own orientations or to seek additional information. Thus, it has been suggested above that increased valuing of good interpersonal relationships and a more prevalent appreciation of personality development as a naturalistic phenomenon are probably necessary stages in the modification of mental health practices by means of mass media.

In discussing the use of printed materials for parental education, it was suggested that effectiveness would depend upon: (a) extent of readership, (b) degree of acceptance of information presented, (c) extent of modification of behavior by virtue of the material read, and (d) the long-term consequences of such modification of behavior. In any program designed to give information, it is relatively easy to sample the population in order to ascertain whether or not the material is being read and its message is being communicated. It is more difficult to determine whether or not such information is accepted, both intellectually and emotionally, as a basis of guidance. To some extent this can be done, however, if the interviewer seeking the information is not identified with the source of the educational materials. Perhaps more effective assessment of this type can be obtained from careful observation of what happens in a discussion group where the materials form the basis of discussion.

There have been very few studies which have attempted to observe systematically the changes in interpersonal behavior brought about through the medium of educational materials. This task can seldom be done by asking the subject about his behavior, especially when the subject knows what is approved and what is nonapproved behavior. In dealing with such matters as change in nutritional practice, described above, it appears that one may accept mothers' reports as reasonably reliable. However, when the question involves a mother's reaction to negativism in her child or a supervisor's handling of a hostile action from an individual supervised, interview data seem far less satisfactory. Behaviors in these situations can, nevertheless, be categorized both with respect to the overt action and with respect to the emotional overtones apparent to an observer, and in many situations it would seem feasible to obtain the requisite observational data. Such data may be secured by questioning individuals having frequent contact with the subject or by strategically planned direct observation.

The long-term effects of various educational programs upon mental health itself are very difficult to assess. Let us assume, for a moment, that 10 per cent of the parents in a group which has been subjected to a program of education with respect to child-rearing practices actually modify their behavior and attitudes in the direction desired. Let us assume, further, that there exists an adequate control group whose members were initially similar in all important respects to the parents subject to the educational program and that there is no consistent change in the pattern of child-rearing practices of this group over the period of study. The change by 10 per cent of the patients in the program group simply means that the educational materials had some effect on certain behaviors; it does not mean that 10 per cent of the children are likely to experience better mental health than if no program had existed. Yet this latter formulation is the crux of the evaluation problem.

There are several possibilities open to the investigators who seek to establish the effect of a program on mental health. The most costly and slowest to yield data involves long-term follow-up of both experimental and control group members, categorizing them with respect to various indices of mental health, good and bad. If one's objective is to study the effect of a program on the incidence of psychosis or neurosis, no other approach can be relied upon to answer the crucial question. It may be noted that in such instances, where incidence of the disorder in the population is relatively low, one must be prepared to include hundreds or thousands of cases in the groups under study.

One alternative entails assessing the incidence or prevalence of relatively minor disturbances in interpersonal relations and the ways in which they are being handled fairly soon after the completion of the program. Those behavioral difficulties which seem frequently to be precursors of neurosis or psychosis might be of particular interest, but general personality assessments and even subjective reports of tensions and tendencies in interpersonal relations can be used. Here again, ideal data would approximate what a therapist would secure, although it does not seem probable that the ideal can be attained except for very small, select groups.

In part, at least, the rationale for many a program will have to be the validity of the theoretical principles incorporated into the program. That is, if longitudinal studies or analyses of clinical data representative of a definable population segment have established the relationship between particular influences and experiences and particular tendencies in personality and interpersonal behavior, other factors being relatively constant, this may be accepted as presumptive if not crucial evidence that in a similar population the modification of the influences and experiences will bring the desired changes in interpersonal behavior. Whatever approach is attempted in evaluation studies of mental health programs, it is to be hoped that the objectives will be stated broadly enough to permit assessment of the ways in which change was brought about and not merely the end results achieved. Studies that seek to analyze the dynamics of change are much more likely to have some carry-over value to other programs where similar principles are utilized with similar populations.

Summary

The present paper has attempted to show the nature and present status of public mental health work. It also has considered some of the ways in which the lessons to be learned from psychotherapy can be applied to this field. The essential elements in individual psychotherapy that tend to produce improved interpersonal relationships were identified as (a) the provision of a nonthreatening situation, (b) the assistance of the psychotherapist in validating for the patient new formulations and understandings that he achieves, and (c) assurance that the patient will ultimately deal with relevant and meaningful experience and psychogenic materials instead of plausible but spurious explanations of his difficulties. Group psychotherapy was indicated as having the additional value of providing group support for accepting new beliefs and ways of behaving and a situation in which reality testing for new insights and behaviors can occur in a meaningful context.

The belief that effects similar to those coming out of psychotherapy can be achieved, essentially through educational methods, rests upon the assumptions (a) that most individuals desire to improve their interpersonal relationships, (b) that a large percentage of the population are psychologically capable of changing their interpersonal patterns, and (c) that the material and information available in the field of mental health and interpersonal spheres are sufficient to justify extensive efforts to help individuals improve their ways of dealing with others.

The objectives of mental health educational efforts have been described as (a) increasing the interest of individuals in the possibility of improving interpersonal relationships and a belief in the importance of this goal; (b) producing more widespread acceptance of the fact that personality and behavior are understandable and naturalistic phenomena; (c) increasing the ability of all individuals, particularly of parents and teachers, to make discriminations and judgments concerning behavior and development that are compatible with those of the professionally trained person; (d) making individuals aware of the relationship between their own needs and motivations and the way they treat others; and (e) assisting them to gain some degree of insight into their own value systems.

The actual educational approaches available were reviewed with the purpose of showing their utilities or possible utilities for reaching the objectives just mentioned. The mass media appear capable of increasing the value placed upon good interpersonal relationships and of promoting the naturalistic concept of personality development. To some extent radio and television have the ability to present material which can possibly lead to family discussion that can lead to new percepts of one's self and of others. Television has the potentiality for providing demonstrations of good interpersonal handling of children and others. Mental health films, if used for the purpose of promoting group discussion among the viewers, appear to show considerable promise for mental health education.

Group activities appear to represent a more powerful way to influence interpersonal behavior than do the mass media. Prenatal conferences, well-baby clinics, mental health institutes, group dynamics workshops, classroom settings, industrial situations, and parent-teacher organizations offer possibilities for achieving new self-percepts and for promoting changes in the ways school and work situations are handled that will ease interpersonal tensions.

Continued progress in promoting mental health through the public health approach requires that research be directed toward (a) careful determination of the personal, social, and cultural correlates of personality development, involving both individuals with inadequate interpersonal patterns and those who have good relationships with others and (b) evaluation of the effectiveness of public mental health activities in terms of their immediate effects upon individuals and the long-term influences that they exert on personality development.

PART II
RESEARCH METHODS AND RESULTS

CHAPTER 9

RESEARCH PERSPECTIVES IN CLIENT-CENTERED THERAPY

By Julius Seeman, Ph.D., *and* Nathaniel J. Raskin, Ph.D.

In the decade or more since the appearance of Rogers' book *Counseling and psychotherapy* (Rogers,* 1942), a considerable body of research literature on client-centered therapy has come into being. This body of literature is the subject matter of the present chapter. However, we do not wish primarily to discuss the present status of research-gained knowledge about client-centered therapy. What we should like to do, rather, is to consider this research from a historical-developmental perspective, as the case history of a research program in being. In this period of interest and ferment regarding ways of looking at the phenomenon of therapy, such an approach may be useful not only as a stock-taking enterprise in its own right, but also in terms of the models it may provide for research in any form of therapy. In this connection we should like to indicate the research directions which have thus far been roughed out in client-centered therapy and to extrapolate from these into areas still to be explored. In so doing, we shall be talking about not only the contributions of research in client-centered therapy, but also its problems and unfinished business. Because other reviews have discussed the literature of play therapy (Dorfman, 1951) and group therapy (Hobbs, 1951), we shall confine our discussion to research in individual adult counseling.

As a way of defining the present task, we suggest two frameworks within which we can organize our thinking about therapy. The first pertains to the bidimensional nature of research in therapy, and the second relates to the role of theory in shaping research plans and directions. With reference to the dimensions of therapy research, we can take our cue from the dimensions of psychological research in general. Here we can see two dimensions—first, the dimension of internal events or processes and, second, the external dimension which seeks to find correlates ("outcomes") to help explain the processes we are interested in studying. The internal dimension exists whether we are studying the process of therapy, the process of concept formation, or the process of maze learning in rats. In therapy research we may arbitrarily define the internal dimension as the interview behavior of client and therapist. Within this dimension of internal observation we can look either through the

---

* References are to the bibliography at the back of the book.

eyes of the subject (the internal frame of reference) or utilize concepts which interpret the events from some other frame of reference. In any event, we are seeking through this dimension to discover the orderly and lawful relationships inherent in the data of the therapeutic process.

The second dimension of therapy research turns to the correlates of the process of therapy; its main task is to teach us more about the process of therapy by teaching us about the concomitant behaviors associated with therapy. This second and external dimension of therapy research has the double task of discovery and demonstration. Its search for independent measures of therapeutic process and outcome leads not only to discovery of new facts about therapy, but also to the classical validation function of verifying hypotheses about therapy.

We started the organization of our thinking about therapy by suggesting two frameworks, one of which was the dual aspect of research in this field. The second framework, the consideration of the role of theory, we can best discuss as we consider the specific research studies. However, it may be well here to restate what the title of this book already presumes, namely, that a structure of theory is a powerful force both for the organization of existing knowledge and for the structuring of directions in which to search out new knowledge. The inexorable direction of science is relatedness; a theory simply cooperates with nature in this respect.

We may turn now to the detailed consideration of the existing research and the directions they imply for further inquiry. We shall discuss first the studies which are encompassed by the internal dimension of research, the searching out of lawful relationships in the therapeutic process.

The Internal Dimension of Therapy Research

The First Formulation of the Process of Nondirective Therapy. —In 1940, prior to the publication of his book, *Counseling and psychotherapy,* Rogers proposed that there was an orderly process in the course of therapy, which he outlined as follows:

1. Rapport established
2. Free expression of feeling on the part of the client
3. Recognition and acceptance, by the client, of his spontaneous self
4. The making of responsible choices
5. The gaining of insight through assimilated interpretation
6. Growing into independence—with support

Rogers received corroboration for the view that such a process did characterize psychotherapy from an investigation conducted by Lewis (1943). In a detailed analysis of six cases involving disturbed adolescent girls, she discovered the following patterns:

Items classified as "Explanation of psychologist's role" were most frequent in the first and second deciles of treatment.

Items devoted to exploration of problems made up approximately 50 per cent of the client items and occurred for the most part during the first two deciles.

Encouragement by the counselor to explore problems was frequent during the early deciles, and reached a peak during the fifth.

From the fifth to the eighth decile, there was a sharp rise in client statements in which relationships were seen between various aspects of information given. This verbal expression of perceived relationships rose to a peak in the eighth decile, giving way in frequency in the last two deciles to statements involving planning—new steps, new decisions, plans for future actions.

Allied to the latter were statements telling of results of actions taken; these reached a peak in the last decile.

Rogers' formulation of therapy just cited, together with the research by Lewis, marks a sort of prenatal period in the development of nondirective therapy. Lewis' research, while based on careful records, did not make use of the more exact and complete method of electrical recording of interviews, nor was the formulation of method yet crystallized in the form in which it was later to appear.

Early Studies in Client-Centered Therapy.—The next stage in the development of client-centered therapy was marked by three steps: (a) the formulation of the process of nondirective therapy by Rogers in a talk at the University of Minnesota and in his book *Counseling and psychotherapy;* (b) the development by Covner (1942) of a technique for phonographic recording of interviews; and (c) the research studies stimulated by these two developments. The early studies varied in the degree to which they made demands upon theory, but in the main they were exploratory and descriptive. Rogers' book was essentially a clinician's book. In it he presented a detailed definition of one form of therapy and differentiated it from other methods currently in use. The book and its concomitant thinking inevitably helped to shape the course of research at the time. In consequence, much of the early research was directed toward the delineation of those processes of therapy which could be observed in the clinician's office during the therapeutic hour. To the extent that the research emphasized this task of surveying and defining the territory of therapy, it neither demanded nor gave an explicit structure of learning or personality theory.

In the first published study on client-centered therapy, Porter (1943) sought to establish a classification system which would describe counseling procedures and bring out the systematic differences which existed among methods. To this end he devised a set of categories which defined counseling procedures along a directive-nondirective continuum and assigned weights on this continuum for each category on the basis of pooled professional judgments. Through the analysis of recorded interviews, he found that such a classification system could be used with significant reliability and that it could differentiate counseling methods.

Although he was primarily interested in this task of differential classification, Porter's questions about the self-consistency of counselors led him to study methods at different stages in therapy and thus to raise questions about possible regularities in counseling at a longitudinal level.

Snyder's study (1945) made its strongest contribution in the development of a similar line of inquiry. He turned his attention to nondirective therapy alone and studied both counselor and client data. He found, first, that the nondirective therapist uses a clearly defined method of counseling and, second, that there is a predictable process of therapy for the client. Snyder's categories were consistent with the current formulations of the process of therapy, and his findings supported this formulation. Specifically, he found that the release of negative feelings was followed by expression of positive attitudes; that following the expression of problem statements, there was the emergence of insight; and that toward the end of counseling, the client increased his planning activity.

One immediate extension of the lines of research set forth by Porter and Snyder is to be found in a study by Gump (1944). He sought to assess the degree to which nondirective methods and psychoanalytic methods could be differentiated; his findings affirmed the differences which one would predict from the literature descriptive of these methods, namely, that the psychoanalytic methods involved a greater proportion of interpretation and the nondirective methods emphasized reflection of feeling. It is of interest to note that in both methods of therapy the client did more than 70 per cent of the talking.

At this point, nondirective therapy was relatively new, but its research already had clear implications for therapy as a process of learning in human beings. It proposed, and presented data in the studies by Snyder and by Curran (1945) to support the view, that learning is an integral part of the process of therapy or readjustment. Of what does this learning consist? Rogers pointed to three aspects of the insight which occurs in counseling: (a) seeing old facts in new relationships; (b) the gradual increase in self-understanding; and (c) recognition and acceptance of aspects of the self formerly defended, denied, distorted, or repressed. The content of this learning was seen as an individual matter, to be arrived at by each client through his own efforts and his own way as he seeks to unravel the confused patterns of his own unique experiences and being. In an intensive study of one case, Curran charted this pattern of learning as it occurred in a therapeutic situation. He buttressed the view of insight stated above by finding "a high content of negative emotion factors in the beginning interviews and then their gradual falling off with the corresponding rise of insight factors in later interviews." He made a more unique and significant contribution by studying in detail the "perception of relationships" aspect of insight. He found that, in the case of Alfred, "at the beginning of the counseling the client came with twenty-five distinct problems which he stated as unconnected and about which he was extremely confused. By the tenth interview he was much less confused, and relationships between problems were appearing. . . .

By the end of the counseling, in the twentieth interview, he had a co-ordinated picture of his various problems, their interrelation and main causes. . . ." Thus, Curran developed one method of studying in detail what any given client learns in the course of therapy.

We have said that the research of this period placed relatively less emphasis upon theory than did the later studies. The clearest exception was the study by Raimy (1948). It is worth while to highlight the significance of Raimy's study as a promising model for the study of psychotherapy as it relates to personality theory. Raimy ordered his work thus: he undertook a detailed theoretical consideration of a single construct in therapy and personality theory; he then derived postulates from his theory, made predictions from these postulates with reference to therapy and personality change, and tested these predictions by empirical means. The construct with which he was concerned was one which has come to have a central place in the personality theory associated with client-centered therapy, that is, the construct "concept of self." Raimy described his thinking thus: "The Self-Concept is the map which each person consults in order to understand himself. The approval, disapproval, or ambivalence he feels for the self-concept is related to his personal adjustment. A heavy weighting of disapproval suggests distress or disturbance. When successful personality reorganization takes place we may also expect a shift from self-disapproval to a self-approving balance." His results supported his hypothesis; cases judged successful showed predicted shifts while in cases judged unsuccessful such shifts were not found.

The main significance in Raimy's study is probably not to be found in his empirical results but rather in the comprehensive formulation of an important aspect of self-theory. Raimy focused on learnings about the self as being the key type of learning in therapy. He saw the self-concept as functioning both inductively and deductively. "It serves to regulate behavior and may serve to account for observed uniformities in personality." At the same time, it "is itself altered and restructured by behavior and unsatisfied needs." Like George Mead (1947), Raimy believed that the self-concept "undoubtedly has its source in the social interactions of the person beginning with the immediate family and continuing on through life. The evaluations which each individual makes of himself . . . are clearly social in origin. These evaluations tend to produce organization when they are positive and may produce disorganization when they are negative."

Time now permits us to bring some perspective to a survey of the work of this early period of research in client-centered therapy. Of its contributions, it is likely that beyond any substantive addition to knowledge which these studies made, their value lay in the demonstration that the methods of science could be brought successfully to bear upon the data of therapy. Yet, with all this, the findings themselves cannot easily be set aside as an integral part of the contribution of this period. For it was not only the utilization of scientific method which compels attention for these studies, but the fact that through the use of this method striking regularities were revealed in the therapeutic process. It was both the methods used and the order found which opened the way for further research and understanding in this field.

When all this has been said, we may state with equal confidence that if the studies demonstrate anything, they demonstrate, too, that research as a process of successive approximation to truth is long, slow, and laborious. For these studies show their youth in details of research method, in their degree of statistical sophistication, and in the concepts used. In these studies reliability percentages in the 80's and 90's can be found, but so too can they be found in the more equivocal regions of the 40's and 50's. What the studies teach in this regard is that reliability, which in studies of this sort is essentially a meeting of minds about concepts, can best be obtained by clear definitions and clear communication about the definitions among those who are participating in the studies.

With regard to the conceptualizing process which sought to explain the nature of therapy, the two threads of major relevance which will continue to appear in therapy studies were already in evidence—the concepts which derive from personality theory, as in Raimy's study, and the concepts which derive from learning theory, as in Snyder's and Curran's studies. Snyder began the task of defining therapy as learning in the pair of categories which turned out to provide the most discriminating index of change in therapy, the categories *statement of problem* and *insight*. At the same time, these categories define the unfinished business of therapy-process research, for they are in effect the two end points on the learning curve. It yet remains to explore the complex mental-emotional processes by which these points are spanned.

Another set of concepts with which the early studies dealt were those which related to counselor method. We may judge the power of a concept by asking to what extent it deals with central components of the phenomenon it seeks to define and to what extent it can be used for predictive purposes. If we use these criteria for judging the concepts used to study counseling methods, they do not fare very well. In the main, these concepts were oriented toward the differentiation of procedures on a directive-nondirective continuum. While this continuum may have been useful in underscoring differences in methods, it is not likely to be our most fruitful one for the assessment of counselor behavior or the prediction of therapeutic outcome in relation to this behavior. The subtler interplay of more central factors which go to create a therapeutic atmosphere are probably to be found elsewhere, and they are likely to cut across the procedural lines used in these studies. Of this, we shall have more to say as we discuss studies which come later in research development.

Development of the Phenomenological Approach in Theory and Research.—For several years after the appearance of the early studies there was a hiatus in research activity. This intervening period was characterized by increasing attempts to order and explain the phenomena observed in clinical practice through the intensification of the theory-building process. From this period of rethinking came the statements which sought increasingly to organize the data of the therapeutic process within the broader context of personality theory. The first organized expression of this theoretical position was given by Rogers (1947) in a paper entitled "Some Observations on the Organization of Personality." The points which he emphasized and which helped to shape further research may be summarized as follows:

1. *The crucial element in the determination of behavior is the perceptual field of the individual.* This postulate stresses the individual's internal frame of reference as a vantage point for the understanding and prediction of behavior. This vantage point has come to have an important place in research in client-centered therapy. It may be noted parenthetically that the individual's internal frame of reference also has a clinical centrality; it is this aspect of the person which the client-centered therapist attempts to understand in the therapeutic hour.

2. *Given certain conditions, the individual has the capacity to reorganize his field of perception, including his perception of self; a concomitant or resultant of this perceptual reorganization is an appropriate alteration of behavior.* Here we find a definition of the therapeutic process which follows from the first postulate. The content of this perceptual reorganization was spelled out to some extent in Rogers' address and more completely later on in his book (1951). Its focal point was the construct: *the self.*

Much of the process research which followed this formulation dealt with hypotheses derived from such postulates as those cited above and took various aspects of the construct, the self, as the point of departure of study. In two closely related studies Sheerer (1949) and Stock (1949) took as their point of departure the hypothesis that psychotherapy modifies the characteristic ways in which an individual views himself and others (see Chapter 13). Sheerer studied those aspects of attitudes toward self and others which could be subsumed as "acceptance of self" and "acceptance of others." She set up a five-point scale expressive of varying degrees of acceptance and rated each relevant item for each interview in ten cases. This procedure resulted in a trend analysis for each case, so that one could observe from the data the systematic variations which occurred during the therapeutic process. Sheerer found that in nine out of ten cases the clients improved increased acceptance both of self and others as therapy proceeded. Stock utilized a broader but comparable base for her analysis of self-regarding attitudes and attitudes toward others, and her results corresponded closely to those of Sheerer.

It will be recalled that one of the postulates advanced by Rogers defined a relationship between perceptual reorganization and behavior change. Hoffman (1949) made a beginning in the direction of studying this relationship by assessing the behavior described by clients while therapy was still in progress. He rated each behavior reported by clients on a three-point scale from immature to mature, and found that cases rated successful or unsuccessful on other grounds could be differentiated on this reported-behavior continuum; the cases judged more successful showed a significantly increased maturity of behavior, while in cases judged less successful no significant ·change occurred (see Chapter 11).

One of the key postulates of self-theory in regard to therapy is that through therapy a person comes to rely more and more upon the evidence of his own senses in establishing a basis for behavior, and less and less upon values and attitudes set by others but not reinforced by his own sensory experience. Raskin (1949) made this postulate a point of study and used the construct "locus of evaluation" to describe this process. He hypothesized that in therapy a client would shift his locus of evaluation from relative emphasis upon others as a source of evaluation to relative emphasis upon self as a relevant evaluator of experience and behavior. He set up a "locus of evaluation" scale which ranged from maximum reliance upon self as evaluator to maximum reliance upon others as evaluator, and applied the scale to ten cases; he found that through the course of therapy a significant shift took place in the direction of greater emphasis upon self as evaluator of experience.

Another aspect of self-theory which has come in for more recent attention is the relation between various aspects of the self. It has been a clinical observation that, typically, early in the therapeutic process there is a considerable discrepancy felt by the client between what he feels he is and what he would like to be. During the course of therapy this gap appears to be reduced, either because the client alters his view of his "present self," because he alters his view of the "desired self," or because of both. Rogers has summarized the studies which bear upon this question and has stated a series of propositions with regard to changing aspects of self in therapy (Rogers, 1951). Two studies by Aidman (1951) and Bowman (1951) were designed to investigate the relationships between these aspects of self during the course of therapy. Their prediction was that there will be increasing congruence between the two aspects of self as therapy proceeds.

When all of these studies on the self are taken together, they begin to form a coherent pattern of empirical study with regard to self-theory and the therapeutic process. Many blind spots remain to be filled in, but through the stimulus of these studies and their theoretical background it is likely that investigations into the self will continue to be a nuclear point of research for client-centered therapy.

Increasing Variety of Studies of Interview Behavior During the Therapeutic Process.—If the foregoing studies in the process of therapy represent a focal point of research in client-centered therapy, they do not by any means exhaust the possibilities for inquiry into the therapeutic process. As a matter of fact, the scope of the studies completed in the past few years are only illustrative of the richness and variety of the hypotheses open to test through the records of therapy. In this connection, there has been some discussion of the utility of the phenomenological approach in the understanding of behavior. Whereas the foregoing studies illustrate an emphasis upon this approach, those which follow employ a variety of reference frames; the additional knowledge thus derived indicates the value of using diverse approaches at this juncture in our knowledge about therapy.

It is worth noting that though the studies cited below have a broad range of content they have this point in common, that each of them is concerned with a form of behavior which the client is exhibiting implicitly in the interview itself as contrasted to the noninterview behavior which he is reporting or talking about. These behavior studies include, among other things, an assessment of the flexibility-rigidity of the client's evaluation processes, a study of defensiveness in the interviews, an assessment of the tension state of the client as inferred from his vocabulary (the Dollard-Mowrer *DRQ*, 1947), and studies of the formal properties of language construction used during the interviews.

Kauffman and Raimy (1949) applied both the discomfort-relief quotient (*DRQ*) and Raimy's self-attitude instrument to a group of seven cases and found that the measures traced changes in the therapeutic process in similar fashion. Other studies of the *DRQ* by Assum and Levy (1948), Cofer and Chance (1950), N. Rogers (1948), and Zimmerman (1950) all confirm the finding that, in cases considered successful, the balance between discomfort and relief changes in the direction of less discomfort and greater relief (see Chapter 11).

Haigh (1949) utilized a concept of defensiveness formulated by Hogan (1948) and applied a measure of defensiveness to the interviews of nine cases which were studied by other measures discussed earlier in this chapter. When he compared the defensive behavior of the first and second halves of therapy, he found a decrease in defensiveness in the latter half of therapy, significant at the 5 per cent level of probability. When the measure of defensiveness was compared with positive measures for the same group of cases (e.g., self-acceptance, insight), the correlations turned out in the predicted negative direction, ranging from —.34 to —.55 and indicating that, on the average, defensiveness reduces as statements of self-acceptance and insight increase. Actually, this correlation was contributed by seven of the nine cases, two being in the reverse direction. Such findings indicate the value of cross-comparisons of separate process measures on the same cases as ways of securing a more comprehensive view of the total process of therapy.

In a study which sought to test a hypothesis related to general semantics, Kessler (1947) investigated the evaluational processes of three clients in terms of the flexibility-rigidity of evaluations or conclusions and of the extent to which the clients explicitly saw themselves as making evaluations. Her evidence was consistent with the prediction that the therapeutic process reflected three stages in the evaluation process: (*a*) evaluations rigid and not explicitly recognized as evaluations, (*b*) evaluations rigid but recognized as evaluations, and (*c*) evaluations recognized as such and flexible in character. This study involved only three cases and can only be considered evidence in a descriptive sense, but it seems sufficiently promising to indicate a fruitful way of looking further at behavior in therapy.

There are two studies which deal with formal aspects of client language in therapy. Seeman (1949) studied the use of tenses in the counseling series in relation to expression of positive and negative attitudes. He found the following relationships: for positive attitudes, there were significant shifts in the direction of an increasing proportion of present-tense expressions as compared with past-tense expressions as therapy proceeded; for negative attitudes, the opposite held true— that is, the negative attitudes that were expressed were expressed increasingly in the past tense as therapy continued. Grummon (1950) undertook an intensive study of grammatical and psychogrammatical language categories used in therapy. He defined approximately two hundred and fifty linguistic categories and studied their relative frequencies of use early and late in the therapy of four clients showing different degrees of improvement as judged by tests and counselor ratings. The linguistic categories which turned out to be most promising in their differentiating power were as follows: (*a*) changes in the type-token ratio, an index of the number of different words in a given size word sample, showed that active vocabulary size increased from early to late in therapy; (*b*) clause length showed increase; (*c*) adjective-verb ratio showed change in the direction of increased proportion of adjectives. In his discussion, Grummon related these findings to psychological properties of language use and their implications as measures of personality integration. One specific observation which he noted was the tendency for spoken language to become more like written language at the later stages of therapy, and he utilized this phenomenon to develop a concept of language efficiency (see Chapter 17).

Studies in the Psychological Climate of Therapy.—Thus far in our consideration of studies in the therapeutic process we have focused our attention mainly upon the process as it affects the client. There are a number of studies which deal with the role of the therapist and the interaction between therapist and client; these studies not only add much to our understanding of psychological climate in therapy but also raise critical issues with regard to those variables which make a difference in the therapeutic effect of a counseling experience.

We have already pointed out the early work done on counselor methods by Porter, Snyder, and Gump. The later phases in the development of client-centered therapy have laid more stress upon the attitudes which underlie the effective use of techniques. This is a variable difficult to assess, and thus far little research has borne directly on the question of counselor attitudes, but there are three studies which provide leads in this direction.

In a study which deals with a counselor training program, Blocksma (1951) has provided an instrument of potential use in process studies. In analyzing the changes produced in a course of client-centered counseling among a group of Veterans Administration personal counselors, he classified the techniques used by these counselors according to whether they were thinking *with, for,* or *about* the client. He found that the training courses effected an increase in the degree to which counselors thought *with* clients, as measured by role-playing situations before and after the course.

Along with the increased attention being devoted to the attitudinal orientation of the counselor, there is an implication in a study by Seeman (1949) of the interdependence of attitude and technique. Seeman utilized Snyder's system of counselor response categories on a later group of nondirective cases and found a definite change in the direction of a more consistent use of client-centered techniques, such changes being concurrent in time with increased emphasis upon attitude. A striking comparison shows one hundred and seventy-two examples of "approval and encouragement" in the six early cases analyzed by Snyder and just one instance of this category in the ten cases investigated by Seeman.

Bergman (1950) chose for study a particular point in the therapeutic process, namely, that point at which the client asked for a definition of the therapeutic relationship, for advice, or for some other type of counselor intercession. His purpose was to determine by sequence analysis which kinds of counselor response to such client requests had a facilitating effect upon further client exploration and which did not. Bergman developed his design at a time when clinical evidence seemed to suggest increasingly that counselor structuring did not facilitate the therapeutic process as it had earlier been thought to do. His findings were as follows: structuring and interpretation were significantly associated with abandonment of self-exploration by the client, while reflection of feeling was significantly related to continued client self-exploration or insight responses.

In choosing this particular point in therapy for study, Bergman has selected a point which can undoubtedly be most threatening to the counselor. What Bergman's study may be saying is that those counselors who are most secure in the use of client-centered therapy can continue to attend to the underlying attitudes and needs which prompt client requests for intercession, and that such communication facilitates therapy. In this connection, Bergman's study also has implications for differential counselor method, comparing as it does the consequences of various kinds of counselor responses. This phase of the study may be relevant for what it does not say as well as for what it says. For example, the fact that interpretation led to abandonment of exploration

and reflection of feeling increased exploration may also refer back to
the counselor's security in the use of these methods; it does not lead
to a generalization about the relative merits of these response types
beyond the context of client-centered therapy. For a general test of
differential counseling methods we must study the methods in their
natural setting.

Lundy (1950) studied counselor-client interaction in one case where
the client had interviews alternately with two counselors using different
therapeutic methods. He posed this problem: "Given two different
conditions of stimulation, what differential effects are observable in the
behavior of the client?" He first established that the counselors differed
in the therapeutic situation provided for the client and then studied
client responses in several ways (e.g., DRQ, Raimy's method, etc.).
He found that, in terms of the measures used, the client's reactions to
the two situations were essentially similar, thus suggesting the existence
of a general set in the client. He also reported that differences in tempo
and affective intensity of the interaction were evident in the records,
but that they required instruments more sensitive to these areas of
interaction to measure the observable variation. This study is useful
in pointing up the problems of instrumentation, for it is an insistent
reminder that we have a long way to go before we can measure the
more subtle but potent factors in therapeutic interaction.

In the area of psychological climate a series of studies have turned
to the nature of the relationship created by therapists of differing
theoretical orientations. These studies have been interpreted by Fiedler
(in Chapter 12), and they will be reported here more briefly as instances
of a particular trend in therapy research. A recent study by Fiedler
(1949) exemplifies this approach. Fiedler stated that his investigation
"derives from the theoretical position that psychotherapeusis is in the
main the function of a good interpersonal relationship between the patient and his therapist." His main hypothesis was that experts of
different schools of psychotherapy will be more successful at establishing an ideal therapeutic relationship than nonexperts and that the experts
of different schools will be more alike in this respect than experts and
nonexperts with the same theoretical orientation. He had judges listen
to the recorded interviews of experts and nonexperts of the psychoanalytic, nondirective, and Adlerian schools and then rate the success
of the relationship they established in each interview by sorting seventy-
five descriptive statements, such as:

The therapist's own needs completely interfere with his understanding
of the patient.
The therapist's comments are always right in line with what the
patient is trying to convey.
The therapist is hostile toward the patient.
The therapist is interested but emotionally uninvolved.

The therapist treats the patient with much deference.
The therapist tends to look down on the patient.

Fiedler's results supported his hypothesis that experts, independent of their orientations, are successful and similar in establishing therapeutic relationships. He concludes that "the most important factors which differentiate experts from nonexperts are related to the therapist's ability to understand, to communicate with, and to maintain rapport with the patient." Fiedler's study was based upon recorded interviews where both counselor and client content were available.

In a related study, Quinn (1950) sought to determine whether estimates of the therapeutic relationship could be made on the basis of therapist expressions alone. He provided a series of discrete expressions by therapists of different orientations and degrees of training and secured judgments as to whether the quality of the therapists' communication was likely to impede or facilitate a therapeutic relationship. He concluded that "the quality of therapist communication is of critical significance in the determining of relative excellence or non-excellence of therapeutic relationships."

Heine (1950) studied the relation between the theoretical orientation of therapists and therapeutic process and outcomes as viewed by clients of these therapists. He presented each client with two scales, one consisting of one hundred and twenty statements describing changes (both favorable and unfavorable) and the other consisting of one hundred and twenty statements describing therapeutic factors which in the clients' experience seemed responsible for any changes which occurred. In terms of changes reported by clients, Heine found that "clients from the psychoanalytic, nondirective, and Adlerian schools do not differ one from the other in a way that is attributable to their having been treated by therapists of different schools." With reference to factors which the clients associated with change, the total results indicated that clients tended to refer to factors regarded by authorities of each school as important. However, Heine also found that for clients who reported the greatest changes the factors were similar irrespective of the type of therapy used. We seem to have here the inference that greater awareness of the technique aspects of therapy is associated with a feeling of minimal progress in therapy.

For a long time formulations about client-centered therapy have stressed the therapeutic atmosphere which the counselor could provide. Recently, however, some client-centered therapists have placed greater emphasis than formerly upon the relationship aspects of therapy. In an investigation now in progress, and one which reflects this emphasis, Bown (1951) is studying the development of therapeutic relationships in client-centered therapy. He is presenting separately to clients and counselors at frequent intervals early in therapy a series of statements descriptive of the possible aspects of a relationship. He will thus secure both client's and counselor's perceptions of any given relationship and be in a position to assess both the degree of congruence of these perceptions and the nature of the perceptions. Examples of his items will indicate the conceptual framework through which relationships will be assessed:

1. The counselor knows much more about the client than he is ever willing to admit.
2. The client thinks about or "talks to" the counselor between interviews.
3. The client would like a closer, more personal relationship with the counselor.
4. The counselor's calmness is most reassuring.
5. The client feels that he owes it to the counselor to change or grow.

We have mentioned earlier our feeling that the central determinants of therapeutic effectiveness are likely to be found more nearly in these studies of the quality of client-counselor interaction than in studies of counselor method in its technical aspects. We have had little or no research in counselor personality and this is an area where research is needed. Yet we are not primarily interested in counselor personality as such, but rather in those qualities which differentiate degrees of effectiveness as therapists. Studies of the kind we have just discussed, providing as they do the view of the person-as-therapist, seem to be the logical testing ground for hypotheses about the personal qualities which contribute to therapeutic effectiveness.

General Significance and Limitations of the Studies in the Internal Dimension of Research in Therapy.—As we consider the contribution which this dimension of research can make to our knowledge of therapy and personality organization, we are at once surprised by the degree to which we have come to take for granted the very records of therapy upon which this sphere of research is based. Recording in the Counseling Center at Chicago is part of the essential fabric of staff activity, and it is on the increase at many centers in the country; thus one comes to regard as a settled and commonplace fact the existence of data which provide an immeasurably valuable source of hypotheses and knowledge about therapy. As to the ways in which the material is used, it seems often true that research in the therapeutic process is just one step away from the counselor's office; it is a means of corroborating the observations and hunches of the clinician, and the hypotheses advanced are a direct expression of the insights of the investigator.

One of the outcomes of this type of research is the objectification and refinement of clinical knowledge. Because the research procedures can usually operate more impersonally and systematically than our own private perceptions (and because they are consequently more complete and less selective), they can not only help us discard fruitless hunches, but also provide a more rigorous quantitative basis for building new concepts. It is this fact which states for us both the contributions and the delimitations of process research. In large measure, the process studies are studies in conceptualization; they have helped build ways of looking at therapy which have added much to the theory-building process. At the same time, it is necessary to draw a distinction between conceptualization and verification as two distinct phases in research. Frequently in process research we are interested in concepts which refer to noninterview behavior, as for example Sheerer's study of acceptance. For such studies, and to the extent that we wish to make inferences about nontherapy behavior, the translation from hypotheses to fact must follow the usual course of verification through independent measures of these phenomena. Thus the studies are not to be regarded as self-contained validity studies of therapy. These studies, then, represent stages in the acquisition of knowledge—stages which undoubtedly will provide much of the content of what we can ultimately know about the therapeutic process.

Studies in Outcomes of Therapy

We shall consider in this section those studies which comprise the second of our two dimensions in therapy research, that dimension which turns attention to the correlates of therapy and seeks to measure those concomitant behaviors which are likely to yield a better understanding of psychotherapy and its effect upon the individual. Although in some respects the preferred method of presentation here would be to group these studies according to the kinds of hypotheses they test, we shall instead group them according to research method or instrumentation, since it was with this emphasis that research in outcomes saw its early development.

In our discussion of the process studies we referred to the emergence and increasing emphasis upon theory-oriented research. This same trend is evident with regard to outcome studies, and it finds its clearest expression in studies now in progress. However, it is also discernible in an earlier progression, and we can point up the trend as it can be seen most clearly in studies using the Rorschach Test as a criterion of outcome.

Outcome Studies of Personality-Test Behavior.—Muench's study (1947) was the first to evaluate client-centered therapy by means of the Rorschach Test. His stated purpose was to go beyond process measures and client self-evaluations in assessing the outcomes of therapy, and to gauge these effects by some more nearly independent external criterion. His total design involved the use of three tests at three points on the structured-projective test continuum: the Bell Adjustment Inventory, the Kent-Rosanoff Free Association Test, and the Rorschach

Test. Each of the tests was given before and after therapy. In analyzing the Rorschach, Muench used a quantitative scoring system involving signs of adjustment derived from Rorschach theory. Muench analyzed each case in considerable detail in a descriptive way, but he did not attempt to relate process and outcome through the use of systematic concepts common to both—that is, he did not attempt to articulate process and outcome at a theoretical level. His group comparisons revealed that differences with all tests between pretest and posttest findings were significant and in the direction of improvement.

In another study several years later, Haimowitz (1948) used the Rorschach Test to investigate outcomes of client-centered therapy. Her work showed development both in design and hypothesis-testing. At the methodological level, the advances involved use of a control group, a larger number of cases, and a follow-up for part of her cases. At the hypothesis-testing level her design placed a stronger emphasis upon the analysis of concepts related to the theory of therapy, as for example, acceptance of self and others, acceptance of emotionality, spontaneity, and the like. By way of a check on this form of analysis, she also used the Harrower-Erickson method of neurotic sign analysis. On both the Harrower-Erickson system and the conceptual system which Haimowitz developed, the experimental group showed significant changes in the direction of improved adjustment, while the control group showed no change. In ten cases retested a year after therapy, six showed continued gain beyond the posttest period and four did not. It is of interest to note that these same six individuals also showed greater gain from pretest to posttest than did the other four; a logical inference here is that if a significant process is set in motion through therapy, it does not stop when therapy is formally completed.

A third Rorschach study, by Jonietz (1950), shows further the trend toward relating outcome studies to a starting point of theory. Using as a point of departure one of the central propositions of client-centered therapy, namely that psychotherapy is a process of perceptual reorganization, Jonietz argued that if perceptual processes were modified in therapy, such modifications should be reflected in changes in perceptual behavior. To study this hypothesis, she used the Rorschach Test as a method of assessing the perceptual behavior of the individual. She found that the therapy group, in contrast to the control group, kept fewer percepts the same, altered more percepts, and added more new percepts. Within the therapy group the cases judged more successful on other grounds showed these trends more markedly than those judged less successful. These findings indicate greater perceptual modification for the therapy group, but they do not yet tell us about the nature of this modification. Jonietz analyzed the percepts for information on this question. She found that the therapy group showed an increase in human percepts and sexual percepts and a decrease in static percepts. Jonietz also studied a group of percepts which are presumed to refer to an individual's concept of himself in relation to his environment; specifically, she analyzed those responses in which a perceptual object was passively receiving behavior, often hostile, or attempting to hide or flee from aggression. For this group of percepts she found the following results:

	Pretest	Posttest
Control	32	29
Experimental	81	31

The chi-square result for this analysis was significant, and Jonietz suggested that the changed proportion of these percepts for the experimental group reflected a decrease in feelings of vulnerability in regard to their environment. One result of the study similar to that of Haimowitz and significant in its implications for the continuity of the learning process in connection with therapy is that, in a retest six months after the completion of therapy, the experimental group continued to show as many new percepts as they did during the therapy period.

There are two further studies which are relevant to this section of our discussion. One is the study by Carr (1949) which essentially repeated Muench's study, using the same method of Rorschach analysis on a new group of clients, and the other is a study by Mosak (1950) which was designed as a study of tests as criteria of therapeutic outcomes. Carr's results showed that on the basis of quantitative sign-analysis no significant differences could be observed between pretest and posttest for a group of clients; on the basis of a qualitative analysis (global judgment), four records showed slight or moderate improvement and five showed no significant change. These results are in general contradictory to those of the foregoing studies; when taken in conjunction with other considerations, they make clear the crucial position of the interpretive framework used for assessing test behavior. For example, eight of the nine cases used by Carr were also used in Jonietz's study, yet with a different framework for viewing the data Jonietz obtained different results.

The purpose of Mosak's study was to make a comparative analysis of three distinct types of test assessment of therapeutic outcome. For this purpose he used two self-rating scales (the Hildreth and the Bell), a structured personality test (the Minnesota Multiphasic), and a projective test (the Rorschach). For the Rorschach Test he used both a quantitative sign analysis and a global rating scale. In analyzing the results, Mosak found significant positive changes in all instruments. The group results for the Minnesota Multiphasic showed significant changes in five of the nine diagnostic categories; for individual results, five profiles reflected much improvement, eleven showed moderate improvement, and twelve showed no improvement. The Rorschach results are interesting in their implications for the use of the sign-analysis. The quantitative analysis of the Rorschach revealed no significant shifts from pretest to posttest. However, in the global ratings four showed much improvement, ten moderate or some improvement, and thirteen no improvement. The Rorschach global ratings of change correlated more highly with the other test changes than did the Rorschach sign-analysis. For example, the correlation of the sign analysis with the Multiphasic was .09, while the correlation of the judgments with the Multiphasic was .44. Mosak offered these results as evidence for the relative sensitivity of the total-rating approach as compared with the sign approach. One further result which is of interest in connection with the problem of criteria is that while both counselor judgment and Rorschach ratings showed positive changes, these changes were not correlated with each other— that is, the two measures showed changes for different people. On the other hand, the Multiphasic changes were correlated with both of the other measures, indicating that it assessed a range of attributes sufficiently broad to hold variance in common with two widely disparate measures of personality change.

We may summarize this section by saying that there is much evidence in it which argues for the hypothesis that psychotherapy brings about personality reorganization. For some of the studies, we can describe with some degree of clarity the nature of the modifications. Yet, in general, a personality test often means a "shotgun" approach to personality measurement. It is perhaps in this area, in the pinpointing of hypotheses and the consequent refinement of observations, that we can make our greatest future advances in the use of personality tests.

Studies of Attitudes Toward Self and Others.—We have already pointed out how the theory development which uses the self as a focal construct influenced research in the therapeutic process. This same influence had its effect upon outcome studies, though its implementation here came somewhat later. In an intensive study of one case, Hartley (1951) set forth one kind of a model useful for the investigation of changes in the concept of self. Though her results are not complete, we can sketch her methodology here. Her purpose was to study a client's attitudes and values toward self and others and the changes in these attitudes and values resulting from therapy. To this end she secured self-descriptions from the client through the use of a population of one hundred and fifty self-referent statements placed on an eleven-point rating scale in a forced normal distribution. Hartley set up three frames of reference for defining self-attitudes: the "present self," the "ideal self" or "desired self," and the "unhappy self"; in addition she secured the client's perception of the average person or of other persons in general. These ratings were secured before therapy, during therapy, and after therapy and were treated by correlation analysis and obverse factor analysis (Q technique).

A study by Butler and others (1952), as part of the University of Chicago Counseling Center research program, uses the same general methodology but sets more refined predictions as to outcome. The sample consists of twenty-five clients and an equal number of controls, and the purpose of the study is not only to assess the changes in concept of self through therapy, but also to determine whether clusters of similar attitudes—i.e., attitude typologies—can be observed. Such attitude typologies, if they exist, will be related to any observed differences in the course of therapy. Partial results are now available for this study; these results suggest that clients before therapy most typically report a wide discrepancy between present self and desired self and that after therapy they report a closer correspondence between these two aspects of self. It is intended in Butler's study to check such findings by other outcome instruments and interview analysis, as well as through control group procedures.

The Q sorting instrument used in the foregoing studies provides an efficient method of securing a large number of ratings which can be compared from person to person. Because of its consequent convenience and utility, it has found increasing application in these and other studies. On this ground it is important to be clear on what the instrument measures. In the case of the foregoing studies, the self-ratings do not provide direct access to the measurement of an individual's concept of self, but to his report of his self-concept—that is, to the self-picture he will communicate to others under the particular social situation in which he is asked to make the ratings. It is legitimate to deal with the data as such, as a reported self-concept, without further steps in verification. To the extent that one wishes to make inferences from the report to the phenomenon itself, the further verification step becomes necessary (see Chapter 13).

An extension of this area of attitude study may be found in those studies which deal with prejudice and its modification in therapy. In general, the argument of these studies is that ethnocentric attitudes are a direct function of personality organization and that if personality reorganization occurs in therapy, ethnocentrism should show a corresponding modification. There are two studies in client-centered therapy which deal with hypotheses of this kind.

M. Haimowitz (1950) used an interview technique to evaluate ethnic attitudes before and after therapy. He conducted intensive interviews of approximately two hours in length, in a setting designed to keep these interviews and the therapeutic experience as separate as possible. The interviewer was not a member of the counselor group. Haimowitz evaluated his results in two phases; first, he undertook to determine the degree of personality reorganization reflected in the differences between pretherapy and posttherapy interviews. He did this through a Q sort rating method applied by an independent judge, and found that of his fifty subjects, twenty-eight were rated improved and twenty-two unimproved. His second step was to determine the degree of attitude change reflected in the interviews. He found an increase in expressed friendliness toward Negroes ($p = .05$) but no progression in favorable attitudes toward other minorities. He concluded that his evidence was more negative than positive with regard to ethnic attitude changes in therapy.

A second study along these lines, by Gordon (1952), had as its general purpose investigation of the effect of therapy upon attitudes toward others; within his design he has studied the interrelationship of various kinds of attitude changes, including both ethnic attitudes and more general attitudes and reactions to others. His instruments included the Sanford-Levinson scale, the Thematic Apperception Test, and a role-taking situation (to be described at greater length later in this paper). Such a design permits the assessment of similar phenomena through multiple means, thus providing a relatively firm basis for the generalizations to be made.

Studies in Situational Behavior.—A further line of development in client-centered therapy research is that sphere of investigation which relies upon situational behavior, as distinct from verbal test behavior, for its assessment of individuals. This sphere of measurement has at least three advantages—first, it widens the range of behaviors open to our observation; second, it provides the possibility of checks upon verbal behavior; third, many of the propositions in personality theory refer to behavior *in vivo,* and situational behavior offers the chance for the most nearly direct observation of the behaviors relevant to the testing of these propositions.

One aspect of situational behavior which is widely recognized for its importance but which has thus far received limited experimental attention involves the physiological concomitants of therapy (see Chapter 19). The only study on this problem in relation to client-centered therapy is one by Thetford (1949). He argued that if therapy resulted in increased capacity for adaptive behavior on the part of an individual, such a change should be reflected in physiological response to a stress situation. Specifically, he postulated that an individual after therapy would show greater tolerance for frustration in the form of reduced autonomic reactivity and quicker recovery of basal autonomic activity after a situation designed to be frustrating to the individual. In using an experimental control group design, he found that the therapy group showed significant increase in recovery speed on the galvanic skin reflex, while the control group did not; similarly, he found reduced variability in heart rate for the experimental group and not for the control group. Thetford concluded that the findings of his study were consistent with the theory that the organism is able to discharge more rapidly and completely the effects of experimentally induced frustration as a result of therapy. A study of this kind represents exploration into a field which deserves more attention. There are several levels at which inquiry into the physiological basis of behavior modification in therapy can contribute to the building and verification of theory. On the first level, if an objective of therapy research is to arrive at an understanding of the ways in which therapy impinges upon the organism, then we must look to the physiological behavior of the person as an integral part of his total behavior. Secondly, increased knowledge of the physiological components of therapy should serve to reduce present ignorance regarding the kinds of experience which an individual is presumed to undergo in therapy. We frequently attempt to distinguish between the intellectual-cognitive aspects of therapy on the one hand and the experiential-affective aspects on the other. The distinction now is based on observed distinctions between certain classes of verbal behavior and on gross observations of overt behavior. Refined physiological measurement should contribute to clearer placement of the role of emotion in the therapeutic process.

The third kind of contribution which physiological research can make is in the spelling out of particular relationships between verbal and nonverbal behavior. We are pretty clear by now that verbal behavior cannot be taken as a direct surrogate of nonverbal behavior; we also know that there is neither a unitary nor a random relationship between the two. The result of this knowledge is that we frequently operate at the level of a generalized skepticism regarding the trustworthiness of verbal behavior. Actually, however, what we need to know are the laws which mediate the relationship between verbal and nonverbal behavior. Psychoanalytic theory has already suggested the kinds of laws which may exist when it refers to such phenomena as reaction formation, rationalization, and the like. It would help immeasurably in our understanding of the process of human communication if we could spell out these laws more fully in experimental fashion. The simultaneous measurement of verbal and physiological behavior in therapy may well lead us in this direction.

Within the broad area of situational behavior, one method which has been used increasingly for assessment purposes is the role-behavior type of situation. Such a method has the potential advantage of offering observations about a person in direct behavioral interaction with others. This does not reduce the experimenter's responsibility to check his inferences against other evidence, but it does enlarge the range of observations possible for any given individual. The study by Gordon, previously referred to, suggests one kind of use which may be made of role-behavior observation. His purpose is to test the hypothesis that as a result of therapy an individual will be more accepting both of himself and others. His instrument is a series of situations in which the subject is asked to put himself in some designated role for each situation and respond in a way which he considers appropriate to the situation. The situations are so devised that the subject is asked to respond to a wide variety of behavior over the total test, including instances where status differences are evident, where the subject has to cope with aggressive or attacking behavior, and the like. Such instruments have wide possibilities for further use because the malleability of the stimulus situations makes it possible to present a broad range of stimulus behaviors and a range of complex stimulus behaviors. The chief problems would seem to lie, first, in the practical fact that they are expensive in terms of personnel as participants and observers and, second, in the need to develop sensitive and valid interpretive frameworks for viewing the data. The second problem is not unique to situational behavior measures, but simply highlights the fact that raw behavioral data of whatever richness are of little use in themselves.

The two studies in client-centered therapy which thus far come closest to assessing client behavior in its natural habitat are, first, a study by Bartlett (1949) and, second, a study at the University of Chicago Counseling Center (1952). Bartlett's study was a follow-up survey of client adjustment in an educational and vocational setting; judgments were made by Veterans Administration training officers regarding improvement or nonimprovement in trainee adjustment six months or more after referral for counseling. Of a total of three hundred and ninety-three cases judged, 17 per cent were regarded as showing no improvement and 83 per cent as showing some or much improvement. The training officers based their evaluations on observations which were varied in nature, and the judgments represent a mixture of environmental and intrapersonal criteria, such as academic grades, number of shifts in training objectives, efficiency in study habits, and apparent worry or nervousness. In sum, the judgments probably come much closer to the layman's perception of adjustment than to any systematic psychological definition.

The study at the Counseling Center was designed to secure judgments from clients and best friends regarding the emotional maturity of individuals before and after therapy. For this purpose the Willoughby Emotional Maturity Scale was completed by the client and two friends designated by him before therapy, after therapy, and again six months later. Each person is instructed to complete the scale independently and without discussion of the scale, though actually no checks are available regarding the independence of the information.

One question which arises in connection with the use of this scale relates to the manner in which "best friends"—laymen for the most part—define emotional maturity. A study by Dratwa (1951) indicates that judgments by laymen regarding emotional maturity reflected in specific behaviors correspond closely with judgments by psychologists, psychiatrists, and social workers. Correlations in judgment among these professional groups and between professional and nonprofessional groups are of the same magnitude, about .70. These data suggest that there is a fair amount of consensus in the definition of emotional maturity.

The significance of this study probably lies less in the particular instrument used than in its orientation toward securing judgments about the person in a situation far removed from the milieu in which therapy takes place. One of the problems inherent in a design of this kind lies in the unknown effects of the friends' possible knowledge that the client has been in therapy and that the investigation is in some way related to the therapeutic experience of the client. One solution to this problem would be to work with clients who are also members of some well defined social group (e.g., class in school, recreation group, dormitory group, or fraternity) and to institute sociometric measurements as well as other measures among the whole group. This would provide an evaluative setting more nearly neutral with respect to the variable of therapy and would elicit measures of individuals as group members rather than clients. Such a procedure also offers the advantage of providing control data in the form of ratings for the group members who are not in therapy.

Some Possible Lines of Development

Thus far in this review we have indicated from time to time the next steps which seemed to emerge from a consideration of the present status of any given area of therapy research. For the remainder of this review we should like to turn more exclusive attention upon the lines of development which are implied in the current picture of research in client-centered therapy.

On Research in Therapy as Program Design.—When we think in terms of the continuing development of therapy research, it is quite useful to use the concept of program design. Marquis (1948) has discussed this concept in the context of the orderly development of knowledge and has defined it as "the planning of an integrated series of research activities, focused on a central problem, and involving a number of scientists for several years." The explicit recognition and organization of research activity on a program design scale will facilitate comprehensive planning of related studies with similar aims. Such a framework has the critical advantage that in it individual studies are not likely to remain isolated points of knowledge surrounded by ignorance but will rather find their place in an organized scheme which will give them more meaning than they could possibly have of themselves.

The research program in client-centered therapy may be defined in its minimal terms as an inquiry into the nature of psychotherapy and personality ; a full and reasonable answer to this inquiry implies the continued threefold division of effort we have thus far seen : attention to the interplay of communication which is the therapy process itself, to the consequences of this process in terms of therapeutic outcome, and to the development of an explanatory structure which organizes these two dimensions in the context of the organization of personality. It is probable that this third aim, that of theory development, is the most necessary single requirement of program design, and it is precisely in this realm that perspective comes hardest. We can agree on problems of experimental design, on requirements for validity testing, and the like, but agreement on interpretation of events is another thing, as the history of theory development readily indicates. What we are more certain to find is diversity in ways of formulating concepts which at a sheer observational level are quite similar in their raw materials. As we move away from phenomena and toward conceptualization—that is, toward abstraction— the materials of experience may be grouped into an almost infinite number of combinations and hence lead toward the discovery of many different meanings. What we know of the history of knowledge tells us that the integration of concepts, and consequent agreement at the abstract level,

comes late in the progress of knowledge. In the preintegration period
the variety of theoretical formulations exerts a centrifugal force which
frequently creates communication problems among scientists who are
trying basically to discover the same facts, but who must do considerable
translation of abstractions in order to understand each other. We can
expect progressive reduction of the ambiguities of this situation through
the rules of the scientific game, which insist that concepts must finally be
stated in testable terms as a condition for their acceptance into the community of ideas. Yet it will also remain true that creativity and testabil-
ity do not always meet at the same point in time, and each person will
inevitably set his own level of tolerance for the gap which lies between the
two.

Beyond the problems inherent in theory construction, the planning of
program design involves consideration of such other aspects of research
as experimental design, criteria of success in therapy, the test of particular
hypotheses, instrumentation, and problems of sampling. We should like
to give brief consideration to each of these topics.

Extensions in Experimental Design.—One of the immediate
extensions of present research trends in terms of design lies in the combination of process and outcome research. Earlier research in psychotherapy has centered upon either the process of therapy as it is reflected
in interviews or upon the outcome of therapy as it is reflected in the
comparison between pretherapy and posttherapy test behavior. Such
designs have their fragmentary aspects. The process studies provide
conceptual frameworks for viewing the course of therapy, but they do
not tell us about the impact of the process upon posttherapy behavior;
similarly, the outcome studies provide measures of behavioral modification and information about individual differences in such modification,
but we know no more than before about the nature of the intervening
experience which produces the differential changes. A research model
which is required for advancing our knowledge of the relation between
the process of therapy and its effects is one which brings the study of
both process and outcome within the compass of a single design. In a
design of this kind, we should expect to center our attention upon one or
more concepts relevant to our theoretical formulations about therapy and
study each concept in terms both of process and of outcome, with a view
toward determining the contingencies between the two. Such a design
makes possible the formulation of predictions relevant to the confirmation
or revision of theory.

Let us illustrate such a model within the theoretical framework which
views therapy as social learning. We may choose here from among a
large number of hypotheses, but let us take an example from Harlow's
hypothesis (1949) that learning is facilitated by the development of a "set
to learn" and from Magaret's speculation (1950) that this particular
learning may characterize successful therapy. Our basic experimental
design then involves four steps: (a) developing an instrument by which

to assess an individual's "set to learn" and administering this instrument before and after therapy; (b) developing a classification system which will allow us to extract from the therapeutic interviews all instances of the development of this "set to learn" as manifested in verbal interview behavior; (c) assessing the interaction of process and outcome measures —i.e., determining the power of the process measure to predict outcome change and vice versa; and (d) applying the predictions to a new sample of cases. Perhaps as much as anything else this model indicates the complexity of the process by which new facts are gained. For, having done this much, we would have added but one point of knowledge to our theoretical system; and it would still remain to study the conditions which facilitate or retard this growth in generalizing ability, the variations due to basic personal predispositions among individuals, and finally the contingencies between this concept and other concepts in our theoretical structure. However, it is an approach of this kind which offers us not only a pattern for studying psychotherapy, but also one answer to the problem of establishing criteria for measuring therapeutic outcome. This point we shall develop at further length.

The Problem of Criteria in Therapy Research.—Discussions about criteria in psychotherapy tend to be pessimistic; they are likely to emphasize not only the necessity but also the difficulty of securing adequate criteria of success in psychotherapy. They point out that symptom reduction is a treacherous criterion, that verbal reports of change are notoriously untrustworthy, and that observations of gross behavior are not only unreliable but hard to interpret. We should declare immediately that we are more optimistic than all this about the question. Further, we think it likely that one factor in particular has contributed a major and unnecessary complication to the thinking about this question. This is the very emphasis upon the concept of "success" as the content to which the criterion addresses itself. We are not arguing here that the concept of success is inappropriate. Psychotherapy is a significant social enterprise, and its value aspects are of prime importance. What we are arguing here is that this very fact introduces the problem of value judgments too soon in the scheme of our research and confounds two sources of criteria which might best be kept distinct, that is, the value aspects on the one hand and the detailed behavior description aspects on the other.

The pragmatic emphasis has shown itself in two ways—in the kinds of designs we have had and in the places we look for criteria. As to the designs, we have most often had studies which choose one or another personality test and administer it before and after therapy. If changes are found (let us assume a control group design), then therapy can be considered to have had a desired effect. Such a design is a kind of market research in psychotherapy; it increases our confidence in the value of our product, but it adds little understanding of the nature of its content. As to the places where criteria are to be found, this pragmatic view emphasizes the individual's behavior in the "outside world": that is, upon an individual's later job adjustment, social adjustment, marital adjustment, academic adjustment, and the like—in short, upon sociologically oriented criteria of successful adjustment.

The foregoing criticisms already suggest the emphasis which we consider more fruitful for criterion derivation. The combined areas of learning theory and personality theory have much to say not only about behavioral acts per se but also about their modes of development and the conditions necessary for their modification. It is in the propositions which lie within this structure that the most fruitful sources of criteria would seem to lie. Thus, we can talk about particular behaviors and set up specific hypotheses with regard to them. For example, within the sphere of problem-solving behavior, we can set situations to measure such things as:

Degree to which irrelevant cues are disregarded on the one hand or are distracting on the other.

Speed with which hypotheses are rejected when the evidence for them becomes negative.

Number of different hypotheses which are formed.

Such examples as these could be multiplied. If we can translate behaviors such as these into efficient-inefficient problem-solving behavior (and we think it feasible), we are then on the way to studying properties of individual behavior which can serve as criteria of therapeutic outcome.

Extensions in Hypothesis-Testing.—In this section we wish to suggest some next steps which research in client-centered therapy can logically take; some of the steps are brief extensions from present research, while others are further removed. In most cases we have already named the subject matter in our previous discussion, but we wish here to focus the discussion more particularly around the question of hypothesis-testing. In this connection we may consider the subject matter of therapy from the standpoints of perception, learning, and communication.

With regard to perception, we have already seen a beginning in Jonietz's study. We may again use as a starting point the proposition that therapy is a process in which an individual modifies his characteristic ways of perceiving himself and his environment. We can see in this formulation the interrelation of perception and learning. When we state the argument this way, we are saying that therapy is a learning process, and we are also identifying a particular content of learning, namely, the learning of new modes of perceptual behavior.

If we follow the design type discussed earlier, we shall need two kinds of instruments; first, we shall need a classification system by which to identify the amount and kinds of perceptual reorganization which take place during the therapeutic process. Second, we shall need measures of perceptual behavior to be given before therapy, after therapy, and preferably again after a year or more. There are a number of instruments available for which there are varying degrees of experimental and normative data; the growing number of studies on perception and personality provide many leads regarding the personality variables inherent in perceptual tasks. One caution which we should wish to observe refers to the broadening definition which perception has come to assume in recent years, particularly with reference to social perception. Our own preference would be to attempt to define some sort of gradient which runs from social perception-cognition at the one end of the continuum to the more classical structural-perceptual tasks on the other, and to measure several points on this gradient. One could then learn whether therapy has a differential effect upon these different kinds of perceptual-cognitive behavior.

With regard to tests of therapy as learning, we have already suggested the spheres of problem solving and the set to learn, or the generalizing power of the person. Another and quite related phenomenon is that of discrimination or differentiation. In discussing the importance of this activity for therapy, Mowrer (1948) suggests that therapy consists, in part, in "helping the patient correct overly extended generalizations by means of appropriate discriminations." Snygg and Combs (1949) consider that learning is essentially an increased differentiation of the perceptual field. These formulations seem to be sufficiently central to the learnings of therapy to receive high priority for further inquiry. We may conceptualize this phenomenon with regard to therapy in the following way: an individual in therapy learns two related kinds of differentiation. First, he learns to differentiate more clearly the intraself stimuli—that is, he learns to identify more easily his own needs and emotional status; his anger can become more readily symbolized as anger rather than some vague stirring in the pit of the stomach. The second area of differentiation is in the self-nonself distinctions; we may say here that a person learns to identify more clearly his own boundaries and can distinguish better between his own needs and feelings and those of others. This form of differentiation reduces the perceptual distortions which come from incomplete differentiation (e.g., projection, displacement, and the like). The research task in studying this phenomenon, as in the others, is the creation of adequate instrumentation at both the process and outcome level. Preliminary inspection of therapy protocols indicates the feasibility of such a task at the process level.

Therapy as communication can readily be considered within the framework of therapy as social learning, and we single it out here because it seems a particularly significant learning in therapy. We may visualize this kind of learning in therapy as consisting precisely in the new behaviors which the client experiences as part of the therapeutic process. This way of thinking about learning in therapy seems particularly apropos when we consider the client as learning new ways of communicating, since that is what he is doing constantly in therapy. What is he learning that becomes significant for integrating behavior? The importance of the symbolizing process in the psychological economy of the individual has been considered elsewhere by Angyal (1941), Rogers (1951), and others; verbal communication can be considered as a special case of the symbolizing process. Thus, for example, if a client should say, "I have been angry with my child," this symbolization not only adds meaning to an inner state but facilitates appropriate behavioral consequences. It is suggested here that these symbolizing experiences in themselves provide new ways of behaving which the client generalizes to nontherapy situations. The excerpt below is illustrative of the point we are making, and also of the kind of material which one would seek in therapy records to test a hypothesis of the sort we are suggesting.

[It is the beginning of the interview, and the client takes his seat, stretching out in the chair in an almost reclining position.]

STUDENT: Whew! It feels good to just sit down.

COUNSELOR: Feeling kind of limp, huh?

S.: Yes, limp, but in a peaceful kind of way. [Pause.] I've just come from talking with Jim. We had it out, and I told him where I stood with him. He took it surprisingly well, too. Funny how scared I was when I approached him—nervous and half shaking. And yet I had to talk to him—couldn't hold it in. Those two days that I stewed getting up nerve were torture. Sometimes I felt I'd explode with all that feeling inside.

C.: It was tough to do, but it just plain had to come out, didn't it?

S.: It sure did. No two ways about it. [Pause.] Funny, how it just kept pushing till I said it. [Pause.] So different from the way it was with Hal and me, back in the old days. He was like Jim in a lot of ways, and I felt the same way about him too. But it was a duller feeling; I kept it in me for half a year instead of blowing off, and finally it just died by itself.

This excerpt provides clear expression of the learning upon which the client has acted, and also helps to clarify the concept of communication as we use it here. By communication we do not simply mean interaction with another; in the latter sense talking about the weather is communication too. Perhaps what we are talking about is a two-step process which first involves communication with oneself and then expression to another. Thus, in the foregoing excerpt the client refers to his earlier experience as a "duller feeling" in contrast to the later one which seemed so sharply defined. One learns both increasing recognition and more adequate expression of feelings; the kind of communication we are talking about refers to both facets of this process.

Problems of Instrumentation.—We have been optimistic in evaluating the possibility of identifying criteria by which to assess behavioral modification in therapy, but here our optimism stops; we cannot be nearly so hopeful in our view of the present status of instrumentation by which to measure the criterion behaviors we have so readily identified. Nor does the problem lie merely in the relative crudity and tenuous validity of present personality tests, for, even if one could be more confident of present test validity, our problems would not yet be solved. The research structure which we have set forth requires that we continually ask of each instrument, "Validity for what?" In other words, since we are setting out to measure quite particular behaviors, our greatest single need is for instruments with known characteristics with reference to these behaviors. To satisfy this need, what we require of an instrument is that a given score or rating will assign some particular quantity or intensity of the behavior in question. We shall need instruments to measure a great variety of behaviors, and this fact sets the magnitude of our task. When one adds to this the fact that our instruments will not be general-purpose instruments, the size of the instrumentation task takes on long-term proportions.

What this means to individuals interested in studying psychotherapy is that they have the choice of improvising upon present instruments and taking crude approximations as a result or of creating (and validating) the instruments they need. Since therapy research is in a relatively early stage, improvisation can still tell us more than we now know. But this will become progressively less true, with the likely consequence that instrumentation will become the chief limiting factor in research unless the alternative of accelerated instrument creation and validation is employed.

In this picture of the status of criterion instruments there is one instrument which should not be overlooked, namely, the judgment of the therapist as a criterion of behavior modification in therapy. On one side we may raise immediate questions about the therapist's involvement and his consequent capacity for objective judgment; on the other, we can argue that there are probably few other persons who are permitted as deep a view into a client's emotional life as his therapist.

The evidence to date regarding the therapist's judgment is in a positive direction with regard to indications of validity, though it also has its equivocal aspects. In the process studies the preponderance of evidence shows significant relationship between counselor judgment and process measures. Thus Raimy's study showed differential processes corresponding with differential counselor ratings, Seeman's study showed a correlation of insight rise with counselor rating, Sheerer's study showed a more marked increase in acceptance for cases rated more successful, and other studies showed similar trends.

In such studies one can raise a question as to the independence of process measures and counselor judgment, since a counselor undoubtedly bases his judgment at least in part upon insight rise, increase in self-acceptance, and the like. Thus if the evidence regarding counselor judgment were limited to process studies it would not be very convincing. However, there are positive indications with regard to nonprocess measures also. In Muench's study, for example, the correlation of counselor rating with Rorschach score improvement was significant at a 10 per cent level of confidence. We have already mentioned Mosak's study, in which counselor rating correlated with Multiphasic change, and Jonietz's study, in which perceptual modification was related to counselor judgment. But the evidence is not all in the same direction; we have already indicated that in Mosak's study counselor rating was not correlated with Rorschach change, and the same absence of relationship was true in N. Haimowitz's study. Perhaps the conclusion which best fits the data is that in counselor judgment we have a criterion of definite promise, and one which bears further serious consideration and refinement.

Sampling Basis of Generalizations.—If the raw materials of theory construction lie in direct observation, then we must raise the question as to the kinds of phenomena which are being observed and upon which generalizations are based. In the case of psychotherapy, the raw material is the experience with clients. For many therapeutic settings, particularly before the advent of the Veterans Administration clinical program, the most common situation was one of selective representation of groups in our culture, with heaviest weighting in terms both of high income and high motivation for therapy. If we take seriously the findings of the social anthropologists, we may ask whether this representation affords an adequate base line upon which to construct generalizations about personality and therapy. There is some evidence for systematic differences in personality constellations in the various subgroups of our society. What this implies is that we shall need eventually not only a more systematic sampling approach in our study of therapy, but also a more comprehensive description of individuals with regard to personality variables. Such an emphasis will offer practical difficulties in clinics which have a service orientation, and it may be that the task will ultimately be done by the creation or strengthening of clinics which have primarily a research orientation. In any event, the need which we refer to here is but one of an interrelated series of needs which, when approached through an integrated pattern, will have much to do with implementing the research directions which we have indicated in this paper.

CHAPTER 10

A METHOD OF MEASURING TENSION IN WRITTEN DOCUMENTS [1]

By John Dollard, Ph.D., *and* O. Hobart Mowrer, Ph.D.

This paper deals with a new measure of tension called the *DRQ,* that is, Discomfort-Relief Quotient. This measure yields a relatively reliable, graphic picture of tension change in a social case record, and conceivably also in an autobiography, psychoanalytic history, or other personal documents.

The Problem

The Committee on the Institute of Welfare Research of the Community Service Society of New York wished to have a study made of the nature, costs, and results of the casework process as applied at different times with varying types of clients. At first glance it seemed possible that the pattern of tension movement *might* be related to the "progress," or "success," of a case. High tension levels at the end of the case might be prognostic of failure or of the likelihood of having to reopen the case. Rapidly falling tension levels might be correlated with what the client learns or with the value of the Society's service to him. With these possibilities in mind, the researchers felt it worth while to attempt to work out a tension measure.

The scientific frame of reference used in this paper is that of modern learning theory. Learning theory holds that responses are incited by drives—primary and secondary. In a learning dilemma, these drives produce novel responses. In the earliest learning situations, responses are connected directly to drives, under the pressure of reward. Reward is viewed as drive reduction. In most complex learning situations drives acquire cue properties; that is, lesser strengths of drive can elicit a response. Similarly, other cues (often external) become patterned with drives and drive cues as a condition of evoking a response.

In the sense of learning theory, thoughts, ideas, and plans are all special cases of habits which are mediated by sentences. These sentences may be hit upon directly by the learner or may be taught (through rehearsal) by a teacher. In the situation of casework therapy, for example, a client can invent or borrow from the caseworker those sentences which

[1] This chapter is reprinted, with permission, from the *Journal of abnormal and social Psychology,* 1947, **42**, 3-32.

will later serve as hunches and plans for most adaptive action. Indeed, it is this acquisition of plan in the casework situation which is at the center of attention.

The community which supports casework is especially interested in two aspects of the worker's task. It is well aware that in *emergency situations* immediate relief must be given. In cases of urgent need, it may not be possible to stop and consider what the client is learning. In these cases the worker must act with speed if she is to follow the behest of the compassionate community.

The wider community is yet more interested in what persists after casework is finished as learned behavior which leads to independence and self-support. It is concerned with what the caseworker teaches and what the client learns. We have studied "tension" as one of the factors which might be operative in this teacher-learning situation.

Private casework seems clearly conscious of its responsibility for character development. Thus, when "Katie Andrews," a thirty-year-old colored woman who had been attempting to support herself, two children, and two elderly women on the ten dollars a week which she received as a maid, presented a request to the Harlem District Office of the Community Service Society for help, she was told, in substance, by the worker, ". . . the money we gave was in order to help a family work out a plan . . . so that they could get along without our help after a short time. We were not certain whether this was the sort of help Mrs. A. needed. We spoke of there being other agencies that could give help on a long-time basis . . . and added . . . that the specific task of our agency was to plan with our clients and while doing so to help them financially."

The casework approach to the client seems parallel in many respects to that of the learning theorist. In a volume produced by the Community Service Society (1940), there are many suggestive statements and references to the interpretative, educational approach of "modern casework." "Treatment," it is said, is a form of "teaching." One client referred to the job of private casework as "teaching people to have common sense" (p. 48). It is further noted that "the workers help the client . . . to learn some new ways of thinking and acting" (p. 33). The parallels between a learning analysis and a casework analysis are further indicated by such phrases as "relieving strain," "reducing tension," "solving problems," "rewarding experiences." It would seem that the notion of learning under the impact of tension is more or less familiar to caseworkers and that there is no real discrepancy between their analysis and that of learning theory.[2]

The problem is nicely pointed up by the attitude of the caseworker-clinician toward the giving of money to the client. In the usual case, money is to be given to reward socially adjustive habits and not the habit of coming to the Community Service Society for more money. In the

[2] Although casework researchers have not dealt with the problem of the tension index, they have thought and written extensively on other aspects of casework problems.

atypical case, subsistence needs must be met for longer or shorter periods of time. The modern caseworker is essentially a teacher, and the client a learner. Her chief value to the client lies in the fact that she is likely to be a better predicter of the kind of habits that will be rewarded in real life than is the client himself.[3]

Tension in Different Types of Cases

Many different types of cases come to a social agency. We have fixed attention on three groups which bring into clear light the importance of the tension factor. These groups are "social-class" cases, "orientation" cases, and psychological cases. A brief description of these types follows:

"Social-Class" Cases.—These might be thought of as humiliated people. They are people of good habits who have suffered loss of income, friends, or preferred occupation and are forced thereby into a relative isolation. This isolation and loss of status are perceived as painful. The loss of the usual satisfactions of community living tends to weaken the work and family habits of persons so afflicted. Frequently, gifts of money will enable the client to maintain some of his usual preoccupations.

"Orientation" Cases.—In general, these people may be thought of as the ignorant, the ill, and the unsophisticated. They are frequently of recent immigrant stock. They are persons who "don't know their way around in the society." To such, health resources can be pointed out, aid in acquiring social skills can be given, and community resources can be indicated.

Psychological Cases.—These are the lonely, frustrated, ineffectual, or driven people. They have acquired "bad" emotional habits, usually in early life. They show anxiety, helplessness, character weaknesses, passivity, misestimation of reality.

Frequently, all three types of problems are revealed in the same case, although clear examples of each type can also be found.

Banal as it may seem to emphasize this point, the social agency is a door of the society to which the troubled individual or family may come. Downward social mobility, lack of orientation, or psychological difficulties result in tension, depression, anxiety, feelings of pressure or illness. The aim of the good society is to keep tension levels relatively low—low enough, at least, to be tolerable for the masses of people.

Whatever our culture may eventually evolve in the way of drive management, it is a fact that clients today come to a social agency excited, pressed, conflicted, driven. Sometimes their excitement is open and vociferous; again it expresses itself in outward apathy or in a tense shyness and silence. In the ideal case, such a client should emerge from

---

[3] When a learner discovers the helpfulness of his teacher's efforts, he begins to display behavior which has been variously designated, according to the nature of the teacher-learner relationship, as "rapport," "identification," "constructive relationship," "suggestibility," "faith," "confidence," etc.

treatment more relaxed, hopeful, and planful. It is the tension factor in this movement from conflict to plan which we are attempting to measure.

Is It Moral to Reduce Tension?

When we talk of "tension reduction," many persons immediately read a kind of moral issue into the problem. They say, "Doesn't reducing tension make people slack, lazy, and careless, or even immoral?" "Isn't tension a good thing? Why do we want to reduce it?" To these persons, and to ourselves when we perforce make these objections, we answer:

It is not the object of casework to reduce tension forthwith and without demands. As repeatedly said, caseworkers create a situation which puts on the client the demand to form new habits. They, further, speak for the community and its demands on the individual. They do not sanction immediate reduction of tension in situations where later suffering is bound to result through drawing upon the client the moral censure of the community or economic discomfort. Caseworkers, therefore, stand for an intelligent or rational policy of life, i.e., the *lowest tension levels* over the *longest periods of time*. Reflection may easily induce a person to bear tension *now* in order to avoid greater tension later. It is just such "realities" which casework teaching emphasizes. We think that the point of view here proposed is, therefore, not only scientifically sensible but also ethically sound.

Two Problems of Measurement

In laboratory research on learning, the two major variables, "trials" and "time," are precisely quantifiable by the simple expedients of counting and watching a clock or stop watch. But in attempting to reconstruct a learning curve solely on the basis of the contents of a social casework record, the situation is by no means so favorable; and we find nothing in existing casework literature to assist us.[4] In the case record, the behavior of the client, or subject, is not nicely fractionated into "trials"; and if there is any reference to the timing of his behavior, it is vague and unsystematic.

However, by re-examining the typical learning curve and more carefully scrutinizing its meaning, we arrive at a promising way of escaping from this predicament. Science is always concerned with the determination of cause-and-effect relations, or, said differently, with the "function" which exists between an independent variable and a dependent variable. In the investigation of learning, the cause, or independent variable, is the

[4] Familiar as caseworkers are with the role of teaching and learning in the casework process (cf. Bertha Reynolds, *Learning and teaching in the practice of social work*, New York: Rinehart & Co., Inc., 1942), they have not attempted to cast their operations into the quantitative form of a learning curve. Many studies of "evaluation" have been undertaken, but all which have come to our attention proceed along quite different lines. Nor are the various types of "content analysis" in current use satisfactory on this score.

"problem situation" which is applied, or represented, in the successive learning "trials" to which the subject is exposed. Similarly, the effect, or dependent variable, is the change in behavior which is reflected, for example, by a reduction in the time required to make a given response to the problem situation.

In laboratory learning we are usually dealing with a problem situation which is intermittent, recurrent; and the learning is on an independent, trial-and-error basis. But in social work, the circumstances are different. The problem situation is more or less chronic, and, by the very nature of the case, independent, unaided learning has largely broken down. The independent variable, or causal factor, which is introduced when the casework process begins is therefore the caseworker's *professional skill*. Assuming that this is applied evenly throughout a given case, it should be possible to use successive interviews or any other subdivision, e.g., pages, of the case record as the unit for quantifying the application of the independent variable.

But the problem of quantifying the *effect* of casework treatment is not so easily solved. As we have seen, casework recordings pay no systematic attention to the factor of time. It was evident, therefore, that the dependent variable would have to be quantified with some other unit of measurement. In this connection it is relevant to note that although the ordinate of a laboratory learning curve commonly represents time, the area under the curve also represents amount of unresolved drive, or tension, endured by the subject. We asked ourselves whether, in the absence of a reliable temporal unit, we might not nevertheless arrive at some unit of drive-tension experienced by the client at various stages in the casework process. It seemed that the report of a successful case ought to begin with "gripes" and end with "smiles," that is, move from high to low tension levels. Why not, then, make a count of the *tension, or discomfort, words* appearing in the successive units (pages or interviews) of a conspicuously successful case record and see if the resulting curve does not in fact move downward, as a good learning curve should?

The DRQ (Discomfort-Relief Quotient)

In attempting to isolate and quantify the element of drive-tension in a case record, we faced a problem reminiscent of the one which Binet and his successors encountered when they attempted to measure "intelligence." They found that actual performance on a given test was a function not only of the innate intellectual abilities of a child but also of the child's age. It was essential, by some means, to partial out the influence of the age factor. This they very neatly did by defining intelligence as the ratio between demonstrated performance ("mental age") and chronological age. The result is the well-known IQ.

A similar expedient seemed promising in the present research. We felt certain that the number of "discomfort" words (identified by the common sense of intelligent people) appearing in successive pages or interviews of a case record would vary, not only according to the degree of discomfort experienced by the client, but also because of other factors. For example, neither pages nor interviews could be expected to be of precisely uniform length, and it also seemed likely that interviewers would vary, both among themselves and during the course of a single record, in the extent to which they used evaluative terms, as contrasted with "process recording." We therefore decided upon the following procedure. The total number of discomfort words on a page was counted. Only words which would stand alone, out of context, as indicating drive-tension were included. The total number of reward, or relief words, was similarly determined. The intensity of the client's discomfort was then represented as a quotient, i.e., as total discomfort words divided by total discomfort and relief words combined. The formula looked like this:

$$\frac{\text{Discomfort words}}{\text{Discomfort plus relief words}} = DRQ$$

A series of such quotients was obtained for the successive pages of a specimen case record and an appropriate graph was made. The result was the irregular curve shown in Figure 6. As anticipated, this curve has an over-all downward slope. (For an analysis and critique of the rationale of the DRQ formula, see Butler, 1952.)

Does the Tension Index Make Sense?

If the tension index is to be useful as a shorthand description of a case, it should "make sense." The index should go up when the reader of the case feels that things are going badly and should go down when matters are going better. In order that the reader may judge this issue for himself, we call attention again to Figure 6. In the text below we offer parallel comments on the events of the case record. The case in question is that of the "Cellini" family. Various high points and low points of the tension curve are labeled from A to G. Herewith is a description of the events occurring at these various points.

High Point A.—Curve begins at a high level representing the severe pressure under which the members of the family lived. The father was unemployed; the wife psychotic and in a mental hospital; the ten-year-old son, a truant; and the three daughters, discouraged and anxious. Mr. Cellini claimed that he and his four children had no food, no clothes, and no money.

Low Point B.—Treatment consisted of temporary relief, improvement of home and school situation, aid in budgeting and planning, attempts to aid the father and the older girls in securing employment.

The son liked school better and was less often a truant. The daughters were taking more interest in the home and looking forward to the eventual return of the mother from the mental hospital.

High Point C.—The swings in the curve illustrate the characteristically episodic nature of treatment and therapeutic movement. Mr. Cellini told of the death, some years earlier, of their nineteen-year-old hobo son in a railway accident and of Mrs. Cellini's hysterical reaction to the event. She blamed herself for his death, became depressed, and was eventually committed to a state hospital. Mr. Cellini also complained of his inability to find work after long and repeated trying.

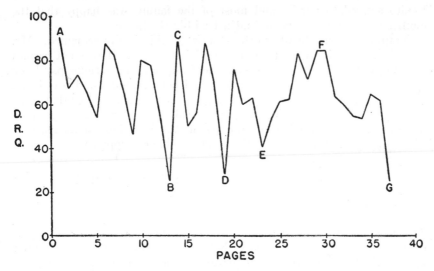

Fig. 6.—Curve showing the pattern of tension movement in the Cellini case. The curve represents an average based on seven independent scorings. The high and low points, *A* to *G,* are explained in the text.

Low Point D.—At this point Mr. Cellini seemed in better spirits. He was pleased that the truant son, Benito, was doing better in school and was staying home more during the evenings. Benito was also seen, and he seemed happy in his ungraded room. Benito's friends all had roller skates and he felt badly that he had none. The worker arranged to give him money for the roller skates. Benito's teacher also reported that the boy was making an effort to keep himself clean and that he was quite responsive to praise and attention.

Low Point E.—Complaints from the Cellini home were much fewer. The family seemed to be getting along well. The girls were working and helping to contribute to the family. One of the older girls had decided to announce her engagement. Thanks to the worker's influence, Mr. Cellini no longer interfered with the courtship of his daughter.

High Point F.—Angela, the oldest daughter, had become ill. She felt pursued, chained, and persecuted. Her talk was confused and scattered. Her psychotic episode appears to have been due to strong feelings of unconscious rivalry precipitated by the mother's return from the hospital. Mr. Cellini also complained of financial difficulties, saying he could not live on the $18.00 a week he was earning.

Low Point G.—The psychotic daughter was given casework help and also psychiatric consultation. These were probably instrumental in helping her to adjust to the new situation. The gains made by Benito seemed to persist and most of the family was happy that the mother was able to return and adjust within the home.

Naturally, many threats to the security of this family remained. Mr. Cellini's meager income was a source of frustration. It was not certain that the oldest daughter was immune from a more serious psychotic episode. The mother had merely outlived her psychosis and was in no way barricaded against a recurrence of it. Still, it may well be that some persons survive and maintain their social composure by very small margins of help and affection and that it was just these small margins which the caseworker was, in this situation, able to supply.

Reliability of Scoring by the Word Method

The counting of tension and reward words as a method of measuring tension may sound plausible enough, but is the scoring reliable? Will duplicate scorers count the same number of tension and reward words on the same page and therefore derive an identical or closely similar *DRQ?* And if they succeeded in getting similar scores for the same page, would they do so for succeeding pages and therefore arrive at the same curve representing tension change? We have put this matter to the test. Using the Cellini case discussed above, we arranged the thirty-seven pages of this record in random order so that the scorer could not follow the "story" of the case by simply reading it. A one-page set of instructions for scoring was attached. No verbal supplementation of these instructions was given, nor were any training sessions held. The scorers did not discuss the case among themselves or compare notes as they were scoring. In Figure 7 the curves showing the scores of eight different persons are represented. The average intercorrelation for the eight curves is +.80. Though such a correlation is regarded as relatively satisfactory in psychological and sociological research, it is very crude in comparison with the exactitude of measurement in the physical sciences. Of course, the fact that the scoring of tension level can be done relatively reliably is no evidence that this measure is related to casework "success." The relation of the tension measure to some measure of success or failure is an entirely separate problem. At the moment, we are concerned with establishing the reliability of this measure.[5]

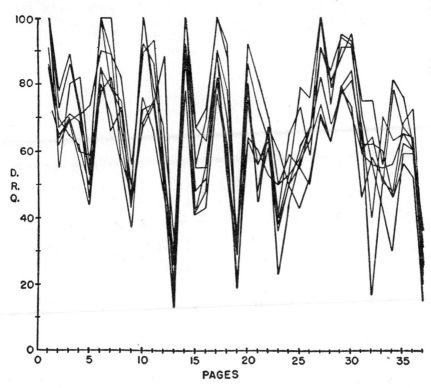

FIG. 7.—Curves showing Cellini case as scored by word method. The scoring on which these curves are based was carried out by eight different persons. The average intercorrelation for the eight curves is +.80.

Reliability of Sentence-Scoring Method

In spite of its relative reliability, the method of scoring a case by isolated words always seemed to us arbitrary and strange. The natural unit of communication is the sentence rather than the word. With the success of the word-scoring method as a stimulus, it occurred to us that the same logic of scoring could be applied to the sentence. We, therefore, tried out a method for scoring sentences. New instructions for scoring were devised. Drive-arousing sentences were scored minus, drive-reducing sentences were scored plus; the neutral sentences were scored zero. The DRQ was computed as earlier described. The ques-

[5] In addition to the "successful" Cellini case already discussed, which did indeed show a downward trend of the curve, we secured a notably "unsuccessful" case from Community Service Society. In the latter case the tension curve remained level, and in so doing expressed the judgment of the social worker concerning the case, which was that "severe environmental difficulties had prevented a real solution."

tion then arose as to whether different scorers could reliably use this method. Figure 8 shows the curves produced by eight scorers, again using as an object the Cellini case. The average intercorrelation for these eight curves is +.81. The persons who did the scoring of sentences are the same as those who scored the word-units just discussed. Had it not been for one peculiarly deviant scorer, the intercorrelation of these scores

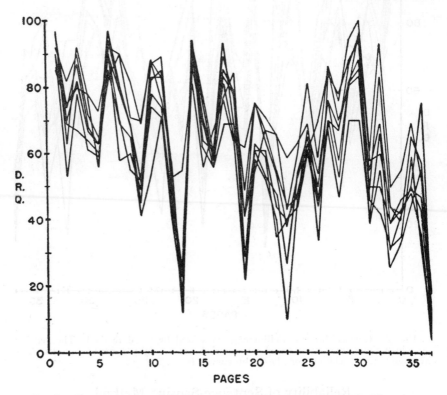

FIG. 8.—Curves showing Cellini case as scored by sentence method. The average intercorrelation for these eight curves is +.81. The persons whose scoring results are shown here are the same as those who did the scoring which is represented by the curves shown in Figure 7.

would have been appreciably higher. It is evident that a relatively high degree of reliability can likewise be reached when the sentence is used as the unit of scoring tension.

Reliability of Clause or "Thought-Unit" Scoring

A number of our scorers objected to using the total sentence as a unit for scoring. They observed that frequently several propositions are compacted into a single sentence in a casework record. One of these propositions might indicate discomfort and another relaxation.

The scorer was then called upon to "weight" the drive and reward elements and to judge which predominated. This dilemma led us to the supposition that we might use the grammarian's "independent clause," or "complete thought," as the scoring unit. In using this method, the scorer has to break each sentence down into its component clauses, which are then scored. More elaborate instructions were devised, and preliminary training sessions were held. In these training sessions the

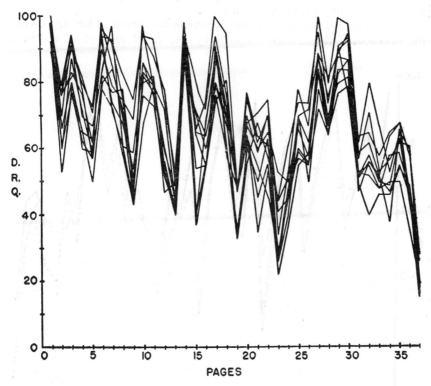

FIG. 9.—Curves showing Cellini case as scored by clause, or thought-unit, method. The average intercorrelation for these ten curves is +.88. None of the scorers with whom this method was tried out participated in the earlier tests.

scorers worked in small groups, scored pages, compared sample scores with each other, and discussed underlying theory with the researchers. In the actual scoring of the Cellini case, each scorer worked independently. Ten new scorers were enlisted for this test.

Figure 9 shows the Cellini case scored by the clause, or thought-unit, method. The curves are obviously similar to those derived from word and sentence scoring. The average intercorrelation for the ten curves is +.88. This is somewhat higher than the coefficients obtained by the word- and sentence-scoring methods (+.80 and +.81, respectively). It would seem that the thought-unit method of scoring is superior in that it eliminates certain sources of confusion inherent in the other two methods. Probably, also, the introduction of the training sessions made the habits of the scorers more stable.

We feel that the results of the thought-unit scoring are significant in that they remove the suspicion that our first group of eight scorers was composed of eccentric geniuses who, just by chance, could score reliably. Since we have been able to train ten additional scorers to score thought units reliably, we can probably train any intelligent person to score according to this method.

In Figure 10, we present three composite curves. One represents the average of the results obtained by the *word* method of scoring;

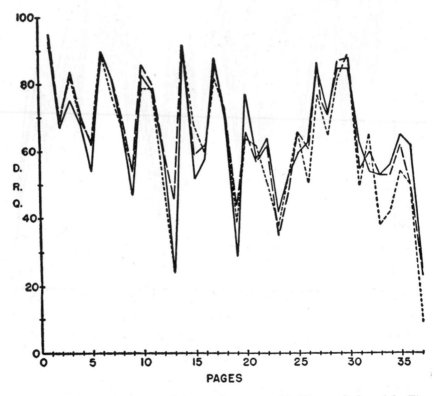

Fig. 10.—Composite curves of the results presented in Figures 7, 8, and 9. The results for word-, sentence-, and thought-unit scoring are shown, respectively, by the solid, the broken, and the dotted lines.

another, a composite of the results obtained by *sentence* scoring; and the third, the results obtained by *thought-unit* scoring. It seems indubitable that something "real" is being scored when results so similar are obtained by three somewhat varying methods.

Correlation Versus Coincidence of Curves

The similarity of the results obtained by these three methods is indicated not only by the parallelism of these three curves, which is estimated by their intercorrelation, but also by the extent to which they coincide. The correlation between the thirty-seven points which determine the "word" curve and the thirty-seven points which constitute the "sentence" curve, in Figure 10, is $+.90$; between the "sentence" curve and "thought" curve, $+.90$; and between the "word" curve and the "thought" curve, $+.93$.

The important consideration is that all three curves—obtained by three different methods and by two sets of scorers—not only closely parallel (i.e., correlate with) each other but, save at a few points, also have almost exactly the same absolute value (i.e., coincide).

The further problem arises as to which type of scoring yields the greatest degree of coincidence as between scorers. We have obtained a formula [6] for determining the degree to which a group of curves actually tend to coincide. Without giving the details of this method, we may say that when it is applied to the word-scoring technique, a value of 0.01000 is obtained; for sentence scoring, 0.00786; for clause scoring, 0.00569. The smaller the value, the greater is the degree of coincidence. Hence, it appears that the method of clause scoring produces at one and the same time the greatest parallelism and the greatest coincidence between curves of this type.

Accuracy of Clause Identification

Preliminary tests had seemed to indicate that different persons could identify the independent clauses, or thought units, constituting a page of case record material relatively accurately. It was nevertheless desirable to make a more systematic check in this connection.

The first step was to ascertain the total number of pluses, minuses, and zeros scored by each scorer on each of the thirty-seven pages of the Cellini record. Since each clause was supposed to be scored either as plus, minus, or zero, the sum of these scores corresponded to the number of clauses which the scorer identified on a given page.

This procedure brought out the fact that the consistency with which different scorers identified clauses was considerably lower than we had initially believed. Figure 11 shows the average curve (solid line) for all

[6] Through the courtesy of Dr. Daniel Horn of Harvard University. The formula is:

$$ S\left[\frac{(SX)^2 - \dfrac{(SX)^2}{n}}{N(n-1)}\right] $$

where S = "sum of," X = score obtained by a given scorer on any given page of the case record, N = number of pages in case record, and n = number of scorers.

eighteen scorers [7] in terms of the number of thought units identified on each of the thirty-seven pages of the Cellini record. The upper and lower limits of variation are indicated by the dotted lines. The average intercorrelation for the eighteen scorers was +.64.

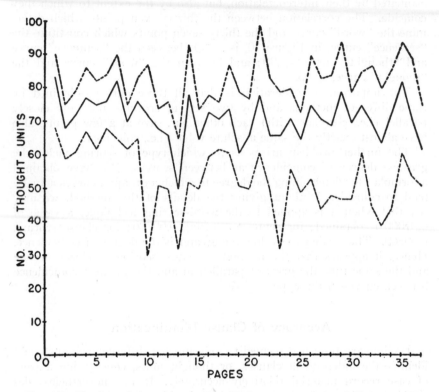

FIG. 11.—Number of thought units identified on pages of the Cellini case. The solid line shows the average number of thought units identified by eighteen scorers. The upper and lower limits of variation are indicated by the dotted lines. The average intercorrelation of the eighteen scorers was +.64.

These results raise a puzzling question: How can the *DRQ* scores be so relatively consistent (with a coefficient of reliability of +.88) for different scorers when the identification of the items which are scored has a reliability coefficient of only +.64? The answer seems to be as follows: It will be remembered that the *DRQ* is a ratio, obtained by dividing the total number of pluses and minuses on a given page (or any other unit of a case record) into the number of minuses. This means that the *absolute* number of pluses and minuses recorded on a

---

[7] After a first test with ten scorers, eight additional scorers were added for the sake of making a test not reported here. All eighteen, however, scored the Cellini case by the thought-unit method, and we are thus enabled to use the results of the eighteen scorers at this point.

given page does not affect the *DRQ* for that page. Thus, forty-five pluses and forty-five minuses will give a *DRQ* of .50, as, for example, will thirty-eight pluses and thirty-eight minuses.

The results just presented indicate that our scorers did not identify the clauses on a given page very consistently, but they evidently did not differ in distinguishing clauses that were to be scored *plus* and clauses that were to be scored *minus*. This meant that, although the absolute number of clauses identified on a given page differed considerably from person to person, the *relative* number of plus and minus clauses remained fairly constant, thus giving the high coefficient of reliability for the scoring method as a whole. If each scorer obtained a slightly different, but nevertheless adequate, sample of the drive and reward units on the page, the *DRQ* could yet be constant. This seems to be what actually happened.

It would have been neater if our scorers had identified the clauses, or thought units, with a higher degree of consistency; but for the reasons just given, it is probably not very important that they did not. If it had seemed urgent to obtain greater agreement in this connection, improved consistency could almost certainly have been obtained by more rigorous instructions and training.

Scorer Anxiety

Each *DRQ* scorer has shown marked anxiety lest his results would not correspond with those of other scorers. The method seemed so tenuous and individual that it was hard for each scorer to believe that his judgment would be anything like typical. Scorers have been literally astonished (as well as relieved) when they compared their list of *DRQ*'s with those of others.

The Psychology of DRQ Scoring

Possibly the psychological transaction involved in *DRQ* scoring can be indicated as follows: The scorer rehearses the sentence. As he does so, the sentence or thought unit produces tensing or relaxing responses in the scorer, or he experiences no change in tension level. The scorers are then required to make a verbal response to the cue produced by tension change. This verbal response is the score. He says "drive" in case tension is increased; "reward" in case tension is reduced and "zero" if rehearsal has produced no change in tension level. Usually this rehearsal transaction occurs so rapidly that it is described by the scorer as "intuitive."

The reliability of judgment concerning the *DRQ* gives evidence of the fact that the rise and fall of human tensions are well registered in common speech and that likewise this speech is sufficiently widely disseminated so that a considerable number of persons can make accurate judgments in respect to tension movement. The scorers in this test were limited to very intelligent persons of college education and some professional training. At lower educational levels, limitations of reading and rehearsal skill might cause the measure to be less reliable.

Configuration Scoring

The problem of configuration scoring arose early and proved troublesome. Some of our scorers felt that it was unwise to score each sentence or thought unit in its own terms and suggested instead that each sentence should be scored in the light of all succeeding sentences in the record. If, for instance, a client "wanted very much" to go to college, this would not be scored by itself as an evidence of drive; according to the configurational method, one would have to "look in the back of the book" for the answer and see whether wanting to go to college actually turned out well as far as the client was concerned. If it did, his apparent wish would be scored as "positive," or "constructive"; otherwise, as "negative," or "destructive." The effect of this method of scoring would be to destroy the independent clause or thought as a unit, since each unit would have to be scored first in its own terms and then in the light of other units or paragraphs on other pages of the record. The unit to be scored would thus be exceedingly and impossibly complex.

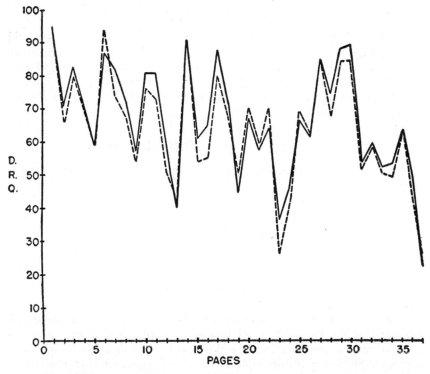

Fig. 12.—Scores of a highly efficient scorer (dotted line) in relation to the average curve (solid line) for the Cellini case.

After much debate on this difficulty, we decided to leave matters alone and let each unit stand by itself. If "wanting to go to college" had a favorable result, this would appear in the scoring of later sentences. We therefore adopted the rule: "Score units as you see them," and let later parts of the record give their own evidence as to increase in, or reduction of, discomfort.

Individual Differences in Scoring

Interesting individual differences sometimes showed up in the way in which a scorer corresponded to, or deviated from, the average. Some scorers were rather consistently accurate. Figure 12 shows the scores of a highly efficient scorer (dotted line) in relation to the average curve (solid line) for the group as a whole. Another scorer (Figure 13) showed a fairly consistent tendency to score too high when the average went up and too low when the average curve went down. It would be interesting to know whether this exaggeration of reaction was char-

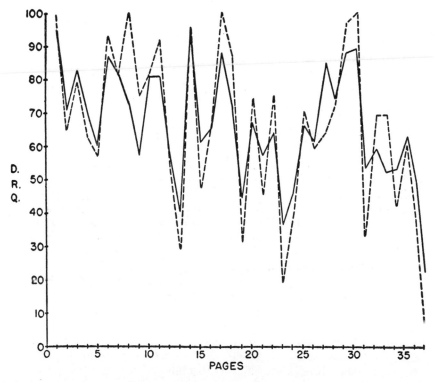

Fig. 13.—Curve of a deviant scorer (dotted line). This scorer showed a more or less consistent tendency to score too high when the average curve (solid line) went up and too low when it went down.

acteristic of this person in other life relations, but time did not permit us
to pursue such fantasies.

Use of the Zero Category

It occurred to us that the use of the zero category might be in some
way related to the deviance of the scorer from the average of his group.
Possibly those who used it most frequently might be those who also
showed great deviations, or vice versa. This suspicion was not supported by the facts. We computed the "sum of the squares" as a measure
of the extent to which the DRQ scores for different scorers deviated
on a given page. Next we added the page deviations to get a single
score for each scorer for the entire record. We then added the total
number of zeros used by each scorer throughout the entire Cellini record.
Finally we correlated these two series of scores, the total deviations
with the total number of zeros. When we did this, we obtained a coefficient of correlation of $+.08$. It seems that there was no relation between
the number of zeros each person scored and the extent to which his DRQ
scores approximated the group average.

DRQ Scores Derived by Chance

In looking at a curve representing the course of a case as determined
by the DRQ method, one might ask: How meaningful, statistically, are
the successive ups and downs in the curve? How significant is the over-
all change from beginning to end? How likely is one to obtain such
a curve purely on the basis of "chance"?

One way of attacking this problem is to construct a comparable
curve on the basis of chance and see what it looks like. Figure 14 shows
such a curve. Letting 1 and 2 stand for zero, 3 and 4 for plus, and 5
and 6 for minus, a die was cast as many times as there were thought
units on each page of the Cellini case record. The total number of pluses
and minuses thus obtained for each page was divided into the number
of minuses alone, and in this manner a value comparable to the DRQ
was obtained. The first curve thus obtained is represented by the solid
line in Figure 14. We see that the curve may fluctuate 10 points above
or below 50 on the graph but rarely beyond that. Nor is there any
consistent trend of the curve upward or downward from left to right.

This curve teaches two things: that the DRQ is not likely to fluctuate
more than 15 or 20 points from one page to the next on the basis of
"chance," and that it is extremely unlikely that there will be any over-all
downward or upward trend in a curve. Therefore, if, as in the Cellini
case, one obtains shifts of 30, 40, or even 50 points from one page to
the next, such changes are almost certainly "significant," i.e., exceedingly unlikely to occur on the basis of "chance"; moreover, a general
downward drift such as is noted in the Cellini case is also extremely
unlikely to occur if chance alone is operating.

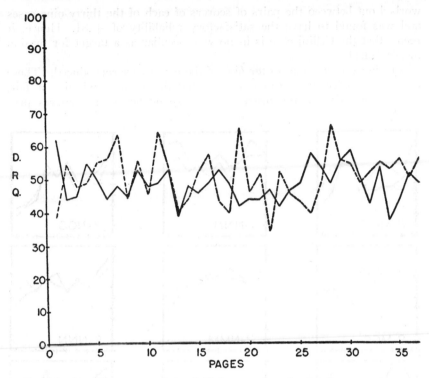

Fig. 14.—Tension pattern of the Cellini case when the *DRQ*'s were determined by chance, that is, by throwing a die. Note that the range of fluctuation is limited and that the curves show no downward or upward trend. The two curves were derived by separate castings of the die.

The dotted line in Figure 14 shows a second curve obtained in exactly the same way as the first one. As was to be expected, the fluctuations in the first curve show no discernible correspondence to those of the second. In this connection, "chance" means that the variable of caseworker skill is applied at random, rather than discriminately as in the actual case. Presumably the real life effect of skill applied by chance would be exactly that pictured in the curves of Figure 14, i.e., no change in tension levels.

Is the Cellini Case a Peculiarly Fortunate One?

It is possible, though hardly likely, that we were lucky in selecting the Cellini case for *DRQ* scoring. It is necessary to show, therefore, that reliable scoring can be done by the thought unit method on other cases. With this in mind, thirty-nine cases were requested from the Family Service of the Community Service Society. Each of these cases was independently scored by two scorers. A correlation coefficient was

worked out between the pairs of scorers of each of the thirty-nine cases
and was found to have the satisfactory reliability of +.81. Hence, it
seems that the Cellini case is in no way peculiar as a target for tension
measurement.

In Figure 15, the curves for nine of these cases are reproduced. These
cases were selected at random from the thirty-nine and give a fair,
visual impression of the degree of correspondence of the curves pro-

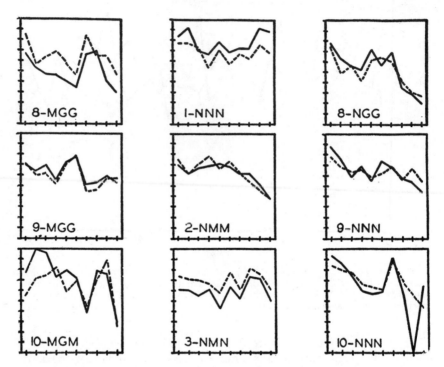

Fig. 15.—Tension curves of nine different cases. Each case was scored by two
persons. These cases give a fair picture of a group of thirty-nine cases as to
parallelism and coincidence of curves. In all except one case (10-NNN), the parallelism is striking. In all cases the slopes of the curves are similar.

duced by each pair of scorers for the same case. The curves naturally
vary in the degree of parallelism and coincidence. The damaging deviations are, of course, those where one curve goes up and the other goes
down. It is clear, however, that a line representing the slope for each
pair of curves would be very similar throughout the nine cases. Examination of the cases showed that very short cases, say those under twenty
pages, were the ones in which deviation between the pairs of scorers
was most likely.

Limitations of the DRQ

1. The *DRQ* does not tell us what kind of drive is operating—whether sex, hunger, fear of status loss, fear of food deprivation, paranoid fears, or what.

2. The drives operating may be unitary or multiple. What is given in the *DRQ* is a summation of all drives operating.

3. One drive may replace another in the course of the time span of the case; the *DRQ* may represent high sex anxiety at one point and high status anxiety at another.

4. The *DRQ* does not distinguish between primary drives, such as hunger, and secondary drives, such as ambition.

5. The *DRQ* does not distinguish between the drives of the client and those of other family members.

6. The *DRQ* does not distinguish between client's drives and the community "drives" (the latter usually represented in the caseworker's comments or opinions).

7. In short, the *DRQ* just measures drive—primary or secondary, single or summated, continuous or serial, that of the client or of any other individual; it is a record of all the tensions that creep into the case record.

Does the Tension Index Indicate Learning?

In and of itself the tension index does not give evidence that learning has taken place in a given client. It does, however, picture whether or not there was a chance for learning to take place. In a case which shows a great drop in the tension line, adjustive learning could take place, provided the caseworker has done her job properly—i.e., provided she has taught the adaptive habits and reserved her rewards for habits acceptable to the community as a whole. If, of course, she has rewarded the client for learning to malinger, it is malingering behavior that will have been learned.

Other Scientific Uses of the Tension Index

The tension index has not been tried out by these researchers on any other kind of written data. Possibly students of the autobiography will find it useful. Perhaps Rorschach protocols or the results of the Thematic Apperception Test can be studied from this standpoint. Full recordings of successful psychoanalyses may show characteristic tension lines. It would seem that the tension measure would be useful in investigations involving any kind of data analogous to the case record.

Does the Tension Index Measure "Success"?

The answer to this question must be somewhat equivocal. We certainly do not claim that it does; nor can we, as yet, be certain that it does

not. As repeatedly emphasized, the behavior of the caseworker is of
great importance in any situation where learning can take place. Some
cases present such momentous difficulties that merely keeping the client
"treading water" may be a considerable achievement. Nevertheless,
the tension line in such cases might be level or might even rise.

If a reliable measure of "real life success" of the client could be
invented, and if this measure proved to correlate highly and positively
with the *DRQ,* it would be possible to determine from the movement
of tension in a particular case what the future outlook of the client
would be. There is, indeed, no certainty that such a reliable measure
can be developed or, if it could, that it would be positively correlated
with a drop in tension index. These are risks, however, which all
researchers must take. The sponsors of the research can determine
the area in which a measurement attempt is to be made. The researchers
can then determine whether or not such a measure can be constructed.

A Caution

We must, for the moment, caution caseworkers and boards of phil-
anthropic organizations against the impulsive assumption that the tension
index measures "movement" in a case or the efficiency with which casework is carried on. (Further research bearing upon this question is
reported in Chapter 11.)

Further Problems

At this stage of the research a whole chain of interrelated problems
appears. At one end of the chain is the question, "Is the case record
like the case in those particulars which are relevant to the eventual
outcome?" At the other end of the chain is the question, "What is
the measure of real life success?" It will be the function of further
research to inquire into these problems, and particularly into the question of whether the amount of drop in the *DRQ* is positively correlated
with caseworkers' ratings of movement.[8]

[8] For scoring instructions and annotated bibliography, see issue of *Journal of
abnormal and social Psychology* cited at the outset of this chapter.

CHAPTER 11

FURTHER STUDIES UTILIZING THE DISCOMFORT-RELIEF QUOTIENT

By O. Hobart Mowrer, Ph.D., J. McVicker Hunt, Ph.D.,
and Leonard S. Kogan, Ph.D.

Since the publication, in 1947, of the study which is reproduced in this volume as Chapter 10, a number of other investigations have been reported which carry forward the same line of inquiry. In the present chapter these studies will be reviewed and evaluated, with special reference to the meaning and validity of the *DRQ* method.

Community Service Society Studies

As indicated in the preceding chapter, the discomfort-relief quotient was developed and first used as a device for measuring "movement" in social casework carried on under the auspices of the Community Service Society of New York City. Shortly after completion of the work reported in Chapter 10, this line of research was taken over by J. McV. Hunt and L. S. Kogan and further elaborated in a number of other studies. One of the first questions to which these investigators turned their attention was that of the *validity* of the *DRQ*. Dollard and Mowrer had shown that the method has a relatively high reliability, and they had set the stage for a validity study by collecting from each of the thirteen branch offices of the Community Service Society three case records which were submitted as representing, in the judgment of workers at the branch offices, great movement, little or no movement (or even deterioration), and an intermediate amount of movement. One of the thirty-nine cases thus collected had to be eliminated, thus leaving thirty-eight. Values were computed which represented the difference in the *DRQ* obtained for the first tenth and for the last tenth of each case record, and these values were correlated with the high, low, and intermediate ratings given to the cases by the caseworkers. The obtained figure was low, of the order of .20, thus indicating that the *DRQ* is probably *not* a valid measure, at least when casework judgment is used as the basis for judging validity.

One possible interpretation of the low validity index thus obtained was that the social workers were unreliable in their judgments of casework movement. A next logical step was therefore to make an empirical check on the degree of consistency which caseworkers might show in rating the same cases. Hunt * (1949) has described this investigation as follows:

It was the failure of the caseworker judgments of improvement to show higher correlation with change in the *DRQ* which led us to test their reliability. In this test we sought at once to determine how well workers would agree and whether professional training and experience would be associated with degree of agreement. We had the movement in our sample of [38] cases judged on a five-step verbal scale by five district secretaries, representing the most training and experience in casework, by a random sample of ten professional workers, by five students at the New York School of Social Work who were in their third quarter of practice, and by five of my students at Brown University. The means of the intercorrelation coefficients for these various groups were respectively +.78, +.70, +.64, and +.59. The amount of agreement among professional workers was surprising, and this trend showed clearly that professional experience contributes to higher agreement. Moreover, the averaged judgments of the district secretaries, which correlated +.94 with the averaged judgments of either the odd or even five of the professional workers, still showed only the +.20 correlation with the *DRQ*. Clearly unreliability of caseworker judgment could not be held responsible for the small size of this correlation (p. 75; see also Hunt, 1947).

Since all of the Community Service Society studies had involved the use of dictated case records rather than verbatim interview recordings, a possible explanation of the discrepancy between *DRQ* results and caseworker judgments was unreliability of the records. In a recent study by Kogan (1951), this problem has been posed as follows:

The present study was carried out to investigate the degree of correspondence between *DRQ*'s derived from a set of dictated interview records and the *DRQ*'s derived from the verbatim interviewee statements in the same set of casework interviews. As is readily apparent, this question is but one very limited aspect of the larger problem of the reliability of the case record, or, more precisely, the problem as to whether the case record is like the case (p. 3).

A sample of thirty-six electronically recorded casework interviews was obtained along with the dictated summaries of these interviews, and the *DRQ* was determined for each of the interviews and each of the summaries.

The product-moment *r* was then computed between the corresponding pairs of *DRQ*'s for the thirty-six dictated and verbatim interviews. This *r* was found to be .64, which, although significantly different from an *r* of zero, is not remarkably high. This degree of correlation might, nevertheless, warrant the use of dictated records for obtaining *DRQ*'s in a large-scale study of *DRQ*'s for casework interviews (p. 5).

* References are to the bibliography at the back of the book.

Another study (Hauser, 1951), using the same thirty-six interviews mentioned above, has been directed at assessing the clinical *meaningfulness* of the *DRQ* content-analysis approach. Among the clinician's criticisms of the *DRQ* method is one that hits at the heart of the basic assumption made by practically all content-analysis methods, namely, that by adding together judgments of component subunits of a document, e.g., single clauses, one can arrive at an over-all index representative of the diagnostic import of the document. For example, the fact that a client mentions one problem ten times and a second problem just once does not necessarily mean to the clinician that the first problem is ten times as important to the client. The clinician may thus feel that an over-all impression or judgment made by an experienced worker or therapist yields a more accurate index of the "true" situation than does an index based on the fractionating and combining sequence of content analysis.

The major topic of investigation in the study just cited was to compare the expression of distress-relief by the client as measured by the *DRQ*—a content-analysis method—and as measured by an over-all judgment procedure which utilized an eleven-step scale, ranging from a possible judgment of *1*, where the client was judged to be maximally relieved or satisfied, to a rating of *11*, where the client was judged to be maximally distressed or unhappy. The latter judgments are referred to as *DRR*'s (Distress-Relief Ratings) to distinguish them from the *DRQ*'s arrived at by the Dollard-Mowrer scoring method. In brief, it was found that the correlation between *DRR*'s and *DRQ*'s for the thirty-six verbatim interviews ranged from a maximum of .60 for the last third of the interviews to a minimum of .22 for the first and second thirds of the interviews. The correlation between *DRR*'s and *DRQ*'s for the interviews as a whole tended to be in the neighborhood of .50. Inasmuch as all of these interviews were initial interviews, loaded on the distress side of the continuum, it seemed probable, owing to "restriction of range," that these *r*'s would be higher for a random selection of casework interviews at all stages of casework progress. The prediction, of course, remains to be empirically verified, but even the present evidence indicates a statistically reliable intrinsic relationship between the "clinical" over-all judgment of distress relieved and the "objective" content-analysis measure of distress relieved The fact that judgmental measures of distress relieved correspond with the *DRQ,* while caseworkers' judgments of "movement" do not, calls into question whether these latter two variables are as much related as theory would suggest.

Still another effort has been made by the CSS researchers to test the validity of the changes in the *DRQ* as a measure of the results in social casework. This has involved relating the differences between the *DRQ* values for the first and last tenths of the case records (*DRQ*-differences) to the valuations ex-clients make of the help they received during their contact with their caseworkers and the agency. These valuations were obtained from the individual members of the 38 families concerned in the original validation study of the DRQ some five to seven years after their cases were closed (Kogan, Hunt, & Bartelme, 1953). Two methods of measuring the ex-client's valuation of the casework help he had received were employed. One consisted of reflecting back previously scaled statements after the ex-client had talked freely in response to the follow-up interviewer's question as to whether or not the casework experience had been helpful. When this method yielded an extremely high preponderance of very positive valuations, a second method was devised as a check. This second method consisted of identifying all the valuative statements which were made by the ex-clients in the follow-up interviews and which got recorded, having them judged on an eleven-step scale, and using the median of these as the measure for each individual's valuation, and the median of those from all the individuals within a family as the measure for the family. These two methods of measuring the ex-clients' valuations of the help received agreed well. The product-moment correlation between them was $+.82$. On the other hand, both measures showed only zero-order correlations with the DRQ-differences ("scaled valuations" with DRQ-differences, $r = -.09$, and mean of "free valuations" with DRQ-differences, $r = +.08$). It should be mentioned that caseworker judgments of movement in these clients also showed similarly low correlations with these ex-client valuations of help received ("scaled valuations" with "movement" judgments, $r = +.17$, and "free valuations" with "movement" judgments, $r = +.11$). Thus, the degree to which ex-clients value their casework experience in retrospect is not predicted by *either* change in the DRQ or by caseworker judgments of "movement." Inasmuch as several clients whose situations deteriorated, or at least failed to improve, during their casework contacts were among those reporting that they "could not have lived without the casework help," it seems probable that they were valuing the experience of having someone "understand" and "listen to their plight" during a crisis rather than saying that as a consequence of it they had been changed or their plight had been changed by the experience.

We leave the studies from the Community Service Society with the following facts and their implications: (1) Changes in the DRQ show very little if any correlation with caseworkers' judgments of "movement," the latter defined as changes in the client with respect to his "adaptive efficiency," "disabling habits and conditions," "understanding," and environmental circumstances. (2) The absence of positive correlation expected from theory between these two variables cannot be attributed to unreliability of caseworker judgments of movement for typical interjudge reliability approximates $+.8$. (3) There is probably fairly high correlation between DRQ's for interviews recorded verbatim and DRQ's for the same interviews as dictated by caseworkers. The one obtained for such a series was $+.64$, but it is probably spuriously low because it was obtained from a series of intake interviews all from the upper half of the potential DRQ range. This fact implies that selectivity in recording can account for only a small share of the absence of correlation between "movement" judgments and *DRQ* changes. Although the theoretical argument that the factors defining "movement" as judged by caseworkers should be associated with changes in distress is exceedingly attractive, these three sets of facts serve to call it into question. It may well be that the records of family agencies, containing as they do the stories of the lives of a number of individuals, some of whom are not directly touched in the casework contact, constitute a poor place in which to test the validity of this theoretical relationship. Verbatim records from psychotherapy with individual clients would probably be more appropriate. These studies show also (4) that neither *DRQ* changes nor caseworker judgments of "movement" predict what clients will *say* about the value of the help they receive five years after their cases are closed; but, again, what the ex-client may be valuing is not the amount of distress relieved in the course of his contact nor the degree to which he changes but rather the experience of having someone attentive and concerned about him and his plight during a time of crisis.

Studies by Assum and Levy, Kauffman and Raimy, and Cofer and Chance

In the years 1948, 1949, and 1950, there appeared three studies which throw new light upon the meaning and applicability of the *DRQ*. The first of these, by Assum and Levy (see Figure 16), was based on a

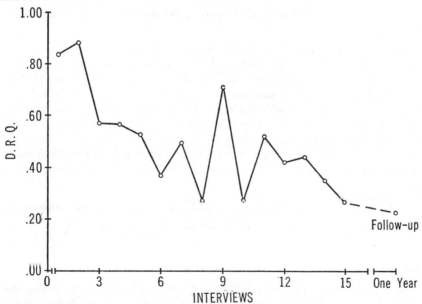

FIG. 16.—Graphic representation of tension changes occurring in a case of non-directive counseling (Assum and Levy, 1948). This study was the first in which the *DRQ* method was applied to verbatim transcriptions of electronic interview recordings.

single case of counseling carried out at the University of Chicago Counseling Center. These writers summarize their study as follows:

Presented in this article are the abridgments of a series of fifteen interviews and a rather complete presentation of a recorded follow-up interview held one year after the close of counseling. An attempt is made to show some of the longitudinal feeling and attitude patterns evidenced in the series. Also included is an analysis of the series using the *DRQ,* which indicates a marked reduction in tension.

The writers feel that, on the basis of the materials presented in the preceding sections, this case can be evaluated as a successful one. . . . Although problems still remain in the family relationships area, Ellen has gained considerable confidence in her ability to handle them, as indicated in the follow-up interview.

The evaluation of this case is not one imposed by the counselor or observers, but is derived from the client's statements with a minimum of interpretation. We accept Ellen's remark in the follow-up interview, "I consider myself to be one of your successful cases," as a valid indicator of how she now sees herself.

We realize that the *DRQ* as an analytic tool contributes no additional knowledge of the client's progress, as the scorings are based upon her own verbalizations. However, it seems to have value in providing a picture of progress which may be lost in merely reading the successive interviews (p. 89).

In an earlier section of their paper, Assum and Levy make these observations:

The Discomfort-Relief Quotient is suggested by Dollard and Mowrer as a measure "which yields a relatively reliable, graphic picture of tension change in a social case record, and conceivably also in an autobiography, psychoanalytic history, or other personal documents" (p. 3). This indicated that the *DRQ* might be a valuable device for the measurement of tension changes in the protocol of this series of nondirective counseling interviews. A casual reading of the interviews, especially the first and last of the series, gives the impression that marked changes in tension have occurred. It was the attempt to quantify these changes, giving a more precise picture of such changes, that led to our applying the *DRQ* (p. 87).

The impressions of the authors, plus the remarks of the client herself, suggest that this was a successful case; and the dramatic decline in the *DRQ* index favors the assumption that the method is valid, i.e., that it measures what it is supposed to measure. This assumption is further confirmed by these observations:

It is interesting to note the marked rise in *DRQ* in Interview 9. During the interval between Interviews 8 and 9 Ellen moved into Co-op house, which constituted a major break with her home. Interview 9 was concerned primarily with the expression of the discomfort she felt and the problems she faced in her new environment. The equally marked falling-off in *DRQ* in

Interview 10 to her previous low level of discomfort might indicate that her equilibrium had been only temporarily disturbed and that she sustained her increased capacity to cope with new problems (p. 89).[1]

As will be recalled from Chapter 10, Dollard and Mowrer noted in the Cellini case a similar tendency for DRQ fluctuations to be meaningfully correlated with the course of the case. Observations of this type support the inference that the DRQ is valid, and they sharpen the question as to why this method correlates so poorly with caseworker judgment.

Kauffman and Raimy (1949) introduce their study as follows:

Two methods of measuring changes in personality based on longitudinal changes in interview protocols have recently been suggested. In 1947, Dollard and Mowrer reported the application of "A Method of Measuring Tension in Written Documents" stemming from the hypothesis that a comparison of alterations in "tension" in casework records would reveal the progress being made. Their results seemed to justify their hypothesis. In 1948, Raimy reported a study, condensed from a more detailed dissertation [Raimy, 1943], which purported to show that by measuring changes in self-evaluation in counseling interviews, the progress of counseling could be traced quantitatively. Although derived from different theoretical positions and applied to different kinds of material, both methods of analysis have the same goal of measuring changes in personality. The present study is a report of an investigation which attempts to study the relationship between the results of the two methods when both are applied to the same verbatim protocols of counseling interviews (p. 378).

The other method of analysis referred to above is the $PNAvQ$, which Kauffman and Raimy describe thus:

This quotient is obtained by having judges classify all counselee responses (the unit here is all words spoken by the counselee between two responses of the counselor) into one of the following categories: P—positive self-reference; N—negative self-reference; Av—ambivalent self-reference; A—ambiguous self-reference; O—nonrhetorical questions. The $PNAvQ$ is then obtained, like the tension index DRQ, by dividing the number of N units plus the number of Av units by the number of N units plus Av units plus P units. The range of possible quotients, like that of the DRQ, is between and including 0.00 and 1.00 with a quotient closer to 0.00 indicating greater self-approval or, in DRQ terms, greater relief from "tension" (p. 380).

Because of the scarcity of published psychotherapeutic recordings, Kauffman and Raimy used a somewhat heterogeneous assortment of materials which they describe in the following paragraph:

[1] The exact method used by Assum and Levy in computing the DRQ was somewhat different from the one employed by Dollard and Mowrer, but there is no a priori reason for supposing that the results were much altered by this change in procedure.

Typescripts of seventeen almost verbatim interviews were available. All were taken from recorded counseling cases. Seven different cases and five counselors were represented. There were two complete series of three interviews apiece, two follow-up interviews, two isolated interviews, and a selection of seven interviews (including two follow-up) from a single case. The problem of sampling all varieties of counseling interviews could not be handled systematically in this study because of the lack of materials. Although interviews were selected from both successful and unsuccessful cases and from initial and final phases of counseling, the sampling is admittedly inadequate, being overweighted with interviews which occurred during the earlier phases of counseling where negative or discomfort statements are most likely to be found. . . . The greatest departure from random sampling is to be found in the fact that all the interviews represented nondirective counseling, since as yet no protocols from other approaches are available. It is doubtful that this selection factor had much influence on the results of the comparison as identical protocols were classified by both *DRQ* and *PNAvQ* procedures (pp. 380-81).

These investigators trained different persons in the use of the two methods and had them independently score the interview materials described above.

The most dramatic illustration of the coincidence resulting from the application of *DRQ* and *PNAvQ* to the same seventeen interviews is shown [in Fig. 17]. Some differences are clearly evident but the over-all impression is one of very considerable similarity. Inspection reveals that the greatest difference tends to be found in those interviews in which there is a preponderance of positive self-reference or relief (pp. 381-82).

When the raw score form of the rank-difference method of correlation was applied, it was found that the results obtained by the two methods had a rho of .838. A different, perhaps less justifiable method of correlation results in an *r* of .961. As the authors remark, these correlations are "in line with the expectations of simple inspection and with the other statistical results" (p. 382).

After discussing a number of differences of detail, Kauffman and Raimy say:

Despite the differences revealed by a comparison of the two methods of studying changes in personality during longitudinal contacts, it would appear that both methods produce essentially similar results. The differences may be important in selecting the particular method to be used in a given investigation, but the similarity revealed raises a number of theoretical issues.

Each method was derived from a different set of postulates, since the originator of *PNAvQ* makes no mention of "tension" in his rationale for classifying self-references but advocates instead an evaluation dependent upon the client's manifest self-approval or self-disapproval. Dollard and Mowrer make no use of these concepts in their instructions for classification or in their theoretical postulates. Instead, they depend upon concepts referring to "dis-

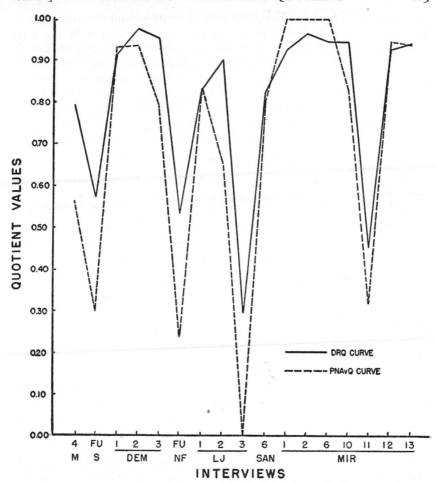

Fɪɢ. 17.—Results obtained by applying two different methods of objective analysis to the same interview materials (Kauffman and Raimy, 1949). It should be noted that the seventeen interviews here represented are selected from a variety of cases. The above curves do not, therefore, depict the course of therapy in a single case. They are drawn as continuous only as a means of making possible a clearer comparison of the two methods employed: the *DRQ* and the *PNAvQ*.

comfort and relief," although their basic postulate is primarily dependent upon "tension" as a construct for *understanding* the changes which take place. Thus they assume that a reduction in tension is accompanied by learning which accounts for "success" in casework and presumably in personality reorganization (p. 384).[2]

After further analysis, Kauffman and Raimy conclude that the two methods, despite different conceptual presuppositions, are *operationally*

[2] In the Dollard-Mowrer study there was an implicit assumption that learning occurs when and only when a drive is reduced and satisfaction or relief is experienced. For a two-factor conception of learning, see Mowrer (1950).

very similar. Despite different theoretical premises and different instructions to the judges or scorers, the two methods give virtually the same results (see Figure 17)—a fact which suggests that in both instances we are measuring something substantial and real, whatever its ultimate significance or meaning may prove to be. At first it might seem that the coincidence of the two sets of findings reported by Kauffman and Raimy constitutes a kind of validation of the DRQ; but if, as now seems probable, the two methods are operationally much the same, all the coincidence of results does, really, is to afford further proof of the reliability of this type of measurement.

Some possible clarification of the Kauffman-Raimy finding of high relationship between the DRQ approach and the $PNAvQ$ approach, despite different presuppositions, is afforded by a study recently carried out at the Community Service Society (Horowitz, 1951). This study was initiated as a check on whether the high r between $PNAvQ$ scores and DRQ's would also hold in the casework setting. In order to carry out this repetition of the Kauffman-Raimy study, Raimy was asked, and kindly consented, to supply his exact instructions for scoring the "self-concept." Perusal of these instructions clearly brought out that positive and negative self-references, as so defined, were not limited to statements expressing approval or disapproval of the self (as indicated in the published articles). Thus positive self-references, according to Raimy, were defined so as to include all expressions of happiness and satisfaction, while negative self-references were defined so as to include expressions of sadness and worry. With this broad interpretation of positive and negative self-references, the DRQ and $PNAvQ$ procedures obviously tend to score the responses in a highly consistent fashion, even though the unit scored is "clauses" for the DRQ and "statements" for the $PN\ AvQ$. This is a suggestive finding.

In addition, therefore, to following up Kauffman and Raimy's study with thirty-six casework interviews, it was decided also to score only those self-references which denoted the dimension of self-approval and self-disapproval. These latter scores were designated as SAQ's (Self-Approval Quotients). In brief, the results were these: The r between DRQ's and $PNAvQ$'s was found to be .38, a "statistically significant" departure from an r of zero, while the r between DRQ's and SAQ's was found to be .14, which was "not statistically significant." The fact that the DRQ's and $PNAvQ$'s correlated to a markedly lower degree than was found by Kauffman and Raimy for nondirective counseling interviews is attributed to several factors, among which is the "restriction of range" previously mentioned. However, the most important factor in connection with this discrepancy is the possibility that in the casework material much of the client's concern is centered around the problems and circumstances of *other family members,* this concern being reflected in the DRQ as distress but not necessarily in the $PNAvQ$ as negative self-attitude. The lack of significant relationship between DRQ's and SAQ's is interpreted as due to the understandable fact that expression of distress does not necessarily parallel expression of self-disapproval, nor does expression of relief necessarily coexist with self-approval.

A study by Cofer and Chance (1950) represents another attack upon the troublesome problem of validity. After noting the apparent face validity of the *DRQ* method but also the failure of Hunt and Kogan to validate the method against social casework judgment, Cofer and Chance say:

In the present study, the DRQ measure was applied to the client's statements in five published nondirectively counseled cases and to one published case which was treated hypoanalytically. In all of the cases, the treatment seems to have been regarded by the therapists as reasonably successful; hence the *DRQ* should show a change consistent with this outcome. Further, the application of the measure to a psychoanalytically treated case and to nondirectively counseled cases may allow for comparisons between the two types of treatment (p. 220).

A preliminary test of the reliability of the method showed that: "The interjudge reliability thus obtained for the *DRQ* based on independent clauses is comparable to that reported by Dollard and Mowrer and seems high enough to justify its further use" (p. 220). The reliability coefficient obtained by these investigators was 0.83 (sigma .07).

Cofer and Chance present their results in tabular form. These have been translated into curves that are reproduced here in Figures 18 and 19. The four curves appearing in Figure 18 all represent cases taken from Snyder's *Case-book of nondirective counseling* (1947); curves for

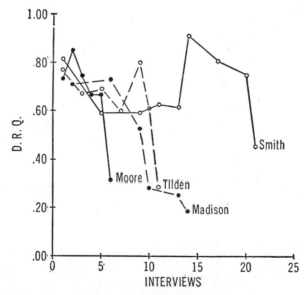

Fig. 18.—Curves based upon data (published by Cofer and Chance, 1950) representing the course of the *DRQ* in four cases of nondirective counseling. These cases were selected from Snyder's *Case-book* (1947).

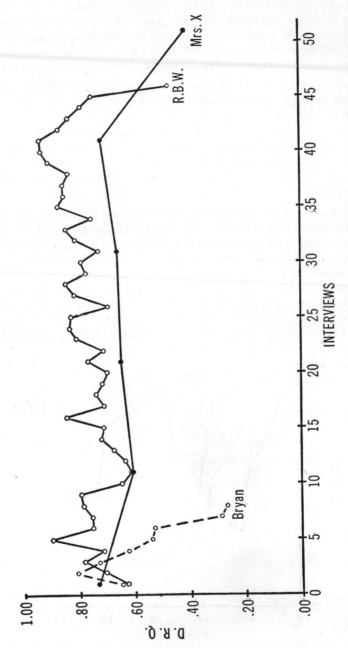

FIG. 19.—Curves representing three cases of psychotherapy: Rogers' (1942) client, "Bryan"; Lindner's (1944) patient, "R.B.W."; and a "Mrs. X," treated by Mowrer. The curves for the first two cases are based upon data reported by Cofer and Chance (1950); the latter upon data collected by Rollins and Twaite (1950).

Rogers' (1942) well-known case of "Bryan" and Lindner's (1944) "Rebel Without a Cause," are shown in Figure 19.

In summarizing the results of their analysis of these six cases in terms of the DRQ, Cofer and Chance say, in part:

It is evident from this study that the expected decline in DRQ has been found for every case. Although it is important to test this method on published cases in which treatment was unsuccessful, so far at least the DRQ has, in general, behaved as it should (p. 223).

Here, then, is presumptive validity, which is further substantiated by the following remarks by the authors:

[In the case of Smith], the counselor comments that other problems arose late in the counseling sequence [cf. rise in DRQ]. The later peak in the other case (Tilden) seems to be associated with the introduction by the client of attitudes toward family members which previously had not been emphasized. In respect to the Tilden case, the counselor reported a setback some time after counseling ended and expressed doubt as to the final outcome. In the Smith case, the client later stated that he probably terminated counseling too early. None of these reservations is made by either counselor or client in the other three [nondirective] cases. The judge in this study noted that, in general, when the client stated that he felt no progress was occurring the DRQ likewise showed a plateau (p. 221).

The DRQ curves for Rogers' "Bryan" and Lindner's "Rebel Without a Cause" (RBW) have been put together in Figure 19 in order to emphasize the differences between the two cases—and possibly the differences between the two therapeutic procedures involved. That the course and magnitude of the cases were strikingly dissimilar is immediately apparent. But the comparison is confounded by the fact that there is represented here not only a difference in therapeutic theory and method but also, quite possibly, a difference in the type of case involved. Still another possible source of "variance" is the individuality of the two therapists. As Fiedler shows elsewhere in this volume (Chapter 12), even though two (or more) individuals profess to belong to the same school of therapy, they may differ more (as judged by certain criteria) than do therapists nominally representing different schools.

Assuming for the moment that "Bryan" and "RBW" represent cases of equal seriousness and complexity and that the experience and proficiency of the two therapists were approximately the same, then the Rogers case is far and away the more successful. Not only does this case involve only eight interviews as contrasted to forty-six in the other, but the therapeutic end point, as determined by the DRQ, is considerably lower (indicating greater gain) in the Rogers case than in the Lindner case.

In the preceding paragraph, we have interpreted the difference between the two cases (as reflected by the curves) in the way optimally favorable to the nondirective case. Let us now give the analytic argument the benefit of all doubts. The commentary might go something like this: "The therapy shown in the case of 'Bryan' is no therapy at all! If the man had a real neurosis, it was never touched, much less cured, by the nondirective procedure. In the Lindner case, the picture is different. Here it appears that the patient came into full relationship with the therapist, with manifestation of resistance, transference, and the other painful experiences associated with 'depth therapy' and that, with the forty-first interview, a crisis was reached which led to a restructuring of the personality and progressive consolidation of gains."

But this argument leaves unanswered the question as to why the same index which is accepted as meaningfully reflecting the course of therapeutic progress in the one case does not do so in the other. If the DRQ is significant in the one case, why is it not in the other as well? If, in other words, the terminal drop in DRQ in the Lindner case is taken as signifying therapeutic success, why is not the much earlier and more spectacular drop in this index in the Rogers case similarly interpreted? The rejoinder might be as follows: " 'Bryan' merely discovered that there was no potency in the nondirective approach and swiftly talked himself *out* of therapy. If, by his own report, he soon began to feel fine, then he was 'through' and there was no point in his continuing the interviews." Here, as indicated above, the assumption would be that radical therapy is impossible unless patient and therapist "work through the transference." In the case of "Bryan" there is no indication that this occurred, the common assumption of the nondirectivists being that successful and significant therapy can occur without transference and that, indeed, transference reactions may do more to get in the way of therapy than to facilitate it.

Or, in the same skeptical vein, one might argue the issue on very different grounds by holding that the problems involved in the two cases were probably entirely different: In that of "Bryan" it might be supposed that his problems were of a more superficial, practical nature and proved capable of resolution within the course of a few interviews, whereas in the case of "RBW" the problems were far more deep-seated, more endogenous, and truly psychological; hence the more protracted treatment required.

It is interesting to compare the DRQ curve for Lindner's patient, "RBW," with the curve for "Mrs. X," a patient treated by Mowrer (Figure 19). Both of these therapies were "hypoanalytical," or "analytically oriented," they lasted for about the same length of time, and the DRQ curves for the two cases are remarkably similar. The curve for "Mrs. X," reproduced from a preliminary study by Rollins and Twaite (1950), is based upon DRQ values obtained for every tenth interview. It is therefore less fully delineated than is the curve for "RBW," but it is striking how closely parallel the two curves are in over-all pattern. Many of the same kinds of observations might thus be made regarding the relationship between the case of "Mrs. X" and "Bryan" as have already been suggested with respect to "Bryan" and "RBW."

A noteworthy feature of the curves reproduced both in Figure 18 and Figure 19 is that most of the drop in DRQ occurs between the next to last and last interviews. This is strikingly true in the cases of Moore, Tilden, and Smith, in Figure 18, and of "RBW" and "Mrs. X," in Figure 19. (The effect is less marked in the cases of Madison and "Bryan.") Here there is at least a suggestion that the DRQ for the last interview is lower precisely because both patient and therapist know it is the last— and are trying to put a good face on their labors (cf. the "hello-good-bye" effect" of Hathaway (see Chapter 13). On the other hand, it might be maintained that the "last" interview need not, in most instances, necessarily be the last, since therapeutic contact can, by mutual consent, be either continued or subsequently renewed; and it can also be appropriately noted that once a patient has obtained alleviation of his suffering, it is the most natural thing in the world for him to remove himself immediately from the degrading (and perhaps expensive) position of being in treatment. To be sure that treatment has really "taken," we should, of course, have a series of interviews with the patient after the major drop in DRQ has occurred and, ideally, one or more later follow-up interviews. Some approximation of this check is achieved in the cases of Madison and "Bryan" (cf. also the Assum-Levy case, Figure 16). Here, obviously, is a matter which needs to be controlled. While the available evidence does not by any means indicate that the terminal DRQ drops are necessarily due to the "good-bye" effect, neither does it exclude this as an important possibility in some instances.

Still other speculations may occur to the reader, but the one fact which rises out of the discussion thus far is this: nothing like a well designed experiment has yet been carried out which would unequivocally indicate the greater therapeutic efficacy of one technique or approach over another. More than this, although there is some evidence for the validity of the particular method of measurement which is here used, its validity is still open to question. However, it would appear that we are almost ready to design investigations in this area which, though not so neatly controllable as laboratory researches, may nevertheless have considerable methodological sophistication and may lead to convincing results (see Hunt, 1952).

Psychological Tension in Nondirective Counseling: Studies by Natalie Rogers

In an unpublished paper entitled "Measuring Psychological Tension in Nondirective Counseling," [3] Natalie Rogers has reported some extraordinarily interesting results which were obtained by means of the DRQ technique. Rogers summarizes her work as follows:

[3] This paper appeared in *The personal counselor* (hectographed, 1949), pp. 237-63 (E. H. Porter, Jr., ed.).

The purpose of this study was to explore with a modification of Dollard and Mowrer's *DRQ* technique the likelihood of using such a technique in measuring psychological tension in nondirective case material. No critical statistical methods were used which would yield bases for saying with what level of confidence the results and comparisons might be judged as reliable and valid. Visual inspections of graphic comparisons between the variations in *DRQ*'s obtained in three cases and (*a*) the counselors' judgments of case success, (*b*) measures of acceptance of self obtained by Sheerer, (*c*) measures of attitudes toward self obtained by Stock, (*d*) measures of problem-statements, planning, and insight obtained by Seeman *et al.*, and (*e*) measures of behavior-maturity obtained by Hoffman all suggest that the *DRQ* very likely does contain a measure of validity which it would be worth while to determine with exactitude.

It is interesting to note that the comparisons made suggest the possibility of a high intercorrelation between measures of quite different personality expressions, the possibility that a unitary factor may be at the basis of the personality changes which occur in therapy (p. 263).

Rogers describes the general design of her research in these terms:

Three recorded and transcribed [nondirective] cases were chosen out of ten such cases on the basis of their varying degree of success. The cases have been titled for convenience with false names so as to be identified easily. Those chosen were Miss Vib, Mrs. Sim, and Mrs. Dem. These cases have been rated on a counselor rating scale from 1 to 9, with the higher numbers indicating an estimate of greater success. Each counselor rated his case as to its degree of success. The following ratings were given to each case:

Miss Vib: 9, considered a success

Mrs. Sim: 7, considered fairly successful

Mrs. Dem: 1, considered a failure

The case of Miss Vib consists of 9 interviews, Mrs. Sim 7, and Mrs. Dem 3. The total number of statements analyzed for the Discomfort-Relief Quotient was 3291.

There were definite purposes in selecting cases with ratings of various degrees of success. The first purpose was to determine if the *DRQ* varied with the rated success or failure of each case. The second purpose was to determine if the *DRQ* correlates with other measures of success of the counseling process, *i.e.*, is discomfort evident when negative feelings about the self are present and is relief evident when positive feelings about the self are expressed (pp. 240-41).

The procedure used in this investigation consisted of judging only statements made *by the patient* and of using sentences, rather than words or independent clauses (see Chapter 10), as the basic research unit. In an attempt to make the *DRQ* as precise as possible, Miss Rogers decided to use only those statements made in the *present tense* (although a preliminary test indicated that the results are not much different if both present and past tenses are used—see Chapter 17). Preliminary tests also indicated that the one person who did most of the scoring in this investigation did it reliably, since her results, on selected interviews, compared favorably with those of a second scorer.

The results thus obtained are shown in Figure 20. The *DRQ* curve for "Dem," the unsuccessful case, shows the least change; the curve for "Sim," the moderately successful case, shows greater change; and the

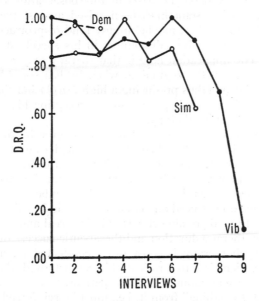

Fig. 20.—Curves derived (by Natalie Rogers, 1949) from the analysis of three cases of nondirective counseling by means of the *DRQ* method. "Vib" was judged, in advance of this analysis, to have been a highly successful case, "Dem" a very unsuccessful case, and "Sim" an intermediate case.

curve for "Vib," the most successful case, shows the greatest amount of change. The changes in *DRQ* from first interview to last interview in each of these three cases are, respectively: —.05, .21, and .88, values which correspond moderately well with the counselor ratings of 1, 7, and 9. These findings, says Rogers, provide the basis for "further inference of the validity of the *DRQ* as a measure of tension" (p. 250).

A limitation of these results, in addition to the small number of cases, is the fact that the judged success of the cases is correlated, or "confounded," with *case length*. There is nothing in the three curves reproduced in Figure 20 which indicates that they necessarily differ in any respect save in extent. All three start at about the same level and, so far as they go, all follow about the same course. Therefore, in the data themselves, there is nothing to counter the assumption that if the first two cases had lasted as long as the third one did, the resulting curves would have been essentially similar. In other words, all that the curves show unequivocally is *how long* each of the three patients stayed in therapy—three, seven, and nine interviews respectively—and a tendency for the curves to drop as therapy continues.

We may thus infer, since number of interviews correlates so highly with counselor judgments of success (1, 7, and 9), that at least one of the factors which counselors took into account (consciously or otherwise) in judging therapeutic success or failure was how long the patient stayed in therapy. And on the basis of this observation one can voice an objection which has sometimes been raised against the *DRQ* technique (or similar methods) : maybe, in any kind of protracted conversations, a person ceases to show discomfort in his speech, if he just talks long enough! The implication here is that therapy may be quite useless and that the patient in the beginning, when he has some hope of help, describes his problems (thus producing a high *DRQ*) but that as therapy (?) continues, he loses this hope and stops presenting his problems and, sooner or later, also stops therapy.[4]

These objections can be answered in some degree by the observation that, with therapy duration "held constant," [5] one does find instances (see Figure 19, also Figure 87 in Chapter 18) in which the *DRQ* curve follows markedly different courses for different patients, thus indicating that such a curve may reflect something more than the number of interviews involved—which we do not need an elaborate statistical analysis to give us! But at the same time, there almost certainly is a real and important relationship between therapy duration and therapeutic success or accomplishment. Since psychotherapy is most often conducted on an outpatient basis, with the patient free to terminate his contacts with the therapist at will; and since we may assume that the patient, to continue in therapy, must be "getting something" from it, i.e., must be reinforced (in terms of learning theory) for making the responses involved in therapy, then it would indeed be surprising if there were no relationship between the duration and the "success" of cases.

However, this line of thought immediately poses another problem: A patient may be "getting something" from therapy, but what he is getting may not be what he needs for genuine therapeutic progress. A patient may, for example, enjoy the sedatives, reassurances, or other opiate experiences which physicians may provide (cf. the "deep narcissistic regression" which Alexander and French (1946) have suggested that certain types of psychoanalysis provide) without the patient learning

[4] For a discussion of results regarding the course of the discomfort-relief quotient during a single interview, see the concluding section of this chapter.

[5] This expression is put in quotation marks to indicate that in psychotherapy, unlike laboratory research, it is only a manner of speaking to say that the duration of therapy can be held constant while other factors are systematically varied. We cannot, for example, deliberately vary the skill of the therapist and yet expect patients to stay in therapy exactly as long as they would if this factor were not varied. If, with two widely different degrees of skill on the part of the therapist, two different patients stay in treatment for equally long periods of time, we would be led to expect the presence of at least one other major variable, *viz.*, the nature or seriousness of the individual's neurosis (i.e., his diagnostic type, readiness for therapy, or the like). This is a nice illustration of what happens to "experiments" when the subjects themselves have some control over the relevant variables.

anything, except to return for more of the same treatment. It is not, of course, essential that in bona fide therapy every interview must end with a feeling of relief or accomplishment on the part of the patient; but it would seem clear that, in general, unless the therapy is progressing— unless, as Harry Stack Sullivan was fond of saying, the patient is *learning something useful about himself*—he will not continue to come to therapy indefinitely. This problem will be discussed again below (see also Chapter 18).

The next phases of Miss Rogers' investigation involved a comparison of the *DRQ* curves obtained for patients "Vib," "Sim," and "Dem" and the curves obtained by means of Sheerer's (1948) index of "acceptance of self." Quoting Rogers,

The degree of self-acceptance is the extent to which the individual recognizes and admits the facts of his experience and the facts about himself and his attitudes, feelings, and abilities; the extent to which he considers himself a worth-while person with the capacity to deal with his problems. When a client is accepting of himself it means that he is aware of his own abilities and liabilities and, accepting them as such, he deals with them as a part of his whole being. One who does not accept himself is likely to be defensive, unable to view himself realistically, dissatisfied with self, and tends to live by others' values rather than his own (p. 249).

It so happened that Sheerer, with the aid of four judges, had already scored all the interviews with "Vib," "Sim," and "Dem" on a five-point scale of self-acceptance; comparison of the resulting data with the *DRQ* data was therefore a simple matter. The three pairs of curves which resulted from this comparison are shown here in Figures 21, 22, and 23. Rogers' appraisal of these results follows:

It will be noticed, in the case of "Vib," that the two lines remain very nearly parallel throughout the entire scale. When acceptance of self is low, tension is high. When the person is accepting himself, tension is decreased. The case of "Sim" evidences a similar relationship: when acceptance of self is at its low ebb, tension is at its high peak. A sharp drop in one is accompanied by a sharp change in the other.

Although the case of "Dem" suggests the same relationships between the two measures, there was actually very little change in the measures of tension or in the measures of the acceptance of self. This visual comparison holds further inference of the validity of the *DRQ* as a measure of tension (p. 250).

A somewhat similar comparison was made by Rogers of the index of change provided by the *DRQ* and by an index developed by Dorothy Stock (1948) of patients' "attitudes toward self." Rogers' comments in this connection will be quoted in full:

Stock made a study containing, among other things, data on the change of attitudes toward the self during counseling. Attitudes toward the self include all feelings about one's personality characteristics, intelligence, ability, be-

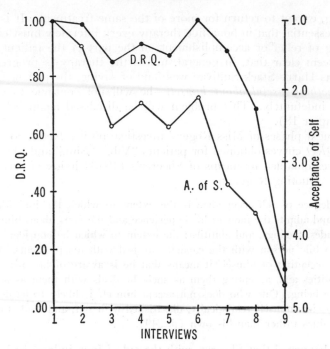

FIG. 21.—Comparison of curves obtained by *DRQ* technique and a measure developed by Sheerer (1949), for Client "Vib." Note that although there is a difference in absolute level, the two curves not only follow the same general course but also have, with minor exceptions, the same inflections. These curves, like the others reproduced in this section, are based upon data reported by Miss Natalie Rogers.

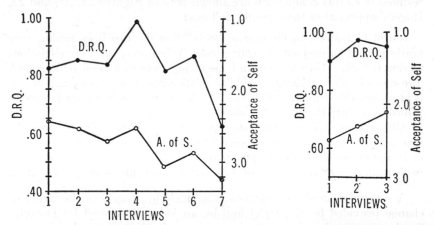

FIG. 22.—Comparison of *DRQ* curve and acceptance-of-self curve for client "Sim." Here, as in Figure 21, the two curves show the same general course and identical inflections.

FIG. 23.—Comparison of *DRQ* curve and acceptance-of-self curve for client "Dem." Here the absolute difference is marked, but both curves show an upward trend.

havior, etc. Stock developed a rating scale which was applied to each client statement that contained attitudes toward the self. The following is the scale used:

5. A positive expression of attitude toward self which is highly emotional.
4. A positive expression of attitude toward self which is intellectual in emphasis.
3. An expression which is objective or neutral.
2. A negative expression of attitude toward self which is intellectual in emphasis.
1. A negative expression of attitude toward self which is highly emotional.

It should be pointed out that this scale does not run from a highly undesirable rating to a highly desirable rating. Both extremes, ratings 1 and 5, indicate a high degree of emotion. A less tense individual presumably would be rated somewhere between 3 and 4. Evidence of the *DRQ* as a valid measure was sought by comparing the high *DRQ*'s with ratings 1 and 5, and *low DRQ*'s with ratings near 3.

The data for each of these three cases were obtained from Stock's study and graphed in relation to the *DRQ*: [see Figures 24, 25, and 26]. These figures suggest again a strong relationship between the *DRQ* and a differently determined evidence of tension. In the case of "Vib" as the *DRQ* increases or decreases, so does the rating of attitudes toward the self increase and

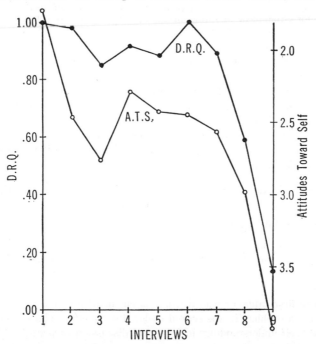

Fig. 24.—Curves showing the course of counseling in case of "Vib," as determined by *DRQ* and by attitudes-toward-self (Stock, 1948). The general similarity of the two curves is evident.

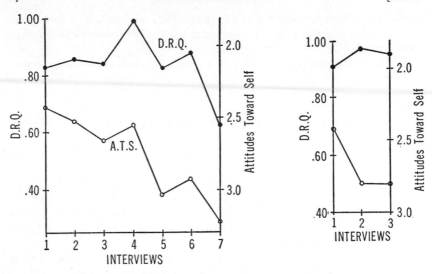

Fig. 25.—Course of counseling in case of "Sim," as indicated by *DRQ* and attitudes-toward-self. Note similarity of inflections, as well as general downward course in both instances.

Fig. 26.—Course of counseling in case of "Dem," as indicated by *DRQ* and attitudes-toward-self. Here the curve obtained by the former method agrees with the counselor's judgment of rating of therapeutic nonsuccess better than does the curve obtained by the latter method.

decrease. As attitudes toward the self become positive (but not highly emotional) so, too, is the measure of tension lower. The same is true with the case of *Sim*. We notice that the case of *Dem* does not follow the same pattern as the two more "successful" cases. Here the tension remains relatively the same in all three interviews, yet the attitudes toward the self become somewhat more positive. These same tendencies appear evident, however, at the outset of the longer cases and might possibly be typical of the initial phase of counseling (pp. 250-53).

Rogers carried out a comparison of the *DRQ,* for the three cases considered above, with certain "content" categories as identified by Seeman and others (1948). She says:

Seeman *et al.* made a study which, among other things, determined the various patterns of client content during the course of therapy. Client statements were analyzed and categorized according to their content. The data from two of these categories [have here been] compared with the data of the *DRQ*. The first category was titled, "statement of problems." Any time the client stated a problem it was scored under this column. The second category was titled "self-understanding, insight, and discussion of plans." These three things were grouped together into one category because increase in these categories has been shown previously to be associated with successful therapy. It was again judged that validity of the *DRQ* might be inferred should the

DRQ decrease when statements of problems decreased and as insight and positive planning increased.

The data for these comparisons is graphed in [Figures 27, 28, and 29]. It will be noticed in each figure that the number of problems stated by the client appears to parallel closely the trend of feelings of discomfort. That is, as fewer problems are stated, lower *DRQ*'s are obtained, and as a greater number of problems are mentioned, the *DRQ*'s are higher. As would be expected, discussion of plans, insight, and self-understanding has an opposite

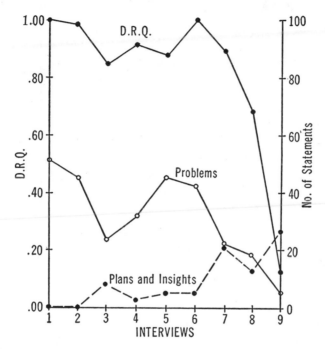

Fig. 27.—*DRQ* curve for "Vib" compared with Statement-of-Problems and Plans-and-Insights curves, as computed by Seeman *et al.* (1948). The *DRQ* and Problems curves decline together as the Plans-and-Insights curve rises.

trend to statements of problems and *DRQ*. Here, too, there appears to be a systematic relationship between the *DRQ*'s obtained and the measures of planning and insight, with the relationship being inverse. To the extent that statement of problems can be taken as evidence of psychological tension and to the extent that planning and insight can be taken as evidence of lack of tension, it would appear that the *DRQ*'s obtained did measure the relative presence and absence of tension (pp. 253-56).

Rogers' final study consisted of a comparison of *DRQ* scores for the three reference cases with measures of "maturity" developed by Hoffman (1948). Again Miss Rogers' remarks will be quoted in full:

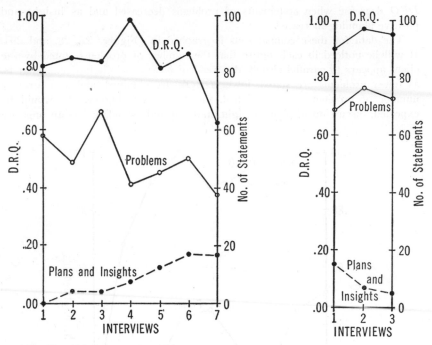

Fig. 28.—*DRQ* curve for "Sim" compared with curves for Statement-of-Problems and Plans-and-Insights. The same relationship is evident here as is shown in Figure 12.

Fig. 29.—*DRQ* curve for "Dem" compared with curves for Statement-of-Problems and Plans-and-Insights. In this unsuccessful case, there is the same tendency as noted in Figure 27 and Figure 28 for the *DRQ* and Statement-of-Problems curves to move together in one direction (in this instance, upward), while the curve for Plans-and-Insights goes in the opposite direction.

Hoffman studied the amount of change in the maturity of reported behavior during counseling. The following rating method was devised. Behavior references were classified into three categories.

Rating Scale:

C. The individual is behaving with little or no control over his environment; he is immature and not responsible.

B. The individual is exercising some control over his environment; he is manifesting some maturity and some responsible action.

A. The individual is behaving with a good deal of self-direction, maturity, and responsibility.

The total number of client statements falling into these categories was determined and totaled for each interview. This gives us raw data for A, B, and C behavior. In order to compare this data with the *DRQ*'s, these three types of behavior were weighted and an average for each interview was found. "A" behavior was given a weight of 3, "B" behavior a weight of 2, and "C" behavior a weight of 1. This gives a range from 1 to 3 indicating the relative maturity of behavior, 3 being a rating of highly mature.

It would seem reasonable to assume that more immature behavior might be associated with more tension, more mature behavior with less psychological tension. Figures [30, 31, and 32] suggest that if the assumption is essentially correct, once again the *DRQ* seems to measure psychological tension as evidenced by its apparent relationship to behavior maturity (pp. 256-63).

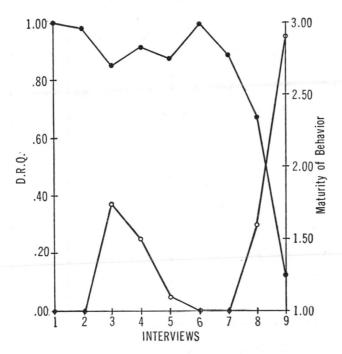

Fig. 30.—Comparison of *DRQ* curve for "Vib" with the maturity-of-behavior curve obtained for the same case by Hoffman (1948). Although the latter curve is somewhat erratic, it presents, as might be predicted, a rough "mirror image" of the *DRQ* curve.

These observations on the relationship between the *DRQ* and personal maturity, limited and tentative as they are, are extremely suggestive. As the reader will have noted, all the studies reviewed in the second and third sections of this chapter are consistent with the assumption that the *DRQ* is reliable and, very likely, valid. At the same time, it will be recalled that in the first section evidence has been reported which indicates that the *DRQ* consistently correlates poorly with the judgment of social case-workers regarding the goodness or success of social casework.

One might at first conjecture that there is a basic difference between psychotherapy and case work, with the latter being quite as much, or more, preoccupied with the administration of financial and other forms of physical "relief" as with personality change. As is well known, social work began as a "helping process" in the charitable sense but matured into a process of "helping others help themselves" which, as commonly implemented in contemporary casework practice, is often not essentially different from counseling and psychotherapy. While it is true that caseworkers in a large agency like the Community Service Society will view the giving of financial "relief" on occasion as part of their professional responsibility, they are usually more concerned about "relief" in the psychological sense.

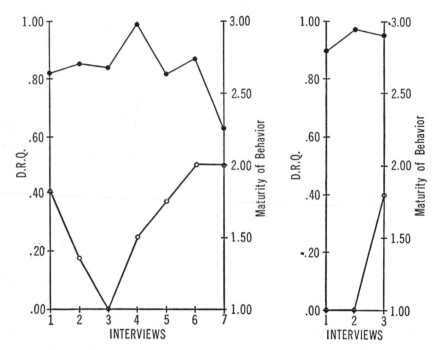

FIG. 31.—Comparison of *DRQ* curve for "Sim" with maturity-of-behavior curve. While the former moves downward, there is a tendency for the latter to rise.

FIG. 32.—Comparison of *DRQ* curve for "Dem" with maturity-of-behavior curve. Here, in contrast to Figures 30 and 31, the two curves tend to move in the same direction. One may conjecture that the rise in the maturity-of-behavior on the third interview in this case is spurious.

We cannot, therefore, assume that either the goals or the methods of casework and psychotherapy are so very different; and even if there be a difference along the lines just suggested, there is no reason to suppose that the *DRQ* would be differentially sensitive to psychological relief. Indeed, a possible criticism which might be leveled against the method is that it would not enable one to distinguish, on the basis of a nicely descending curve, whether such a change reflects real learning and greater capacity to cope with day-to-day problems or whether these problems, by outside aid or intervention, have been artificially eased and simplified. On the premise that social workers today have a higher regard for casework which provides psychological relief than for the giving of mere financial assistance or other forms of situational manipulation, it might be inferred that caseworker judgments and *DRQ* results correlate poorly (among other reasons—see above) because the *DRQ* measures both of these effects indiscriminately. On the other hand, the last of the studies carried out by Rogers suggests that the *DRQ* correlates rather closely with growth in personal maturity, rather than merely with gain in personal comfort. However, this is a point on which the data are by no means conclusive and one which may, with further investigation, prove useful in accounting for what now stands as a baffling inconsistency.

DRQ Changes Within Individual Interviews

Thus far in this chapter we have been concerned with the use of the discomfort-relief quotient as a means of charting tension change throughout the course of an entire psychotherapy or social casework record. The question which we now wish to ask is: Can the same measure be used to chart the course of tension change during a single interview and, if so, with what results?

In connection with the comparison of verbatim intake interviews and dictated summary records which was referred to in an earlier section, Kogan (1951) has made a preliminary attempt to answer this question. He says:

A second exploratory aspect to the study was directed toward a trend analysis of *DRQ*'s in the initial casework interview. For this purpose the thirty-six verbatim interviews were broken down into three successive sections, each section containing roughly the same number of client statements. A client statement was defined as the total response of the client occurring between two successive responses of the worker. An analysis of variance of the *DRQ*'s was carried out which resulted ultimately in a test of the significance of differences between mean *DRQ*'s for each of the three successive portions of the interviews. The mean *DRQ* for the first section was 86.2; the mean *DRQ* for the middle section was 79.8; the mean *DRQ* for the last section was 82.6. The P value for the difference between the first section of the interviews and the middle section fell at a confidence level of less than .01, while the other two differences were "not statistically significant." This suggests that the distress expressed was relatively lowest in the middle portion of these intake casework interviews. It was felt that no attempt should be made to interpret this finding in terms of the content or casework process of the initial interview until future study would confirm that this "dip" in expressed distress is a genuinely consistent phenomenon (pp. 6-7).

Boder (1951) has used the *DRQ* for analyzing the course of tension during single interviews with persons who had undergone life in concentration camps in Nazi Germany (see his book, *I did not interview the dead,* 1949). The resulting curves are shown in Figure 33. Dr. Boder has generously supplied the following comments to accompany his curves, which are previously unpublished.

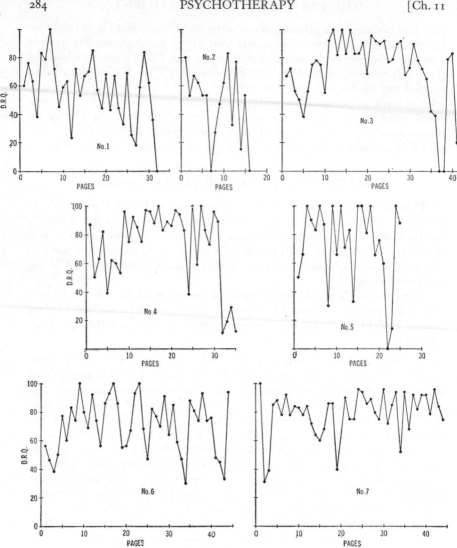

Fig. 33.—Seven curves, obtained by the *DRQ* method, which represent tension changes during the course of interviews conducted by D. P. Boder with "displaced persons." Although each of these curves is based on the scoring of one person, each of the interviews was independently scored by three persons; but the results, according to Boder, were so similar that "averaged" curves were only slightly different from those here reproduced.

The article by Dollard and Mowrer on the *DRQ* as a technique for the analysis of tension in verbatim recorded reports appeared in January, 1947, when the author was working on the first analysis of the autobiographies of displaced persons, collected shortly before in the D.P. camps of Europe. During the actual interviews and by listening and relistening to the recordings, the investigator could not help observing the fluctuations in language dynamics and expressive vocalizations (weeping, shouting accompanied at times by pounding on the table, whispering, and sighing) of the interviewees. It became apparent in many cases that, as the interview progressed, narratives of great emotional impact were being alternated either with reports of insignificant events or with reports of occurrences no less tragic than the preceding ones but invested in language reflecting in tone and choice of vocabulary a great deal of composure and matter-of-factness. It appeared to the investigator that these alternations might be interpreted as fluctuations either in selectivity of memory or in expressive dynamics, and that the emotional drop in the narrative represents in some way a phenomenon of fatigue or refractory phase brought about as a consequence of preceding intensive emotional display. One could not help observing at times in the behavior of the interviewee a component of embarrassment capable of toning down the force of the report, as if the interviewee was expecting some expression of sympathy or encouragement from the interviewer before proceeding with other high points of his recollections. Our observations indicate that these fluctuations of emotional impact within the interview are readily reflected in the DRQ values.

It is possible that the "process of therapeutic learning" to which the authors of this chapter refer is substantially enhanced during such phases of emotional plateaus when the interviewee, emotionally exhausted or blunted, comes to discuss his problems with less "feeling" and consequently with greater "non-inhibited" insight. Of course, not all interviews for which the DRQ's were computed present such drops at the end of the interview. This however does not contradict in any way the assumption made that where these drops of DRQ's do occur they may be indicative that a therapeutic factor is in operation.

The investigator, as well as the research assistants who engaged in the computing of the DRQ's of the interviews with displaced persons, could not help observing that a spurt in the DRQ is readily produced by some remark of the interviewer. In spite of the intention to make the interviews with the displaced persons as nondirective as possible, the interviewer felt compelled at times to interpose some questions or remarks which, on many occasions, would arouse an unexpected burst of statements of intense emotional import. This is precisely akin to the situations, pointed out by the authors, wherein social workers initiate "further exploration" after the story, as such, has been told by the client.

The curves shown in Figure 33 have been arranged to form a progression from the one with the greatest downward trend to the one with the least downward (actually some upward) trend. Dr. Boder has volunteered the information that this type of variation in the curves corresponds roughly to his impressions concerning the psychological status of the persons interviewed: the persons whose DRQ curves tend to go down during or at the end of the interview gave independent evidence, he felt, of being better adjusted at the time than did those persons whose curves did not drop or actually rose. The former type of person may have gone through some very terrible experiences, and as he relates these his DRQ

will be high; but now things are better, the story has had a happy ending, and everything is going to be all right—hence the terminal drop in the curve. But let us suppose that the interviewee has been so traumatized, so disorganized, so degraded by his experiences that he continues to suffer, not realistically, but emotionally, neurotically; let us suppose that he is *still* miserable. As the account of such a person comes up to the present, there being as yet no happy ending we would not expect his discomfort-relief quotient to drop in any very substantial way.

It was this type of interpretation of the data which Boder had in mind when he reported the impression that the descending curves come from well-adjusted interviewees and the curves that remain high throughout (e.g., curves 6 and 7) come from persons much less well adjusted. Here is a crude kind of validation of the DRQ as a measure of psychological tension, but the criterion against which the validation is made is so impressionistic that only limited confidence can be placed in it.

The foregoing discussion suggests another point which should be considered. Boder's subjects undertook the interviews with the understanding that they were merely to have an opportunity to tell their story with respect to concentration-camp life, and what happened to them before and afterwards. They were neither promised nor given any form of help, emotional or material; and the interviewer was almost entirely passive, except for occasional questions of fact. Certainly the interviews had no avowedly therapeutic motive, yet the DRQ curves often look as if there had been a kind of therapeutic effect.

Two considerations appear relevant here. We know that it is a not uncommon experience to find relief in just "talking out" one's troubles to another person even though that person does nothing more than indicate that he has heard and, at least partially, understood. This sort of thing may have occurred to some extent in Boder's situation. But it is also probably true that the DRQ tended to drop as the interview proceeded merely because the subjects, as suggested above, had nothing more very terrible to relate. They had, in other words, "talked themselves out," both emotionally *and* factually, historically. We thus see the possibility that the DRQ may reflect not only the *current* emotional status of the subject; it may also *tell a story,* a story of "ups and downs," of adventures and misadventures, but a story of events which are now *past.* To the extent that the DRQ is thus confounded, it might be a desirable refinement, when we are trying to get at current psychological status, to use, let us say, only statements of discomfort and relief which are couched in the present (or possibly future) tense. The fact that a person has *been through* bad times and experiences does not mean that he is necessarily *now* uncomfortable or unhappy. As T. H. Blau has suggested, in a personal communication, a rise in the DRQ may mean merely "a rehashing of former tensions expressed largely in the past tense." Differentiation between statements made in the present and in the past tense might, at least in some circumstances, constitute a desirable innovation in DRQ methodology.

But why, we may now ask, did not the *DRQ* curves obtained by Kogan for intake interviews show a similar downward trend? Why did they move downward reliably from the first to the second third of the interview and then point back up again? It may have been that, in the casework situation, the worker was largely passive during the first part of the interview but then became *more active,* in turn *activating the patient* and causing the upturn in the *DRQ* curve. This supposition is highly tentative, but it would fit with the fact that Boder was passive throughout his interviews and obtained curves that, in general, continued to decline right to the end, whereas the social workers, instead of merely thanking and dismissing their clients after they had "told their story," initiated further exploration and planning with them.

In the light of some of the ambiguities just discussed, it would be useful to know what regular therapeutic interviews look like in terms of the discomfort-relief quotient. Do they, for example, show any consistent trend from beginning to end? Or do they vary greatly in this respect from session to session? The only data known to the writers which are relevant here are those collected by Rollins and Twaite (1950) from the case of "Mrs. X," already briefly referred to. These investigators determined the *DRQ* for the first ten minutes and for the last ten minutes of the 1st, 11th, 21st, 31st, 41st, and 51st (last) interview of a fully recorded psychotherapy. The results are shown in Figure 34. As will

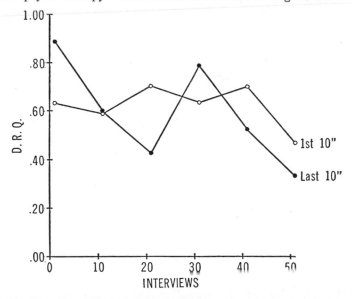

Fig. 34.—Two curves showing the relationship of psychological tension, as measured by the *DRQ,* during the first and last ten minutes of six psychotherapeutic interviews (the 1st, 11th, 21st, 31st, 41st, 51st and last). As will be noted, the tension level for the first ten minutes shows only a slight downward trend throughout the course of treatment, whereas the tension level for the last ten minutes declines markedly. These curves are reproduced from an exploratory study by Rollins and Twaite (1950).

be seen, the results were inconclusive in that, in three of the six interviews chosen for analysis, the DRQ was higher at the end than at the beginning, whereas in the other three interviews the reverse was true.

Attention has already been called to the relationship between a patient's continuing or discontinuing psychotherapy and the amount of relief or discomfort experienced therein. However, on the earlier page where this problem was mentioned, reference was made only to the overall trends in such a measure as the DRQ. Here let us ask a somewhat different question: How important is it that patients should, in general, have the experience of "feeling better" when they end an interview than when they started it? If there is commonly a downward trend in discomfort during individual interviews, the responses involved in therapy would presumably be rewarded and the patient would be inclined to continue making them; but if, on the other hand, there is usually an increase in discomfort during individual interviews, therapy would be a punishing experience and the patient would have a tendency to terminate it.

However, there is more to the problem than this. Not all the rewards and punishments connected with therapy are experienced during the course of the therapeutic hour. Patients report that between interviews they often "do a lot of thinking," and their attitude toward therapy will be somewhat influenced by whether their therapy-centered activities between interviews are, in general, clarifying or confusing, rewarding or punishing. An eminent psychiatrist once remarked that "every interview with me is a stress interview," thus implying that his patients probably quite regularly left his office less tranquil than when they entered. If this were indeed the case, then most of the reinforcement which kept patients in treatment with him (when this was not supplied by coercion) must have come from the clarification, insights, and satisfactions experienced between interviews. Here we can do no more than indicate the nature of this engrossing problem; it is discussed more systematically in Chapter 18.

To return briefly to Figure 34, there is one interesting trend to be noted: Whereas the DRQ for the initial ten-minute period remains relatively constant during the entire course of the therapy, the DRQ for the terminal ten-minute period shows a downward trend. With such fragmentary data as are here available, generalizations are hazardous; but it would not be surprising if further investigation shows that interpretation, reflection, or other technically determined behavior on the part of the therapist are somewhat "upsetting" to the patient during the early stages of therapy but that, as therapy proceeds, they come to be more and more tranquilly accepted and effectively utilized by the patient. If this were true, one would perhaps expect a tendency, of the kind evident in Figure 34, for the DRQ to rise or remain constant during early interviews and to drop during the later interviews. But here, however, we are venturing into a no man's land in which plausible-looking explanations may be merely booby-traps for the unwary.

The foregoing discussion raises one other problem which should be briefly noted. If, as therapy proceeds, it becomes an increasingly agreeable experience (save for the complexities of transference), one may reasonably ask: Why does anyone ever *leave* therapy? Why does it not become a kind of addiction? Two considerations are relevant here. In the first place there is nearly always an element of inconvenience, and thus ambivalence, involved in therapy. One might think most immediately in this connection of the cost, but it is doubtful if free therapies (if properly conducted) ordinarily last much longer than do fee therapies, for there are nearly always additional elements of inconvenience and humiliation. Moreover, as therapy proceeds, if it is successful, it means that the patient's therapeutic needs diminish. Functions which initially have to be performed by the therapist become self-functions (see Chapter 3), and the patient becomes able to "take with him" that for which he had, in the beginning, to go to the therapist. In short, we may suppose that the dynamics of therapy (disregarding the transference, which one can never do entirely) would go as follows: The factors which tend to drive persons out of therapy (fees, inconvenience, humiliation, etc.) tend to remain relatively constant, whereas the forces that drive them into therapy diminish, with the result that when a point of diminishing returns is reached, they stop.[6] There would thus appear to be no serious difficulty in reconciling the fact that patients eventually leave successful therapy with the inference that as therapy proceeds it becomes (at least up to a point) an increasingly satisfactory experience. In simplest terms, it is as if the patient comes to therapy with intense drives (anxiety, depression, inferiority feeling, etc.) which he does not know how otherwise to reduce; in therapy he learns to do so and then eventually finds that he no longer has any impulsion, or need, to continue "in therapy." What he has learned, i.e., "the therapy," has become a way of life!

Application of the DRQ to Psychotic Verbalizations

A study recently reported by Meadow, Greenblatt, Levine, and Solomon (1952) raises a number of interesting questions regarding the significance and utility of the Discomfort-Relief Quotient, which should be examined in some detail. These investigators summarize their findings in these words:

Two experiments designed to test the validity of the use of the DRQ as a measure of psychological tension and adjustment are described. Thirty-five chronic schizophrenic patients randomly selected from a pre-lobotomy schizophrenic group at the Boston Psychopathic Hospital were used as subjects.

⁶ Another interesting, though somewhat tangential, question arises here: What, in terms of the foregoing discussion, is the difference between a therapy which is terminated ("prematurely") by the patient because he feels it is a failure and a therapy which is terminated by the patient (perhaps at a much later date) because he feels that it has been a success? The difference, one would suppose, might be roughly the same as that between a rat's ceasing to push a "Skinner bar" because expected food was not forthcoming (extinction) and a rat's ceasing to push such a bar because the pushing had "worked" and the food thus obtained had fully satisfied the rat's hunger (satiation).

In the first experiment, the *DRQ*'s derived from the protocols of a newly devised free verbalization test were correlated with clinical ratings of tension made by a psychiatrist. The test-retest reliability coefficient for the *DRQ* was +.82; interscorer reliability for the quotient was +.77. The reliability coefficient for two independent raters of tension was +.78. The results indicated a zero correlation between the *DRQ* and the rating of clinical tension.

In the second experiment the *DRQ* was correlated with three groups of measures of adjustment—namely, a series of abstraction tests, an index of "looseness of association," and a clinical rating of "personality integration."

Test-retest reliability coefficients for the measures of abstraction ranged from +.89 to +.94; for the looseness of association index the test-retest reliability coefficient was +.78. Interscorer reliability coefficients for the tests of abstraction and looseness of association ranged from +.89 to +.97.

The results indicated a positive relationship between the *DRQ* and all measures of adjustment.

The results of both experiments are interpreted to indicate that a relatively high *DRQ* cannot be used as a valid measure of tension but may be used as an indicator of good adjustment in schizophrenia.

To interpret the positive correlation between a relatively high amount of expressed discomfort and relatively good adjustment, we hypothesize that the more serious maladjustments in schizophrenia are accompanied by intensified defensive processes that prevent the conscious recognition and verbal expression of feelings of discomfort.

The assumption of previous investigators that a relatively low *DRQ* is indicative of low "tension" state, good adjustment, and therapeutic success is challenged by the results of the present experiments (p. 661).

On the basis of this summary, a possibility immediately suggests itself for reconciling the findings of Meadow *et al.*—or at least some of them— with the results previously discussed. With the exception of the Community Service Society studies, the investigations reviewed in this chapter fairly consistently support the view that the *DRQ* is positively correlated with psychological tension and that both tension and *DRQ* drop as successful therapy proceeds. In the Meadow study, on the other hand, evidence is advanced which shows a reverse trend: the better "adjusted" the individual, the *higher* the *DRQ*. But the population here, we must remember, was a peculiar one: it consisted of psychotics whose disorganization was so extreme as to seem to warrant psychosurgery. And it need not surprise us in the least if psychotic subjects show a trend with respect to the *DRQ* which is unlike or even the reverse of that of normal and neurotic subjects. Normal persons represent the ultimate in reality orientation; and neurotics, even though under great stress, are likewise still "hanging onto reality." But the psychotic has "let go." Perception, speech, and other aspects of his behavior are distorted in the interest of reducing inner tensions; and in schizophrenia speech is notoriously subject to deterioration, serving, as we say, autistic rather than communicative functions.

Meadow and collaborators make this same point when they remark:

Every clinician is familiar with the type of schizophrenic patient who, by his constant grimacing, restlessness, and rapid pulse, reveals considerable inner emotional turmoil, though he may not express any of this turmoil in the manifest content of his verbalizations. *The breakdown of interpersonal communication which characterizes schizophrenia perhaps makes the spoken word a relatively unreliable indicator of internal state in this group of subjects* (p. 660, italics added).

In order to get a more tangible frame of reference in which to review these findings, let us imagine a triangle the base of which represents a continuum from good (normal) personality organization, at the left, to extreme personality disorganization, at the right. And let us suppose that the height, or vertical dimension, of the triangle represents psychological tension. Let us now further assume that the *left* side, or leg, represents the region of "neurosis" and that the *right* side, or leg, represents the region of "psychosis." In other words, what our diagram then suggests is that as human beings move from normality into neurosis (on the left side of the triangle), they experience both increased tension (the vertical component) and increased personality disorganization (the horizontal component). But then, if the disorder is progressive, the individual reaches a "turning point" (apex of the triangle) at which, while still moving toward further personality disorganization, he *reverses* his direction as far as the tension dimension is concerned.

There is, we discover, some clinical support for conceptualizing the domain of psychopathology in this way. Certainly the relatively intractability of psychosis suggests that its treatment, i.e., the task of bringing the individual "back to normality," is an "uphill proposition." Since the defenses involved in psychosis are likely to become highly efficient in managing anxiety and other tensions, it may be extremely difficult to get the affected individual to give them up and move back into a region of heightened suffering.[7] Moreover, this schematization conforms to the common perception of a "qualitative" difference between neurosis and psychosis. As long as a person is still in realistic contact with his environment, we say he is merely neurotic, even though under great stress; but when he "breaks" with reality, he has, we say, "gone psychotic."

There would appear to be some justification, therefore, for making a qualitative distinction between normals and neurotics, as persons who try to use speech realistically, objectively, communicatively, and psychotics, for whom speech becomes primarily a means of coping with internal turmoil with splendid disregard of its conventional interpersonal functions. Thus we feel that the findings of Meadow *et al.*, while important in their own right, do not necessarily call into question, as these authors

---

[7] Psychotherapy with neurotics also, as we know, involves "resistance," but not in such extreme degree. Neurotic symptoms are not so "severe" as are psychotic symptoms, nor are they, presumably, so "successful" and hence so tenacious.

suggest, the reliability of the results of other studies employing the *DRQ* with essentially normal or neurotic subjects. They say:

Previous workers who have used the *DRQ* have assumed that it measured tension and that it was related inversely to good adjustment. The present research, which indicates clearly that the assumption does not hold for a clinically schizophrenic group, raises the question of its validity in neurotic patients. The further use of the *DRQ* in studies of neurotics, without further experimental justification, would appear to be unwarranted (p. 661).

As indicated in preceding sections of this chapter, there are indeed some grounds (see especially the Community Service Society investigations) for questioning the validity of the assumptions underlying the use of the *DRQ* with normal or neurotic subjects; but we are not convinced that the findings reported by Meadow and coworkers constitute such grounds. Rather do they provide a useful extension of the application of the *DRQ* method to a *new type* of subject, namely psychotics; but their findings are consistent both with what we already know about such persons (as regards their use or, rather, abuse of language) *and* with prior assumptions concerning the *DRQ,* providing that we make the allowance suggested above for the fact that in psychosis there is a kind of verbal disorganization that we do not find in neurosis. Indeed, such disorganization is one of the distinguishing and differentiating criteria of psychosis! Need we be surprised, therefore, if in making such a radical change in the type of subject studied we find that the *DRQ* performs differently?

One other major feature of the Meadow study justifies further comment. As just indicated, we do not at all agree that the results reported for psychotic subjects necessarily call into question the results previously obtained through use of the *DRQ* with neurotic patients. However, in terms of the hypothetical triangle suggested above, it is interesting to take a second look at the findings of this investigation. One of the variables which Meadow *et al.* studied in their subjects (first "experiment") was *tension,* i.e., the variable represented by the *vertical* dimension in our triangle. And the other variable which they studied (second "experiment") was "adjustment," which they defined as something ranging from "personality integration" to "impairment in abstraction, looseness of association, and personality disintegration" (p. 660), a continuum certainly reminiscent of the organization-disorganization baseline of the triangle.[8]

We may now restate the Meadow results, in terms of the triangle, as follows: The *DRQ* was found to be reliably correlated in their psychotic subjects with the variable ("adjustment," "organization") repre-

[8] One might be prompted to wonder how much range or variation there was in the "adjustment" of these subjects, since the plight of all of them was deemed sufficiently desperate to warrant lobotomy. Presumably they were all at the "end of the line" as far as clinical evaluation and manageability were concerned. The fact that there was nevertheless considerable spread in these patients in respect to the particular tests of "adjustment" administered to them suffices for purposes of the reported inquiry.

sented *horizontally* in the triangle analogy but *not* with the variable (tension) represented *vertically* in the triangle. This finding poses a provocative problem.

For neurotics we would expect goodness of adjustment or personality organization to be *negatively* correlated with the *DRQ,* because neurosis is represented by the *left* side, or leg, of the triangle. Here as one moves toward better personality organization (i.e., to the left) the function represented by this side of the triangle drops, and a downward trend means lowered tension. Since the *DRQ* is purportedly a measure of tension, then these are the results to be expected—and the ones obtained by various investigators previously cited.

Likewise, for psychotics, we would expect goodness of adjustment to be *positively* correlated with the *DRQ,* because psychosis is represented by the *right* side, or leg, of the triangle; and here, as one moves toward better personality organization (i.e., to the left) the function represented by this side of the triangle rises, and upward movements mean heightened tension. Since the *DRQ* is purportedly a measure of tension, these are, again, the results expected—and obtained by Meadow *et al.*

Up to this point there is no problem. Everything is exactly as would be predicted on the basis of the triangle. *Here* is the rub: If the inference demanded by our triangle is valid that in psychosis the better adjusted individuals are, the more tense they will be (since the right, or "psychotic," leg of the triangle points left *and up*), then we ought to find the *DRQ* correlated not only with empirical measures of adjustment but *also* with empirical measures of tension. This was not found by Meadow and his colleagues to be the case. Here are the comments of these investigators:

The correlation between the psychiatrist's clinical rating of tension and the *DRQ* derived from the free verbalization protocol was +.05. The data, therefore, indicate no direct relationship between the verbalization of tension and the over-all clinical tension level of the patient.

In further examining the *DRQ*'s and clinical ratings of tension of individual patients, possible reasons for this lack of correlation were suggested. There was one small group of patients whose hands perspired freely, whose voices quivered tremulously, whose entire mien betrayed a state of intense excitement. These patients received a very high psychiatric tension rating but appeared to be unable to verbalize either discomfort or relief and consequently achieved a relatively low *DRQ*. Other patients received a similarly low *DRQ* score but their calm, placid behavior led the clinicians to rate them as very low in tension. One group of paranoid patients received both a high psychiatric tension rating and a high *DRQ* score. A second paranoid group received an equally high psychiatric tension rating but extremely low *DRQ*'s on the basis of such verbalizations as "There's nothing wrong with the lower parts of my body, they are beautiful; I am the heavenly mother."

It appears clear from these examples that the tension of some patients is directly expressed verbally, in other cases it is not expressed at all, and in still

other cases an emotional state is expressed verbally which is the direct opposite of the behavioral picture. When all of these patients are combined into
one group the net result is the zero correlation which appears in the data.

All the foregoing seems reasonable enough, but it does not explain the
dilemma cited above. As already indicated, it is not surprising that the
correlation between the *DRQ* and "adjustment" turns out to be negative
for normal and neurotic subjects and positive for psychotic subjects;
while one might not have been able necessarily to predict this outcome,
it is certainly easy to justify *post hoc*. But what is puzzling is that while
the *DRQ* and "adjustment" correlate positively and so significantly in
the Meadow subjects, the *DRQ* and "tension," instead of likewise correlating positively (as the triangle analysis would suggest), correlate not
at all. This paradox must remain in our minds, at least for the present,
unresolved. But this finding does not, we repeat, necessarily impugn
the assumption that tension and the *DRQ* are positively and significantly
correlated in normal or neurotic subjects.

Summary

Investigations which were reviewed in the first section indicate that
discomfort-relief quotients derived from casework records, while reliable,
do not correlate very impressively with criterion measures derived from
social caseworkers' judgments of "movement." It has been established
that this failure of validation is not due to inconsistency between, or unreliability of, caseworker judgments. Nor is it due to distortions of the
case which are introduced by dictation of the record by the caseworker.
Neither *DRQ* changes nor caseworkers' judgments of "movement" predict the value ex-clients will put on the casework help they received five
years after their cases were closed.

In the second and third sections a number of other studies are reviewed
which show that *DRQ* values derived from psychotherapeutic and counseling records correlate relatively highly both with therapists' estimates
of therapeutic success and with a number of other objective measures of
personal change during therapy. While still largely in the exploratory
stages, this line of research tends to show that the *DRQ* is not only a
reliable measure but also a meaningful and valid one, i.e., that it measures
something which is an important part of the personality change which
purportedly occurs in therapy.

If the *DRQ* thus proves to be valid for psychotherapy but not for
social casework, one of two inferences would seem to be in order: (*a*)
either the processes involved and the changes brought about in therapy
and casework are different, or else (*b*) psychotherapists and caseworkers disagree in a rather systematic way about what they believe to be the
essence of the treatment process. In both casework and psychotherapy,
it is evident that the *DRQ* measures something *real;* this is shown by its
repeatedly confirmed reliability. The essence of the discrepancy lies in

the fact that psychotherapists seem to believe that the "something real" which the *DRQ* measures is an important variable in determining therapeutic success or failure; social caseworkers feel, on the other hand, that this same variable is not very significantly related to what they regard as "movement" (i.e., success or failure) in the casework process.

The discussion in these three sections is based upon results obtained by applying the discomfort-relief quotient to *entire* case records or psychotherapies. In the fourth section some preliminary data are reproduced which bear upon the question of what happens, typically, to the patient's level of tension, as reflected by the *DRQ*, during the course of a *single interview*. While these data are by no means definitive, they point up some interesting issues as to what therapy means to patients and what determines whether they will persevere in or abandon the therapeutic enterprise (see Chapter 18).

Finally a study is reviewed in which the *DRQ* was correlated with psychiatrically assessed tension and "adjustment" as measured by certain special tests in a group of schizophrenic subjects who were awaiting frontal lobotomy. The fact that the *DRQ* was found to be uncorrelated with tension in these psychotic subjects is interpreted by the original investigators as casting doubt upon the assumed correlation between the *DRQ* and tension in neurotic or normal subjects. Because there is a qualitative shift in the way psychotics (particularly schizophrenics) use, or rather *abuse,* language, it is here held that the findings of this particular study, while important in their own right, do not have any necessary bearing upon results previously reported with normal or neurotic subjects. Further analysis of the results of this study point up an interesting paradox which the present writers are not able to resolve.

CHAPTER 12

QUANTITATIVE STUDIES ON THE ROLE OF THERAPISTS' FEELINGS TOWARD THEIR PATIENTS

By FRED E. FIEDLER, Ph.D.[1]

A great deal of knowledge has accumulated about the nature and function of patients' feelings toward therapists, which have been a focus of interest for psychoanalysts ever since Freud's classical papers (Freud,* 1922, 1935a). However, relatively little has been written about the therapist's feelings toward his patient. The reason for this one-sided interest is partly historical. But also, therapists naturally find it easier to be objective about their patient's feelings toward themselves than their own feelings toward the patient. A greater degree of experimental and statistical control is therefore necessary to minimize the effects of bias and the therapist's involvement. It is hoped that we can utilize the vast fund of psychoanalytic experience as well as the experience of later schools, such as the nondirective and the Adlerian, for example, and apply the knowledge gained about patients' feelings to the exploration of therapists' feelings.

We shall assume, in common with most present-day theories of psychotherapy, that the patient's feelings toward the therapist are an integral part of treatment, and that the therapist's way of dealing with these feelings, the "handling" and "resolution of the transference neurosis" is the essential part of treatment (Alexander, 1948). For the purposes of this paper it is unimportant to specify whether the transference is to be interpreted or, for example, accepted by reflecting the patient's feelings. We shall not assume, with present texts on psychoanalytic treatment or other therapies, however, that transference "develops spontaneously as the result of continued contact with the therapist" (Appel, 1944; Alexander and French, 1946) and that it develops provided the therapist remains passive and encourages the patient to express himself freely and without reservations. The major hypothesis of this paper is (a) that all psycho-

---

[1] The writer wishes to express his appreciation to Drs. D. W. Fiske, H. F. Hunt, W. F. Soskin, D. Campbell, and J. G. Miller for their critical suggestions. The theoretical orientation of this approach emerged in group thinking in which initially Drs. R. W. Heine, R. D. Quinn, and H. A. Blumer, and later Dr. D. W. Fiske, Mr. K. S. Isaacs, and Miss Sarah Counts, played a major part.

* References are to the bibliography at the back of the book.

therapies have as their effective core the interpersonal relationship rather than specific methods of treatment, (b) that the relationship is created by the therapist, and (c) that the therapist's conveyed feelings rather than his methods are the prerequisites to the formation of a therapeutic relationship.[2] This hypothesis is, of course, far from new. We shall attempt to support it here by evidence from recent investigations.

Very briefly, some of the assumptions and rationale underlying this chapter are as follows: Many therapists see psychological maladjustment essentially in terms of maladjustment to "significant" other persons, be they real or imaginary. The patient's psychological disorder is thus caused by disrupted interpersonal relationships in childhood or later life. The patient consults a psychotherapist so that he may be aided in re-establishing sound interpersonal relationships with others on whom the patient depends for his emotional satisfactions. In order to get well, the patient must then in some manner acquire the capacity to form such relationships. Presumably he does this as a result of psychotherapy, and it is hypothesized that this capacity is acquired by actually forming an interpersonal relationship with his therapist. Moreover, successful and unsuccessful therapists [3] presumably do not differ for intellectual reasons in their ability to "tell the patient" how to accomplish his goal; they probably differ because their concomitant feelings and emotions toward the patient differ. According to a number of writers in the field (Appel, 1944; Benedek, 1946; Freud, 1935a; Horney, 1945; Kubie, 1950), the therapeutic relationship develops with little or no effort on the part of the therapist. But those who have supervised neophytes or who look back upon their own early attempts will recall that some patients never develop a relationship with their therapists. Inasmuch as this occurs very infrequently in the case of some therapists, but with undue frequency in the case of others, it seems very likely that the therapist's own feelings toward the patient are involved in the process. We shall explore in this chapter some of the feelings which are found in good therapists as contrasted with those found in poor therapists, and we shall attempt to delineate the functions which these feeling reactions fulfil.

---

[2] While this is clearly an oversimplified and artificial distinction, we shall for the purposes of this paper define "relationship" broadly as the spontaneous interpersonal interaction between the therapist and his patient It is dependent on rapport, trust, and confidence and upon communication on the basis of feelings as well as words. In contrast, we shall define "methods" as techniques of therapy which are acquired in the course of formal training. This includes such acts as interpretation and analysis of dreams, free associations, and the life style, as well as reflections of feelings and "acceptance" in the Rogerian sense of the word, or the maintenance of silence. In other words, when the therapist asks himself, "What shall I say or do now?", he is about to apply a "method" or "technique" at his disposal. In general, the therapist's way of relating is not to be learned from books, while his methods *can* be learned in this manner (Thompson, 1950).

[3] Inasmuch as we do not have an operational criterion of the "good" or "successful" therapist or the "poor," "unsuccessful" therapist, we must rely on reputation as a criterion. Hence, when we speak of good or poor therapists in this chapter we mean reputedly "good" or "poor" therapists or reputedly "successful" or "unsuccessful" therapists.

Therapeutic Relationship as Basic to Therapy

Our first question, it will be recalled, was whether the therapeutic relationship is primarily a function of the therapist's competence or of the therapist's methods and orientation.

If we can show that the therapeutic relationship is basic to the therapeutic process, it would suggest that skill in applying the right methods at the right time is not the factor which determines whether or not patients will get well. While many therapists have stated that the relationship is important, textbooks have tended to place more emphasis on the technical competence of the therapist: The Adlerian therapist must learn how to interpret the patient's life style, the nondirective therapist must learn how to reflect feelings and attitudes, the psychoanalytic therapist must learn how to interpret dreams and free associations. But we assume that the patient consults a psychotherapist because his interpersonal relationships arouse, rather than allay, his anxieties. It seems more likely therefore that the patient must learn new ways of relating to others if his therapy is to be successful. This he probably learns by relating to his therapist. Almost all major writers in this area are agreed that the therapeutic relationship is highly important; but therapists of different schools feel (a) that their school creates a different relationship and (b) that the relationships created by their school's methods are better than those created by therapists of other schools (Adler, 1929; Alexander, 1946; Freud, 1922; Rogers, 1949; Shoben, 1949; Thorne, 1948).

In view of the differences in methods and theory which exist among various schools, we might assume that the therapeutic relationship does indeed vary widely from school to school. If it does not vary, however, then the theoretical differences as to the most efficacious therapeutic relationship are semantic in character and the different methods all lead to the same relationship. On the other hand, if the differences in theory are not artifacts caused by different vocabularies, then we shall find that therapists of different schools will view different relationships as maximally effective even when semantic differences are minimized.

In order to explore this issue, the writer asked a number of therapists of various schools and various degrees of reputed competence to describe in a Q technique investigation [4] what they considered to be the ideal therapeutic relationship. They were asked to do this by sorting a set of qualitative statements, all descriptive of therapeutic relationships. The statements were to be sorted so that the most descriptive statements were on one extreme of a forced normal distribution and the least descriptive statements were at the other extreme. The entire distribution obtained from each therapist was then intercorrelated with those obtained from every other therapist, and the matrix was factor-analyzed. Two different sets of statements were used, and two groups of therapists cooperated. The therapists were drawn from the psychoanalytic, nondirective, and

---

[4] For description and discussion of this technique, see Chapter 13.

Adlerian schools, as well as including some who considered themselves to be eclectics; several nontherapists also cooperated. The results of this investigation clearly indicated the following:

1. A single factor was found in the concepts of different therapists as to the nature of the ideal therapeutic relationship. This suggests that therapists of different schools see essentially the same elements in the relationship as important, and differences in school and method do not lead them to attempt the creation of a relationship which differs in essence from those which therapists of other schools attempt to create.

2. Nontherapists described the ideal therapeutic relationship in terms no different from those of therapists, and (if we use factor saturations as a criterion of accuracy) with as much precision as some therapists, even though they had had no experience with therapy. This apparently indicates that the therapeutic relationship is not unique to psychotherapy but can be found—or at least imagined—by those who have never experienced therapy.

3. Therapists who were reputed to be experts agreed more highly with experts of different schools than with nonexperts within their own school. This seems to indicate that the therapeutic relationship is primarily a function of expertness rather than school, although relationships of different schools may vary in the more peripheral aspects (Fiedler, 1950c).

The results of this study only indicate, of course, that therapists of schools with Freudian heritage *attempt* to create the same therapeutic relationship, and one might argue with considerable justification that the actual use of different methods will even here create different relationships. While the goals may well be alike, differences in treatment methods, such as exist between the tutorial, directive Adlerians and the nondirective therapists or psychoanalysts, would lead to different relationships. In order to determine whether therapeutic relationships are more basic to therapy than therapeutic methods and techniques, it was therefore necessary to ask (a) whether good therapists of different schools do create relationships more like those of experts of other schools than like relationships created by nonexperts within their own school and (b) whether better therapists create better therapeutic relationships.

A further study was therefore undertaken (Fiedler, 1950b, 1950c). The writer obtained one wire-recorded therapy interview from the early part of the treatment from each of ten therapists. Four of these therapists practiced psychoanalytic therapy, four nondirective, and two Adlerian therapy. One half of the group of therapists in each school were nationally recognized therapists, the others were nonexperts. (Here "nonexperts" are beginning therapists who had been practicing for some time and who had received all or part of their practical training.) The wire-recorded interviews were presented to one judge with psychoanalytic training, one with nondirective training, one who had received some psychoanalytic and some nondirective training, and one completely untrained judge who had studied dramatic interpretation. The judges were asked to describe each of the interviews by means of seventy-five statements which had previously been used to describe the ideal thereapeutic relationship. The statements were so selected that twenty-five fell on a dimension of communication, understanding, and rapport, twenty-five dealt with the emotional distance between the therapist and his patient, and twenty-five were concerned with the status role which the therapist maintained toward his patient.

· Again each judge's description of the ten therapy hours were intercorrelated and factor-analyzed. Correlations were also obtained between each described therapy hour and a composite description of the ideal therapeutic relationship. The results of this investigation supported the findings of the study of the ideal therapeutic relationship:

1. Expert therapists created relationships more like those created by experts of different schools than like relationships created by nonexperts within the same school.

2. Relationships created by expert therapists correlated significantly more highly with the composite ideal therapeutic relationship than did relationships created by nonexperts. (The differences between experts and nonexperts in the ratings of the trained judges were beyond the .05 and .01 level; and in the untrained, thus least biased, judge's ratings they were well beyond the .001 level of confidence.)

The data here obtained were corroborated by a Q technique study by Heine (1950) in which eight patients in treatment with therapists of the psychoanalytic school, eight in nondirective therapy, and eight with Adlerian therapists were asked to describe the changes they had experienced as a result of therapy and the factors in treatment to which they attributed the changes. He found that patients of therapists from different schools tended to describe the factors leading to change in terms of *different treatment methods* but nevertheless in terms of the same *atmosphere* (relationship). It is thus clear that the essential similarities in the therapeutic relationships exist not only in the eyes of the therapists (as evidenced by their concept of the ideal relationship) and in the eyes of outside observers listening to recorded sessions, but also in the eyes of the patients who undergo treatment. We assume that all major schools may justifiably claim that they have helped patients to adjust (Shoben, 1949), while all have had to admit failures. We assume further that reputedly good therapists do good therapy (i.e., help their patients more in a shorter time than therapists who are not reputed to be experts). We may then reason as follows:

1. Psychotherapy is a process based upon the therapeutic relationship and the methods and techniques of psychological treatment.

2. The studies cited suggest that good therapeutic relationships are primarily a function of expertness and are independent of school, therefore are correlated with good therapy but not methods. We know from anecdotal and clinical evidence, however, that patients can be successfully treated by a variety of methods, some of which are considered, on theoretical grounds, to be poor. The competent application of specific meth-

ods and techniques alone is therefore not related to successful treatment, although it may well enhance the therapist's security and in this way contribute to a better relationship.

3. We may thus infer that the essential aspects of the therapeutic relationship are a more elemental component in therapy than methods or techniques. Perhaps the therapeutic relationship may then best be envisaged as a vehicle of various treatment methods, or as the context within which treatment methods can be effective.

But if we assume that the therapeutic relationship is a basic component in therapy, we find ourselves caught on the horns of an apparent dilemma: Since good therapists create good relationships, the patient apparently plays no part in it. From clinical evidence we know, however, that certain patients do indeed seem untreatable by psychological methods. We must therefore inquire as to the respective parts the patient and the therapist play in the relationship.

Therapist's Part in Determining Nature of Relationship

The previously mentioned studies leave little doubt that the therapist does play a large part in determining the nature of the relationship. Still the possibility remains that the patient plays an equally important role in this respect. If the latter possibility is true, then a description of the therapist's part alone will not be sufficient to describe the relationship as accurately as would be the case if the therapist's and his patient's contributions were available; and secondly, assuming that each patient is different, each therapeutic relationship would also be different. On the other hand, if the therapist primarily determines the nature of the relationship, judgments about the relationship based only on his part would suffice for describing the entire relationship, and his relationship with one patient would be highly related to his relationships with other patients.

A recent study (Quinn, 1950) investigated this aspect of therapeutic relationships. Quinn utilized the same ten cases and the same set of statements as were used in connection with this writer's investigations. The main difference between his and the writer's study was, however, that Quinn presented his judges with wire recordings from which all patient statements had been erased. The judge was thus able to hear what the therapist said, but not what the patient responded or what caused the therapist to make the statement. His judges were also asked to rate each of the therapists in terms of the emotional investment and rapport, as well as the therapist's understanding of the patient which the wire recordings revealed. In general, this scale is highly related to the communication dimension in the set of descriptive statements used by the writer.

Quinn found that the therapeutic relationship could be described with fairly high interrater agreement. Moreover, in most cases, the agreement between his group of judges and the judges used in the writer's study was as high as the agreement within the groups of judges. In other words, his judges could do as good a job in predicting merely from the therapist's statements as my judges were able to do on the basis of both therapists' and patients' statements. He also found that experts could be differentiated from nonexperts by his rating scale, which dealt only with understanding and emotional communication.

The hypothesis that the therapist plays the determining part in shaping the relationship receives additional support from incidental, but not definitive, findings in connection with the writer's investigations on the reliability of wire-recorded interview ratings (Fiedler, 1949). Several therapists had permitted the recording of several hours with different patients. Judges were asked to re-rate the same therapy hour, rate an additional hour with the same patient, and rate one hour which this therapist conducted with a different patient. It was found that hours with two different patients correlated as highly as two hours with the same patient, or a rejudging of the same hour. In one case, for example, a correlation of .83 was obtained on rejudging the same hour, .85 for two different hours with the same patient, and .81 for hours with different patients. These findings, particularly in conjunction with those of Quinn's study, suggest that the therapist's attitudes are quite stable from patient to patient and are not affected by differences in the content of the hour or differences existing between patients.

How can we reconcile this, however, with the fact that some patients are "more difficult" or "impossible" to work with? Surely, "more difficult" or "impossible" implies the existence of a different, poorer relationship. If the foregoing results are not due merely to chance, the patient's contribution to the relationship must be of such nature that it does not enter into the determination of the quality of the relationship. This would seem consistent with the previously described results only if we consider the patient to be a limiting factor; he may determine whether or not a relationship will come into existence, or how profound and stable the relationship will be, but the character of the relationship will be determined by the therapist alone.

This solution is suggested by the findings of Fiedler and Siegel (1949), who studied drawings of human figures by patients who improved in psychotherapy and those who did not. The improved and unimproved groups came from a population of eighty mental hygiene clinic patients with diagnosis of psychoneurosis. Improvement was determined by two judges who read through the progress notes and rated the patients independently in terms of five areas of adjustment. Drawings of only the most improved fifteen and the least improved nineteen patients were utilized. The results suggested that patients who failed to improve in therapy also did not draw a face, or drew the face in a highly immature manner according to Goodenough's scoring criteria. (Whether or not the patient would improve could not be predicted merely by the fact that the face was drawn in a mature manner.) According to Machover

(1949), the patient who omits facial features "is one who is evasive about the frictional character of his interpersonal relationships. . . . Superficiality, caution, and hostility may characterize the social contacts of such an individual." If this hypothesis is correct, then it would follow that certain patients who do not improve (at least under mental hygiene clinic conditions) make it impossible for their therapists to develop a sufficiently good interpersonal relationship with them. On the other hand, patients who have the capacity to form good interpersonal relationships, as evidenced by the quality of their drawings, might still not improve because of unfavorable environmental conditions or because they came under the care of a poor therapist. In addition, therapists differ, of course, in their ability to deal with various types of patients.

It thus appears that the therapist determines to a considerable extent the character of the therapeutic relationship. We have also in some measure accounted for the fact that patients of even the best therapists may have a poor relationship or no relationship with their therapists. From these findings we may hypothesize that the therapist alone determines the character of the relationship, but a final demonstration of this proposition must await further research: e.g., asking judges to describe the relationship only on the basis of the patient's statements, or shifting the patients experimentally from therapist to therapist and comparing the extent to which interactions between the patient and his various therapists remains the same.

Nature of the Therapist's Feeling Reactions

We have seen that the therapist's ability to create a good therapeutic relationship seems to be a prerequisite to the use of various therapeutic methods. We have also seen that the relationship is created primarily by the therapist. But what do we mean by relationship?

It will be recalled that the writer asked a number of expert and nonexpert therapists to describe the ideal relationship. A composite description was constructed which utilized the descriptions of the four experts, representing three different schools and having factor saturations of .88 or above. This composite concept of the ideal therapeutic relationship will here be illustrated by listing the eight most and the eight least characteristic statements by which it was described.

Most Characteristic
The therapist is able to participate completely in the patient's communication.

Highly Characteristic
The therapist's comments are always right in line with what the patient is trying to convey.
The therapist is well able to understand the patient's feelings.
The therapist really tries to understand the patient's feelings.

The therapist always follows the patient's line of thought.

The therapist's tone of voice conveys the complete ability to share the patient's feelings.

The therapist sees the patient as a co-worker on a common problem.

The therapist treats the patient as an equal.

Highly Uncharacteristic

The therapist cannot maintain rapport with the patient.

The therapist's own needs completely interfere with his understanding of the patient.

The therapist feels disgusted by the patient.

The therapist is punitive.

The therapist is very unpleasant to the patient.

The therapist acts in a very superior manner toward the patient.

Least Characteristic

The therapist shows no comprehension of the feelings the patient is trying to communicate.

These statements, then, represent a general, very stereotyped description of how therapists would ideally like to feel and act toward their patients. (Lest the reader think that some therapists do not act in an "uncharacteristic" manner, let him consider that judges' descriptions of the relationships created by some nonexperts correlated with the ideal as low as $-.77$!)

It is interesting to compare these statements with those used by patients in Heine's study (1950) to describe their therapists. It will be remembered that three groups of eight patients with therapists of three different schools were asked to describe the factors in treatment leading to changes toward adjustment. We thus obtain an estimate of relationship aspects which the patient sees as most productive. Heine presents the ten statements which patients considered to be most conducive to treatment and the ten they considered to be most deleterious. They are here presented in the order of importance they have in the patient's eyes:

Most Conducive to Treatment

The therapist never let me feel that he rather than I was to take responsibility for solving my problems.

The therapist got across the feeling that we were really working together to understand my problem.

There was definitely a feeling of mutual trust in my relations with the therapist.

The therapist was a very natural, unaffected sort of person.

Aside from anything else, the therapist was a likable fellow.

I had the feeling that here was one person I could really trust.

The therapist always seemed to know what I was trying to get across to him.

I never had the feeling that the therapist was in over his depth in trying to help me.

The therapist was anything but cold and distant.

The therapist seemed to be in pretty good control of himself at all times.

Most Deleterious to Treatment

It seemed to me that the therapist didn't take his work too seriously.

The therapist seemed to want me to maintain pretty close control over my emotions when I was with him.

I had the feeling the therapist was so sympathetic that he couldn't really be helpful.

I somehow caught the feeling that the therapist couldn't regard me as an equal.

It seemed as if the therapist always lapsed into wordy explanations when he might have let me finish.

I never had the feeling that the therapist really understood what I was trying to get across.

The therapist often seemed to be lost in his own thoughts rather than attending to what I said.

I always had the feeling that I was just another patient as far as the therapist was concerned.

I often felt, "I'd better not tell the therapist that."

I was a little afraid really to tell the therapist what I thought about myself.

The reader will note that many of these statements deal with understanding and rapport between the therapist and his patient, and the security which the patient wants to see in the person who treats him. The patient wants the therapist to be genuinely interested in him, to be well disposed toward him, and to treat him as an equal. Essentially the same traits are found important in differentiating experts from nonexperts on the basis of wire recordings. The statements which all the trained judges in the writer's study rated as most differentiating between experts and nonexperts are the following:

More Characteristic of Experts Than of Nonexperts

The therapist is well able to understand the patient's feelings.

The therapist is never in any doubt about what the patient means.

The therapist's remarks fit in just right with the patient's mood and content.

The therapist is interested but emotionally uninvolved.

The therapist maintains a friendly, neutral attitude throughout.

More Characteristic of Nonexperts Than of Experts

The therapist cannot maintain rapport with the patient.

The therapist shows no comprehension of the feelings the patient is trying to convey.

The therapist somehow seems to miss the patient's meaning time and again.

The therapist's own needs completely interfere with his understanding of the patient.

The therapist often misses the point the patient is trying to get across.
The therapist finds it difficult to think along the patient's lines.
The therapist is hostile toward the patient.

The trends obtained in this study are further corroborated by the factor
patterns which were obtained from the descriptions the writer's judges
made on the basis of wire-recorded therapy sessions. We find no factors
which clearly differentiate all therapists of one school from those of other
schools, but experts and nonexperts are differentiated on factors related
to the therapist's security, his ability to understand the patient, and his
capacity to show warmth without becoming overly involved.

Finally we can obtain some information from the way in which the
therapist perceives the patient in relation to himself (Fiedler, 1951b).
This provides us with an objective and quantifiable measure, the "feeling reaction pattern" of the therapist's unconscious feelings toward the
patient, although we are as yet not able to interpret the exact meaning of
such apparently unconscious feelings with confidence. In grossly oversimplified manner, the rationale and method are as follows:

The therapist's prediction of the patient's feelings may be viewed as
one measure of his ability to perceive the patient objectively. Misperceptions or distortions are presumably caused by the therapist's unconscious
feelings toward the patient. We can therefore ask the patient to describe
himself with a set of qualitative statements (the writer used statements
suggested by the need-press variables in Murray's *Explorations in personality*) (Murray, 1938). We then ask the therapist to predict how
the patient will describe himself with these same statements. We also
ask the therapist to describe himself and finally to describe how he would
ideally like to be. A purely objective attitude on the part of the therapist
would manifest itself as follows: The therapist would predict the patient's self-description with a high degree of accuracy, and he would
predict the patient's self-description to be neither more nor less different
from his own self-description than it actually is. Similarly, the patient
would be perceived as neither more nor less similar to the therapist's
ideal than he actually is. If the therapist assumes (or predicts) the patient's self-description to be much more similar to himself, we may infer,
in line with projective theory, that he desires the patient to be *more like
himself* (more human, more equal?); but if he assumes the patient to be
less similar than the patient actually describes himself to be, we may
assume that the therapist wants his patient to be *more different from
himself* (less "good," psychologically more distant?). If he perceives the
patient to be more like his ideal than the patient actually is, we may
interpret this to mean that the therapist will also unconsciously demand
that the patient live up to the therapist's expectations (of emotional
gratification?). Seeing the patient as less like his ideal probably means
that he sees the patient as more poorly adjusted, thus in need of help
and succorance. While we cannot be certain that these interpretations
are correct, we find that good therapists see their patients as more like

themselves (rho's of .52 to .68 with supervisory rankings, N's of 10-17) and that good therapists assume their patients to be more similar to themselves than to their ideals. This will be called a *favorable feeling reaction pattern*.

These data suggest that feelings of closeness (empathy), respect for the patient, an undemanding attitude, security, and the ability to understand the patient are related to therapeutic skill. Unfortunately, Heine's study does not permit us to divide the patients into those treated by good therapists and those treated by poor therapists. It is highly probable that such data would have permitted us to find differences between descriptions of good and poor therapists' patients similar to those obtained in Quinn's and the writer's studies.

We have spoken much about the therapist's feelings; yet we have seen again and again that the therapist's understanding of the patient is mentioned as being of utmost importance. But understanding might depend on the therapist's ability to know what the patient is thinking and feeling; this is an objective, intellectual task. May it not be, therefore, that the therapist who has the most understanding of his patient's feelings, who has the most adequate personality theory, is also the more competent therapist? While this would not contradict the findings by the writer that good and poor therapists can be differentiated on the basis of the relationships which they establish, it would mean that the basic component of the therapeutic relationship may be primarily objective understanding by the therapist rather than certain of his feeling reactions.

In order to investigate this possibility, let us define intellectual, objective, diagnostic understanding operationally as the ability to predict the patient's feelings toward himself. While this is clearly not all that diagnosis implies, it is probably a reasonable task for the clinician; and, to judge from the importance generally attached to the self-concept or self-perception, a task generally representative of diagnostic work. Most importantly, however, it is a diagnostic task which we can validate objectively.

Good therapists, according to Quinn's, Heine's, and the writer's studies, are said to understand their patients in the therapeutic sense of the word. If understanding in psychotherapy is the same as the intellectual, objective understanding in diagnosis, we shall expect that good therapists will also be able to understand their patients better in the diagnostic sense of the word. We should also expect that diagnostic tests, providing additional understanding, would increase the therapist's prediction of his patient's self-description.

Our results do not indicate, however, that diagnostic and therapeutic understanding are the same (Fiedler, 1950c). We find that good therapists predict their patient's self-descriptions only slightly better than poor therapists (correlations of .13 and .19 for two small samples between reputed therapeutic competence and prediction), and neither of these correlations is significantly different from zero. Incidentally we also find that good therapists predict no better than poor therapists or laymen on a test requiring them to listen to a wire-recorded therapy session which is periodically interrupted with requests for predictions of the patient's subsequent reactions. This study is further supported by Luft's recent findings (1950). The fact that the therapist has seen diagnostic reports on the patient also does not seem to raise his ability to predict the patient's self-concept significantly.

Corroboration for these findings can also be found in a recently completed investigation by Taft (1950) at the University of California. Taft studied various personality traits which are associated with ability to predict others. He summarizes his findings as follows: "The following characteristics appear related to the possession of this ability [to judge others] : . . . being a student in the natural sciences rather than the social sciences, having an oversolicitous mother, high intelligence, academic ability, possessing an organized, socially passive, serious, unemotional and realistic personality, being task-oriented rather than socio-oriented, and being liberal but not extreme in political attitudes.

"The following characteristics that are usually believed to be possessed by good judges of others were not found: artistic ability, ability to play social roles, sociability, femininity, and ability to judge self . . . good judges of others are extraceptive persons possessing a hard-headed attitude toward their peers, while the poor judges are intraceptive persons who *view other people in terms of their relationship with themselves; they are socially dependent and err in the direction of being overgenerous in rating their peers"* (italics added).

Good therapists seem to be much more like the poor predictors in Taft's study—cf. especially the finding related to overestimation of the similarity between the patient's and the therapist's self-descriptions. On the basis of Taft's and the writer's findings, it seems quite likely that therapeutic and diagnostic understanding are different processes, and that therapeutic understanding is not related to the therapist's knowledge about the patient. It seems much more probable that the therapist's "understanding" means that the patient feels understood, i.e., empathized with. Therapeutic understanding may therefore be a feeling reaction on the part of the therapist in the same sense that feeling benign, feeling sympathetic and tolerant toward the patient, or regarding the patient as an equal is a feeling reaction.

Function of the Therapist's Feelings Toward the Patient

In the preceding sections of this paper we have described several methods which permit quantitative measurement of some of the therapist's feelings. We have presented evidence to suggest that these feelings tend to be correlated with therapeutic competence and, therefore, presumably affect the therapeutic process. Let us now explore the ways in which the therapist's feelings affect the course of treatment.

The two prevailing, and not necessarily contradictory, views regarding the dynamics of cure are (*a*) that the patient improves as a result of discussing and reliving his emotional difficulties in therapy (Alexander and French, 1946; Bergman, 1949; Shoben, 1949) and (*b*), held by analytic writers, that the patient's cure is effected as a result of the handling and final resolution of the transference (Appel, 1944; Alexander, 1948; Freud, 1935*a*). If these theories have validity, we will expect the therapist's feelings (*a*) to play an important role in facilitating (or inhibiting) the expression of feelings by the patient, and (*b*) to exert similar influence on the development and depth of the patient's feelings toward the therapist. No less important, of course, is the handling and resolution of transference; but, inasmuch as we do not as yet have relevant data on that phase of therapy, we shall not be able to deal with this aspect of treatment at this time.

The terms "expression of feelings," "feeling reactions," "transference," and "countertransference" are at present so variously defined that it seems impossible to satisfy all definitions which are current in the field. The operational definitions which will be used here are therefore to be seen as covering only one part of the more comprehensive definitions which might be advanced. While it is hoped that the operational measures will satisfy the essential aspects of current definitions, we shall attempt to make them sufficiently explicit so that the phenomena can be interpreted in terms other than those used in this paper.

Let us first consider the ways in which the therapist's feelings might affect the expression of feelings by the patient. To do this we have utilized the method developed by the present writer (Fiedler, 1950*c*) in connection with evaluation of therapeutic competence of the VA project on the selection of clinical psychologists (Kelly and Fiske, 1951). It is based on the content analysis of the progress notes which therapists keep for their own records of therapy hours. These notes generally give a short account of the topics which the patient discussed during the hour, and usually also the interpretations by the therapist and observations which the therapist made but did not communicate to the patient. These notes are customarily not seen by anyone else, although they are clinic property. While they are sometimes utilized by the therapist to relate to his supervisor the happenings of the previous hours, these notes have not generally been used for evaluative purposes. It is reasonable to assume therefore that most therapists are not interested in distorting the notes, but, on the contrary, attempt to keep an accurate account of the hours. This assumption is supported by Covner's investigations (1942), which showed that most of the important events are accurately recorded, even though minor events are usually left out. The rationale of the method which will here be presented rests on the generally accepted notion among therapists that patients must talk about their problems in order to be helped in solving them eventually. In addition, the generally accepted psychoanalytic theory of the development of transference holds that the free expression of feelings is a necessary precondition for its development (provided, of course, that the patient has the requisite capacity to form any relationships). In other words, the basic working tool of the psychotherapist depends on the fact that the patient is able to express his feelings freely and therefore eventually develops transference. Thus, Horney (1945) states that transference develops "because of free associations, interpretations by the analyst, and his attitude of tolerance," but others (Appel, 1944; Alexander, 1948) have ascribed the development of transference essentially to the fact that the patient expresses his feelings freely.

We have assumed that disrupted interpersonal relationships play a large, if not the major, part in the psychological illness of the patient. Unless the patient discusses and attempts to solve problems concerned with his interpersonal relationships, he is not really tackling his problems in the most efficacious way—if he is tackling them at all. But he must work within the framework of the therapeutic relationship; and the further afield he goes in discussing his problems, the less are the chances that he will be able to solve problems which pertain to his interpersonal life. A discussion of his feelings either toward himself or toward the therapist during the hour will thus be the most direct attack the patient can make upon his problems: in both cases all the responsible participants are present and can interact in the therapeutic situation. Moreover, they are responsive to the feelings which the patient expresss. The therapist is responsive by pointing out the meaning of the attitude, by accepting it as such, or by interrelating it in the light of the patient's other problems; the patient is responsive to his own feelings because he can change his perception of himself and others as a result of them. A somewhat less direct approach to his problems involves discussion of his relationships with persons who are significant in his emotional life: those on whom he primarily depends for emotional satisfactions, such as his parents, his siblings, his children, or his spouse. Finally, revealing to the therapist intimate details of his life, such as antisocial acts, his sexual habits, and the like, indicates that his relationship with his therapist is such that he trusts and confides in him. The discussion of his symptoms or a discussion of other topics, such as sports, work relationships, financial troubles, etc., is probably far removed from immediate solution of his problems—essentially it is a reassertion of his defenses. Although these last-mentioned topics might well have meaning to the patient, the discussion is not likely to be highly productive as far as therapy is concerned unless he is capable of tying these meanings in with his core problems.

In purely mechanical terms, the method entails categorization of every topic on which the patient is reported to have spoken. These topics are then differentially weighted, and a ratio is obtained of weighted topics (important topics) over total topics. This apparently loose procedure gives rather high reliabilities and is fairly consistent from case to case. It has already been discussed in greater detail in a report on the VA project on the selection of clinical psychologists (Kelly and Fiske, 1951). As further evidence on the validity of the measure here called the "relationship index," we might mention at this point that this index correlates .52 to .72 with supervisory ratings of therapeutic competence in several samples and correlates .55 and .47 (N of 9) with previously mentioned measures. (While the measure is based on what the therapist reports the patient as saying and thus introduces some distortion, it also permits us to use the therapist as a screen which lets only presumably important events emerge in the record.)

If we accept this relationship index as a measure of the amount and quality of feelings which the patient expresses during the hour, we can attempt to answer some of the questions which we have previously posed.

We have said before that we shall expect the therapist's feelings toward the patient to affect the amount of feelings which the patient expresses. In some measure this hypothesis has already been supported, since we have shown that the index obtained from the content analysis of the progress notes correlates relatively highly with supervisors' judgments of therapeutic competence. This does not mean, however, that the therapist's own feelings need be involved. It might as easily be argued that the poor therapists don't let their patients talk because of the methods which they employ. On the other hand, if the low relationship index found with patients of poor therapists is primarily a matter of poor methods, then we would expect that these poor methods would tend to become more and more apparent as therapy progresses. In other words, if it is primarily a matter of methods, then patients of good therapists ought to increase the relative amount of expressed feelings per hour, while patients of poor therapists ought to decrease the amount of feelings expressed over the course of treatment. It is relatively easy to test this hypothesis, albeit the size of the samples and the crudeness of measurement make the conclusions highly tentative. If we rank-order the hours in treatment for one patient and similarly rank-order the indices obtained for these hours, then we should find a high correlation coefficient if the patient expresses more and more feelings with each successive hour. This is what we might expect to happen in the case of good therapists. If, however, the relationship indices become lower and lower with each succeeding treatment hour which we rate, then the correlation coefficient should be highly negative. This procedure was undertaken for two samples, consisting of sixteen psychoanalytically treated cases and nine cases treated by psychologists in a mental hygiene clinic. In both samples of cases, the median rank-order correlations were low (.13 and .19 and ranging from .54 to —.86), which seems to indicate no systematic increases or decreases in terms of the feelings which the patient expresses over a period of time. To be certain that the lack of systematic increases or decreases does not occur either in the beginning or in the later phases of treatment, the first sample of sixteen cases was treated as follows. Several hours from the early part of treatment, some from the middle part, and several hours from the last part of therapy were rated and ranked. The ratings thus sampled hours from all phases of treatment, including some hours after the hundredth or two hundredth interview in lengthy cases. In the sample of nine cases, treated by psychologists, only the first nine treatment hours were rated (excluding the first interview, which is usually a history-taking session). Inasmuch as no systematic increases in expressed feelings occurred here either, it might be hypothesized that the therapist's feelings make themselves felt at an early point in treatment and continue rather consistently throughout. However, this raises the question as to whether good therapists' cases behave differently from cases of poor therapists. The therapists in each of the two samples were therefore ranked in terms of their reputed competence, and this rank-order was compared with the ranked magnitude of the correlation coefficients obtained from their cases. In other words, we first obtained a correlation coefficient indicating whether the patient expressed more or fewer feelings as treatment went on, and then in turn we compared this correlation coefficient with the competence of the therapist, in order to find out whether patients of good therapists tended to express more feelings as time went on while patients of poor therapists tended to express fewer and fewer feelings. We find that the correlation coefficients for the two samples of therapists are .01 and .04 respectively. What does this mean? Keeping in mind the small sample statistics which were used, we might suggest the following very tentative interpretation of these data:

The therapist may have a certain set of attitudes toward the patient which is fairly general and which thus makes itself felt throughout the course of treatment. This would account for the fact that we find no significant increases or decreases in relationship indices, i.e., in the amount of feelings which the patient expresses during his time in treatment. We might further postulate that therapists have a certain tolerance for the amount and intensity of feelings which their patients can express without making the therapists feel anxious and insecure. The therapist's unconscious attitudes will thus regulate how far the patient may go in each hour to express his feelings freely. (This interpretation finds additional support in the reliability studies undertaken in connection with the VA project. Unless we assume such a regulating factor to be present, it would be difficult to explain why different patients with the same therapist would only rarely exceed a certain relationship index.)

How does all this fit in with the notions of therapy which have here been advanced? We might see these results as the manifestations of the patient's needs to express his feelings and relive his past traumatic experiences in order to get well. The more feelings he is free to express, the more abreaction takes place per hour and the more quickly the cumulative effect of such experiences will permit him to tackle more basic problems in his psychological make-up. If the patient can express only a minimal number of feelings, the cumulative effects of such experiences may be outweighed by other traumatic experiences which occur in his life at the time.

Still the critical reader will say with justification, "Why are we talking about the therapist's feelings and not his feelings and methods? It has not yet been shown that methods are not as important as the relationship." This is unfortunately true. Our evidence, albeit suggestive, is inconclusive. We know from the study of free drawings that certain pa-

tients will probably not be able to develop a relationship with their therapists. We cannot expect, therefore, that a good therapist will be successful with every case he treats. On the other hand, the implicit hypothesis
of this chapter has been throughout that certain favorable feelings on the
part of the therapist toward his patient are necessary prerequisites to good
therapy. If we divide the number of therapists for whom "feeling reaction patterns" are available into those with favorable attitudes and those
with unfavorable attitudes and divide the patient group into highs and
lows on the basis of the relationship index (or feelings which the patient
expressed), we obtain a fourfold table (see Table 1) which supports the
hypothesis. Not one of the patients whose therapist falls into the low
group is himself in the high group. In other words, in order to have a

TABLE 1

RELATIONSHIP OF "COUNTERTRANSFERENCE PATTERNS" TO THE "RELATIONSHIP
INDEX" FOR FIFTEEN THERAPISTS [5]

Feeling Reaction Patterns	Relationship Index	
	High	Low
High	7	2
Low	0	6

patient who expresses his feelings freely, one must be a therapist who has
favorable attitudes toward his patient. A similar result is obtained when
we substitute reputed competence for the relationship index. Combining
the middle and low categories for reputation, the Fisher-Yates Test shows
significance at the 1 per cent level. When reputation is dichotomized,
the results are significant at the 5 per cent level (see Table 2). Inasmuch
as these indices tend to find their level right in the beginning of therapy,

TABLE 2

RELATIONSHIP OF "FEELING REACTION PATTERNS" TO SUPERVISORY
RATINGS OF THERAPEUTIC COMPETENCE [6]

Feeling Reaction Patterns	Rated Therapeutic Competence		
	High	Medium	Low
High	7	5	?
Low	0	2	6

[5] Significant at the 5 per cent level according to the Fisher-Yates Test for 2x2 contingency tables.
[6] Transformation into a 2x2 contingency table, with medium and low categories of therapeutic competence combined, yields a table which is significant at the 1 per cent level
according to the Fisher-Yates Test. Dichotomizing rated therapeutic competence into high
and low groups yields a table significant at the 5 per cent level by the same test.

it appears that the patient is almost immediately aware of the therapist's feelings toward him.

A very similar phenomenon also occurs when we consider the patient's feelings on a more global scale, that is, in terms of one aspect of transference. Freud (1935a) has spoken of it in one context as follows: "Now in [transference] with our male patients, there at least we might hope to be spared the troublesome element of sex attraction. Well, the answer is much the same as with women. The same attachment to the physician, *the same overestimation of his qualities,* the same adoption of his interests . . ." (italics added). While this is by no means the only definition, nor the entire meaning of transference in its current usage, and while it is possible to define operationally more of these terms, let us consider here only the italicized part of the statement, especially inasmuch as other aspects are dynamically related to it. We can measure overestimation of somebody's qualities (i.e., idealization) by asking our subject to describe (e.g., by means of Q technique) how he would ideally like to be. We can then ask a patient to predict how his therapist will describe himself, and we can actually ask the therapist to describe himself. We thus obtain three descriptions which can be intercorrelated: the correlation between the patient's ideal and the therapist's self-description gives us the actual similarity of the therapist to the patient's ideal; the correlation between the patient's ideal and his description of the therapist gives us an estimate of how similar the patient assumes the therapist to be to his ideal, i.e., how ideal a person the patient assumes the therapist to be. After squaring the correlations, we can subtract the real from the assumed similarity and obtain a measure of the overestimation of the therapist's qualities by the patient. This measure correlates .49 with therapeutic competence in a sample of fifteen therapists; thus, it suggests that the ability to evoke such attitudes on the part of the patient is related to therapeutic skill. Again we may now ask whether this measure is related to the therapist's attitudes toward his patient. Therapists' as well as patients' descriptions and predictions were obtained (Fiedler and Senior, 1952) for a sample of fifteen therapists and their patients. A sixfold table of "high" therapists and "low" therapists, in terms of their feeling reaction patterns and

TABLE 3

RELATIONSHIP OF "FEELING REACTION PATTERNS" TO IDEALIZATION OF THE THERAPIST AS MEASURED BY OVERESTIMATION OF THE THERAPIST'S QUALITIES ON THE PART OF THE PATIENT [7]

Feeling Reaction Patterns	Idealization		
	High	Medium	Low
High	5	3	0
Low	0	3	5

[7] Combining the medium and low categories for transference, we obtain a 2x2 contingency table which is significant at the 5 per cent level according to the Fisher-Yates Test.

the upper, middle, and lower third of the patient groups in terms of over-estimated similarity of the therapist to the patient's ideal reveals again that patients whose therapists have unfavorable feeling reaction patterns do not overestimate their therapists' qualities to a large extent. In other words, in order to develop transference as manifested by this symptom, favorable attitudes of the therapist toward his patient again seem to be a prerequisite (see Table 3).

Summary

In this chapter we have reviewed research on the role which the therapists' feelings play in the therapeutic relationship. Good therapeutic relationships appear to be essentially similar in three different schools which employ different methods of treatment and which operate on the basis of different personality theories. We have also presented evidence suggesting that the therapist is primarily responsible for the character of the therapeutic relationship and that the patient exerts a limiting or constraining force in the relationship. We have finally indicated that certain feelings on the part of the therapist seem to be prerequisite for the free expression of patients' feelings and for the development of idealization of the therapist. We have not attempted to interrelate the data presented in this chapter with eventual outcome of treatment, partly because criteria of successful treatment are highly tentative at present, and partly because the fragmentary evidence which has been obtained up to this time cannot be interpreted with any confidence. It might be stressed, however, that generalizations from "successful therapists" to "successful therapy cases" are decidedly not warranted until further evidence can be gathered.

CHAPTER 13

"Q TECHNIQUE"—DESCRIPTION, HISTORY, AND CRITIQUE [1]

By O. Hobart Mowrer, Ph.D.

We are beginning to see the publication of what will probably be a crescendo of studies employing a method of personality evaluation known, somewhat ambiguously, as "Q technique." Reference to such studies is made in three other chapters (9, 12, and 14) of this book; and reports on numerous other investigations, now in progress, will appear shortly. The method involved is one which has considerable promise; but it is predicated upon a number of assumptions which need to be critically examined and which have many implications that invite exploration. Furthermore, its background and early exposition have resulted in uncertainty and controversy as to precisely what Q technique is and is not. In this chapter we shall therefore first identify the method operationally, then dip back into its history for further understanding, and, finally, evaluate its significance and potentialities in the context of current personality theory, related testing procedures, and the logic of psychological inquiry generally.

In order to help the reader see the organization of the chapter and follow the general argument more easily, an outline is given below:

SOME EXAMPLES OF Q TECHNIQUE
    Example I
    Example II

HISTORY OF Q TECHNIQUE AND ITS RELATION TO FACTOR ANALYSIS
    Phase I : 1912-35
    Phase II : 1935-42
        A. Contributions of Stephenson and Thomson
        B. Review and Evaluation
            1. Inverted Factor Analysis and Type Psychology
            2. Scaling Aspect of Q Technique
            3. Potentialities of a General Approach

[1] The writer has benefited from criticisms and suggestions made by a number of persons on the basis of a preliminary draft of this chapter. To all these persons he is extremely grateful. The nature of their respective contributions will, in most instances, be evident at appropriate points in the text. However, for particularly detailed and helpful comments, special indebtedness should here be acknowledged to Drs. Donald W. Fiske, Wilfred A. Gibson, Starke R. Hathaway, and Paul E. Meehl.

Phase III : 1942 and After

SUMMARY

Inclusion of a chapter of this kind in a book on psychotherapeutic theory and research is justifiable on the grounds of specific applications which will be indicated in the following pages. No attempt will be made here to enter into the more strictly statistical aspects of Q technique (see Chapter 14) ; in fact, technical statistical issues in this connection are hardly in point at all. As Stephenson once remarked in a personal communication to Davies * (1939) : "There is nothing *statistically* novel about Q technique . . . ; but the *psychological* implications . . . have never been clearly appreciated" (p. 411). It will be our purpose here to try to extend both appreciation and critical understanding of this method.

Some Examples of Q Technique

"Q technique," as we shall shortly see, is a term with a checkered history and an uncertain future. However, before going into terminological matters, it will be useful to give two illustrations of the sorts of problems and procedures which are currently associated with this expression. The first example is a study carried out by Hartley, at the University of Chicago, and the second is a study now being conducted by Ewing at the University of Illinois.

Example I

In Hartley's study, a woman who was about to undergo counseling was presented with 150 (the absolute number is not critical) 3x5-inch index cards on each of which was written a statement such as the following ones :

* References are to the bibliography at the back of the book.

At times I get so terribly depressed that I just don't want to attempt anything.

I don't want to be an average person. I want to *do* things.[2]

The array of statements or items used in Q technique can be derived in any of a variety of ways—from personality inventories, statements occurring in conversation, newspapers, plays, books, or elsewhere—but in the research under discussion they were selected from the protocols of persons who had previously undergone counseling or psychotherapy.[3]

After the cards were presented to the subject, she was told to *sort* them into eleven different categories or piles. She was told to place each card in one or another of the categories (numbered 0-10) according to whether the statement printed on it was completely inapplicable to her, completely applicable, or intermediate in applicability. The completely inapplicable statements go into the category at the extreme left, the completely applicable statements at the extreme right (or vice versa—the direction of the gradient is unimportant), and the intermediate statements go into the intermediate compartments.

In this type of procedure, the only other requirement which is made of the subject is that he or she sort the 150 cards so that they constitute a *normal* distribution.[4] This takes the form of the subject's being told *how many* cards there be in each of the piles or categories. The subject is, however, entirely free to determine *what* cards go into each of the eleven categories. The subject is also free to sort and re-sort the cards until satisfied with their arrangement.[5]

The sorting of the cards under these instructions has been called a "Q sort." For reasons which will be developed below, it is suggested that

[2] Examples taken from an unpublished paper by Dr. Margaret W. Hartley (1950) entitled "Q Technique: Its Methodology and Application."

[3] For further discussion of item selection, see page 358.

[4] For discussion of the advantages and disadvantages of a "forced-choice" method in this situation, see page 370 and Chapter 14. See also Travers (1951).

[5] The *number of cards* used—150—was a compromise between a very large number (which would, in principle, insure maximal reliability) and a very small number (which would be desirable in terms of the test tolerance of the subject and the experimenter's time). The number of categories employed in the sorting of the cards was more arbitrary. There seems to be no a priori reason why one could not use either a simple rank-order method (in which event there would be as many "categories" as cards) or merely two categories (true and false) or any intermediate number of categories. Nor is it imperative in using eleven or some comparable number of categories that the distribution of items therein be statistically normal. However, as a matter of computational efficiency and convenience, it is desirable that the cards be normally distributed and that the number of categories lie somewhat intermediate between rank-order and dichotomy. In some of his early studies, Stephenson (1935b, 1939) used eleven as a convenient number of categories, and that has become more or less standard. (The writer is indebted to Dr. L. L. McQuitty for calling attention to the following footnote in Edwards (1947): "It should be pointed out also that the formula for r is based upon measurements taken by pairs. The calculation of r from a correlation table results in a slight loss in precision. This, however, is negligible if there are twelve or more class intervals and if N is approximately 50 or greater" (p. 98). For a study using only two categories, see Moore, Stafford, and Hsu (1947), cited under "Implications and Comments," below.)

this procedure be referred to instead as an "S sort" or as "S procedure." When sorting is done on the basis of the applicability of the statements to *oneself,* this particular type of S sort is known as a "self sort."

It will be immediately evident that the same cards can be sorted under a variety of instructions. The subject may be told, for example, to sort the cards, not in terms of what he, as a person, *is,* but in terms of what he *would like to be.* This type of S sort is known as a "self-ideal sort," or simply as an "ideal sort." Or the subject may be instructed to sort the cards in terms of their applicability to *other persons, social stereotypes,* etc. The possibility will also suggest itself of having other persons sort the cards *for the subject.* As will thus be apparent, the flexibility and possible applications of the method are considerable (see Chapter 14).

In Dr. Hartley's study one variation from the self-sort was to have the client sort the cards, not only in terms of the kind of a person she perceived herself to be, but also in terms of the kind of person she would like to be. Repetitions of these two performances, the self-sort and an ideal sort, might be called for at stipulated intervals during the course of counseling; there might be follow-up sorts, or there might be only a before-treatment and an after-treatment sort. But for purposes of simplicity, let us suppose that in the example under discussion there were only the before- and after-treatment sorts.[6]

Now it is evident that the pretreatment self-sort and the pretreatment ideal sort can be correlated. In order to do this, all that is necessary is to number the cards (for purposes of identification) and then set up a table showing the results for the two pretreatment sorts as shown in Table 4.

There would probably be universal agreement among psychotherapists, regardless of training or theoretical persuasion, that prior to treatment a disturbed, puzzled, suffering person would show a discrepancy between his description of himself as he *is* and as he *would like to be.* This discrepancy will be reflected by a *low positive* or a *negative* correlation between the values assigned to the 150 cards on the two sortings. In the Hartley study, the actual correlation between the pretreatment self-sort and the pretreatment ideal sort was found to be $r = .18$.[7]

---

[6] The total procedure employed by Hartley was as follows: "The subject was required to sort a population of 150 statements along a subjective continuum from *least characteristic* to *most characteristic* according to their significance for each of the concepts (a) the self, (b) the ideal, (c) the unhappy self, and (d) the ordinary-other. The counselor, in addition to describing his own self and ideal, performed predicted and diagnostic self-sortings for the client. The subject performed the four sortings mentioned above three times—at the commencement of therapy, at the ninth interview, and at the termination of therapy. The counselor described his self and ideal once, and gave his sortings for the client twice—after the third interview and at the termination of therapy" (Hartley, 1951, p. 1). There was also a set of follow-up sortings made by the patient eight months after the termination of therapy.

[7] In granting permission for the publication of this and the following correlational values, Dr. Hartley has asked that they be "presented as the kind of raw data one achieves by correlating any two score arrays" and has emphasized that in her study "conclusions were not drawn on the basis of single or paired correlations as, in my opinion, the methods of factor analysis are indispensable for the proper analysis of a large group of interrelations" (personal communication).

TABLE 4

HYPOTHETICAL RESULTS FOR A PRETREATMENT SELF SORT AND A PRETREATMENT
IDEAL SORT, SHOWING THE READINESS WITH WHICH SUCH RESULTS
CAN BE CORRELATED

The numerical entries in the Self-Sort and the Ideal-Sort columns correspond,
respectively, to categories or compartments (numbered from left to right or right
to left) into which each of the 150 cards has been placed on the two sorting
procedures.

Card No.	Self Sort	Ideal Sort
1	7	4
2	10	9
3	7	4
4	2	0
5	6	10
Etc.	Etc.	Etc.

There would likewise be general agreement that as a result of successful therapy the discrepancy between the self sort and the ideal sort should
decrease, as indicated by a posttreatment correlation between the self sort
and the ideal sort which is higher than the pretreatment correlation
between the self sort and the ideal sort. This expectation is again confirmed; the correlation between these two sorts, posttherapy, was found
to be $r = .81$.

Here, then, we have the exciting possibility of obtaining a simple,
quantitative index of "movement" in any given instance of psychotherapeutic endeavor! The greater the change in the correlation between
self-sort and ideal sort, pretherapy and posttherapy, the greater the presumptive improvement; and the more nearly the posttherapy correlation
approximates 1.00, the more nearly the therapy may be said to have
brought the individual to the ultimate in "normality." [8]

But this is not the end of the method's possible usefulness. In the
particular application of the method which is here being used for illustrative purposes, there is the possibility of obtaining, not only the two correlations just described, but also a correlation between the pretreatment
self sort and the posttreatment self sort, on the one hand, and a correlation between the pretreatment ideal sort and the posttreatment ideal sort,

[8] In his recent book, Rogers (1951) has suggested that the neurotic or poorly
integrated person can be represented by two circles which are only slightly congruent; after successful therapy in the case of such a person, the two circles are
assumed to have a greater degree of congruence. The latter figure "pictures the
end point of personality development as being a basic congruence between the
phenomenal field of experience and the conceptual structure of the self—a situation
which, if achieved, would represent freedom from internal strain and anxiety, and
freedom from potential strain; which would mean the establishment of an individualized value system having considerable identity with the value system of any
other equally well-adjusted member of the human race" (p. 532). For a somewhat
related way of representing neurosis and normality in a different frame of reference,
see Mowrer (1951). It is also interesting to juxtapose this type of thinking upon
the work which has been done regarding "level of aspiration."

on the other. Here we would seem to have a possible means of ascertaining, perhaps with considerable precision, whether therapy achieves its results mainly by modifying the self, the self ideal, or both.

To the present writer, this method for quantitatively analyzing the results of psychotherapy has a special significance. It will be recalled from Chapters 3 and 6 that the orthodox Freudian position has been that a neurotic is always a person whose superego, or conscience, is "too severe." This position could be extensively documented, but the two following quotations will sufficiently illustrate the kinds of statements which have been commonly made in this connection:

No sooner have we got used to the idea of this superego, as something which enjoys a certain independence, pursues its own ends, and is independent of the ego as regards the energy at its disposal, than we are faced with a clinical picture which throws into strong relief the severity, and even cruelty, of this function. . . .

If the parents have really ruled with a rod of iron, we can easily understand the child developing a severe superego, but, contrary to our expectations, experience shows that the superego may reflect the same relentless harshness even when the upbringing has been gentle and kind, and avoided threats and punishments as far as possible (Freud, 1933c, p. 87 and p. 90).

If one accepts this conception of neurosis, then the mandate to the psychotherapist is clear: try to help reduce the "severity" of the patient's superego! For reasons developed not only in the chapters cited but elsewhere (Mowrer, 1950), it is the writer's position that the neurotic suffers less from superego severity ("false guilt") than from *ego immaturity* and that it is the therapist's responsibility to help the ego to grow up to the usually quite reasonable and proper standards of the superego, rather than to attempt (usually unsuccessfully, if not hazardously) to weaken or lower these standards. In other words, this conception of neurosis and its treatment holds that where there is a gain in intrapsychic integration it consists of the ego's coming into line with superego demands, not of the superego's being scaled down better to suit the ego. Children grow up and develop personally by learning to meet the demands of their parents and other adult members of society, not by ignoring or neutralizing or outwitting those demands. Since the ego and the superego are the internal equivalents of the child and his parents at an earlier stage, the analogy would suggest that in therapy it is the ego rather than the superego that shows the change and "growth." [9] Therefore, any method which offers the possibility of reliably determining whether therapy does, in fact, involve mainly a modification of the ego or mainly a modification of the superego is of special interest.

---

[9] As indicated in the preceding footnote and in numerous other passages in his last book, it would seem that Rogers' position in respect to this important issue is closer to that of Freud than to that of the writer. However, because of differences in concepts and phraseology, this matter is difficult to determine and will be reverted to again presently.

The results of the Hartley study on this score were as follows:

The views of present self changed markedly from the beginning to the end of therapy: $r = .15$.

The views of ideal self changed little during this same interval: $r = .71$.

Here is a very tentative indication that therapy results primarily in a change in the ego, or "present self," rather than in the "ideal self," or superego. And the same empirical picture, though with a somewhat different interpretation, is reported by Roger (1951b) for a more extensive study using the same general approach:

At the present writing, further investigation is being made of this problem, using the Q technique developed by William Stephenson. This permits a detailed analysis of the perception of self before and after therapy, as well as the self-ideal as it is perceived before and after therapy. Results from the first few cases indicate that the self-ideal changes somewhat during therapy, perhaps in the direction of a more realistic or achievable ideal. The perceived self changes even more markedly, and in a direction which brings it closer both to the pretherapy ideal and the posttherapy ideal. The correlation between self and ideal is initially low, but becomes much higher as a result of therapy due to the changes in a converging direction in both self and ideal. Thus the result of therapy would appear to be a greater congruence between self and ideal. The self and the values it holds are not so disparate. These statements are highly tentative and may be much altered by completion of the researches under way (pp. 140-41). [More recently, Rogers (1952) has published detailed results for one case, obtained by use of this methodology. These results conform, in their over-all pattern, to those alluded to in more general terms above.]

The findings of both Hartley and Rogers thus indicate, tentatively to be sure, that the "self," as defined by the S sort procedure, tends to change more during the course of psychotherapy than does the "self-ideal," or "ideal self," similarly defined. What are the systematic implications of this finding? Can it, for example, be legitimately taken as opposing the Freudian view that psychotherapy is largely a matter of lessening the "severity" of the superego, i.e., as confirming the view that recovery from neurosis involves growth in ego maturity rather than superego modification? Here the objection might be made that the "self ideal," the self that the patient would *like* to be, is not necessarily the same as what Freud denoted by the term "superego." However, it is instructive to recall that, before Freud coined the term "superego," he used the term "ego ideal" to refer to precisely the same concept. The first use of this term seems to have occurred in the following passage, taken from *A general introduction to psychoanalysis:*

I also told you that by analysis of the narcissistic disorders we hoped to gain some knowledge of the composition of the ego and of its structure out of various faculties and elements. We have made a beginning toward this at one point. From analysis of the delusion of observation we have come to the conclusion that in the ego there exists a faculty that incessantly watches, criticizes, and compares, and in this way is set against the other part of the ego. In our opinion, therefore, the patient reveals a truth which has not been appreciated as such when he complains that at every step he is spied upon and observed, that his every thought is known and examined. He has erred only in attributing this disagreeable power to something outside himself and foreign to him; he perceives within his ego the rule of a faculty which measures his actual ego and all his activities by an *ego-ideal,* which he has created for himself in the course of his development. . . . We recognize in this self-criticizing faculty the ego-censorship, the "conscience"; it is the same censorship as that exercised at night upon dreams, from which the repressions against inadmissible wish-excitations proceed. When this faculty disintegrates in the delusion of being observed, we are able to detect its origin and that it arose out of the influence of parents and those who trained the child, together with his social surroundings, by a process of identification with certain of these persons who were taken as a model (Freud, 1935a, p. 371).

Although Freud thus first used the term "ego-ideal" to refer to what he later called the superego, it is not yet certain whether this is necessarily the same as the function which is measured by a "self-ideal" S sort. What a person would *like* to be may or may not correspond closely to what he feels he *ought* to be; and if to this we add the notion that for the neurotic a part of the problem is that he has actually repressed not so much the forces of the id as those of conscience itself, then we become still less sure that in a "self-ideal" sort one is necessarily getting at superego functions.

In a personal communication, Professor Rogers has commented upon this problem as follows:

The self-ideal is what the person wants to be, which is in many instances very different from what he feels that he should be. In fact, I have proposed that we undertake a study to discriminate between the wanted self and "should be" self. I am convinced that we would find quite a difference and at the end of therapy the person is more like his wanted-self and probably further removed from his superego or should-be self.

It is apparent that the problem is, in part at least, one of interpretation. For Rogers, an ideal sort is one in which the subject describes his "self-ideal," but not necessarily his "ideal self." This may at first seem to be a distinction without a difference, but in the passages just quoted it is clear that for Rogers an ideal sort provides a picture of the individual's ideal, most desired conception of himself rather than of an outside or foreign (parental, social) conception of him. Rogers is thus saying, in effect, that an "ideal sort" is more of a function of the ego than of the superego. This may be the case; but it remains to be shown, empirically, how much these two functions would in fact differ in a person seeking therapy; and it will be recalled that when we speak of "the self and the values it holds" it is not immediately evident, a priori, that we are not dealing with superego functions, with the "should" area of the personality.

What stands out, then, from the foregoing discussion is this: that Q technique, as applied by Hartley, immediately takes us into some of the most important and controversial areas of psychotherapy and that it not only raises vital issues but, more importantly, holds promise also of help-ing to resolve them! [10]

Example II

The second example of so-called Q technique which will be used here for illustrative purposes is a study undertaken by Ewing (1952) at the University of Illinois. In it, persons who have just started personal counseling at the Student Counseling Bureau are given (after the second interview) 150 cards on which are printed descriptive words or short phrases such as "Bashful," "Dominating," "Ill at ease," "Feeling of in-feriority," etc. The clients are then asked to sort these cards into six categories. (This smaller number of categories is being used in order to simplify the mechanics of sorting; and an *even* number of categories is employed in order to make the results more readily amenable to the briefer statistical treatment which can be carried out by tetrachoric cor-relation.) The subjects are asked to do five different sorts: a *self sort,* an *ideal sort,* a *father sort* (a sorting of the cards so that they characterize the sorter's father), a *mother sort,* and a *counselor sort.* The sortings of the various "trait names" are in terms of an applicability-inapplicability continuum, just as in the Hartley study; and the subjects are again required to sort the cards into a normal distribution.

[10] The writer is indebted to John M. Butler, of the University of Chicago, for calling attention to a remarkable anticipation of this type of inquiry, by Lennig Sweet, in *The measurement of personal attitudes in younger boys* (1929). Follow-ing earlier leads by Goodwin Watson, Sweet asked his subjects to check certain questionnaire items four ways: I. "How you feel"; II. "How you think you ought to feel"; III. "How your group feels"; IV. "How most boys feel." "Six categories were supposed to be investigated. These were, together with the manner of scoring them: (A) *Peculiarity of Interest*—the total difference between the rating which the boy gives Column I (Self) and the Model Rating. (B) *Peculiarity of Ideal*— the total difference between the mode in each question of Column II (Ideal) and the boy's ideal on each question. (C) *Self-Conflict*—the total difference between the boy's self-rating on each item and his ideal on each item (Column I-Column II). (D) *Criticism of the Average Person*—total difference between the boy's rating of items in Column II (Ideal) and Column IV (Most Boys). (E) *Self-Esteem*—total criticism score minus total conflict score. (F) *Insight*—total difference between items in Column IV (Most Boys) and the mode in Column I (Self). A low score measures a high degree of insight" (p. 13). The parallelism between Sweet's study and the work of Hartley is at once apparent and striking. Hartley's investigation is distinctive in two important respects: (*a*) it uses the more refined scaling pro-cedure advocated by Stephenson (see below) and a correlational rather than additive statistical procedure; and (*b*) it makes measurements *through time,* i.e., studies the effects of therapy, rather than attempting merely to get a static, one-shot picture of the individual. However, the basic idea of getting at individual "adjust-ment" ("integration" is a better term) by studying the relationship between per-ceptions of the self, the ideal, and other frames of reference is certainly made very explicit in the Sweet study and, together with Watson's contributions, constitutes a landmark in this type of inquiry.

In so far as it proves feasible, all subjects will be asked to do the same set of five sortings after about ten interviews (approximately half-way through counseling) and again at the end of counseling.

Thirty-four unselected undergraduate college students have already been asked to sort the 150 trait-name items in terms of the "cultural ideal," i.e., in terms of what they believe to be *generally regarded* as desirable or undesirable personal characteristics. Average values have been obtained for all items on this type of rating so that these values can be directly compared with those assigned to each of the items by any given subject.

In Ewing's study, fifteen comparisons thus become possible for the results obtained from each set of sortings of the cards.[11] Many other comparisons are, of course, possible, such as those between the before-, during-, and after-counseling sorts and between different subjects.

This study, more strikingly than the first one, suggests that Q technique is a research tool which may prove useful not only in clinical but also in *social* psychology. As Ewing has observed (personal communication), earlier writers (Le Bon, McDougall, and others) have posited that each social group has a "mind," made up of an integration of the minds of the individual members of the group. The investigation here described suggests the converse thought: that each individual mind is made up of a "group," i.e., is composed very largely of experiences with and attitudes toward *other persons* who have played particularly significant roles in the life of the individual (cf. Sullivan, 1947).[12]

A feature of the Ewing study which is of special interest is the opportunity it would seem to afford for studying the phenomenon of *identification* in personally conflicted individuals and the changes which occur in this respect during the course of therapy. As indicated elsewhere (Chapter 3), there is considerable evidence for believing that in many (perhaps all) neuroses there is a basic conflict between masculine and feminine strivings (values, identifications); and if this be true, one would expect a change during successful therapy in the direction of greater congruity between the patient and the like-sexed parent.[13] Incidental observations to this effect will be recalled by every experienced therapist. For example, one male patient observed to the writer toward the end of therapy: "I have noticed that the lines of my father's face as I remember him seem to have softened in recent weeks," thus indicating a *rapprochement* of the son and the dead father in terms of interpersonal values and affective

[11] Counting the cultural ideal sort, there are six sorts. Using the familiar formula $\dfrac{(N)\ (N-1)}{2}$, we see that there are fifteen possible correlations.

[12] For a related suggestion concerning the psychology of groups, see below, "History of Q Technique and Its Relation to Factor Analysis." See also Chapter 12.

[13] This prediction might be expected to be verified only in those cases where the like-sexed parent is a reasonably adequate and representative specimen of masculinity or femininity. Where the like-sexed parent is in some degree inverted, successful therapy would be expected to follow another course (Mowrer, 1950, chap. xxi).

relationship. Life experiences commonly seem to have a somewhat similar effect, as suggested by Mark Twain's classical remark, made as he approached middle life: "I have been amazed to discover how much *my father* has learned in the last ten years!"

It is interesting that Stephenson in a general way anticipated this use of Q technique in one of his early (1936a) papers, when he said:

> We have here a suggestion that Q technique will supply a potent tool for experimental work on the similarities of siblings, twins, members of the one family, etc. (p. 354).

The possibilities in the Ewing study for investigating other psychologically and socially important problems are very numerous, but enough has been said to show the versatility of the method and to indicate further its general usefulness.

History of Q Technique and Its Relation to Factor Analysis

Today one hears the question asked increasingly: "What *is* Q technique?" Two examples have just been given of procedures to which the term is being currently applied, and one soon discovers that it has also been used to refer to still other procedures.

The purpose of the present section is to trace the history and interrelation of these other procedures and thus lay the groundwork for showing that the term "Q technique," as commonly employed at present, is too inclusive and should be supplemented by additional terms. In this way much of the current ambiguity and confusion can be eliminated and the way cleared for the more precise and efficient application of a group of related methods.

As one studies the investigations and theoretical papers out of which Q technique, in its varied meanings, has emerged, one finds three relatively distinct historical periods or phases. These will be discussed in the following pages.

Phase I: 1912-35

If one gives a number of tests to a number of persons, one obtains a *score matrix* of the type shown in Table 5. Early factor analysis, as it was developed by Spearman, called for the correlation of the results for each test with the results of every other test; and the resulting correlations were arranged in a *correlation matrix* of the kind shown in Table 6. On the basis of such data, factor analysis of the conventional type is then carried out.

But as one views Table 5, it is apparent that one can correlate the entries, not only by columns, but also *by rows*. What would such a procedure mean? One of its meanings, or possible uses, is very familiar. In Chapter 10 an example is given of eight persons being asked to score each of thirty-seven pages of a social case record. In order to see how *reliably*

TABLE 5

CONVENTIONAL ARRANGEMENT OF A SCORE MATRIX, GIVING THE RESULTS
OF MANY TESTS APPLIED TO MANY SUBJECTS

Tests	A	B	C	D	E	Etc.
Persons						
1	x	x	x	x	x	x
2	x	x	x	x	x	x
3	x	x	x	x	x	x
4	x	x	x	x	x	x
5	x	x	x	x	x	x
Etc.	x	x	x	x	x	x

these persons did the task assigned to them, the scores or ratings which
each individual gave to each of the thirty-seven pages were correlated
with the ratings assigned to the same pages by the other scorers. In this
situation, each page of the case record was a kind of separate "test," and
it was therefore possible, by correlating "rows" instead of "columns," to
obtain a correlation matrix comparable to that shown in Table 6. By
averaging the resulting correlation values, it was then possible to obtain

TABLE 6

CONVENTIONAL ARRANGEMENT OF A CORRELATION MATRIX, GIVING THE RESULTS
OBTAINED BY CORRELATING EACH OF THE COLUMNS IN TABLE 5
WITH EVERY OTHER COLUMN

Tests	A	B	C	D	E	Etc.
Persons						
A						
B	x					
C	x	x				
D	x	x	x			
E	x	x	x	x		
Etc.	x	x	x	x	x	

a figure which represented the agreement, or consistency, in terms of an
average correlation value, with which the scorers were able to do their
work. Thus, by *correlating persons,* rather than tests (i.e., pages of the
case record in this instance), we arrived at a "coefficient of reliability"
for the group with respect to ratings which the individual members of
the group were all asked to make.

This is a very old and very familiar procedure, and it may be said to
be the first application of the "correlation of persons." [14] If Q technique

---

[14] One of the early uses of "correlation of persons" as a means of establishing
the reliability of a test is that reported by Thomson and Bailes (1926), in "The
Reliability of Essay Marks." These investigators had six teachers mark essays
written by thirteen children, and the resulting score matrix was correlated "hori-

is defined simply as the "correlation of persons," as opposed to the "correlation of tests," then *this* is Q technique.[15]

But even during the period between 1912 and 1935, another use was seen for the correlation of persons. If "tests" can be subjected to factor analysis, then it is apparent that the same can be done with respect to "persons," i.e., correlations can be computed either vertically or horizontally in a score matrix such as that shown in Table 5; and at an early point it was seen that whereas the correlation of tests leads to the isolation of personality traits, or "factors," the correlation of persons will lead to the identification of personality *types*.

As Burt (1940) has observed: "Almost from the outset . . . correlations have been calculated between persons; and from time to time such correlations have been expressly studied from a factor standpoint" (p. 169). In a study reported by Burt and Moore (1912), implications of this procedure for type psychology were explicitly noted (see especially p. 251).[16] And later that year Burt, in collaboration with Davies, conducted a study in which the possibilities already noted were put into effect. Davies, in her 1939 review, says:

The earliest use of the method appears to be that of Burt and Davies in 1912 for a study of imagery types among school children; and the first table of this kind to be printed in full and examined from the standpoint of factor theory is that discussed by the former in his 1921 Report on *Mental and scholastic tests* and based on data obtained with tests of intelligence. . . . In 1926 . . . Thomson and Bailes published three tables of correlations between teachers' marks; though they do not actually work out saturation coefficients by the summation method, they give (according to a common practice at that time) correlations with the average or total order, which amounts to much the same thing. Some of the most interesting data are "consistency coefficients" obtained from one and the same individual with one and the same set of test material. From 1922 onward, first at the National Institute of Industrial Psychology, and later at University College, Burt and his research assistants, following a fairly systematic program, have used the method for investigating temperamental types, aesthetic appreciation, and the like (p. 410).

---

zontally." The authors conclude: "These correlations are, on the whole, high, and point to a considerable measure of agreement—in excess of what is commonly held to be true. And in spite of the individual inconsistencies, one can, we think, draw the same conclusion throughout, that the correlations obtained by judges of essays are fairly satisfactory, *considering the great difficulty of the task*. But considered as reliability marks for two markings of the same work, the correlations are very low" (p. 91).

[15] As we shall see shortly, Stephenson has maintained from the outset that Q technique is *not* merely the correlation of persons but the use of the values thus obtained for the carrying out of a factor analysis. He says: "I have just inferred that if two persons estimate a population for the same trait, the correlation between the two series of estimates is sometimes called the 'reliability coefficient' of the trait. Q technique, for such data, would begin with the factor analysis of the correlations of this kind for *many* persons" (Stephenson, 1936b, p. 359).

[16] Burt says that, as early as 1911, Stern had referred to correlations that are carried out " 'horizontally' instead of 'vertically' " (Burt, 1940, p. 171).

Burt himself summarizes this early work on the correlation of persons as follows:

In particular it [the "new technique"] appeared especially suited for numerous incidental problems in education and vocational guidance—e.g., for studying the preferences of children and adults, for assessing the agreement among school or university examiners, for estimating the reliability of psychological observers, for analyzing the nature of alleged temperamental and clinical types, and generally for all those inquiries in which the performances of the persons examined had to be compared with a subjective rather than with an objective standard, i.e., was itself a set of personal reactions or judgments (Burt, 1940, p. 172).

Here no attempt will be made to review all of the early work which involved the "correlation of persons," for Davies has already done this admirably. But we should not omit reference to a study by Beebe-Center which apparently represents the first use of the method in this country. This writer says:

If the considerations above be legitimate, the application of Spearman's method to hedonic tone enables one not only to judge the legitimacy of assuming a general hedonic factor in the case of a given class of stimuli, but also to ascertain the degree of generality of such a factor. This degree of generality is clearly equal to the proportion of unselected observers whose hedonic ranking of the stimuli when intercorrelated yields coefficients of correlation which satisfy the tetrad equation. Should it be found that any group of observers chosen at random satisfied these conditions, the general hedonic factor may be considered to be entirely general.

But further—provided always that our theoretical considerations be correct —the application which we are proposing for Spearman's method enables us to ascertain the degree to which the general hedonic factor is operative in the judgment of any given observer [or hedonic "type"?] and its value in the various individual stimuli.

It might be added that this line of thought suggests a ready means of distinguishing aesthetic hedonic value from nonaesthetic hedonic value, [the value] being considered aesthetic in proportion as it is general in the sense in which the term is used above. It also suggests a means of distinguishing between the aesthetically sensitive and the aesthetically dull. [Here is an unmistakable reference to typology!] Given a set of aesthetic objects, i.e., objects to which there have been assigned entirely general hedonic values in the sense in which the term is used above, the aesthetic sensitivity of an individual to these objects could be considered a function of the correlation between the hedonic value assigned by him to the objects and their general hedonic values. [Italics added to emphasize the use by Beebe-Center of a subjective continuum.]

What results are yielded by the actual application of Spearman's method to appropriate hedonic data? In the course of an experiment upon hedonic habituation carried out at Harvard in 1925-26, I had occasion to determine the hedonic rank-orders of fourteen olfactory substances for each of eight observers [by the method of paired comparison]. Intercorrelation of these rank-orders yields the Spearman coefficients given in the table below (Beebe-Center, 1932, pp. 202-3).

The specific outcomes of this study are of no immediate interest here. Rather is it important to note that the *method* used by Beebe-Center involved three important features: (*a*) "horizontal" as opposed to "vertical" correlation; (*b*) use of a scale or continuum which avoided the problem of "disparity," or "heterogeneity," of items (see below); and (*c*) clear, if limited, perception of the implications for personality typology. These considerations, as we shall presently see, occupy an important place in what was shortly to be designated as Q technique.[17]

Phase II: 1935-42

A. Contributions of Stephenson and Thomson.—In the light of the facts which have just been reviewed, developments which took place in 1935 and subsequently are somewhat puzzling. Godfrey Thomson and William Stephenson date the inception of Q technique from that year, and Stephenson, especially, feels that it marks a radical departure from all previous conceptions. On this score Thomson (1950) says:

The first explicit references to correlations between persons in connection with factor technique seem to have been made independently and almost simultaneously by Thomson (1935, July) and Stephenson (1935a, August), the former being pessimistic, the latter optimistic. But such correlation had actually been used much earlier by Burt and by Thomson, and almost certainly by others (p. 199).

Thomson's 1935 reference to the "new" method was restricted to a footnote which runs as follows:

The above matrix of correlations R has *t* rows and *t* columns, and the correlations are between tests. Although it would be out of place to digress into the matter in the present article, I would like to call attention to another matrix obtainable by standardizing the matrix of raw scores by columns

---

[17] At least three other American foci of interest in this approach should be noted. The earliest and most important of these has been at Catholic University, in Washington, D. C., from which has come a number of papers by Moore (1939, 1941, 1946), Moore, Stafford, and Hsu (1947), Stafford and Hsu (1947), Hsu (1946, 1949), and others, (see Hofstaetter, 1941). In 1942 Carlson and Harrell, at the University of Illinois, published a paper entitled, "Voting Groups Among Leading Congressmen Obtained by Means of the Inverted Factor Technique." And Winch (1947), a sociologist, has written on "Heuristic and Empirical Typologies: a Job for [Inverted] Factor Analysis." Among the first group of investigators to profit from direct contact with Stephenson since his arrival in this country are Fiedler (1949, 1950b) and Fiske (1950). However, none of these investigators took the step that is a central feature of the two examples of Q technique which have been presented in the preceding section (see "Summary," p. 343).

instead of, as here, by rows. If we call it in that case Y instead of Z, then we have

$$Y'Y = Q$$

where Q is a p-square matrix of q-correlations, each correlation being between *two persons,* not between two tests. Sampling error would mean error because we had not used the whole population of tests on the two persons, just as ordinarily it means that we have not used the whole population of persons on the two tests.

The attempt, however, to standardize the matrix of raw scores by columns [18] forces our attention on to the fundamental question of mental units, which I think has tended to be neglected in the recent work on psychological correlations. When I standardize the matrix of raw scores by rows in the usual way, I am of course assuming that whatever the raw units may be, at any rate the same unit is used along any row, on the different persons. This gives the matrix Z.

If I want to standardize the matrix of raw scores by columns, I can only do so if I can assume or ensure that the raw units used in any one column are all the same. That is, I have to be able to say that a person does better in a test i than he does in a test j, and this raises hosts of difficulties, the consideration of which, however, will make anyone who studies this matter rather careful how he talks about scores in tests without facing the question of what units are being used, consciously or unconsciously (pp. 75-76).

Stephenson's first published statement regarding Q technique appeared as a note in *Nature,* entitled "Technique of Factor Analysis," and is so brief that it can be quoted here in full.

Factor analysis is a subject upon which Professor G. H. Thomson, Doctor William Brown and others have frequently written letters to *Nature.* This analysis is concerned with a selected population of n individuals each of whom has been measured in m tests. The $(m)(m-1)\sqrt{2}$ intercorrelations for these m variables are subjected to either a Spearman or other factor analysis.

The technique, however, can also be inverted. We begin with a population of n different tests (or essays, pictures, traits, or other measurable material), each of which is measured or scaled by m individuals. The $(m)(m-1)\sqrt{2}$ intercorrelations are then factorized in the usual way.

This inversion has interesting practical applications. It brings the factor technique from group and field work into the laboratory, and reaches into spheres of work hitherto untouched or not amenable to factorization. It is especially valuable in experimental aesthetics and in educational psychology, no less than in pure psychology.

It allows a completely new series of studies to be made on the Spearman "central intellective factor" (g), and also allows tests to be made of the Two-

[18] Thomson is here speaking of a score matrix in which the columns are headed "Persons" and the rows labeled "Tests," rather than the other way round. Thus, when he refers to "raw scores by columns," he means all the scores for each person, i.e., "raw scores by rows" in terms of the more conventional type of table or matrix (see Table 5).

Factor Theorem under greatly improved experimental conditions. Data on these and other points are to be published in due course in the *British Journal of Psychology* (Stephenson, 1935a, p. 297).

The article in the *British Journal of Psychology,* just cited, has to be consulted in order to gain anything like a complete picture of what "inverted" factor analysis meant to Stephenson at this juncture. The following excerpts will give some of the highlights and the general tenor of his thinking:

> In the following paper I am to describe some consequences of a new factor technique which, I believe, should do for general and type psychology what Professor Spearman's original work has done already, and will continue to do, for individual psychology. Factor analysis in the past in the hands of Spearman, Thurstone, Hotelling, and others, has concerned itself with *individual differences;* its variables have been estimates or tests, its populations are groups of persons. The analysis I am to describe serves a very different, yet complementary purpose: its variables are *persons,* whilst its populations are groups of tests or estimates. This very simple inversion of all previous factor theorems and techniques leads unexpectedly to many new fields of experimental work . . . .
>
> In the current technique, tests are variables, whilst in the inverted technique persons are variables instead, and we deal with the correlation between persons (Stephenson, 1936a, 344-45).

In this article, Stephenson, for the first time, calls the method something other than "inverse," or "obverse," factor analysis. He says:

> Following Professor G. H. Thomson's suggestion, I shall use Q as the sign for correlations between persons, so distinguishing them from correlations such as *r* between two tests (p. 345).

Burt had previously used P to designate much the same procedure, but Stephenson's vision of the method seemed to him so different from the conceptions of his predecessors that he felt a new term was needed, to distinguish his method from "the old P procedure."

On the next page of the article Stephenson reverts to Godfrey Thomson's question of the legitimacy of correlating items in a raw score matrix which are not on the same scale and which, even though mathematically equalized by the method of standard scores, still cannot be thought of as being comparable for the reason that they represent disparate, noncomparable dimensions or qualities. Thus, if one test yields a score for a given individual of 1.14 for "intelligence" and another test gives a score of, let us say, 26 for "emotional stability," the question of how to make these scores mathematically comparable is really insoluble; for there is no exact way of determining how many units of "intelligence" equal or are *worth* one unit of "emotional stability." This is the old and familiar problem of trying to add, multiply, or otherwise mathematically manipulate "apples and oranges." One can, of course, compare such unlike objects with respect to some *common quality* such as weight, but here our unit ceases to be either apples *or* oranges and becomes *pounds*. This is actually the solution which Stephenson adopted,[19] but the method by which he rationalized this expedient was as follows:

These measurements are indeed incomparable so long as we consider measurement to be the prerogative of individual psychology, or the psychology of individual differences as this is understood today. But such measurements can be rendered comparable and homogeneous if they are thought of from the point of view of *type* psychology. Thus, we say that the *common-sense* type of person has a preponderance of W factor over G factor; that is, the heterogeneous factor measurements W and G *are put in an order of significance for the individual, and this order is compared with the orders of other individuals. If, then, any list of heterogeneous measurements or estimates can be arranged in an order of some kind, or in a scale, for their representativeness or significance for the individual, they may be held to be made homogeneous with respect to that individual.* This last sentence opens the way to many applications of Q technique (p. 346).

Elsewhere in the same article Stephenson makes much the same point in different words:

In a paper elsewhere [Stephenson, 1936b] I have shown that past work on personality traits and orexis generally is readily open to investigation anew by way of Q technique. It seems likely that such work is best approached by way of this technique. The procedure is uniformly as follows. A population of traits is selected; *these are put in an order of representativeness for the individual,* those most characteristic of him being given high scores, whilst those least characteristic are scored low. The procedure is otherwise the same as that followed in the above examples. The selection of traits can be made on many grounds, some to suit general, and others only particular purposes (p. 357).

So far as I know, no one had previously used the technique completely, or with full understanding (p. 352).

In conclusion Stephenson says:

In the above pages I have introduced a factor technique which is an inversion of all previous factor work. Following Professor G. H. Thomson, I have used the term Q for correlation between persons, just as *r* is used for

---

[19] For a discussion of the same problem from a somewhat different standpoint, see Burt (1937). He says: "Several investigations carried out both at the Institute of Education and at University College by research students and myself appeared to confirm the value and the validity of the procedure in this field. There is, for example, no way of knowing whether A really gets as much pleasure as B from looking at Picasso's *Clown;* but A can certainly tell us whether he prefers Picasso's *Clown* to Watteau's. Thus, we can get a group of persons to rank a selected set of pictures or other aesthetic stimuli in order of preference, and then correlate their rankings either with each other or with an empirical or an a priori standard" (p. 63). In the same paper, Burt gives a good review of his early (antedating Stephenson's) uses of Q technique.

correlation between tests. Certain elementary theorems have been described, and some applications of Q technique instanced, notably its use as an essential instrument for general and type psychology for isolating types of persons and supplying indices of such types. I briefly describe anew the kind of factor analysis which, I believe, best fits workaday conditions, namely the inverted form of Spearman's two-factor theorem. A few examples of Q technique have been worked, but many others could just as readily have been included.

I have concluded that Q technique serves general and type psychology, just as r technique is for work on individual differences, and this dichotomy would seem to be a fundamental one (Stephenson, 1936a, pp. 360-61).

B. Review and Evaluation.—Against the historical background which we have now reviewed, it will be useful to examine the contributions of Stephenson and Thomson as of the middle 1930's. As we have seen, the possibility of "correlating persons," as well as tests, had been recognized for nearly a quarter of a century prior to 1935; and the method had been put to practical use in studying the reliability, or consistency, of raters and test-markers, in the determination of personality types,[20] and in other connections. As we have likewise seen, subjective scaling as a means of avoiding the problem of heterogeneity of test scores had also been previously employed, by Burt, Beebe-Center, and others.

Three considerations remain, then, as the ones for which Stephenson and Thomson deserve credit as of this period:

1. INVERTED FACTOR ANALYSIS AND TYPE PSYCHOLOGY. The two investigators just cited were certainly among the first to propose that factor analysis be applied to correlations between persons, as it had already been applied to correlations between tests. How large a place the investigation of personality types occupied in Stephenson's early conception of Q technique is indicated in the following passage:

This, then, completes what I set out to say. . . . Several contributions to psychometry have been outlined, notably that which offers to bring type psychology within the folds of scientific psychometry, and which results in the interesting conception of a standard or typical person for a population of traits, this standard being merely a true estimate of the *nature* of a factor discovered by correlations and inverted factor theorems. It seems highly gratifying that the much abused and ancient viewpoint in psychology, that of personality and physical types, after many vicissitudes and misconceptions, has at last become crystallized into postulates and methods which render a scientific account of it, and which will make of it, surely, an unchallengeable feature of psychology. It seems to me a fascinating matter that type psychology is statistically merely the obverse of present-day psychometry, and that, after all, we can emulate the physicist and measure persons in terms of standard persons (Stephenson, 1936c, p. 304).

[20] "In my *Memorandum* [1936] I stated that 'generally, the correlation of tests or traits leads to an analysis of the human mind in the abstract; and the correlation of testees leads to an analysis of the concrete human population,' i.e., to the study of individuals and their grouping into types" (Burt, 1940, p. 185).

Writing in 1940, Wolfle made the following observations on this score:

The problem of isolating personality types, with types defined in terms of the possession of a given pattern of traits, has been investigated by Stephenson with what he called the "inverted factor technique." It is not a new method of factor analysis but a new use. Ordinarily one correlates the scores on one *test* with those on another and factors the resulting correlation table. In the inverted technique, one correlates the scores of one *person* with the scores of another person, so that the correlations are between persons instead of between tests. This table of correlations between persons may then be factored by any appropriate technique. The obtained factors are not traits of personality but types of individuals. It is possible to give to each individual a score which indicates his degree of approximation to, or his correlation with, the most typical person.

Stephenson has presented several short examples of the application of the inverted technique (1935b, 1936a, 1936b). In one study (1936a), eighteen persons rated themselves as to the applicability of thirty "moods." One general type characterized the normal person. The more usual a person is, the higher is his saturation with this factor. The second factor showed similarities with Kretschmer's cyclothymic-schizothymic distinction, with some individuals having positive and others negative weights on the factor. This factor, Stephenson adds, becomes very large in psychiatric patients.

The inverted factor technique has not been given sufficient trial to justify any final judgment on its usefulness. Thomson (1939) thinks the method is suitable for such tasks as comparing the different graders of a set of examination questions but warns that it is not applicable where the several measures on each individual are in different terms. Dunlap (1938) considers it "the best method yet proposed for locating types" (pp. 37-38).

Perhaps because of the inherent difficulties in the type conception of personality, so-called "inverted" factor-analytic studies have not proved very fruitful to date. Hofstaetter (1951), for example, has summarized the current situation as follows: "Intuitively established typologies have been practically abandoned in the modern scientific psychology of individual differences, and the more recent attempts to replace them by statistical type-notions ('Q technique'), though promising, have not yet been applied widely enough" (p. 99). The value of Q technique, in the sense of factor-analytic study and isolation of personality types, thus remains in the balance.

2. SCALING ASPECTS OF Q TECHNIQUE. The problem of heterogeneity of test scores as it applies to the "correlation of persons" had already been solved, in principle, well before 1935. However, Stephenson did much to put this solution into practical effect and introduced, in addition, an important computational aid. By means of the forced-choice technique according to which subjects are required to sort items into a normal distribution (see Examples I and II above), the *mean* of the distribution automatically becomes the same for each subject, as does the

sigma thereof, a fact which greatly simplifies the calculation of correlation coefficients. However, as Stephenson has himself remarked, "such distributions are matters of convenience only" (1936*b*, p. 355) ; and, as will be pointed out later, this gain in convenience is achieved at the expense of informatio. which for some purposes may be quite essential (see page 370).

3. Potentialities of a General Approach. Although Stephenson and Thomson both advanced the notion that personality types might be objectively identified by means of "inverted" factor analysis, the former has been the more energetic in pushing and publicizing the research implications of this and a related group of ideas which he has collectively christened "Q technique." Stephenson's writings in this connection, while sometimes unsystematic and partisan, are always stimulating and characterized by lively imagination and an infectious enthusiasm. Stephenson's early work along these lines was interrupted by the Second World War, but he has more recently returned to this area of inquiry and some of his current contributions will be alluded to in later pages of this chapter.

Phase III: 1942 and After

At this juncture the reader may be struck by the disparity between Examples I and II of Q technique (pages 317-26) and the historical denotations which have emerged thus far in the present section. This disparity becomes particularly clear when one tries to identify the common elements involved.

It is obvious that the use of "inverted" factor analysis is not an essential feature of Q technique, since it is not involved, or not necessarily involved, in Examples I and II. Nor is even the "correlation of *persons*" a common element, since correlation of the performances (S sorts) of one and the same person at two different times has also been termed "Q technique." By a process of elimination, we are thus left with only the method of scaling and standardizing data which is described above (i.e., the S sort) as the distinguishing feature of Q technique. But if we use the latter term exclusively for denoting this procedure, we have no special designation either for the correlation of different persons on the basis of a single set of test results or for the correlation of the same person on the basis of two or more sets of test results obtained at different times. It is common practice at present to refer to this method of scaling and standardizing data as a Q sort, but for reasons which have already been touched upon and will be elaborated later (page 343), it seems preferable to use the designation "S sort" for this purpose, as has been the practice throughout this chapter.

It is thus apparent that we do not yet have a proper perspective for resolving the various semantic and logical problems which are implied by the term "Q technique." Happily there is another series of investigations, not previously cited, which promises to deliver us from these difficulties and to provide a framework into which the various special methods ambiguously defined as Q technique can be systematically fitted.

A. The Emergence of O Technique and P Technique.—In 1943, Bordin published an article, entitled "Factor Analysis in Experimental Designs in Clinical and Social Psychology," based on a doctoral thesis written in 1942 at Ohio State University under the direction of H. A. Edgerton. A preliminary report of the study was presented at the meeting of the American Psychological Association, at Evanston, Illinois, in the fall of 1941.

These details are important for the reason that in Bordin's study we find, for the first time, recognition of the unique research possibilities which arise when one starts repeating, not persons or tests, but *occasions*. Prior to Bordin's study, factor-analytic researches had been restricted, as already indicated, to attempts to arrive at the components, or *traits*, of personality (traditional factor analysis) or at the characteristic ways in which these components combine in particular persons to form personality *types* ("inverted" factor analysis). Both trait psychology and type psychology are essentially static or nondynamic, and both importantly stress, in their underlying presuppositions, the element of nativism or innateness. But when one begins to repeat occasions, new possibilities open up for the study of personality movement, of *change;* and it is here that Bordin's study blazes a trail which will lead us back to a fuller and more orderly understanding of investigations such as those previously described in this chapter.

Bordin begins by criticizing conventional factor analysis on the grounds that: "A study of this sort cannot be truly said to produce scientific facts, but merely to demonstrate that data can be manipulated to fit a preconception" (p. 421). And, in keeping with the thesis that the preoccupation of Stephenson and other British psychologists with more or less immutable traits and types had limited their vision, Bordin says: "It would seem that these men are so preoccupied with biological hypotheses that they have overlooked other approaches to the data" (p. 423).

The study which Bordin carried out consisted of soliciting ratings from forty-one college students with respect to their "degree of participation" in 119 types of social recreation. This inventory was given to the students as freshmen, during the first two weeks of school, and again during the middle of the sophomore year. The data obtained made possible a study, through correlational methods, of the "influence of the college environment" upon students by showing the changes which were produced by such influences. If the way in which the students rated the 119 items referring to recreational participation on the first occasion correlated highly with the way they rated them on the second occasion, then the college environment had produced little change, but if the correlation between the first and second ratings was low, then change had manifestly occurred.

Since certain collateral information was not available for all subjects, Bordin felt that his study fell short of achieving its fullest possible significance, but he remarks: "Yet the shortcomings of this experiment merely serve to emphasize the latent power of this experimental design" (p. 425). And in a truly prophetic vein he adds:

Thus we see that this experimental design permits an effective co-mingling of the statistical and clinical methods in such a manner as to permit of more systematic and public demonstration of the tenability of various hypotheses and yet retains that proximity to the raw data of psychology which clinical psychologists have so rightly emphasized. Further, this type of experiment, by its very proximity to the raw data, can stimulate the development of further insightful hypotheses about the behavioral phenomena under observation (p. 426).

Bordin clearly foresaw the possible applicability of his method to personality research along the life-line of the individual, which Murray (1938) has emphasized, to the "nature-nurture problem," and to the study of "the development of attitudes and the conditions fostering their changes" (p. 428). Bordin fails to make explicit mention of the possibility of using this method to investigate the effects of psychotherapy—probably because he was continuing to think in terms of using it with many persons rather than with a single individual—but what is unmistakable is that here is the first clear appreciation of the "dimension" or "universe" of *occasions,* in addition to those of *tests* and *persons.*[21] Hartley's study is apparently the first to repeat occasions with a single subject, but it will be seen that this technique is implicit in Bordin's study, since it involves essentially the same procedure with *many* subjects. Instead of giving many tests (each of the 119 items can be regarded as a "test," just as can each of Hartley's 150 cards) to one subject on two (or more) occasions, as occurred in Hartley's study, Bordin gave many tests to many subjects on two (or, potentially, more) occasions. In this and other respects which will become evident upon reading this paper, Bordin approximated the kind of social-personality research suggested by Pepinsky *et al.* (see p. 342). It also anticipated Cattell's growing interest in the relationship between "personality" and group "syntality" (Cattell, 1950*a*).

Shortly after the publication of Bordin's study, Cattell (1946, 1947) began to experiment with another type of correlational procedure involving the repetition of occasions (for a detailed account of this procedure and its history, see Chapter 15). Given a multiplicity of tests and a multiplicity of occasions, it is obvious that one can correlate in either of two ways, just as one can with a multiplicity of tests and a multiplicity of

[21] Bordin (personal communication) points out that "either Anastasi or Garrett or both had carried out factor analyses (in this case, of R technique correlational matrices) at about the same time in which occasions were involved. Occasions were represented by the analysis of the factor structure of a set of tests at different age levels. This is not exactly equivalent to my design in that I do not think the same people were used. However, it is close . . . ." (Cf. Anastasi, 1932; Balinsky, 1941; Garrett, 1946.)

persons. Bordin was apparently the first to correlate results obtained by giving many tests on two (or more) occasions; whereas Cattell was the first to see the possibility of correlating the results obtained by giving two (or more) tests on *many* occasions. To the latter procedure Cattell has given the name "P technique"; and to the former we can, in like manner, apply the term "O technique."

If correlation of the results obtained by giving two (or more) tests to many persons on one occasion is known as R technique, and if correlation of the results obtained by giving many tests to two (or more) persons on one occasion is known as Q technique; and if the giving of two (or more) tests to one person on many occasions is known as P technique; and if we then refer to the correlation of results obtained by giving many tests to one person on two (or more) occasions as O technique, it is apparent that Examples I and II of Q technique (pages 317 and 324) are not examples of Q technique at all, properly speaking, but of *O technique*. The author agrees that a rose by any other name would smell as sweet, but the distinction between Q technique, as the correlation of persons, and the procedure used by Bordin, Hartley, Ewing, and now many others is so real and so important that we obviously need different terms for the two operations.

B. Cattell's Covariation Chart.—At this point a graphic device developed by Cattell comes to our assistance as a means of showing the systematic relationship between the four correlational procedures which have just been identified and two more which will be discussed shortly. In *Description and measurement of personality* (1946), and again in a more recent volume (Cattell, 1950*a*), this writer presents a "covariation chart" which is here reproduced as Figure 35. In describing this chart Cattell * says:

The search for functional unities by R, Q, and P techniques begins in each with correlation coefficients worked out on a *series* peculiar to each. In R technique a correlation is between two tests (or symptoms) on a series of persons; in P technique [22] it is between two tests on a series of days or occasions, and so on. While we are thinking of the general theory of manifestation and of the method of discovery of functional unities, it is instructive to glance at the covariation chart. . . .

This is a device, discussed in greater detail elsewhere [Cattell, 1946], reminding us that there are essentially *three* fundamentals, or, rather, series of fundamentals, among which the relations of correlations can be established in psychology. They are: people (or organisms); tests (or behavioral performances of any kind); and occasions (on which tests or people interact). The series in each of these constitute the three dimensions of the chart. Whenever two parallel lines are drawn on or through the parallelepiped, there exist two correlatable series. Thus the band running . . . horizontally to

* By permission from *Personality: a systematic theoretical and factual study,* by R. B. Cattell. Copyright, 1950. McGraw-Hill Book Co., Inc.

[22] Not to be confused with the "old P [really Q] technique" of Burt.

the right [in Figure 35] starts with two tests (each represented by a dot in the vertical line of test series). The length of each line is represented by a series of persons—a projection upward of the series of persons along the bottom edge. The band lies in a single vertical plane, corresponding to a single-occasion lamina (the first one) from the series of occasions represented

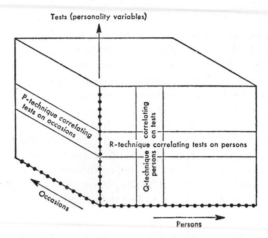

FIG. 35.—The "covariation chart" of Cattell (1950a), which might equally well be called a "correlation cube." It shows, systematically, the interrelationship of three types of statistical procedures: correlations that are carried out with a universe of *tests* (R technique), correlations that are carried out with a universe of *persons* (Q technique), and correlations that are carried out with a universe of *occasions* (P technique).

by dots along the left lower edge. In short, it is an R technique band, representing the correlation between two tests administered on one occasion to a series of people.

As the student who cares to play with this diagram will find, it directs to many untried and novel possibilities of correlation series, each capable of throwing light on functional unities in a new context. It presents approaches beyond P, Q, and R techniques, such as the correlation of occasions; but the three most relevant to personality study remain the R, Q, and P methods, as indicated by parallel tracks on the diagram (Cattell, 1950a, pp. 31-32).

Study of Cattell's covariation chart indicates that O technique occupies much the same position with respect to P technique that Q technique occupies with respect to R technique. In R technique tests are correlated, with persons held constant; in Q technique persons are correlated, with tests held constant. In P technique, in its simplest form, two tests, on the same person, are administered many times; in O technique, in its simplest form, many tests, on the same person, are administered two times. If many tests were repeated on the same person, not twice, but many times, the data obtained would make possible both an O technique and a P technique analysis; likewise, if many tests are given just once to many persons, the data needed for both Q and R technique analyses are obtained.

Enough has thus been said to indicate that the type of correlation involved in Examples I and II (pages 317 and 324) are neither Q technique nor P technique (as defined by Cattell) but a distinctive type of correlational procedure here termed O technique.[23] From the foregoing discussion it is also evident that on the top side of Cattell's figure there is the possibility of *two more* correlational techniques. However, the way in which Cattell has drawn this figure does not make it particularly well suited for discussing these two techniques. Accordingly, essentially the same chart has been redrawn and is presented as Figure 36. Here we

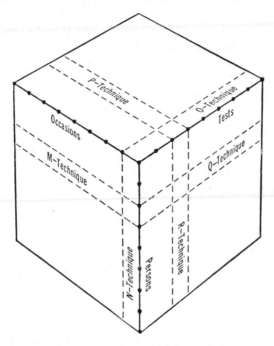

Fig. 36.—A modified and expanded version of Cattell's covariation chart (see Figure 35). Here three "new" techniques are indicated: O, N, and M. For discussion of these and their relation to techniques R, Q, and P, see text.

clearly see all six of the correlational techniques which are logically possible. These can be defined as follows:

R Technique: Correlation of results obtained from many persons taking two (or more) tests on one occasion

Q Technique: Correlation of results obtained from two (or more) persons taking many tests on one occasion

P Technique: Correlation of results obtained from one person taking two (or more) tests on many occasions

---

[23] Since the above was written, Cattell, in a new study (1951*d*) has likewise introduced the O notation. See also Cattell (1952*b*).

O Technique: Correlation of the results obtained from one person taking many tests on two (or more) occasions

N Technique: Correlation of the results obtained from many persons taking one test on two (or more) occasions

M Technique: Correlation of the results obtained from two (or more) persons taking one test on many occasions

N technique will be immediately recognized; it is, for example, the familiar procedure followed in establishing the test-retest reliability for a test. M technique is less easily recognized perhaps, but it turns out to be of unusually great interest and will be discussed at length below (see pages 349-53). Just as R and Q technique and P and O technique have certain logical and mathematical relationships, so, obviously, do N and M techniques. It is clear that by giving one test to many persons on many occasions, one would obtain data that could be subjected to correlational or factor-analytic procedures along the lines of either N or M technique. So far as the writer is aware, however, no one has systematically exploited this possibility.

The total possibilities for correlational and factor-analytic procedures which are suggested by Cattell's covariation chart may be summarized, then, as follows:

R and Q Techniques: Many persons, many tests, one occasion

P and O Techniques: One person, many tests, many occasions

N and M Techniques: Many persons, one test, many occasions

Many persons given many tests on many occasions would yield comprehensive data which would make possible all six kinds of correlation and all six kinds of factor analysis.[24]

It might appear that in this way we exhaust the possibilities offered for correlational studies in the field of personality, but this may or may not be true, depending upon how one resolves the enigma which arises in trying to fit into the covariation chart all the operations involved in Q technique as represented in Examples I and II (pages 317-26). It will be recalled that before therapy the self sort and the ideal sort were correlated, and that the same was done after therapy. Is *this* Q technique? This term should, as we have seen, be reserved for the *correlation of persons*. The issue, then, is whether in the case under discussion, there are one or two "persons" involved. In the physical sense, one person does both the self sort and the ideal sort; but in the psychological sense,

[24] A recent study by Pepinsky, Clyde, Olesen, and Pielstick (1950), entitled "Individual Personality and Behavior in a Social Group," suggests the possibility that in group therapy (or any other study of "social action") it might be desirable to give many persons many tests on many occasions and thus create a more systematic way of studying the individual and social changes occurring in such a group. (The number of correlations which would thus become possible and necessary is appalling, but electronic computers would perhaps obviate this difficulty.) Cf. Chapter 14.

two persons might be said to be represented: the present, existent person and an imaginary, ideal person into whom the present, real person may eventually change. From one standpoint, we might rationalize this type of procedure as Q technique; and, in the same sense, we may be said to correlate "persons" and thus to use true Q technique if we had one person do Q sorts for a number of objectively different persons and then correlated the results.

It may be objected, however, that this resolution of the problem is based upon a semantic dodge, a kind of pun on the word "person." An alternative would be to assume that Cattell's chart is incomplete and that yet other dimensions (in "hyperspace") are needed for variations in what might be called *instructions* or *set*. Under "Implications and Comments" below, more will be said about this variable (see pages 365 and 373). It would still seem that the difference in results produced by the same person when acting under different instructions can be legitimately handled on the assumption that different "persons" are involved—the person-you-are, the person-you-would-like-to-be, the person-your-spouse-thinks-you-are, etc. Therefore, in the Hartley study, we may say that Q technique was employed when the pretherapy self sort and ideal sort were correlated and when the posttherapy self sort and ideal sort were correlated. But when the pretherapy self sort was correlated with the posttherapy self sort and when the pretherapy ideal sort was correlated with the posttherapy ideal sort, this, properly speaking, was not Q but O technique. The fact that the S sort procedure was employed in all instances for collecting and standardizing the data should not confuse the issue with respect to the kinds of correlations which were carried out.[25]

Summary.—From the foregoing historical review, it is clear that the term "Q technique," as defined by Stephenson (following a preliminary suggestion by Thomson), is a loose designation for a number of distinct, though functionally related, procedures which need to be more precisely defined. One of these procedures is the method of scaling and standardizing data here termed the S sort.[26] While the rudiments of this procedure had been previously adumbrated, the writings of Stephenson in the mid-1930's did much to publicize the procedure.

Another of the procedures loosely subsumed under the term "Q technique" is the correlation of persons (as contrasted with tests) and, optionally, factor analysis of the resulting data. This general approach had

[25] Since the above was written, C. E. Osgood has pointed out (personal communication) that in addition to the three universes identified by Cattell—persons, tests, and occasions—there is a fourth related universe: that of *scales*. This observation has many interesting implications which Osgood will develop in a future publication. Cattell (1952*b*) has also recently referred to what may, for some purposes, be regarded as two additional universes: *scales* and *observers*. (See discussion of the Subjectivity-Objectivity Dichotomy, pp. 353-58.)

[26] It is suggested that this procedure, for which a distinctive name is clearly needed, be termed "S sort" or "S procedure" for the reason that *S* stands for *self* psychology, for *subjective* scaling, and for *Stephenson*.

also been anticipated by earlier workers, but the publications of Stephenson, along with those of Thomson, did much to stress the special characteristics of what may be called "correlation in the second dimension" (or "transverse" correlation) in contrast to the more traditional ("vertical") type of correlation.

With the advent of Bordin's work, in 1942, the next logical step was taken of extending this type of inquiry into the "third dimension." Cattell's P technique was a complementary development, and N technique and M technique follow axiomatically once the three dimensions of tests, persons, and occasions have been identified and systematically related by means of Cattell's "covariation chart."

The observation has often been made that while correlational methods isolate *common elements,* they do not identify *causes.* This statement is certainly true as it pertains to what has here been termed R technique and Q technique (in the restricted sense). But the exciting thing about O technique is that it introduces a correlational method in which time, and therefore "causes," in the sense of independent variables (like therapy), can operate and produce measurable effects. It opens up promising new possibilities for studying personality *changes,* and in this respect it marks a significant departure from both conventional and "inverse" factor-analytic methods. More attention will be given in later pages to the implications and potentialities of the P, N, and M techniques.

Implications and Comments

When first planned, indeed even in first draft, this chapter seemed to be on a subject which was nicely delimited and readily manageable. But further exploration has caused the topic to ramify in a most unruly manner. It could easily expand into a whole volume, and still leave inviting issues unexamined. What follows is therefore more in the nature of a series of appendices than a unified and orderly set of conclusions. The chapter, in current jargon, is decidedly "open-ended."

I. Psychology and Scientific Method

This chapter takes us into the very heart of the question of scientific method in psychology. For many persons the question of proper method largely determines their concept of the content and aims of psychology, and since there have been two relatively distinct and seemingly opposed types of methodology, we have tended to have two kinds of psychologists. Departments have sometimes split on this issue; and, at the present time, after the reorganization of the American Psychological Association less than a decade ago in the hope of unifying the academic ("scientific") and applied ("professional") aspects of psychology, there is still talk of "fission." Many still view the new organization with distrust and alarm. The "experimentalists" tend to dismiss other psychologists with remarks such as the following (actual) one: "Whatever else Professor Blank may be, I know this: he is not a scientist!" And the more "professional" members of the discipline are inclined to reply somewhat to this effect: "Whatever else Dr. X. is, I know this: *he* is not really a psychologist!"

The central issue in this controversy is between the study of *principles* and the study of *persons*. In the former type of inquiry we try to hold all other factors constant, vary *one* independent variable (cause) and note the changes in one (or more?) dependent variable (effect). So ingrained is this conception of science that every bright schoolboy learns it; but more than one psychologist has questioned its adequacy in the study of personality or personology. For example, in the same issue of *Character and Personality* in which Stephenson gave the first extended description of Q technique, P. E. Vernon wrote as follows:

> This dilemma is fundamental. We see the individual personality as an organized structure, but have to acknowledge that our notions of it are subjective and unscientific. We try to investigate it scientifically, but its essential nature disappears in the process, and we are left with comparatively meaningless strings of test-scores and standard deviations, and correlations between the scores of large groups of persons. . . . We must admit also that the whole conception of the total personality and its structure is at present very indefinite. . . . We cannot expect to achieve a systematic view of personality until scientific investigation is able to contribute more to our knowledge of it than it has done so far (Vernon, 1935, p. 3).

The classical method of scientific inquiry calls for the study of *one* cause-effect sequence, or principle, in *many* subjects, with the result, say the critics of the method, that we lose sight of concrete, specific individuals. The reply commonly is that after we discover all these isolated principles, we can then "put them together" and understand and predict the workings of total personalities.

But there have been many doubts expressed with regard to this approach. Freud is said to have once remarked that he would rather have 100 hours with one subject than one hour with each of 100 subjects. This puts the difference in approaches very succinctly. In this country, G. W. Allport has been one of the most persistent advocates of studying persons-as-such, as well as principles (Allport, 1937).[27] And we find some interesting remarks in this connection in Stephenson's writings. For example:

> The above process [R technique] still involves traits as units of measurement, and therefore, according to Gestalt notions, there must ensue an inevitable distortion of the *whole* individual. Man, we are reminded, is more than any sum of such traits. . . . The technique now to be described does, I believe, counter these objections to a large extent. All measurement becomes a matter of the relative significance of traits *within the individual;* the individual is his own standard of reference; and one need only compare the separate person,

---

[27] For recent discussions of this problem, from two quite different approaches, see Rosenzweig (1950) and Lorenz (1950).

as a pattern or type, with other separate individuals (Stephenson, 1936b, p. 361).

Type and individual psychologists have been divorced in the past, the latter believing that there are no such things as mental types and the former expressing their abomination of psychometry and all its works. The truth is, however, that there is no need for this separation. Type psychologists have grasped an important matter when they remind us that abilities and traits can be considered relative to the individual himself, and that only by so doing can the individual, so to speak, be maintained whole and intact. "The true characterological significance of the trait," says Stern, "becomes evident only when we investigate its role in the total scheme of X's character." It is precisely such an investigation that Q technique affords (Stephenson, 1936a, pp. 351-52).

These early statements were somewhat complicated by Stephenson's concern with *type* psychology, but it is clear that he was working toward the study of personality in the fully integrated sense. A more precise and explicit analysis of his approach follows:

It is probable, indeed, that if the mental tester's concern in the past had been with sheep, or goats, or any other animals, instead of with the personalities of human beings, a distinction would have been observed from the outset between species or types based upon the orderliness of their *parts* relative to the animal as a whole, and the mere over-all sizes of any of the separate components of the whole as such. A big sheep, for example, or a little one, an old one or a young one, is still of the type *mouton,* and a large or a small goat likewise of the species *bouc.* If I were to represent animals in general by a universe of linear measurements taken, say, about 1,000 lines fixed by the morphology of vertebrates, the *relative* sizes of these skeletal parts within each animal would enable me to distinguish sheep from goats, whatever their age or condition; and any "mixed" species would be as distinct and as unequivocal as any pure type itself. Only a butcher is primarily interested in the individual differences in sizes of sheep (Stephenson, 1950a, p. 27).

Stephenson has made a real contribution along these lines, but there has been a notable delimitation. By thinking in two dimensions rather than in three (see pages 330-44 above), he has failed to establish the systematic relationship between the "multivariate" (persons) approach to psychology and the "univariate" (principles) approach (see pages 349-53 below). In the article just cited, he moves tentatively in this direction and then retreats. He says:

But, similarly, ever on the search for the *causa finalis,* there are psychologists who wish to reach into personality, into inner structures and cores of steady motivation, which *cause* behavior to be what it is. The essence of personality, according to this view is found in "perpetual motives," and not in traits, nor in behavior per se (p. 29).

Here we see the concept of causation touched upon but then immediately canceled out by the assumption that a person's *motives* are really fixed and enduring, uninfluenced by experience through time (learning). From this standpoint, a personality type has not only *pattern* but also *permanence*. What Bordin, Hartley, and other American investigators have in effect done is to adopt, from Stephenson and others, the concept of pattern but not the assumption of permanence; and the use of methods which Stephenson has himself strongly advocated is proving the justification of this altered point of view.

Although Freud hardly ever used the term "learning," it is probably correct to say that Freud really introduced learning (the "life history" axis) into personality theory. Certainly in his emphasis upon childhood experience and upon the possibility of carrying out radical therapy, i.e., producing marked personality change, in adults, Freud was thinking in the "third dimension," i.e., developmentally.

As we have already seen (page 340), Cattell's covariation chart provides a framework into which a number of different psychological approaches can be meaningfully integrated. The relationship of those investigative methods which stress *principles* and those which stress *persons* will be further elaborated in the following pages.

II. The Atomism-Wholism Issue: an Analogy

Students of personality have commonly disparaged the "atomism" of ordinary scientific methods and insisted that what is needed is a method, or methods, which will give a "picture" of the *whole* person, instead of focusing upon only a limited aspect, or part, of *many* persons. In their impatience, they have commonly rejected all "quantitative" methods and gone over to purely "qualitative," intuitive, or descriptive ones. But it is now evident that there is no inherent incompatibility between atomistic and wholistic approaches in psychology, provided they are seen in proper relation to each other.

An excellent analogy (for which the writer is indebted to Philip Du Bois of Washington University) is provided by the problem of communicating the "information" contained in an ordinary photograph. For centuries it seemed unlikely that one person could ever convey to another any very precise impression of what another person "looks like" by means of such "atomistic" symbols as words. The difficulty, as it turned out, was that we were not willing to be atomistic enough![28] The solution to the problem, as it has been developed in recent years, actually requires only two words, "yes" and "no"; but it requires that these words be used so many times that only a machine is likely to have the requisite patience and speed. If we think of a binary system of communication (a "scale of two") in which "yes" is represented by a dot and "no" by no dot, we have the essential feature of the present-day means by which highly accurate physical likenesses of persons (or anything else) can be trans-

[28] Cf. the analogous problem of communicating the infinite variety of human speech by means of twenty-six exceedingly atomistic units. See Miller and Selfridge (1950).

mitted, around the world if need be, by Wirephoto. Here, by the process of "scanning" an original photograph, i.e., analyzing or dividing it into a very large number of small units, a machine makes a succession of yes-or-no decisions regarding the density of the photograph at successive points; and when these decisions are reproduced at the other end of the communication system simply as dots and no-dots, the result is a very good approximation of the original photograph.

The S sort, as a method of portraying personality, is somewhat analogous to the Wirephoto method of transmitting pictures. The reason that we had not previously been able to communicate a physical picture of the "whole person" was that we were trying to use elements, such as descriptive adjectives, that were too global, too molar. Likewise, the reason we have not been able to get a very good personality "picture" is that we had been trying to do so by means of too few items of information, i.e., scores on only a *few* tests or traits; whereas what is needed, as the Wirephoto analogy clearly suggests, is a method which will give us information regarding a *great many* limited aspects or facets of the person. S procedure does this, or at least it makes the feat possible in principle. If we were sure that the items on an S sort were sufficiently numerous and representative (see pages 358-61) and if we were sure that our subjects sorted them with the proper set or attitude (pages 365-68), we would be assured of getting for each person a combination of ratings or values which would be unique and which would reliably differentiate each person from every other person.

As already indicated, an S sort can be conducted on the basis of a dichotomous or "binary" distribution, as well as with an eleven-point scale. Likewise, by complicating (to a quite unnecessary degree) the Wirephoto method, one could employ a series of eleven dots ranging from black, through intermediate grays, to white. In television a somewhat similar system is, in fact, used. But for present purposes, let us think of a simple binary system in both cases, i.e., simple yes-no judgments. The analogy between S procedure and Wirephoto will then become further apparent if we note that, instead of using a visual comparison of photographs for two persons, we might actually use a correlational method. If the yes-no, or dot-no-dot, decisions used in Wirephoto were coded as 1 or 0, then we would have, for each of the hundreds of spaces, or cells, comprising a photograph sent by wire, a series of entries in a very long column, and these entries might be correlated with comparable entries in another column representing a second picture. Identical pictures would, of course, correlate perfectly. Dissimilar pictures would correlate imperfectly, in proportion to the degree of dissimilarity (presupposing that the pictures were equated for size, were properly centered, etc.).

It so happens that we can, of course, make purely visual "correlations" of two pictures and agree, in most instances, upon the identity or difference of persons shown in two photographs. In getting a "personality picture," we have no comparable visual habits and must let our perceptions of likeness and difference rest upon statistical devices, such as correlation. But in principle the two methods are very similar and point the moral that to see, depict, or "measure" the *whole* person it is essential to move in the direction of *greater* "atomism," not less!

Perhaps one of the severest limitations of factor-analytic methods of studying personality is that they are too molar, i.e., they try to single out highlights, or nodal points, in the personality and, by measuring these, portray the total personality. The foregoing discussion suggests that perhaps what would be most useful in this connection is a method which would evenly "scan" the whole person, i.e., a collection of items, or "little tests," that would give information about every significant aspect of the person, every cell or facet, instead of concentrating, or lumping, the information around a few personality features or "factors." The inspiration of the Wirephoto method is that there is absolutely no duplication of information but, on the other hand, no absence of information. The "coverage," in other words, is "thin" but comprehensive. This method is so uniquely appropriate for catching the *pattern* of the data that each individual item of information can be exceedingly crude: dot, no-dot; yes or no; 1 or 0. But because the possible combinations of yes and no, when sequential order is added, rapidly mount toward infinity, it is still possible to transmit an enormous amount of "information" relatively efficiently.

III. Multivariate and Univariate Methods, with Special Reference to M Technique

On pages 341-42, attention is called to M technique, a procedure which involves giving one test to two (or more) persons on many occasions and correlating the results obtained. At first, this method seemed to be little more than a scientific curiosity. One saw that it could be used to determine whether two (or more) persons are living in the same environment and being affected in the same way by weather, nutrition, wars, technological change, etc. If the results for two persons on a given test fluctuate together through time, i.e., if there is "correlation of persons on occasions" (as opposed to "tests"), then it is clear that the same external influences are impinging upon them. But we hardly need an elaborate statistical procedure to tell us whether two persons live close together or far apart. Conceivably the method could be used to study socioeconomic "distance" or "proximity," but here again we would not expect it to reveal anything which is not already known, or at least knowable, from a common-sense standpoint.

In conversation, John C. McGregor has suggested to the writer that if one were to find, as a result of applying M technique to a social group or society, that most members thereof were having common experiences, and if these were *new* experiences, then one might expect *cultural change* (coordinated social learning) to occur. But it remained for Benjamin Fruchter of the University of Texas to bring home the fact that it is M technique that takes us also into the psychology of learning as a laboratory discipline. Despite the writer's preoccupation with the latter type of research, he was oblivious of this connection until it was pointed out by Fruchter.

As we have already seen, neither R nor Q technique ordinarily involves any assumptions about time or causation. It is assumed, tacitly or otherwise, that personality traits and types are relatively static affairs and that one needs only a two-dimensional surface to represent both types of correlational procedure. In P technique, as developed by Cattell, the dimension of time or occasion importantly appears, but here the variations which occur within a given individual with respect to his repeated test performance are assumed to occur "spontaneously," i.e., no external or independent attempt is made to influence the subject during the course of the tests or observations. One might say that only *internal* or *natural external* causes are assumed to be operative in P technique research.[29]

In N technique, as employed, for example, to determine test-retest reliability, we assume that the subjects will, of course, vary from one occasion to the next but that this variability will be random (rather than systematic) and that it will "cancel out" from individual to individual. Learning, as a systematic source of variation, is either disregarded or (by using split-half controls or some other method) its effects are excluded.

Therefore in R, Q, P, and N techniques, the phenomenon of orderly psychological change, i.e., learning, is almost wholly disregarded; and it is in O technique that, for the first time, we suddenly find "dynamic," i.e., cause-and-effect, thinking. Here an *independent variable* is introduced and its effects systematically measured. Here *therapy* (or some other systematic influence) is brought to bear upon the subject between the first and the second application of a test battery (S sort); and the dependent variable, i.e., personality change (or learning), is measured (inversely) by the amount of correlation between the first and second (before and after) administrations of the battery. Here, for the first time, we are approaching something that looks like an "experiment," as opposed to *in situ* (descriptive, naturalistic) research, but a "control group" is clearly wanting. And this observation leads us back to a consideration of M technique.

It will be remembered that M technique calls for at least two persons (or other types of subjects), and here we can see the possibility of using "differential treatments," i.e., having an experimental group and a control group. We can, for example, expose one subject (or group of subjects) to an independent variable and not so expose the other subject (or group of subjects); and with this development we find that we have, so to say, rediscovered the conventional pattern of "scientific," or *univariate*, research!

[29] Cattell has spoken of this type of research as being carried out with the person or persons *in situ* (in the sense in which geologists use this expression), i.e., undisturbed with respect to their normal life situation. This type of research is sometimes referred to (in geology, astronomy, etc.) as "descriptive" or "naturalistic," as opposed to the "experimental" approach, wherein variables are deliberately manipulated.

Re-examination of Figure 36 will help visualize the place of this type of investigation in the covariation chart. If we imagine a horizontal mid-line dividing the upper and the lower halves of the N-M face of the cube, we can think of the persons (or animal subjects) falling in the upper half as, let us say, the "experimental" (treatment) group and of the persons in the lower half as the "control" (no treatment) group.[30] Moreover, by further subdividing these two groups, we can introduce the possibility of investigating the effects of one, two, three, or more other *independent* variables; i.e., we can have a "factorially designed" experiment, in the manner of R. A. Fisher.[31]

It is true that in experimentation, whether of conventional or factorial design, we do not ordinarily use a coefficient of correlation as a means of showing differences between differently treated groups; and for this reason it may appear that such research has nothing in common with M technique. But here we are raising the question of the most efficient way of evaluating results rather than one of research design. If, for example, we plot curves for two differently treated groups in a study of learning, we have, in effect, an indication (which is open to inspection) of the cor-relation between the results obtained from these two groups. From such results one can, of course, obtain a coefficient of correlation; but such a value is not a very efficient measure for the reason that it will not show different *absolute levels* in the two curves, only similarities or differences in pattern (see pages 347-49). In this dimension of inquiry, absolute levels are usually thought of as more meaningful than are pattern differ-ences, and for this reason "measures of significance," such as the t test, or F test are commonly employed. But in "personality" research, pat-terns are of the essence, and it is here that the correlational methods are uniquely important.

To make explicit a point which is suggested in the foregoing discus-sion, it should be observed that "tests of significance" are particularly applicable to "univariate" (including factorially designed) research, whereas correlational methods are peculiarly useful in "multivariate"

[30] The expedient of making one and the same group of subjects serve as its "own control" is interesting in this context. In terms of the covariation chart, it consists of M technique, essentially, with the subjects being alternately treated and untreated with respect to the experimental variable; or, said differently, it involves "moving" the subjects alternately back and forth with respect to the space above and below the imaginary mid line mentioned above. A somewhat comparable effect could be produced in using O technique by alternately applying and withholding, with respect to a single individual, an independent variable such as therapy.

[31] In one sense, a factorially designed experiment may be said to constitute "multivariate" research, since it involves the use of more than one independent variable; but there is normally only one (measured) dependent variable, and, in actuality, by the use of different "cells," the independent variables vary "one at a time," thus preserving the basic conception of univariate research. Otherwise, "confounding" is said to occur. But in Q and O technique the picture is very differ-ent; here one measures (i.e., asks the subject to sort or evaluate) a *great many* items and, in O technique as exemplified by the Hartley study, it is the influence of a single independent variable, therapy (actually a very complex phenomenon), upon *all* these items or dependent variables and their interrelationship (*viz.*, "personal-ity") that is of greatest interest to us.

research. However, as we have just seen, it is not a question of one of these approaches being "right," "legitimate," or "scientific" and the other one not; they are *both* valid and may be used alternatively, depending upon our data and purposes. Perhaps we may even say that the truly "unscientific" frame of mind is one which affirms one of these approaches and rejects the other, regardless of which *way* the affirmation and the rejection apply.

In one of his early articles, Stephenson (1936*a*) has remarked that "type and individual psychologists have been divorced in the past," and adds: "The truth is, however, that there is no need for this separation" (p. 351). As we have seen at the outset of this section, the same fission, on a still grander scale, exists today, but there is, indeed, "no need for separation." By appropriate elaboration of Cattell's chart, we can see that there is a "place for everything" and that partisanship is more an expression of poor vision than virtue.

In a suggestive article entitled "A Synthesis of Experimental Designs in Program Research," Royce (1950) has recently developed, on the basis of a different approach, a very similar point of view. The following paragraphs indicate the general tenor of his thinking:

It should be obvious by now that the writer is demanding that we attack multiple variable domains with multiple variable techniques. After sufficient exploration by factor analysis and extensions by analysis of variance, it should be possible to return to the fundamental single variable experiment. Lest the writer be misunderstood, it will be explicitly stated that our purpose should not be to get around the single variable experiment, but rather, to permit us to get to it (p. 298).

The writer [summarizing] has attempted a synthesis of designs for experimentation at different phases of research. The single variable experiment demands rigidly controlled conditions to which much psychological research cannot conform. The reason stems largely from ignorance of the multiplicity of sources of variation which are operative in a given domain. It has been pointed out that in such situations the experimental designs involved in factor theory are appropriate. Once the basic unities have been identified, the factorial designs of Fisher can be appropriately utilized in order to extend our knowledge of the effects of one thing or another on these fundamental variables. Finally, with the clarification derived from multiple variable investigations, it may be possible to set up rigidly controlled single variable experiments which will give us quantitative empirical confirmation of mathematically rationalized theories of behavior (p. 302).

Similar suggestions are beginning to emerge in some of the newer books on statistics and research methodology.

The fact that almost the entire issue of the *Journal of Clinical Psychology* for January, 1949, was devoted to a symposium on "Statistics for Clinicians" is also indicative of the energetic efforts that are today being made to bridge the gap between "experimental" and "clinical" psychology, and there is every indication that this attempt will brilliantly succeed. Many of the papers in this symposium justify careful study, and the article by Horn especially shows how different lines of inquiry are beginning to converge on common conclusions and methods. There are many features of the Horn paper which invite comment, but here we shall remark on only two, the first being a proposed method of personality research which is very similar to O technique and which is also suggestive of the method described in this book by McQuitty (Chapter 16).[32] The relevant section of Horn's paper reads as follows:

Method B: Classification of the test items according to the shift in response from a first to a second administration of the test. If *Yes, ?, No* constitute the possible responses, one might search for a congruence of meaning among those items to which the response is the same in both tests (*Yes-Yes, ?-?,* and *No-No*), . . . Or again, one might classify the items on which there was a shift in response according to shift from certain to uncertainty (*Yes-?, No-?*) . . . .

In using Method B, we assume a relationship between the personal interpretations of the stimuli. . . . If there is a change in response from one test administration to a second, there has been a change in interpretation of the stimulus, presumably reflecting a change in the intensity of the need or needs involved. If the interval between tests is short, this probably reflects a temporary (reactive) shift in intensity; if the interval is long, it may reflect either a temporary or a fairly permanent shift (Horn, 1950, p. 45).

And in the following passage Horn refers to something very similar to Cattell's P technique.

If we must administer a personality questionnaire four times and still be faced with the possibility that Method B is inapplicable due to the unreliability of the pattern of changing responses, we might as well administer it ten, or twenty, times and study the covariation of responses over a respectably long series. This approach, Method C, we have named the Repeated Questionnaire Technique (p. 46).

These and many other excerpts which might be quoted from the symposium indicate the creative exploration and imagination which today characterize the thinking of statisticians with some degree of clinical interest and sophistication, and of clinicians with statistical capabilities. A new consolidation of psychological methodology is surely in the making.

IV The Objectivity Subjectivity Dichotomy

If it be agreed that we have correctly identified Q technique, in the overall picture of research possibilities provided by Cattell's chart, as the "correlation of persons," we may then turn and examine, separately, the

---

[32] For discussion of still another related method, developed by Osgood, for studying the "total personality," see Chapter 17.

issues raised by S procedure. A quick way of characterizing this method is to say that it makes a virtue of what, in ordinary scientific inquiry, is regarded as an evil. The point can be perhaps best made by using, not a scientific, but a practical example. If a number of teachers are asked to mark the same set of examination papers, variation in the performance of the students is taken as a matter of course, but variation in the *performance of the teachers* is likely to be regarded by others as indicating a "lack of objectivity" and to prove a source of embarrassment to the teachers themselves. In such a situation, the teacher variation, or "error," is likely to be conveniently masked by the use of a pooled, or averaged, mark for each paper, although Thomson (1946), among others, has clearly shown the dubious assumptions involved in such a procedure. He says:

We may wish the "idiosyncrasies" . . . of a certain examiner to be given great weight. It clearly would not do, for example, to exclude Examiner A from the above team *merely* because he is the most different from the common opinion of the team, without some further knowledge of the men and the purpose of the examination. The "different" member in a team might, for example, be the only artist on a committee judging pictures, or the only Democrat in a court judging legal issues, or the only woman on a jury trying an accused girl (p. 205).

But as Thomson goes on to say:

In noncontroversial matters, if all [judges] are of about equal experience, it is probable that this system of [equal] weighting, restricting itself to what is certainly common to all, will be most generally acceptable as fairest (p. 205).

At the same time it is clear that, if we have any reason for wishing to do so, we can use the examination marks as a means, not only of learning something about the students, but also of learning something *about the teachers.* We can, in other words, turn about and investigate the very thing that hampers our getting a thoroughly "objective" measure of the students, namely, the "subjectivity" ("personalities," "individual differences") of the teachers. That is to say, when one group of persons (the teachers) reacts to the reactions (test responses) of another group of persons (the students), we can take either of two different points of view: we can look at the same results from the standpoint of what they tell us ("objectively") about the persons in the one group or from the standpoint of what they tell us ("subjectively") about the persons in the other group. More specifically, we may say that the "subjective" approach involves "looking backward" at the "judges" when they are ostensibly giving us information only about the "subjects" (or, more properly, the "objects").

One of the most illuminating passages on the matter of objectivity-subjectivity in correlational studies has been written by Burt (1940) and is reproduced below:

Consider once again the type of inquiry I have been describing—for example, one of the many experiments in which a number of persons are asked to rank a series of English compositions in order of merit, and the rankings are correlated by persons. What do the results reveal? Do they indicate the literary appreciation of the judges, or the literary merits of the compositions judged? If the compositions are children's essays, and the judges school examiners, then we shall probably regard the figures as grading or classifying the compositions judged. If, however, the judges are children and the compositions extracts from authors differing widely in literary skill, then we may use the figures to grade or classify the judges according to their powers of appreciation. The truth is that with both experiments what our measurements really express are in the first instance neither the qualities of the judges by themselves, nor the qualities of the test stimuli by themselves, but the interaction between the two. Which of the two interacting qualities we treat as constants and which we treat as variables will depend upon the question we set out to study and upon the way the experiment has been planned (pp. 204-5).

Godfrey Thomson in his book, *The factorial analysis of human ability* (1950), has a chapter on "Exchanging the Roles of Persons and Tests," in which the principal example deals with the marks which six examiners gave to Latin examination papers written by fifteen students about sixteen years of age. These marks, taken from an earlier study by Burt, are given in Table 7. Here it is apparent that, if one so desires, in situations where there are multiple judges or markers of responses made by a number of subjects, one can, by correlational methods, study either the agreement of the subjects or the agreement of the judges. And Thomson proceeds to show how, in the latter instance, one can further determine, not only who are the good "students," but also who are the "good" and who the "poor" markers. This is a particularly good example of the relativity of "data" in psychological inquiry.

While showing very clearly that one can use the same set of data either to make an "objective" analysis of one group of persons or to make a "subjective" analysis of another group, Table 7 at the same time raises an interesting question about the adequacy of Cattell's covariation chart. This cube has no surface on which to superimpose Table 7. However, the difficulty is easily resolved, with interesting implications. One immediately sees that what was first done in the Latin examination was this: one examination was given to fifteen students on one occasion. If the resulting fifteen examination papers had been scored by a single marker or if the marks for a group of judges were averaged, the results could be represented in a single vertical column on the right-front surface of Figure 36. However, what happened was that the fifteen examination papers were, so to speak, rotated counterclockwise through 90°, thus making the examination paper of each of the fifteen students *a test* for each of the six markers or examiners. Thus, strictly speaking, in Table 7 "Candidates" are really "Tests," for what was "response" in one situation (the examination-taking) becomes "stimulus" in another situation (ex-

TABLE 7

MARKS GIVEN BY SIX EXAMINERS TO LATIN EXAMINATION PAPERS WRITTEN
BY FIFTEEN ENGLISH SCHOOLBOYS ABOUT SIXTEEN YEARS OF AGE

This table, reproduced by Thomson (1950) from an earlier study by Burt, shows
that the same data can be used, in such a case, to study, by correlational means (see
text), the similarities and differences in the performance (personality) of either
the individuals who took the examination or those who marked it.

Candidates	Examiners					
	A	B	C	D	E	F
1	39	43	52	37	43	40
2	39	44	50	43	43	46
3	44	51	55	47	46	46
4	37	46	43	44	40	43
5	38	47	55	35	43	45
6	45	50	54	45	45	49
7	42	52	51	45	44	46
8	43	49	53	47	46	46
9	32	42	49	34	36	38
10	37	40	48	37	39	42
11	38	42	47	39	36	39
12	40	44	50	41	36	42
13	38	43	50	36	34	41
14	35	45	49	37	40	40
15	32	38	41	38	34	34

amination-marking). We therefore find the covariation cube to be
entirely adequate to accommodate this type of data, and one does not
readily find other data which fail to fit into the scheme which the cube
suggests.[33]

We thus see that what is a test-response for one person can become a
test-stimulus for another person. When an item is being treated *as a
response,* and when its marking is supposed to tell us something about
the maker of the response, the procedure is said to be *objective;* but when
the same item is being treated *as a stimulus* and when its marking is used
to tell us something about the marker of the item, the procedure is said
to be *subjective,* or *"projective."*

Stephenson has formulated the same point of view as follows:

In Webb's work all the persons of a population were estimated for traits
such as perseverance, trustworthiness, and the like. Each trait was a variable,
the population was the group of persons estimated, and the estimators were,
so to speak, outside the picture, little account being taken of them, except to
give the so-called reliability coefficients of the traits. . . . Now by Q technique we could investigate the estimators rather than the estimated persons.

[33] See, however, footnote 25 above.

We could not hope thereby to learn much about these estimate persons, but only something about the estimators (Stephenson, 1936b, pp. 358-59).

In the Thomson example of Latin examination papers, we have no problem of item disparity or heterogeneity if we decide to correlate the examiners; but if, for instance, each of the schoolboys had taken an examination on a different subject matter, so that the "tests" (examination papers) which the examiners were asked to score were qualitatively different, the problem of item disparity would reappear. It was to meet this problem that Stephenson (following earlier investigators) proposed the device which, for purposes of clarity, we have termed S procedure. While it may be effectively used as a means of *obtaining data* which are later to be subjected to Q technique proper (or to O technique, as in the Hartley example), S procedure is something apart therefrom, as indicated by the fact, just demonstrated by the Thomson illustration, that Q technique can be employed with data collected *without* the use of S procedure. S procedure may, in other words, be used in conjunction with either Q or O technique in the restricted and more exact sense of these terms; but it is not an essential feature of Q technique, and, as we shall later see (pages 370-75), Stephenson's special version of S procedure is not even essential to O technique.

By way of summarizing what has just been said, we may usefully quote again from Horn, who says:

It is useful to distinguish between *parameters of personality* in which variation occurs as we go from one individual to the next and *variables of personality* in which variation occurs as we sample an individual's behavior at different times and under varying conditions. The bulk of statistically sophisticated research in the field of personality and clinical investigation has depended upon an analysis of the parameters of personality—upon the determination of a single score to identify each individual on each measure. This may be the reason for the barrenness of the psychometric portrait of the individual. Barren, that is, until the competent clinician organizes with intuition and skilful artistry his material with, at best, only a dim awareness of the reasons for this organization (p. 43).

From the standpoint of the parameters of personality, personal variability, as defined above, simply contributes to "error" or "error variance" and lowers the significance of the supposedly more significant sources of variance. But when we change our frame of reference from "objectivity" to "subjectivity," what was previously "unreliability" of items becomes, as Horn has pointed out, "sensitivity." And it is precisely "among these items that our technique permits the study of relationships in terms of covariation of the several items" (Horn, p. 46).

To this we may add the observation that in "objective" testing (data-collecting) procedures, the subject *makes* the responses and the investigator marks them (against some composite or group norm), whereas, in S procedure, the investigator makes the response (provides the items) and the subject *marks* them, i.e., rates them on a subjective, self-referential continuum.[34]

V. The Problem of Item Selection

A common feature of both Q and O techniques is that they employ a "universe of tests," just as R and N techniques employ a "universe of persons" and P and M techniques employ a "universe of occasions." But whereas much attention has been given to the logic of sampling universes or populations of persons, little attention has been given to sampling theory where test or occasion universes are concerned. This is due, presumably, to the fact that techniques R and N are very familiar and much used, whereas techniques Q and O and P and M are less so. As Burt (1940) remarks:

> The influence of selecting persons is now fairly well recognized. The influence of selecting tests is more frequently overlooked. The technique of correlating persons demonstrates very clearly how the special selection of tests or traits can twist the whole factorial pattern (p. 208).

> We must specify our standard population and our standard set of tests. In the case of general intelligence, this has already been attempted, though not always with a clear consciousness of the reasons. There the idea of a typical sample of the populations, with typical standard deviation, and a typical test-scale, like the Binet-Simon series, has already been adopted for practical purposes. The same principle would be explicitly accepted for other traits and for theoretical work; and the best provisional conventions might thereupon be discussed and defined (p. 209).

There can be no doubt that, just as there are different "universes" of persons, so are there different "universes" of tests or test items. And just as we use now one, now another universe of persons (or animal subjects), depending upon our particular purpose (see Chapter 14), we might also think of the possibility, indeed the necessity, of using, in Q and O techniques, one or another of various possible test populations, according to the questions we wish to ask and answer.

It will doubtless already have occurred to the reader that the results obtained by the use of these techniques may vary widely with the nature of the universe of statements (or trait names) from which items are selected. Let us make the point in its most extreme form by taking the following example. Suppose that one selected items from the universe of universally applicable and universally inapplicable statements, such as:

---

[34] This discussion is reminiscent of one engaged in by G. W. Allport and Mark May some years ago (see Mowrer and Kluckhohn, 1944). May held that "personality" is definable and identifiable only in terms of its "social stimulus value," whereas Allport held that "personality" is what the person "really is." According to May's position, one would presumably conclude that the only legitimate way to find out what a person is like, in the present context, would be to have others do S sorts for him; whereas Allport's position would imply that the self sort is the more authentic and meaningful. Comparison of self sorts and sorts-by-others may throw new light on this old problem; cf. the technique of *sociometry*.

"I usually walk in an upright position," "I eat recurrently," "I frequently hold my breath for as much as ten minutes," etc. By thus composing an S sort of what Kluckhohn and Mowrer (1944) have called "panhuman" characteristics (and using a dichotomous distribution), one could insure the finding that different persons correlate highly, i.e., are quite *homogeneous*. If, on the other hand, one selected highly "idiosyncratic" characteristics, such as place and date of birth, address of present residence, and full name of spouse as items, one could insure the finding that the correlation between persons is very low, i.e., that persons are very *heterogeneous*. Or, by selecting characteristics, such as society-bound characteristics or role-bound characteristics (see Kluckhohn and Mowrer), which fall in between in the matter of universality, one could insure results which would group, or "factor," individuals into societies or into special roles (such as professions, religions, political parties, etc.).

This inference, that the selection of items is important in Q technique, has been objectively demonstrated by Moore, Stafford, and Hsu (1947) in a study which they summarize as follows:

One hundred and twenty-eight personality traits were used to test 56 junior and senior students in a woman's college. The subjects are believed to be very homogeneous in almost every measurable and observable respect. Each person was correlated with each of the others in terms of the traits commonly claimed or denied, or differentially claimed or denied by each pair of persons compared. The correlations were computed for two separate analyses, each comprising 1,540 correlations in all. In order to use the tetrachoric correlational technique, an assumption was made that one individual's traits are normally distributed according to the frequency of their occurrence in his whole life. This assumption seems logical, yet challenges further experimentation and verification. Then each correlation matrix was subjected separatively to a Thurstone centroid analysis. The first analysis brought out 9 factors and the second 11 factors. Out of the 9 factors, 3 can be interpreted easily after rotations. They were identified as a cycloid factor, a schizoid factor, and a suspicious factor. The rest of the 9 factors were not easily interpreted. There was, however, a super-factor which reflects the homogeneity of the sampling. After the 128 trait items were examined from the point of view of their relative frequency of positive answers from the subjects, 38 items were omitted; these either had less than 6 positive answers or more than 50, out of 56 subjects. The 90 traits so selected were used as the statistical population for the computing of the second correlation matrix, which consists of another set of 1,540 correlations. After rotations the 11 factors of the second analysis seemed all real, and none was residual. They were identified as follows: (1) an adjustment factor, (2) a romantic factor, (3) a factor of inferiority, (4) a factor that is not very clear-cut, (5) an extrovert factor, (6) a frustration-romantic factor, (7) a schizoid factor, (8) a prepsychotic "paranoid" factor, (9) a jealousy factor, (10) a factor not very clear-cut, possibly an adjusted introvert type, and (11) a prepsychotic "simple or catatonic schizophrenia" factor. It was pointed out that the first type of analysis is more suitable for the problem of ascertaining the homogeneity of the sampling, while the second type of analysis, in which only traits with high validity and differential value are used, is more suitable for the problem of analyzing the configuration of traits into syndromes of finer differentiation and variation. Therefore, factors in factor analysis should be regarded as *relative,* not only depending on the persons used, but also on the traits [tests]. No factor can be identified in absolute terms unless the factor has been consistently isolated and identified from different studies (pp. 46-47).

Against these background facts, let us pose the question, perhaps more sharply than before: How does one know the correct universe from which to draw items for an S sort which is designed for use in research on psychotherapy? A reasonable, but not necessarily the only possible, inference is the one made in connection with the Hartley example, namely, that the items should be drawn from the universe of statements which people make while undergoing psychotherapy. But it is at once evident that such a universe will be too large, since it will contain both universal and idiosyncratic statements (and perhaps others), which, for reasons already given, will be nondiscriminating. We can therefore narrow our selection to the universe of statements made by persons undergoing therapy which refer to characteristics with respect to which individuals are likely to *change,* i.e., characteristics which are likely to be affected by *learning.* These statements, it turns out, are likely to fall into two categories: interpersonal statements and intrapsychic (introspective, self-referential) statements, i.e., statements indicative of *"social* adjustment" and statements indicative of *"personal* adjustment."

After the item universe is thus defined, the items selected should be tested in a preliminary way to make sure that they are understandable, representative, etc. The question arises as to what population or universe of persons should be used for making such a test; but this is an intricacy with which we need not be concerned here.

Cattell (personal communication) has suggested the desirability of performing a conventional (R-type) factor analysis on the items used in S procedure as applied, for example, to the study of therapy, in order to make sure that all of the personality variables which have now been isolated by the R-type factor analysis are represented. This is a reasonable suggestion, perhaps, but it remains to be seen whether this method of selecting and validating items is preferable to one which is guided by the premises of psychoanalysis, projective psychology, self-psychology, or some other "dynamic" school of thought.

Cattell has also suggested the desirability of using, in Q and O technique studies, not only the frankly subjective data obtained by means of an S sort, but also data obtained by more objective measures—physiological measures, ratings by others, etc. (see Chapter 15). The difficulty here is that introduction of this type of data revives the old problem of disparity or noncomparability of values obtained on "separate tests." It is this problem that S procedure was specifically designed to obviate; and since, as noted previously, the use of standard scores does not really meet the issue, the use of a single subjective continuum (S procedure) seems to be the only alternative.

In summary, then, we may note that while using an S sort it may look as if we are studying "the whole personality," but we are actually not, since we do not have a random sample of items drawn from all possible items relevant to any given individual. Rather are we using (if we have proceeded rationally) a sample of items drawn from a more circumscribed universe which has, or is thought to have, special cogency with respect to our immediate purposes. This may seem like a retreat from the "multivariate" approach, but it is probably no less justifiable in theory than it is essential in practice. However, the whole matter of item selection where trait-universes are involved is as yet very incompletely explored and will profit from further inquiry. This is even more true of the problem of "item selection" where we are dealing with a universe of occasions.

VI. R and Q Techniques Compared

There is a large and controversial literature on an issue which has thus far not been considered in this chapter, namely, the question as to whether a factor analysis which is carried out on the basis of correlations between tests (R technique) yields information different from or essentially similar to the information obtained by carrying out a factor analysis on the basis of correlations between persons (Q technique). Since this chapter is mainly concerned with correlational techniques which stop short of factor analysis, this issue is not of central importance. However, it will be useful to indicate the nature of the controversy at least in outline.

Stephenson's position on this score is summarized in the following excerpt from his 1936 article in *Psychometrika:*

I have clearly stated that systems (1) [the correlation of persons] and (2) [the correlation of tests] can be quite independent, but it will be better to state explicitly that I regard the two as, by very definition, statistically independent of one another in general.

System (2) in general is not to be regarded as the direct obverse or mere transpose of data already analyzable by way of system (1); nor is it the case that these two systems are merely two complementary ways of analyzing one and the same original matrix of data, the results being no less complementary or deducible one from the other (p. 206).

Burt has stated his position in these words:

With this modification [correlation of persons] of the usual procedure, the roles of persons and traits become interchanged or *transposed*. To talk of *inverting* the factors or the theorems is misleading alike to the mathematician and to the logician; and the use of the term has prompted a good deal of criticism that is really irrelevant to the principle essentially involved. As I have often pointed out, the theorems required for analyzing correlations between persons are not "inversions" of those required for the older procedure; they are formally identical with them, and materially their analogues. Similarly, the matrix of measurements with which we start is not the *inverse* of, but a *transpose* of, that which is correlated in the usual way (the rows are merely rewritten as columns, and if necessary restandardized). And to describe the resulting factorial matrices as inversions of each other is incorrect, except in certain special cases (Burt, 1940, p. 169).[35]

"Q technique," we are told [by Stephenson], "is pre-eminently a method of isolating types. . . . In the past, type psychology could not be subjected to factor analysis." Now, as I shall endeavor to show later on, in virtue of the principle of reciprocity, the type-factors obtained by correlating persons are, in theory at any rate, virtually identical with those obtained by correlating traits (p. 191).[36]

Broadly speaking, we correlate persons rather than tests when we are concerned with the complex resemblances between total personalities (or aspects of those personalities) rather than with the more limited resemblances between particular traits or their tests (p. 197).

Once again I find it difficult to imagine that, by Q technique, I can obtain a factor-saturation describing a set of persons as a type, and yet, in principle, be entirely unable to reach the same figure by correlating the relevant traits: it is like saying the name JONES can only be found in the telephone directory by hunting for the word as a whole, and that if I look first for J, then for the O's under J, then for N, E, and S, I shall never find Jones. The equivalence of the two procedures, however, is a matter that I shall defend more fully when I deal with the so-called "reciprocity principle" (p. 201).

Thus, when we correlate tests or persons, we must regard our factors as being principles for classifying tests or traits quite as much as principles for classifying persons (p. 203).

The solution to the paradox is not far to seek: at bottom what we are really classifying are neither the minds, on the one hand, nor the tests or traits or school subjects, on the other, but the *relations* between the two (p. 203).[37]

Godfrey Thomson (1950) has taken a somewhat intermediate position in this respect. He says:

In short, all the methods of Parts I and II of this book . . . used on correlations between tests may be employed on correlations between examiners. The tests have come alive and are called examiners, that is all (p. 208).

[35] Burt gives the mathematical basis for these statements in an earlier study (Burt, 1937). See also Burt and Stephenson (1939).

[36] For a comparison of the trait factors and the person factors which have emerged from recent factor-analytic work, see Cattell (1952a, 1952b) and Moore, Stafford, and Hsu (1947).

[37] The position of R. B. Cattell seems to be very similar to that of Burt (Cattell, 1952a). P. E. Vernon likewise agrees with Burt. He says: "Such factorizations of persons are shown by Burt to be complementary to the straightforward factorization of tests. Indeed the scores obtained by an individual on a set of test-factors would be identical with his loadings in respect to a set of types or person-factors. Hence the choice as to which of the two approaches should be used depends simply on the kind of test scores or psychological material that is available" (Vernon, 1938, p. 40).

Since Stephenson has found numerous negative correlations between persons, and since few negative correlations are reported between tests, we seem here to have an experimental difference between the two kinds of correlation, and if ever correlations between persons come to be analyzed as minutely and painstakingly as correlations between tests, it would seem that the free admission of negative loadings would be necessary (p. 211).

After detailed consideration of Burt's principle of reciprocity, Thomson says:

Indeed, even for doubly centered matrices of marks, this simple reciprocity holds only for the analysis of the covariances and not for analyses of the matrices of correlations. Except by pure accident (and as it happens, Burt's example is in the case of test correlations such an accident), the saturations of the correlation analysis will not be any *simple* function of the loadings of the covariance analysis (p. 218).

All of the foregoing discussion, and much more, has centered around the issue of whether the results obtained by factor analysis based upon correlational technique R gives results essentially the same as or different from those of factor analysis based upon correlational technique Q. It is not our purpose here to protract this controversy, which, from one standpoint, is a matter for the statisticians and mathematicians.[38] But it can be pointed out that, potentially, the same questions exist with respect to P and O techniques and with respect to N and M techniques, since each of these techniques implies the other, just as in the case of R and Q techniques. Thus far in this chapter, P, O, N, and M techniques have looked as if they were all quite distinctive; but this, we may now surmise, is only because we have not thought in terms of applying factor-analytic methods either to the P-O surface of the covariation chart or to the N-M surface. But if we consider factor analyses on these two surfaces, i.e., in order to make the relatively many correlations which factor analysis requires, we have to have, on the P-O surface, a considerable number of tests given to one person on a number of occasions, and on the N-M surface one test given to a number of persons on several occasions. When score matrices of this kind are obtained, we face, mathematically, the same questions which have already been noted in connection with the R-Q type of matrix (see Table 5).

[38] An interesting development has recently been reported by Louis Guttman (in a lecture at the University of Illinois, May, 1951). Using a "new form of factor analysis," he finds, when correlating tests, a single factor of *complexity* running through them, with no indication of discrete common factors. In other words, the tests, as a result of this procedure, align themselves on a *complexity continuum* and only in this way. If, now, the same data were to be correlated by "rows" rather than by "columns," i.e., by persons rather than by tests, it would seem likely that persons would be differentiated, not on the basis of "complexity," but on the basis of their capacity to *deal with* complexity, i.e., their *ability*. The two continua thus identified would really be nothing more than mirror images of each other, thus re-emphasizing Burt's reciprocity principle and reminding us of his contention that "at bottom what we are really classifying are neither the minds, on the one hand, nor the tests or traits or school subject on the other, but the *relations* between the two."

Cattell (1951) and Saunders (1951) have recently written papers on the possible applications and meanings of factor-analytic procedures carried out on these two surfaces. Whether such procedures will prove relatively fruitful or sterile remains to be determined, since only the most tentative and exploratory studies of this kind have as yet been actually attempted. But these uncertainties need not affect the main inferences drawn in this chapter, since we have been primarily concerned with correlational methods short of factor analysis; and at this simpler level, it is surely clear that R, Q, P, O, N, and M techniques are meaningful and distinctive operations. For further discussion of these and related issues, see Cattell (1952b) and Stephenson (1952).

VII. Statistics of the Individual

Neither R nor Q technique, conceived respectively as correlation of tests and correlation of persons, gives us a "statistics of the individual." As already noted, R and Q techniques both presuppose a minimum of *two* persons (and the factor-analytic extensions require a good many more). As Horn (1950), among others, has clearly indicated, one of our great scientific needs in psychology is for a statistical method that can be validly used with *one* person. O technique, when combined with Stephenson's method of scaling, provides such a method, and so does Cattell's P technique. Osgood (1952) has devised a related method, which will be exemplified in Chapter 17; and still another method, developed by McQuitty over the last two decades, is fully described in Chapter 16.[39]

All these developments point to the conclusion that a momentous new step is today being taken in psychology as science, a step which will mate-

[39] In an article entitled "Alternative Views on Correlations Between Persons" (Burt and Stephenson, 1939), Stephenson remarks, somewhat paradoxically it would seem, that: "Laws in *r* technique derive from large numbers of cases (persons) and from individual differences; laws in Q technique can derive from work on *one* person only, and are independent of individual differences" (p. 273). And this despite the fact that the paper is on "correlations between *persons*"! Certainly there is no indication in this paper as to precisely *how* Q technique can be used to study "*one* person only." That remained to be demonstrated by Bordin. In a recent paper, Stephenson (1951) describes an extension of his own thinking regarding Q technique which replaces "the present largely inductive methodology in factor analysis by one orientated more towards hypothetico-deductive directions, and outlining the rationale for dealing statistically with the single person, the "single case" as it is sometimes called (p. 1). And again: "Q, in its own terms, can delve instead into the 'single case,' as we said in 1935, without reference to individual differences" (p. 16). That this investigator is beginning to think more dynamically, more causally is suggested by his reference elsewhere in this paper to "effects," "dependent variables," and to the possibility of personal change ("Factors are never immutable entities"—p. 27). Yet he is reluctant to concede that *time*, or *occasions*, (see Cattell's "covariation chart") is a new, third dimension, comparable in importance to that of *tests* and *persons*. Without acknowledging the time dimension in a systematic way, it is difficult to see the meaning of "work on *one* person only." Stephenson says: "Cattell, indeed, confuses psychometric matters with mere *applications* of these. For example, Cattell introduces *time* into his adumbrations. But we could as readily add 'state of hypnosis,' or 'state of drunkenness,' and call for the complete repetition of his systems in terms of two new domains, H and D for everyone in a state of hypnosis (H) in the one case, and all of them drunk (D) in the other" (p. 13).

rially advance clinical research and which will systematically articulate it with the more traditional research methodologies employing a "statistic of groups." As Horn (1950) has said: "A more general application of this kind of approach to other materials turns, in effect, each individual into a statistical research problem for the clinical definition of his personal structure in his own terms" (p. 44). We indeed stand on the threshhold of an exciting era!

VIII. Some Misgivings Regarding O Technique

In principle, O technique, as originated by Bordin and now widely used by others, is a genuine methodological innovation and is undoubtedly "here to stay." However, it suggests a number of questions which must be considered:

A. The Problem of Conscious and Unconscious "Sets."—One of the most disturbing criticisms that might be made of O technique as exemplified in Examples I and II (pages 317 and 324) stems from the now well-established fact that the attitude or set with which a subject approaches a test may markedly influence his performance on the test, without any necessary imputation of wilful deception. We need to remind ourselves that a person who is a candidate for psychotherapy (particularly in a situation where the therapy, if forthcoming, will be free of charge or virtually so) will tend to behave on a test *like* a candidate-for-psychotherapy. And it is clear that a person who behaves in this way will hardly be inclined to "put his best foot forward." If he is personally miserable and feels that he is in need of psychological help, he will think of himself as, and behave on a test like, a person who is suffering, inadequate, and far from the kind of person he would like to be.

At the same time, such a person will be prompted to hold up high standards for himself, both in terms of the level of personal integration and comfort he wishes to achieve and in terms of common cultural values. It is only common sense that a neurotic person should wish to be psychologically healthy (except for the resistances which will be mobilized when therapy actually begins); and every candidate wishes to be thought well of by his prospective therapist in terms of his social ideals and worthwhileness as a person, for otherwise there would be the danger that he would be regarded as a "psychopath" and dismissed as a poor therapeutic risk.

The work of Hathaway and others with the Minnesota Multiphasic Personality Inventory has shown that wide variations in scores for the nine clinical scales constituting this test can often be obtained by administering it to the same persons under varying circumstances; and similar findings have been reviewed by McQuitty (1941) for other "personality tests." [40]

[40] For other reviews, see Meehl and Hathaway (1946) and Gough (1947).

Earlier in this chapter, attention has been called to the possibility of obtaining differences in performance on an S sort as a result of differences in instructions or set which are supplied by the experimenter. Here we are considering the differences in test performance which may be due to differences in instructions or set which are supplied *by the subject*. Mc-Kinley, Hathaway, and Meehl (1948) have discussed "the influence of attitudes toward the test situation" (as revealed by the K score on the Minnesota Multiphasic Personality Inventory), with special reference to "faking good" and "faking bad." Meehl (1945) has an earlier paper in which he considers "the possibility of conscious as well as unconscious 'fudging.'" The essential point of both papers is well illustrated by a story told by E. Lowell Kelly regarding air-cadet selection during the Second World War. According to Kelly, the most discriminating item in a long questionnaire was: "Do you tend to get dizzy when you look over the edge of a high building?" The men who replied "No" were the ones most likely to "wash out" in cadet training. The item was therefore not a test of adjustment to high places, but an indicator of security or insecurity in admitting a "weakness" common to most persons—and of a desire not to be turned down for this elite military service. As Meehl observes, it is not only the "projective" tests that give insight into the core of personality; "structured" tests, if properly interpreted, may often provide precisely the same sort of information. He says:

In summary, a serious and detailed study of the MMPI items and their interrelations both with one another and [with] nontest behavior cannot fail to convince one of the necessity for this kind of approach to question-answer personality tests. That the majority of the questions seem by inspection to require self-ratings has been a source of theoretical misunderstanding, since the stimulus situation seems to request a self-rating, *whereas the scoring does not assume a valid self-rating to have been given.* It is difficult to give any psychologically meaningful interpretation of some of the empirical findings on MMPI unless the more sophisticated view is maintained.

It is for this reason that the possible differences in interpretation do not cause us any a priori concern in the use of this instrument. Whether any structured personality test turns out to be valid and useful must be decided on pragmatic grounds, but the possibility of diverse interpretations of a single item is not a good *theoretical* reason for predicting failure of the scales. There is a "projective" element involved in interpreting and responding to these verbal stimuli which must be recognized, in spite of the fact that the test situation is very rigidly structured as regards the ultimate response possibilities permitted (Meehl, 1945, p. 299).[41]

It would therefore seem incumbent upon persons using O technique to determine to what extent the obtained discrepancies between pretherapy self sorts and pretherapy ideal sorts are a product of test-taking attitude and to what extent a product of therapy proper. It would, for

---

[41] For a further development of this point of view, see the volume edited by Abt and Bellak (1950).

example, be most useful to know what the same subjects would do by way of an S sort if they were required to take this test in connection with their application for a job or admission to college or a professional school.

A study which is of special relevance here is that reported by Gough (1947), entitled "Simulated Patterns on the Minnesota Multiphasic Personality Inventory." He refers to Ossipov's definition of a malingerer as "an actor who portrays an illness *as he understands it*" and cites a study by Bordin which indicated "that students acquainted with the occupational groupings included in the Strong [Vocational Interest Test] were able to simulate certain specified occupational types, even though they were unfamiliar with the mechanics of scoring" (p. 215). He also reports that "Benton had nine homosexuals who were positively identified on the Mf scale [of the MMPI] retake the test and try to conceal their femininity. Six of the nine were able to bring their Mf scores within normal limits" (p. 216). Gough summarizes his own investigation as follows:

A military group of eleven persons, consisting of three psychiatrists, three clinical psychologists, three psychiatric social workers, and two personnel consultants, took the Minnesota Multiphasic Personality Inventory in three ways: first, giving frank self-appraisals; second, attempting to simulate severe psychoneurosis; and, third, attempting to simulate paranoid schizophrenia. The simulated records were compared with a neurotic criterion of fifty-seven severe psychoneurotics, and a psychotic criterion of thirteen paranoid schizophrenics (p. 224).

Figure 37 reproduced from Gough's paper, shows the remarkable voluntary approximation of the normal group to the neurotic group on the nine standard scales of the MMPI; only in terms of the special scales, K and F, did the simulated neurotic scores differ from the genuine ones. The simulation of the psychotic profile was somewhat less successful, but even here the two psychotic profiles (real and faked) were much closer to each other than either was to the normal profile. To be sure, the persons who were asked to engage in this project were psychiatrically sophisticated, and less sophisticated subjects would probably not have been quite so skilful in "portraying the illness" (see also Weisskopf and Dieppa, 1951; Kelly and Fiske, 1951, p. 14 and p. 20; and Gough, 1952) ; but the results dramatically make the point that instructions, attitudes, and purposes are important determinants of the type of behavior we elicit from human subjects in any kind of testing situation. Until controls are available for research of the kind exemplified by the Hartley and Ewing studies, the findings must be interpreted very cautiously indeed.[42]

[42] Since the above was written a study by Wesman (1952), entitled "Faking personality test scores in a simulated employment situation," has come to the author's attention. Seventy-three students were given the Bernreuter Personality Inventory on two different occasions, once with instructions to imagine they were applying for a position, which they badly wanted, as a salesman, and later with instructions to imagine they were applying for a position, which they equally desired, as librarian. Says the author: "The table [of results] speaks eloquently for itself.

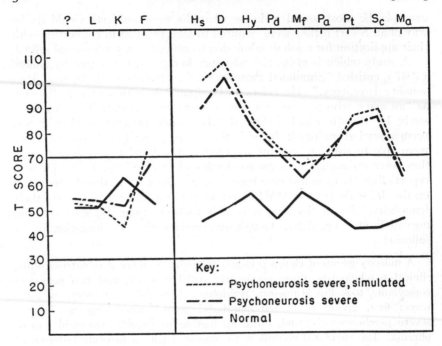

Fig. 37.—Profile curves, reproduced from Gough (1947), showing how closely a group of eleven clinically sophisticated normal persons can come to simulating the performance of severe psychoneurotic patients (N = 57) on the ten clinical scales (*Hs* to *Ma*) of the Minnesota Multiphasic Personality Inventory. The nonsimulated (normal) performance of these same eleven persons is shown below the other two curves. However, two of the four nonclinical scales, K and F, tend to differentiate not only the normal performance of the nonpatient group from their simulated performance but also their simulated performance from the performance of the true psychoneurotics.

B. Flight into Health.—There is, of course, the fact to be considered that in the studies reported by Hartley and by Rogers, clients show a uniform "upward" trend in their self sorts from beginning to end of therapy; and this finding might be said to constitute a kind of intrinsic validation of the test employed. This argument may be sound, but it calls for substantiation. In psychoanalytic circles there is a familiar phenomenon, called "flight into health," which is most likely to display itself after ten or fifteen interviews, just at the point where the patient's deepest resistances are being activated and where negative transference reactions are most pronounced. There is always a considerable risk that patients will attempt to leave analysis at this point, and one of the commonly exhibited strategies of escape is that of "feeling fine" and expressing no further need for analysis.

If one saw these distributions without foreknowledge of how they were obtained, he could only conclude that they represented two quite different groups of people. . . . The demonstration seems to the author sufficiently dramatic to point up the susceptibility to faking of personality inventories in the industrial situation" (pp. 112-13).

Since the therapeutic philosophy embodied in the Chicago studies is, in certain respects, different from that of psychoanalysis, there is no guarantee that patients necessarily exhibit the same types of mechanisms in the two types of treatment; but the flight-into-health strategy is so familiar to analysts that they are likely to be suspicious of marked therapeutic gains which are reported after a number of interviews which, by analytic standards, would constitute only the beginning phase of intensive treatment.

What has just been said should not be construed as a defense of orthodox psychoanalytic theory or treatment procedures (see especially Chapter 18) but only as a word of caution against a too literal interpretation of patients' reports of progress. Patients, even though in the midst of a painful transference reaction, are rarely willing to take direct and full responsibility for discontinuing treatment and often show great ingenuity in inventing justifications for such a course of action. What better reason, then, than an abatement of symptoms, even though the underlying conflicts and difficulties of living remain essentially unmodified!

C. Malingering.—Another artifact which may arise from quite a different mechanism is the following. Some patients may be prompted to report therapeutic gains where there are none, not because of flight-into-health (which is consciously experienced as a real improvement),[43] but because of having simply become discouraged with therapy. However, they may be too "polite" to say how little help they really feel they have obtained from the therapist. "After all, poor man, he tried! So why hurt his feelings by telling him what a failure he has been?" If this possible objection to an uncritical acceptance of the improvement scores of patients on S sorts (or any other pencil-and-paper type of test) seems improbable, one has only to read diagnostic or therapeutic protocols for patients who have previously been in therapy or who have perhaps been hospitalized to be impressed with how great a discrepancy there may be between a patient's true state of mind and what he may report for purposes of expediency. There may also be, in some cases, a kind of self-deception, based upon a desperate desire to *believe* that one has been helped.[44]

D. Spurious Stability of the Ideal Sort.—Early in this chapter, passing reference was made to the fact that the "idealness" of an ideal sort can be interpreted in two ways: It may refer either to the, perhaps quite egocentric, wishes of the patient as to what he *would like* to be, or it may refer to cultural prescriptions as to the kind of person one *ought* to be. In either case, the ideal sort might be expected to show considerable stability, but for different reasons. As has been pointed out, the anchorage of moral standards *outside* the individual, within the group, would lead us to predict but slight changes in this area as a result of psy-

---

[43] For a discussion of the exchangeability of symptoms and the defense strategies of the negative transference, see Mowrer (1950, chap. xviii).
[44] Cf. Hathaway's (1948) discussion of the "hello-goodbye pattern."

chotherapy. In the final analysis, therapy is a method of *individual* treatment and would not be expected to change society, or even to alter, necessarily, the individual's preception of the standards of the group. This reasoning, if substantiated, would explain the stability of the ideal sort. Less significant would be the influence exerted by the fact that *everyone* wants to be "comfortable," "happy," "healthy," "effective," etc. If the items which give ideal sorts their distinctive "weightings" are in any marked measure items of the kind just cited (egocentric items), then the stability of the ideal sort would be spurious and relatively useless research-wise. Perhaps the upshot of this discussion is that a thorough analysis needs to be made of just what items are given distinctive ratings in ideal sorts. It should then be possible to answer some of the questions here posed.

IX. S Procedure and the MMPI Compared

Before now it will very likely have occurred to the reader that there are many similarities between an S sort and various other personality inventories and questionnaires. In principle, there is no difference between the sorting of item cards into designated categories and the checking or rating of listed items. Actually some tests—for example, the Minnesota Multiphasic Personality Inventory—are available in two forms, one involving cards which can be sorted, and another which calls for the checking of a questionnaire. Whether one uses only two (e.g., "Yes" and "No") or many (e.g., 0-10) scale steps is usually a matter of computational convenience or special requirements; and there is also no inherent reason why the *nature* of items used in an S sort and in other tests should necessarily differ.

As a subject "goes down the line" checking or assigning scale values to test items—as, for example, in the MMPI, in the McQuitty test of personality integration (Chapter 16), or in the Osgood "semantic differential" test (Chapter 17)—there is only one way in which the results differ, essentially, from those obtained by means of an S sort: In the latter case, there is a *forced normal distribution,* which has the advantage (for computational purposes) of automatically equalizing all means and standard deviations, whereas in most other testing procedures the subject is given complete freedom to put as many items in any given category as he wishes.

The disadvantage of the S procedure is that over-all average differences between individuals are lost. On most tests it is possible, with respect to some attribute which the test purportedly measures, to say whether one individual is "above" or "below" another individual and to say how both individuals fall with respect to the mean performance of some standard population, or norm. We thus see the meaning of the statement which is sometimes made that in S procedure we "throw away the means" for each individual and thus eliminate the possibility of comparing, in absolute terms, different persons with respect to the attribute which is under investigation.[45] We cannot, in other words, say whether one person is "better" or "worse" than another—only whether, on the basis of a correlation coefficient, the two persons are *similar* or *dissimilar*. Likewise, when an S sort is given to the same person on two occasions (e.g., before and after therapy), we can measure only *change,* and not improvement or deterioration (at least not directly).[46]

Perhaps the most striking illustration of the difference would be in terms of what would happen if there were a change in the *absolute intensity* of personality components but no change in *pattern.* It is, for example, obvious that there might be a marked absolute discrepancy between two series of test scores arranged as a "profile," and yet the relative position or rank order of the scores might remain virtually unchanged, giving no change in correlation, but certainly not proving that "nothing had happened." This point is illustrated by Meehl as follows:

Multiphasics of persons sober and slightly drunk show marked similarity in form, even when the elevation changes, and even when individual items change a lot. That is one of the most interesting findings we have. Give the

[45] In a recent paper, Stephenson (1951) has remarked "Galton long ago realized that we could only deal systematically with individual differences by replacing the multitudinal and vastly different units of mental tests and the like with standard scores, that is, with pure numbers. This, in effect, is what we do when we correlate normal variates: we reduce the previously diverse units of each variate to pure numbers, such that their mean is zero and their standard deviation is 1. Moreover, for mental tests it is probable that we throw away no important information by this procedure, as Thurstone has been careful to point out. The *means* for different mental tests in R technique are in a systematic sense arbitrary matters, depending upon how long the tests are made, the difficulty of the items, and so forth. The same applies to Q technique, where we can standardize *intra*-individual operations, and where, indeed, we could use no other statistical procedure known to us at present. For what on earth could the *mean* score of one person's self-description "mean," and what kind of information is contained in the statement that X's mean score is larger than Y's for their respective operations on their self-notions? The great power and elegancy of the correlational technique, in both R and Q, lies precisely in the fact that not only can it represent data without throwing away any pertinent information with respect to *means,* but also, as Galton first discovered, that all scores can be reduced to pure numbers by standardizing the vastly disparate units of the numberless variates that can exist in the two systems" (pp. 15-16).

[46] Improvement (or deterioration) can be inferred only by an extension of the method, in terms of the coincidence or discrepancy between an S sort for the self and for the ideal, or between other personality aspects along lines first suggested by Watson and Sweet (Sweet, 1929). Repeated application on different occasions of the *same* S sort may show more or less *change* in a person, but it gives us no basis per se, for inferring either progress or the reverse. It is only by giving at least two different kinds of S sorts on two or more occasions and noting whether the results for these are becoming more or less similar, that a legitimate inference concerning therapeutic achievement can be made. We thus make psychological illness or health, not a matter of an individual's absolute position with respect to some external norm, but instead a matter of how well he "fits together," how well *integrated* he is. Now, to be sure, one of the things he has to make fit is the "voice of the community," or at least that part of it which has been internalized; but, to repeat, the basic consideration is integration, not conformity. A person cannot, of course, be integrated without a substantial degree of conformity (not, that is, unless he becomes, psychologically if not physically, a social isolate); but conformity itself cannot be the measure. This is another way of approaching the problem of how meaningful is a mean or an interpersonal norm when considering such matters; cf. footnote 45 above. For a different approach to the problem of integration, see Chapter 16.

Multiphasic, then give somebody two or three good strong cocktails and let him take the Multiphasic over again, and he gets a very similar pattern though he may have as little as 45 per cent overlap in his significant item responses (Meehl, 1950a, p. 26).

As will be shown by the investigations of Osgood (Chapter 17) and McQuitty (Chapter 16), there are many other useful things which one can do with personality data when one does *not* throw away the means, and the fact that this is regularly done in an S sort may constitute a limitation. In S procedure one can, of course, make a study of the numerical fate of a particular item or of a group of items; i.e., the value(s) assigned to a given item or item cluster may change markedly from one administration of a test to another, and if such items are known (or believed) to be "saturated" with some special psychological significance, then such changes could be dealt with in terms of differences, mean differences, or the like. Contrariwise, it is also possible to correlate results obtained by methods other than S procedure. Lewis E. Drake of the University of Wisconsin now has under way a study in which he plans to correlate the MMPI scores or profiles of students before and after counseling. Meehl (personal communication) has expressed some specific reservations about the use of the MMPI in such correlational studies, but in principle there is no difficulty.

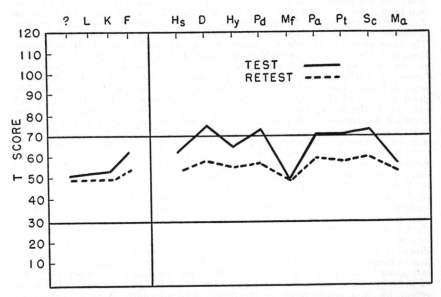

Fig. 38.—Profile curves, reproduced from Schofield (1950), indicating mean scores on the fourteen scales of the MMPI of twenty psychotic patients before and after hospital treatment which included electroshock convulsions. Most of the differences in the mean scores on the clinical scales (*Hs* to *Ma*) are statistically significant. Results produced on other groups of patients included in the same study by means of psychotherapy were much less striking.

Since we are here basically interested in methods of measuring the results of psychotherapy, it is pertinent to note two attempts which have been made in this connection with the MMPI. The first of these is a study conducted by Schofield (1950). In this study, test and retest results on the MMPI for a group of twenty-five neurotics who were treated at the University of Minnesota psychiatric clinic on an out-patient basis show only a shade of change, but the psychotics who received in-patient treatment made more notable gains (see Figure 38).

More recently Kaufmann (1950) has reported a study of a similar nature, conducted in the Student Health Department at the University of Wisconsin, the major results of which are shown in Figure 39 and

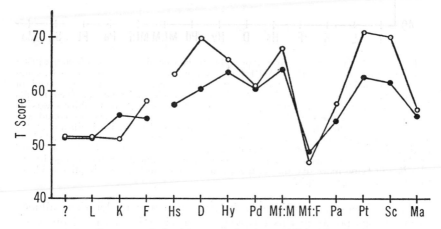

Fig. 39.—Profile curves derived from tabular data published by Kaufmann (1950) showing mean scores on the MMPI for fifty-one students before (open circles) and after (filled circles) psychotherapy in a university health service. Of the four non-clinical scales, two (K and F) show mean differences significant at the .01 level of confidence. Of the ten clinical scales, five (*Hs,* D, *Pa, Pt,* and *Sc*) give mean differences which are significant at the same level of confidence. Some of the other differences are significant at the 0.5 level.

Figure 40. Of particular relevance here are the author's comments on changes in the K score of the two groups. He says:

The patient group scored significantly lower than the control group on this scale in the pretest. This significant difference between the two groups disappeared in the posttests . . . .

A group of psychiatric patients may reasonably be expected as a function of emotional disturbances to be more critical in a self-blaming sense than a normal group. Since guilt feelings are often a powerful factor in emotional maladjustment, it is easy to see why such patients should present themselves in a more self-critical manner than normal individuals [thus earning lower K scores and heightening their over-all neuroticism]. . . . Lastly, it is not inconceivable that patients who willingly submit to psychotherapy may *want to impress the therapist with the seriousness of their difficulty.* While this may not be a matter of crude deception, it may nevertheless be a factor in increasing the intensity of the patient's self-criticism [i.e., in increasing his "plus-getting" and lowering his K score] (Kaufmann, 1950, p. 461, italics added).

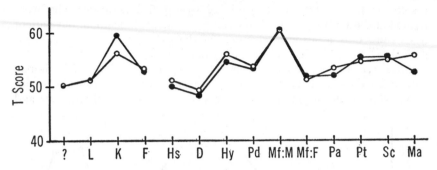

Fig. 40.—Profile curves derived from tabular data published by Kaufmann (1950) showing mean scores on the MMPI for fifty-four college students selected as no-therapy normal controls for the fifty-one students referred to in the legend of Figure 39. On the ten clinical scales, the only sizable difference between results for the first and second administration of the test to these control subjects was on the *Ma* scale, and this difference is significant at only the .05 level of confidence. The mean difference on one of the four nonclinical scales, K, is significant at the .01 level. The control subjects give profiles, for both the first and second administration of the test, which are, in general, considerably below the "before" and "after" profiles for the treatment group. However, the treatment group moves in the *direction* of being more like the control group, a fact which is presumptive evidence that the therapy was helpful.

These observations take us back once again to considerations alluded to at various points in this chapter and specifically discussed on pages 369-70. Until it is clearly shown that the discrepancy between performance on an S sort, pre- and posttherapy, is not significantly influenced by a greater motivation to "plus-get" in the beginning than at the end, we must interpret the results of O technique investigations employing this method of gathering data with caution. Since the work of Hathaway, Meehl, and others on the effects of the test-taking attitude forcibly calls our attention to such a probability, this work is very valuable. Nevertheless, O technique is an extremely promising approach, being admirably suited in theory to show personality changes (especially of an organizational kind) and to provide, by virtue of its self-referential character (as opposed to the use of group references or norms), the requisite degree of *sensitivity.*

Perhaps one of the reasons that it is easy to overlook the possible effects of "faking" in connection with tests administered before and after psychotherapy is that we are accustomed to think only of "faking good," i.e., of the tendency on the part of persons to make themselves appear *better,* i.e., less neurotic, than they actually are. Experience in the selection of military personnel has shown us that this is one situation in which at least some individuals will try to make themselves appear *worse,* i.e., more neurotic, than they actually are. Perhaps a person who is a candidate for free (or at least relatively inexpensive) psychotherapy may have a similar tendency to "plus-get."

Summary

Because this chapter is long, involved, and deals with a variety of issues, no attempt will be made to summarize it in the usual sense. However, we may state here, in brief form, some of the inferences which it suggests.

1. The expression Q technique, as it has been used since 1935, is highly ambiguous, inexplicit, and confusing. It refers, we find, to a number of different concepts and operations which need to be carefully distinguished and independently evaluated.

2. Contemporary researches in the field of personality, including those employing "Q technique," show that we are moving rapidly toward the development of a true and valid *statistics of the individual*. One of the innovations which has made this development possible is the realization that we can deal quite as legitimately with a population of tests as with a population of persons.

3. Analysis of these developments shows further that there is still another population or universe which is statistically meaningful and psychologically important, namely, that of *occasions*. Consideration of the universe, or "dimension," of occasions, especially in the context of Cattell's covariation chart, leads to an over-all, integrated conception of psychological inquiry which systematically relates and unifies the more strictly "experimental" methods with specifically "clinical" approaches.

4. Many intriguing possibilities, as well as pitfalls, are suggested by this type of analysis. Some of these are explored in a preliminary manner, with special reference to the problem of measuring the outcomes of psychotherapy.

CHAPTER 14

CORRELATIONS BETWEEN PERSONS AS A RESEARCH TOOL [1]

By Lee J. Cronbach, Ph.D.

Correlation between persons has been suggested repeatedly in the literature, at least as far back as 1925. Many of the papers treat of it in connection with factor analysis, William Stephenson being the principal advocate of the method (Stephenson,[*] 1950a, 1950b). One of the earliest American papers was Zubin's discussion of like-mindedness, in 1938 (Zubin, 1938).

Except for a few studies by Stephenson himself, practically no use was made of this type of correlation until 1948, at which time Stephenson joined the staff of the University of Chicago and came in contact with its vigorous clinical research group. Some sort of spontaneous combustion occurred, and studies using Q technique, as he calls his procedure, erupted right and left, many in Rogers' group (Rogers, 1951b) and others being done independently, including those published by Fiedler (1950b, 1951a). Interest in the method is now spreading rapidly.

I think the basic reason why we were so slow to recognize the aptness of correlating persons is that the method was introduced in terms of factor analysis. In particular, Stephenson was first impressed with the possibility of factoring people into types. While this is one way the method can be used, American psychologists are not very warm to the idea of types and would prefer other ways of formulating clinical research problems. The early papers also said, strangely enough, that correlation

---

[1] This chapter is based upon a paper delivered at Washington University, St. Louis, on March 10, 1951, as part of a symposium on research method in clinical psychology. The program was supported by the U. S. Public Health Service.

During the period while this chapter was in press, thinking on this problem has been greatly extended. Our own recent research has demonstrated such severe limitations on the specific techniques of correlation and Q sort (Cronbach and Gleser, 1952; Warrington, 1952) that many statements herein should be more carefully qualified. Specific qualifications have been inserted into the chapter, but an over-all rewriting to reflect the trend of recent work has not been feasible. In general, such methods of assessing similarity as applying the D formula to profiles based on cluster of items will probably replace the methods discussed in most detail here. Professor Stephenson himself has shifted his focus away from Q correlation; his most recent proposal for "factorial design" employs cluster scoring of the Q sort, and he no longer computes correlations (Stephenson, 1952).

The general logic and potential value of studies of similarity stand as stated here, even though the technique is modified.

[*] References are to the bibliography at the back of the book.

between persons was a method for studying general characteristics common over all groups, and not designed to study individual differences. Bordin may be right in his guess that the early proponents of the method were preoccupied with biological models and so overlooked its relevance to social hypotheses (Bordin, 1943). The recent uses of the technique put little emphasis on factor analysis. As it is now being used, correlation between persons is a device for translating into operations many of the current concepts of personality, social psychology, and phenomenological theory. Since those fields have sadly needed operations, the method promises to be a great contribution.

There has been considerable controversy regarding the precise use and significance of correlation between persons. Sir Cyril Burt (1940) has disagreed with Stephenson on several significant issues. The relation of their positions, as I see it, has been that Burt has taken a sounder view of the logical and mathematical questions in this field, but Stephenson has contributed admirable imagination in finding ways to use this type of correlation. While this paper departs from Stephenson's procedural suggestions in several respects, the ingenuity with which Stephenson developed his ideas is not to be minimized.

Stephenson's cheerful belligerence is at least matched by the gusto with which R. B. Cattell has entered the arena. In a most recent discussion of Stephenson's work, Cattell (1951) manages to be simultaneously outraged and outrageous. I would agree with Cattell that no technique should be used without constant recognition of its meaning and assumptions, but I can accept neither his outright dismissal of the Stephenson proposals nor his unlimited enthusiasm for other factor analysis methods. There are sound issues in Cattell's argument, but to tease his reasoning out of its emotional context and consider each point is not here appropriate. A constructive examination of these issues may better follow completion of ongoing sympathetic studies of psychometric theory in this area.

Before describing the technique, I shall enumerate types of studies to which the techniques of Q sort and correlation between persons are apropos. First, the Q sort invented by Stephenson provides a flexible method for obtaining a qualitative description (or self-description) of the individual in a form for rigorous manipulation. The Q profile is halfway between the idiosyncratic, highly personalized sketch a clinician might write, and the formal diagnostic profile from the Wechsler or some other test which "measures" the person on a limited number of scales. Second, the Q sort permits comparison of many different personas which coexist as features of the same individual. To take a simple illustration, we can correlate a person's self-description with his description of certain roles; and so we can say which role he thinks he fits most nearly. Third, correlation between persons provides a basis for studying the homogeneity of groups. To examine whether one group is more homogeneous than the population from which it is drawn, we need only examine the similarity measures for pairs within the group, compared to pairs drawn at

random from the population. In general, hypotheses regarding homogeneity of groups should be tested by the Fisher discriminant function
or an equivalent test, instead of basing the analysis on Q correlations
directly. Such a procedure differs from the usual analysis of variance
because it studies not homogeneity in a single variable, but resemblance
between relatively large segments of the personality. The fourth present
use of correlation between persons is to study changes, especially in
therapy. There is hope that in properly designed studies these correlations report changes in the configuration of personality, whereas former
objective methods have been restricted to changes of certain scores. If a
patient moves so that his configuration is more like a normal standard and
less like his pretreatment makeup, therapy has been to some degree
successful.

Q Sort as a Forced-Choice Device

In current studies, data are gathered by a special procedure known as
the Q sort. Then Q sorts made by different persons, or at different times,
or under different instructions, are correlated with each other. The
method of correlation between persons is completely general, however,
and can be applied to almost any data. The only inviolable restriction is
that all variables are measured on the same scale. That is, we must be
able to give sensible meaning to the statement, "Variable a is greater than
Variable b, for this person." The card-sorting method is practical and
frequently appropriate, and for that reason it is being widely used.

The Q sort is obtained in a manner like this. A pack of fifty statements is handed the subject. He is told to sort them into eleven piles,
putting in the extreme right-hand pile the statement which fits him best,
and in the extreme left-hand pile the statement which is least true for him.
Then he puts the next most applicable statements in the next pile, and so
on until the residue which are neither true nor false for him go in the
middle. The subject is told before he begins how many statements must
go in each pile: 1 in the end piles, 2 in the next, then 4, 7, 7, and 8 in
the middle pile; or some other pattern. This means that the subject has
been forced to arrange the statements in a somewhat normal distribution,
from those which fit him best to those which fit him least. The procedure
can be used with other numbers of statements, and with a greater or lesser
number of piles. Any statement may be used in the sorting, depending
on the problem. To study interests, an item might be "I do crossword
puzzles regularly"; to study social relations, "I find it easy to make
friends."

In the Q sort, we have a variant of the forced-choice procedure which
has so many psychometric advantages. For one thing, this method of
interrogation is much more penetrating than the common questionnaire
where the person can say "Yes" to all the favorable symptoms and "No"
to all unfavorable ones. The method is free from those idiosyncrasies of
response which cause some persons to respond "Cannot say" twice as

often as others, and so make their scores noncomparable. The forced choice requires every person to put himself on the measuring scale in much the same manner. Since more statements are placed in the middle piles, the subject is freed from many difficult and rather unimportant discriminations he would have to make if he were forced to rank every statement. And the fact that discrimination near the center of the scale is difficult is reduced in importance by the fact that in product-moment correlations the end cells receive greatest weight.

There is a continuum of complexity from the two-item paired comparison to the full Q sort. Kuder's preference tests call for sorting three items at a time on a three-point scale. We could provide five items, from which the subject selects the most and least applicable, or seven alternatives, or any higher number until mechanical complexity becomes a deterrent. This complex forced choice is a powerful method. A set of three items, to be ranked in three piles, tells us in effect how the subject answered on three different paired comparisons: *ab, ac,* and *bc.* If thirty-six statements are grouped in twelve triads, the subject tells us his choice on just thirty-six paired comparisons. Yet if we take only *twelve* statements and require the subject to put them into a six-pile quasi-normal distribution, we automatically get answers (not, however, experimentally independent) to fifty-eight paired comparisons. With the larger number of statements used by Stephenson, the total number of comparisons mounts amazingly. And, with so many items, the number of configurations of responses is incredibly high. For just twelve statements which are uncorrelated and which have maximum variance, division into six piles permits over thirteen million configurations.

The forced-sort method has drawbacks. Travers' (1951) recent review of the forced-choice rating scale makes the point, very properly, that careless item-writing will confront the subject with logically meaningless choices. Also, forced-choice devices are somewhat resented because the subject is required to condemn himself. If he puts "I beat my wife frequently" in the end pile—saying, "This definitely does not fit me"—, he has left in his hand some other incriminating card which he must put in a pile signifying "This is false, but not quite so false."

There are other reasons for believing that the forced distribution may not in the end be most advantageous for many studies. The forcing methods eliminate from consideration possible differences in level of elevation of profiles. In some investigations this factor may represent an undesired response set (Cronbach, 1950), but in other studies this may be a type of individual difference worth studying. Another effect of the usual Q sort is that differences in scatter within profiles are eliminated from consideration. This may be psychologically indefensible, if there is reason to think that persons differ in their variability over traits. Moreover, such equalizing of scatter vastly increases the error of measurement in Q correlations for persons who have little true variability (flat profiles). Cronbach and Gleser (1952) have discussed the situations in which Q sorting and correlation between persons is disadvantageous, and have suggested procedures which permit the investigator to use the information which Stephenson's technique loses. One of their major suggestions is the introduction of D, a measure of distance between persons, which is more general than Q correlation. It is possible that *unforced* sorts will be found a superior procedure for most investigations.

So far as present research indicates, almost any set of statements can be the basis for investigations of correlation between persons. One set often used is based on Murray's list of needs. One could use statements expressing self-concepts taken from therapy protocols, statements of values, political attitudes, or descriptions of overt behavior. These statements define the chunk of personality to be investigated. We need more research than we now have regarding the selection of statements. Until we penetrate the problem more deeply, I can suggest these criteria. First, statements, while logically bearing on the same domain, should represent a large number of continua. Correlating persons seems to have no advantage if we present items which all fall into one scale dealing, say, with age or weight. Second, statements being compared should have about the same average degree of desirability, over the entire population. If statements range from black to white, the sorts by different persons will be about the same, and the method becomes insensitive. Third, each statement should have substantial variance, in that different persons put it in different piles.

In both conventional measuring scales and Q sorts, items are a sample from a universe. In the test where an interpretable score is sought, the universe is one in which all items are positively correlated. Loevinger (1947) notes that such tests are based on a "Principle of Equivalence." In obtaining data for correlating persons, it is essential that items have some logical similarity, but correlation is generally undesirable. Here, as in the Strong Blank, the tester makes use of that kind of test design which Loevinger called the "Sampling Principle." There is some merit, for correlating persons, in the lumpy test composed of groups of correlated items—a sort of cluster-sampling principle which permits important variables to take on substantial weight.

Attention is called to the fact that the selection of variables makes a great difference in the results obtained. People who are relatively similar on one set of items will generally not be similar on other sets, unless both sets deal with the same segment of personality. We cannot therefore speak without qualification of two persons as being similar. They are similar within a certain domain, on certain variables or factors.

While the sorting method is of special value in many problems, I repeat that it is not necessary to restrict correlation between persons to such data. Any set of data whatsoever may be used, although the method leads to absurd results unless all data are expressed in logically comparable units. Those units may be metric units, as in the case where numerous measures of length are taken as variables, or the units may be standard-score units which express the individual's standing in the group.

Correlation between persons may be based on test-score profiles, facts from a case history, or any other data.

Correlation Between Persons

Once we have our data, we correlate one person with another. Correlating one person with another isn't half so exotic as it sounds. We do it all the time. Professor Smith makes out a test and gives it to Student Jones. Then each one fills out an answer sheet with the answers he thinks correct. Smith lays his sheet over Jones's and counts one point for every agreement. This scoring operation is logically identical to correlating the two answer sheets, even though we do not express the score as a correlation.[2] We could get a correlation from this fourfold:

		Smith marks	
		+	0
Jones marks	+	24	11
	0	6	33

Jones's score is 57 points out of 74. His correlation with the teacher is .55. Because the teacher's answers are regarded as God-given, we don't speak of our examinations as an investigation to see how closely the student's pattern corresponds to the teacher's. Yet that is what they are, and this is particularly evident in tests which require judgment and the weighing of complex evidence.

Strong's Vocational Interest Blank correlates the answers of the subject with the answers of a group, such as lawyers. In his method he partials out the correspondence of individual and group to men-in-general. The Minnesota Multiphasic Personality Inventory correlates the subject with the composite response of a group of diagnosed patients, such as manics. On the Stanford-Binet Test, the subject's responses are correlated with the responses given by relatively mature children; the more like them he is, the higher his score. What is now being done with data gathered through Q sort, one could also do by appropriately treating almost any test, as Zubin originally showed. The advantage of Q sort is its special mechanical efficiency.

Correlation would be measured by any product-moment formula. The most efficient formula for the case where all profiles have the same mean and variation, as in the forced sort, is

$$Q = 1 - \frac{\Sigma d^2_j}{2nV_x}$$

Here d is the difference between the scores on a given statement for the two persons, and V_x is the variance over all n statements for any person.

[2] The usual score is number right; the phi correlation is approximately number right minus chance expectation, divided by possible rights-minus-chance.

The distance formula of Cronbach and Gleser, to be preferred when information about differences in elevation and scatter are to be considered in the similarity measure, is

$$D = \sqrt{\sum_j d^2}$$

which is a simple function of Q for the forced-choice condition. The paper where this is introduced discusses several variant formulas for special purposes. The D measure closely resembles in its properties the r_p formula proposed by Cattell (1949). It has been suggested independently in a recent paper by Osgood and Suci (1952).

In studies of similarity, great importance should be placed on determining the reliability of a person's profile. Comparisons will give quite misleading impressions if the profiles are unreliable, and unreliability is to be expected from many of the profiles now being compared in psychological work. Suppose a person's profile is unreliable, because his response to the several variables is unreliable. Then his location with respect to other persons is unreliable, and his similarities might be quite different on a repeated test. In Q sort or other correlational methods, the reliability is substantially different for different persons. Such reliability can be estimated by correlating two profiles obtained for the same person, using two measurements on the same variables. At present, there is no suitable correction method for taking the information about reliability into account, but the investigator is warned to interpret with caution if reliability is low for some cases. Falsely high or low Q correlations can be obtained when one or both profiles compared are unreliable.

Studies of Social Relations

The most common directions for studies using Q sort are to arrange the statements from those which fit you best to those which fit you least well. This gives the *self sort,* a self-report picture of the individual. Correlation between self sorts is involved in any number of research questions. Are happily married couples more alike than the unhappily married? Do couples grow more alike during marriage? Does the therapist have the best results with patients more like himself? In sociometric choice, do people select others who are like themselves?

If self sorts are obtained for a large number of persons, we can correlate and factor analyze to divide the people into types. This method has been especially often used by Stephenson, but factor analysis may not be the best method for treating interpersonal data. The mean correlation within a group is a direct measure of homogeneity.

Now we approach the most intriguing aspect of the Q sort methodology: a given person embodies many different personas. We have obtained his self sort. Now let us ask him to sort for another person.

How would your therapist sort these cards? Or, therapist, how would your patient sort them? We have five correlations:

>   similarity
>   assumed similarity (2)
>   accuracy of prediction (2)

The sixth correlation (P/T vs. T/P) is unimportant in this relation. The accuracy of prediction is a validity coefficient; it tells us how good a diagnostician the therapist is. If an assessor studies the Rorschach protocol and sorts the cards as he thinks the patient will, we have obtained

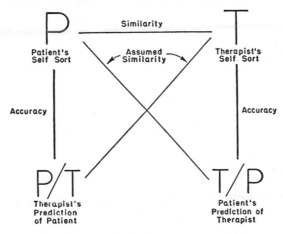

Patient's Self Sort

Therapist's Self Sort

Accuracy

Accuracy

Therapist's Prediction of Patient

Patient's Prediction of Therapist

Fig. 41.—Q sorts by therapist and patient.

an estimate of the validity of the Rorschach as this man uses it. If you object to the self sort as a criterion, we can obtain a criterion by asking a supervisor or a therapist or someone else who knows the subject to sort the cards according to his behavior. Besides validating diagnoses, the accuracy correlations permit other research. Do good leaders perceive members of their groups more accurately than poor leaders? Do subordinates who get high ratings perceive their superiors insightfully?

Since I have proposed a different method of qualitative validation (Cronbach, 1948), I mention the difference between that method and this. My allowing an assessor to write a free statement regarding the man permits him to point to idiosyncratic features encountered in no other record in the group. This is a valuable type of prediction and should be validated. In Stephenson's method, the assessor must use a standard list of statements. But since the list can be long, and since statements that do not apply to a case or for which criterion data are lacking fall into the middle piles and have rather little influence on the validity coefficient, Q sorting does test diagnostic efficiency with considerable flexibility.

Assumed similarity is an index of the extent to which you think the other person is like yourself. In Fiedler's work, it appears to be a sign of warmth and acceptance when the therapist says, in effect, "This guy is much like me; there, but for the grace of God, go I." Some such attitude is particularly involved when the assumed similarity is much higher than the real similarity. It appears, from Fiedler's work with small samples, that this tendency to identify with the other person marks the superior therapist (Fiedler, 1951*b*).

Now we introduce another sort: "What kind of person would you like to be?" Or, if our investigative appetite is for studies of the superego, "Put in this pile those things which *ought* to be true of you," etc. And we can introduce an ideal for the other person: "What ought *he* to be?" Figure 42 shows a pattern you can trace for yourself; almost every line you can draw between two points has an important psychological significance.

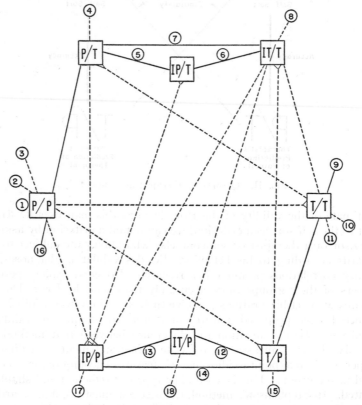

Fig. 42.—Ideal sorts by patient and therapist. Letters to left of slant line denote directions given sorter; letter to right indicates the sorter. Sorters P and T may be patient and therapist or pupil and teacher, etc. Sorts: P—"What is P like?" IP—"What is P's ideal?" Then, for example, IT/P is the patient's sort to indicate his perception of the therapist's ideal.

Transference appears in the relation of T/P and IP/P (line 14). If these are similar, the patient is saying, "I want to be like the therapist."

Here is a tool for studying identification with heroes, formation of ideals, and other aspects of character development. With suitable modification of questions, we can inquire into the goals of leaders, the goals of leaders as perceived by their groups, and the extent to which those goals are held by the group members.

The correlation of self sort P with ideal IP/P (line 3) is an index of claimed self-satisfaction. It would not do to assume that this is an infallible measure of adjustment, but it is important in therapy. According to some views of therapy, there should be an increased correlation between self sort and ideal sort before therapy is completed; others would want the self sort to become more like an observer's sort (the insight correlation, line 16). Keeping records during the course of therapy of the satisfaction correlation, the transference correlation, and others should tell us a good deal about the process of therapy.

One of the most useful concepts in current social psychology is role. There are vocational roles, age roles, sex roles, status roles. We can define aspects of these roles operationally in several ways. Consider the role of the professor. We can ask people to sort a set of cards according to how professors act. The *objective status,* what professors do, is a composite of sorts made by trained observers. The *stereotype,* "What do people expect of professors?" is a composite of sorts made offhand by the man in the street. Of course there are students' stereotypes of professors, and professors' stereotypes of professors, too. The professor's self sort may differ radically from his perception of professors in general. We can correlate the self ideal, what the person is trying to do or his perception of his responsibility, with what others in his social field expect of him. Some people fit the roles to which they are assigned. Others take up statuses with which their characteristic behavior has a low correlation. The techniques we are discussing may be useful in singling out these cases in order to study their social adaptation.

The Place of Correlation Between Persons in Science

Having examined the procedures of current studies, we can back off and take a comprehensive view of the place of correlation between persons in a science of behavior. This discussion might be regarded as an answer to the recurrent question, "How does correlation between persons relate to the old method of correlation between tests? Does it do anything different?" There is a short and easy answer to this question, that under certain circumstances the results are very similar and in that case they are alternate procedures. But a more complicated answer is of considerable interest.

The problem of the scientist studying behavior is to find organizing principles (dimensions, rubrics, etc.) for describing the matrix composed of all the organisms in the world, and all the behaviors of those organisms. This grand matrix is a set of data which are to be placed in a comprehensible order. Order is found in covariation; when, knowing one entry, we can predict other entries, we begin to have generalization. Natural observation, unaided by any refinements of method, intuitively perceives a certain order within this matrix. We recognize certain configurations of anatomical structure or behavior appearing in many different organisms, and we set up categories like horse, dog, lion, man. The use of such groupings involves an implicit assumption that describing animals in their groups accounts for more of the variance within the table than setting up categories of behavior and stating laws without reference to species. We cannot, for example, account for speed of locomotion by a formula based on age when we take all species together. Young rabbits run faster than old bears; mature horses move faster than young beetles. But we can account for speed of locomotion fairly accurately just by knowing the species. Within species, there remains variance to account for by age and other variables. Whether we use natural observation or careful principles of taxonomy, we are performing an operation of correlation between organisms, grouping those which have greatest similarity. This method can become extremely refined, as in the processes of experimental genetics where a category like *Drosophila* is finally subdivided into strains having common genes. In other fields, where it is impractical to perform breeding experiments to test the hypothesis that organisms are alike, one may use such statistical procedures as Fisher has developed. His discriminant function, for instance, is applied to the problem of arranging specimens of iris into groups which resemble each other, i.e., which constitute species. In these cases the primary basis of classification is physical measurements, but the logical problem is the same as in the use of behavioral data.

The psychologist takes as an implicit assumption that some organisms are more alike than others. He performs experiments on rats or on dogs or on people. I know of no instance where a study has been based on an indiscriminate mixture of chimpanzees and people. The psychologist has always implicitly correlated his organisms, sorted them into groups, and worked with one group at a time.

This is not to say that transspecies laws cannot be found. At certain times the scientist must raise his eyes to look for these. The Linnaean principles for organizing species into a hierarchy were arrived at precisely by working across the table following certain behaviors across many species, rather than working within species. The paleontologist generalizes in a similar fashion. He reports, in effect, that many characteristics are correlated over many species, and that this correlation can be accounted for by a "factor," lateness of appearance of the species. In psychology, we are familiar with the cephalocaudal principle of maturation. This is a law which accounts for variance, predicting accurately which of two behaviors will emerge first. To arrive at a good prediction, however, we must supplement this law relating behaviors with some laws stating resemblances among organisms. The Gesell norms for infants tell us that bodily locomotion for this species develops during the latter half of the first year after birth; someone else's study of salamanders gives the generalization that locomotion is virtually complete at the time of hatching. To predict any entry in our grand table, we must know both the species groupings and the principles which relate one behavior to another. Sometimes the behavioral principle is the same over all species. At other times, due to the limited state of the science, the laws found for different species are different. Psychology is suffering today from the necessary difficulty that relations found in rat learning do not apply, in their present form, to much human learning; and from the difficulty that relations which hold true for patients so disturbed as to require treatment do not have the same validity when applied to a nonclinical sample.

The essential procedure of science is to break down the grand matrix by alternate application of correlation between organisms and correlation between characteristics. The psychological experimenter stratifies his sample of organisms according to species (and then usually makes his study in only one stratum; but the experimental design could be repeated over many species when the time is ripe). Having decided to use people, he then usually turns to the problem of subdividing behaviors. This division, too, is commonly based on intuitive rather than deliberate observation. An investigator decides that, say, anthropometric traits constitute a homogeneous field for study. He operates on a hunch that these go together. Current convention divides variables into groups such as intellectual, emotional, social, and physical. An investigator may break across these lines, but often this comes gradually and reluctantly. As an example, I can point to Thurstone's recognition, over the last fifteen years, that the Word Fluency factor is more an expression of a style of performance or a temperamental variable than a measure of intellectual power. It was first introduced into factorial studies on the assumption that it was part of an intellectual domain.

Sometimes we have lost sight of the fact that correlations among characteristics are relative to the sample and that we can make better sense of the matrix of human traits if we group organisms within species. The obvious example here is grouping by cultures. We tried grouping by races once, but found this an unproductive way to account for behavioral variance. Grouping by cultures is constructive. Behaviors that correlate within one culture often do not correlate at all within another. As soon as we start writing laws that apply within a culture, explicitly recognizing that these are not general human laws, our minds are freed to look for the more basic organization of characteristics that transcends cultural lines. Once it was thought that "the male is naturally dominant." This "law" was false. But it is not false to state that sex roles are defined in any culture and that those persons who do not conform to the sex-appropriate pattern are punished.

The present-day social scientist operates in the belief that species, and within species cultures, are appropriate groupings for his purpose. Moreover, he recognizes that people may appropriately be subgrouped according to age and sex, because age and sex account for much behavorial variance in many cultures. Within such a frame, one turns to a problem of discovering psychological principles for white American young adult males. It is at this point where psychological theories are especially incomplete, for they do not reduce this grouping in any logical way. There are psychiatric classifications, with which no one is content. There are theories along the lines of Kretschmer, Sheldon, Jung, or Lloyd Warner, to take a few examples; none of these is very satisfactory as a way of accounting for variation. One of the vigorous current suggestions is that behavior can be accounted for largely in terms of the role in which the person perceives himself. If role proves a fruitful way to account for much currently unexplained behavior, we can deliberately pursue the next step of seeking to explain individual differences among those in the same role.

The scientific process, viewed in this way, becomes a matter of saying: Organisms which are alike in a certain way show the following correlations in their behavior. The continual endeavor is to find broader organizations, hence more sweeping laws. But the basic datum for a higher-order law is a lower-order relation, and nonchance relations cannot be perceived when fundamentally different organisms are shuffled together in a sample. The inquiry that seeks correlations among persons aims to reduce the population under study to one where relations between behaviors become more visible. It is not necessary to define a typology in mutually exclusive boxes like biological species. It is profitable for scientific purposes to study a relatively homogeneous group, and we need not fool ourselves into thinking it sharply demarcated and internally uniform. "The American culture" is a helpful concept, but we are not deluded into ignoring its diversity. The view here outlined does not argue that the product-moment correlation technique is the only way to establish similarities. There are many alternative modes of analysis which work better as one attains greater insight in an area; as a first approximation, the D measure of similarity seems good enough to recommend. The configurations that link persons, and the configurations of personas in a person or a social group, are well worth study.

CHAPTER 15

INTRAINDIVIDUAL REPETITIVE MEASUREMENTS (P TECHNIQUE) IN UNDERSTANDING PSYCHO-THERAPEUTIC CHANGE [1]

By Lester Luborsky, Ph.D.

Introduction and Aims

In the clinical field, we stress the importance of the single case in deriving our understanding of personality. The principles we discover are dependent not only upon the frequency of identical behavior or traits in a number of persons (as in cross-sectional studies of common behavior), but also upon the way behavior varies from time to time within a single person under different external and internal conditions (along the longitudinal, intraindividual dimension). The clinician may note, after it occurs once or twice, the concomitance of a patient's depression with his anger at his wife or therapist. But the clinician may miss some of the manifold, simultaneously varying dimensions of, for example, the patient's energy level, dependence, fluency, mood, and autonomic equilibrium. The techniques of intraindividual measurement to be described here offer a feasible method of studying these manifold changes in a single case.

A type of factor-analytic treatment of repeated intraindividual measurements has been termed "P technique" (developed by Cattell,* 1943). It begins by measuring a person repeatedly at intervals on the same battery of tests or variables; when the series of measurements is long enough to give an adequate "population of occasions," the measurements are correlated. Thus, if two symptoms fluctuate together from day to day, a high correlation will be obtained between them; and we can suspect they spring from the same dynamic source. If no significant correlation is found, we may infer the behaviors are dynamically remote or unconnected. The factor-analytic procedure, then, extracts from the correlations the major groupings of tests or variables.

P technique is one of six systematically defined methods of correlation and factor analysis. Other investigators have used P technique (without

[1] The author wishes to express his appreciation for critical reading of the manuscript to Drs. Robert R. Holt and Robert Wallerstein. Permission has been kindly granted by *The Journal Press* to reproduce parts of the earlier article by Cattell and Luborsky (1950). Tables 8 and 9 and the 5 conclusions beginning on p. 5 are reproduced with only minor changes. The author is especially indebted to Dr. R. B. Cattell with whom the research in the earlier article was cooperatively executed.

* References are to the bibliography at the back of the book.

calling it that) in its purely correlational form. Here, the method is extended, with clinical material, to its factor-analytic application.[2]

The aims of this article are: (a) to demonstrate selected results from the employment of the P technique method with a peptic ulcer patient in psychotherapy; (b) to assess the present study so that future studies utilizing this method can be more fruitful; (c) to suggest possible applications of P technique (and allied versions of it) to research in personality structure, especially psychosomatics and psychotherapy; and (d) to evaluate the way in which a statistical (factor-analytic) and a clinical approach supplement and inform each other. Since both methods are used on the same case, we have an unusual opportunity for delineating the merits and drawbacks of each.

Case Demonstration of the Method and Selected Results

Procedure and Choice of Variables.—In determining procedure, one patient was seen by the author for two hours each day for fifty-four days over a period of twelve weeks, beginning in March, 1946. Each session included an hour of repetitive testing and an hour of recorded discussion of dreams and free associations. The variables that were finally used in the factor analysis are listed in Table 8. These variables include only a small part of the possible scorable material—this is especially true in the realm of the dreams and free associations—and none of the tests, which for a variety of reasons had to be discontinued,[3] are included.

The choice of variables was guided by these considerations:

1. The major dimensions of variability for this patient were to be established by sampling a large segment of the personality. This involved using tests in the exact manner of previous studies of personality trait structure by the usual correlation techniques (Cattell, 1946, 1947) and then keying the findings into the structure of existing findings. It was more difficult to choose a sample of the physiological than of the psychological variables, since there are fewer large-scale factor studies of the former.

2. In the choice of measures, three realms or levels of observation commonly studied by different specialists were to be covered. These were (a) objective personality measures, (b) physiological tests, and

---

[2] A description of the six methods is given by Cattell (1946); see also Chapters 13 and 14. Other investigators who have employed forms of the P technique are cited under "Applications" below. Two studies have been reported in which P technique was used on normal subjects. This is the first in which P technique is combined with clinical material.

[3] A slightly more detailed description of procedure is given in Cattell and Luborsky (1950). A detailed description of all forty-six procedures may be obtained from the American Documentation Institute of Washington, D. C., by ordering Document No. 3353.

TABLE 8
Classified List of Variables

Number	Variables
Physiological: Biochemical	
30	Glucose concentration in the blood (Shaffer-Hartman-Somogyi method)
31	Calcium level (serum calcium; Clark Collip method)
32	White corpuscle count (absolute)
33	Red corpuscle count (absolute)
44	Neutrophil count per cent of total white from blood smear
45	Lymphocyte count per cent of total white from blood smear
11	Salivary pH (alkalinity of saliva)
12	Salivary quantity (secretion in two minutes)

Physiological: Total Organism

Number	Variables
15	*PGR* mean magnitude of deflection to stimuli (as per cent fall)
14	*PGR* initial resistance (absolute) of skin
13	*PGR* frequency of spontaneous deflections in three minutes
not used	*PGR* magnitude of upward drift in relaxing after shock
41	Frequency of urination
42	Frequency of stomach awareness, i.e., of reported pains and discomfort
17	Negative after-image; length of duration after standard exposure
40	Hours of sleep

Psychological: Objective Measurement

Number	Variables
8	Myokinesis, mean length of movements intended to be 1″
9	Myokinesis, mean length of movements intended to be 2″
10	Myokinesis, drift in either direction from intended line of drawing
5	Speed of writing and multiplying (correctly)
6	Perseveration (disposition rigidity) by visual motor test
7	Inability to acquire new mental set (substitution multiplication)
2	Reaction time to light, mean of twenty reactions with regular and irregular
1	Reaction time ratio; time for regular warnings over time for irregular
discontinued [a]	Suggestibility sway test
3	Fluency of association, verbal; sentence completion and two T.A.T. cards
4	Fluency of association, drawing (unrestricted nonverbal fluency)
37	Amount of dreaming recalled, indicated by number of words of description
38	Feeling at end of dream, scored low for happiness, high for frustration or fear
39	Completeness of dream, extent to which dream action seemed achieved, scored low for completeness
43	Frequency of recorded laughter during daily interview
19	Funniness of jokes as rated by subject (twenty two jokes)
16	Number of words remembered from a word list; deliberate memorizing
not used	Ratio of emotional to nonemotional words recalled
discontinued [a]	Reversible perspective speed
not used	Endurance of shock, magnitude voluntarily endured
46	Serial order number of test session

[a] See explanation for discontinuing, p. 401.

TABLE 8 (*continued*)

Number	Variables
	Psychological Rating
19	Cooperativeness vs. obstructiveness
20	Emotionality vs. calmness, steadiness
21	Attention-getting behavior vs. self-sufficiency
22	Self-confidence and aggressiveness vs. retiring submissiveness
23	Cheerful contentedness vs. worryingness, anxiety
24 [b]	Persistent in desires, strong-willed vs. not insistent, quitting
25	Friendly interest in people vs. shyness, caution
26 [b]	"Lively," jumpy, restless vs. quiet, poised
27	Vigor, orderly mind vs. languidness, absent-mindedness
28	High intellectual interest vs. lack of interest in work and discussion
	Psychological Self Rating
29	Distractible, dependent vs. absorbed, self-sufficient
not used	Subject's attitude to therapist
34	Strength of interest in food
35	Strength of interest in sex activity
36	Strength of interest in social activities

[b] Variables 24 and 26 were intended to represent respectively G factor (as persevering vs. quitting, fickle) and I factor (as sensitive, jumpy vs. stolid, poised) but the meanings given by the raters were found to be as now labeled. The daily raters included three friends of the patients and the writer.

(*c*) introspective materials including free associations, dreams and self-observations.

3. Measures were to be chosen that are suitable for repetitive testing in this unusual context where ordinary assumptions of reliability and validity may not hold. Here it was necessary to deal with acclimating effects,[4] to find tests which were sufficiently brief, and to select measures which bore on a particular personality segment. For many measures, especially the physiological ones and those which were selected from the free association sessions, these difficulties did not enter in. And, for many of the tests we were able to construct approximately equivalent forms, e.g., fluency of association, power of memorizing, disposition rigidity. Practice effects on some tests can be separated from other fluctuations as a trend factor. More work is necessary on (*a*) the types of tests which show promise and (*b*) the assumptions underlying repetitive methods of intraindividual measurements where the interest is in the meaningful test "unreliability."

Results on Personality Factor Structure.—A total of forty-six usable variables (Table 8) were extracted from the tests, the dreams, and the free associations. Scores on these were intercorrelated, and the

[4] One known study describes the use of many equivalent forms on six intellective tests to avoid memorization of the test responses (Guetzkow and Brozek, 1947).

correlation matrix was factorized by the simple centroid method into nine factors (which were rotated to simple structure positions). In an earlier article (Cattell and Luborsky, 1950), a preliminary identification and interpretation of these factors was attempted in relation to (a) two other P technique studies on normal subjects (Cattell, Cattell, and Rhymer, 1947; Williams, 1949); (b) the results of more usual cross-sectional correlation factor studies, i.e., R technique (Cattell, 1946, 1947); and (c) general psychological and physiological knowledge.

The factors in Table 9 are arranged in descending order of their contribution to the variance of all variables. The capital letters before the tentative factor name refer to the R- or P-technique factors of previous studies to which the factor appears most similar.[5] The factors are presented here without individual discussion, but most of them will be considered in later sections as they bear on other aims of this article, e.g., if they change grossly during treatment.

Conclusions regarding the use of P technique in arriving at the patient's personality factor structure:

1. Most of the nine factors contain variables from all three levels of personality expression—psychological ratings and tests, physiological measures, and free associations.

2. The general hypotheses which provoked this study are, in part, confirmed. First, the daily variations show functional connections and are large enough to correlate and factorize. Second, the factors or source traits obtained are, in the main, matchable with the common factors obtained in R technique and in two previous P technique studies using some variables in common, although more uniqueness occurred than had been expected. Third, the symptoms in a clinical case can, by P technique, be positively locked into the general structure of personality factors.

3. Only four of the eleven or twelve known R-technique factors—A, C, F, and H—appear with tolerable certainty here, while E appears less certainly and with resemblances to G. These are the same five factors that appeared in the first P-technique study and most clearly in Williams' study, so that the intraindividual *variances* of factors are apparently systematically different from those in interindividual studies, in reducing the roles of B and K especially.

4. The four factors here, not matchable with R technique, are either new factors or familiar factors which cannot be reliably identified because of insufficiency of behavior ratings in the loadings. They are (a) a

---

[5] Factor letters referred to in this article:
F— = desurgency
H+, H— = adventurous cyclothymia vs. withdrawn schizothymia
E+, E— = dominance vs. submissiveness
G— = Immature dependent character (the opposite of positive character integration)
C— = general emotionality
A+ = cyclothymia

TABLE 9

THE NINE PERSONALITY FACTORS EXTRACTED FROM SCORES ON THE FORTY-SIX DAILY MEASURES

Variable	Correlation [a]	Direction and Name of Variable [b]

Factor 1 F—, or (E+, F—)[c]: Modified Desurgency vs. Surgency

39	—92	Dreams reported to be complete
5	—70	Low speed of writing and multiplying
36	—63	Low strength of interest in social activities
18	—55	Low rating of funniness of jokes
6	—54	Low disposition rigidity (perseveration) in motor test
40	51	Long hours of sleep previous night
9	—44	Large movements in myokinesis (two inches)
2	—41	Quick reaction time

Factor 2 or (E—, G—): Submissiveness, Dependence vs. Dominance, Drive

39	72	Dreams reported to be incomplete
22	—58	*Retiring, submissive, not self-confident* [d]
43	57	High frequency of laughter in interview
20	56	*High general emotionality, not calm or steady*
28	—44	*Low intellectual interest in work and discussion*
45	42	High lymphocyte count (per cent)
3	41	High verbal fluency of association

Factor 3 or C—: General Emotionality vs. Emotional Stability, Maturity

7	—67	Ready ability to acquire new mental set
4	56	High fluency of association in drawing
20	51	*High general emotionality, not calm or steady*
24	51	*Persistent in desires, insistent, not quitting*
8	45	Large movements in myokinesis (one inch)
45	42	High lymphocyte count (per cent)
21	38	*Attention-getting, not self-sufficient*
25	38	*Sociable interest in people, not shy or cautious*
16	36	Few words remembered in memorizing

Factor 4 or H: Adventurous Cyclothymia vs. Withdrawn Schizothymia

37	70	Dreams described in many words, long and frequent
15	68	Large *PGR* deflection responses
30	—52	Low glucose concentration in blood
25	49	*Friendly, interested in people, not shy*
27	44	*Vigorous, orderly-minded; not languid*
14	40	High initial resistance on *PGR*
17	—38	Brief negative after-image duration
29	—35	Absorbed, self-sufficient, not distractible or dependent

[a] Correlation of each variable with the factor.
[b] These names of the variables take account of signs and are directly interpretable.
[c] Capital letters refer to the most similar factors in cross-sectional studies. Capital letters in parentheses refer to greater tentativeness of the matching.
[d] The combined psychological ratings of friends and the writer are identified by italics.

TABLE 9 (*continued*)

Variable	Correlation	*Direction and Name of Variable*

Factor 5 or A: Cyclothymia vs. Schizothymia

37	69	Dreams described in many words, long and frequent
16	—58	Few words remembered in memorizing
1	55	High ratio on warned to unwarned reaction times
45	48	High lymphocyte count (per cent)
39	—39	Dreams described as complete
19	35	*Cooperative, not obstructive*
29	—37	Absorbed, self-sufficient, not distractible or dependent
8	30	Small movements in myokinesis (one inch)

Factor 6: Relaxation, Parathyroidism vs. Hypoparathyroidism

38	—70	Happy feeling tone at end of dreams
43	51	High frequency of laughter in interview
1	47	High ratio on warned to unwarned reaction times
31	42	High calcium level in blood serum
41	41	High frequency of urination
14	40	High initial resistance on PGR

Factor 7 or F—: Desurgency vs. Surgency

26	—57	*Poised, quiet, vs. lively, jumpy, restless, easily embarrassed*
42	—54	Low frequency of awareness of stomach pains
37	48	Dreams described in many words, long and frequent
32	—46	Low white corpuscle count in blood
7	42	Low ability to acquire new mental set
38	—37	Happy feeling tone in dreams
33	36	High red corpuscle count in blood
2	—35	Quick reaction time
11	—33	Acid trend in salivary pH
23	—32	*Worrying, depressed, anxious, not cheerful*

Factor 8: Therapeutic Trend

46	60	Serial order number of session
38	57	Unhappy feeling tone to dreams
45	46	High lymphocyte count (per cent)
39	45	Dreams reported to be incomplete
29	44	Distractible, dependent, not absorbed or self-sufficient
3	42	High verbal fluency of association
31	37	High level of calcium in blood serum

Factor 9: Fatigue or Vagotonia

34	—81	Low strength of interest in food
35	—64	Low strength of interest in sex
32	—47	Low white corpuscle count
29	44	Distractible, dependent, not absorbed or self-sufficient
44	—42	Low neutrophil count (per cent)
41	41	High frequency of urination

second factor of surgency-desurgency; (b) relaxation, parathyroidism vs. hypoparathyroidism, which has some resemblance to I factor; (c) a factor of fatigue or vagotonia, which has some resemblance to J factor; (d) a trend factor, tied up with the temporal sequence of sessions in the therapeutic interviews and characterized by physiological stress. This trend factor reveals the only substantial correlation found among factors, namely .54 with the hypoparathyroid factor.

5. The factor patterns are still not accurately enough determined to show how much of the divergence of a given subject's source trait patterns from (a) common source traits (R technique) and from (b) the unique source traits of another individual (P technique) is real, and how much is error of measurement. Cattell (1951) suggests the value of P technique in revealing Allport's unique traits.

6. The main symptom, stomach pains, has some relation to the waxing and waning of general emotional integration (C factor), and to the schizothyme factor (A—), but its outstanding association is with the principal source trait involving anxiety—the surgency vs. desurgency factor. This association, however, is clearly in the direction of greatest stomach upset in times of surgency ($r = -0.54$).

Results on Personality Factor Structure and the Patient.—To the extent, then, that the measures chosen for factorization are representative aspects of his personality and that the psychological assumptions of the statistical method of factor analysis are valid,[6] these factors are the major dimensions of the patient's personality variability during the treatment period. Many psychologists, particularly clinicians who might agree that such findings have important research values, would raise questions of meaningfulness: (a) the results are expressed in unfamiliar factor and trait terminology; (b) the level of abstraction of the traits appears to have little to do with facets of personality that can be used to help a therapist understand what is going on in his patient; and (c) the "major dimensions" may leave out "minor" dimensions because they do not comprise enough variables to make up a "major dimension." [7]

In this section we take a first step in the direction of establishing such "meaningfulness" by a clinician's sketch of (a) the patient; (b) the applicability of the factors to the aspects of personality referred to in the free associations; and (c) the nature of the treatment.

The patient, Paul R., was a twenty-five-year-old white male, a university student who at the beginning of this study had completed two semesters and had just been dropped from school for low grades. On entering the university, his ACE (1940) total score for the College of

---

[6] The reader who wishes further information on this point can find it in Thurstone (1948), English (1948), and Cattell (1950a, chap. ii).

[7] Salivary secretion may be an example, since it did not fall in any factor. The work of Szasz (1950a, 1950b) would lead one to expect its involvement in ulcer symptoms.

Commerce was in the 70th percentile, with a Q (quantitative) in the 65th percentile and L (language) in the 85th percentile. He was apparently physically robust [8] and of athletic build. However, he had been rejected from the army a year before with a diagnosis of peptic ulcer. He was the oldest of four children who were brought up on a small farm in a north central state. His parents were both American born of Bohemian and Czechoslovakian origin. The family was Catholic, but just prior to the experiment Paul left the church and joined a Protestant sect.

Paul had been an unusually successful farmer on a farm of his own. He had sold out completely (land, house, barns, tractors, and airplane), against his family's advice, to get a higher education, although this meant starting afresh at "the bottom of the ladder." He was very active in campus activities, especially the YMCA and church groups, in which he held a very large number of small offices. During his first two semesters he made average grades. In his third semester, his grades were low and he failed a course in accounting because he "could not seem to remember the stuff long." The teacher ("like my father") did not care whether he got it or not and would not answer any questions, or "take arguments."

The patient impressed most people, particularly casual acquaintances, as being a genial good mixer, cyclothymic, friendly, and self-assured. His passage across the campus was typically interrupted by more than an average number of warm greetings to friends.

Paul received more responsibilities and criticism than his younger brother and two sisters, and the parents tended to favor the brother. Although all members of the family were strongly loyal to each other, they failed to establish warm relationships. The mother had demanded payment from Paul for food consumed and rent during visits home after the age of twenty-one, saying, "My own mother never helped me any." During his early childhood, Paul recalled, his mother kept him tied up with a rope on the porch while she did her work. There was a great deal of friction between the father and mother which Paul partly attributed to the father's patriarchal conception of the wife's role in the family.

The patient's purpose in volunteering for this unpaid,[9] difficult experiment grew partly out of his having been dropped from school. He visited the Guidance Bureau for counseling and was referred to us. In return for helping us with our research project, he was to have the opportunity to profit from treatment. He said that he was especially concerned about his school work and hoped that he would be readmitted the following

---

[8] He had had difficulty all his life with heartburn and gas, especially when he was called upon to take charge of something or on dates. His medical history (five years earlier) notes constipation and "impression of spastic colitis" and requests of the doctor for hay fever injections and a Wasserman test.

[9] The results of this research on a "patient-subject" needing therapy have advantages of wider application than results on a paid subject. The motivations of the subject necessarily influence his test results, particularly on those tests eliciting largely dynamic personality trends rather than static traits. We felt that if the method were to have any later use for experimental analysis of therapeutic procedures, we would get relatively fewer insights into the values of this procedure from a paid subject.

semester. He was glad that he could "make a contribution to science." He revealed in his associations that he tried to "find the sources of help on the campus," "make contacts with people," "make myself stronger," and otherwise socially affiliate himself.

In terms of Paul's unconscious needs, the writer (who was also his therapist) suggests that he had strong needs to be dependent and to have problems solved for him (but had great defenses against these needs); that he enjoyed the position of sole recipient of so much attention; that he enjoyed the legitimacy given his interest in looking at himself by our interest in him; and that he was strongly masochistic.

The stomach trouble was not mentioned as a motive for treatment before he started, but he expressed concern about it often during the treatment. He would interrupt his associations or dreams with a surprised, pained, self-annoyed observation, e.g., "right now my old stomach is kicking around." These self-reports were tallied for each session and used as a manifestation of the kind of disturbed gastrointestinal functioning that had led to his ulcers about a year and a half before when X rays showed "superficial ulcers" and he spent two weeks in the hospital and "took about fifteen months to regain anything like my former endurance. Of course the endurance is not nearly what it used to be."

My *impression* of the applicability of the factors to the content of his free associations may be of interest since material is too voluminous to be presented here. In general, topics which seemed to go with the factors were very prominent, although my categories for classifying the behaviors might have been very different without knowledge of the factors. The patient frequently referred to his state of "equilibrium," energy level, strength of striving (Factor 1, 7?); "masculinity," "drive," "confidence in myself," "optimism," "want to help *others* out," "everyone is crying for help" (Factor 2?); much or little "stick-to-itiveness," "difficulty in remembering things" (Factor 3?); and state of "tiredness," "rest," "relaxation" (Factors 6, 9?).

In the treatment period, Paul was instructed to try to say whatever came to his mind. There was almost no reflection of feeling or interpretation, except for a few nondirective statements and clarifying questions by the therapist (T) toward the end of each free association session. To a too large extent, therefore, Paul was to get whatever benefit he could from his own unguided free associations, and the therapeutic relationship. He was given somewhat more guidance in interpreting his dreams. Each dream he brought in (always written out) was first repeated without recourse to the written version, and then the patient (P) associated to the main elements. T then always asked last for P's best possible reconstruction of the meaning of the dream. T then accepted the interpretation no matter how far he felt it to be from his own interpretation of the latent content. It was surprising how P, who was very unsophisticated psychologically, often gave fairly good interpretations (i.e., convincing to T). The import of these was somewhat vitiated by his disbelief in dreams and other resistances to treatment.

There were several deficiencies in the treatment, some due to the inexperience of therapist, some to the interference of the double goals—therapy and science. In most sessions (as the examples beginning on page 406 illustrate), P was too concerned over making decisions about immediate problems to try to understand the feelings or hidden assumptions on which he acted. He spent most of the time deciding rather unreflectively whether or not he would win his girl friend, get back in school, and compare well with his boy friends and brother; how to get ahead and make money, how to get back to a state of health and rest and how to convince his father of something. During the sessions he devoted much of his energy to the act of looking at his own actions for looking's sake: "I'd like to have a glass door on me to see what it [stomach] looks like." He defended himself by obsessive thinking against the reflection that he might not attain what he desired.

It was a serious resistance to progress that P was permitted to maintain the motivation or "excuse" of making a contribution to science. He wanted and needed help but could hide behind a noble purpose. He also used in the same way permission to learn some of the results after fifty-four days. Although it was often pointed out to him that this direct transmission of information could not help him, that he would get more out of our discussions, it permitted him to postpone changes in himself in expectation of the magical effects of the later test results.

It must be emphasized that what happened as a result of and in the treatment cannot be related solely to the treatment, but is a mixture of products of therapy and largely independent fluctuations. The mixture confuses somewhat all evaluations of psychotherapy. Especially in this case, the responsibility for change cannot be definitely assigned to the therapy. Whereas, before treatment, the patient had just been dropped from school and was in the throes of deciding what to do with his life in the face of this almost catastrophic blow, after treatment he re-entered school and made passing grades. A year later he married, and from external appearances he had continued to do well. To my knowledge he has not had another full-blown ulcer relapse. All this might well have occurred without therapy, and his ups and downs during treatment may have been little influenced by the treatment. To further complicate the problem, after the fifty-four-session "experimental period," he was seen in more active therapy for ten more sessions and then twice in the next two years. As a conservative estimate, the treatment gave him support during a trying period of his life. Although his personality structure appeared unchanged at the end of treatment, there were two likely gains: more clarity about what he wanted in school and in life and slightly more ability to say "no" to people who would impose on his good nature. There is no way of knowing how the factors changed *after* the experimental period.

Changes in the Patient During Therapy.—"Change" during therapy is (*a*) indicated by the changes in factor loadings during the course of treatment and (*b*) inferred from my inspection of the free associations. The former is here dealt with more extensively than the latter.[10] The major changes in factors can best be seen by summing [11] the variables in each factor and plotting these as a curve for the fifty-four sessions. Only those curves which show considerable shift in level from the beginning to the end and weekly are summarized in Table 10.

TABLE 10

Summary of Over-All and Weekly Changes in Factors
During Psychotherapy

Over-All	Week End and Weekly
1 Large rise in "modified desurgency"	
3 Slight rise in "emotionality"	Drop over week end, hump during week
7 Slight rise in "surgency"	Drop over week end
8 Rise in "therapeutic trend"	
9	Rise in "fatigue" over week ends

FACTOR 1. A marked and consistent change was the trend toward increased "modified desurgency" beginning at the week end of the third week. This factor, even though it is one which contributes most to mean variance, has been the hardest to identify in terms of the common factors of cross-sectional (R-technique) studies. It is a good example of the virtue of the P technique in discovering unique factors.

Several variables within the factor were highly correlated with the serial order number of the session and therefore most responsible for the rise: the patient's rated interest in social activities became less and less with time ($-.78$) as did his ratings of funniness of jokes ($-.82$). His movements became progressively larger ($+.82$) in trying, while blindfolded, to make a two-inch line. In this factor context, these changes may mean that he became less concerned about being with people, reacting to (T's) jokes, and being exact about the motor task. Perhaps he was less concerned to please, impress, do well on T's tasks, and more withdrawn into himself (i.e., long sleep, dreams complete, less speedy).

[10] It would be relevant to illustrate the associations of the factor loadings on each day on *all* nine factors with the free association and dream material (a total of approximately 500 typewritten pages). This proved to be impossible because of an embarrassment of riches in the nature and quantity of the free association material. It would be necessary for brevity either (*a*) to score various aspects of the daily free association material and correlate with the factor loadings or (*b*) to read over all sessions and try intuitively to abstract qualities which go with high and low points in each factor or pattern of factors. In the following section we have demonstrated the latter method for a single factor, Factor 7.

[11] The scores on each test were converted into equivalent scores (T scores) in order to add the variables in each factor for each day. The further refinement of a weighting for each test according to its correlation with the factor was considered unnecessary. The self- and friend-rated composite variables in each factor were omitted because of their ambiguous meaning.

FACTOR 3. "General emotionality" declined until the sixth week and then gradually rose. The total rise was very small. It dropped over each week end and humped up during the week.[12] In this factor there was a combination of variables which implied, together with very evident (to himself and others) social striving, that he was more ready to acquire new mental sets, more "fluent in associations," more apt to overestimate line length, more off keel physiologically or fatigued (high lymphocyte count), and less able to retain new words in memory. The factor pattern alone did not give any hint of the nature of the striving except that it involved more "persistence of drives," "attention-getting behavior," and "interest in people." (It would require the type of analysis given to Factor 7, below, to get at this type of explanation.) The pattern seemed to correspond to a clinically observed one in which he would "knock himself out" with work pressure, get into a state of heightened associational fluidity, and find it difficult to retain his studies.

FACTOR 8. This factor, called "therapeutic trend," *as an entity* correlated highest of the factors with the session number (+.60), although, here again only a few items individually correlated with the session number. We can deduce from these items that therapy aroused progressively more resistance (as evidenced by the correlation of +.64 of "dreams reported to be incomplete" with the session number (the higher the session number the less "complete" was the dream) ; rating of more distractible, +.43; and greater verbal fluency, +.42).

Several of the individual tests which did not fall in the factors described above changed in a manner consistent with the trends reported so far. Negative after-images increased in duration (+.67 with the number of the session), which perhaps is consistent with greater persistence of "unsteady states." The amount of dream material recalled decreased (−.55), perhaps along with increased unwillingness to give anything to T. His rated interest in sex increased (+.57), probably as a derivative of his sexual maladjustment becoming more conscious and causing greater resistance. Some other correlations were less easily rationalized: −.50 with the number of PGR deflections, +.57 with the number of words recalled, +.59 with red corpuscle count, etc.

Two of the tests which had to be discontinued are consistent with the hypothesis that the patient was becoming more negative and constricted. The "number of reversals in perspective" of a cube figure was discontinued because he claimed it no longer reversed. After the thirty-first session, at the beginning of the seventh week (at the time when his Factor 3 started to rise again), the reversals ceased entirely and the figure became a "gem head"—a fixed structure. After the twenty-third session (middle of the fifth week) the suggestibility sway test was

---

[12] This may be similar to a picture sometimes seen at the beginning of analytic treatment when "emotionality" declines because of the relief of beginning treatment (or "transference cure") and then builds up over many weeks as old conflicts come nearer consciousness; they build up during the week and diminish with each brief interruption of treatment.

discontinued since his sway had become negligible. Apparently he was reacting to the task as if it were a contest of wills and he had to suppress any evidence of weakness.

These trends seem consistent (after the fact) with clinical impressions of changes which are based on the free associations. But, as stated solely in factor terms, the changes sound like the bare bones of the therapy, however objective a record they are of some aspects of change in the patient's personality. Aspects of the difficulty with this type of description are its dissimilarity with respect to the terms a therapist uses, the level of abstraction of the categories (factors) which encompass variables from several usual "levels," and the inseparable mixture of products of therapy with fluctuations that are independent of the therapy. Finally there must be much real nonoverlap—the factors give only the grosser trait changes, and, of course, one's theory of therapy has to account for both the grosser and subtler ones.

Fluctuations in Factor 7 Understood Through Free Associations.—Factor 7 has the advantage, as a choice for demonstration, of containing three variables which are very closely connected with the free associations—report of stomach pains during free association, length of dreams, and feeling tone of dreams.[13] Furthermore, the immediate free-association contexts in which the stomach pains occurred can then be analyzed (see next section).

1. A first approximation of the meaning of this factor can be derived from inspection of the variables composing it. The name of the factor, "desurgency-surgency," originates from its three "smallest" variables: No. 23, the observer and self-rating combination of the trait "worrying, anxious and depressed"; No. 2, quick reaction time; and No. 11, acid trend in the salivary pH. This triad is similar to one found in other P technique studies (Cattell, Cattell, and Rhymer, 1947; Williams, 1949), but the match is not perfect since inefficiency of memorizing does not come in here as it should according to the first study,[14] and these three variables correlate least with the total factor. The core of this partly unique factor is No. 26, observers' and self-rating combination of traits, "quiet vs. lively, jumpy, restless"; No. 42, low frequency of awareness of stomach pains; No. 37, dreams described in many words, long and frequent dreams; and, to a lesser extent, Nos. 23, 7, 38, and 33. I have summarized below the meanings held in common among the variables in the factor. These meanings were inferred at this stage from an inspection of the variables *before* analyzing the free association material:

[13] Factor 2, which contains "laughter during free associations," was considered for demonstration but dropped in favor of a factor with more obvious relevance to the patient's major physical symptoms. However, the "larger" factors (i.e., those that account for more of the mean variance) very likely are easier to understand in relation to the free associations, as a brief inspection indicates.
[14] But the number of words memorized does correlate with one measure in the factor, the amount of dream recall, —.57.

a) There was lessened pushing of himself, lessened activity (quiet, poised, and low ability in a fluency and speed-of-work task called "substitution multiplication").

b) There was relative autonomic quiescence and physiological equilibrium (the high red and low white count, little stomach disturbance,[15] and quick reaction time).

c) There was greater satisfaction, or acceptance, of major unconscious needs (longer dreams and self-rated happier tone to the outcome of his dreams). Longer dreams require, of course, that the dreams be remembered and brought to the therapist. It is likely that at these times his resistance to treatment was less. It is consistent with this interpretation that the therapist felt that P's resistance became greater from the beginning to end of therapy, as his dreams became shorter with each session.[16]

2. Table 11 summarizes, with examples, some common characteristics of the six free association sessions during which the desurgency factor was highest, and characteristics of the six sessions lowest in desurgency, i.e., high surgency. The method of summarization was to read over each session and pick out categories that might distinguish between high and low points on the factor. Such a method has the subjectivity of much clinical research. Its reliability is difficult to check, and it allows many categories to slip through unnoticed. However, these highest and lowest sessions have several internal and differential consistencies. Moreover, these consistencies are in agreement with the inspectionally derived meanings of the factor's items—as far as the meanings go.

This brief summary points to a tentative psychodynamic formulation:

Desurgency: The patient has a more take-it-or-leave-it attitude to the treatment and T—he does not feel he needs T and can almost tell T "where to get off." (His concern to report his "take-it-or-leave-it" attitude to his girl friend also reflects indirectly his feeling toward T.)

Surgency: He is manifestly keying up his strength, ready to challenge or demand from father figures (especially T) love and care.[17]

---

[15] Two other variables which do not fall in the factor correlate with frequency of stomach pains and further imply physiological (autonomic) vulnerability on the surgency side: (*a*) The larger the percentage deflections of the PGR, the greater the frequency of stomach pains, $r = +.48$. (*b*) The greater the number of spontaneous deflections in the PGR in three minutes of looking into a dark box, the greater the number of stomach pains, $r = +.40$.

[16] Long dreams are often a sign of resistance (see Eder, 1930). For P, the quantity of dreaming recalled seemed to be a sign of how much of a gift he wished to bring; e.g., in Session No. 18, "Today I have something for you"; or when he had no dream in Session No. 15, "When I'm more tired, I have more difficulty remembering dreams."

[17] His longing is expressed almost directly in several sessions. In Session No. 50 he is jealous of my youngster for "the close relationship that exists between mother and child. . . . I'd like to have a mother and baby belonging to me." In Session No. 41 he is jealous of his roommate for a letter from his mother: "I never had a letter like that in my life. . . . I gather she treats him a lot like that when he's home."

TABLE 11

SUMMARY OF CHARACTERISTICS OF SIX MOST AND SIX LEAST "DESURGENT"
FREE ASSOCIATION SESSIONS

"Desurgency"	"Surgency"
1. He feels slightly less inclined to be active: e.g., (Session No. 6) "I was in no mood for it [talking to girl friend] so I went home," or (Session No. 18) he is "not inclined to slate things for the week end," or (Session No. 27) "everything seems to be in equilibrium today."	1. He is more hurried, running, keyed up, off keel, in disequilibrium, megolomanic, trying to convince himself of his own power. In consequence he sounds somewhat less contemplative, with more mere reporting of plans. He spontaneously comments on being more shaky and disturbed by the electric shock and needle in three of the six sessions.
2. He tries to talk himself into a re-signed "take it or leave it" attitude, unsure of how she feels about him. (Mentions her in all six sessions; the above applies clearly in four.)	2. He is more sanguine about his chances with his girl friend (three sessions) or doesn't mention her (three sessions).
3. He has more doubt about the treatment being of use to him (clear in five of six sessions). He even feels free enough (of fear of T?) to poke fun at our work together by a parody (Session No. 18): "Well, what are you thinking about today? Oh, just free associate"; or (Session No. 27) "Do you have anything in particular you'd like to ask me today?" (Laughs.) He refers to T's colleague's advice to him to be a salesman: (Session No. 31) "I don't have any appetite for it." (Yet he brings in much dream material in these sessions.)	3. He is more concerned about his relationship with men. He wants to please them more, yet is jealous, competitive, angry, resentful of what they give him or withhold. He is more concerned about measuring up. In all six "surgent" sessions vs. one session in "desurgency" he wants the results of our tests. In two sessions he reports incidents of fighting with siblings or older men. (He brings little or no dream material.)
4. He reports stomach pains in only one of the sessions.	4. He reports stomach pains in five of the six sessions.

He fears yet longs to be weak, dependent, feminine, powerless, giving in, and taken advantage of. One of his main defenses against the latter impulse is denial of weakness through developing conventional symbols of strength: "building masculinity," "muscles," "on my toes," "masculine glamor," leadership, independence, administrative ability of a "big executive" type, "plans to make money."

Certainly these are garden-variety dynamics, although the intensity of the conflicts is more common in peptic ulcer patients (Alexander, 1950, p. 102), and it is not entirely surprising that stomach pains occurred on his surgency side as a physical expression of the "hunger" and not on his desurgency side ($r = -.54$ of stomach pains with desurgency). Paul's first really noticeable stomach trouble came when in second-year high school. "I was always letting off gas, especially when I sang solos" or was "leader of 4-H group." Nor was it unexpected that he emphasized intestinal fortitude in his adolescent poems: "For it's the fellow with guts that gets ahead." He almost literally wore his guts out trying to "get ahead."

But can we go further in translating our tentative knowledge of the psychodynamics of his "surgent" states into a sequence of psychological events which immediately results in his stomach disturbance?

Analysis of Immediate Free-Associational Contexts of Stomach Pains.—The method of studying the common elements in the free-associational contexts in which the patient reported awareness of stomach pains yields further clinical insights.

The method assumed the following:

1. The context of free associations contains etiological elements—a tenable assumption since free associations are likely to give much of the thought context (to the extent the patient can and will report "whatever comes to mind"). However, there is no reason to expect (just as with dreams) that *all* reported contexts will alone give enough of the thoughts to make the meaning clear.

2. The awareness of disturbance is reported at the time it occurs. There was no proof of this except in the manner of the patient's verbalization, e.g. "there goes my stomach," as if it had just occurred.

Two more assumptions may be required that are not as essential to the psychological as to the physiological level of comprehension of the "stomach" variable:

3. The "awareness of stomach disturbance" corresponds to some largely unitary disturbance rather than a wide variety of dysfunctions all introspectively reported as the same. There can be no proof of this since no concomitant physiological measures of stomach action or contents were taken. Again there was only the verbalization and introspective description of the disturbance to go on; but it is enough to lead me to conclude that a largely unitary (i.e., the same from time to time) set of physiological effects were repeated. These seem to be: hypersecretion ("a squirting," "foaming") and hypercontraction ("my stomach is kicking again").

4. This reported stomach disturbance was similar to that which led to the patient's earlier stomach ulcers. The assumption of the ulcer-stimulating nature of the phenomena he reported is common in previous clinical studies (see Alexander, 1950, p. 106). The method (and results) therefore may have greater value for psychosomatic medicine.

The method consisted, then, in abstracting from the verbatim transcript of the sessions the 100-200 words in the main topics immediately before and after the patient's report of his stomach pain and then going

over these contexts to find common elements.[18] Every instance in
the fifty-four sessions was examined (twenty-six occasions, in sixteen
sessions)—almost half of the reports were in the six sessions of highest
surgency. The stomach pains reported in the sessions with highest
surgency occurred in contexts similar to those in other sessions. The
typical context structure was as follows:

1. HIS STRIVINGS. These were to win his girl friend, to get "appreciation," to get ahead in school, to attain high public position, and
to acquire a lot of money (i.e., to get dependent or narcissistic satisfactions).

2. CONSEQUENCES OF HIS STRIVINGS: These were (a) a fear (or
wish) to use up (or not have enough of) his energy, money, or power
and to be left weak and vulnerable to being taken advantage of; and (b)
a renewed effort to convince himself of his power, energy, optimism,
worth, and morality.

3. THE DISTURBANCE OF HIS STOMACH. Immediately before the
stomach pain was reported he was stewing in the aftermath of the
intruding anxious thought that he was weak, that he might not win
out in his manifest striving—his armor might be perforated. He usually
reported the stomach pain with a mixture of hurt, complaining curiosity,
and reference to it as kicking him—i.e., as if he were the passive object
kicked around by the stomach. (This perception of weakness is clearly
stated or inferable in seventeen of the twenty-six instances.)

4. LATENT MASOCHISM AND DEFENSES. Thereafter, he usually gave
way further to latent masochistic, submissive feelings, complaining of
and proving his weakness—or defenses against these feelings by competitive aggression or obsessive moral self-justification. It was almost
always clear that the person whom he wished to please, to convince of
the purity of his motives was a father figure against whom he consciously
expressed competitive and resentful feelings.

Three examples taken from two sessions of high surgency have been
analyzed within this framework (Examples 1 and 2, Session No. 19).

T. If you could get the lady situation, as you call it, cleared up you
would feel better.

P. I think that would tend to be so—I know that there would be the
problem just the same; but if I could find the fellowship or com-

---

[18] Interjudge checks are desirable here as well as in the previous analysis of
the surgency sessions. The checks might be easier if it were possible to define some
categories for quantitative scoring, such as "the number of oral words" or "the
number of words with a depressed tone." An ingenious method of reliability for
use when one's aim is to demonstrate the unique qualities of a context without
having to define all its contents for scoring is reported by Brenman, Gill, and Knight
(1952) in a paper on changes in ego states in hypnosis. They set expert judges
the task of distinguishing contexts in which the patient had made the statement, "I'm
going deeper," from contexts that never contained the statement. The "stomach"
contexts can be similarly tested.

radeship, you might say, the appreciation or give-and-take I'm hoping for—I don't believe I'm hoping for too much—and then have that possibility of not winning; but as long as you know you are still in the running—running in a contest for a long time, just begin to wonder how the darned thing is going to work out—[*Example 1*] *there goes my stomach again*—largely seems to be a matter of sharing things—I share things with people all around me—that's one thing that people say about me—I believe it's so, might as well admit it [laughs]. Usually add something—like a discussion or just a social gathering; and I enjoy sharing things with people— I wish I had someone closer to me personally to share things with— things have more meaning. I've always had the idea for just myself alone—I can't see much in that. Heck, I'd go out and be a beggar or tramp—any number of ways I could get along—a roaming farm-hand or something like that. I've built a lot of things with different people on committee work and various kinds of organizations like that—but it's all so—it's outside in a way—it is close to a person, yet it lacks that personal closeness that it isn't so endearing for one thing either—might go on for a year or two years, something like that—it isn't the close association there—there are times when I met with certain friends of mine, men and women—we have a lot that same thing—after a while for a time I forget almost everything and am interested solely in that one operation—whatever we're doing—discussion or listening to music something like that—as I see it—well, I do get certain satisfactions from things like that—not only satisfaction I go into it for—something to be done, enjoy it, too —go into a lot of committee work to compensate the lack of the other—and yet I don't see how I could leave it even though I would get married—just part of my work really and part of my training— I always figured working was a pretty good thing to keep a person on the track when the going gets rough—at least not standing still— at least getting something done—still you're accomplishing things.

Just happened to be thinking about some of these different tests we're running—wonder what the reports are going to look like—things like that—like to compare my observations of myself with the observations of this experiment and see how closely I've measured— most of the time I've been measuring pretty close—just like to check the mechanical device and see how close I am measuring—just happened to think of [a second-best girl friend]—kind of like to see her again soon ... 22 ... [*example 2*] *my stomach makes me think back* to the Cosmopolitan Club again [laughs] Just happened to think of my hand-wrestling with [roommate] again today—couldn't throw him—just couldn't seem to get—when I do something that is going to take energy I usually kind of throw a switch in my mind —and I couldn't do that the other day—by gosh, couldn't seem to get that connection with my mind, my hand, and my body—today got to fooling around—last week pretty busy week—had some rest,

by gosh, put the old works into that hand of mine [laughs] and
throw him all over the place—still not up to par yet—I was kind of
surprised—I thought I was all done for.

Analysis of Example 1.—1. In this context the patient is manifestly
striving to win his girl friend, who for him is associated with "getting
appreciation" with "give and take." (For him, the food and girl are
repeatedly closely associated verbally, just as his daily rating of need
for food and need for sex are highly correlated.) (The striving is for
a narcissistic gratification, "appreciation," as well as an oral satisfaction.)

2. The striving is not easily acceptable to him. He constantly makes
statements like: "I don't believe I'm hoping for too much," as if to say
he must justify this striving to someone. Another evidence of the
unacceptability (threat) of the striving is the tremendous effort he
must put forward in order to get his end—it is an intensely competitive
striving, "running in a contest."

3. At the point where the opposing sides of the conflict are aroused,
he becomes disturbed and wonders "how the darn thing is going to
work out," and his stomach pains are now noticed. At the point where
his stomach "goes off," he is thinking of the possibility of his being the
weak, forlorn loser, that some other man might win out.

4. At the point after his stomach goes off, he redoubles his self-
criticism, he talks as though he had been accused of being selfish and
paints a picture of his own need by saying: "I'd go out and be a beggar
or a tramp." In answering this self-imputed criticism that he is selfish,
not willing to share things, he rationalizes his striving to the altruistic
level of a need to share things with another person and brings in the
opinions of other people as witness that he usually adds something to
a social group. (This masochistic feeling has become an end in itself
for him and is his way of demonstrating to the criticizing institution
the purity of his motives.)

Analysis of Example 2.—1. This context has much in common with
the first example. At the beginning of the context his striving is for
reassurance that he is measuring up, that he is adequate, that the therapist's findings will agree with his own or perhaps that the therapist
approves of him. The striving immediately before his stomach pain is
to see another girl friend, "kind of like to see her again soon."

2. His difficulty in accepting the striving is shown in its association
again with measuring up or being inadequate.

3. The conflict then again involves his stomach.

4. After his stomach "goes off," he thinks of an incident of competitive hand-wrestling with his roommate in which he was shown to be
the weaker. Just before the incident, he refers to the group of boys

with whom he eats. Perhaps it is not too much to say that he is illustrating how he resolves the conflict by competition with men in which he needs to lose.

Example 3, Session No. 26:

P. . . . buying her flowers and candy here and there—it all adds up to a heck of a big sum—cut some of it anyhow—huh—at least won't do it unless I get results [laughs]. I don't mind to spend it, I don't believe so much in cutting down—getting it done—it can be done— why should a fellow always go backward and have a negative attitude —waste money sometime, and it will go as far—I think I can swing it—almost feel like going out and getting her a ring now—I feel in a way—I won't do it for a while—I know the size to get [laughs]. I took care of that a long time ago [laughs]. Need to get myself some more sleep—["Y" director] was so generous and all that ["Y" director] is so generous—I had a piece of steak about that big around—beans, potatoes, hot rolls, and salad—about finished that up and came to second course—doggone, almost plead with him— I didn't want it in the worst way—*there goes my stomach again*— he gave me another piece that big—dropped a lot of broccoli and beans and potatoes on my plate [laughs]. That will never do—got to do this right—gave me a big potato—think that threw me off— have to get a certain amount of raisins—or I get out of kilter—seems to give me some bad by-products somehow—doesn't leave me feeling good. I felt good after eating it but I thought it would do something, though—oh well—time to go—that was it—get that from Southerners—heard it . . . 30 . . . I really feel better about this church situation—my brother wrote me today and was rather sorry to hear about it in a way—he still has a fatherly attitude—he agrees with me all down the line—this attitude isn't exactly right and that one isn't quite right, and then he comes down to the end and says there's just one religion for the spirit—right down to spirit that counts and so on—the Catholic is the religion so on so forth—I'd just as soon drop the subject—just don't care to talk about it especially— that's the way it is to be done.

Analysis of Example 3.—1. His problem at the beginning of the context is whether to continue spending so much money on his girl friend or to cut down. His striving, manifestly at least, is "almost feel like going out and getting her a ring now."

? The way in which he deals with the striving is well shown by the incidents he thinks of immediately following the above. In addition to fearing that he is using up all his money (i.e., becoming poor) on the girl, he tells himself that he needs to get more sleep (he is using up all his energy); and then he tells of the stomach-disturbing incident in which he is having dinner with one of the directors of the "Y" where he works and wants to get ahead. The man wants to feed him or, as he feels it, overfeed him, and yet he cannot say "no." He cannot accept his manifest wish for the girl, and he cannot accept the man's wish to feed him.

3. When the thought becomes apparent to him that he had to give in to the man (or more likely, wanted to), his stomach "goes off" again.

The "fear" of accepting is explained after the stomach goes off in terms of a fear that his bowels will get out of order, and very likely he rationalizes his acceptance by the obligation to be polite. He becomes concerned about right and wrong and whether he felt good or bad after the stomach disturbance, and then he describes an argument with his brother about the "right" religion in which his brother took a fatherly attitude toward him and reproved him for deviation from the Catholic religion.

The formulations at this stage of analysis have much in common with Alexander's (1950) (if our use of language is the same). What I have called "weakness" at the time of the report of stomach pain is often recognizable as what Alexander refers to as "infantile dependency" followed by "inferiority feelings." In the case of Paul, his wish to be taken care of, fed, and helped (often by a man), becomes dangerous when he reacts to it as a demonstration of his weakness. His self-criticisms can often be paraphrased as, "I should have been, or am, by God, strong enough to reject what was offered, or do without what I do (or shouldn't) want." What follows (in terms of Alexander's "defense" language) is a rejection of these feelings and a "renewed effort" to deny or otherwise overcome them.

Summary, Applications, and Discussion of Methods

The nature of the P technique method has been described and demonstrated with selected results on a patient in psychotherapy. We have penetrated into the patient's personality dynamics through various levels of analysis: (a) his nine major dimensions of variability (and the similarity of these factors to those found in cross-sectional studies); (b) the way in which these change during treatment; (c) the yield by combining the symptom-containing Factor 7 with free associations; and (d) the yield by combining the stomach symptom with free associations.

How to evaluate the assets and liabilities of this complex set of methods and their applications? The discussion to follow will consider mainly these questions: (a) What are the applications to research? (b) How does the P technique method compare with other methods for similar purposes, and what modifications in P technique procedures are suggested by this study? (c) How do the factorial and clinical approaches in this study complement and supplement each other?

Applications to Personality Research.—As discussed above, the method gives an objective personality diagnosis in terms of more unique individualized factors than those of cross-sectional factor studies (see Cattell, 1951).

Recently a much simpler way of making the calculations has been worked out by Woodrow.[19] Future studies will not require, as did ours, as much statistical effort as a large-scale cross-sectional study.

Applications to Psychotherapy Research.—The three principal ways in which the processes of change and end products of therapy have been approached in other studies are: (a) cross-sectional type of testing before and after therapy, (b) analyses of the verbal content of the therapy sessions, and (c) clinical conceptual analysis of the patient's responses to treatment.[20] The P technique is a valuable addition to these. As used in this study it takes off from a combination of (b) and (c). It gives both beginning and end profiles as well as progress of change on the same objectively determined dimensions and therefore should help in comparing the therapy of different patients.

However, as to the immediate help to the psychotherapist on the particular case being treated, it must be stated emphatically that it has little to offer. For one thing, the factor analysis is not likely to be done until after a major segment of the therapy is completed. Moreover, the avenues for effecting change have little to do with the therapist's knowledge of his patient's fluctuation in a host of variables. It has more to do, for example, with the therapist's setting up an atmosphere where the particular patient can develop.

The fact that the treatment occurs in a research setting may be used by the patient as a resistance and must be dealt with like any other resistance. As a practical recommendation, it is suggested that less resistance might be aroused if a person other than T administers the daily test procedures as part of his job, e.g., in a case with physiological symptoms, a physician rather than the therapist should do the physical tests.

Application to Psychosomatic Research.—These methods were able to tie together, in factor syndromes, variables from the physiological and psychological levels. The major physical complaint, stomach pains, was tied in with material from other levels.

The method of analyzing free-association contexts (above) was not a necessary product of the P technique. It was more similar to the type of clinical analysis that is done in psychosomatic studies of the etiology of peptic ulcers.[21] But the results could then be set into the factor results. Thus, it was concluded that not only are the stomach

---

[19] Personal communication by Dr. R. B. Cattell of unpublished study by Dr. Herbert Woodrow

[20] Excellent examples of each are: (a) and (b) in combination, Rogers and associates, major study in progress (1949 and 1950); (b) Hunt (1948), using Dollard and Mowrer's distress-relief quotient; (c) Pious (1950).

[21] The method of "analysis of behaviors in free-association contexts" is somewhat unusual in (a) choosing for study an introspective report of a physiological disturbance and (b) trying to discover the etiology within the sequence of immediately preceding and following thoughts. This method may have application to the study of other behaviors, e.g., laughing, coughing, wheezing, twitching.

pains the product of a conflict of dependent strivings and defenses, but they are also one usual component of a "surgent" syndrome.

The latter method suggests a simpler variation of the P technique for patients in psychotherapy and psychosomatic research: Choice of only a few variables which can be conveniently measured throughout therapy, variables which one expects have a bearing on the patient's illness. It is preferable to choose known measures of some function, e.g., blood pressure. Then the scores on such measures can be inter-correlated with chosen aspects of the psychotherapy sessions, and the correlations can then be factorized.

About the near relatives of P technique: Many psychosomatic studies have made use of the basic idea of physiological measures con-current with interview and psychotherapy sessions, but without the type of statistical analysis suggested here.[22] Lasswell's (1935, 1936) study is most similar to the present one. He plotted time series of four indicators: PGR, pulse, words, and visible movements, against trial psychoanalytic interviews and drew conclusions about "the con-nection between (unconscious) tension and acute (conscious) affect." Intraindividual correlations without factor analysis (or only with cluster analysis) may be useful in many types of clinical problems as suggested by Horn (1950) and Baldwin (1950) and well illustrated by Holt (1950). These three writers also provide intuitive and statistical analyses of the problems of interpreting intraindividual correlations.

Factorial vs. Clinical Approach.—The factorial and clinical ap-proaches as used in this study certainly gave more together than they would have separately—and their togetherness on a single case provided a rare opportunity for discerning the contribution and limitations of each. My results are in partial disagreement with one of the criticisms of factor analysis (MacKinnon, 1944, p. 39) that it cannot describe the single case. I accept the fact that both methods can get at a kind of "truth." The factor approach in *personality* research gives "truth" in the usual scientific sense with more demonstrable certainty, but it is difficult to see how the statistical manipulations eventuate in clinically meaningful end products. Although the clinical approach as used here is considerably more rigorous than most, it suffers from greater dif-ficulties in validation than the factorial. The clinical approach's value, of course, is in revealing information which is more immediately under-standable and usable to clinicians. The level of abstraction of the factors often bears little relationship to what a clinician wants to know. A clini-cian (especially psychotherapist) may or may not have any need to know what are the patient's major source traits.

A major lack lies in the nonoverlap. Not enough variables that measure clinically important qualities were included in the present

---

[22] The following is a good sample of these: Mirsky, Kaplan, and Broh-Kahn (1950); Alexander (1939), Mittelman and Wolff (1939); Mittelman (1942, 1943); Benedek and Rubenstein (1939); Meyer, Bollmeier, and Alexander (1945); Holmes, Goodell, Wolf, and Wolff (1947); Margolin et al. (1950).

factor analysis. The factor-analytic method as typically used in personality research unnecessarily begins with a paucity of hypotheses and clinical insights. This deficiency usually results from overreliance on easily scorable tests and aspects of behavior (e.g., "length of dreams"). It would have increased the value of the present research as a study in changes during psychotherapy if more measures had been taken from the free-association and dream material, preferably after an intuitive psychodynamic analysis. After such an analysis one can set up measures to get closer to the phenomenon in question. For example, our measure of stomach disturbance—"frequency of occurrence"—was very crude, since it did not account for strength or other qualities. If the dynamic analysis of the free-association contexts had been done first, it could have been converted to scorable categories for inclusion in the factor-analytic mill.

But for clinical research the P technique factor patterns have a major contribution to make in providing an objectively derived structural backdrop of source traits whose strength and fluctuations can be measured and which interlock with variables within the clinical material. When given important variables, the P technique can arrange these with dexterity into possible "syndromes" or factors. The factors suggest aspects of the clinical material to be explored, and the yield can then help in the job of naming the factors. In the present case, a clinician unaided by these statistical arms might not have been able to pick out so many covarying patterns in such complex material—e.g., he might have missed some of Factor 7 and the other expressions of Factor 7 in the free associations. But, the interesting consistencies in my findings with those of Alexander, although not all of my Factor 7 variables had counterparts for comparison in Alexander's work, indicates that convergence of results can be obtained by the two approaches. The P technique method, as combined in this study with clinical material, provides an alternative route to the verification of clinically derived hypotheses.

CHAPTER 16

A STATISTICAL METHOD FOR STUDYING
PERSONALITY INTEGRATION [1]

By Louis L. McQuitty, Ph.D.

The clinician is concerned with the personality organization of the individual. Therapy is designed to improve that organization. Our knowledge of individual personality organization, and the concept of improvement in relation to it, is limited because of the lack of statistical methods specifically designed to study the interrelationships within the individual. Allport * (1937) has stated this limitation in reference to factor analysis as follows: "... the products of factor analysis, determined by an extension of correlational methods, are empirically self-consistent. But they too pertain only to the abstract average man, and not to single individuals" (p. 356).

The present paper outlines a revised factor-analytic design. The design involves an application of association indices which is intended to make them more representative of the individual subject. Instead of interpreting each individual's behavior in terms of the characteristics of abstract average man, it compares each individual successively with those categories of individuals who are most like him in certain characteristics and thereby arrives at an interpretation intended to be more appropriate to the individual.

Clinicians and personality theorists have given us an abundance of theories and hypotheses concerning the organization of personality, but many of the theories and hypotheses do not lend themselves readily to conventional empirical investigation. They have often been revised in various ways in an effort to make them more amenable to conventional modes of inquiry (Sears, 1944, p. 306). An alternative approach is to attempt to revise and develop research methods so as to make them more appropriate for investigating the theories and hypotheses pertaining to individual personality organization.

If we are to apply the latter approach to quantitative research methods, it means that we need a system of statistics specifically designed

[1] Appreciation is expressed to Research Professor Raymond B. Cattell, of the University of Illinois, who studied this chapter and made many helpful suggestions. Much of the research on which this article is based was supported financially by the U. S. Public Health Service and by the Research Board of the University of Illinois. Appreciation is expressed to both agencies and to the research assistants: Russell J. Jessen, Mrs. Gail Rowan, Thomas Rowan, and Allan Gottneid.
* References are to the bibliography at the back of the book.

for the study of the personality organization of the individual: a kind of *statistics of the individual case*. The method outlined in this paper is one development in this direction. Other developments are the O and P techniques of factor analysis, described in Chapters 13 and 15 of this book, and the profiles of factor standings for individuals, which result from R technique, i.e., the usual factor-analytic method. The revised method to be described differs from all three of these techniques in fundamental ways. In the R technique, the individual profiles are in terms of common factors. In P, O, and the new technique, the factors themselves, are more or less peculiar to the individual. P, O, and R techniques analyze responses as reflective of postulated underlying, linear continua. The revised method, on the other hand, analyzes responses as indicative of the presence or absence of elemental characteristics. These contrasts among methods and techniques can be portrayed more clearly after the revised design has been outlined.

Revised Factor-Analytic Design in Relation to Clinical Theories

The revised factor-analytic design herein outlined, together with empirical results, can be introduced by a consideration of clinical theories concerning the organization of the personality in the individual. The revised design was developed specifically for the investigation of these theories. Certain of these theories will be briefly reviewed. We will then show how the revised factor-analytic design is appropriate for the investigation of these theories, and later we will report some results obtained from preliminary applications of the design.

Most, if not all, psychoclinicians concern themselves with two types of interpretations. These are (*a*) individually oriented interpretations and (*b*) generally oriented interpretations. The first pertain to the organization of the personality within a particular client. The generally oriented interpretations concern themselves with principles and processes in the abstract, i.e., with the organization of personality within an abstract or average man.

These two positions are represented in the following quotations from Freud (1935*a*), the first quotation illustrative of the general theory and the second illustrative of hypotheses in reference to the behavior of specific individuals.

. . . our insight into the causation of the neuroses is thus enlarged. First, there is the most general condition of privation, then the fixation of the libido (forcing it into particular channels), and thirdly, the *susceptibility to conflict* produced by the development of the ego having repudiated libidinal excitations of that particular kind. The thing is therefore not so very obscure and intricate—as you probably thought it during the course of my exposition. To be sure, though, after all, we have not done with it yet; there is still something new to add and something we already know to dissect further (p. 308).

In the above quotation Freud is outlining theories that are, in general, applicable to the development of neurosis. In this sense, they apply to an average, abstract man. In order to arrive at this abstraction, much behavior as it expresses itself in individuals is necessarily summarized under generalized captions or even entirely eliminated. The portions lost by the process of abstraction are presumably of lesser significance for the understanding of behavior than are those retained. This point emphasizes the importance of the method of abstracting. In factor analysis the method is clear, and for the possible exceptions of rotation, will produce the same results no matter who factors the data. In many studies, the factors are the same or similar with test items which appear to be quite different, in some ways. This point is well illustrated by Cattell in his book, *Description and measurement of personality* (1946, pp. 469-96).

Even though the abstract variables, i.e., the factors, of factor analysis are arrived at by more objective methods than are the analogous variables of psychoanalysis, clinicians have applied the latter much more widely in practice. This suggests that criteria, in addition to those of objectivity, would be helpful in arriving at abstractions which would be readily applied in clinical practice. One such additional criterion is here suggested. It is as follows: *In arriving at general interpretations of behavior, those methods are best which suppress or ignore least individual behavior.*

A more specific statement of this principle is as follows: *A method of abstracting which retains both qualitative and quantitative variables in its process is more fruitful than one which retains only quantitative variables.*

It is suggested that factor analysis, as now generally applied (i.e., R technique) and as illustrated by Spearman (1927), Thurstone (1947), Mosier (1937), Guilford (1936, pp. 457-513), and Cattell (1946), emphasizes quantitative differences to the relative neglect of qualitative ones. In addition, it is suggested, clinical practice in general emphasizes qualitative, as well as quantitative, differences—but in a less exacting way than does factor analysis. We will outline how the R technique of factor analysis somewhat neglects qualitative differences. Then we will illustrate with a quotation from Freud that the clinician applies qualitative and quantitative description.

The R technique, it is true, results in factors, which themselves are qualities, but they are common qualities, i.e., qualities of an abstract or average man. The interpretation of individuals is in terms of different quantitative standings on these common qualities. This provides for qualitative differences in the configurations of standings, but no inquiry is made into the possibility that behavior components are organized into different factors, or qualities, for different individuals. In this sense then, R technique does not investigate individual differences in the organization of behavior into different factors or qualities for different individuals. The revised factor-analytic design, to be later outlined, attempts to do just this.

The clinical-practice approach in the study of behavior is illustrated in the following quotation from Freud (1935a), where he is hypothesizing causes for differences in the behavior of two hypothetical girls:

The differences which ensue in these two destinies in spite of the common experiences undergone, arise because in one girl the ego has sustained a development absent in the other. To the caretaker's daughter sexual activity seemed as natural and harmless in later years as in childhood. The gentleman's daughter had been "well-brought-up" and had adopted the standards of her education. Thus stimulated, her ego had formed ideals of womanly purity and absence of desire that were incompatible with sexual acts; her intellectual training had caused her to depreciate the feminine role for which she is intended. This higher moral and intellectual development in her ego has brought her into conflict with the claims of her sexuality (p. 309).

In this quotation, Freud emphasizes qualitative differences in the egos of the two individuals. ". . . in one girl the ego has sustained a development absent in the other. To the caretaker's daughter sexual activity seemed as natural and harmless in later years as in childhood. The gentleman's daughter had been 'well-brought-up' and had adopted the standards of her education." In other words, Freud emphasizes qualitative concern by stating in effect that the egos of the two girls have different characteristics and qualities. On the other hand, Freud illustrates quantitative concern by stating that the one girl reached a "higher moral and intellectual development" than the other.

This quotation is illustrative of hypotheses relating to particular individuals. It, in conjunction with the earlier one which is illustrative of general theories of an abstract man, points up another suggestion, namely: Having built up generally applicable hypotheses, the interpretation of individual behavior is limited somewhat by the variables developed as appropriate to the understanding of an abstract man. Freud's interpretation of the causes of the differences between the two girls is in terms of differences in their egos, a variable treated by Freud as significant for general theories. The theories of a composite man serve as the framework within which we view and interpret the behavior of the individual.

The psychological meaningfulness of the abstract structure for understanding the behavior of particular individuals is dependent upon the restrictiveness of individual differences. If individual differences are large in extent and many in numbers and kinds, the meaningfulness of abstract interpretations is less directly applicable to the understanding of the dynamics within the individual than if the reverse is true.

In addition, some of the individually significant variables may be obscured, or completely obliterated, by analysis in terms of the variables appropriate to an average or abstract man. This condition would generally result when causal influences are randomly distributed from individual to individual. If the abstract framework does not include the significant variables operative in the behavior of the individual, then the interpretations of the behavior of the individual in terms of the framework are barren and discouraging and, in fact, do little to assist us in the prediction and control of individual behavior, or in developing psychotherapeutic techniques and methods.

Descriptions of frameworks for understanding behavior depend to a major extent on the methods of abstraction used in developing them. One reason that Freud and factor analysis, as represented by R technique, arrive at somewhat different frameworks is because they use different methods. We have suggested two criteria to guide us in developing methods for arriving at frameworks. They are as follows: (a) A method should be objective. (b) It should minimize the losses which occur when we abstract.

One way to minimize the losses as we abstract is to perform the operation on a series of subuniverses of persons who have something in common. An individual's behavior can then be interpreted in relation to any one or more of several averages. The clinician often uses this approach. Our quotation from Freud concerning the development of neuroses referred to a subuniverse which has in common the development of neuroses. Many authors, Burnham (1924, pp. 55, 207, 208), Lecky (1945, pp. 137, 139-40, 151-52), Rogers (1947, pp. 364-65), and Snygg and Combs (1949, p. 136) have abstracted primarily on the basis of observing the behavioral characteristics of the subuniverses which appear to them to include only healthy-minded, or adequate, personalities. The same thing can, of course, be accomplished statistically. What is needed is a statistical method which will automatically pick out the most fruitful subuniverses from which to abstract. Just such a statistical method is hereinafter described, and findings obtained with it are reported in relationship to its specific utility for measuring changes in clients undergoing psychotherapy.

Abstraction is, of course, in terms of generally applicable variables. One criterion that may assist in isolating fruitful variables in terms of which to describe individual differences is as follows: first select groups of individuals who seem to differ in a wide range of behavior and then search for a variable which appears to characterize the difference in whatever mode or area it expresses itself.

In an effort to apply this criterion, we have selected community persons and mental-hospital patients as groups of persons who differ in a wide range of behavior and have hypothesized for investigation that they differ in an operationally definable variable of harmony or integration of responses.

The Statistical Method

The method of assessment which we have applied in the study of harmony of responses has the following characteristics:

1. It is objective.
2. It treats both qualitative and quantitative individual differences.

3. It compares individuals with various subsamples within the universe. These subsamples differ in harmony of responses.
4. It enables us to factor-analyze the responses of a single individual in order to determine their degree of harmoniousness.

It will perhaps be helpful first to review some of the results obtained with this single-individual, factor-analytic design in relation to clinical theory and then describe it in relation to group factor-analytic methods and in relation to its potential for measuring progress in psychotherapy.

A quotation from Bernard Hart (1925) serves as a helpful frame of reference within which to view the results achieved by factor-analyzing the responses of single individuals, some of whom are community persons and the others, mental-hospital schizophrenic patients. The quotation from Hart is as follows:

It [the patient's mind] no longer represents a homogeneous stream progressing in a definite direction toward a single end but is composed of more or less isolated mental processes, each pursuing its own independent development, unaffected by the presence of its fellows. The patient believes that he is the king, and he is also aware of facts which totally contradict that belief; but although both these things exist together in his mind, they are not allowed to come into contact, and each is impervious to the significance of the other. They pursue their courses in logic-tight compartments, as it were, separated by barriers through which no connecting thought or reasoning is permitted to pass. Similarly, the patient's belief is unaffected by our scientific demonstration of its impossibility. He understands perfectly each point of our reasoning, but its significance is not allowed to penetrate the compartment which contains his delusion; it glides off as water glides off a duck's back (pp. 56-57).

If such logic-tight compartments are present, they should reveal themselves as facts in factor analyses of single individuals. Such components, on the basis of clinical evidence, would be expected to be more developed in mental-hospital patients than in community persons. For the purpose of investigating such propositions as these, we have developed a method for factor-analyzing the test responses of single individuals. Since the results deriving from this individually oriented factor analysis can be reasonably well understood by analogy to those deriving from factor analysis as usually applied, it seems wise to report some of the results before describing the method, so that the results may be used as background material for later outlining the method.

The results can be seen by referring to Figure 13, which shows the number of factors in the responses of each of four persons, two of them community persons and two of them schizophrenic patients, as determined by Stewart (1951, pp. 42-60) in his application of the new type factor-analytic technique suggested by McQuitty (1950a, pp. 478-80). Community person A reveals but one factor and community person B shows two factors. Mental patient C reveals four factors and patient

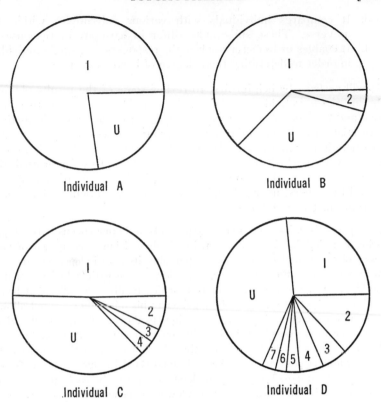

Individual A   Individual B

Individual C   Individual D

FACTORS

		1	2	3	4	5	6	7	Unique
INDIVIDUALS	A	0.77							0.23
	B	0.63	0.05						0.32
	C	0.48	0.09	0.04	0.03				0.36
	D	0.27	0.11	0.06	0.05	0.04	0.03	0.03	0.41

Fig. 43.—Personality factor structure within the individual. (As determined by a new factor technique applied to twenty-seven objective items.) The numbers in the circles and at the top of the table refer to the factors which derive from the four factor analyses of the individuals, A, B, C, and D. The numbers in the body of the table show what proportion of variance in each analysis is attributed to various factors where one equals maximum variance.

D, seven factors. These results derived from a method of analysis designed to give orthogonal factors, i.e., the complete centroid method.[2]

[2] However, the loadings on the first and second factors, only, for individuals B, C, and D are correlated negatively. This does not require that the factors themselves be correlated. The correlations probably derive from the nature of the test instructions in conjunction with the nature of the analysis and the index of association. (The test instructions request that each individual give one, and only one, of three answers for each item.) Solutions to these problems are discussed later herein.

They are probably as independent of each other as are the logic-tight compartments described in the above quotation from Hart. In these factor-analytic results on individual patients, we have exactly what theories of conflict, dissociation, and independent selves within the individual would lead us to expect. These results, then, give impressive objective support to the clinical theories. The methods and techniques on which they are based represent powerful potential tools for the advancement of clinical inquiry, including, of course, changes with psychotherapy. In the study of changes with psychotherapy, one could factor-analyze the responses of the client at successive intervals during the course of therapy.

Relation to Other Methods of Personality Assessment

The analysis that we have just reported is a structural one as distinct from a content analysis. It is a structural one in the sense that it deals rather exclusively with individual differences in the ways and extent to which responses are interrelated without concern, as yet, for the ideas contained in the test items to which the responses are made. It will become, in addition, a content analysis, if we name the factors isolated. We have not, as yet, done this because the naming of factors is usually preceded by rotation of the factor structure, and to do this for each of several individuals is very laborious. Later, we will report a way of reducing the labor tremendously.

Factor analysis, as usually applied (R technique) also represents a structural analysis, as well as a content one (because the factors are usually named), but it is not designed to investigate the possibility that responses are organized into different factors for different individuals.

The above quotation from Hart implies both content and structural analyses and individual differences in the logic-tight compartments or factors that make up the structure.

A content analysis is one which concerns itself with the ideas that are expressed by responses. Various ideas are taken as reflective of various degrees of personality adjustment. This content approach, as represented by Woodworth and reported by Symonds (1931, p. 174), by the Thurstones (1930), by Bernreuter (1933), and by Hathaway and McKinley (1940), for example, has the advantage of being objective, but at present possesses shortcomings in validity as brought out in the following quotation from Ellis (1946). "It is concluded that group-administered paper-and-pencil personality questionnaires are of dubious value in distinguishing between groups of adjusted and maladjusted individuals, and that they are of much less value in the diagnosis of individual adjustment of personality traits" (p. 426).

Those approaches concerning themselves with structure as well as content, such as the projective methods, remain to be objectified and quantified in ways that can be demonstrated to represent relatively high validity (Cattell, 1946, pp. 462-63 and Cureton, 1951, p. 651).

Hypotheses of the Revised Factor-analytic Design

The method, to be described herein, i.e., the factor analysis of data which is somewhat characteristic of the single case, retains the objectivity of the personality inventory and investigates, to some extent, individual difference in the organization of responses into factors. The method is based on several hypotheses, which have undergone preliminary investigations with substantiations (McQuitty, 1938, 1941, 1949, 1950a, 1950b, 1951, 1952a, 1952b, 1953; Grzeda, 1948; Helper, 1951). Two of the hypotheses are as follows: (a) There are individual differences in harmoniousness of responses. (b) Harmoniousness of self-descriptions is less for mental-hospital patients than it is for community persons.

A key problem here is how to measure the harmoniousness of responses. The method of measurement decided upon will determine what is meant by harmony. There are probably various hypotheses that could lead to the same method. However, a description of the hypotheses that led the author to the present measurement approach may help to highlight and clarify the approach. The hypotheses are as follows:

1. Man lives in a world of ideas.

2. These ideas are lawfully interrelated in the sense that to accept some of them encourages both the acceptances of additional ones and the rejection of other ideas. Mathematics represents an extreme illustration of this point. For example, if you accept the facts that $2 \times 4 = 8$ and that division is the opposite of multiplication, then you tend to accept that $8 \div 4 = 2$ and reject that $8 \div 4 = 3$.

3. Man does not comprehend immediately, or even eventually, all of the interrelationships of the ideas which he accepts.

4. Ideas may be accepted as harmonious and then later lead to conflicts in subsequent considerations. This process is realized and utilized in geometry. The following quotation from a high-school geometry textbook outlines the method (Seymour and Smith, 1941): ". . . certain relationships are proved to be false by first assuming them to be true and showing that such assumptions lead to contradictions of what is known to be true" (p. 100).

In the situation covered by the quotation, the relationship that is assumed to be true does not immediately reveal itself to be inconsistent with other, already accepted, ideas. It is only after we make certain deductions from the assumption that we discover it is inconsistent with other ideas and this only in the sense that it leads to relationships in obvious contradiction to already accepted ideas.

There are important differences between this special procedure as applied in geometry and mental activity as it often proceeds in daily life.

In geometry, we accept the relationship to be true, provisionally, often for the explicit purpose of showing that it is false because it leads to contradictions with ideas already accepted. In everyday mental activity, we often accept a proposition as true because: (a) it is obviously consistent with certain ideas which we accept (for example, it may be

accepted because it is stated by one whom we regard as an authority—
or by one whom we admire) and (b) no immediate inconsistency with
other previously accepted ideas is realized. The proposition may come
to serve as the basis for other conclusions. Successive conclusions may
be derived over a period of years until the starting point may be
forgotten. The process may lead eventually to conclusions that are
realized to be inconsistent with other conclusions—from other forgotten
starting points. When this awareness of inconsistency arises, we feel
frustrated and anxious and are often at a loss to know why we feel as
we do. In geometry we are usually readily able to trace back and reject
the false proposition. In everyday life, it would appear that some special
technique is required to accomplish this. Such techniques as catharsis,
directive and nondirective counseling, dream analysis, and free association have been proposed and found somewhat helpful, i.e., according to
clinical interpretations of their influences.

5. There are various ways of reacting to conflict. In some situations,
even in daily life, we can trace back and reject a proposition which has
led us into conflict. In other situations, we in some way dissociate the
groups of ideas that conflict, one from the other, and still entertain both.
This may be a mild dissociation or a logic-tight one. We have this process
expressing itself to some extent in mathematics, in the case of Euclidian
versus non-Euclidian geometry. Each group of ideas is internally self-
consistent but not consistent with those of the other group. In our
geometric interpretations of the world we work exclusively with one
group of internally consistent ideas—not jointly with two or more contradictory systems. We often consciously treat the two or more systems
as logic-tight compartments.

6. The harmoniousness among ideas entertained by an individual is
less to the extent that logic-tight compartments are involved.

If an index of harmoniousness of ideas can be developed it might
turn out to be related to the prevalence of logic-tight compartments and
to mental health. That such an index can be developed is implied by
our second hypothesis. The hypothesis states that ideas are lawfully
interrelated in the sense that to accept some of them is to encourage both
the acceptance of additional ones and the rejection of other ideas. This
hypothesis suggests that man's acceptance and rejection of various ideas
might be developed into a quantitative index of the interrelationships
or degrees of harmony among ideas. If such an index could be developed,
it could be applied first to many individuals as a method for determining
the interrelationship among many ideas. Next, the framework of the
interrelationships among ideas could be used as an instrument for evaluating the degree of harmony reflected by the ideas endorsed by an individual.
This is accomplished by asking the individual which of the ideas he
endorses. He endorses only some of them. The ones he endorses could
then be referred to the framework of interrelationships for evaluating
their degree of harmony. This would give an index of harmony for the
individual in the universe of ideas sampled.

It is presumed that all categories of ideas are not equally significant for an evaluation of mental health or psychotherapy. It is here hypothesized, for the purpose of investigation, that the harmoniousness of self-descriptions is related to mental health, and consequently varies from mental hospital patients to community persons (see page 422 of this chapter and McQuitty, 1949 and 1950b).

Emotional Considerations in the Approach

Before outlining the details of the method for measuring harmoniousness of self-descriptions, it may be helpful to specify one sense in which emotional considerations are involved in the approach. This can be done by reference to categories of ideas. Ideas are probably more emotionally toned to the extent that they are self-referential (Sherif and Cantril, 1947, p. 93). Other things equal, self-descriptions, as a group, probably represent our most emotionally toned category of ideas. In this sense, our studies pertain to the degree of harmony in our most emotionally toned system of ideas, the self-centered ideas or self-descriptions.

Measuring the Degree of Harmony of Self-descriptions

Our approaches to the measurement of the degree of harmony of self-descriptions may now be outlined in more detail. There are several phases in our approach. There is the problem of the sample of self-descriptions. What is the universe of self-descriptions, and how can it be sampled without bias? Our solution to this problem is based on the following hypothesis: *If harmoniousness of self-descriptions is a sufficiently abstract and broadly applicable variable to discriminate between community persons and mental-hospital patients, then it probably expresses itself widely and approximately equally in quite different areas of self-descriptions.*

From the point of view of this hypothesis, in relation to an effort to develop an index of harmony which will discriminate between community persons and mental-hospital patients, it is relatively immaterial as to whether or not the self-descriptions chosen for study are representative in every respect of the universe of self-descriptions.

Our initial approach to the investigation of the above hypothesis was to study harmoniousness of self-descriptions in two quite different areas: (a) the area of interests, as represented by the Strong Vocational Interest Blank, and (b) the area of adjustment, as represented by the Bernreuter Personality Inventory.

Before stating the degree of relationship that we found between the measures of harmony in these two areas, it will be helpful to describe the method of measurement in more detail. As we outline the method of measurement, we will specify the ways in which it possesses the characteristics indicated earlier in this chapter.

We have hypothesized that the acceptance of ideas encourages both the acceptance of additional ones and the rejection of other ideas. If this hypothesis is true, then groups of ideas vary in their degree of inter-attractiveness among the ideas. If we can obtain an index of degree of mutual attractiveness among ideas, it could be investigated as a harmony coefficient in relation to mental health.

To simplify the problem, suppose that we want to know the extent to which ideas a and b are mutually attractive. We could search for manifestations of the presence of each idea and obtain a ratio of the extent to which the ideas occur together vs. separately, as a measure of their mutual attractiveness or harmoniousness. We would not need to concern ourselves with searching in places where neither idea exists.

We could repeat the above process for all the pairs of ideas of a group and thus develop a framework indicating the harmony among the ideas.

So far we have discussed ideas in the abstract. If we wish to obtain an empirical index of the mutual attractiveness, or harmoniousness, of ideas, we may turn to a realm of their expression, namely the responses of people to questions, such as represented by the endorsements of items in a personality inventory.

In order to outline an empirical index, suppose we have the tabulated responses of a sample of individuals to a personality inventory.

Let the following letters represent the following tabulations:

$a =$ the number of persons who endorse idea a
$b =$ the number of persons who endorse idea b
$ab =$ the number of persons who endorse both ideas, a and b

Then the concomitance index [3] is

$$\frac{ab}{\sqrt{a \times b}}$$

The persons who endorse neither a nor b are ignored. They tell us nothing about the interassociation between the ideas. This point is emphasized by an example. Suppose in trying to discover the degree of interassociation between two ideas x and y, we ask members of a group of subjects if they endorse x and if they endorse y. Suppose all subjects respond negatively. The results tell us nothing about the degree of inter-association between the ideas. In order to obtain information about the interassociation between the ideas, we have to find either (a) subjects who endorse the ideas or (b) ideas which are endorsed by the subjects we do have. In these cases, the subjects who (a) endorse both ideas and (b) the subjects who endorse only one of two ideas furnish information about the interassociation of ideas.

[3] This formula represents an atypical adaptation of the common-elements coefficient of correlation. The two ideas represent the variables, and the persons endorsing each idea are treated as if they are the elements of which the variable is composed. For an interpretation of the Personian coefficient of correlation in terms of a common-elements formula, see McNemar (1949, pp. 117-18).

Even in the above cases, the subjects who endorse neither furnish information only if we assume a relationship between endorsing and failing to endorse. The present approach recognizes that most test instructions force a linear relationship of opposites when they specify the number of responses the subjects are required to give. This is accepted as desirable in order to standardize conditions. However, the relationship forced by the instructions usually pertains to each idea, only. For example, if a subject endorses idea x, he cannot simultaneously fail to endorse it. But, nevertheless, it is still possible for him to react to subsequent items in a manner which denies the forced relationship of opposites. For example, he may react in two different ways to subsequent items: (a) With respect to some of them, he may react as did most of the subjects who endorsed x and (b) with respect to others of them, he may react as did most of those who did not endorse x. These possibilities may be such as to deviate significantly from chance. If this should occur, it would then indicate that to endorse x is not necessarily the opposite from a failure to endorse it. In the present approach we assume that the endorsements are discrete, and we study the interassociationship between them, using only those subjects who (a) give one of two endorsements, or (b) both of two endorsements.

Suppose now that we have the following two questions from a personality inventory, which can be answered in the three ways indicated after the question:

1. Are you often lonely?   Yes   Between   No
2. Are you a selfish person?   Yes   Between   No

Each of these questions solicits one of three answers: "Yes," "Between," or "No." "Between" is defined as representing an answer intermediate between the two extremes indicated by "Yes" or "No." Each answer represents a self-expressed idea about the endorser.

Each of the two questions solicits one of three answers. The answers represent the framework for investigating the degree of relationship between nine pairs of ideas about oneself, as follows: Yes 1 — Yes 2, Yes 1 — Between 2, Yes 1 — No 2, Between 1 — Yes 2, Between 1 — Between 2, Between 1 — No 2, No 1 — Yes 2, No 1 — Between 2, and No 1 — No 2.

The concomitance index for Yes 1 — Yes 2 equals:

$$\frac{\text{Number who answer both Yes 1 and Yes 2}}{\sqrt{\text{Number who answer Yes 1 times number who answer Yes 2}}}$$

An analogous formula can be written for determining the degree of concomitance between each of the other eight pairs of ideas represented by the eight pairs of answers.

If we had an inventory of, say, twenty questions, each with three answer alternatives, we could then investigate the degree of concomitance between a large number of pairs. We could, for example, investigate the nine pairs of answers between questions 1 and 2, also between 1 and 3,

1 and 4, etc., then between 2 and 3, 2 and 4, etc., then between 3 and 4, 3 and 5, etc., and so on. If we exhausted all these possibilities, we would have the following number of concomitance indices between ideas:

$$\frac{9 \times 19 \times 20}{2} = 1710$$

There are at least three interrelated ways in which these concomitance indices can be treated for the assessment of personality integration. The three methods may be labeled as follows: (a) factor analysis of the individual personality, (b) a measure of personality integration, and (c) a rapid factor analysis of the individual personality. Each of these three methods will be outlined. The first two methods have been applied in a number of studies (McQuitty, 1938, 1941, 1949, 1950a, 1950b, 1951, 1952a, 1952b; Helper, 1951; Stewart, 1951), and they give considerable promise. A limiting consideration in their utilization grows out of the fact that they consume a great deal of time in statistical computations. Efforts to overcome this limitation have led to the third method. An outline of the first two methods, together with a review of some of the results achieved by them, will prepare us to grasp the significance and potentialities of the third method. This last method appears to possess all of the promise of the first two methods, and in addition, requires a remarkably brief amount of time in its assessment of the individual personality, i.e., after elaborate preliminary computations have been completed.

Factor Analysis of the Individual Personality

Using the concomitance index, an individual's personality structure can be objectively assessed with results analogous to those deriving from clinical appraisals.

If a subject gives one answer to each of the twenty questions of an inventory, there would be $1/9 \times 1,710$, i.e., 190 pairs of answers resulting from his endorsements. All the pairs of answers, i.e., pairs of ideas about self, have indices of interrelation, as determined by the concomitance index outlined above. These indices fit into a twenty-by-twenty matrix, resulting in a table of interassociations which can be factor-analyzed to investigate the personality organization of the individual as represented by his responses. This is the approach from which the individual factor results already reported herein derived, in which we found objective quantitative support for clinical theories of conflict, logic-tight compartments, and selves within the individual, in the sense that the association matrices of the two schizophrenic patients were found to represent four and seven orthogonal factors respectively; while those of two community persons were found to represent only one and two orthogonal factors respectively. In addition, the unique factor variance was found to be much greater for the patients than for the community subjects (Stewart, 1951, pp. 42-60).

We have some supplementary evidence on the degree of generality that can be ascribed to the factor analysis of single-case matrices. J. O. Neuhaus, a graduate student at the University of Illinois, factor-analyzed another matrix for one of Stewart's subjects. As reported earlier herein, Stewart factor-analyzed, using our new approach, the matrices for four individuals A, B, C, and D. The first two are community subjects and the last two schizophrenic patients. Neuhaus used an entirely different set of twenty-seven personality items and factor-analyzed the matrix resulting from the responses of subject C to them. Neuhaus found that the matrix required the postulation of four factors, just as had a matrix for the same subject based on twenty-seven different items as analyzed by Stewart. In both cases, Tucker's criterion (Thurstone, 1938, pp. 65-72) was applied to determine the number of significant factors. Results from these applications are shown in Table 12. In each study the criterion for the fifth residual matrix has approached very near to the Tucker limit thus indicating that only the first four factors are significant.

TABLE 12

APPLICATION OF TUCKER'S CRITERION

Residual Matrices	Objective Items (Analysis by Stewart)		Subjective Items (Analysis by Neuhaus)	
	Criterion (ϕ)	Limit $\left(\dfrac{n-1}{n}\right)$	Criterion (ϕ)	Limit $\left(\dfrac{n-1}{n}\right)$
I-II	.722	.962	.945	.963
II-III	.887	.962	.893	.963
III-IV	.924	.962	.897	.963
IV-V	.935	.962	.953	.963

The twenty-seven personality test items used by Neuhaus in his study have been characterized as "subjective" and those used by Stewart as "objective;" both characterizations were suggested by McQuitty on the basis of previous research by him (1949, 1952a). In fact, the items used by Neuhaus and Stewart were at the opposite extremes of an objective criterion applied to a total of 190 items.

Objective items are characterized as such in the sense that the cues on which answers to them are based appear to be equally observable by both the examinee and others. In the case of subjective items, the cues appear to be available to the examinee through introspection in a manner in which they are not available to the observation of others. In this sense, the first and second questions below would be regarded as objective and subjective, respectively:

Do you laugh often?
Do you have disturbing thoughts often?

Two matrices, one from each of these two categories of items, resulted in the same number of factors for a single mental hospital patient. The results are shown diagramatically in Figure 44. These diagrams are interpreted in the same manner as are those of Figure 43. It is interesting to observe that the two diagrams of Figure 44 for the one

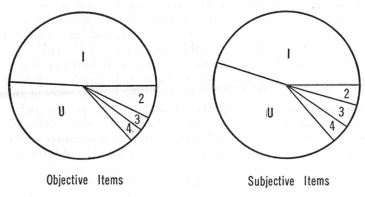

Objective Items   Subjective Items

FACTORS

TESTS	1	2	3	4	Unique
Objective	0.48	0.09	0.04	0.03	0.36
Subjective	0.41	0.04	0.05	0.04	0.46

Fig. 44.—Personality factor structures from two tests for one subject. The numbers in the circles and in the top row of the table refer to the factors which derive from the two independent factor analyses of individual C. The numbers in the body of the table show what proportion of variance in each analysis is attributed to various factors where 1 equals maximum variance.

subject, using different items, are much more alike than any two of the four in Figure 43, for four different subjects with identical items. *This result is consistent with the view that our revised factor-analytic design produces organizational interpretations of the single personality that are in general characteristic of it.*

A Measure of Personality Integration

To factor-analyze a matrix for each member of a group of individuals would be a long and laborious task. It is fortunate that a less time-consuming score of personality integration can be computed which seems to conform closely to the results of factor analysis. A score of personality integration can be computed in any one of several ways. If we consider the twenty answers that a subject has given to the twenty items of a personality inventory, we then have 190 pairs of answers out of a pool of 1,710 pairs, i.e., in a test composed of items with three answer possibilities. Each of the 190 pairs of answers has a concomitance index.

A mean of these indices gives a score of personality integration in the sense that scores thus computed discriminate between groups of community persons and mental-hospital patients, as reported elsewhere (McQuitty, 1938, 1950b).

In the above reference studies, instead of taking a mean of the indices for all possible pairs, we restricted ourselves, because of the labor involved, to a systematic sampling of them, i.e., to successive pairs, as represented by items 1 — 2, 2 — 3, 3 — 4, etc., making a total of nineteen pairs in a twenty-item test rather than a total of 190 pairs.

We have found that the efficiency of our tests is increased if a correction is incorporated in the scoring which is designed to eliminate an influence related to individual differences in the various pairs of answers, i.e., individual differences in the number of (a) yes-yes pairs, (b) yes-between pairs, (c) yes-no pairs, (d) between-yes pairs, etc. The efficiency of the tests is increased in the sense that integration scores from two tests of different item content (the Strong Vocational Interest Blank and the Bernreuter Personality Inventory), have a significant correlation only when the correction is incorporated (McQuitty, 1938). Also, the differentiation between community subjects and mental hospital patients achieved by results from tests of personality integration is probably increased by the correction (McQuitty, 1938, 1952a).

The above finding of a significant correlation between the integration scores determined from the Strong Vocational Interest Blank and the Bernreuter Personality Inventory indicates that the variable of personality integration has breadth in the sense that it is revealed in two quite different test item areas.

The above correlation is also pertinent in evaluating the generality of meaning of the results obtained when the matrices of single individuals were factor-analyzed, as reported earlier herein. These factor results were derived from tests containing items similar to many of those contained in the Bernreuter Personality Inventory. In addition to the factor results, integration scores were obtained. There is a close relationship

TABLE 13

A COMPARISON OF INTEGRATION SCORES AND INDIVIDUAL FACTOR STRUCTURE

Individual	Integrative Score	No. of Orthogonal Factors	Unique Variance	Common Variance
A	Highest in a sample of community subjects	1	23%	77%
B	Average in a sample of community subjects	2	32%	68%
C	Average in a sample of schizophrenic patients	4	36%	64%
D	Lowest in a sample of schizophrenic patients	7	41%	59%

between the integration scores and the factor results as indicated by Table 13.

The individuals with the scores indicating less personality integration have matrices reflecting more factors, more unique variance, and less common-factor variance. In other words, the relatively disintegrated persons of the study reveal more independent influences in their responses and act as if there are independent "selves" determining their answers. This result, in conjunction with the significant correlation between integration scores on the Strong and Bernreuter inventories, suggests that similar factor patterns would have been obtained for individuals A, B, C, and D if we had studied matrices deriving from the Strong Inventory in lieu of the Bernreuter type items.

An Interpretation

The above results appear to be more meaningful if we review them in the light of some of our hypotheses and certain characteristics of the methods used in obtaining them.

Two of the fundamental hypotheses out of which the methods developed are as follows:

1. Individuals differ in the harmony of their self-descriptions.

2. Self-descriptions are a particular category of ideas, and ideas are lawfully interrelated in the sense that to accept some of them encourages both the acceptance of additional ideas and the rejection of other ideas.

If we did not have some such hypotheses as these, there would be no meaningful reason for pursuing the mathematical manipulations that we have outlined herein.

The outcome of the mathematical manipulations supports the hypotheses. The hypotheses seem to superimpose a particular viewpoint concerning behavior dynamics. They tend to suggest that much overt behavior can be explained in terms of the ideas that individuals entertain. In this sense the role of emotions as causal factors may be regarded as minor; the ideas appear to be the determining factors in behavior.

The emotions may have value for indicating which ideas are significant for the assessment of personality integration. It may be that emotionally toned ideas are most valid for this type of measurement. This possibility would seem to indicate that the significance of ideas for the assessment of personality integration varies from individual to individual—since, as we know, the relative emotionality of ideas varies in this respect. This suggestion can be investigated and partially corrected (if need be) by further application of the methods of this chapter. Subjects could be requested to rate the relative emotionality of the items on which they are tested. For each subject, the items could be divided into groups according to rated emotionality. The groups of items would probably vary at least some and maybe considerably from subject to subject. Each group of items could be scored for each subject and the scores studied in relation to some criterion of personality integration. It is here suggested that the degree of harmony of the most emotionally toned ideas would be most closely related to personality integration.

If the interpretation just offered is correct, it would indicate that emotionality remains relatively constant, while degree of harmony of ideas varies in direct relation to personality integration. This would mean that the degree of interrelationship of ideas is more closely associated with personality integration than is the degree of emotionality of ideas.

Another interesting possibility derives from the interpretations of this chapter. We have indicated that the emotionally toned self-descriptive ideas are most valid for the measurement of personality integration. An index of harmony is applied in this measurement. By using different test items and by redirection of our measures of harmony to institutions rather than to individuals, we might be able to evaluate a significant characteristic of institutions. We could compute the harmoniousness of ideas that one entertains about an institution. We could do this for many individuals about the same institution and take a mean of the individual scores as an index of the harmoniousness of the ideas which are incorporated in the reported characteristics of the institution. We could apply the approach to several institutions and, perhaps, obtain a basis for comparing institutions as to the harmoniousness of the ideas reported as characteristic of them. More specifically, this approach could be applied to the labor-management relationships in various companies and might prove to be an effective index of their degree of harmony. The harmoniousness of the labor-management picture could then be studied in relation to such things as conflict-cooperation between labor and management, production, personnel turnover, etc.

For our present purposes, it is helpful to consider the point of view of this chapter in relation to psychotherapy. Psychotherapy, as generally applied, may be regarded as reviewing one's experiences until all of one's ideas have been so changed that they are more harmoniously interrelated. This process involves a conflict for the client, and the conflict within this process is more severe for the more disturbed patient. The conflict within this process seems to grow out of an effort on the part of the client to interrelate all ideas which he consciously accepts. He appears to do this, in part, by refusing to accept new ideas which are obviously in conflict with those that he has already accepted. In a similar manner he finds it difficult to recall ideas which appear to be in conflict.

It may be possible to lessen the efforts to integrate during the time that the patient is attempting to reconstruct his past. The use of free association, hypnosis, catharsis, and nondirective counseling may have this effect. Explicit structuring of the counseling situation along the following lines might help facilitate counseling and lessen emotional upheaval. The client could be encouraged to disregard his respect for integrated material temporarily; instead he could be encouraged to seek after disintegrated material in an effort to discover ways of integrating it.

A New Type of Composite Factor Analysis

In discussing the relation of our revised factor-analytic design to psychotherapy, we have treated it as applied to the single individual. The individual matrices can be combined into a composite one and analyzed. Results from this approach, in conjunction with those from the individual matrices, have significance for psychotherapy.

Stewart analyzed composite matrices for both eighty-four community persons and seventy-two schizophrenic patients, each group treated separately (Stewart, 1951, pp. 27-42). The composite matrix for each group was obtained by first preparing the matrix for each individual. This gave eighty-four matrices for the eighty-four community subjects. In order to obtain the entry for cell 1 of the composite matrix, a mean was taken of the cell 1 entries of all the eighty-four individual matrices.[4] Other cell entries for the composite matrices were computed in an analogous manner.

Stewart (1951, pp. 27-42) factor-analyzed four composite matrices, two for community people and two for schizophrenic patients. The same two tests were used for community subjects and schizophrenic patients. One of the tests was composed of twenty-seven "subjective" items and the other of twenty-seven "objective" items (p. 21). Despite the fact that the four matrices for single individuals resulted in one, two, four, and seven factors respectively, the four composite matrices each resulted in but one factor with the exception of one of the two matrices for schizophrenic patients, which resulted in two factors, with the second factor accounting for only 2 per cent of the total variance.

The above results indicate that a great deal of data significant for the understanding of the behavior of the single case may be lost when it is interpreted in terms of a reference frame of average or composite man exclusively. On the other hand, it may be impossible to obtain generally accepted interpretations of behavior of individual cases unless they are on the basis of comparisons with the behavior of others. The approach outlined in this paper has achieved a compromise solution to this dilemma. This is accomplished in the following ways:

1. Instead of comparing the individual with an average man representative of the population, it compares him successively with *many* average men, each representative of a subuniverse within the population.

2. The particular method of test construction isolates many categories of people. When a subject gives any two answers, *a* and *b,* to an inventory of items, he is treated by the method as having placed himself in three categories of people: those who give answer *a,* those who give answer *b,* and those who give both answers,

---

[4] Before the mean was computed, the cell entries or concomitance indices were converted to Fisher's z's (Fisher, 1948, pp. 197-201). The mean of the z's was computed and the result converted to a mean index.

a and *b*. His answers, *a* and *b,* are assumed to reflect the same amount of integration for him as they do for all people who give them. The amount of integration reflected by them derives from a ratio. The numerator of the ratio is the number of persons who gave both answers. The denominator is a mean of the numbers of those who gave each answer (see pages 425-27).

3. When all the answers a person has given to an inventory are considered, he can be treated as having placed himself in many categories of people. The categories deriving from pairs of answers, such as *a* and *b,* give the subject an index of integration.

4. The different answers that various individuals give reflect different degrees of personality integration. Factor analysis represents one way of evaluating the degree of personality integration. In applying this approach we found, as reported earlier, that mental patients reveal less integration than do community persons in the sense that they reveal more factors, less common variance, and more unique variance.

5. Another measure of integration is a corrected mean of the indices of integration, i.e., of the concomitance index. We have found that this gives significant differences between groups of community persons and mental hospital patients (McQuitty, 1938, 1950*b,* 1952*a*).

6. Still another measure of integration is possible. Instead of taking a corrected mean of the indices, one might take a measure of dispersion of the indices on the basis of the hypothesis that degree of integration would reflect itself as well, or even more definitely, in the degree of scatter.

Individual vs. Group Factor Analysis

There is another indication that individual factor analysis loses less of the data than does group analysis. This evidence derives from intercomparing the common factor variances for the coefficients of the composite matrices, the individual case matrices, and a usual type matrix. If the common factor variances are relatively high, then relatively little is lost in the analysis. The usual type matrix chosen for the comparison is one reported by Cattell (1950*b*). The items from which this matrix derived were selected by Cattell because there was a basis for believing that they would be highly loaded with already discovered factors. Cattell attempted to include items to represent all "important psychological areas of personality," including of course "all putative personality inventory item factors." His second factorization (the one with which the present analysis is concerned), after rotation, yielded nineteen oblique factors, "none of which exceeded quite moderate degrees of obliqueness."

This usual type factor matrix was chosen for the present comparison because it was felt that it maximized the opportunity for common variance

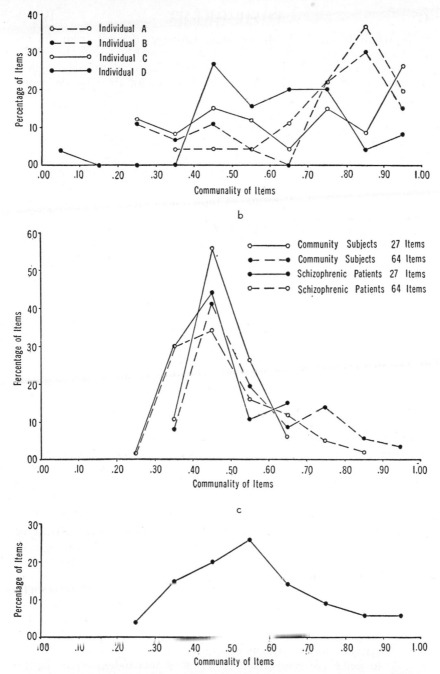

Fig. 45.—The communality of items accounted for in three methods of analysis; *a* shows the communalities for four individuals derived from the individual factor analysis method; *b* shows the communalities for four composite matrices derived from the composite factor analysis method; *c* shows the communalities derived from the usual type of factor analysis.

to be relatively large. If the common variances derived from the revised factor-analytic design, herein outlined, should be larger than those reported in the usual type matrix under study, it would strongly suggest that less of the data is lost by the revised design than by the usual approach.

The results of the comparisons are shown in Figure 45, where we have plotted the frequencies of common variance for all items in each matrix. Figure 45a shows the results for the four individual matrices; Figure 45b, for the four composite matrices; and Figure 45c, for the usual type of matrix. The frequencies are in terms of percentages, i.e., each frequency was divided by the number of items in the matrix from which it was derived. Percentages rather than cardinal numbers were used because the matrices vary in the number of items, and it was desired to make the curves comparable. There were eighty items for the usual type matrix, sixty-four for each of the composite matrices, and only twenty-seven for each of the individual matrices. The matrix with the largest number of items has the greatest chance for high communalities, other things equal.

The common variance is higher for the individual matrices than for either type of composite matrices. *This result is consistent with the surmise that less of individual behavior is lost in individual factor analysis than in the two types of group factor analysis here represented.*

The new-type, composite matrix resulted in lower common variance than did the usual type of matrices. This may be due either to differences in the methods of building up the matrices, differences in the items, or differences in the number of items. Differences in the number and kinds of items were not accepted as an explanation of the difference in common variance for the individual versus usual-type matrix because they would seem to have favored the reverse finding, based on the fact that the items for the usual type of matrix were greater in number and derived from a selection based on much previous research.

There are at least four possible explanations of why the individual matrices produced more common variance than the group-type matrices.

1. The first of these applies to the comparison of individual-type matrices with the Cattell group-type matrix but not to the comparison of the individual-type matrices with the new-type, composite matrices.

   The Cattell matrix is composed of tetrachoric coefficients. The individual-type matrices are composed of concomitance indices. In order for the comparison to be entirely satisfactory for the purpose at hand, it would be necessary to have an index of association which is equally appropriate to the two applications and to make the comparison in terms of this index. Some of the difference in the comparison may be due to different characteristics of the indices of association used. However, all the difference is probably not due to this, for, if it were, we would have ex-

pected less difference between the individual-type matrices and
the new-type, composite matrices.

2. The usual type of factor analysis superimposes the assumption
that the three alternative answers to an item reflect various
amounts of an underlying linear continuum. The revised factor-
analytic design avoids this assumption by applying the concomitance index and by using it to compute the degree of association
between answers as distinct from that between items. For example, the usual approach computes the correlation between items
1 and 2 by treating the three responses to each item as if they lie
along a continuum. The revised design computes the degree of
association between each: Yes 1 and Yes 2, Yes 1 and Between
2, Yes 1 and No 2, Between 1 and Yes 2, Between 1 and Between 2, Between 1 and No 2, No 1 and Yes 2, No 1 and Between 2, and No 1 and No 2.

The revised design might possibly be applied to investigate the assumption of linearity superimposed by the usual approach. One possibility
would be to factor-analyze the type of matrix shown in Figure 46, which
could be filled in from the indices obtained in applying the revised design.

A problem would arise in determining the numerical values to be
entered in such cells as $Y_1 - Y_1$, $Y_1 - B_1$, $Y_1 - N_1$, $B_1 - B_1$, $B_1 - N_1$,
$N_1 - N_1$, $Y_2 - Y_2$, $Y_2 - B_2$, $Y_2 - N_2$, $B_2 - B_2$, $B_2 - N_2$, N_2 N_2,
$Y_3 - Y_3$, $Y_3 - B_3$, $Y_3 - N_3$, $B_3 - B_3$, $B_3 - N_3$, $N_3 - N_3$, etc. This is
a technical problem which can be solved. A solution to it is required in
a rapid method for obtaining a factor pattern for the individual subject
(to be outlined later in this chapter) as well as for the present problem.
Since the solution is primarily technical, it is outlined in the appendix
section of this chapter.

If the assumption of linearity is tenable, the interrelationships within
each Y_1, Y_2, Y_3, etc.; B_1, B_2, B_3; and N_1, N_2, and N_3 in the factorial
matrix should be analogous.

Another approach would be to set up three separate matrices, one for
each set of Y, B, and N answers, and then to compare the three factor
structures. If the assumption of linearity for item responses is tenable,
then the factor structures for the three matrices should be similar.

3. Another reason for the differences in the amount of common
variance between group and individual matrices may be related
to the distribution of factors. Factors, themselves, may be randomly distributed among individuals. In fact, our results support
this conclusion. It may be that the factors from group matrices
exist only as abstractions in the average man. They may be
abstractions from the more or less randomly distributed and more
fruitful and significant factors of the single case. Our results,
as already indicated (page 433), support this conclusion. Additional research is, of course, needed with both approaches in
order to further clarify these issues.

4. A third reason why the individual analysis may account for more of the variance than the group methods is related to the fact that it selects out of the data for group analyses those concomitance indices which are most appropriate to the description of the particular individual under study. This point can be clarified by reference to several matrices of concomitance indices. Our discussion will show how the individual technique selects out the concomitance indices most appropriate to the individual and will introduce us to a new and rapid method of determining a factor pattern for the single individual.

	Y_1	B_1	N_1	Y_2	B_2	N_2	Y_3	B_3	N_3	Y_4	B_4	N_4	Y_5	B_5	N_5	etc.
Y_1	...	...	...	...	...	...	...	...	...	...	...	...	...	...	...	...
B_1	...	...	...	...	...	...	...	...	...	...	...	...	...	...	...	...
N_1	...	...	...	...	...	...	...	...	...	...	...	...	...	...	...	...
Y_2	...	...	...	...	...	...	...	...	...	...	...	...	...	...	...	...
B_2	...	...	...	...	...	...	...	...	...	...	...	...	...	...	...	...
N_2	...	...	...	...	...	...	...	...	...	...	...	...	...	...	...	...
Y_3	...	...	...	...	...	...	...	...	...	...	...	...	...	...	...	...
B_3	...	...	...	...	...	...	...	...	...	...	...	...	...	...	...	...
N_3	...	...	...	...	...	...	...	...	...	...	...	...	...	...	...	...
Y_4	...	...	...	...	...	...	...	...	...	...	...	...	...	...	...	...
B_4	...	...	...	...	...	...	...	...	...	...	...	...	...	...	...	...
N_4	...	...	...	...	...	...	...	...	...	...	...	...	...	...	...	...
Y_5	...	...	...	...	...	...	...	...	...	...	...	...	...	...	...	...
B_5	...	...	...	...	...	...	...	...	...	...	...	...	...	...	...	...
N_5	...	...	...	...	...	...	...	...	...	...	...	...	...	...	...	...
etc.	...	...	...	...	...	...	...	...	...	...	...	...	...	...	...	...

FIG. 46.—A concomitance matrix (group-type).

Rapid Analysis of the Individual Personality

The method of selecting out the association indices most appropriate to the description of a particular individual derives from a group concomitance matrix. We will first consider a usual-type correlation matrix and show how the concomitance-type matrix differs from the usual-type matrix. We will then show how our method of factor-analyzing the test responses of the single case accomplishes this by selecting out for analysis from the group concomitance matrix the indices most appropriate to the individual under study. We will describe an original method whereby the factor pattern for the individual can be read directly from a group factor matrix, by extracting from it the factor pattern indicated by the answers given by the particular subject. Next, we will outline how the association matrix is derived from a response matrix, as distinct from a test-item matrix. After this, we will show that all the factor techniques, i.e., R, Q, P, O, M, and N, are applicable in our approach and, in fact, are less time-consuming in computation and are probably more meaningful, particularly in the case of R, O, and Q. Then, we will compare our research design with the more usual factor-analytic research design and outline how our research design avoids some of the assumptions inherent in the usual design.

Interpretations of factors deriving from our method can be in terms of configurations of any kind if the analysis so indicates; the factors are not as much restricted to common linear continua as they are in usual-type factor analysis. The factors can vary in configuration from individual to individual, and can be present in some individuals while absent in others. This allows for a qualitative difference between individuals in the interpretation of our quantitative data. Further investigations with our factor-analytic design may justify calling the method configurational analysis on the basis of the interpretations that derive from it. In the meantime, we will refer to the method as "configurational analysis," primarily to distinguish it from the usual factor-analytic design, only in the sense that it superimposes less restriction on the variables between which correlation coefficients are computed and, therefore, allows for a greater breadth of results and interpretations.

A usual-type correlation matrix is shown in Figure 47. The entries in the cells of this table, here represented by dots, are the correlation coefficients of every test with every other test, each coefficient listed twice—except those for communalities of the tests.

The new-type matrix is shown in Figure 46. Instead of listing successive tests or test items in the left column and top row, it lists the three answer possibilities, Y, B, and N, to each of the successive test items. The entries represented by dots in the cells are concomitance indices, which were described earlier in this chapter (pages 425-27). The chart is here referred to as a concomitance matrix, and as a group-type one, the latter designation to distinguish it from a concomitance matrix for the individual, which is to be described next.

It is from the group-concomitance matrix that the indices most descriptive of an individual are derived. The ones that are extracted depend on the responses that the subject under study gives to the items of the test. Suppose, for example, that a particular subject answered Y_1, N_2, B_3, N_4, etc. His individual concomitance matrix would then be

Tests or Test Items	Tests or Test Items										
	1	2	3	4	5	6	7	8	9	10	etc.
1	...	...	...	...	...	...	...	...	...	...	...
2	...	...	...	...	...	...	...	...	...	...	...
3	...	...	...	...	...	...	...	...	...	...	...
4	...	...	...	...	...	...	...	...	...	...	...
5	...	...	...	...	...	...	...	...	...	...	...
6	...	...	...	...	...	...	...	...	...	...	...
7	...	...	...	...	...	...	...	...	...	...	...
8	...	...	...	...	...	...	...	...	...	...	...
9	...	...	...	...	...	...	...	...	...	...	...
10	...	...	...	...	...	...	...	...	...	...	...
etc.	...	...	...	...	...	...	...	...	...	...	...

FIG. 47.—A usual-type correlation matrix.

as shown in Figure 48. This matrix lists the answers the subject has given to the questions of a test in both the top row and the left column of the matrix. The dots refer to the concomitance indices between the answers. These indices are extracted from the group-concomitance matrix. The subject under study gives the answers Y_1 and N_2, for example. The concomitance index between these two answers is shown in $Y_1 - N_2$ cells of the group matrix. It is entered in $Y_1 - N_2$ cells of the individual matrix. Other cells of the individual matrix are filled in

	Y_1	N_2	B_3	N_4	etc.
Y_1	...	...	...	...	...
N_2	...	...	...	...	...
B_3	...	...	...	...	...
N_4	...	...	...	...	...
etc.	...	...	...	...	...

FIG. 48.—An association matrix (individual-type).

in an analogous manner. This is the type of individual matrix from which different factor patterns were obtained for patients and community persons, as reported earlier in this chapter (pages 419 and 420).

To analyze the matrices for each of several persons is very time-consuming. It is fortunate that we have been able to develop a method for obtaining a factor pattern for the individual which is practically instantaneous, i.e., once certain group data have been analyzed. All that is necessary is to analyze, using the usual factor methods, a group-concomitance matrix. This gives us the number of factors represented by the matrix and the loadings of each answer for each factor, together with the common and unique variances, if required. An example of a factor matrix of this kind is shown in Figure 49. It is here referred to as a

Answers	\multicolumn{13}{c}{Factors}		
	1	2	3	4	5	6	7	8	9	10	11	12	etc.	h^2	u^2
Y_1	...	...	...	...	...	...	...	...	...	...	...	...	...	...	...
B_1	...	...	...	...	...	...	...	...	...	...	...	...	...	...	...
N_1	...	...	...	...	...	...	...	...	...	...	...	...	...	...	...
Y_2	...	...	...	...	...	...	...	...	...	...	...	...	...	...	...
B_2	...	...	...	...	...	...	...	...	...	...	...	...	...	...	...
N_2	...	...	...	...	...	...	...	...	...	...	...	...	...	...	...
Y_3	...	...	...	...	...	...	...	...	...	...	...	...	...	...	...
B_3	...	...	...	...	...	...	...	...	...	...	...	...	...	...	...
N_3	...	...	...	...	...	...	...	...	...	...	...	...	...	...	...
Y_4	...	...	...	...	...	...	...	...	...	...	...	...	...	...	...
B_4	...	...	...	...	...	...	...	...	...	...	...	...	...	...	...
N_4	...	...	...	...	...	...	...	...	...	...	...	...	...	...	...
etc.	...	...	...	...	...	...	...	...	...	...	...	...	...	...	...

FIG. 49.—A concomitance factor matrix (group type)

concomitance factor matrix, group-type, to distinguish it from an individual-type factor matrix, to be described next. The top row shows the several factors. The left column lists the answers, as Y_1, B_1, N_1, Y_2, B_2, N_2, Y_3, B_3, N_3, etc. The dots opposite the answers and under the factors are the loadings for the answers in the factors.

Just as an individual's concomitance matrix can be extracted from a group concomitance matrix, so an individual's concomitance factor matrix can be extracted from a group concomitance factor matrix. Figure 50

Answers	Factors														
	1	2	3	4	5	6	7	8	9	10	11	12	etc.	h^2	u^2
Y_1	...	...	...	...	...	...	...	...	...	...	...	...	...	...	...
N_2	...	...	...	...	...	...	...	...	...	...	...	...	...	...	...
B_3	...	...	...	...	...	...	...	...	...	...	...	...	...	...	...
N_4	...	...	...	...	...	...	...	...	...	...	...	...	...	...	...
etc.	...	...	...	...	...	...	...	...	...	...	...	...	...	...	...

FIG. 50.—A concomitance factor matrix (individual type).

shows an individual matrix. It was prepared by first referring to the answers which an individual gave to a test. Suppose that these are Y_1, N_2, B_3, N_4, etc. These answers are listed in the left-hand column of the individual factor matrix. The factors listed at the top are the same as those listed in the group matrix. The loadings entered in the body of the individual matrix are taken from the group matrix and are for the answers given by the individual under study. The same result could have been obtained by merely checking on the group matrix the answers that the particular subject gave.

At the extreme right of the top row of each matrix, the symbols for common and unique variance are shown; they are determined by the same operation as applied in factor analysis and have analogous meanings. The h^2 refers to common variance, and the u^2 designates unique variance.

Factor analysis of a group-type concomitance matrix involves two difficulties, for which we have at least partially satisfactory solutions: (a) There is the problem of estimating the communalities for the several answers of any one item. One rather lengthy solution to this problem is given in the appendix. Another solution is to use unities for like answers of the same item (such as $Y_1 - Y_1$) and zeros for unlike answers of the same item (such as $Y_1 - B_1$, $Y_1 - N_1$, and $B_1 - N_1$). (b) The other difficulty derives from the forced-choice nature of the responses to each test item and has been pointed out by Guilford (1952) in other situations. The answer alternatives to each item are in the forced choice pattern in the sense that the subjects are requested to endorse only one of the three answer alternatives to each item. This forces a zero interassociation (as measured by the concomitance index) between the unlike answers to any one item, for to give one answer is to avoid giving the other two answers, insofar as the subjects follow the test directions. A result of this condition is a negative correlation between the first and second factor loadings for the answers.

A suggested solution to this latter difficulty is to break the matrix of concomitance indices down, under specified principles, into three submatrices in such a way that each submatrix contains one and only one response to each item. Each of the three submatrices can then be factorized separately.

The matrices can be broken down so that the first submatrix represents the most highly interassociated pattern of answers, the next submatrix the next most, and the third one the least. Or, in other words, if the degree of interassociation of answers can be accepted as directly proportionate to personality integration, then the three submatrices are assembled according to the relative amounts of personality integration they reflect, as measured by the concomitance index. This approach allows us to realize several advantages.

This method of solving the second difficulty gives us a better solution to the first. The primary problem in the first difficulty was to estimate the communalities for such answers as $Y_1 - B_1$, $Y_1 - N_1$, $B_1 - N_1, \ldots$, $Y_2 - B_2$, etc. The test instructions require these to be zero (as computed by the concomitance index) but the subject's reactions to them in comparison with his reactions to other items may indicate them to be other than zero (see page 426). Item pairs of this kind disappear when we break down the group type matrix into submatrices. The only unfilled cells in the submatrices are the diagonals which may be estimated in one of the ways customarily used in factor analysis. For example, any diagonal cell may be filled by using as its entry the highest value in its column.

The manner of breaking down the matrix, according to the degree of interassociation of their answers, is as follows:

  a) Consider the group-type matrix of Figure 46.
  b) Consider column Y_1 in this matrix.
  c) Consider the relative sizes of the concomitance indices for $Y_1 - Y_2$, $Y_1 - B_2$, and $Y_1 - N_2$.
  d) Underline the largest of these three indices.
  e) Compare the indices for $Y_1 - Y_3$, $Y_1 - B_3$, $Y_1 - N_3$ and underline the largest.
  f) Proceed on down column Y_1; compare the three indices for each item and underline the largest.
  g) Omit the indices for item one when proceeding down the column of an answer to item one.
  h) Sum the indices underlined in column Y_1.
  i) Repeat steps (b)—(h), inclusively, for the other columns. In each column omit the three indices which are for the same item as the answer of the column being studied.
  j) For each item, select the answer column which has the highest sum of underlined indices. The answers for these columns constitute the variables of the first submatrix. The first submatrix is

prepared by (a) lifting these variables and the concomitance indices between them from the group-type matrix and (b) assem-
bling them in a submatrix.

The second submatrix is obtained in an analogous fashion from what
is left of the group-type matrix after the first submatrix has been lifted.
The third submatrix is what is left in the group-type matrix after the
second submatrix has been lifted. Each submatrix is factorized separately.[5]

The approach just outlined assumes that the loading for each answer
has the same meaning and remains relatively invariant for all individuals
who give it. An analogous assumption is involved in the usual factor-
analytic approach. There is, however, a fundamental departure from the
usual factor-analytic design (i.e., when the concomitance index is analyzed); not all subjects in the sample of a configurational design are
involved in determining the loading for an answer. This is because the
degree of association between two answers is determined exclusively by
those persons who give one or both of the two answers. This approach
would seem to allow for the loading of any answer to be more representative of those who give it than is the case in the usual factor-analytic
design, where the loading is determined by all persons of the sample. In
this sense, it is relatively consistent with clinical theory. Clinical theory

[5] Since this chapter was written, the author has realized that steps analogous to
those outlined for the group-type matrix can be applied to investigate patterns of
responses. In this application, the steps enable us to select out, from the many
theoretically possible patterns of answers to a test, those which occur empirically.
Thus far, the method has been applied to (a) hypothetical test results which derived
from hypothetical subjects, each subject being characterized by one of six response
patterns and (b) test results from mental-hospital patients and community persons
on five items of a personality inventory. In case (a), the method reproduced the
patterns and determined which subjects were "typed" by them, both operations with
100% accuracy. In case (b), the method gave promising differentiation between the
two categories of subjects on a cross-validation study.

The method can be applied to a table which shows the frequency of responses for
(a) single answers, (b) pairs of answers, or (c) triads of answers, etc. The more
concentrated patterns can usually be selected quite adequately from frequencies for
single answers. As the patterns become more diffuse, they may require that frequencies be tabulated for combinations of successively greater numbers of answers,
e.g., first for pairs, then triads, then tetrads, etc.

When a pattern is tentatively recognized, certain of the subjects are scored for the
pattern in order to determine just which subjects manifest the pattern. Only those
subjects with the smallest frequency for an answer, or combination of answers, of
the pattern are scored. No subjects other than these can manifest the complete
pattern. The subjects are scored by assigning a value of one for each answer of the
pattern given by the subject. Those who make a perfect pattern score are said to be
"typed" by the pattern. The responses of the "typed" subjects are subtracted from
the frequencies, and the resultant frequencies are searched, as before, for other patterns. The process can be repeated until all subjects are "typed."

This method of frequency pattern analysis has critical significance for both (a)
the differentiation between members of different groups and (b) the investigation of
pattern- and type-theories. It enables us to investigate (a) whether or not "types"
exist and (b) whether or not a given set of test items differentiates between all
members of two samples. In this latter case, if some subjects from different groups
have identical patterns of responses, then no method of item response weightings can
differentiate them. This method of pattern analysis will be described more completely in subsequent publications.

often insists that some test items have different meanings to various subjects and that like responses often have different diagnostic significances, depending on the other responses with which they occur. This clinical theory led us to revise factor analysis in the manner just described so that it would be more consistent with clinical theory and might therefore prove to be a more valuable tool in clinical research.

As illustrated above, by factor-analyzing a group concomitance matrix, as distinct from the usual-type correlation matrix, we automatically obtain factor patterns for each of all the possible matrices for single individuals. This would give us factor-analytic results for as many individual matrices as there are combinations of answers. In a three-answer alternative test of twenty items, there would be 3 to the 20th power, or 3,-486,784,401 matrices. Having factor-analyzed a group concomitance matrix deriving from a twenty-item test of three-answer alternatives to each item, we would have individual factor patterns for approximately three and a half billion potential individuals, all of whom differ in their answer patterns. In other words, once we have the group concomitance factor matrix, we can read an individual's factor pattern from it in a matter of seconds instead of spending weeks or months to factor-analyze the individual's concomitance matrix. We can, of course, do this for any and all individuals who take the test which has been factored for the group.

The above approach should result in striking differences in personality structure between community persons and mental-hospital patients. This statement is based on evidence from Stewart's study (1951, p. 58), where it was reported that individual factor analyses for schizophrenic patients reveal more factors, more unique variance, less common variance, and less first-factor variance than do those for community persons, and on the results from our studies in the measurement of personality integration (McQuitty, 1950b), where we reported evidence that mental patients are less integrated than community persons.

There is one reason why the individual factor patterns derived from the group concomitance factor matrix might be more meaningful than those derived from the analysis of individual concomitance matrices. Those from the group-factor matrix might reduce the amount of unique variance. This is because each answer therein would have been analyzed in relationship to three times as many answers as it would have been in the individual correlation matrix.

If this revised form of individual factor analysis should continue to develop in the manner in which it gives promise of doing, it is not difficult to see its tremendous potentialities for psychotherapy. Here we have, for the first time, an objective method of investigating an individual's personality structure in a few minutes. In addition, we have objective evidence, as earlier reported herein, of the ways in which mental patients seem to differ in personality structure from community persons. It appears, then, that we can evaluate objectively the client during the course of therapy in a very short time and specify whether or not the results give evidence of change and whether the direction of the change, if present, is toward or away from mental illness. Additional research is, of course, needed on these points.

Potential Contributions

The potential contributions of the approaches outlined in this chapter are not in any sense limited to the area of psychotherapy. They have many other potentialities in psychological theory, test-construction theory, and practical endeavors. It may be helpful to indicate some of the possibilities in each of the areas.

Psychological Theory.—The methods, together with the results thus far achieved and the hypotheses out of which they developed, would seem to suggest a compromise between Gestalt and purely atomistic interpretations in the understanding of behavior. We began with the study of ideas as elements and investigated the ways in which they are interrelated. We found that they are not static elements, but rather that they are dynamic: i.e., they seem to grow and develop in the sense that they fit into factors and become more meaningful to the extent that they are interrelated with more ideas.

The factors, themselves, would seem to be dynamically interrelated with observable behavior in the sense that our evidence indicates that mental patients are characterized by individual factors different from those of community persons.

From the point of view of the theoretical position just outlined, the most healthy-minded individual is one whose ideational life is composed of but one self-descriptive individual factor; he is one who has achieved an interrelationship among all his ideas about himself. This would suggest that he lives a self-satisfying life in the sense that all of his ideas about himself are very meaningful to him and understood by him. If it should turn out on further research that all of his ideas, not merely his ideas about self, are representative of a single individual factor, it might be appropriate to suggest that he lives a very "enriched life" in the sense that his ideas are very meaningful to him by virtue of being so completely interrelated.

Test Construction and Psychological Theory.—Eisenberg (1941, pp. 19-49) and Hutt (1949, p. 60), in their critical considerations of personality inventories, have pointed out that items have different meanings for different subjects. *This point of view, that items have different meanings for different subjects, is an implied hypothesis deriving from the theoretical frame of reference for our research design.* Just how it is implied by our frame of reference will now be outlined. We will show also how the hypothesis can be investigated and how it is, in part, substantiated by the results that we have already obtained.

We hypothesized that ideas are interrelated in the sense that to accept some encourages both the acceptance of additional ideas and the rejection of other ideas (page 422). This hypothesis would have been more definitely stated if it were not for our opinion that identically stated ideas have different meanings for different people. The hypothesis would have been more definite in the sense that it would have substituted some such word as "causes" for "encourages" and the hypothesis would have read: The acceptance of some ideas causes both the acceptance of additional ones and the rejection of other ideas.

One reason that the interrelationships between ideas are not highly obvious is that people lack a communality of ideas with exactly the same meanings for all persons. We approach a complete communality of understanding of ideas in mathematics; the elementary interrelationships there are more obvious to those who are especially well trained in mathematics. The interrelationships of elementary mathematical ideas, as measured by concomitance indices applied to well-trained mathematicians would be relatively high. In this sense, the interrelationships would be more obvious than they are in material commonly used in personality inventories. If the ideas used in personality inventories carried exactly the same meanings for all subjects, the interrelationships as we measure them would be higher.

Before outlining the meaning of these conditions for test-construction, it is interesting to consider the significance of what we have said for the psychology of error. From our point of view, the child does not make a psychological error when he says that 4×3 is 7. The interrelationships of his ideas produce the answer 7. This is because his interpretation of the situation, including *his* ideas of 4, 3, $\times$, and 7, is different from that intended by the teacher; other ideas in *his* interpretation of the situation may include, for example, fear of the teacher, a conviction that a numerical response is required, a realization that $3 + 4$ equals 7, and a belief that $\times$ and $+$ mean the same thing. The child may not be familiar with the ideational aspect of 3 and 4 which involves multiplication. In this sense, then, there is no psychological error. There is no chance response. There is complete determinism. The dynamics of the ideas involved determine the answer that is given. The only reason that persons give different answers is because different ideas are involved.

From the point of view just outlined, items on ability tests, as well as personality tests, have different meanings for different subjects. The different meanings produce different answers, sometimes the "generally accepted" or "correct" answer and sometimes the "abnormal" or "incorrect" answer. Both are caused by the interaction of dynamic ideas, and have the same principles of explanation. No hypothesis of chance reaction or psychology of error is required for an interpretation of the dynamics within the individual. However, in order to objectify conclusions about behavior, psychologists often interpret the behavior of the individual in relation to the behavior of others. In doing this, we superimpose constructs on data that seem to represent the data tolerably well—but never exactly. We always obtain deviations from the superimposed constructs. We often explain these by means of the chance hypothesis.

In the approach outlined in this paper, we have attempted to minimize the extent of dependency on the chance hypothesis. We have done this (a) by comparing the individual successively with many stratified groups, each time with that subsample which seems to be most like him in respect to responses under study (page 433) and (b) by avoiding restriction of interpretation in analyzing the data (pages 413-18 and 426).

If it be granted that the items of psychological tests are differently interpreted by different subjects, and that these differences of interpretation reflect themselves in answers, test-construction methods should take cognizance of these hypotheses. One way to take cognizance of them is to present several alternative answers for all items, based on trial runs of open-ended questions. Another way is to avoid the assumption of linearity of item responses in studying the interrelationships of answers. Our application of the concomitance index has avoided this restriction. When our group matrices of concomitance between answers (Figure 46) as distinct from correlations between tests is factor-analyzed, it is expected that the various answers to some items will have different factorial structures. This result would tend to support the hypothesis that items are interpreted differently by various subjects. They are interpreted differently in the sense that answers to them have different patterns of interrelationship with other answers. This is what was found in the four individual factor analyses reported earlier in this chapter.

Practical Endeavors.—Having mentioned some of the potential contributions to psychological theory deriving from the methodological approach here outlined, we may now indicate some of the more immediately obvious practical possibilities. *We may have here the basis for rapidly and objectively screening out people as unsuited for military service and as being in need of further diagnostic study and therapy. In addition, we may have the basis for developing an objective nosological system of mental diseases and personality types in general, together with a battery of tests for diagnosing mental diseases and personality types.*

One does not need to restrict one's self to structural analysis in his application of the configurational approach; he can include efforts toward content analysis if he wants to become concerned with methods of rotation. The simple-structure method of rotation (Thurstone, 1947, pp. 319-45) is probably applicable to the individual concomitance factor matrix to the same extent as it is to the usual-type factor matrix of factor analysis. It may even be that individual-configurational analysis may offer an approach for investigating the validity of the simple-structure approach to rotation. Rotated individual factor matrices could be compared with clinical analyses on the same subjects. Such investigation might offer some support to the theory of simple structure, or it might suggest other theories of rotation. In any event, it would seem worth while to pursue such investigations.

It is very possible that the simple-structure method of rotation is not appropriate to the group concomitance factor matrix. This is because the group concomitance factor matrix represents an overlapping assemblage of individual concomitance factor matrices. Rotation of each of these individual matrices by itself might give different results than would be obtained if the group matrix were first rotated and the individual matrices read directly from the results without further rotation. This is a problem which can, of course, be investigated. If it should turn out that simple-structure rotation is not appropriate to the group concomitance factor matrix, it might be possible to develop methods that would be appropriate.

Several Configurational Techniques

All the factor techniques, i.e., R, Q, P, O, N, and M, may now be shown to be applicable in the configurational approach. Evidence of their applicability can be introduced by referring back to the group-association matrix and showing the source out of which it is constructed.

The group concomitance matrix derives from a response matrix as distinct from a score matrix out of which the usual type of correlation matrix is constructed. A response matrix is shown in Figure 51. The top row lists the three answers to each of the successive test items. The left column lists the persons who responded to the test. The pluses indicate the answers which the persons gave, and the negatives the an-

Persons	\multicolumn{13}{c}{Answers}
	Y_1	B_1	N_1	Y_2	B_2	N_2	Y_3	B_3	N_3	Y_4	B_4	N_4	etc.
1	+	−	−	−	+	−	+	−	−	−	−	+	−
2	−	+	−	+	−	−	+	−	−	−	+	−	−
3	+	−	−	+	−	−	+	−	−	+	−	−	−
4	+	−	−	−	−	+	−	+	−	−	+	−	−
5	+	−	−	−	+	−	−	−	+	−	+	−	−
6	+	−	−	−	+	−	−	−	+	−	−	+	−
7	−	+	−	+	−	−	+	−	−	+	−	−	−
8	−	−	+	−	−	+	−	−	+	−	−	+	−
9	−	+	−	−	−	+	+	−	−	−	−	+	−
10	−	+	−	+	−	−	+	−	−	−	−	+	−
etc.	−	−	−	−	−	−	−	−	−	−	−	−	−

Fig. 51.—A response matrix.

swers that they did not give. These are the raw data from which the
concomitance indices are computed to give the entries for a group concomitance matrix. For the purpose of contrast, a score matrix is shown
in Figure 52. Instead of listing the answers in the top row, it lists the
tests or test items; the answers are listed in the cells of the matrix.

	Tests or Items			
Persons	1	2	3	4
1	Y.	B	Y	N
2	B	Y	Y	B
3	Y	Y	Y	Y
4	Y	N	B	B
5	Y	B	N	B
6	Y	B	N	N
7	B	Y	Y	Y
8	N	N	N	N
9	B	N	Y	N
10	B	Y	Y	N

FIG. 52.—A score matrix.

Reference to these matrices in relation to Cattell's covariation chart
(1946, p. 96; 1950a, p. 30; 1952b) will enable us to show how all the
factor-analytic techniques are applicable in the configurational approach.

Mowrer's redrawing of Cattell's covariation chart is shown in Figure
36, Chapter 13 of this book. Our analogous chart, a concomitance chart,
is shown in Figure 53. The R technique surface of the covariation chart
derives from score matrices like those illustrated in Figure 52. The R
technique surface of the concomitance chart, on the other hand, derives
from response matrices like those illustrated in Figure 51. As a result
of this difference in derivation, the two charts differ in nomenclature
along the top, right hand edge of the chart. In the covariation chart, this
edge is labeled "Tests." In the concomitance chart, it is labeled "Answers." The covariation chart represents different ways in which the
covariations in variables may be investigated. The concomitance chart
represents different ways in which the relative tendency of elements to
occur together in stratified samples may be investigated.

Before showing that all the factor-analytic techniques are appropriate
to our configurational approach, it is helpful to consider a difference

between these charts. This difference emphasizes a fundamental way in which the configurational approach departs from the usual factor-analytic research design.

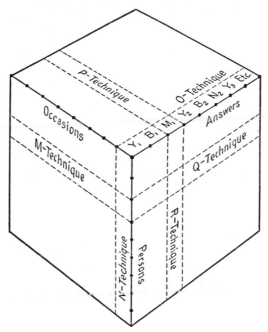

Fig. 53.—Concomitance chart based on Cattell covariation chart (Cattell, 1946, p. 97).

In the covariation chart, the investigator is concerned with how much of each variable, as measured by each test, is present in each subject. In factor-analytic studies, indices of the covariation are obtained. The indices used usually require that the test-item responses be reflections of underlying linear continua. In the case of tests of many items, it is required that the items of each test meet some criterion of linearity, or it is merely assumed that they do, and items not found to meet an objective index, or thought not to meet the conditions of linearity, are excluded. The tetrachoric coefficient of correlation, for example, involves the assumption that the dichotomized responses to each item are reflective of an underlying linear continuum.

In the case of the concomitance chart, on the other hand, the investigator is concerned with the relative tendency of attributes to be present together; he is not concerned with their tendency to be absent together. The attributes may be manifested by any category or categories of responses whatsoever. No requirement is superimposed by the concomitance index that the several answers to each item must be treated as reflective of any underlying linear variable in order that the item may be included in the study. In other words, the concomitance index superimposes less of a requirement concerning the nature of what is being reflected by a response to a test item. Consequently, results of our configurational approach may result in any type of configurational interassociations of responses and are less limited by an initial assumption.

We may now return to show that all the factor-analytic techniques are applicable to our approach. The factor-analytic techniques are outlined earlier in this book by Mowrer (Chapter 13). The analogous techniques for configurational analysis are labeled on the surface of the concomitance chart in Figure 53. They are described below as based on concomitance indices:

> R technique: between two answers as determined by the extent to which they are jointly given versus separately given by each of many individuals on one occasion
>
> Q technique: between two persons as determined by the extent to which they give identical answers versus different answers to many questions on one occasion
>
> P technique: between two answers as determined by the extent to which they are jointly given versus separately given on each of many occasions by one person
>
> O technique: between two occasions as determined by the extent to which one subject gives identical versus different answers on the two or more occasions to many questions
>
> N technique: between two occasions as determined by the extent to which many people give a particular answer on both occasions versus only one occasion
>
> M technique: between two persons as determined by the extent to which they agree in giving or failing to give a particular answer to a question on several occasions

R technique will be considered in some detail later in this chapter in a general comparison of configurational and factor-analytic analyses. Before doing this, it would seem appropriate to mention some of the potentialities of some of the other techniques when considered from the point of view of the concomitance chart which derives from concomitance indices.

It will be helpful if we first point out that a concomitance index can derive from a number of test situations other than the type with which we have thus far concerned ourselves, i.e., a list of items, each with a three-answer alternative. Our methods are appropriate to any situation where elements, i.e., responses, may be treated as present or absent. An example that will help us in talking of the Q technique is a situation in which we have, say, twenty-five personality adjectives that may be representative of some area of personality. We may request each of two persons to pick from the list of twenty-five adjectives the ten that are most descriptive of him. Suppose that the two selections contain eight duplications. Q technique, by the concomitance approach, would give an index of 0.80 for the relationship between these persons on the universe of personality sampled by the adjectives. This approach has several advantages:

1. It is very rapid.
2. It avoids the problem of mental units of measurement involved in the factor-analytic Q technique. The problem of mental units in factor-analytic Q techniques is well brought out by Mowrer in his quotations from Thomson (Chapter 13, page 331).
3. It would appear to have greater potentialities for a psychology of types, advocated by Stephenson, than does Stephenson's factor-analytic Q technique, because our Q approach avoids the linearity restrictions involved in the Stephenson approach. Instead it deals in the presence or absence of elements, i.e., responses. Through application of R-configurational technique we can isolate significant factors and learn how to sample these in application of the Q technique.

If the application of the above suggestions should prove fruitful, it might be possible to set up a group concomitance factor matrix deriving from the Q technique, from which personality types could be read in a manner somewhat similar to that in which individual factor patterns can be read from the R technique group concomitance factor matrix of Figure 49. The suggested Q technique concomitance factor matrix from which individual structure could be read might turn out to be something like the one suggested in Figure 54. This might be called a personality types matrix.

The personality types matrix might be used jointly with an R technique group concomitance factor matrix to investigate, rapidly and objectively, an individual's personality type—or "diagnosis" in the case of mental patients. We have already outlined how a personality factor pattern may possibly be read rapidly from an R technique concomitance factor matrix as a result of the person having completed a short test. The factor pattern serves as the basis for reading the particular personality type from the personality types matrix. All that is necessary is to check the subject's factor loadings in the body of this matrix. If the personality types matrix is complete, so as to represent all types, the checks would all be in a single row, and the subject would be the type represented by that row as labeled in the extreme left column. In order for this approach to be practical, there would have to be some limit in actuality on the great number of patterns of responses theoretically possible.

Personality type could be expected to be reliable in the sense that they would probably reappear even if the analysis were repeated with a different sample of personality items from the same universe. Evidence for this point derives from the finding, reported earlier (pages 428-29), to the effect that the personality structures of individuals, as here determined, remain relatively the same even though the test-items used in portraying them vary rather widely.

Types of Persons	Factors														
	1	2	3	4	5	6	7	8	9	10	11	12	etc.	h²	u²
1	...	...	...	...	...	...	...	...	...	...	...	...	...	...	...
2	...	...	...	...	...	...	...	...	...	...	...	...	...	...	...
3	...	...	...	...	...	...	...	...	...	...	...	...	...	...	...
4	...	...	...	...	...	...	...	...	...	...	...	...	...	...	...
5	...	...	...	...	...	...	...	...	...	...	...	...	...	...	...
6	...	...	...	...	...	...	...	...	...	...	...	...	...	...	...
7	...	...	...	...	...	...	...	...	...	...	...	...	...	...	...
8	...	...	...	...	...	...	...	...	...	...	...	...	...	...	...
9	...	...	...	...	...	...	...	...	...	...	...	...	...	...	...
10	...	...	...	...	...	...	...	...	...	...	...	...	...	...	...
etc.	...	...	...	...	...	...	...	...	...	...	...	...	...	...	...

FIG. 54.—A personality-types matrix.

Potentialities of some of the other factor-analytic techniques can be realized by analogies with those which we have indicated above. One will, for example, realize immediately that O technique in configurational analysis avoids the necessity of a linear continuum of answer alternatives and requires only a very short time to compute. It will, however, be helpful to consider in some detail a comparison between the configurational approach and the usual factor-analysis research design as they pertain to R technique.

Configurational Analysis vs. Factor Analysis

The concomitance chart derives from the fact that configurational analysis concerns itself with the interassociations between answers, rather than between tests, as described earlier (page 450). This type of analysis represents a significant departure in methodology from the usual factor-analytic approach. It derives from a different hypothesis concerning the most fruitful manner in which to conceive of the organization of behavior.

This difference in hypothesis can be better appreciated if we first introduce a scientific consideration common to the two approaches. Thurstone (1947), in his book on *Multiple factor analysis,* states that "This volume is concerned with the methods of discovering and identifying significant categories in psychology and in other sciences" (p. 51). Our new method has the same concern.

The two methods differ in their conceptualization of the behavioral entities investigated. Factor analysis, as generally applied, treats responses as if they are reflective of variables which are characteristic, in various degrees or amounts, of all individuals. Configurational analysis, on the other hand, investigates responses as if they are reflective of elements which are either present or absent in the characterization of individuals, as indicated by whether or not the responses are given. In addition, the type of configurational analysis with which we have thus far been concerned assumes that those individuals who give one or both of two responses are the only ones who furnish information about the degree of relationship between the responses.

The two methods also differ in portraying the organization of behavior in the individual. Factor analysis, as generally applied, determines factors of average man by analyzing coefficients of correlation which are representative of man in general. The organization of behavior in each individual is portrayed by stating where he stands on each of the factors of average man. Configuration analysis, on the other hand, selects out those indices of association which are more or less peculiar to each individual and analyzes them to obtain factors which are presumably somewhat peculiar to the individual. Each individual's factor pattern is stated in terms of these potentially more individualized factors.

In configuration analysis, the extent to which the factors are individualized is, in general, lesser when an individual's factor pattern is determined from a group-type factor matrix rather than from the individual's matrix of indices of association. Nevertheless, the pattern is still probably more individualized than it would be if it were determined by the usual method of factor analysis.

Factor analysis results in individual differences in standing on a relatively fixed system of factors. Configurational analysis probably results in individual differences in both the nature of factors and the proportionate influence of whatever ones turn out to be common to several individuals.

Qualitative differences in factor analysis, as generally applied, are limited to individual differences in the configurations of standings on the factors. In configurational analysis, it is at least potentially possible to obtain qualitative differences between individuals in the nature of factors themselves and consequently, of course, in the factor pattern.

It would appear then that configurational analysis provides a new and perhaps very fruitful approach to the statistical study of both qualitative and quantitative differences in behavior.

Both factor analysis and configurational analysis agree in expressing responses as a linear function of primary causes, i.e., factors. This is inherent in the factor-analytic operations applied by both approaches. In this sense, then, configurational analysis is dependent on the achievements of those who have contributed so much to factor theories, methods, and techniques, especially to Spearman (1927, Appendix) and Thurstone (1931, 1935, 1947).

Types of Configurational Analyses

We have pointed out that the type of configurational analysis with which we have thus far been concerned assumes that those individuals who give one or both of two responses are the only ones who furnish information about the degree of relationship between the responses. An alternative assumption results in another type of configurational analysis, with all the technical possibilities of the first type.

The alternative assumption is that both those who fail to give responses and those who give them furnish information about the interrelations of responses. Application of the tetrachoric or some other coefficient, which conceives of the two or more responses to each item as reflective of an underlying and continuous variable, as represented in so many factor-analytic studies, represents a restricted approach to the possibilities here present.

An untried variation is to allow for more than two categories of responses to each item and to determine the interrelationship between all pairs of responses on a "given"-"not given" basis for each response. This approach, unlike the usual factor-analytic approach to categorized data, could result in studies of the single individual, just as the first type of configurational analysis can. It would, in fact, represent a second type of configurational analysis. We may think of the first type as *response-oriented configurational analysis* because in computing indices of association between pairs of responses it is concerned exclusively with those individuals who give one or both of the two responses. The other application of configurational analysis we may call *population-oriented configurational analysis* because it considers all members of the population, as represented by the sample, in computing indices of association between pairs of responses.

In *population-oriented,* just as in *response-oriented,* configurational analysis we could probably obtain individual differences in both the nature and number of factors, in the loadings, and in the factor patterns. The difference between *population-* and *response-oriented* analysis would derive from the fact that the association indices involved in the population analyses pertain to an *average of the population.* In the other type, the association index for each pair of responses derives exclusively from those persons who give one or both responses of a pair. In other words, the individuals involved in computing each coefficient are those who are somewhat more like the subject than is the population as a whole. This approach assumes that appropriately selected samples of subuniverses of people are best for computing the degree of integration reflected by a pair of responses. Population-oriented analysis, on the other hand, assumes that the population as a whole is best for determining the degree of relation reflected in pairs of responses.

Based on the two tentative conclusions of a previous study by Mc-Quitty (1953), the two alternative methods, *population* and *response,* would appear to be fruitful for the assessment of personality integration in different areas of test content. The two tentative conclusions from which this expectancy derives are as follows:

a) Maximum personality integration is achieved in the objective realm by reflecting majority opinion.

b) There are various combinations of material representing relatively high integration in the subjective realm. To achieve maximum integration here does not require that one reflect majority opinion.

The terms "objective" and "subjective" from the above quotation are used with the same meanings as defined earlier in this chapter (pages 428-29). The quotations suggest that response-oriented configurational analysis would be fruitful for the study of personality integration in the subjective realm, and that population-oriented configurational analysis would be fruitful in the objective realm.

Rotation methods applied to individual factor matrices from population configurational analyses might give results quite similar to those obtained by first rotating the group-factor matrices and then reading the individual-factor matrices therefrom.

Potentialities of Configurational Analysis

Configurational analysis treats each answer alternative to each item of a psychological test as reflective of the presence or absence of a behavior characteristic, depending, of course, on whether or not the alternative is endorsed. Factor analysis, on the other hand, restricts the interpretation of the data by assuming that the successive alternatives (or some dichotomy of them) are reflective of various amounts of an underlying variable, usually treated as a linear continuum in computing coefficients of correlation. That the configurational approach may be fruitful in personality studies is indicated by the fact that personality studies which incorporate the restriction of factor analysis have resulted in relatively low common factor variances, i.e., low compared with those for intelligence test items (McQuitty, 1942). That elimination of the restriction may be helpful is indicated by our analyses of the single individuals which produced relatively high common variances for personality items (pages 433-38).

We have referred to a study which compared common-factor variance accounted for on intelligence and personality test items to indicate that configurational analysis may be more fruitful than factor analysis in the study of personality. This does not mean that we are of the opinion that factor analysis is more fruitful than configurational analysis in the study of ability. In fact, our expectation is the reverse. Our expectation is based on the following conditions:

1. Much of the variance determined by factor analysis in many ability test items is unique, i.e., error variance and reliable variance peculiar to the specific test (Demaree, 1950). It may be that, by avoiding the above indicated restriction of factor analysis, we could account for more of the variance in a more meaningful way, such as in terms of common variance rather than error or specific variance.

2. Successive answers to an ability test item, in order to be reflective of an underlying linear continuum, have to tap areas in which all subjects are relatively equally familiar. This is usually accomplished by preparing items from areas frequently experienced by all subjects, or, on the other hand, from areas seldom, if ever, experienced by any of the subjects. It would seem that, in order to obtain items reflective of linear continua, we have usually restricted ourselves to areas in which individual differences in experience are minimized. Test items from the opposite type of areas may prove more fruitful for psychological research if we are able to supply methods more appropriate to their investigation. Configurational analysis gives promise of being one such method, in the sense that it imposes less restriction on the interpretation of the data; it is not limited to the interpretation of individual differences in standings on common factors; it can investigate the various ways different individuals interrelate characteristics to produce factors.

One reason that results on most psychological tests seem to have so little relationship to what people do in everyday life may be that the restrictions of usual methods of measurement force a search for items relatively uninfluenced by individual differences in experience. Without the limitation of such restrictions, we might be able to construct tests more closely related to the behavior of people in everyday life. Support of this interpretation is contained in our measures of personality integration as a means of discriminating between community persons and mental-hospital patients (McQuitty, 1938, 1941, 1942, 1949, 1950a, 1950b, 1951, 1952a, 1952b, 1953) together with Stewart's results (1951) from application of our configurational analyses to the study of patients and community persons.

Garrett (1946) has maintained that intellectual ability of the young child is relatively undifferentiated and that it becomes differentiated as the child has experiences. Studies of abilities by Thurstone (1938) and others have shown that these differentiations can be isolated as factors by the methods of factor analysis. It is our hypothesis that they can be more adequately represented by factors if configurational analysis is employed. One reason that we have scatter on intelligence tests may be that we attempt to describe the responses of the individual in terms of a linear continuum which is appropriate to the abstract average man but not to the individual. These suggestions can, of course, be investigated by applying both factor analysis and configurational analysis to the same data.

Configurational analysis can be expected to incorporate experience-influenced test items more effectively in its study than can factor analysis as usually applied. This is because the approach does not exclude those items whose answers do not reflect a linear continuum. Many investigators (Stoddard, 1949, pp. 340-92) have reported evidence that certain experiences are associated with increases in the IQ. Since configurational analysis is adapted to the study of items influenced by experience, it might be helpful in investigating the influence of experiences on the IQ. It is here suggested that it might be possible to discover differences in the ability-factor patterns of individuals who have had quite different experiences in those areas maintained by many investigators to influence the IQ.

A configurational analysis of ability data in conjunction with personality data might reveal that personality factors develop out of ability factors and deviate more from linearity in their manifestations than do ability factors.

The hypothesis that personality factors develop out of ability factors, i.e., are an extension of them, is suggested by some of the other hypotheses, results, and interpretations outlined earlier in this chapter. The results of our configurational analyses reported herein, giving personality structure differences for patients and community persons, developed out of the study of the interrelationships of ideas. It is our tentative interpretation that these ideas have bases in the intellectual factors of the persons concerned. This interpretation suggests that psychotherapy involves intellectual learning, i.e., the discovery of integration through intellectual activity. Some material is much more difficult for certain persons to learn than it is for others of equal general intelligence. This may be because such material is more inconsistent with the ideational configurations of some people than of others. Lecky (1945) has pointed out the influence of consistency versus inconsistency in the development of ideas. Our configurational methods of investigation may result in findings which will give objective quantitative support to Lecky's position.

Our configurational approach might serve as a basis for assisting in directive methods of counseling. If we can isolate the ideational, or attitudinal, factors of clients, we may be able to offer therapeutic suggestions that are more likely to be accepted by the client. One advantage that client-centered counseling may have over most directive methods may grow out of the possibility that self-suggestive integrative solutions are more internally consistent with all the personality factors of the client. If we can assess these personality factors more adequately—and configurational analysis promises that we can—we may be able to become more effective with the directive methods of counseling.

The above paragraphs have outlined some of the potentialities of configurational analysis. These as well as other possibilities can be investigated by the approach outlined in this chapter. The approach was outlined in relationship to the hypotheses which suggested it and in conjunction with results from preliminary investigations. These results support the hypotheses and give evidence that the approach represents an objective and meaningful method of appraising personality. *If* these promises continue to be borne out and *if* the approach is developed further, then the method should be particularly helpful in psychotherapy, personnel selection, and education from both the scientific and the practical points of view. In addition, the general approach would then appear to have the possibility of contributing significantly to theory in the fields of personality and test-construction in particular and also of psychology in general.

Appendix: Estimating Communalities for an Association Matrix

This appendix is concerned with estimating the numerical values to be entered in such cells as $Y_1 - Y_1$, $Y_1 - B_1$, $Y_1 - N_1$, $B_1 - B_1$, $B_1 - N_1$, $N_1 - N_1$, $Y_2 - Y_2$, $Y_2 - B_2$, $Y_2 - N_2$, $B_2 - B_2$, $B_2 - N_2$, $N_2 - N_2$, $Y_3 - Y_3$, $Y_3 - B_3$, $Y_3 - N_3$, $B_3 - B_3$, $B_3 - N_3$, $N_3 - N_3$, etc., of the response concomitance matrix of Figure 46. A form of the following solution to the problem was first developed by Roger Stewart.

	Y_1	B_1	N_1	Y_2	B_2	N_2	Y_3	B_3	N_3	Y_4	B_4	N_4	etc.
Y_1	...	...	...	...	...	...	...	...	...	...	...	...	...
B_1	...	...	...	...	...	...	...	...	...	...	...	...	...
N_1	...	...	...	...	...	...	...	...	...	...	...	...	...
Y_2	...	...	...	...	...	...	...	...	...	...	...	...	...
B_2	...	...	...	...	...	...	...	...	...	...	...	...	...
N_2	...	...	...	...	...	...	...	...	...	...	...	...	...
Y_3	...	...	...	...	...	...	...	...	...	...	...	...	...
B_3	...	...	...	...	...	...	...	...	...	...	...	...	...
N_3	...	...	...	...	...	...	...	...	...	...	...	...	...
Y_4	...	...	...	...	...	...	...	...	...	...	...	...	...
B_4	...	...	...	...	...	...	...	...	...	...	...	...	...
N_4	...	...	...	...	...	...	...	...	...	...	...	...	...
etc.	...	...	...	...	...	...	...	...	...	...	...	...	...

FIG. 55.—A frequency-response matrix.

We will first outline the logic of the solution and then report the statistical details.

The values of concern are unknown because the entries for corresponding cells of the frequency of response matrix shown in Figure 55 are unknown. Each cell of this latter matrix shows how many subjects of the sample give both of two responses. Cell $Y_1 - N_2$, for example, lists the number of subjects who responded "yes" to the first item of the test and "no" to the second item. If any of the cell values of either matrix can be estimated, the estimates for them can be applied to compute the corresponding values of the other matrix. In addition, if the cell values for $Y_1 - Y_1$, $B_1 - B_1$, $N_1 - N_1$, $Y_2 - Y_2$, $B_2 - B_2$, $N_2 - N_2$, $Y_3 - Y_3$, $B_3 - B_3$, $N_3 - N_3$, etc., i.e., the diagonals, of the frequency matrix are known, then the other values of concern are determined, provided we assume that the numbers of persons giving each response, Y_1, B_1, N_1, Y_2, B_2, N_2, Y_3, B_3, N_3, etc., is constant for equal-size samples of the same universe. Now the diagonals of the concomitance matrix can be estimated as in factor analysis. The usual method there is to accept the highest entry in the column as the best estimate of the diagonal entry. The diagonal estimates can be used to compute the diagonal frequency entries of the frequency-of-response matrix. All that is necessary is to solve for $\overline{aa}$ in the following formula:

$$Caa = \frac{\overline{aa}}{\sqrt{a \times a}}$$

where

$a =$ the number of individuals giving any particular response,

$Caa =$ estimate of communality for the response as given by the highest index that the response has with any other response of the study, and

$\overline{aa} =$ number of persons who would be expected to give a both the first and second time if all of the reliability of the response is determined exclusively by factors which it has in common with other responses of the study.

By transposing the formula,

$$\overline{aa} = Caa \times \sqrt{a \times a}$$

By application of this formula, to responses Y_1, B_1, N_1, Y_2, B_2, N_2, Y_3, B_3, N_3 etc., we can estimate the entries for the diagonals of the frequency matrix. Once these are known, the others are determined and can be computed as shown below:

Let:

a) $\overline{YY}$, $\overline{BB}$, and $\overline{NN}$ equal the estimated values, as computed from the above formula for any item;

b) Y, B, and N equal the number of subjects who give each of the three answers, respectively, to the items; and

c) $\overline{YB}$, $\overline{YN}$, and $\overline{BN}$ equal the unknown cell entries to be computed for the item.

Then:

d) $\overline{YN} = Y - \overline{YY} - \overline{YB}$

e) $\overline{YN} = N - \overline{BN} - \overline{NN}$

f) $\overline{YB} = B - \overline{BB} - \overline{BN}$

Subtracting (*e*) from (*d*):

g) $0 = Y - \overline{YY} - \overline{YB} - N + \overline{BN} + \overline{NN}$

h) $\overline{YB} = Y - \overline{YY} - N + \overline{BN} + \overline{NN}$

Adding (*f*) and (*h*):

i) $2\,\overline{YB} = B - \overline{BB} + Y - \overline{YY} - N + \overline{NN}$

j) $\overline{YB} = \dfrac{B - \overline{BB} + Y - \overline{YY} - N + \overline{NN}}{2}$

Analogously:

k) $\overline{YN} = \dfrac{N - \overline{NN} + Y - \overline{YY} - B + \overline{BB}}{2}$

l) $\overline{NB} = \dfrac{B - \overline{BB} + N - \overline{NN} - Y + \overline{YY}}{2}$

Formulae (*j*), (*k*), and (*l*) can be used to compute the missing values of the frequency matrix, Figure 55, and these plus the estimated diagonals in conjunction with a concomitance index can be used to compute needed vacant cells of the response concomitance matrix, Figure 46.

CHAPTER 17

CHANGES IN VERBAL BEHAVIOR DURING PSYCHOTHERAPY

By O. Hobart Mowrer, Ph.D.

Oratio imago animi.—Language most shows a man: Speak, that I may see thee. It springs out of the most retired and inmost parts of us, and is the image of the parent of it, the mind. No glass renders a man's form or likeness so true as his speech.

Ben Jonson, Timber, 1641

Neurosis as Communication Pathology

Language: Some Definitions and Theory.—Language, in even its most sophisticated developments, is dependent upon the primitive process of signaling, i.e., upon the making and understanding of *signs.* And signs, we quickly discover, are of two kinds: inadvertent and intentional. The odor which an animal emits or the shadow which a hawk makes as it soars across the sky is a sign of the first type; they occur, so to say, automatically, unavoidably, and the organism responsible for them would often be better off without them. But where signs are *made,* i.e., where they may be said to be an aspect of *behavior,* they fall into the second category, and it is this type of occurrence from which language, as we know it at the human level, springs.

Using a different phraseology, Zipf * (1949) has made the same distinction, as follows:

If ages ago an individual made a stereotyped outcry of pain or flapped a fin with spontaneous joy at the sight of food, and if some other individual of the same [or a different?] species inferred therefrom what kind of action was happening or impending, then speech, in the above restricted definition, will have occurred. . . . This view is essentially that of the "bow-wow" theory of speech, and all animals with stereotyped cries (or smells or gestures) indulge in speech. In our usage in later chapters we shall call this the language of the species, or the *language of physiology* (p. 151).

On the other hand, as soon as a dog barks, or lifts up his paw, for example, in order to evoke a particular kind of response, and if the bark, or paw-lifting, is not the result of an automatic physiological act, then *cultural speech* has occurred if any other individual understands it correctly. Thus when the dog

* References are to the bibliography at the back of the book.

barks in order to beg for his supper, and his master understands, then the two have a cultural vocabulary in common, and *cultural speech* has occurred (p. 152).

We can avoid the teleology implied by Zipf's use of the phrase, "in order to" (and likewise the voluntarism suggested above by the term "intentional") by saying simply that signs in the second sense are items of behavior which are perpetuated, not as incidental products (like odors and shadows) of other processes or actions, but as responses which are likely to prove rewarding, or functional, in the context of social interaction.[1] While no harm is probably done by referring to these two types of signs (the inadvertent or "physiological" and the intentional or "cultural") as "speech," we make a serious error, however, if we equate either of them to *language* as we know it in human beings. De Laguna (1927) has cogently observed that it is only when an organism begins to *combine* two (or more) signs of the second type in a particular way that true language emerges. This special manner of combining signs is the phenomenon which grammarians refer to as *predication* and can be illustrated in a number of ways.

True language, or predication, is operating when, for example, one organism influences the subsequent behavior of a second organism with respect to a third organism (or thing or place) when the latter is *not present*. Thus, if A says something (makes signs) to B about C which causes B's subsequent behavior with respect to C to be modified, it is clear that A must have been able to make, and B to understand, a sign which "stood for" C. In order to accomplish this feat, an organism must be able to use and understand a special type of sign, one which, so far as we know, has been mastered only by man. A mother hen can cry the chicken equivalent of "is dangerous" when a bird of prey swoops overhead, or she can cluck alluringly, and thus imply "is good," when she has discovered food; but she has no sign for "hawk" or for "food"—or for any other *thing*. Various animals make signs which function as the equivalents of verbs, adverbs, adjectives, exclamations, and possibly other "parts of speech," but they have no *nouns,* and they are thus forever barred from the special type of signaling activity which occurs so prodigiously among human beings. The only "sentence" which an animal can make is one wherein a signal which serves as predicate is tacked onto a "subject" which is present physically, rather than symbolically. Thus, in order for a mother hen to teach her chicks the proposition "A hawk is dangerous," the best she can do is to wait until a hawk is visibly present and then cry, "is dangerous!" She cannot, in other words, quietly and in advance of actual danger instruct her chicks in the hazard of hawks some leisurely afternoon when the sky is clear and there is no immediate threat from such creatures.

---

[1] All signs which occur in the inanimate world, even though perceived and usefully reacted to by living organisms, thus fall into the first category.

Perhaps the most concise way to describe this limitation in the use of signs by infra-human organisms is to say that they cannot *abstract,* in the sense of having signs which can be used to *re-present* other organisms, things, and events in their absence. A moment's reflection will show that with the development of this capacity, man's remote ancestors took a momentous step forward which no other organism has yet negotiated. As Susanne Langer (1948) colorfully observes, "Between the clearest animal call of love or warning or anger, and a man's least, trivial *word* [particularly if that word be a *noun*], there lies a whole day of Creation—or in modern phrase, a whole chapter of evolution" (p. 83).

It may be that some unusually intelligent pets or domestic animals become capable of *understanding* a few simple sentences, and it is almost a certainty that under laboratory conditions two initially neutral stimuli could be conditioned to separate meanings so that when combined they would function as the subject and predicate of a true sentence. There is, however, no indication that any organism other than man ever *makes* such a meaningful combination. Even in the so-called "talking birds," where sentences or even series of sentences may be learned and repeated ("parrot-like"), the indications are that these entertaining performances are merely elaborate substitutes for the social chattering and singing that go on in a state of nature with other members of the same species. Thus, when a certain versatile parakeet says the first stanza of "Mary had a little lamb," [2] the bird is certainly not *telling* us anything about either "Mary" or a "lamb" but is instead merely expressing, conjecturally, its desire for some sort of response or attention on the part of its trainer or others or is perhaps merely entertaining itself in the autistic manner described in detail elsewhere (Mowrer, 1950, chaps. xxi and xxiv, 1952e, and 1953b).

The unique quality of human language, namely meaningful predication, has been missed by a number of writers. For example, no less a student of such matters than Zipf, in the context of the passages already quoted, has said:

The difference between physiological and cultural speech may be a fine line, but it is an important line, since once the second step of emitting a *conventional* signal has occurred, then there is no dynamic difference between that single conventional signal and the most highly elaborated syntactic speech of man, except for the size of the *n* number of different signals (p. 152).

As we shall presently see, Zipf has concerned himself long and usefully with researches on the variety and numerousness of human *words*; and it is therefore not surprising if, in his preoccupation with them, he has missed the special importance of sentences.[3] But it has now been

---

[2] A commercial recording of this performance can be purchased through *All-Pets Magazine.*
[3] In the book cited, there is no reference whatever to sentences in the index.

established by a number of investigators that although human words, taken singly, are often not much different (except probably for "nouns") from the signs which are made and meaningfully reacted to by lower animals, the articulation of words into sentences is a phenomenon not to be found anywhere below the human level.

Neurosis and the Communicative Process.—Language, as just defined, may serve either of two different functions; one of these leads to psychological and social health, the other to psychopathology.

In the preceding section it has already been implied that the principal function of language is *communication,* and it goes without saying that in order for this function to be maximally serviceable from a social standpoint it must be *realistic,* i.e., there must be maximal congruence between verbal statements and the phenomena to which they refer. From their earliest years, children are schooled in *honesty,* verbal misrepresentation being seriously disapproved. And well it may be, for a society of language-using organisms cannot operate effectively if its members are continually "crossing-up" one another by statements which are untrue. Even a single inaccuracy in directions or information may be a cause of very considerable inconvenience, not to say disaster; and the injunction not to bear "false witness" was certainly a familiar one long before Moses visited Mount Sinai.

Since language is a complex affair, we would expect, in any event, that children would have some difficulty in learning to use it with fluency and precision; but there is a source of difficulty which is incomparably more serious. As we have already seen, the principal, certainly the *approved* use of language is that of communication; but language can be used, or rather abused and perverted, to another type of purpose. Language may be used not only to communicate but to confuse and deceive, in which event purely private, short-term ends may be served, but at the expense, in many instances, of social ends—and indeed also of the long-term interests of the individual.

Used in its appropriate social context for purposes of communication, language is ordinarily rewarding, to maker and responder alike. For one thing, it effects a stupendous saving of effort. This point was brought home to the author many years ago by the following incident. A little boy of five had had such an anomalous and disorganized upbringing that he either would not or could not use speech, yet he seemed to have normal native intelligence and speech organs. One morning, at the institution where he was under treatment, he did not wish to have cereal put into his bowl. He pushed it away repeatedly and, while pointing to his bowl, made various grunts and expressive (but unintelligible) facial and eye movements. Presently the attendant said: "Peter, *show* me what you want," and the little boy promptly led her some distance, through two adjoining rooms, to a refrigerator. When this was opened, the child pointed to a bunch of bananas and was perfectly content when one of them was taken back into the dining room and sliced into his bowl. How very much simpler—both for him and the attendant—it would have been if he could have *told* her what he wanted![4]

This illustration, multiplied a million fold, may convey some sense of the phenomenal social utility of language. But there is a different sense in which language may be "useful": it may be used to conceal, to *keep* information, rather than to make it common, or communal. Language can, in other words, have powerful *subjective* uses which may or may not be consistent with its objective uses. And it is therefore not the imperfections or errors in language usage which occur on a mere trial-and-error basis that cause most trouble, but the temptation every child (and adult) experiences deliberately to misuse language in the interests of protecting himself or herself from consequences which would follow if language were used accurately, honestly.

The noncommunicative or subjective functions of language cover a considerable range. It has been shown elsewhere (Mowrer, 1950) that in talking birds, and probably also in human infants, the first utterance of words is on a purely autistic, rather than upon an instrumental or communicative basis. At this stage, word noises are made, not because they tell anyone anything, but because they *sound good*, i.e., are comforting and interesting, to the user. In poetry, song, and fiction there may be, in adults, a reversion to this primitive level of language functioning; but here we are warned, implicitly if not directly, that we are just *playing* with words, simply having fun with them, and that in this context they have little or no necessary reference to "truth" in the sense of objective reality. And likewise in dreams, whether by night or by day, things are "said" primarily because of the satisfactions they bring the user, rather than with the exacting, business-like objectivity of real life.

Now these autistic or "artistic" functions of language are different from, though not wholly unrelated to, the abuse of language that occurs in calculated deception. In the latter case language is used with a definitely social purpose, but the purpose is not the normal one; it is not to inform or instruct the hearer realistically, but rather to mislead or deceive him in such a way as to make life easier for the speaker than it might otherwise be.[5] At an early age almost every child discovers independently, if not by example, and experiments with, the possibility of reporting that he has done things which he has not done or that he has not done things which, in fact, he has; and so great are the possible gains in this type of behavior that it can be effectively discouraged only when parents and others penalize it and themselves set a good example in this respect. The temptations to use language in this socially perverse

---

[4] Kasanin (1946) quotes Sullivan's definition of language as a means of "getting what we want and saving us experiences we do not want."

[5] As we have already seen, language normally serves to reduce effort and pain; its abnormal use may be said to involve an attempt to extend this function beyond its natural limits. See Mowrer (1953a and 1953b).

way are very great, and the issue as to whether the child will surmount or succumb to them is of central importance for subsequent character development.

A preliminary view of the problem suggests that in the life history of every neurotic person there has been considerable social deception; but it should be noted at once that deception does not necessarily lead to neurosis. Deception is not pathogenic when, because of guilt, it is either confessed to or is apprehended by others and is followed by its "natural consequences." Nor is it pathogenic, in the sense of leading to neurosis, when the misrepresentation occurs in a setting in which parents have not been much concerned about honesty and the individual has himself internalized no very exacting standards on this score. But where high standards have been held up to, and internalized by, the child, deception, if not confessed or apprehended, is likely to weigh heavily upon conscience. The child may have succeeded by his misrepresentations in averting the social consequences of his actions (or inactions), but he does not avoid the internal, *psychological* consequences; and it is at this point that the individual faces a fateful choice. He may, on the one hand, decide (depending upon past experience, intelligence, etc.) that the guilt feelings are intolerable and that the only practical solution is to make a clean breast of the whole matter and "take one's medicine." Or the child may feel that this course of action would be too painful, that he would be treated unfairly, or that all the fuss about honesty is, after all, of no importance and conclude that the logical solution is to turn and *attack* the internal source of discomfort, namely the conscience proper. In Chapter 3 detailed attention has already been given to the course of events that is likely to transpire when such a campaign of conscience repudiation is embarked upon (see also Mowrer, 1950, chaps. xix, xx, and xxii). Suffice it here to recall that, as the strategy of conscience dissociation or repression is consolidated, the seeds of neurosis are firmly planted.

Neurosis, we thus discover, can be defined, simply and precisely, as a *disturbance in communication.* It starts (quite universally, it seems) with social deception which is succeeded, sooner or later, by a breaking of relations with conscience. Ego and superego, or conscience, are no longer on "speaking terms." No longer can conscience make itself "heard" by merely "whispering" to the ego; it is now silenced (at least for the time being), and when at length it again succeeds in speaking, it is in the (to the patient) unintelligible, bizarre, and frightening language of neurotic affects and symptoms. Since conscience is the individual's most intimate link with parents and with human traditions and values in general, it is not surprising that the individual who has established an "iron curtain" between ego and superego soon begins to feel isolated, cut off, alone, lost, frightened.[6]

---

[6] The neurotic also often complains of a sense of "unreality." But this "unreality" is of his own making, reality having been progressively delimited and distorted by his evasions, deceptions, rationalizations, and dissociations.

The current view which is most widely held is, of course, that neurosis arises when a person breaks, not with the moral or social aspects of his heritage, but with his *biological* heritage. Particularly by Freudian analysts—whose influence on general thought has been enormous—is it assumed that the neurotic is a person who has been so thoroughly, indeed so excessively civilized or "humanized" that his animal needs suffer to the point that he is psychologically crippled, if not incapacitated. And in support of this position it is common practice to cite the fact that "sex" seems to be involved in virtually every instance of neurosis. However, there is a possibility here of causal misattribution. Sexual episodes may be so generally associated with neurosis, not because sexual impulses fall under too powerful inhibition, but because —how shall we best say it?—because the chances are so good that deception with respect to tabooed sexual activity will be successful! The sexual escapades which one finds with such great regularity in the life history of neurotics may be pathogenic, not because they result in "fixations," "inhibitions," "frustrations," or any of the other hypothetical states which the Freudians have popularized, but because these episodes mark the inception of strategies of parental deception and ensuing repudiation of conscience. Other persons, persons who do not become neurotics, have almost certainly had many of the same experiences as far as sexual activity itself is concerned, but they have missed neurosis either because they were apprehended, themselves reported these experiences, or had so little character that there was no internal protest from conscience because of the act and/or the attendant deception. The specific source of pathology is thus located, not in sexual behavior as such, but in the practices with respect to communication and concealment into which the person may be driven by such behavior. We thus pass from a *sexual* theory of neurosis to a *deception theory*.

If one steals (anything, that is, except information), something of a physical nature must be transferred from one point in space to another; and while it may never be found, it will almost certainly be missed and vigorously searched for. Murder, likewise, is something that cannot be committed in the abstract, without leaving a *corpus delicti*; and the fact of arson is only too painfully apparent, however unavailable the arsonist himself may be. But many proscribed forms of sexual behavior can be engaged in—solitarily, with animals, or with other human beings—with no very tangible or obvious results. In many instances, it is only conscience that is in a position to persecute the sexual transgressor; and it is therefore most often in the control of sexual activity that neurotic, i.e., deceptive and dissociative, tendencies have their beginnings and find their most powerful reinforcement. But, be it noted, the basic pathology is moral (interpersonal) rather than "libidinal." Disturbances in sexual functioning—frigidity, impotence, precocity of ejaculation, obsessive thoughts of incest or homosexuality, etc.—may appear symptomatically, as a consequence of neurosis, but only rarely, if ever, as its fundamental cause.

Another way of describing current conceptions of neurosis is to say that it is caused by an individual's *believing too much*. Freudians have taken the position that in the neurotic the superego is "too severe," i.e., makes the individual feel that certain impulses and actions are "wrong" when, by common standards, they are not. General semanticists have charged the neurotic with overgeneralizing, with either-or categorizing, and with reification of words (see page 538). And learning theorists, when they have ventured into the realm of psychopathology, have most commonly portrayed neurosis as a failure of extinction and discrimination, i.e., as a tendency to make responses long after they cease to be realistic and rewarding. But in all instances there is a common emphasis upon a learned *excess* of some sort—too much fear of punishment, too much confidence in words, or too great "habit strength"—responsibility for which is commonly laid at the door of parents and other socializers of the young.

However, in the frame of reference we are here exploring, it is not believing too much that makes human beings neurotic; it is instead their tendency to *report too little*! Because honest and precise use of words sometimes leads to painful (though, in the end, usually useful) consequences, there is, as we have seen, a tendency to use words dishonestly and unprecisely; and when this strategy is followed by uncomfortable *internal* consequences, there is likely to ensue a battle with conscience which, if successful from the standpoint of the ego, institutes the condition termed "neurosis."

Here we need not pursue the question of whose responsibility or "fault" it is if a child becomes such a self-defeating evader, rather than a healthy accepter, of consequences. Whatever one's theory of neurosis, parents are undoubtedly important, and good ones are better than poor ones. But it is nevertheless of some significance whether we see neurosis primarily as a matter of what has been *done to* the patient or as an expression of what he himself is *doing*, or *failing to do*.[7] Whoever or whatever it was that started any given individual on a neurotic career, ultimate responsibility for recovery rests with the patient himself (assuming that he is now an adult, rather than a child, and that the individual has not become so disorganized as to require institutionalization). For just as neurosis itself is more properly characterized as

[7] This line of thought has an obvious bearing on the question of whether it is in the *past* or the *present* that one finds the causation of neurosis. Of this much we may now be sure: no one ever has a neurosis who is not *currently* practicing dissociations and deceptions. In this sense, the causation of neurosis lies in the present; but if one is to identify the circumstances which disposed an individual to take the path of evasion rather than that of consequence-facing-and-taking, one must, of course, go back along the life-history dimension. The extent to which it is necessary thus to explore and understand "the past" for the patient to recover from neurosis is arguable. In principle, neurosis can be eliminated simply by helping an individual to move from essentially dishonest personal and interpersonal strategies to honest ones, with or without analysis of developmental experiences. In practice, however, it appears that such an exploration is commonly helpful, perhaps indispensable. Cf. Chapter 3, especially those passages dealing with transference as "therapeutic regression."

something which the patient himself does, rather than the product of what has been done to him, so is therapy much more a matter of what the patient himself learns to do and not to do than of what the therapist, by way of "treatment," does for or to him. In short, both neurosis and therapy are *active* processes from the standpoint of the patient, and in both instances the processes involved are intimately related to the phenomenon of *communication*.

This is not the place to elaborate a comprehensive theory of psycho-pathology, but the perception of neurosis as a form of communication pathology highlights the rationale of treatment in some interesting ways. One of these is shown in Figure 56 and Figure 57. In the first of these

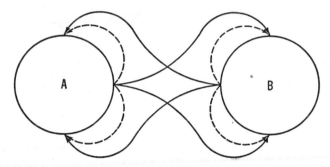

Fɪɢ. 56.—Schematic representation of two persons (A and B) engaged in normal conversation. The solid lines represent the flow of sound from the mouth of each speaker to the ears of the other person. The broken lines represent the flow of sound from the mouth of each speaker to the speaker's own ears. Two types of "feedback" thus operate in the case of each speaker: (*a*) from speaker to listener and back to speaker (solid lines) and (*b*) from speaker directly back to speaker (broken lines). There is, of course, also the possibility of purely internal or neural feedback from what one is saying—or merely thinking. But no attempt is made here to represent the circuits of "association pathways" thus involved.

figures we see, schematically, the relation of two persons engaged in *normal* conversation. When individual A speaks, he is heard not only by individual B but also by himself (see the broken lines); and likewise, when individual B speaks, the sound waves fall upon his own ears as well as upon those of A (broken lines). In ordinary discourse we are thus, in a sense, "talking to ourselves" quite as much as to others, and we are continually responding to our own verbal behavior as much as (indeed sometimes more than!) others do.[8]

But in neurosis this picture is altered, in the manner indicated in Figure 57. Here, because of the dissociations and defensive barriers which the neurotic has erected, the individual does not allow himself

[8] Fairbanks (1951) has reported a preliminary study with human subjects in which a brief delay is introduced in the "feedback" from mouth to ear, with results which show how continuously we "listen" to ourselves while speaking. The neurotic, of course, hears his own speech well enough in the physical sense; but it is at the psychological level, at the level of having relevant associations and making indicated inferences (see page 544), that intrapsychic communication breaks down in his case.

to "hear," in the sense of associating fully to, what he himself is saying (or thinking); and it becomes the function of the therapist to listen attentively—with what Reik (1948) has termed the "third ear"—and then, little by little, by means of interpretations, "make the unconscious

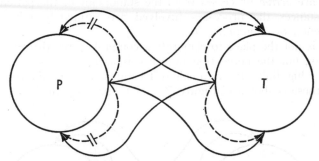

FIG. 57.—Schematic representation of a neurotic person (P) and a therapist (T) engaged in therapeutic conversation. This diagram is the same as the one shown in Figure 56, except that there is a barrier which prevents the patient from "hearing"— in the sense of clearly perceiving the implications of—what he himself says. (This barrier is, of course, *within* the patient, but it is here shown as external to the patient for the sake of simplicity.) Therefore, in order for such a blocked or "dissociated" person to recover the ability to associate freely and to understand fully what he himself says (or thinks), someone else (the "therapist") has to listen and then talk back (interpret) to the patient in such a way as to circumvent the defenses and barriers which the patient has erected.

conscious." The therapist, in other words, sees ("hears") connections which the patient will not allow himself to see and wages a campaign of association, in opposition to the patient's dissociative trends. The therapist in a very real sense *undoes* the patient's dissociations, bypasses his defensive barriers, and in this way performs a function for the patient which the latter has become unable to perform for himself. Step by step, with the therapist's aid and support, the patient recovers this ability and in so doing moves from neurosis to normality, from chronic, irreversible dissociation to determined, consistent association.[9]

[9] At this point we find ourselves on the horns of a dilemma. In the preceding pages emphasis has been placed upon the extent to which "responsibility" for neurosis and recovery therefrom rests with the patient; and we have just now had occasion to stress the role of the therapist in opposing the patient's dissociative trends. Without such opposition the confirmed neurotic is presumably unable to "help himself" and is therefore *not* "responsible," not response-able. How can this seeming contradiction be reconciled? First of all, it is our objective (and that of the healthy part of the patient's own personality) to replace the habit of dissociation by the habit of association. Our goal is therefore not to change other persons or the patient's physical environment in order to make him more comfortable *as he is;* it is rather to produce change *in the patient,* but in that part of him which has to do with *habits,* with the methods of solving problems. Much current thinking stresses the patient's conditioning, his emotions and feelings; and these are seen as the product of things that have happened to him. In the latter frame of reference it becomes the therapist's responsibility to give the patient new, more benign experiences, new conditioning, comfortable emotions to replace the negative, hampering ones. The present approach, by contrast, stresses the shortsighted, self-defeating habits or personal and interpersonal strategies which the patient has learned and,

We must not lose sight of the fact that management of internal conflict by dissociation is rewarding, just as in the use of deception in situations involving a potential clash of interpersonal interests. But this reward, or "reinforcement" in the sense of learning theory, is likely to be a short-term affair in both instances, with ensuing social and psychological pathology. When the strategy of deception and dissociation has begun to "backfire" on an individual, the discomfort, interpersonal and intrapsychic, may be very great; and it is these sources of discomfort which the therapist, in favorable cases, is able to rely upon as "therapeutic motives," as the forces which can be pitted against the immediate satisfactions provided by dissociation.[10] Therapy is therefore an operation which is shot through with ambivalence, for the reason that the therapist's interpretations, associations, inferences ("interferences," from the patient's standpoint) deprive the patient of the satisfactions which dissociative solutions have provided; but they may also bring profound relief in the sense of making once again intelligible to the patient situations which had been "parataxically distorted" (Sullivan's term) to such an extent that he or she could no longer understand them rationally or cope with them realistically.

---

consciously or unconsciously, is "using"; and the task of the therapist is, in large measure, to place the patient in a "learning situation," by blocking old habits and creating circumstances in which more permanently satisfactory ones can be acquired. (For fuller development of this analysis, see Chapter 6.) Reduced to its simplest terms, the solution to the dilemma cited above goes as follows: The therapist cannot acquire new habits (of honesty and consistency) *for* the patient; he cannot, that is to say, implant or bring about, by surgery, drugs, or any other kind of "treatment," the necessary neural changes. But what he *can* do is to bring to light (by interpretations) the self-defeating character of old habits, help the patient understand their nature and origin, and then stand, with upraised, warning arm, in the path of the patient when he subsequently starts to revert to these strategies. Thus we come to see that "therapy" is genuinely a matter of "client-counselor collaboration" (Perry and Estes, Chapter 4). Neither counselor nor client can do the job alone; there must be an appropriate *division of labor*. It is therefore not a question of the therapist being active ("directive") and the patient passive or of the therapist being inactive ("nondirective") and the patient active; instead *both* must be active, both must be "doing therapy," both must be working at the collaborative task from the standpoint of the particular part of the task which *each* has to perform.

[10] It used to be the practice, in psychoanalytic circles, to distinguish between neurosis and "character neurosis." It goes without saying that in the present setting there is no such distinction. In the writer's experience, *every* neurosis involves basic character problems, for reasons which have been sufficiently indicated above. Not every character problem or defect necessarily leads to neurosis; such problems may, for example, lead simply to personal demoralization or psychopathy, without neurosis. But the reverse relationship seems invariant. No problem of character (morality, ethics, integration, interpersonal relations), no neurosis! (From this statement it might be inferred that therapy involves trying to "strengthen the superego." This does not follow. The neurotic has a sufficiently strong superego; his neurosis is testimony enough of this. The "character problems" here referred to are mainly in the ego region of the personality and importantly involve denial, repudiation, dissociation of the superego. The therapist does not need to strengthen, weaken, or otherwise modify the superego. His task is rather that, and solely that, of opposing the dissociative trends within the patient and between him and other persons; when this function is effectively carried through, the "strength," and also the specific content, of the superego will take care of itself.)

All of this is well illustrated by the following excerpts from the forty-second interview with a young married woman. At the beginning of therapy she suffered from what was to her a totally incomprehensible inability to go out alone or to shop, save under the most restricted circumstances. The details of the case need not be given here except to say that the symptom, upon analysis, turned out to be an expression of the patient's self-criticism, self-condemnation, and guilt on the score of evasion and duplicity which she had long practiced. More specifically, it became evident that she was being a poor mother to her five-year-old daughter, was being somewhat rejecting of her, and often felt "just *hateful*" toward her. The source of this hostility, it developed, was the patient's own self-anger and shame at behaving so immaturely herself while supposedly setting a model for her little girl to follow. The powerful negative feeling she had toward this child was really projected self-hate and contempt. Said otherwise, the child and the mother role this young woman felt obliged to play threw her into an intolerable conflict with both external authority and her own conscience, a conflict which she had never fully worked through and reconciled. By the end of the forty-second interview the picture was clear, at least in outline, and the patient immediately returned to it at the outset of the forty-third interview in these words:

> Last time, towards the end of the session, it just came out that the reason I felt so anxious about going downtown was some difficulties with Josephine. Well, I thought about it quite a bit; and I, I just hadn't admitted it to myself, but I clash, we *clash* a great deal. Sometimes, well, I, I even get afraid of my feelings, because they are so *strong* toward her, in a negative way. I mean, it, it's so hard for me to say because I, I don't even like to admit it to myself, and because I know it's such a wrong thing to do, and it's bad; but, well, sometimes I just, I just feel she's in my *way* and she makes me nervous! And I don't want to *bother* with her. Sometimes I'm real nice to her because I feel so terrible *guilty,* that I've done something *wrong* with her, that I haven't treated her right; and I buy her things and do things for her, in a very superficial way. Sometimes even my feelings toward her feel like they don't come from within me; they don't come from my heart at all. They're just *put on,* because I feel that I haven't been treating her right. She even sometimes asks me, "Do you like me, mother?" or "You haven't been nice to me today, and I haven't been bad." And she makes me feel so terribly guilty, too, and, and for good reason! Sometimes when she strikes me the wrong way, I just get, I just get, I'm *afraid* of my feelings, they're so terribly strong! I just get so *furiously* mad [an explosive sigh] that sometimes I really have to control myself. Then I, she is [sobbing] just an innocent little child as yet, and she hasn't done anything against me. I brought her into this world, and here I, well, I don't know what to say about it.

After verbalizing the feeling that, now her little girl is getting older, motherhood places certain "demands" upon her, the patient continues:

> I suppose the minute demands are put upon me, I clash against them or I can't carry them through. And I've always—particularly now that I've been going through therapy—I realize that I've clashed with anything that's forceful, or that's demanded upon me, or that's asked of me in a forceful way, and I can't—. She [Josephine] was all right and I loved her, and everything, when she was a baby; . . . but as she gets older, I realize my shortcomings and that I fail in my, uh, position as a mother, and so of course, it makes me very irritable. And, well, I become very impatient, and sometimes I just really feel *hateful* toward her. I don't know exactly why, and I don't want to really admit it to anybody, or even to myself, because it's, I *know* it's the wrong thing to do.

The patient expresses the feeling that the problem of her relationship with her daughter has become increasingly acute since the birth of a second child, another little girl. She says:

> I have noticed I *have* been neglecting the older one due to the fact that the little one [who does not yet make the same moral demands upon the mother] substituted in her place. And I have good reason to, when I go downtown now, I know now I have a very good reason to feel guilty. I just overlooked that completely, and I just pushed it out of my mind. . . . I just completely *disregarded* these feelings, and I haven't *admitted* them. But after the last session and my realization that I didn't want to take Josephine downtown and didn't want to explain to her my difficulties, I realized that, that I just felt *ruthless* about the whole thing. . . . I didn't at all realize my responsibility toward the children; and, well, in a way, I also feel that I'm just emotionally not mature enough even to know how to handle it the right way. [Patient finds herself in the type of "learning situation" described in footnote 7.] Anyhow it's [laughing], it's something entirely new; I've never even thought about that, and it's, it's, I always thought everything was perfectly all right there. I just *told* myself it was.

At this point there was a pause and the therapist remarked:

> It's evident that these feelings and thoughts have a lot of meaning and, and power for you; and the fact that you could come in at the beginning of the hour today and turn immediately to them and go to work on this is, I think, a sign of real growth.

The patient then resumed, and it is in the following that the mixture of pain and relief which is so characteristic of the breakup of dissociations is most dramatically portrayed:

Well, it, it, they upset me *terribly,* because I [sobbing], well, I, I just disregarded it entirely. I just didn't think it, uh, I didn't *want* to think that I was that kind of a person. Well, I, I'm terribly happy that I can come in here and talk about it, because it's been on my chest, and I would like to get it off. I don't know exactly *how,* but I'm terribly glad that I can finally *talk* about it and, and that I even *know* what it is! I just always said to myself everything was all right there and never realized, or didn't *want* to realize that, that it wasn't all right. I was really, or am really, afraid of my feelings because sometimes I just get really terribly hateful feelings that I, that I know I shouldn't have. So I right away say to myself, "Well, I'll push them away; they aren't really there. I don't have those feelings; they're all *wrong.* A mother *can't* feel that way toward her child. It's impossible! It's improper and immoral!" I don't know, I just say to myself how *wrong* it is! And I just haven't exactly figured out what brought them on or why I should feel that way toward her, except one reason: I know I do feel resistive. She demands certain things which I know I wasn't, or am not capable of giving her, so—uh. Maybe she [laughing], maybe she bothers my conscience too much, which irritates me.

The lengths to which human beings will sometimes go in attempting to deal with powerful internal conflicts is again illustrated in the following excerpts from the third interview with an unmarried woman in her early thirties who had had a great deal of difficulty with masturbation. Toward the end of the interview, in summarizing his associations to the patient's productions during the hour, the therapist commented as follows:

So the mixup that you've gotten into can be very simply described as follows: You have very high standards for yourself as a person, in terms of integrity and consistency and honesty and so forth. You believe that honesty is, is important; and yet in a number of areas, in a number of situations, mostly apparently having to do with sex, you have not taken the consequences of your actions. You have not done a thing and admitted it and taken the consequences; but you have, in order to avoid consequences, you have gone *against* a very definite set of values in yourself, namely those of honesty and consistency and courage and so on; and I think the self-condemnation, the self-reproach, and this kind of loss of satisfaction in living, loss of respect, self-respect, self-confidence has come, not from any of these particular incidents that you have related, but from the loss of respect in connection with the way you've handled them.

Now this, again, is not anything unique at all. It's a quite regular pattern in the development of neurosis. One can state it quite simply as follows. I'm now convinced that *every* neurosis is preceded by deception and evasion, by *interpersonal* deception and evasion. Well, as I say, that alone may not lead to neurosis. First of all, the person may not, his conscience may not bother him, or he may get caught. But, in the event that he does *not* get caught and his conscience *does* bother him, then he has the problem of what to do about conscience now. And fighting with a well-developed conscience is, is pretty tough. You can't very well run off from it, because it goes with you. And it's not an easy thing to cope with, so that real neurosis starts at the point the person begins to deny conscience, begins to repudiate it or dissociate it or repress it. And it's not clear whether your difficulties have ever gone over into neurosis, full-fledged neurosis, because it's not clear that you have succeeded in denying your guilt very successfully at any time. You've certainly struggled with it and *tried* to live it down or deny it, ignore it; but I'm not sure how successful you've been in the strategy of dissociation or denial, conscious denial of these feelings.

At this point the following brief but eloquent exchange took place between patient and therapist:

P.: Uh, uh [clears throat], uh, in connection with this masturbation, I, I couldn't *stand* myself afterward. I thought I was too horrible, and I finally, it was, I was really doing my *utmost* to stop it and to, I don't know, it, it dawned on me more and more that I just *couldn't* stand myself. It was just repulsive to me! I couldn't, I *hated* myself for doing that. And I got so I would think of myself as two people, one, the person that did those things and then me, myself, I wasn't really that way. Of course, I knew all the time I was kidding myself, but I tried to put it out of my mind that way.
T.: You tried to dissociate in that way, by attributing certain values to one person and another set of values to another, separating them in this way.
P.: Yes, it sort of helped. It, it made life bearable, but it wasn't something that I could forget, anyway, really. It went through my mind all the time.

Another patient, a male graduate student (not in psychology), some months after successful completion of therapy, returned spontaneously for a visit with the therapist, who asked him if he would mind describing what therapy had meant to him, how he now perceived it. These are his words:

P.: Well, I'm sure that I can't state it very clearly, but I think that I would call therapy a slowly regained sight for a blind person, as an analogy. When I first went into therapy, I had no understanding of my problems. I couldn't state them; and if I could state them, I, uh, I couldn't *isolate* them from the emotional context. I could not look at myself, or anything else, logically and *clearly*. All I would see would be a jumble. It's a miracle to me how I ever got through the first couple of years of graduate school; and I think I did it by a very mechanistic business of just simply rote memory, without stopping to *think* about things. And I think my analogy of the blind slowly regaining sight is good from another respect, from another angle, because—let's see how I want to put this. It's like you're living about a tenth of a life when you go into therapy. You are afraid to experiment in life—afraid to experiment with friends, with people, with situations, especially *social* situations. In other words, you can't *see* what's going on, and, not being able to see, you have really no conception of what is missing.

T.: You have the insecurity of the blind man, as well as his—.

P.: Yes, exactly. And I would say that would be a definition of the first part of therapy. And during the middle stretches, there is, as far as I could tell in myself, there is merely an enhancement in my willingness, my ability to talk about myself, but still without much understanding. . . . And then, *very* slowly, a little light leaked in, a little bit of understanding, a little bit of assimilation; but still a period of reliving unhappy experiences, with a little understanding of it, but just enough to make myself want to understand more. And, all of a sudden, I was sort of over the hump. Come the revelation! And yet it wasn't like any bolt of lightning. It was like pulling a cloud from my mind, and *there* were all the thousands of pieces, fragments of personality, lying around; but now they could be seen, now they could be understood, now they could be reassembled. And the great joy of everyday discovering a little something new, and a new correlation. "Well, this fits in *here* and this is why *this* happened." Not nearly as clear as that, of course. But, all of a sudden, therapy, instead of being quite painful, quite disturbing, became a very pleasant experience. . . . Then, at the end of therapy, was where another piece of learning had to be done. I had to come to some conclusion, that, although these hours were very pleasurable, the time was fast approaching when I was wasting both our time, and that I was just coming back hour after hour because it was a pleasurable experience. . . . I think making the decision to end therapy is almost the most important step in therapy. . . .

T.: Therapy is a curious thing. . . . It's as if you were looking at some sort of irridescent stone, and you hold it in one light and it has one color and you put it in another light and it has a different color. And as one's experience in this field grows, one keeps seeing different possible angles from which one can look at therapy. One that has interested me recently is one that I think squares pretty well with your perception of therapy. . . . I had an experience this fall when I got back from the East that illustrated it. Under the pressure of other duties, last year there were a number of things around my office that I didn't get done and that I might usefully have done, like filing things and getting things tidied up; and I found that when I actually got around to doing these things I located a number of things that I had misplaced or lost track of. And I had the feeling of being better "organized," of *knowing* now where things were, of having them *accessible* and *usable,* and at hand. Thus your description of the blind man getting so he could see seems to me quite parallel. The neurotic is a person who, in the past, has preserved himself by sort of progressively destroying himself. Whenever something bothered him, he would lop it off, so to say, throw it away, discard it, push it under the rug. But that process can apparently go only so far until it tends to backfire. Certainly one of the aims of therapy is to help recover these bits of self that have been—not destroyed, since they're recallable—but have been ignored, pushed aside. And, of course, you ignore enough of these things and you get to the point that there's not much of "you" left, and you don't function very well.

P.: Yes, I think that's what I meant by using the analogy of the blind man. His field of experience, as compared to the field of vision, becomes *so* small, as more and more experiences become painful, or nonpleasurable, that when, in spite of himself, he has to deal with something outside this deliberately restricted field of experience, then he definitely shows neurotic behavior, and is unable to cope with situations, situations which have perhaps been a part of his personality before they were lopped off. . . .

I've noticed, in myself, quite often, that the first tendency of mine, when a situation comes up that formerly brought forth a neurotic reaction, is toward that neurotic reaction; and then, immediately, I catch it and back off from it. . . . And I really think that is what therapy is for, to teach a person to cast sort of an amused, skeptical eye on himself and say, "Oh-oh, watch this; this is no good."

T.: . . . Yes, I feel that the therapist has a very definite responsibility to attempt to locate, to interpret, to attempt to explain, and to pose really these, well, I can't think of any better term than *self-defeating,* short-term strategies, strategies that have a short-term gain and a long-term loss.

P.: I can give you a very clear example of this from my own experience with therapy. I would go off on these rambling, incoherent statements about nothing in the first few weeks of therapy, and you would say: "Now I may be wrong, this is just a sheer guess, but I think that perhaps this is what you're saying." Now this interpretative business is very important, because if the patient sees, early in therapy, that he can couch his emotions and statements in almost any language he pleases and still the therapist will have enough intuition, enough experience in these matters, to really see what he's talking about, then the tendency to be vague, the tendency to evade the responsibility for one's statements will be less. In other words, my first few weeks or months of therapy, I used to feel quite resentful, *very apprehensive* when one of these, "Now, I am not sure, this is a sheer guess, but here is what I feel about it." But, in the last few months of therapy, I used to await these things, with very pleasant expectations, to see where my own reasoning had gone wrong and how to straighten it out. In other words, it's the difference between the very emotional outlook of the patient early in therapy and the more rational outlook later on. . . .

T.: In other words, in the beginning the interpretations are threatening [P. Yes, very!], [11] but then as the patient begins to gain some satisfaction and strength from the associative tendency, then he begins, as you say, to look forward to these, and to utilize them, instead of feeling threatened by them.

It will be a long time before our objective research in the area of psychotherapy becomes as deeply revealing as a direct perusal of our patients' own words. But verbatim accounts of the transactions between patient and therapist leave much to be desired. For one thing, these, in their entirety, are voluminous and scrutiny of them is extremely time-consuming. Therefore, we very much need devices—graphs, ratios, indices, and the like—which will enable one to see at a glance something of the over-all course of therapy. This, of course, becomes especially important if one wishes to make a systematic comparison of many different therapies. Moreover, we now have growing evidence that in the course of therapy certain changes occur which neither patient nor therapist directly perceives. Nor are these changes apparent to another person who, as he reads interview protocols, focuses upon the *meaning* or communicative function of language. They become evident only when one looks at language specimens analytically, quantitatively—one may almost say, *mechanically*. The second half of this chapter will be devoted to a consideration of such approaches.[12]

---

[11] The immediate reaction of patients to interpretations, to the re-establishment of old, painful connections, is well illustrated by the following comment, made by another male patient toward the end of the eighteenth interview. The therapist had just interpreted a bit of transference behavior and had put it into the context of the patient's claustrophobia. Said the patient, after a pause: "I found that suggestion rather gruesome. It, uh, momentarily I had an increase in apprehension. Uh, in terms of, Would I appear foolish if I were to get up and walk out? This business of, Are the halls lighted, and is the stairway? Could I get downstairs and outside? Just, just as you were talking." Under similar circumstances a woman patient recently remarked: "It makes me extremely angry to hear you say that, yet I know it's true." And another: "That sounds perfectly horrible! I don't *want* to control him, yet I'm doing it, in some ways."

[12] In the foregoing pages neurosis has been identified as a form of communication pathology, and therapy has been seen as an effort to improve communication between the patient and others and between different areas of his own personality. But no attempt has been made to liken this approach to the type of formal communication, or "information," theory developed by Shannon and Weaver (1949), among others (see, however, pages 536-44). Recently Cronbach (1952) has used the Shannon-Weaver approach as a basis for discussing the rationale of diagnostic testing, with interesting results. How much relationship, if any, exists between our references here to neurosis and therapy as problems in communication and Cronbach's discussion of testing remains to be explored.

Empirical Studies of Language in Psychopathology and Psychotherapy

Whitehorn and Zipf (1943), in a study which will be considered in more detail presently, have written an admirable introduction to the second half of this chapter. They say:

> Considered simply as behavior . . . speech productions are impeccably objective. Indeed, for the study of behavior, speech has one striking advantage—it can be subdivided into specific and definite acts with great certainty. Words are almost universally recognizable and identifiable as distinct and separate actions. No other type of behavior lends itself so well to unequivocal report and analysis (p. 831).

There is likely to be a flowing, almost liquid quality about nonverbal behavior which makes it very difficult to quantify in its totality. We can isolate specific "acts"—such as a rat's getting through a maze or pressing a Skinner bar—but much of the concomitant behavior is lost, save as the experimenter makes observations which he himself is likely to characterize as "incidental," "unsystematic," or "qualitative." But as the writers just cited imply, in language the ongoing sequence of activity is fractionated relatively fully and automatically into conventional units, namely *words*—a fact which enormously facilitates the problem of quantification.[13]

Yet the quantitative approach to language behavior has been very slow in developing. By the turn of the century, many of the basic present-day methods for the study of nonverbal behavior (especially in animals) had been delineated, but it is only within the past decade that there has been a real burgeoning of quantitative approaches to verbal productions. On the writer's desk is the last issue of one of our psychological periodicals, in which four of the eleven articles comprising the issue are devoted to some aspect of quantitative language inquiry. Such a high incidence of interest in linguistic problems is not generally found in our psychological journals today, but articles of the kind cited are certainly much more common than they were a decade ago.

The line of development is especially germane to research on psychotherapy, for here our data are pre eminently verbal. As Brody, Newman, and Redlich (1951) have recently observed, in psychotherapy "verbal behavior is of paramount importance," and the gradual perfection of electronic recording over the years has at last made this source of data fully available for scientific scrutiny. Our task, now, is to

---

[13] Whitehorn and Zipf, in stressing certain objective approaches to the study of language, acknowledge that words have meanings as well as purely behavioral properties. They say: "We do not intend to imply that the content of speech—what one means to say—is of no consequence, but we are reporting here on interesting characteristics of form—ignoring content" (p. 832). As we shall see later, there are indications—cf. the work of Osgood (p. 530 ff.)—that even the subjective aspects of language may now be yielding to relatively precise quantification.

discover fruitful means of processing these data. A number of promising possibilities have already been reported in this connection, and these will be reviewed and supplemented here by reference to some new, previously unreported methods or possible new applications of older ones.

Zipf's Contributions to Language Analysis.—Over a period of twenty-five years of unremitting research, just ended by his untimely death, George Kingsley Zipf has probably done more than anyone else to implement the belief that language can be studied "with the same dispassionate objectivity with which one is wont to study, say, the social behavior of bees, or the nest-building of birds" (Zipf, 1949, p. v). Here it will not be possible, or relevant, to attempt anything like a comprehensive review of his work, but its main lines can be quickly grasped. Many of Zipf's major inquiries have as their point of departure the extremely simple—and obvious (after someone else has provided the example)—procedure of systematically counting and comparing the relative frequency of different words in any given verbal production.

To give concreteness to this procedure, let us take as a specimen the four paragraphs which constitute the introduction to the second main part of this chapter (pages 481-82, excluding the footnote and the quotation). Operationally, the procedure consists merely of listing each new word as it appears and of putting one tally after it and an additional tally for each subsequent repetition. When one is through, one has as many words listed as there are *different* words in the specimen, and by adding all the tallies one obtains the *total* number of words.

This type of procedure is likely to prove surprisingly interesting and instructive. One of the first things that becomes apparent is that the words on which one first begins to get repetitions are, in general, very short ones. For example, in the present specimen, the word which first appears a second time is "in"; this repetition is found in the beginning sentence. And as a counterpart to what has just been said, one finds that as one gets toward the end of the specimen, the only new words are relatively long and, necessarily, less common ones. Immediately below are given the first ten and the last ten words in the list, with the frequency of their occurrence indicated by the tallies:

Whitehorn /	reviewed /
and ⁄⁄⁄⁄ //	supplemented /
Zipf /	reference /
in ⁄⁄⁄⁄ ⁄⁄⁄⁄ /	new //
a ⁄⁄⁄⁄ ⁄⁄⁄⁄	previously /
study //	unreported /
which ⁄⁄⁄⁄	possible /
will //	application /
be ///	older /
considered /	ones /

It is clear from inspection that the last ten words are, on the average, longer than the first ten; and actual count shows that the average length of the first ten words is only 4.5 letters, whereas the average length of the last ten words is 8.0 letters. It is also apparent that most of the latter words occur only once in the specimen, while some of those in the first ten occur many times.

The tendency for the frequently used words to be short and for the less frequently used ones to be longer is shown even more strikingly by the two columns reproduced below. These two columns are, respectively, the first ten words and the last ten words in the list of all words used in the present specimen, arranged in the order of their frequency of occurrence (see numbers in parentheses). Words which occur only once in the specimen, or which tie for frequency of occurrence at any other level, are ordered in terms of the sequence of their occurrence in the specimen itself.

of	(21)	connection	(1)
the	(19)	reviewed	(1)
in	(11)	supplemented	(1)
a	(10)	reference	(1)
is	(10)	previously	(1)
to	(10)	unreported	(1)
and	(7)	possible	(1)
which	(5)	application	(1)
behavior	(5)	older	(1)
as	(5)	ones	(1)

As simple computation will show, the average length of the ten words most frequently used is 3.0 letters, while for the last ten words which occur only once in the specimen the average number of letters is 8.7.

Bousfield and Barclay (1951) have shown the same tendency to be operative in a different type of situation. They asked different, but comparable, groups of college students to list, respectively, as many *birds, carpenter's tools,* and *celestial bodies* as they could think of. Part of the results are shown in Table 14. Here it is apparent that the most commonly recalled, and probably also the most commonly used, words within any given category were considerably shorter than the less commonly recalled (used) words. Furthermore, it will be noted that the average length of words representing carpentry tools was 2.08 syllables; for the birds, 2.45; and for the celestial bodies, 2.76—a sequence which probably corresponds, roughly, to the relative frequency with which we have occasion to use words in one or another of these categories. Tools we refer to fairly often; birds perhaps less often; and celestial bodies—unless we are meteorologists, astronomers, astrologers, or lovers—fairly infrequently.

Zipf (1949) gives results obtained from a much larger language specimen which indicates the typicality of the results already cited. In a study by R. C. Eldridge of 43,989 running words taken from a col-

TABLE 14*

MEAN SYLLABIC LENGTHS OF ASSOCIATES AND THEIR FREQUENCIES OF OCCURRENCE

Birds Listed by Group I (100 Subjects)			Carpenter's Tools Listed by Group II (58 Subjects)			Celestial Bodies Listed by Group III (60 Subjects)		
Frequency of Occurrence	Items	Mean Syllabic Length	Frequency of Occurrence	Items	Mean Syllabic Length	Frequency of Occurrence	Items	Mean Syllabic Length
1	105	2.90	1	168	2.77	1	114	3.11
2	35	2.69	2	37	2.32	2	21	2.81
3- 4	30	2.87	3- 4	31	2.16	3- 4	19	3.05
5-10	27	2.26	5- 7	25	2.08	5-14	19	2.63
11-28	27	2.33	8-13	21	1.52	15-59	17	2.18
29-49	26	2.12	14-58	21	1.62			
51-98	21	2.00						
	271			303			190	

* This table is reproduced, with permission of the authors and publisher, from Bousfield and Barclay (1951). It shows that in three classes of words—names of birds, carpenter's tools, and celestial bodies—there is an inverse relationship between word length and frequency of spontaneous recall (and presumably, also, use).

lection of American newspapers, Zipf found that a group of the most frequently occurring words had an average length, in phonemes (a phonetic rather than alphabetical or syllabic unit), of only 2.666, whereas the 2,976 words which occurred least frequently (only once each) averaged 6.656 phonemes in length.

From data of the kind cited, Zipf has formulated what he refers to as "the law of abbreviation of words," which holds that there is an "inverse relationship between the lengths of words and the frequency of their usage" since "the work of uttering a longer word is greater than the work of uttering a shorter one" (1949, p. 63). According to this law, long words, if commonly used, tend to be contracted into shorter ones—e.g., " 'phone" replaces "telephone"—and shorter words tend to replace, and thus become more common than, longer ones—e.g., "car" replaces "automobile." In sum, common words become short and short words become common. Only in the case of relatively uncommon words do we long abide the inconvenience of great length.

It is apparent that in Zipf's law of abbreviation we are dealing with a phenomenon of seemingly great stability and generality. Whether it can be turned to clinical advantage, i.e., whether it will reveal characteristic differences *between* individuals or *within* individuals on different occasions (let us say, before and after therapy), remains to be determined. It is conceivable that neurotic needs may make some persons pedantic and polysyllabic and that, following therapy, their speech would become simpler and more direct. But it is equally possible that neurosis might have a restrictive, stultifying effect on speech and that therapy might release the individual to use more varied, less usual words.

Trends of the kind just suggested might be detected in either of two ways. They might show up, first of all, simply as changes in average word length.[14] While variation in average word length may well occur as a result of therapy, there is no a priori reason to suppose that there would be great consistency in the nature or direction of the resulting changes. This, of course, would be a simple matter to check and might yield some interesting findings.

A second approach, and one more directly related to the law of abbreviation, would involve a study of word length *as a function* of frequency of use. The only study of this kind known to the author which has clinical implications is one recently reported by S. J. Baker (1951). Baker introduces his study as follows:

The present paper proposes to examine the relationship between the words in the word-frequency list of a single individual and the form [length] of

[14] In this connection one might profitably peruse the recent literature on the "Flesch index" (Flesch, 1948, 1951, 1952). Contrary to the intimation of the originator, it has not been found that writers who use the shortest words are necessarily the most intelligible or interesting (Stevens and Stone, 1947). Also related is the work on Basic English (Richards, 1943). Here communication is achieved by means of a few relatively short words, but at the price of much circumlocution. Maximal speech economy probably normally justifies a considerably larger vocabulary containing a good many of the longer and *more specific* words.

those words. . . . In two earlier papers I have drawn extensive statistical evidence from a series of forty-four letters written by a woman named Mrs. Dravoldi to a newspaper editor in the space of slightly more than two months. This correspondence contains more than 45,000 connected words. As part of an analysis of this woman's linguistic habits, I broke down the first 40,000 connected words of her correspondence to establish a word-frequency list. It emerged that Mrs. Dravoldi used a total of 3,081 different words in the course of writing 40,000 connected words. Of this total, 1,492 occurred only once (pp. 235-36).

Fortunately, for purposes which will be discussed later, Baker has published the resulting frequency list, down to (but not including) the words that occur only once. On the basis of these data, Baker obtains the curve represented by the broken line in Figure 58. As the legend explains, the solid line is a comparison curve, based upon normative data gathered by Thorndike (1921) and by Horn (1926). Although Mrs. Dravoldi, on the basis of the content of her letters (which the editor to whom they were addressed neither published nor acknowledged), would be diagnosed as mentally deranged (Baker suggests paranoid schizophrenia), it is striking how closely her writings correspond to those of a " 'normal' cross-section of the writing public" which Thorndike and Horn studied, with respect to Zipf's inverse relationship between word length and frequency of use.

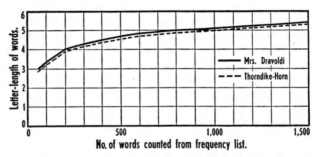

Fig. 58.—Graphic representation of the relationship between frequency of word usage and word length (Baker, 1951). As will be seen, this relationship is almost exactly the same for a mentally disturbed person ("Mrs. Dravoldi") and for a norm established by Thorndike and Horn. Within the limits here tested, the method is manifestly insensitive clinically.

The Baker results, while involving a comparison of only one individual with a standard criterion, suggest that the principle or law of word abbreviation is so basic, so general, so stable that it may have no utility either for diagnostic purposes or for showing the results of change produced by psychotherapy. Certainly if a patient mumbled a single word or phrase repetitively or talked "word salad," the relationship between word length and word frequency would be distorted. But if we remind ourselves that ordinary language is a *conventional* mode of behavior and that it has been *phylogenetically* evolved, it will not be surprising if this index shows no significant individual differences so long as the individual examined is attempting to communicate—and this is virtually a prerequisite for psychotherapy, or at least for a type of psychotherapy from which abundant verbal protocols are likely to be obtained. So long as a patient is sufficiently "in contact" to be able to address remarks to another person, the indications are that the law of abbreviation will apply to his utterances in essentially the same way as it applies generally; and if this be the case, then the prospects are not very good that his utterances will change measurably in this respect as an outcome of therapy.

But the law of abbreviation is not the only induction which Zipf has made as a result of empirical word counting. He has also derived the "law of vocabulary balance." However, unlike the assumptions underlying the law of abbreviation, which are few and simple, those underlying the law of vocabulary balance are more complex and not always fully explicated. Therefore, in order to avoid possible confusion, let us approach Zipf's own discussion of the second of his major principles somewhat obliquely.

Returning to the illustrative specimen taken from the present chapter, we find that after the words are listed in the order of their occurrence and tallied for frequency (see page 482), we can rank-order the 207 different words involved with respect to their frequency. Taking all words with a frequency of occurrence of three or more, we obtain the list reproduced below:

Rank Order	Word	Frequency
1	of	21
2	the	19
3	in	11
4	is	10
5	to	10
6	a	10
7	and	7
8	as	5
9	which	5
10	behavior	5
11	but	4
12	been	4
13	our	4
14	this	4
15	language	3
16	has	3
17	be	3
18	verbal	3
19	are	3
20	data	3
21	for	3
22	have	3
23	quantitative	3

When the words appearing in our specimen are thus rank-ordered, a number of considerations emerge:

1. Once again, we see the popularity of little words. Thus six of the eight most popular words have only one or two letters (none over three), and there is a noticeable increase in word length thereafter, as popularity declines.

2. It is clear that while the very structure of the English language tends to dictate frequent use of certain words, the appearance of other words—in this case "behavior," "language," "verbal," and "data"— are indicative of the topic under discussion. Thus, it is suggested that the relative frequency of words is somewhat influenced (not at all surprisingly) by the nature of the topic or topics under discussion. It is therefore apparent that we should differentiate between *structural* and *topical* determinants of word usage.

3. Likewise, it emerges that some words will have the *same* frequency of occurrence, and that the number of such words increases as the frequency decreases. Thus, we find that in the original frequency list, which is not fully reproduced here in order to conserve space, there are 29 words that occur twice and 155 words that occur only once.

The partial frequency list reproduced above is represented graphically in Figure 59. If the 29 words which occur only twice and the 155 words that occur only once were included in the curve shown in this graph, a very long asymptote would extend out to the right, suggesting a hyper-

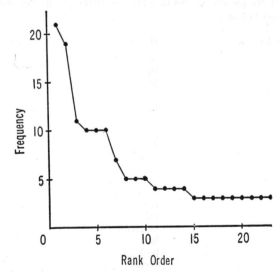

Fig. 59.—Curve showing the relationship between the frequency of occurrence and the rank order (based on frequency) of words in a small sample of scientific writing. In order to save space, this curve is incomplete. As will be seen, there were 9 words in the sample which occurred three times each. If the 29 words that occurred twice each and the 155 words that occurred once each were represented on the curve, it would extend out to the right in a long asymptote, giving the total curve a hyperbolic function.

bolic function of some sort. This suggestion is fully substantiated by extensive studies carried out by Zipf. Using an analysis made by Joos and Hanley of the 260,430 running words in James Joyce's *Ulysses,* Zipf has plotted the rank-frequency relationship in the manner illustrated in Figure 59, with the following results:

If the ranks are plotted on ordinary arithmetical coordinate paper, a sweeping curve is formed closely hugging the axes, something like the familiar pressure-volume diagram of Boyle's law when it is plotted over a wide range (Whitehorn and Zipf, 1943, p. 834).

But the plotting of such extensive data on regular coordinate paper becomes very unwieldly, so that it was a natural step for Zipf to transfer the data to double logarithmic coordinates; and when this is done for the *Ulysses* material the results shown in Figure 60 are obtained. Zipf's comments follow:

In [Figure 60] we present in Curve *A* the data of the entire *Ulysses* thus plotted, and the reader can assess for himself the closeness with which this

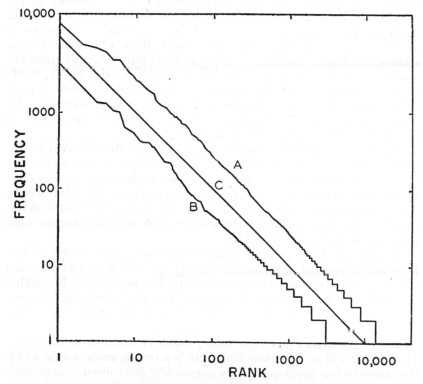

Fig. 60.—Two curves (*A* and *B*) showing how closely the rank-frequency function for words used in English prose (Zipf, 1949) approximates a straight line with a 45° angle (*C*) when such data are plotted on doubly logarithmic paper. The source and further explanation of these curves will be found in the text.

curve descends from left to right in a straight line at an angle of 45°. In order to suggest that the *Ulysses* is not unique in respect to a *hyperbolic rank-frequency word distribution,* we include gratuitously in Curve *B* . . . the rank-frequency distribution of the 6,002 different words in fully inflected form as they appear in a total of 43,989 running words of combined samples from American newspapers [previously mentioned]. Curve *C* is an ideal curve of 45° slope that has been added to aid the reader's eye (Zipf, 1949, pp. 25-26).

Readers who are accustomed to the conventions commonly followed in plotting the results of psychological research are likely to experience some difficulty in interpreting the curves shown in Figure 60. Ordinarily, in psychological research, the variables represented by the two dimensions of a graph are assumed to have some empirical relationship (if the results are "positive"), but no formal, logical, or mathematically determined relationship. This assumption is clearly violated in Figure 59 and Figure 60; for here, as will be immediately evident, the two variables, or dimensions, are interdependent. In an ordinary learning curve, for example, the vertical dimension is likely to be time intervening between presentation of a problem and the occurrence of the solution or "correct" response, and along the horizontal dimension will be plotted the successive occasions or "trials" on which observations or measurements are made. If learning occurs, there will be an inverse relationship between number of trials and the time taken to reach the goal or find the solution of the problem; but this relationship is wholly *empirical,* since it would be entirely possible, mathematically, for no change to occur, for the time to increase rather than diminish with successive trials, or for the curve to have any conceivable shape (so long as it did not double back upon itself).

But in the Zipf rank-frequency type of curve the situation is different. Since the rank position of a word is dependent upon the frequency with which it occurs in the specimen under analysis, it is clear that rank and frequency cannot vary independently. In other words, we see at once that the relationship is not wholly empirical but is determined, at least to some degree, by the very way in which the two variables are defined and derived.

Because the assumption of mathematical independence of variables is so clearly violated in the rank-frequency type of curve, and since the curves shown in Figure 60 are so extremely close to a straight line with a 45° slope, one may be tempted to assume that the "circularity" is complete, i.e., that both the shape and the slope of these curves are given by the formally determined (definitional) relationship between frequency of occurrence and rank order, which is based upon frequency. However, it will soon be clear that there is a certain range within which the curve is free to move, i.e., is empirically determined. Since rank is determined by frequency, we know at once that the curve can never at any point turn upward, since no word having a later rank can have a higher frequency than a word having an earlier rank; if this relation-

ship were violated, it would mean that the words had not been correctly ranked. But there is nothing inherent in the Zipf procedure which
would prevent one from obtaining a perfectly flat line; this would necessarily occur in a language specimen in which all words were used
with exactly the same frequency. Likewise, if a language specimen
consisted of but a single word used repetitively, then the rank-frequency
curve would again be straight but almost vertical, since the word with
the first rank would have a very high frequency and all subsequent
"words" in the specimen would have a frequency of zero. If, in short,
a subject used all words which he used at all with absolutely the same
frequency, then the resulting rank-frequency curve would be exactly
horizontal; and if, on the other hand, a subject used only one word, i.e.,
said or wrote it over and over again, then the rank-frequency curve
would start at an extremely high point and would drop immediately
to the base line. There is therefore, an arc of almost 90° within which
a straight line may vary, as a function of the empirical data; and it is
also theoretically possible for the resulting function to be curvilinear,
i.e., to meander, in an almost infinite number of ways within this arc.
Thus the fact that the two curves shown in Figure 60 are virtually
straight and drop at an angle of almost exactly 45° is, in the words of
the Harvard mathematician, J. L. Walsh (1949), truly a "remarkable
finding."

One further word regarding the nature of the Zipf rank-frequency
curves may be in order before we consider their psychological significance. The reader may at first be puzzled by the rather curious "steps"
at the lower end of these curves. Reference back to Figure 59 and the
attendant discussion will prove useful here. Since the frequency with
which a word occurs in any given sample is necessarily a *whole* number,
whenever the curve drops at all it must drop by a value of at least one,
and as one nears the bottom of doubly logarithmic paper units become
progressively larger, as shown by the height of the steps.

More puzzling, perhaps, is the question of how the top, or surface,
of the steps is derived. As already indicated, in this type of analysis
all the words having the *same* frequency are given, arbitrarily, consecutive rank values. The top of the steps is therefore a reflection of
the number of words which have the same frequency and to which has
been assigned a given sequence of rank values. Some suggestion of the
meaning of these steps, as they appear on ordinary coordinate paper,
will be apparent in Figure 59. The logarithmic scale simply has the
effect of making these steps shorter, particularly toward the right end
of the scale.

Now according to Zipf there are two opposing forces constantly at
work in language. From the standpoint of the speaker, language, he
maintains, would be maximally simple and convenient if it consisted
of only one word; whereas, from the standpoint of the listener, language
is maximally satisfactory and useful when it contains as many different
words as there are meanings to be differentiated. Thus, Zipf reasons,

actual speech always represents a compromise or balance between a tendency toward "unification" (repetition) and a tendency toward "diversification" (variety). In written language, as Figure 60 indicates, this balance is such as to fall, in the selected exhibits, exactly halfway between the two possible extremes (many different words used equally often and one word used exclusively) and to approximate very closely a straight line; and Zipf, in an extended series of other studies, has shown the remarkable generality of this relationship.

But, as we have seen, it is at least theoretically possible for rank-frequency curves to deviate either in the direction of unusual flatness or unusual steepness or in respect to certain other types of irregularity. Let us ask, therefore, what the implications would be if one found a language specimen which showed, let us say, a systematic trend toward either verticality or horizontality. According to the Zipf analysis, deviation toward flatness indicates a sociocentric orientation on the part of the speaker (or writer), whereas marked steepness suggests, by the same token, egocentricity. Since repetition of a single word could not possibly serve the purposes of both speaker and hearer, we may say that a rank-frequency curve that deviates markedly downward is indicative of *autistic* trends in the speaker, whereas a curve that tends to be unusually flat shows unusual concern on the part of a speaker for the convenience and interest of the person to whom the speaker's remarks are addressed.

Against the background of this discussion it is interesting to ask to what extent these theoretical predictions are confirmed empirically. Here the 1943 article of Whitehorn and Zipf is particularly in point. In the introductory paragraph of this paper, immediately following the passage quoted on page 481 of this chapter, appears the following sentence, which shows an awareness of the clinical bearing of Zipf's method:

Furthermore, speech is inherently social or interpersonal, in its historical development and in its learning and primitive use by the person, so that one's speech should somehow reveal, even though somewhat remotely and indirectly, some implications of the development of one's interpersonal attitudes (p. 831).

In 1943, extensive recorded vocal behavior on the part of persons who might be suspected of showing significant deviations in this respect was not available. It is therefore not surprising that Whitehorn and Zipf fell back largely upon the use of personal letters written by more or less disturbed persons. "Margaret C.," a highly educated young woman, was briefly hospitalized with a psychosis in which "childish" behavior was very pronounced. When letters which she wrote to one of her physicians following a period of hospitalization were analyzed, the results shown in Figure 61 were obtained. The only thing very distinctive in these curves is the "bend" at the top of the curves. Of this the authors say:

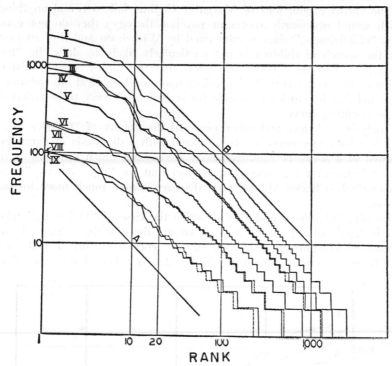

Fig. 61.—"Rank-frequency distributions for Margaret C. (a 'childish' adult) in samples of (I) 50,000 words; (II) 30,000 words; (III and IV) 20,000 words; (V) 10,000 words; (VI and VII) 5,000 words, and (VIII and IX) 2,000 words" (Whitehorn and Zipf, 1943, p. 838). From inspection of the above curves it is evident that, although larger word samples give higher curves on a rank-frequency chart, a small sample (2,000 words) gives a curve with essentially the same shape as the curves derived from much larger samples. This fact suggests that the relationship which is here under examination is an exceedingly stable one but, by the same token, one which may not be of much value for diagnostic or other "clinical" (highly individualized) uses.

This particular bend, which for convenience we shall henceforth term the top concavity, represents nothing more than the fact that the words were taken from letters that were intimately personal, and not formal; in and for itself the top concavity has no necessary connection with abnormality. . . . In this connection we suggest that the presence of a top concavity in intimately personal (i.e., not formal) letters may be ascribed to the fact that the writer and the reader have a certain commonness of experience and hence can dispense with the high degree of articulation that is otherwise necessary in writing to a nonintimate. . . . In brief, the definite articles and other short, highly frequent articulatory words, which are necessary for coherence when one is writing to a person who is a stranger to the topic, become unnecessary in writing to the intimate. It is the substandard frequency of these articulatory words which is found in colloquial and intimate writing (and speaking) and which is reflected in a top concavity (pp. 839-40).

The verbal productions of Margaret C. thus fail to reveal anything which would necessarily represent psychopathology; they do not even show "childishness," since results cited by Whitehorn and Zipf suggest that the speech of children is not particularly likely to show the "top concavity." But these results do show that the rank-frequency distribution of Zipf is not entirely dependent upon mathematical interrelationships and that it is at least possible for stylistic difference to be reflected in the resulting curves.

Analysis of letters and other personal documents of "Charles M.," who was for many years institutionalized with a diagnosis of paranoia, resulted in a series of rank-frequency curves not much different from those of Margaret C., except for the fact that the "top concavity" was less marked—Charles M., we soon discover, was a much more formal person.

Finally, Whitehorn and Zipf describe the case of "Helen B.," who was institutionalized at the age of twenty-three with a diagnosis of paranoid schizophrenia. Analysis of her correspondence led to the rank-frequency curves shown in Figure 62. By a line of reasoning that

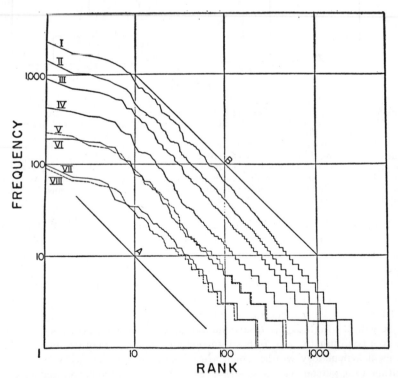

Fig. 62.—"Rank-frequency distributions of Helen B. (with paranoid schizophrenia) in samples of (I) 50,000 words; (II) 30,000 words; (III) 20,000 words; (IV) 10,000 words; (V and VI) 5,000 words, and (VII and VIII) 2,000 words" (Whitehorn and Zipf, 1943, p. 846).

is convincing but too involved to be reproduced here, the authors conclude that the steepness of the curve is a reflection of this patient's tendency toward autism, the tendency, that is to say, to be excessively self-centered and self-referential in her speech and writing and to think of her own needs and interests at the expense of her hearers or readers with respect to ease of comprehension. The following excerpts will serve to expand the authors' hypothesis in this connection:

The abnormality of the autistic person lies only in ignoring the other fellow; that is, it lies in his disregard of the social obligation to make only those changes which are socially acceptable in the sense that they are both understandable and serviceable in the group.

Naturally, once the autistic person pursues his own linguistic and semantic paths of least effort, the result may well appear to his perplexed auditor as a disorder of meanings, or even as a disorder of association. Yet the autistic speaker, in making his own language, without the nuisance of satisfying the auditor's needs, may employ the same principle of linguistic and semantic change as does the normal person, though not with the same care to insure community acceptance (p. 849).

To the series of cases analyzed by Whitehorn and Zipf can be added, by way of further exemplifying the rank-frequency method, that of Mrs. Dravoldi, reported by Baker and already cited in this chapter. Baker provides all of the raw data necessary for making a complete rank-frequency analysis of this woman's productions.

The curve resulting from such an analysis is shown in Figure 63. Here will be seen some interesting peculiarities. Most striking of these is the marked drop in the curve between the fourth and fifth entries. Mrs. Dravoldi's four most frequently used words are "you," "I," "to," and "&." The next four words are "a," "have," "but," and "is." It is almost as if the first four words belong to a distribution or universe which is discontinuous with the next four and subsequent words. Precisely what this peculiarity means is difficult to determine; but it is noteworthy how different these eight most popular words are from the eight words most frequently used in the specimen of scientific writing discussed above. Some of the discrepancies are undoubtedly related to the fact that Mrs. Dravoldi's productions took the form of "personal letters," but it is possible that purely personal predilections may also be reflected here.[15]

The marked convexity or humping of the second, major part of the curve is interesting, but its meaning is not immediately apparent. The steepness of the latter part of the curve is suggestive, in terms of Zipf's type of thinking, of autistic, self-referential trends in this person, but beyond this little can be said.

It is of some interest to glance now at the rank-frequency curve which derives from the word count already done for the introductory

[15] Cf. discussion below of the possibility of correlating word-frequency lists.

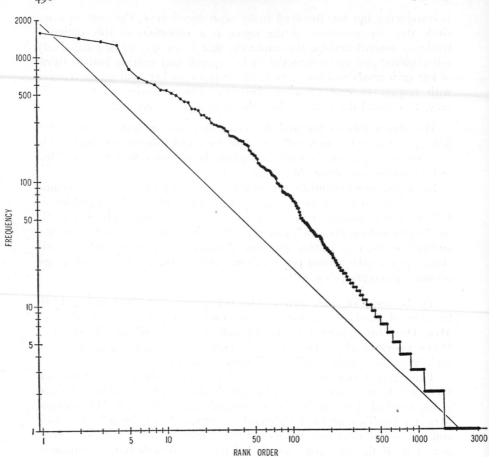

FIG. 63.—A Zipf-type rank-frequency curve based upon written productions (letters) of a "Mrs. Dravoldi," as analyzed and reported by Baker (1951). This curve deviates in a number of interesting ways from the straight line, at an angle of 45°, which is regarded as "normal." For possible interpretations of the eccentricities of the Dravoldi curve, see text.

paragraphs of the second half of this chapter. We have seen how strikingly this small sample of verbal behavior illustrates Zipf's law of abbreviation. In Figure 64 we see what this same material looks like when graphically analyzed for *semantic balance*.[16] Even though the sample is a very small one, the resulting data plot, on doubly logarithmic paper, in such a manner as to give a function remarkably close to a straight line. But there is a perceptible deviation from the standard

---

[16] Our discussion here does not at all exhaust the possible methods of analyzing psychotherapeutic or other clinical productions which are suggested or implied by Zipf. In collaboration with the author, J. Robert Williams (1950) has, for example, obtained some preliminary results which make use of Zipf's concept of "verbal time perspective." This method gives promise of utility in therapeutic protocol analysis, but the findings are too tentative to warrant discussion at this time.

angle of 45° which Zipf found to obtain for *Ulysses* and many other
language specimens he has analyzed. This may be an expression of
the smallness or "unreliability" of the sample; but since inclination of
such a curve toward the horizontal is interpretable, in Zipf's frame of
reference, as implying an effort on the part of a writer to diversify or
"specify" his words maximally, in the interest of reader comprehension,
we can perhaps temporarily accept this comforting interpretation!

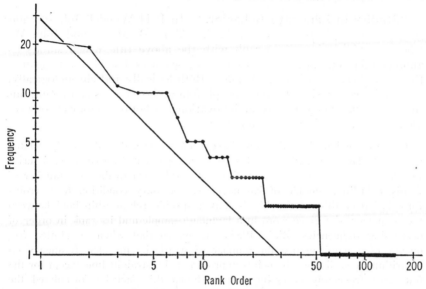

Fig. 64.—A rank-frequency curve derived from the first three paragraphs of the
second part of this chapter and plotted on doubly logarithmic paper. The data are
the same as those from which Figure 59 is derived. Though the number of words
involved is small (only 359), the curve is remarkably straight and deviates only a
little from an angle of 45° (see straight line).

Despite the amount of space here devoted to the question, it is still
difficult to say, in summary, whether either the law of word abbreviation
or the law of vocabulary balance has any very usable clinical applications.
In case of the latter, the underlying rationale might seem to lend itself
rather neatly to diagnostic and other clinical purposes, and such fragmentary data as we have on this score are not entirely unpromising; but
certainly there is at present no basis for great optimism with respect to
either of these laws.

However, from this exploratory analysis of Zipf's methods a suggestion emerges which would appear to be worth a serious trial. It will
have already been obvious that once words are rank-ordered on the basis
of their frequency of occurrence in two or more verbal specimens, they
can be *correlated*. Not all the words that appear in one specimen will
necessarily appear in another, but a great many words—certainly all of
the more common *structural* words and many *content* words—will be

contained in the two samples; and the rank values thereof could thus be compared. This procedure might provide a measure of similarity or difference between persons or of continuity or change, through time, within a given person, much in the manner of Q technique and O technique, respectively (see Chapter 13). Such an approach to the analysis of successive segments of a psychotherapeutic transcription may or may not prove profitable, but it would seem to deserve some exploration (see next section, especially footnote 21).

"Studies in Language Behavior."—In 1944 Wendell Johnson and three of his students, Helen Fairbanks, Mary B. Mann, and John W. Chotlos, published a monograph with the above title which stands as another milestone in the advancement of scientific knowledge regarding the verbal behavior of human beings. Both logically and chronologically, the studies comprising this monograph follow the basic work of Zipf, but they introduce many important innovations. Chotlos' summary of previous work reads, in part, as follows:

Certain previous investigations have been concerned with closely related problems. To begin with, Carroll (1938) has presented an equation describing the relation of the number of different words (D) to the total number of words (N) in a sample of language. A necessary condition to Carroll's formulation of this relationship is that a specific relationship hold between the frequency of a given word in a language sample and its rank in order of decreasing frequencies. Zipf (1935) discovered that when he plotted frequency of a word against the number of words having that frequency on logarithmic coordinates, the points approximated a straight line except for the few most frequently occurring words. From this fact he formulated the harmonic series law of word distribution, in which he states that the most frequent word in a large sample of language makes up 1/10 of the sample, the second most frequent word 1/20 of the sample, the third most frequent word 1/30 of the sample, etc. This formulation can be put in the form of the equation

$$F = \frac{N}{10R}$$

in which F is the frequency of occurrence of any given word in a language sample, R is its rank in order of decreasing frequencies, and N is the total number of words in the sample.

Skinner (1937) has also presented results pertaining to the relationship between F and R. In analyzing the results obtained from 1,000 responses to his verbal summator, he plotted ranks of words in order of decreasing frequencies (R) against frequency (F), as expressed as a percentage of the total sample, on logarithmic coordinates, and found the points tended to fall in a straight line.

A deviation from linearity was again noted in the more frequently used words. Skinner (1937) also reanalyzed the Kent-Rosanoff (1910) data on free association response words in the same manner. He found that when the rank order of words in terms of mean frequency per thousand was plotted against mean frequency per thousand on logarithmic coordinates, the resulting curve was approximately linear for the 100 responses most likely to occur (pp. 77-78).

The studies of Johnson *et al.* are in one important respect more closely related to the work of Carroll than that of Zipf. Zipf, it will be recalled, used the relationship between word *frequency* (F) and *rank* (R) as his basic analytic tool. Carroll, on the other hand, worked with the relationship between the *total* number of words (N) involved in a given sample and the number of *different* words (D) therein. Johnson designated the latter relationship the *type-token ratio*, i.e., the ratio represented by the number of different words (types) over the total number of words (tokens). Chotlos suggests a useful way of keeping in mind the difference between "types" and "tokens." He says:

. . . the unit of language used in this study is the word, and it is generally referred to as a *token* in order to differentiate it from a unit of vocabulary, the *type* (p. 107).

Thus, *every* word, no matter how many times repeated, is a *token* (a "counter"), but only *different* words qualify as *types*. Clearly the sum of tokens is equal to the sum of words (Carroll's N), while the sum of types is equal only to the sum of different words (Carroll's D).

With these terminological relationships established, we are now in a position to ask: How are a Zipf rank-frequency curve and a Johnson type-token ratio related? As already noted, if a subject uses just one word, over and over again, the resulting "language" specimen will give a rank-frequency curve of maximum steepness, representing the absolute limit of verticality in the Zipf system. The same data would result in a type-token ratio of $\frac{1}{N}$, where the 1 represents the only word used (the single *type*) and N represents the total number of words in the sample, i.e., the *tokens*. For a sample of any given size, $\frac{1}{N}$ will obviously be the *smallest possible* type-token ratio. Therefore, maximum steepness of a Zipf rank-frequency curve corresponds precisely to a minimal type-token ratio.

However, the reverse of this relationship does not hold in any simple manner. We have already seen that if all words used in a given specimen are used with exactly the same frequency (highly improbable but conceivable) the resulting rank-frequency curve will be absolutely flat, i.e., it will represent the upper limit which is possible in the Zipf type of analysis. But such a curve would *not* represent, necessarily, the maximal value which is possible for the type-token ratio. Suppose that 50 words were used 100 times each. The rank-frequency curve would be flat, but the type-token ratio (TTR) would be only 50/5000 or .01, and the highest possible value for the latter measure is 1.00. Only in the special case of a language specimen in which no word is repeated would the rank-frequency curve reach its upper limit (flatness) and the type-token ratio *its* upper limit (unity).[17]

These relationships are exemplified in Figure 65, reproduced from a study by Bousfield and Barclay (1951), already cited. These investigators, it will be recalled, asked the students in each of three undergraduate psychology classes (containing 100, 58, and 60 students, respectively) to write the names of as many birds, carpenter tools, and celestial bodies as they could think of. In any *individual* case, the type-token ratio would be 1.00 (since words are not repeated) and the rank-frequency curve would be flat and minimally elevated, since every word occurred with the same frequency and that frequency would be one. Here are the special circumstances under which the *TTR* and the Zipf-type analysis reach the upper extreme together.

The curves shown in Figure 65 are, however, *composite* curves, one for each of the three *groups* of subjects. Frequencies are here computed on the basis of the number of times that the different students in any one class mentioned the *same* bird, tool, or celestial body. In all three situations, there was a large number of items which were mentioned by almost everyone in the respective groups (giving the initial, relatively flat part of the curves), but then diversity began to occur and the curves drop very rapidly. The difference in the absolute level of the three curves represents the difference in the number of subjects in each of the three groups.

That the upper half of all the curves is so nearly level (rather than having the 45° angle which Zipf considered normal) is due to the fact that individual subjects were not allowed to use (list) any one word more than once, which, of course, is contrary to the "rules" governing speech or writing. There is a generally accepted convention that it is not "good form" to repeat words in too rapid succession; but there is certainly no objection to repetition otherwise—in fact, the very nature of language makes repetition, especially of the formal or structural words, a necessity. The enforced rule against repetition used by Bousfield and Barclay thus automatically prohibited the *normal* repetitiveness of language, with the somewhat distorted and artificial results shown in Figure 65. In fact, what we have here is not really *language* at all, but simply a *listing* of certain specified language elements.

---

[17] There is, in other words, a systematic relationship between the height, or *level*, of a rank-frequency curve and the *size* of the *TTR*. As indicated above, when a rank-frequency curve is flat *and* in the lowest possible position, i.e., when each word used has a frequency of only one, the *TTR* is maximal (1.00). And as the level of such a curve rises, the *TTR* will necessarily drop. From this it follows that a "normal" rank-frequency curve, i.e., one that descends from left to right at an angle of 45° and therefore represents words that range from very high to very low frequencies, will tend to have intermediate *TTR* values. Moreover, as results to be reported presently show, when the language sample used is small and the rank-frequency curve, though normal, is lower on the coordinates than when the sample is large, the *TTR* will be higher than when the sample used is relatively great and the rank-frequency curve starts at and descends from a higher point on the ordinate.

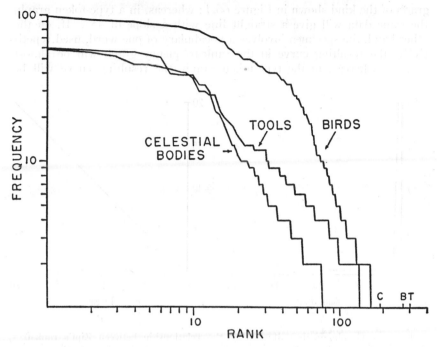

Fig. 65.—Rank-frequency curves based upon lists of birds, carpenter tools, and celestial bodies written out by the members of three college classes (Bousfield and Barclay, 1951). That these curves depart so markedly from what is usually obtained from normal language samples (a straight line with a declination of 45°) is explained by the fact that the specimens from which the curves were derived were not "normal language." They were, for each individual subject, just a list of different words referring to things in some given category. Therefore, if rank-frequency curves had been drawn for individuals, they would all have been flat. The shape of the curves actually obtained comes from the fact that in any given group of subjects, certain words (e.g., certain tools) were listed by nearly everyone and certain other words were listed by only a few persons. The resulting frequency data are thus somewhat like, though by no means identical with, the distribution of words in a specimen of speech or writing from a single subject: some words used many, many times and others (perhaps a good many others) used very infrequently. These data are of principal interest in helping one conceptualize what a rank-frequency means and how it varies with different kinds of data.

By way of further indicating the relationship between Johnson's type-token index and Zipf's rank-frequency type of analysis, it will be useful to compare Figures 66A and 66B. The first of these is a rank-frequency (nonlogarithmic) graph, on which two types of data are plotted, and the second is a type-token graph showing the same data. The data here referred to represent two extreme cases, one in which a language sample includes many words repeated only once, and another which includes many repetitions of but one word. As already indicated, a language specimen in which there is no repetition (as in the Bousfield-Barclay data for individuals) will give a flat-line curve in a rank-frequency graph of the kind shown in Figure 66*A*; whereas, in a type-token graph, the same data will give a straight line with a slope of 45°. If, on the other hand, the specimen involves a vocabulary of one word, used repetitively, the resulting curve in the rank-frequency graph will be almost vertical, whereas, in the type-token graph, the resulting curve will be

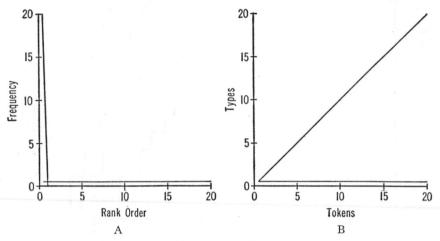

A   B

Fig. 66.—Graphs further illustrating the relationship between Zipf's rank-frequency method of language analysis and Johnson's type-token approach. As indicated in Figure 66*A*, a language sample which involves the repetition of a single word (e.g., twenty times) gives an almost vertical function on a rank-frequency graph, whereas a language sample in which every word is a new word (i.e., *no* repetitions, as in the Bousfield-Barclay lists for individuals) gives a straight-line function at the level of 1 on the ordinate. (Actually, neither of these collections of words is a sample of *language,* properly speaking. Cf. pages 463-66.) As indicated in Figure 66*B,* a language sample which involves the repetition of a single word gives a straight-line function at the level of 1 on the ordinate of a type-token graph, whereas a language sample in which every word is a new word gives an ascending straight-line function with an angle of 45°, since every added "token" also means an added "type." Thus data which give a nearly vertical line on a rank-frequency graph give a low, flat line on a type-token graph; and data which give a low, flat line on a rank-frequency graph give an ascending (45°) straight line on a type-token graph. (If one plotted the type-token *ratio*—types/tokens—for the two samples, still different functions would be obtained; the first sample would give a curve which descended according to these values—1/1, 1/2, 1/3, 1/4, etc., whereas the second sample would give a straight-line, flat function based on these values—1/1, 2/2, 3/3, 4/4, etc.)

perfectly flat. (For further details, see the legend accompanying these graphs.)

Since the two most extreme types of language possible (if they can be called "language") are used in these two hypothetical examples, it becomes evident that they set the limits of possible variation in a rank-frequency graph and in a type-token graph. The possible variability of a straight-line curve in the former will be through an arc of 90°, whereas in the latter case, the range is limited to 45°. Moreover, it should be noted that a type-token curve will always start at the origin of its graph, whereas a rank-frequency curve may start at any point along the ordinate, depending upon the frequency of the most-used word.

Another interesting finding is that when the data represented in Figure 67 (a type-token curve empirically derived by Chotlos, 1944) are transposed to doubly logarithmic paper, the straight-line function shown

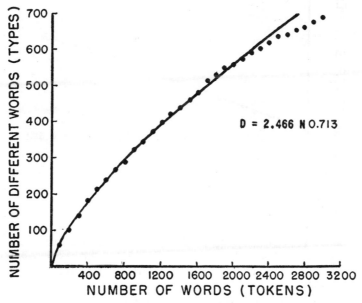

$$D = 2.466 \, N \, 0.713$$

FIG. 67.—A curve, empirically derived by Chotlos (1944), indicating the way in which the number of *different* words (D) increases in a specimen of written language as a function of the *total number* of words used (N). How closely the equation shown on the graph fits the empirically derived function (represented by the sequence of dots) is indicated by the solid line.

in Figure 68 is obtained. This compares in linearity with the Zipf curves shown in Figure 60. However, both the direction and the absolute inclination of these two lines are notably dissimilar, indicating the essentially different nature of the functions involved.

Let us now turn to a consideration of some of the results obtained by Helen Fairbanks (1944) from an analysis of oral language samples, of 3,000 words each, obtained from ten schizophrenic patients and ten college freshmen who were selected because of their high performance on a verbal aptitude test. Each subject was read proverbs and asked to interpret and amplify upon them in any way desired. The experimenter kept presenting proverbs until a speech sample of the specified length was obtained.

Each of the ten schizophrenic language samples and each of the ten normal samples was divided into thirty segments of 100 words each, and the *mean* value was then obtained for the type-token ratios for each of the thirty 100-word segments in each case. These *mean TTR* values ranged from .49 to .62 for the schizophrenic subjects and from .61 to .67

for the normal subjects. Two findings thus emerge: (*a*) the schizophrenic subjects have, on the average, a mean *TTR* which is reliably lower than the comparable value for the normal subjects and (*b*) the schizophrenic subjects show more variability among themselves in this

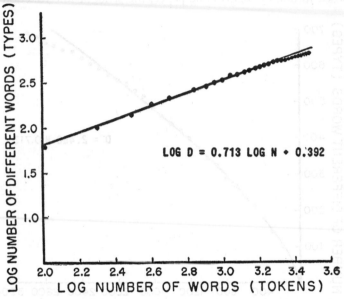

Fig. 68.—The same data as appear in Figure 67, converted to log functions. This conversion, as will be seen, results in a straight line for the values derived by the equation shown in Figure 67 (solid line) and an almost straight line for the empirically determined values (represented by the sequence of dots).

respect than do the normal subjects. On the basis of these findings, Fairbanks says:

In general it may be concluded that the schizophrenic patients tended to have lower mean segmental *TTR*'s than did the freshmen. In other words, the schizophrenic patients employed smaller vocabularies than did the freshmen.

Interpretation of these differences in regard to the *TTR*'s of the schizophrenic patients and the freshmen must necessarily be made with caution because of several variables in the two groups, especially in the schizophrenic group, such as age, time of onset of illness, intellectual level and educational advantages, which the experimenter was not able to control rigidly within the limitations of this study (p. 26).

Such data as were obtainable suggested a slight positive correlation between intellectual level and the *TTR* in the schizophrenic subjects. There seemed, however, to be no connection between *TTR* and diagnostic type. Although there appears to be some confounding due to the influence of intelligence upon the TTR's, it would nevertheless be a reasonable expectation that TTR's would, in general, be lower in schizophrenics than in normal persons.[18] On this score Fairbanks remarks:

Clinically, schizophrenic patients present a tendency to repetition of behavior known as stereotypy which may be of attitude, movement, or speech. When the same word, phrase or sentence is repeated, the stereotypy is known as verbigeration (Noyes, 1934). It is possible, then, that the lower mean TRR's for the patients represent to some degree in a quantitative manner this clinical picture of stereotypy (p. 27).

On the basis of the data reviewed on pages 493-94, it seems that schizophrenic written productions show a tendency to give slightly steeper rank-frequency curves than do the productions of normal subjects (but see Figure 69 and accompanying discussion), and since steepness in such a curve reflects a tendency toward repetitiveness, it would be consistent to discover that schizophrenic subjects have, on the average, smaller TTR's than do normal subjects.

On the basis of the data already described, Fairbanks made an analysis of the relative frequency of the different parts of speech in the two groups of subjects. She says:

From this we may conclude that the schizophrenic patients used significantly fewer nouns, conjunctions, prepositions, adjectives, and articles than did the freshmen, and significantly more pronouns, verbs, and interjections (p. 28).

On the basis of comparable data available for the speech of children, Fairbanks concludes:

Certainly there is no apparent tendency for the schizophrenic patients to regress toward the childhood level with respect to the general grammatical construction of their language, unless it might be in regard to more frequent use of verbs (p. 30).

This finding is in keeping with the general point of view reported by Cameron (1938, 1939), and it is consistent with the conclusions of Whitehorn and Zipf, cited earlier, regarding the case of "Margaret C."

---

[18] Mary Mann, in her section of the monograph under discussion, makes the following interesting comments on this score: "The question as to whether the language of schizophrenics differs, insofar as it does, from the language of superior university freshmen, because the schizophrenics are less 'intelligent' raises an extremely complicated issue. It is not to be lightly dismissed, for example, that the phrase 'highly intelligent schizophrenic' may be in a basic sense self contradictory. The fact that an intelligence test shows a schizophrenic to be superior mentally probably tells, from one point of view, as much about the test as it does about the patient. The schizophrenic offers a means of validating the test quite as definitely as the test offers a means of evaluating the patient. A particularly pertinent answer to the test on which a schizophrenic scores a high 'intelligence quotient' is that, when all is said, the patient is in custody. The issue is not a simple one by any means . . ." (p. 42). For a discussion of the relationship between learning and personality disorders, see Chapters 5 and 6.

Fairbanks made a careful and illuminating study of the relative frequency with which her two groups of subjects used different words. At the top of a list of the 100 words most frequently used by the ten freshmen are the eleven words shown at the left in Table 15; at the right are

TABLE 15

Two Lists Showing the Eleven Words Most Frequently Appearing in the Speech of Ten Normal College Freshmen and the Eleven Words Most Frequently Appearing in the Speech of Ten Hospitalized Schizophrenic Patients (Data from Fairbanks, 1944)

If a word appears in one list but not in the other, the frequency of its use by the opposing group is shown in parentheses. Note that "I" and "not" are used disproportionately by the schizophrenic group, reflecting, inferentially, the negative self-preoccupation of the latter.

Freshmen		Schizophrenics	
Word	Frequency	Word	Frequency
the	1140	I	2501
and	1113	not	942
I	924	and	785
a	788 (365)	the	735
to	779	it	729
is	629	do	638 (304)
it	623	to	635
of	612 (416)	that	633
that	599	is	580
you	562 (392)	well (interjection)	565 (271)
not	484	know	496 (139)

the corresponding eleven words most used by the ten schizophrenic subjects. Fairbanks' comments on the two lists, taken in their entirety, are as follows:

Several interesting differences between the [100-word] list for the schizophrenic patients and that for the freshmen can be noted in regard to the frequencies for various words. For example, the schizophrenics used "not" almost twice as many times as did the freshmen. In addition, "no" and "never" occur in the list for the schizophrenics, while no other clearly negative words occur in the first 100 words for the freshmen. Hence, we have the schizophrenics using these negative words 1,087 times to 484 times for the freshmen. . . . Instead of the "never" used by the schizophrenics, the freshmen used "always" about an equal number of times. Another interesting item is that the freshmen used "very" over three times as often as did the schizophrenics (154 to 46). When the verbs among these 100 most frequently used words for the group were considered, it was found that the schizophrenic patients used eight past tense verbs a total of 1,158 times while the freshmen used six such verbs only 683 times. It is interesting to note, also, that two verbs carrying the connotation of indecision, "suppose" and "guess," occur among the 100 most frequently used words of the schizophrenics for a total of 158 times, while no such words occur in the comparable list for the freshmen (pp. 31-32).

But perhaps the most striking finding in this connection is the much greater incidence of self-referential words in the schizophrenic list. Fairbanks' comments here are as follows:

Another analysis that suggests itself, because of the schizophrenic's self-preoccupation and his tendency to ignore his environment, is the relative frequency of referrals to self and of referrals to others found in the language of the two groups. . . . The most striking fact . . . is that references to self, using some form of the first person singular ("I, my, mine, me, myself") make up 10.42 per cent of the total number of words for the schizophrenic group, while they represent only 3.69 [per cent] of the total for the freshmen. On the other hand the freshmen used the first person plural pronoun in its various forms ("we, our, ours, us, ourselves") three times as often as do the schizophrenics; the second-person pronoun, plural and singular ("you, your, yours, yourself, the, thou"), almost twice as frequently as do the schizophrenics; and the third-person pronoun, singular and plural . . . almost 20 per cent more often.[19]

The schizophrenic patients used a total of fourteen neologisms, or coined words. . . . Neologisms were not found in the freshman samples (p. 34).

From the outset it was apparent that these findings held exciting possibilities for the development of measures sensitive enough to show therapeutic progress; and subsequent work, to be reviewed presently, has given further substance to these hopes. While the possibility could not be wholly discounted that the higher type-token ratios of the freshmen represented merely their superior intellectual and scholastic attainments, such factors would *not,* presumably, account for the differences just described. Here we have strong presumptive evidence that we are dealing with variables directly related to the presence or absence of psychopathology, an assumption which has gained continued support from subsequent researches.

In a study which in many ways parallels that of Fairbanks, Mary Mann (1944) has investigated college freshmen and institutionalized schizophrenics from the standpoint of *written* language productions. There were twenty-four subjects in each category; they were equally divided as to sex and were selected according to roughly the same criteria as used in the Fairbanks study. In all cases the material was obtained by

---

[19] These results are an emphatic confirmation of the clinical impressions commonly reported regarding the schizophrenic syndrome. Goodstein (1951), in summarizing such impressions, cites Cameron as believing that "the essential disturbance in schizophrenia lies in the social disarticulation of the patient, and this reflects itself in schizophrenic speech. The primary function of all language—communication—is gone" (Goodstein, 1951, p. 99). And in like vein he quotes Sullivan thus: "The more completely one becomes self-centered, the more utterly he becomes cut off from integration with other more or less real people, the more utterly novel, perfectly magical, and wholly individual become the symbols which he uses as if they were language" (Sullivan, 1925, p. 29).

asking the subject to write a story of his life. Subjects were encouraged to write until a minimum of 2,800 runnings words had been accumulated.

Mann, following Fairbanks, first computed the "mean-segmental" type-token ratios for patients and students, using "segments" of 100 words each. The range for the patients was from .4600 to .7450, while the range for the students was from .6708 to .7357. The same trends are seen here as in the Fairbanks study—higher average TRR and less variability for the freshmen—but the differences are less striking. When Mann computed the "over-all" TRR's for freshmen and patients, i.e., the type-token ratio for the total sample of 2,800 words for each subject, the range was .1850 to .3932 for the patients and .2689 to .4079 for the freshmen, thus confirming the results for the mean-segmental type of analysis. (The generally lower values obtained for the over-all TTR's than the mean-segmental TTR's represents the tendency for this measure to give smaller values as the size of the sample is increased. Thus, each of the 2,800-word samples would be expected to give an over-all TTR considerably lower than the mean TTR for the twenty-eight 100-word segments.)

On the score of variables other than psychopathology which might account for the results just cited, Mann says:

Comparisons were made to determine the effect of certain variables, among the schizophrenics, on their mean-segmental TRR's. These intragroup comparisons indicated that differences in intelligence test scores, level of educational attainment, and duration of confinement in the hospital had relatively insignificant influence on the TTR's for the patients, and did not adequately account for the differences between the schizophrenic patients as a group and freshman students as a group (p. 71).

With the Fairbanks data available, Mann was able to make a comparison of the TTR's of both normal and hospitalized persons in respect to written as opposed to oral forms of expression. Although this comparison is not as fully controlled as might be wished, it is nevertheless suggestive that the *average* mean-segmental TTR's for the patients were .6559 and .5681, respectively, for the written and the oral productions and, for the students, .7135 and .6416. Thus, as Mann observes, the patients in their written productions just slightly exceed, on the average, the TTR's for the students in their oral productions. The patients are thus reliably inferior to the students in respect to the type-token ratio, but in both groups this value is higher for written than for spoken language.

This finding [says Mann] may be attributed to the fact that, generally speaking, an individual's written language is a more finished product, permitting more altering and rearranging of the words used than in his spoken language (pp. 71-72).

To this might be added the speculation that since written language must function without benefit of gesture, intonation, or observation of the person addressed, it cannot be quite so simple, quite so rudimentary as can spoken language.[20] For a similar interpretation, see Boder (1940).

Mann's analysis of the relative frequencies of different parts of speech in her two groups showed no very impressive differences (in contrast to the findings of Fairbanks in this connection). However, Mann gives a summary of earlier studies which have clinical interest and are suggestive.

Of the relationships between certain parts of speech, the adjective-verb quotient (Avq) is of perhaps the greatest interest, since it, or a variation of it, has been used by other investigators. Busemann, as reported by Boder (1940), recorded in shorthand a number of stories told by children of different ages and found a marked fluctuation of the relationship between "qualitative" and "active" (dynamic) expressions. In the category of qualitative expressions he included not only adjectives, but also nouns and participles of verbs, when used as attributes to any other nouns; in the category of active expressions he included all verbs except the auxiliary. By dividing the number of verbs by the number of qualitative expressions he obtained a measure which he called the action quotient (Aq) of style. Busemann found that a rhythmical increase and decrease of the Aq occurs with increase in age, which he believes to correspond to alleged rhythmical changes of emotional stability during childhood, adolescence, and youth. Furthermore, according to Busemann's theory, these rhythmical variations continue throughout the whole lifetime and reflect rhythmical variations of emotional stability and creative power.

Rorschach, again as reported by Boder, in classifying the interpretations given by subjects to a series of ink blots, calculated the ratio between different types of descriptions made. He found that the predominance of kinesthetic description (verbs) indicates moderate, sluggish motility, introversion, and little adaptability to reality, while the predominance of color descriptions (qualitatives) reflects the excited, but alert, exact, and rapid motility, extraversion, and better adjustment to reality.

Stimulated by the suggestions made in these studies, Boder set out to find whether there exist gross differences of adjective-verb ratios corresponding to differences in subject matter of various classes of writing. He inverted the procedure of Busemann, however, and took the adjective as the numerator in order to obtain a measure which might (if Busemann is right) correlate positively with desirable traits. The ratio he used indicates the number of adjectives per one hundred verbs and is designated in purely grammatical (as opposed to Busemann's behavorial "action quotient") terms as the adjective-verb quotient (Avq). He found that for each of the kinds of writings studied, i.e., plays, legal statutes, fiction, and scientific monographs, the distribution of

---

[20] For these and related reasons, typed transcriptions convey a somewhat less vivid impression of the therapeutic process than do the original recordings, from which the transcriptions have been made. By artful use of punctuation, underlining, indication of pauses, editorial inserts regarding crying, laughing, loudness or softness of speech, and so forth, some of the meaning of the situation which is not carried by words alone can be retained; but some loss and even distortion are probably inevitable in the transcribing process.

Avq's shows sufficiently large differences to prove that as a rule the *Avq* varies with the subject matter of the text (Mann, 1944, p. 65).

In her comparison of the 100 words most frequently used by the students and the 100 words most frequently used by the patients, Mann reproduces a table similar to that of Fairbanks, previously mentioned. In Table 16 are reproduced the eleven words most frequently used by

TABLE 16

Two Lists Showing the Eleven Words Most Frequently Appearing in the Written Language of Twenty-Four Normal College Freshmen and the Eleven Words Most Frequently Appearing in the Written Language of Twenty-Four Hospitalized Schizophrenic Patients (Data from Mann, 1944)

Here the deviations noted in Table 15 entirely disappear. If these data are representative, they suggest that spoken language is much more likely to bring out psychopathology than are written productions, which may have the effect of putting the person on guard and thus eliciting more formal, more stylized verbal behavior.

Freshmen		Schizophrenics	
Word	Frequency	Word	Frequency
the	3,354	the	3,052
I	2,778	and	2,950
and	2,350	I	2,662
to	1,805	to	2,093
was	1,468	of	1,641
my	1,346	was	1,069
in	1,328	in	1,054
of	1,162	my	859
a	844	a	847
it	672 (507)	we	795
we	646	had	646 (603)

Mann's two groups and the absolute frequency of their occurrence. Whereas in the Fairbanks study such a comparison immediately revealed striking differences, it is the *similarities* which are impressive in the Mann study. Of the first eleven words in the two lists, ten are common and have roughly the same sequential order; and the two words which are different in the lists have values which are not markedly different from their values in the opposing lists. Mann found almost exactly the same incidence of first person plural, second person singular and plural, and third person singular and plural pronouns in the two groups; and the schizophrenics showed notably *fewer* first person singular pronouns than did the freshmen: 5.92 per cent of all words as opposed to 7.05 per cent.

The following passage, which deals at some length with this discrepancy between the Fairbanks and Mann results, is quoted from the concluding section of Mann's paper.

Of the measures used in this study the type-token ratios appear to offer the most fruitful means of differentiating quantitatively written language samples of the type investigated. With the exception of the adjective-verb quotient, and perhaps certain other ratios of parts of speech, the grammatical analysis did not prove useful in this respect. From the results reported by Fairbanks as to the frequency of certain types in spoken language, and from observations of clinical manifestations of egocentricity, negativism, and frequency of neologisms, the prediction might logically have been made that an investigation of type frequencies would provide a quantitative differentiation of the language of the groups studied. However, the results of the analysis were contrary to this prediction. It is possible that the formality of the writing situation offers a possible explanation of the relative infrequency of self-reference terms, for example, in the written language of schizophrenics.

. . . Two other considerations may be mentioned in this respect. It could be postulated that the task assigned the subjects in this study, that of writing a "life story," would tend to increase the frequency of references to self. This may actually have operated to increase the frequency of self-reference for the freshmen [inspection of the results shown in Tables 15 and 16 does not support this suggestion], but for the schizophrenic patients this effect may have been counteracted to a large extent by their tendency to enumerate, and to get "off the track" in recounting their life histories by describing certain places, events, or things, with little or no reference to their own relation to such places, events, or things (p. 73).

Assuming reasonably accurate samples in both the Fairbanks and the Mann studies, it is apparent that hospitalized patients with a diagnosis of schizophrenia behave, under the conditions stipulated, much more like a group of intellectually superior college freshmen when they write than when they speak. This greater similarity in written performance is revealed by a general attenuation in differences of the kind reported by Fairbanks for the speech productions of the two types of subjects. Difference in the type-token ratio was still statistically reliable for the freshmen and schizophrenics when written material was used, but this difference was notably reduced, and many of the other differences reported by Fairbanks disappeared entirely.

However, there is a reasonable question regarding the generality of these findings. The request made by Mann of her subjects to *write* about *themselves* may have been much more threatening to the schizophrenic group than was the request which Fairbanks made of them: to interpret and elaborate upon proverbs. Such a possibility is strongly hinted at by Mann's observation that the schizophrenics in her study kept digressing into impersonal areas, almost as if conscious self-description and revelation was so painful that they sought irrelevancies as a distraction. The fact that Fairbanks' schizophrenic subjects, when talking, used the personal pronoun "I" 2.7 times as often as did her freshmen group, whereas Mann's schizophrenics used this pronoun only about half as often as did the first group of patients, shows clearly that something in the Mann procedure dampened the abandon with which Fairbanks' patients used this and related self-referential pronouns. This effect may conceivably also be a reflection of the fact that most persons get, in the course of their schooling, more formal training in written than in oral expression. Hence, the greater similarity found by Mann in the productions of her two groups may be an indication of the greater degree of conventionality or stylization involved in writing.

The two studies just reviewed thus leave many open-ended questions, but they are suggestive as regards methodologies which may be adapted to research in psychotherapy, and present indications are that some of their specific findings are going to be substantiated by other investigations (see below).

Because Fairbanks and Mann both publish the 100 words most frequently used by their normal and their schizophrenic subjects and also give the absolute number of times each word was used, it is possible to make an illuminating comparison, by means of Zipf rank-frequency curves, of these data. The two lower curves shown in Figure 69 represent the language behavior of Fairbanks' normal group (solid circles) and of her schizophrenic group (open circles). Three things are evident:

1. Zipf's rank-frequency analysis gives curves for normal and schizophrenic samples which are remarkably similar, even though the samples are known to differ significantly with respect to the TTR.

2. Both curves show a marked "top concavity," which includes the ten most frequently used words.

3. The excessive use by the schizophrenic group of the personal pronoun "I" accounts for the deviant position of the first point on the schizophrenic curve.

The two top curves in Figure 69 portray the language behavior of Mann's normal group (solid circles) and her schizophrenic group (open circles). The following features of these curves are noteworthy:

1. The parallelism between the schizophrenic and the normal productions is even more striking here than in the case of the Fairbanks results.

2. Again a "top concavity" is to be seen, but it is less extensive, containing only the first three words as opposed to the first ten in the Fairbanks data. This difference is in keeping with Zipf's supposition that the top concavity is a reflection of the degree of language informality. In Figure 59 we have the rank-frequency curve for a piece of formal scientific writing, and the top concavity is hardly perceptible. On the other hand, in the Fairbanks data, representing highly informal language productions (essentially conversational in nature), the top concavity is conspicuous and extensive. And in the case of the Mann data, which were derived from autobiographical written productions and which thus probably represent an intermediate degree of formality-informality, the top concavity is found to be, appropriately enough, intermediate.

But the most important, over-all inference to be drawn from these results is that the rank-frequency type of analysis is probably of very little or no value in differentiating the verbal productions of normal and pathological subjects. Certainly if there is as little difference between the oral productions of college freshmen and schizophrenic patients as the two lower curves in Figure 69 indicate and as little difference between the written productions of similar groups as the two top curves show, it is most improbable that reliable differences would be found by means

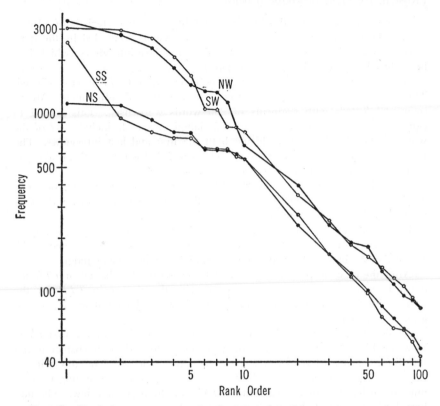

FIG. 69.—Rank-frequency curves for four samples of language: normal written language (*NW*) and schizophrenic written language (*SW*), the two top curves; and normal spoken language (*NS*) and schizophrenic spoken language (*SS*), the two lower curves. It is striking how closely the two curves for normal and schizophrenic subjects parallel each other in the case of both written language (data from Mann, 1944) and spoken language (data from Fairbanks, 1944). The only point of conspicuous deviation in the two pairs of curves is at the beginning of the two lower curves, and this is caused by the tendency of the schizophrenic subjects, in speech, to use one word far more frequently than any other: namely the personal pronoun "I." This interesting deviation is not found in the pair of curves based upon written language. The difference in absolute level of the two pairs of curves is occasioned by the different number of subjects used (ten in each of Fairbanks' two groups and twenty-four in each of Mann's two groups). These curves confirm the conclusion reached earlier in this chapter, namely, that Zipf's rank-frequency type of language analysis is not, in general, clinically sensitive.

of this measure for language specimens of patients before and after they have undergone psychotherapy. On the other hand, it appears that the type-token ratio, though a logically somewhat related measure, has a greater degree of sensitivity and may prove useful in this connection.

Some support for this inference has just been supplied to the writer by Jean M. Roshal, whose own summary of her thesis research, carried out at Pennsylvania State College under the direction of William U. Snyder (Roshal, 1952), is reproduced below:

My research investigated behavior variability as a characteristic of adjustment. The population consisted of forty-two students counseled by the nondirective method. This study used the first and last interviews, which had been electrically recorded and transcribed.

As a measure of variability, the type-token ratio (*TTR*) was selected. This has been described by Johnson as a measure of adjustment. Mean-segmental *TRR*'s with segments of 200 words were used. This served to equate the samples of different size. The language sample included *all* of the words spoken by the patient during both the first and last interviews. The interviews ranged in length from 202 words to 7,342 words, with an average of approximately 3,200 words for each interview.

The principal hypothesis stated: Where improvement resulted from psychotherapy, the *TTR* would be higher for the last interview than for the first interview. This reflects increase of variability.

Improvement with therapy was estimated by a composite score, based on changes from negative to positive feelings, and rating scales completed at the end of therapy by the client, the counselor, and an independent judge.

After the cases were sorted on the criterion score, the change in *TTR* for the thirteen highest cases was compared with the change in *TTR* for the twenty-nine lowest cases. The null hypothesis was rejected at the 1 per cent level of confidence.

As shown in the table below, the mean-segmental *TTR* for the first interview was higher for the low cases than the high. This led to the suspicion that the difference may have been a regression phenomenon. The top thirteen cases were then compared with the thirteen cases from the remaining twenty-nine which had the lowest segmental *TTR*'s for the first interview. The null hypothesis was rejected at the 2 per cent level.

MEAN SEGMENTAL TTR'S

Group	First Interview	Last Interview	Difference
13 high	.5192	.5331	.0139
29 others	.5269	.5219	—.0050
13 low	.5048	.5011	—.0037

While these results are "positive" in the sense that the most successful cases show a gain in *TTR* and the poorest and intermediate cases show a loss, they indicate one of two things: they show either (1) that the type-token ratio changes only vary slightly as a result of therapy or (2) that the effectiveness of the therapy involved in these cases was not great. In any event, it will take more dramatic results than these to demonstrate that the TTR has anything more than theoretical interest in this connection; its value as a practical indicator of psychotherapeutic changes cannot, at present, be said to have been established (see Grummon's results, p. 526 ff.).

At an earlier point (page 497), reference has been made to the possibility of correlating two series of words on the basis of the frequency with which these words have been employed in two language samples. The data of Fairbanks and Mann, discussed above, afford such an opportunity. Taking the 100 words most frequently used by Fairbanks' normal subjects and the 100 words most used by her schizophrenic subjects (in speech), we find that 79 words are common to both lists. When these words are correlated on the basis of the frequency of their use by the two groups of subjects, an r of .738 is obtained. When, on the other hand, one correlates the 83 words that are common to both of Mann's lists (derived from written specimens), one obtains an r of .966.

Here, then, is another indication that schizophrenic language and normal language are more differentiated in speech than in written communication. Moreover, we soon see that most of the difference in these two correlations comes from a difference between schizophrenic speech and schizophrenic writing, rather than from a difference between normal speech and normal writing: the correlation between the 67 words which appear in the list of 100 words most used by Fairbanks' normal subjects in speech and also in the list of 100 words most used by Mann's normal subjects in writing is .814, whereas the correlation between the 64 words which appear in the list of 100 words most used by Fairbank's schizophrenic subjects and also in the list of 100 words most used by Mann's schizophrenic subjects in speech is .683. These relationships are schematically represented below:

Normal Subjects Speech (Fairbanks)	$r = .738$ $(N = 79)$	Schizophrenic Subjects Speech (Fairbanks)
$r = .814$ $(N = 67)$		$r = .683$ $(N = 64)$
Normal Subjects Writing (Mann)	$r = .966$ $(N = 83)$	Schizophrenic Subjects Writing (Mann)

It is thus evident that (a) there is a substantial difference between the words most commonly used by normal and schizophrenic subjects in speech (under the conditions stated), that (b) there is very little difference between the words most commonly used by normal and schizophrenic subjects in writing (under the conditions stated), that (c) there is a difference between the words most commonly used in speech and in writing in the case of both normal subjects and schizophrenic subjects,[21] but that (*d*) this difference is most marked in the case of schizophrenic subjects. These results suggest that the correlational procedure by which they were obtained may be sensitive enough to be applicable in measuring the results of psychotherapy.[22]

Reference has already been made to the contribution of Chotlos to the monograph under discussion in this section, but because his research was largely restricted to a study of 1,000 school children, his findings seem to have less specific bearing upon the problem of measuring psychotherapeutic change than do the findings of Mann and Fairbanks. However, the Chotlos paper will reward careful study, both from the standpoint of content and methodology, and the following remarks are especially noteworthy:

Further qualifications of the present results [including those of Fairbanks and Mann] arise with regard to the fact that pertinent determining factors may have been omitted from consideration. Two such factors may be (1) number of *topics* discussed by each individual and (2) *rate* of verbal output per unit of time (p. 108, italics added).

And later:

Consideration of . . . language structure suggests that perhaps it may be feasible to divide the words of any language sample into two categories. First, there are the interstitial or structural words which form the core of framework structure of language. Since these words carry little meaning beyond the verbal context in which they appear, they may be termed *intensional* words in contrast to the second type of words, the content and action words that have, directly or indirectly, an *extensional* reference. Since the more frequently occurring words are of the intensional type, we have a basis for making an analysis of the language into two parts (p. 110, italics added).

Johnson, in the introduction to this monograph, in an appendix of his book *People in quandaries* (1946), and in a paper entitled "Speech and Personality" (1948*b*), gives a number of other suggestive leads for re-

[21] This difference is almost certainly due, in part, to the fact that the speech specimens and the written specimens were on different topics: comments on and interpretations of proverbs in the one case and the subject's life history in the other. This surmise is substantiated by the fact that when the topic is held constant but type of subject varied, the number of common words is 79 for spoken language and 83 for written language; but when the type of subject is held constant and the topic is varied, the number of common words drops to 67 for normal subjects and 64 for schizophrenic subjects (see footnote 22).

[22] The correlational values given above do not completely reveal the extent of similarity or difference in the specimens in question. As will be noted, the correlations were restricted to the words which are common to any two lists of 100 words. However, it is obvious that the *number* of such words is itself an indication of the similarity or difference between two lists. Since this fact enters only indirectly into the correlational computations here employed, it is clear that a somewhat different statistical procedure is needed to bring out the whole truth with respect to similarities and differences between word lists of the kind under discussion.

search in this field; but many of these are still in the formulative stage
and lack empirical support at the present time. The discussion has here
been limited to procedures which have been empirically tested.

Empirical Studies Based on the Case of "Mrs. X."—In Chapter
11 of this volume reference has already been made to a preliminary analysis of the transcribed therapeutic protocols of a "Mrs. X" from the
standpoint of the discomfort-relief quotient. In the following pages will
be reported the results of a number of other highly exploratory studies
which have been carried out with the same material, primarily as a means
of testing and exemplifying certain research methodologies.

The first of the studies to be reported here was carried out by Zimmerman and Langdon in 1949, using as a point of departure some of G.
W. Allport's (1937) criteria of a mature or normal personality. Allport
points out that, among other attributes, the mature person is only minimally concerned with himself, in the sense of being introspective and self-
centered, and is maximally, or at least optimally, interested in other persons and objective events. From this it would seem to follow that as a
person moves from immaturity to maturity during the course of therapy,
his diminishing self-consciousness may be reflected in the relative frequency with which he uses certain of the common personal pronouns.
Figure 70 confirms this supposition. Here we see, first of all, a general
downward trend in the incidence of the first person singular pronoun
"I."

Such a change in self-reference during the course of therapy is also
consistent with the results of Fairbanks, just reviewed. If severely disturbed, hospitalized patients show a greater tendency (in speech, if not
in writing) than do superior college freshmen to be preoccupied with
themselves and to use the pronoun "I" more frequently, it is reasonable
to suppose that progress from psychological illness to health, during
therapy, will be characterized by a parallel shift in this connection. When
one's automobile is out of order, one is likely to refer to it more frequently
than when it is working properly. When a car or any other piece of
machinery is efficiently performing its intended function, one talks about
it minimally, largely taking it for granted. Likewise, when a person's
psychic equipment is grating and squeaking, it is understandable that
one's attention should be directed toward it much of the time, with a
lowering of attention to and interest in external happenings, persons, and
objects. As the intrapsychic difficulties are resolved, there will be a
growth in "objectivity" and a reduction in "subjectivity."

The I curve shown at the top of Figure 70 dramatically illustrates the
virtue of objective researches as supplements to the direct impressions
obtained of the therapeutic process by therapist and patient. Although
both the therapist and the patient in the present case might have been
able, at the end of therapy, to report that the patient was beginning to
get more interested in things "outside herself," it is doubtful if either of

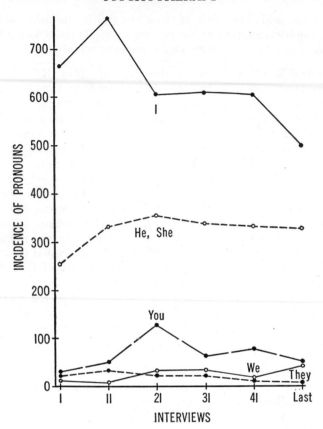

Fig. 70.—Curves showing the relative frequency of the pronouns, "I," "he," "she," "you," "we," and "they," in every tenth therapeutic interview with a "Mrs. X." The most striking change is in the incidence of the first-person singular pronoun "I." These data were analyzed by and are here reported with the permission of Zimmerman and Langdon (1949).

them was aware of the specific change in verbal behavior shown in this curve.[23]

The next three curves in Figure 70, showing respectively the incidence of third person singular, second person singular, and first person plural pronouns, all evidence an upward trend, in contrast to the decrement in the top curve. The three curves just cited all represent or include persons other than the patient, and their upward tendency may therefore be taken as indicative of a growing *interest in others* (cf. Fairbanks quotation, p. 507).

At the bottom of Figure 70 the curve for the pronoun "they" shows a downward trend. What does this mean? On the basis of what has

[23] Growth of this patient's outside interests and activities was especially marked after the therapy had formally ended, as indicated by a series of letters written by her to the therapist periodically over a three-year period.

just been said about the objectification of the patient's interests, it might seem that the decrement in the they-curve represented a contradictory trend; but there is a special consideration which enters here. If a person is going to include himself in groups more and more and thus use the pronoun "we" increasingly, he will, almost of necessity, refer to groups less and less by means of the pronoun "they." May we not, therefore, interpret the reciprocal trends noted in the we- and the they-curve as reflecting growth in group affiliation on the part of the patient, as an increment, that is, in the feeling of group "belongingness"?

The you-curve in Figure 70 has some features of special interest. As will be seen, it rises to a peak at the twenty-first interview and then declines again. Since the patient's resistance and transference reactions were at their height during the period represented by the twenty-first interview, it seemed not unlikely that the patient's greatly augmented use of "you" at this point might be an expression of her accelerated interaction with the therapist, whom she would normally address or refer to by means of this pronoun. Accordingly, Zimmerman and Langdon made a count of references to the therapist during each of the six interviews which are here under consideration; the results are shown in Figure 71. Here it will be seen that from the first to the twenty-first interview there is a marked increment in therapist references, thus, in part at least, confirm-

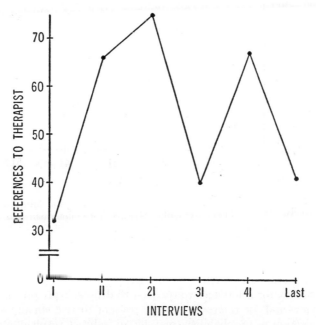

FIG. 71.—Incidence of specific references to therapist by "Mrs. X" in every tenth therapeutic interview. The marked increment, followed by an equal decrement, suggests that the curve may give a rough indication of "transference." The curve is reproduced from a study of Zimmerman and Langdon (1949).

ing the surmise expressed above. At the end of therapy, the incidence of references to the therapist was again relatively low, suggesting perhaps that the transference had been "worked through" and that the patient's attention was turning to other things. However, the low value of therapist references on the thirty-first interview makes the curve decidedly irregular and reminds us of the fragmentary and perhaps unreliable character of these results and the necessarily tentative nature of the interpretation here given to them.

In the second part of their study, Zimmerman and Langdon made a count of the relative incidence of different grammatical tenses. Some of the results are shown in Figure 72. Here, it will be noted, there is an

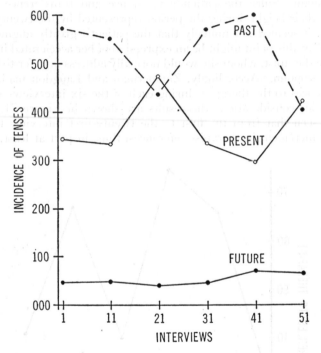

Fig. 72.—Curves showing the incidence of past-, present-, and future-tense verbs in every tenth therapeutic interview with "Mrs. X." (Zimmerman and Langdon, 1949). The over-all tendency for references to the past to decline and for references to the present and the future to increase is evident.

over-all decline in references to the past and an over-all increase in references to the present and the future, as therapy proceeds.

The tendency for references to the past to drop sharply on the twenty-first interview and for references to the present to rise equally abruptly, if not a reflection of unreliability, may be an indirect result of the transference relationship (cf. Figures 72 and 73). This relationship might well be expected to "pull" the patient out of the past into the present by virtue of the fact that she is vigorously interacting with another person in the "here and now." Following the same line of reasoning, as the transference is worked through, the patient reverts, apparently, to her former level of preoccupation with the past (and slight concern for the present) ; but in the end, as the therapy is consolidated without transference, the growth of references to the present markedly increases and references to the past correspondingly decline. These speculations regarding the incidence of past- and present-tense verbs as a function of the transference may or may not be confirmed by further work. However, the generally downward trend in the curve for past-tense verbs and the rise in the future-tense curve is consistent with the findings of Fairbanks, already cited, and with results obtained by Grummon in a study which will be considered shortly.

The curve for the incidence of future-tense statements shown in Figure 72 is of special interest and is reproduced, on a larger scale, in Figure 73.

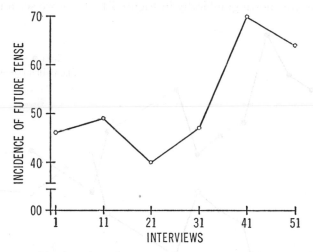

Fig. 73.—Amplification of the future tense curve shown in Figure 72. There are many indications that therapeutic progress is accompanied by increased planfulness— and, hence, increased reference to the future.

The marked rise seen in this curve is consistent, first of all, with results previously reported by Fairbanks; a similar finding has been noted by Seeman in a different connection (Chapter 9) ; and it is also consistent with the findings of Grummon (see below). Growth in future-tense statements is likewise consistent with the growth of "plans and insights" referred to in Chapter 11.

All in all, the results obtained by Zimmerman and Langdon, and complementary findings reported by others, with respect to the incidence of personal pronouns and grammatical tenses constitute some highly promising leads for further and more systematic investigations of therapeutic process.

In 1950 Lazowick and Young, using the same case, undertook a somewhat related study but one which started with a rationale which was more explicitly grounded in the assumption that psychopathology is, ultimately and basically, a disturbance in interpersonal relationships (Sullivan, 1947). The most nearly universal feature of therapy is that it, too, is an interpersonal transaction, and this fact suggests that the therapeutic relationship may be one into which interpersonal problems which have ended in deadlock may be brought and where, with the therapist acting as a mediator of or catalyst for new learning, resolutions are found which, when generalized, produce improvements both in the patient's social life and in his*intrapsychic (notably ego-superego) relationships.

The first step taken by Lazowick and Young was to count all references to *self* and all references to *others* which occurred in some selected interviews in the Mrs. X case which has been previously discussed. The results are shown graphically in Figure 74. Here we see a tendency

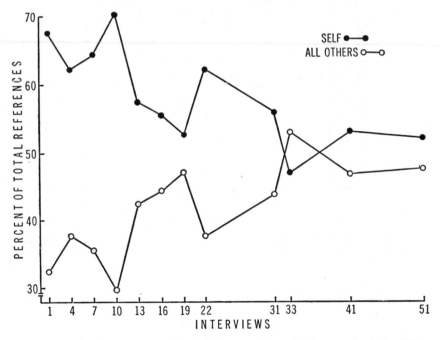

Fig. 74.—Reciprocal curves showing the proportion of references made by "Mrs. X" to herself and to others during the course of psychotherapy. The lessening of self-preoccupation and growth of concern for others are clearly indicated. These curves are reproduced from a study by and with the permission of Lazowick and Young (1950).

for the patient to become markedly more "socialized" in her productions and correspondingly less self-centered. This finding further supports, but does not materially expand, the results previously reported regarding the incidence of personal pronouns. However, Lazowick and Young extend their analysis in a distinctly novel direction when they break down their count of references to others in the manner shown in Figure 75. Here a number of noteworthy trends can be observed. Early in therapy the patient, as the therapist well remembers, made many references to the long-dead father (which, in itself, would heighten the use of past tense verbs), and as therapy progressed preoccupation with the father and her relation to him diminished.

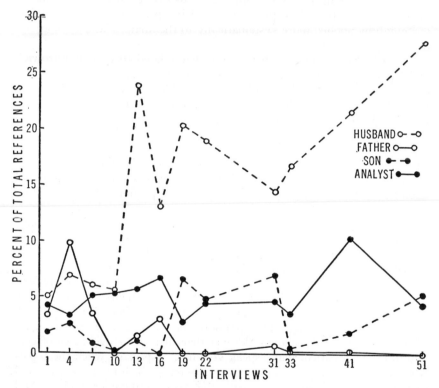

FIG. 75.—Curves showing a breakdown of the composite curve for references to others shown in Figure 74. Growing awareness of and reference to the patient's husband is especially marked. These curves are reproduced from the unpublished work of Lazowick and Young (1950).

As therapy progressed there was some growth, as Figure 75 indicates in the patient's references to her son; but the most spectacular change is in respect to references to the patient's husband, corresponding to the emergence in the therapy of deep disturbances in psychosexual orientation and awareness of serious problems in the role of wife and mother.

Resolution of the patient's "fixation" with respect to the dead father and her growing references to and sense of responsibility for her son and her husband are consistent with common assumptions regarding successful therapy. Only in respect to references to the therapist are the findings at all paradoxical. The results of Zimmerman and Langdon showed a heightening of references to the therapist at the twenty-first interview, when transference was approximately at its maximum. In the Lazowick-Young analysis, no such phenomenon is apparent. A partial explanation may lie in the somewhat different methodologies used in the two studies, and it will also be noted that the latter investigators did not base their analysis upon precisely the same interviews as those used by Zimmerman and Langdon. But for present purposes, this discrepancy is not of major importance. Both studies illustrate promising procedures, which can be meaningfully applied more systematically to the analysis and comparison of subsequent cases.

A method of content analysis somewhat related to that of Lazowick and Young is shown in Table 17. Here we see at a glance the rise and decline of expressed concern with various problem areas as psychotherapy proceeds. Every therapist has the experience of having patients work into certain problems, resolve (or temporarily retreat from) them, and then pass on to new problems, until at length they feel that their problems are no longer overwhelming and that they can cope with them on the basis of their own resources and newfound skills. This phasic or episodic character of therapy is well portrayed in Table 17. This table is based upon the work of Donald R. Gorham and is reproduced here, for illustrative purposes, with his permission.

It would be interesting and perhaps of practical advantage to have a kind of master form or chart on which there would be enough topical headings so that anything a patient discussed might be appropriately entered. In this way, it would be possible not only to get a graphic impression of what problem areas therapy has involved for any given patient but also to make comparisons between different patients and thus bring out both the common and the unique features of therapies in general. This type of analysis might also highlight something that therapists again often sense intuitively, namely the fact that silences or avoidance of certain topics by a patient may "speak volumes," especially when the topics which are being concurrently discussed are ones which might be expected to have collateral associations with the avoided topic or topics. And here we come close to a method of content analysis involving the concept of "contingencies" which is now being developed by C. E. Osgood. However, this work is still in too preliminary a stage to warrant discussion at this time.

V. S. Horvitz, in another unpublished study using transcribed protocols from the therapy of Mrs. X, has made a preliminary attempt to show therapeutic progress in terms of certain frequency measures of the patient's speech. Having selected 100-word samples from near the beginning and the end of the 3rd, 13th, 20th, 29th, and 39th interviews, Horvitz computed the type-token ratio, the number of verbs, the number of qualifiers, and the verb-qualifier ratio for each of these ten samples. No very clear-cut results were found, but there was a suggestion of a drop

TABLE 17

TABULAR INDICATION OF TOPICS DISCUSSED BY A PATIENT DURING THE COURSE
OF FIFTY THERAPEUTIC INTERVIEWS
(Data reproduced through the courtesy of D. R. Gorham.)

THERAPY SESSIONS

	5	10	15	20	25	30	35	40	45	50	55
HOME RELATIONS											
Mother	X	XXXX	XXXXX X	XX	XX X	XX X					
Father	X			X	X				X		
Oedipal Relations			X	X	XX			X	X	X X	
Childhood	XXXX					X					
Matricide Fantasy			X								
PSYCHOSEXUAL											
Incest Feelings										X X	
Homosexual	X					XXX XX		XXX	XX XX	XX	X
Heterosexual				X X X		X	X	X X			
Masturbation	X	X					X	X			
Guilt Feelings	X		X							XX	
Sublimation		X					X	X			
Impotence	XX X				X						
Phobias									X		
Fetishism				X				X			
Bed-Wetting	X										
Circumcision				X							
INTERPERSONAL											
Aggression		XXX		X X	XX XX			X X			X
Independence			XX X	XX			X				
Authority		X				X	X				
PERSONAL											
Vocation				X X	XX	XXX X			X X	X X	XX
Amnesic Recall		X X			X	XX		X X	X		
Drinking	X	XX			X						
Responsibility		X X	XX								
Military Service					X			X	X X		
THERAPEUTIC RELATIONSHIPS											
Progress of Therapy	X	XX	X	XX X	XXX	X	X X	X		X	X X
Relation to Therapist	XX			X		X	XXX X	X X	XX X	X	X
Breaking Off										X	X

in the type-token ratio between the beginning and the end of the interviews. What this study serves to show is mainly that if these and related
measures are to prove useful in quantitative studies of therapy, they will
have to be applied more systematically and with larger samples.[24]

From this and the preceding section it is apparent that the two types
of measures which are most likely to prove immediately practicable in
therapy research are differential frequency of pronouns and differential
frequency of tenses. The type-token and other similar ratios may prove

[24] Cf. The findings of Roshal (1952), previously cited, and those of Grummon
(1950) to follow.

useful, along with differences (measured by some correlational procedure) in the constitution of the frequency lists of words commonly and less commonly used in therapy.

While this type of research has far to go before it will be able to answer questions which are of practical and theoretical import to the actual conduct of psychotherapy, the very possibility of obtaining objective measures of therapeutic change raises an interesting issue, namely, do such changes reflect changes in the patient's "perception of self" (as Rogers would presumably hold), or are they, in themselves, the types of changes on the basis of which the altered self-perceptions come about? Said most concisely, the issue is: Does therapy produce changes in the *perception* of self or changes *in* the self proper? Although objective measures of therapeutic change sharply raise this issue, it is not very likely that they will settle it. A large part of the issue is philosophical, in the most technical sense of the term, since it involves questions both of epistemology and ontology. Therapeutic approaches which stress the transcendent importance of *perception* lean in the direction of philosophical *idealism,* while those that stress the importance of "real" change, due to learning, are inclined toward philosophical *realism* and *materialism.* Since some of the issues here involved are so deeply philosophical, they are probably not answerable on the basis of empirical research, if at all, but this remains to be seen.

Grummon's Research on Language Categories and Psychotherapy.—That some of the trends noted in earlier studies represent orderly principles rather than mere fortuitous findings is made particularly evident by the recent work of D. L. Grummon (1950). The transcribed interviews of four patients who had client-centered counseling provided the basic materials for this investigation. Two of these patients were hospitalized and were receiving electroshock convulsions at the same time the counseling took place. The other two subjects presented less serious problems and were treated on an out-patient basis. Of these four subjects, one showed little or no improvement, a second showed limited improvement, and the other two showed considerable improvement.

For such detailed analyses as were involved in Grummon's study, it was not practical to use all the recorded material available in each case. Instead a sample of 2,000 words taken from an early point in therapy and a like sample from a late phase of therapy for each subject were used. As Grummon remarks, the focus of his research was not upon "the meanings implied in the words and sentences of the speaker [but upon] the form of the linguistic act which serves as a vehicle for the meanings" (p. 1). Some three hundred quantifiable categories were used in this study (cf. Sanford's 1942a study), but the results for only a few of the most significant ones will be considered here. One category, the grammatical negative, was studied on a somewhat greater scale—with a total of sixteen counseling cases—and the results were correlated with Rorschach findings for these cases.

Grummon describes his most salient results as follows:

The Type-Token Ratio. The one-hundred-word Type-Token Ratio, a measure of active vocabulary size, increases significantly upon the completion of treatment. The size of increase for the one-hundred-word *TTR* for individual cases does not appear to be closely related to the degree of therapeutic success as judged by several outside criteria. However, increases for five-hundred-word and one-thousand-word *TTR*'s do seem related to the degree of therapeutic success, although the data here are subject to considerable sampling error. Likewise individual differences in the size of these *TTR*'s are related to individual differences in the overt adjustment status of our subjects (p. 7).

These findings are consistent with expectations generated by the studies of Fairbanks and Mann. These writers, it will be recalled, found that normal college freshmen have a higher type-token ratio than do hospitalized schizophrenics. It would therefore be reasonable (see also the results of Roshal, page 514) to suppose that in successful therapy patients might show an increase in respect to this measure. The somewhat equivocal results obtained by Horvitz may be due to the smallness of his samples and the fact that he was working with a single case.

One of Grummon's most interesting findings has to do with the grammatical negative. On this score he says:

The Negative. When the grammatical negative was studied in ten non-psychotic, self-referred counseling cases and in six hospitalized psychotic subjects, successful treatment was found to be accompanied by a significant decrease in the frequency of the grammatical negative in the counseling protocols, whereas it tended not to decrease in unimproved subjects. Some evidence is presented to show that this decrease may also take place in speech situations other than the counseling situation. Individual differences in negative frequency show a relationship to individual differences in overt adjustment, but prediction for an individual case would be a hazardous undertaking.

In any event, it is of theoretical interest that successful treatment is related to a decrease in negative frequency. The writer interprets this as being related to a tendency on the part of the well-adjusted person to be positively actualizing himself in relation to his environment rather than having avoidance reactions to the environment. The maladjusted person would appear to know what he wants to avoid but fails to know that which will give him positive satisfactions.

Negative frequency did not show a significant correlation with Rorschach estimates of adjustment but did show a high correlation with interview measures of adjustment and therapeutic progress. This suggests to the writer that negative frequency is not related to "basic personality structure" but is related to overt life adjustment status (pp. 7-8).

Here again we see a trend which was adumbrated in the Fairbanks study, where it was found that "schizophrenics used 'not' almost twice as many times as did the freshmen" (p. 30) and that there was also a marked differential for the words "no" and "never." Here, apparently, is a significant indicator of personal adequacy and normality.

On the score of grammatical tenses, Grummon says:

> *Time Reference.* The completion of counseling is accompanied by a significant decrease in predicates referring to past time relative to predicates referring to present, universal, and future time. This finding tends to confirm the clinical observation that the completion of client-centered counseling results in the client being less concerned with the past and more concerned with present decisions and future plans.
>
> The frequency of predicates referring to different categories of time apparently is markedly influenced by factors specific to the speech situation. Therefore, it is difficult to determine from our data the general relationship between personality characteristics and tendencies to emphasize particular categories of time. However, there is some indication that a high frequency of predicates referring to universal time appears in the language of an individual who is attempting to develop a socially acceptable mode of adjustment in the face of, or as a defense against, underlying emotional turmoil (p. 8).

Here is a principle which now appears to have considerable generality. Fairbanks noted a decided tendency for her patient group to use more past-tense verbs and fewer present- and future-tense verbs than the student group. Seeman, in the study already cited (see also Chapter 11), found that growth in plans and insights during therapy is accompanied by a shift from references to the past to references to the present and the future. And Zimmerman and Langdon, using the case of Mrs. X, found exactly the same picture. As therapy progressed, past-tense verbs declined in frequency and present- and future-tense verbs increased. Now, again with quite independent materials and methods, Grummon obtains the same result! As the last-named investigator warns, we cannot yet be sure that some artifact may not be operating here; for example, it may be that if *anyone* talks protractedly, such a change in verb-tense ratio may occur. However, there is no reason why this should necessarily occur, and there are two independent grounds for thinking that the finding is a valid one: (*a*) the Fairbanks study shows that the incidence of past-, present-, and future-tense verbs differs for comparatively small language samples drawn from two groups differing in a known way with respect to normality-abnormality; and (*b*) such a finding makes inherently good sense from the standpoint of general clinical observation and theory.

Another important confirmation Grummon reports thus:

> *Pronouns.* There was a marked tendency for a high frequency of pronouns to be associated with poor adjustment. However, care must be taken in examining this relationship because (1) pronoun frequency is materially influenced by factors specific to a particular speech situation, (2) pronouns serve a variety of different functions in speech, and (3) pronoun frequency

must be interpreted in terms of the psychological meaning of the speech situation of the speaker. A high incidence rate of the first person seems to be associated with a preoccupation with self, but this may or may not be an unhealthy sign depending upon the demands of the situation. Pronouns classed according to referent (such as people other than self, self and others considered together, impersonal, etc.) show promise for studying both personality and the process of psychotherapy. Pronouns having an indefinite or vague reference should be useful for studying the efficiency of linguistic behavior (pp. 8-9).

Another and quite novel finding of the Grummon study is the following:

Clauses. The number of clauses contained in a given length word sample (an indirect measure of clause length) discriminates between both the overt adjustment status of the subjects and changes in adjustment status resulting from treatment. Longer clauses are associated with better adjustment.

With the speech of Vib and Win serving as a reference point, the two psychotics used few subordinate clauses relative to independent clauses at the beginning of treatment but increased markedly in the percentage of subordinate clauses used at the end of treatment. Other clause categories designed to indicate the degree of subordination fit this same pattern. A low relative frequency of subordinate clauses may be related to depression. The writer suggests that the examination of different kinds of subordinate clauses would be useful in studying the relationships between speech and personality (pp. 9-10).

Grummon reports on a number of other measures which are suggestive but have not yet led to very striking results. In appraising the over-all outcome of his research he says:

It is of considerable theoretical interest to know that the *form* of language, which is generally *not consciously controlled by the client,* changed for the four subjects upon the completion of client-centered counseling and, in the case of two subjects, concurrent electroshock therapy. This finding is a valuable supplement to previous findings that the meanings contained in language, more consciously controlled by the client, change between the beginning and end of client-centered counseling.

However, the mere number of speech characteristics that change significantly between the beginning and end of treatment does not appear to be an adequate guide to the amount of change in adjustment status and personality make-up that results from psychological treatment. To obtain this kind of information, it is necessary to learn more about the psychological meaning of specific speech characteristics. This study makes a beginning in this direction.[25]

Other Promising Approaches to the Empirical Measurement of Psychotherapy.—In light of the energetic advances currently being

[25] The foregoing quotations, from the Summary of Dr. Grummon's unpublished dissertation, are reproduced here with the writer's special permission.

made in learning theory, perception theory, and the psychology of language, on the one hand, and the rapidly growing interest in objective research on psychotherapy, on the other, it is not surprising that many suggestions for new methodologies are currently emerging in the psychological literature. In this, the concluding section of this chapter, only a few of these can be described in any detail, while others must be alluded to only in the most sketchy fashion.

1. OSGOOD'S "SEMANTIC DIFFERENTIAL." The first thing to note is that this method starts with an interest in the phenomenon of *meaning* and represents an attempt to obtain objective measures thereof (Osgood, 1952). Obviously, if this method can be perfected, it will be of great use in therapy research, for whatever one's systematic position with regard to therapy theory it is clear that one of the important dimensions of change is that of attitude, perception, meaning.[26] More concretely, if it can be shown that the denotations and connotations of certain key words (concepts) change during therapy, this will provide a new investigatory tool of considerable power.

The essence of the Osgood method derives from the fact that if human beings are asked to place a word, let us say "mother," on each of a series of scales which are bounded by such dichotomous words as high-low, fair-unfair, strong-weak, rough-smooth, etc., they can do so with a relatively high degree of confidence and consistency. (Test-retest correlations are in the neighborhood of .85.) These scales may, in theory, have any number of points or steps, but work by Osgood and his students has shown that for most purposes a seven-point scale is optimal. By this type of procedure it is clear, then, that a word can be given a series of comparable quantitative values, one for each of the scales on which it has been placed, or rated, by the subject.

It is also equally clear that a similar series of values can be obtained for as many additional words as one wishes to investigate. The resulting data (obtained by revolving the concepts and scales "out of phase" with each other so that the subject cannot perceive exactly what he is doing) may then be arranged in a score matrix of the kind illustrated in Table 18. Here it is apparent that two types of correlational operations can be meaningfully carried out (cf. Chapter 13). The data can be correlated horizontally, i.e., by rows, and when each row has been correlated with every other row, a correlation matrix emerges on the basis of which a conventional factor analysis can be carried out. From such a procedure it is possible to determine what scales are independent, i.e., derive distinctive information from subjects, and what scales are redundant and can thus be usefully eliminated. In this way, the battery of scales employed can be "streamlined," with the result that the subject, with a minimum of time and effort, gives a maximum of information about himself.

---

[26] Dr. George Preston, in his little book *Psychiatry for the curious* (1940), has trenchantly remarked that mental disease, or health, is "a matter of attitudes." One might equally say it is a matter of meanings.

TABLE 18

A SCORE MATRIX ILLUSTRATING TWO WAYS IN WHICH RESULTS FROM OSGOOD'S
SEMANTIC DIFFERENTIAL TEST CAN BE TREATED

By correlating the data by rows and then factor-analyzing the results, one can
determine which scales are similar and which are distinctive; likewise, by correlating the data by columns and then factor-analyzing, one can determine which concepts or word meanings are similar ("close" to each other) and which are distinctive (dissimilar, "remote").

Scales	Concepts							
	A	B	C	D	E	F	G	Etc.
1	3	4	4	6	6	7	6	—
2	3	3	1	1	1	4	1	—
3	2	4	5	7	7	4	4	—
4	3	3	4	2	7	6	6	—
5	3	5	7	4	4	4	4	—
6	4	6	7	7	7	6	7	—
Etc.	—	—	—	—	—	—	—	—

A comparable procedure, applied to the *columns* in Table 18, can be
used to show what words are "close to" (correlated with) each other and
which ones are "remote" in terms of what may be called the subject's
"semantic geography" or meaning manifold. Thus it is possible to get
a "picture" of a person at any given point in time from the standpoint of
his or her *system of meanings* and then to compare this picture with those
of other persons or with that of the same person at some later date. Osgood has devised a method for representing a person's semantic constellation by three-dimensional models such as those graphically portrayed
in Figure 76A and Figure 77A.[27] These particular figures are based
upon the results obtained from asking a young man and a young woman,
at the outset of therapy, to rate the following eight words [28] on each of the
accompanying twenty seven-step scales:

Words	*Scales*
God	High _ _ _ _ _ _ Low
Mother	Green _ _ _ _ _ _ _ Red
Father	Weak _ _ _ _ _ _ _ Strong
Baby	Rough _ _ _ _ _ _ Smooth
Me	Active _ _ _ _ _ _ Passive
Lady	Empty _ _ _ _ _ _ Full
Fraud	Small _ _ _ _ Large

[27] Osgood has actually devised several different methods of achieving this end
(cf. Osgood and Suci, 1952). Although demonstrably related to factor analysis,
these methods represent considerable simplification from the standpoint of computation and seemingly greater appropriateness to the data.

[28] These words were only a few of the total number of words which the subjects
were asked to rate on each of the scales. The others were mainly neutral or "buffer"
words, which are not represented in the findings here reported. However, indications are that these neutral words play no essential function.

Words	*Scales*	
Sin	Cold __ __ __ __ __ __ __	Hot
	Clear __ __ __ __ __ __ __	Hazy
	Young __ __ __ __ __ __ __	Old
	Good __ __ __ __ __ __ __	Bad
	Peaceful __ __ __ __ __ __ __	Ferocious
	Sick __ __ __ __ __ __ __	Healthy
	Angular __ __ __ __ __ __ __	Rounded
	Tense __ __ __ __ __ __ __	Relaxed
	Sad __ __ __ __ __ __ __	Happy
	Soft __ __ __ __ __ __ __	Loud
	Wet __ __ __ __ __ __ __	Dry
	Beautiful __ __ __ __ __ __ __	Ugly
	Fresh __ __ __ __ __ __ __	Stable

Some striking similarities will at once be noted between Figure *76A* and Figure *77A*. Most conspicuous is the fact that in both cases there is polarization of "sin" and "fraud" at one extreme and of the remaining concepts "me," "mother," "father," "God," "lady," and "baby" at the other. This finding is consistent with the writer's view (see Chapters 3 and 6) that the neurotic is typically a person who has repudiated his own self-criticisms, repressed his superego, or, in theological phrase, refused to accept his own sense of wrongdoing or "sin." The result is that the self-critical faculty or forces, denied direct access to consciousness, can assert themselves only indirectly, deviously, bizarrely, in the form of so-called symptoms.

By the process of interpretation, the dissociations are gradually undone, with an ensuing readmission into conscious awareness of the self-criticisms which have presumably, at an earlier time, been rejected. That therapy does in fact operate in this manner is suggested by Figure *76B,* based upon results obtained by a second administration of the Osgood test to the female patient after fifteen interviews. The concepts of "me," "mother," and "father" have all dropped decidedly in the direction of "sin" and "fraud," with "God," "baby," and "lady" retaining essentially their original position.

A few weeks after therapeutic contacts (there were forty-four altogether) had been terminated, the test was administered a third time, with results shown in Figure *76C*. "Me" and "mother" have moved back toward the "good" end of the model, but "father" is left down toward the "bad" end. These changes correspond remarkably well to the clinical facts. One of this patient's main difficulties had been her "alliance" with her father against her mother, and we see that in Figure *76A*, "father" is indeed closer to "me" than was "mother." During therapy this situation was explored and repudiated, with a decided "break" with the father and a new alignment with the mother, as shown in Figure *76C,* by the

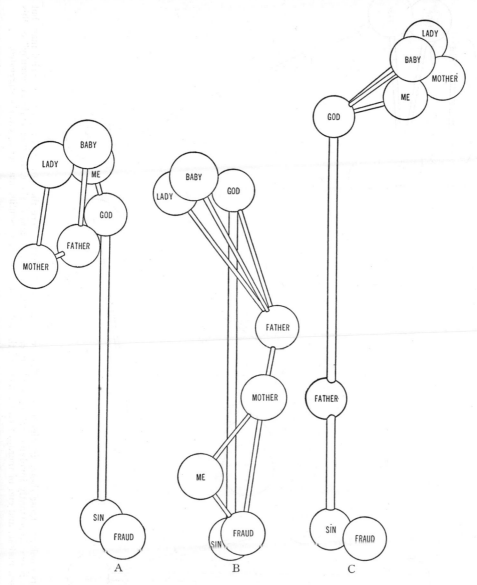

A   B   C

FIG. 76.—Graphic representation of the results obtained by administration of Osgood's Semantic Differential Test during the course of psychotherapy. The three figures, *A*, *B*, and *C*, are two-dimensional representations of geometric models showing the relationship of eight selected concepts in the "mind" of a young woman patient at the beginning, middle, and end of treatment. In the beginning, this patient was experiencing difficulty in playing the role of wife and mother; at the end of therapy, decided gains had taken place in this connection. The models seem to show something of the process whereby the patient renounced her "father identification" and moved in the direction of greater femininity.

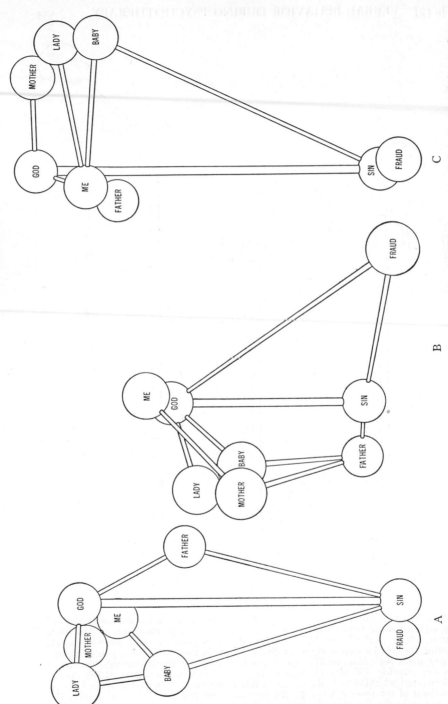

Fig. 77.—Results similar to those shown in Figure 76, obtained with another patient. Here the patient is a young married man, but again the problem is one importantly involving cross-sex identification. Figures *A*, *B*, and *C* show the "semantic geography" of this patient at the outset, middle, and end of therapy; realignment of the patient in a more masculine manner is clearly suggested.

proximity of "me" and "mother" and the distance between "me" and "father."

The second patient with whom this test was used (a young man) like-wise showed, in the beginning, a tendency to be closer to the opposite-sexed parent. This patient spoke very warmly of his mother and in-dicated that he had consciously been relieved when his father had died some years earlier. In the middle of therapy, as represented by Figure 77B, all of the concepts which were initially at the top or "good" end of the model drop, although "me" remains very close to "God." How-ever, this seems to have been a significant type of change, for from it emerged the picture shown in Figure 77C, at the end of therapy (forty-three interviews). Here "me" and "father" are close together, in the general vicinity of "God"; "mother," "lady," and "baby" form another constellation somewhat removed; and the model resumes its original elongated form. These developments conform closely to the clinical events.

There are many reasons for believing that successful therapy involves a kind of crisis which the individual has to pass through in moving toward personality reorganization. The old neurotic pattern has to be aban-doned, with an ensuing period of disorganization and confusion, followed by a restructuring along lines which are consistent and healthy, rather than pathological.[29] This is the general pattern which we see in Fig-ure 76, A-B-C and Figure 77, A-B-C. It may be remarked that at the point of second administration of the test, both patients were beginning to experience symptom alleviation. This fact is reflected, inferentially, by the greater proximity of "me" and "sin" and by a lessening need for the forces of self-criticism to express themselves out of context, dissocia-tively and symptomatically. Ideally, one would like to see the symptoms directly represented in the results of this type of test; but since symptoms may be highly specific to the individual (although in the two cases under discussion they were rather similar, both involving forms of agoraphobia), it may not prove feasible to try to include in a general test items which would be specific enough to catch the highly variable nature of sympto-matic manifestations.

Because of the extremely small number of cases with which this method has thus far been used as a means of measuring the results of psychotherapy (a modified form of the test is now being given to a larger number of patients), no claim can be made for its general validity. How-ever, the findings to date are suggestive. It may even be that the method may prove useful for standard diagnostic purposes. Certainly the test is easy to give and score, and the results can be presented in a form which is highly graphic and communicatively effective.

While the relevance of the Osgood method to research on psycho-therapy is apparent, a question might be raised as to whether it is appro-

[29] These results will be reported in another paper (Luria, Osgood, and Mowrer, 1953), along with an alternative method of analyzing and spatially representing the data obtained from these two patients.

priate to mention it in a chapter on *verbal* changes during therapy. In this procedure the subject does not say or write so much as a word, and the responses which he does make (check marks) are definitely non-verbal. But it will be recalled that the test items to which these responses are made *are* verbal: sentences in the one case and words (concepts) in the other. What the McQuitty and the Osgood procedures (in common with other similar tests) do, in effect, is to provide a situation in which the experimenter makes (or supplies) the test items and the subject marks them, instead of the reverse arrangement, wherein the subject makes the items (answers to questions, spontaneous remarks, or the like) and the experimenter marks them (see Chapter 13). Although one or the other of these two types of procedure may be preferable for particular purposes, it can hardly be said that one is more or less "verbal" than the other.

As far as the Osgood and McQuitty procedures are specifically concerned, it is clear that they pertain to outcome research more than to the investigation of therapeutic process per se; but, as the following section will show, a counterpart of the McQuitty method may be devisable for strictly process purposes, and further inquiry may show the same to be true of the Osgood method. Indeed, the kind of analysis developed by Lazowick and Young, discussed earlier in this chapter, may be thought of as a step which has already been taken in this direction.

2. WINTHROP'S TEST OF ATTITUDE CONSISTENCY. The procedure of Osgood just described is applicable, in its present form, only to "outcome" research in psychotherapy: i.e., one must have the patient's personal cooperation instead of merely the record of his conversations with the therapist. However, it is possible that something of the same underlying logic can be adapted to the purposes of "process" research, and in two papers by Henry Winthrop we find some provocative suggestions to this end.

Winthrop, in his first paper, "Semantic Factors in the Measurement of Personality Integration" (1946), has called attention to the possibility of getting at personality integration in a more formal manner, i.e., by noting the tendency of subjects to endorse statements which are either mutually consistent or contradictory. The items in the test are precisely worded so that the canons of formal logic can be applied to them, and the particular pattern of statements endorsed is interpreted as indicating whether the testee is himself relatively well integrated and consistent or conflicted ("ambivalent") and inconsistent.

The same reasoning, it would seem, might be applied to the statements produced by the patient during the course of therapy. Therapists commonly observe vacillation and self-contradictory tendencies in their patients. Following suggestions made by Winthrop, might it not be possible to derive relatively precise scores of consistency-contradiction in the patient's productions? One would, of course, have to distinguish between what Winthrop, in his second paper (1949), refers to as the "vertical" and the "horizontal" dimension of contradiction, i.e., contradiction between concurrent statements and between statements made at relatively great temporal intervals. If one regards therapy as a form of personal change, it would be almost axiomatic that as therapy progresses there will be changes in respect to the statements that the patient makes. And it is certainly a common observation that what a patient says, often very emphatically, early in therapy will be very different from what we find him saying later in therapy. Insight, by its very nature, is expected to result in changed perceptions, beliefs, and behaviors.

But if we take a briefer span of time, let us say a single interview, we may expect comparatively little change in the patient; and yet we may find highly contradictory statements being made. Sometimes the contradiction is oblique and so subtle that it can be heard only by the clinician's carefully attuned "third ear"; but it is a part of our common store of assumptions that a neurotic individual is necessarily inconsistent, unstable, and vacillating and that as therapy progresses he becomes less so, a trend which ought to be reflected by a greater degree of logical congruence in the patient's verbal productions. In fact, one useful way to define neurosis is to say that it involves a set of beliefs and behaviors which cannot be consistently maintained and that normality, by contrast, involves a system of attitudes and actions which is more permanently workable, i.e., can be consistently maintained for an indefinite period of time.

Enough has thus been said to show the direction in which the Winthrop articles point: to a study of the statements, or "propositions," contained in psychotherapeutic protocols from the standpoint of logical congruence and contradiction. The details of such a method of analysis remain to be worked out, but the possibilities here, from the standpoint of theory, are numerous. Only a few of these can be considered at this time.

First of all, it should be noted that the line of thought pursued by Winthrop is congruent with the point of view taken in the first part of this chapter, namely that neurosis starts as social deception and grows into a process of dissociation which, in order to maintain itself, must frequently be extended, thus giving to neurosis its aura of a progressive, malignant disease. Using a somewhat different vocabulary, Winthrop (1949) appears to be saying much the same thing in the following passages:

A subject will refuse to perceive relations which he is perfectly capable of perceiving because to do so would involve the formation of an attitude which runs counter to certain egocentric or neurotic desires. It is not that the subject will not, cannot, or does not frame such an attitude for himself. He does; but it is left covert, for when it is hidden he can refuse egocentrically to abide by its implications in behavior, above all, evaluative, prospective, socioethical behavior. If, on the other hand, it were made overt, he might be subject to social and family pressure to conform . . . in order to earn or retain the approval and good will of others. . . . When it is true that he insists both upon this approval and upon his egocentric satisfactions, concealment of the attitude is imperative. To reveal it would be to eventually invite conflict, for others would then be in a position to force him either to comply with the domain of the attitude or retain his ego satisfactions and take the consequences of his choice. To avoid such a conflict he resorts to neurotic concealment, that is, he conceals from those from whom he expects approval [or fears punishment, we may add]. . . .

This neurotic concealment takes place by means of *overextensionalizing* [30] devices. The subject refuses to make connections, to classify. Those sets of experiences which could reasonably be integrated under a given, socially workable attitude are compulsively, dishonestly, and sometimes pathologically treated as though they were unique, discrete situations which bore no relationship to one another. . . . As a result of such dishonest *overextensionalizing*, values which are completely incompatible with one another, frequently even for the same context, are allowed psychologically to exist side by side. From such telic chaos only a low order of attitude-consistency can reasonably be expected, so that personality disintegration in our sense of the term may be easily generated. Carried to pathological extremes, so as to become a neurologically irreversible habit, overextensionalization might even lead to the schizophrenic loss of the "categorical" attitude (pp. 213-14).

This point of view is the antithesis of the one repetitively emphasized by the "general semanticists." Winthrop agrees with Korzybski, as probably everyone would, that one can, to be sure, go beyond one's data and overgeneralize ("overintensionalize"), but it is useful to see that the possibility of error is not entirely in one direction. As Winthrop pertinently notes, "A too literal interpretation of semantic literature with respect to the dangers of intentional thinking [generalizing] . . . might seem to suggest that a hopeless schizophrenic is the most desirable type of semanticist" (p. 215) ; and here the author refers to the work of Goldstein on the loss of "abstracting" ability in pathological states and cites, on an earlier page, the findings obtained by Vigotsky, Kasanin, Hanfmann, Cameron, Angyal, and others through the use of concept-formation tests (the so-called *Zuordnungstests*) with schizophrenics and other psychotic subjects.

Winthrop's conclusion in this connection follows:

. . . it should be said that an optimum, semantic adjustment should be neither completely intensional nor completely extensional, even so far as desirable habit formations are concerned. It should always be a balance between the two types of habit formation. Consequently, both in relation to the maintenance of attitude-consistency and its corollary, personality integration, and in relation to their specific interest in linguistic adjustment, the works in

---

[30] This term, a peculiarly unhappy choice from the standpoint of immediately conveying the intended meaning, is used by Winthrop as the reverse of "overintensionalizing" or *overgeneralizing*. "Overextensionalizing" thus means a too specific, too concrete, too discriminating frame of mind, one in which the individual fails or refuses to generalize to a degree which is legitimate and, indeed, logically and psychologically necessary.

general semantics should, in the future, devote some research to the detection and measurement of overextensionality (p. 214).

What the author is saying here is almost exactly what modern statisticians are saying when they point to "errors of the first order," so-called, and "errors of the second order." The former (and more familiar) ones are the errors which come from basing a conclusion or generalization on too few instances, while the latter (and only recently emphasized) errors come from not attaching *enough* significance to the obtained results or observations. To point the parallel in another field, that of learning theory, Winthrop is saying that realistic behavior usually lies somewhere between too rapid learning (jumping to conclusions) and too slow learning (being *too* skeptical, *too* hard to convince). Or, to draw the analogy perhaps more sharply, living organisms can err in their behavior either by trying to generalize (apply past learning) too fast or by trying to be too specific, too particularistic in interpreting the results of past experiences.

Applied most concretely to the theory of neurosis and its treatment, what the foregoing discussion comes to is the suggestion that personality difficulties are probably far less likely to result from overgeneralizing (failure of discrimination, failure of extinction, etc.) than from a refusal to see connections, continuity, or generality where continuity manifestly exists. It is, as noted earlier, not the tendency to *affirm* too much that causes the trouble but an excessive trend toward *denial,* and its expression in deception and dissociation.

But a forceful objection can be advanced at this point. Some of the readers of Winthrop's first article took the point of view that a test of "attitude-consistency" could not possibly reveal basic neurotic or dissociative trends for the following reason. If the trend toward denial has progressed far enough to have produced dissociation, then many, or perhaps all, of the contradictory, inconsistent, conflictful attitudes within the personality will have been excluded from consciousness and will therefore not be tapped by a pencil-and-paper or questionnaire-type test.

In his second paper, in a section entitled "The 'Subconscious' and the Attitudinal *Anlage,*" Winthrop puts the matter in this way:

A common, frequent, but superficial criticism of our procedure was to assert that the *real* attitudinal basis for our behavior is to be found in the mechanism of the "subconscious" and that there is therefore no way of really detecting an individual's attitudes and consequently no way of measuring the extent of his conflicts (pp. 103-04).

The author characterizes this objection as "mystagogic obstructionism." This, in the judgment of the present writer, is not to give the criticism its due and is to miss the correct, and by no means uninstructive, solution to the difficulty. Winthrop's attempt to deal with the problem runs as follows:

If our critics take the position that these "subconscious" attitudes determine only covert behavior, then their position is a nihilistic one, scientifically speaking, for by definition "covert" behavior is indeterminable in principle and in practice and, in the last analysis, is not behavior at all, so that such a stand would be meaningless and not worthy of attention in serious intellectual inquiry. Since all behavior must therefore be overt to be behavior at all, the second line of retreat for our critics would exist in relation to another consideration. Either, it is true that a time-study of the individual's overt behavior is capable of being expressed verbally in the form of hortatory, conative, and optative statements, or, it is not so capable of being expressed. If our critics assert that it is not so capable of being expressed, they take an impossible position. First, they confuse the sense in which they have used the word "determine," for, if the attitudes in the subconscious "determine" overt behavior, by an implication not too obvious to immediate inspection, such a use of the verb "determine" suggests clearly that the expressed attitudes are not ineffable. Second, if in some obscure and inscrutable sense no cognitive liaison could be effected between the determining attitudes of the subconscious and the expressed behavior, the burden of proving that either analytically or empirically such a link *can never be established* would lie with the protagonists of such a position. For these two reasons it seems most reasonable to assert that a time-study of the individual's behavior is verbalizable into sentential assertions of an attitudinal nature. The final line of retreat would then be to assert that, even if the attitudes in the subconscious are verbalizable from a time-study of the individual's behavior, the logical relationships of contradiction and contrariety do not obtain among such verbalizable attitudes. To this last line of retreat, however, we think we have addressed ourselves sufficiently in the preceding sections (pp. 185-86).

There are two more direct ways of dealing with this problem. First we may recall the existence of the so-called "projective" devices, whose intended function is, specifically, to plumb the unconscious regions of personality and to elicit, in language which only the tester can presumably understand, the nature of the attitudes and other energies imprisoned there. Thus, in theory at any rate, all we need to do to develop a test of attitude consistency which will obviate the problem raised by the fact of repression is to have a test with two parts, each with more or less parallel items: one set of items designed to get *conscious* attitudes or values and the other designed to reveal the corresponding *unconscious* (and presumably often quite contradictory) attitudes and values. Some students of projection psychology may lay claim to now being able to conduct such an inquiry, but no such claim has been as yet generally validated. (This is a line of thinking which Winthrop in some measure anticipated.)

The other way of meeting the objection to tests of personal integration or consistency where a part of the personality is excluded from consciousness is as follows: As the present writer has pointed out elsewhere in this volume (Chapter 3), there are good grounds for distinguishing between two aspects or phases of neurosis: the *latent* phase and the *manifest* phase. In the former, dissociations are presumably working well, i.e., the offending, conflict-producing impulses (Winthrop would say "attitudes") are kept successfully out of consciousness, and at this time it would be reasonable to suppose that the repressed energies have no very definite expression or representation in consciousness. Therefore, one might not expect the inconsistency, contradiction, or conflict between the consciously experienced forces and the unconscious forces to be apparent at this stage in a test of the kind described by Winthrop. But, as we know, repression is not likely to be perfectly maintained for a very long period, with the result that, sooner or later, there will be a return or threatened return of "the repressed" with ensuing disturbances of consciousness—anxiety, depression, and inferiority feelings—which the patient may then attempt to cope with by any of a variety of so-called neurotic symptoms. It is at this point that the afflicted individual is most likely to resort to psychotherapy, and at such times it is certainly correct to say that the "unconscious" is by no means completely unconscious. The intruding forces from the realm of the repressed now make themselves felt in the form of neurotic affects and symptom defenses, and it is precisely by listening attentively to what the *patient* (the ego) says, on the one hand, and what his *symptoms* (the forces of the superego) say, on the other, that the greatest advances are made in the direction of discovering the "contradiction" that underlies the neurosis.

What this comes to, then, is that, as long as personal contradictions and conflicts are successfully held in abeyance by dissociations, neither the therapist nor the tester using tests which allow full exercise of the patient's censorial faculties can detect the opposing forces.[31] But when the neurosis becomes manifest, then we can get at the inconsistencies— by the intuitive sensitivity of the therapist, by tests like Winthrop's, or perhaps it can be detected, by careful analysis, in the recorded protocols.[32]

In a section of his second paper, on "The Gestalt Concept of the 'Total Personality' and Personality Integration," Winthrop discusses another matter of broad theoretical importance. There can be no doubt that Gestalt psychologists have been influential in creating the present widespread and healthy interest in *ego psychology*. *Integration* is an ego-

---

[31] Whether the so-called projective tests can do any better at this stage is an open question. If such tests can tap the roots of a successfully controlled, i.e., latent, neurosis, they presumably do so by creating situations, usually in the realm of visual perception, in which the neurosis becomes "manifest" but only to a limited extent, i.e., to the extent of permitting the (specially trained) test interpreter, but not the patient, to perceive or be aware of the neurosis.

[32] When a neurosis becomes transformed into the negative transference relationship, the factor of resistance, opposition, inconsistency, or contradiction becomes extremely clear. At this stage, the patient is saying certain things and the therapist is saying something different, i.e., he is "interpreting"; and to the extent that what the therapist is saying is but an expression, now made fully explicit and overt, of what a submerged, denied part of the patient's own personality has previously been *trying* to say, we can regard the patient-therapist conflict as representing a two-person, diadal version of what has previously been a conflict, or "inconsistency," between different parts, or regions, of the patient himself. For further discussion of transference as an interpersonal version of what was formerly an intrapsychic conflict, see Chapter 3.

psychology concept, and so is *anxiety,* conceived as the psychic pain experienced when the ego's integration, cohesion, systematic structure, or "security" is threatened. But by the emphasis which Gestaltists have put upon such phrases as, "The organism always acts and reacts *as a whole,"* they have quite unnecessarily excluded from their purview a phenomenon which is the *sine qua non* for psychopathology. If Gestaltists had said that the psychologically *healthy* organism always "acts as a whole," they would have been on more solid grounds, for the possibility would have then been open to see psychopathology precisely as a *failure* of wholeness, of consistency, of integration (Mowrer, 1950, chaps. xv and xix).

Winthrop's attack on this problem runs as follows:

In general Gestaltists questioned the significance of a test of "attitude-consistency" and questioned its diagnostic value in indicating psychological conflict precisely because an attitude-consistency test was not a stimulus situation calling for the response of the "total personality." . . .

The phrase "total personality" is used somewhat obfuscatedly and tyrannically in the literature of Gestaltism. . . .

In meeting this Gestaltist criticism of our test of attitude-consistency we should therefore rightfully begin with some operational understanding of what can be meant by the phrases "total personality," no matter how crude and prosaic the content of such a concept may turn out to be (pp. 205-6).

The procedure which Winthrop proposes as an operational basis is factor-analytic in character and can, for present purposes, be omitted; the implications thereof are described thus:

At present the phrase "total personality" is not only used fuzzily in Gestaltist literature but this fuzziness varies somewhat in connotation from one writer to another. Even if there were a standard definition of "total personality," in use by all psychologists, regardless of their particular philosophical positions, it should still be noted that there is probably no test (of any kind) responses to which would involve the "total personality." . . . This being so, by definition, no single member of the battery nor any subset of members, used as a composite test, such as *Zuordnungstests,* can ever be asserted capable of dealing with or measuring the "total personality."

It is for these reasons, we repeat, that our Gestaltist correspondents' dismissal of an attitude-consistency test as being less significant than we have supposed, on the grounds that psychologists must be prepared to deal with the "total personality," cannot be taken too seriously (p. 208).

Likewise, to the extent that "personality disintegration" in our sense of the word "disintegration," as a conflict in values and goals, will become a matter of serious concern for academic and clinical research, we too shall inescapably have to confine ourselves to the detection and measurements *of something less than the "total personality"* (p. 210).[33]

[33] For another discussion of the dilemmas which *Gestalttheorie* faces when it moves into the clinical area, see Paul Schilder's 1932 paper, "Psychoanalysis and philosophy," which is reproduced as chap. i in his posthumous volume, *Psychoanalysis, man, and society* (1951).

Perhaps the problem can be put into most concise terms by posing it as a paradox. Granted that the personality or self-system always *tries* to act or function "as a whole," the fact is that it sometimes finds its wholeness or integration seriously threatened. Here, because of an inability to achieve a high-order synthesis (abstraction) which would preserve the unity of the personality, the self-system sometimes—and here is the paradox—resorts to a deliberate splitting-off of parts of personality, of the kind we term dissociation. Put most simply, *the person divides himself in order that he may remain unified.*

Once put into such a flagrant paradox, the difficulty is easily resolved. With the Gestaltists, we can properly assume that the self-system, if it is to remain a *system,* must be integrated, interconnected, organized, unified. This integration or wholeness is ordinarily preserved by "normal" mental processes, but sometimes human beings fall into the error of using pathogenic mechanisms, notably those of deception and dissociation; and when this occurs unity is preserved (temporarily) by the expedient of creating within the *total* personality, but outside of consciousness proper, one or more fragmented subsystems or lesser constellations which Freud termed "the unconscious" or "the repressed." In therapy, the objective is to help the patient permit a gradual return back into consciousness of the fissioned-off piece or pieces of the main self-system, where the original conflict or conflicts, now reactivated, can be resolved integratively rather than disintegratively, i.e., in such a way as to lead to greater strength and maturity of personality, rather than to neurosis.

There are numerous other issues discussed by Winthrop in such a suggestive manner as to have both practical and theoretical implications. Only two more of these can be alluded to here, briefly. Elsewhere the present writer (Mowrer, 1950) has taken the position that from one point of view a neurosis is a sign of personal strength rather than weakness; it is a sign that the afflicted person—by the very intensity of his anxiety and other neurotic affects—is still striving to achieve an integrated self-system and an orderly, consistent way of life. Winthrop, in keeping with this point of view, notes that although neurotic individuals always have a low index of integration or "attitude consistency," all persons with poor integration are not necessarily neurotic. He says:

The concrete-minded personality, just this side of schizophrenia, can survive with relative ease in a family which is undemanding and more or less concrete-minded, itself, in an occupation in which, in a sense, concrete-mindedness is at a premium, as in many types of unskilled labor and certain types of skilled labor, and in a circle of acquaintance in which the abstract attitude is conspicuous by its absence. Since the writer has had the good fortune to have met many such personalities functioning outside of institutions and who were observably cheerful and apparently happy, a low *index of power* [of abstraction, consistency, integration] clearly does not generate psychological conflict. In fact a case may be made out for the view that a rather high order of intelligence is required for psychological conflict which requires an awareness and a capacity for recognizing the broad dimensions underlying evaluative activity, which one individual who has little of the "categorical" attitude can hope to cope with, but which awareness and capacity are definitely called for in the maintenancy of attitude-consistency (p. 199).

Finally we may note a useful distinction which this author makes between *factual* and *evaluative* statements. As an example of the first, Winthrop gives the following: "Franklin went to Paris." The statement may be either true or untrue, but it is "factual," i.e., purely objective in its reference. On the other hand, the same statement, with only slight modification, becomes evaluative: e.g., "I hope Franklin went to Paris." Slight as this change may seem, it is of great psychological significance. It should be noted, first of all, that the *subject* of these two sentences is different; in the one case it is "Franklin" and in the other case it is "I." And it is likewise noteworthy that the principal verb is now "hope," instead of "went."

The bearing of all this on one of the technical aspects of client-centered counseling is obvious. One of the very common devices in this type of therapy is to repeat ("reflect") back to the patient essentially what he has said, but with the prefix: "You feel (think, wish, fear, hope, suspect, etc.) that. . . ." Superficial and sometimes meaningless as this procedure may appear, it has two persistent effects: it slants the topic of discussion constantly in the direction of the *patient himself* and indicates a continual focusing by the therapist upon how the patient *feels* and *perceives*. While the client-centered therapist eschews "interpretation," by the device just described he is continually making *inferences* and thus going beyond, slightly or greatly, what the patient himself says. As indicated in Chapter 3, it is possible that "nondirective reflection" and "interpretation" may, upon careful analysis, turn out to be less different than they at first appear to be. In any event, we see the utility of looking carefully at the words and sentences used in therapy, not just from the standpoint of their intended or perceived meanings, but also from the standpoint of their syntax, grammar, and logic. To this end Winthrop's papers deserve close examination.

3. OTHER POSSIBLE RESEARCH METHODOLOGIES. As already indi- cated, there is a tendency for psychologists and social scientists to concern themselves increasingly with the various aspects of language and its func- tions. From this widespread and growing concern we can expect the emergence of new techniques, over and beyond those already reviewed in this chapter, for the scientific analysis of the verbal materials produced in the course of psychotherapy. It is not feasible here to pursue all of the possibilities now appearing on the horizon for developing new method- ologies, but some of the investigations and theoretical papers which can be profitably studied in this connection are the following: Arronson (1952), Bales (1950), Bugenthal (1952), Hayakawa (1947), Henry (1951), Donald Johnson (1950), Johnson, Johnson, and Mark (1951),

Katz and Braly (1947), Krout and Ross (1935), Lee (1947), Mead (1947), George Miller (1951), Pickford (1950), Ruesch and Bateson (1951), Sanford (1942a, 1942b), Mapheus Smith (1950), White (1951), and Wischner (1950). The reader will also wish to consult a series of suggestions recently published by a group of investigators at the Washington University School of Medicine (Watson and Mensh, 1951a and 1951b; Watson, Mensh, and Gildea, 1951; Watson, 1952a and 1952b); also Goss (1952) and Wischner (1952).

CHAPTER 18

TENSION CHANGES DURING PSYCHOTHERAPY, WITH SPECIAL REFERENCE TO RESISTANCE

By O. Hobart Mowrer, Ph.D., Bernard H. Light, Ph.D., Zella Luria, Ph.D., and Marjorie P. Zeleny, M.S.

The plan and purpose of this chapter are as follows. In psychotherapy much depends upon the skill of the therapist in understanding and properly dealing with the resistances of his patients. Freud was the first to call attention to this fact, but in certain important respects his discussion of the problem is incomplete and self-contradictory. The first part of this chapter is therefore devoted to a further analysis of the problem and an attempted resolution of some of the paradoxes which inhere in the Freudian formulations.

Carl Rogers and his many followers have long held that resistance, and more particularly transference phenomena, are not inherent features of the therapeutic process but are rather the results of inappropriate technique. In the second part of this chapter the Rogerian arguments on this score are reviewed and evaluated in the context of the modified Freudian position developed in the first part.

Since resistance is not only interesting from a theoretical standpoint but is also of practical significance in evaluating a patient's progress and in predicting whether he will continue in or leave therapy, it has seemed worth while to try to develop means of measuring this phenomenon during the course of therapy. In the third part of the chapter, empirical research with two such measures is reported and the results are collated with another measure previously described, namely the discomfort-relief quotient (see Chapters 10 and 11).

The Enigma of Resistance in Freudian Theory

Freud on Resistance and Repression.—The best theoretical statement on the problem of resistance is that contained in Chapter xix of Freud's * *General introduction to psycho-analysis* (1935a). Here Freud's original observations are described with great clarity and a theory is formulated which still appears to be right up to a point but which now calls for supplementation and correction. Since Freud's chapter is of such central importance, the following discussion will be based upon it al-

---

* References are to the bibliography at the back of the book.

most exclusively, and numerous excerpts will be quoted in order to provide a sure foundation for the criticisms and emendations here suggested.

Freud * dramatically opens this chapter by pointing out the paradoxical character of therapeutic resistance. He says:

When we undertake to cure a patient of his symptoms he opposes against us a vigorous and tenacious *resistance* throughout the entire course of the treatment. This is such an extraordinary thing that we cannot expect much belief in it. . . . To think that the patient, whose symptoms cause him and those about him such suffering, who is willing to make such sacrifices in time, money, effort, and self-conquest in order to be freed from them,—that he should in the interests of his illness, resist the help offered him. How improbable this statement must sound ! . . .

The resistance shown by patients is highly varied and exceedingly subtle, often hard to recognize and protean in the manifold forms it takes; the analyst needs to be continually suspicious and on his guard against it (Freud, 1920, p. 253).

The author then speaks in detail regarding the numerous ways in which resistance may manifest itself, but these strategies are now sufficiently well known not to require enumeration here. More to the point are the theoretical issues, and Freud soon returns to these in his discussion of the relationship between resistance and transference. He says:

The intellectual resistances are not the worst; one can always get the better of them. But the patient knows how to set up resistances within the boundaries of analysis proper, and the defeat of these is one of the most difficult tasks of the technique. Instead of remembering certain of the feelings and states of mind of his previous life, he reproduces them, lives through again such of them as, by means of what is called the "transference," may be made effective in opposition against the physician and the treatment. If the patient is a man, he usually takes this material from his relationship with his father, in whose place he has now put the physician; and in so doing he erects resistances out of his struggles to attain to personal independence and independence of judgment, out of his ambition, the earliest aim of which was to equal or to excel the father, out of his disinclination to take the burden of gratitude upon himself for the second time in his life. There are periods in which one feels that the patient's desire to put the analyst in the wrong, to make him feel his impotence, to triumph over him, has completely ousted the worthier desire to bring the illness to an end. Women have a genius for exploiting in the interests of resistance a tender erotically tinged transference to the analyst; when this attraction reaches a certain intensity all interest in the actual situation of treatment fades away, together with every obligation incurred upon undertaking it. The inevitable jealousy and the embitterment consequent upon the unavoidable rejection, however considerately it is handled, is bound to injure the personal relationship with the physician, and so to put out of action one of the most powerful propelling forces in the analysis (p. 256).

Here, in effect, Freud is saying that the resistance, or opposition, which patients show in therapy is essentially the same as the opposition they have shown, as children, to the attempts of parents and others to socialize them. And it is for this reason that this form of resistance is characterized as *transference:* since therapeutic resistance is but a re-enactment of oppositional attitudes and strategies which have been present in other, earlier interpersonal relationships, it can properly be referred to as "transferred."

In keeping with this implied line of thought, Freud then remarks upon the therapeutic opportunity afforded by transference behavior:

Resistances of this kind must not be narrowly condemned. They contain so much of the most important material from the patient's past life and bring it back in so convincing a fashion that they come to be of the greatest assistance to the analysis, if a skilful technique is employed correctly to turn them to the best use. What is noteworthy is that this material always serves at first as a resistance and comes forward in a guise which is inimical to the treatment. Again it may be said that they are character-traits, individual attitudes of the ego, which are thus mobilized to oppose the attempted alterations. . . . Also you must not carry away the impression that we look upon the appearance of these resistances as an unforeseen danger threatening our analytic influence. No, we know that these resistances are bound to appear; we are dissatisfied only if we cannot rouse them definitely enough and make the patient perceive them as such. Indeed, we understand at least that the overcoming of these resistances is the essential work of the analysis, that part of the work which alone assures us that we have achieved something for the patient (pp. 256-57).

Before proceeding further, let us summarize Freud's argument up to this point. It begins with the empirical observation, which all therapists can confirm, that patients actively resist our efforts to help them. Then comes the proposition, only a little less easily demonstrated, that the interpersonal strategies they employ in this connection bear more than a passing resemblance to strategies they have used as children in opposing the efforts of their parents to train and educate them. It is therefore understandable that the step which Freud next takes is to show that the oppositional forces which are thus mobilized by the patient in therapy are not only the same as those shown, at an earlier stage, to parental authority but that they are also the same as the forces that have been responsible for the phenomenon which Freud made the precondition for all neurosis, namely repression. His remarks on this score follow:

In what way can we now account for this fact observed, that the patient struggles so energetically against the relief of his symptoms and the restoration of his mental processes to normal functioning? We say that we have come upon the traces of powerful forces at work here opposing any change in the condition; they must be the same forces that originally induced the condition. In the formation of symptoms some process must have been gone through, which our experience in dispersing them makes us able to reconstruct.

As we already know from Breuer's observations, it follows from the existence of a symptom that some mental process has not been carried through to an end in a normal manner so that it could become conscious; the symptom is a substitute for that which has not come through. Now we know where to place the forces which we suspect to be at work. A vehement effort must have been exercised to prevent the mental process in question from penetrating into consciousness and as a result it has remained unconscious; being unconscious it had the power to construct a symptom. The same vehement effort is again at work during analytic treatment, opposing the attempt to bring the unconscious into consciousness. This we perceive in the form of resistances. The pathogenic process which is demonstrated by the resistances we call REPRESSION (pp. 258-59).

The Contradiction in Freud's Argument.—All the foregoing is empirically well based and logically compelling. However, it is in one important respect incomplete, and it was in his attempt to supply the missing link that Freud seems to have seriously erred. Implicit in what has thus far been said is the inference (*a*) that in repression one is directing against the internalized voice of parental authority, namely the conscience or superego, the same opposition that one has previously directed against one's actual parents, (*b*) that neurosis arises, once repression has been established, because the forces of conscience, now denied direct access to consciousness, express themselves indirectly, i.e., symptomatically, and (*c*) that when we, as therapists, attempt to "make the unconscious conscious," i.e., when we try to help conscience once again obtain a "hearing" from the ego, we encounter the same negative attitudes and hostile strategies that had previously been directed against parents and which were later turned against the conscience in the form of repression.

But these inferences, which seem to follow so naturally from his stated premises, Freud never made explicit. Instead, at this juncture he gave his reasoning a peculiar twist. It was not, he believed, repression of the internal surrogate of parental (and general social) authority that provides the precondition of neurosis; instead he assumed, for reasons which we will try to understand more fully later, that it was sexuality, *always* sexuality which falls under repression and thus provides the energy behind neurotic symptoms.[1]

That Freud believed repression of sexuality to be the *sine qua non* of neurosis is today so well known as to make documentation unnecessary, except that it will be useful to remind ourselves, once again, of precisely what he said on this score in the chapter which is here under scrutiny. Let us pick up the train of his exposition with the following sentences:

By means of analysis we can always discover the purpose behind the neurotic symptom. This is of course nothing new to you; I have already pointed it out in two cases of neurosis. But, to be sure, what do two cases signify? You

---

[1] Freud (1933c) later modified this position to the extent of conceding that another "instinct" besides sex, namely *aggression,* might also fall under repression and thus become pathogenic; but this was a modification of detail, not of principle.

have a right to demand 200 cases, innumerable cases, in demonstration of it. But then, I cannot comply with that. So you must fall back on personal experience, or upon belief, which in this matter can rely upon the unanimous testimony of all psychoanalysts.

You will remember that in the two cases in which we submitted the symptoms to detailed investigation analysis led to the innermost secrets of the patient's sexual life. In the first case, moreover, the purpose or tendency of the symptom under examination was particularly evident; in the second case, it was perhaps to some extent veiled by another factor to be mentioned later. Well now, what we found in these two examples we should find in every case we submitted to analysis. Every time we should be led by analysis to the sexual experiences and desires of the patient, and every time we should have to affirm that the symptom served the same purpose. This purpose shows itself to be the gratification of sexual wishes; the symptoms serve the purpose of sexual gratification for the patient; they are a substitute for satisfactions which he does not obtain in reality (pp. 262-63).

If Freud felt that the phenomenon of resistance would appear incredible to his readers, how much less probable would these asseverations regarding sexuality seem! That they are incompatible with common intuition and traditional beliefs is perhaps not very relevant, from either a logical or a scientific standpoint [2]; but, more to the point, they are in direct contradiction to what one would expect on the basis of the system of thought which Freud himself created and which has been reviewed in the preceding pages.

Perhaps the quickest way to penetrate to the heart of this contradiction is as follows. If one assumes, with Freud, that sexual inhibition is the neurotic's central problem and that the therapist's main task is therefore to champion the right of such impulses to expression, how illogical it would be to call the patient's resistance to such a campaign "transference"! Certainly this role of the would-be therapist is not a role which parents have formerly played; quite the contrary. If one assumes that parents, conscience (introjected parents), and therapist (substitute parent) are all trying to accomplish the same thing, i.e., to help the patient move from subservience to the primitive pleasure principle toward observance of the reality principle (optimal integration of sacrifices and satisfactions through time), then it is legitimate to see in the neurotic's opposition to one something very like his opposition to the other. But if one posits that the neurotic's parents have produced in him a superego which is unreasonable and unduly harsh and that the proper function of the therapist is to reverse this state of affairs, then it is difficult to see why one would expect the patient to turn against the therapist the *same*

[2] Freud's observation that every therapy leads one "to the sexual experiences and desires of the patient" is sound enough; but, as shown in Chapter 17, there is a quite specific and special reason for this which accords well with the view that repression characteristically goes against conscience rather than against the sexual "instinct."

set of forces as those which have been used to oppose parents and their internal surrogate. If parents have stood for severity, especially in the area of sexuality, and if the therapist stands for permissiveness and indulgence, then in what sense can we speak of the patient's reactions to the therapist in his curative endeavors as "transference"? If the therapist thus aligns himself with the patient's supposedly repressed id, against the patient's superego and, implicitly, also against his parents, would we not rather expect the patient's reactions to such a person to be the antithesis of those which he first directed toward parents and which later instituted repression?

If, on the other hand, one posits that in neurosis it is conscience rather than sexuality that falls under repression, the whole conceptual structure becomes tightly knit and impeccably logical. The therapist, in thus confronting the patient, does not see his task as that of undoing the overzealous work of parents but as taking up those aspects of the patient's socialization which have remained unfinished and, with good fortune, succeeding where actual parents have failed or, at most, have succeeded only partially. That the therapist, approaching his task from this orientation, should encounter the same forces within the patient's personality as formerly opposed both parents and conscience is almost axiomatic; whereas, if the therapist sees his responsiblity as that of opposing conscience, parents, and, to some extent, society in general, the theoretical picture is as blurred as the therapeutic outcome is problematic.[3]

---

[3] A more liberal interpretation of the Freudian position might hold that the therapist "aligns" himself with neither the id nor the superego but rather with *the ego*. In so doing he supposedly gives the patient sufficient "ego strength" to readmit to consciousness id-superego conflicts which had previously been so ominous that the patient's only recourse, at an earlier period, was repression. A few contemporary interpreters of Freud (e.g., Fenichel, 1945, and Fromm, 1947) have suggested that when a weak or infantile ego is faced by such a conflict, the resulting repression may go in *either* direction, toward the id forces, in one case, toward the superego in another. And from this it would follow, as it does not follow from Freud's own stated position and that of most of his followers (but see Mowrer, 1950, pp. 483-86, and pages 561-64 below), that symptoms may represent the energies of *either* the id or the superego. This is not the place for an extended examination of the merits of this position. However, three observations are in order.

1. While we are not prepared to state that neurosis is never based upon a repression of sexuality (or hostility), we believe that in the overwhelming majority of cases (and possibly in all) it involves the opposite strategy, namely superego repression.

2. It is not clear to us exactly what it means, operationally, for a therapist to "align himself" with the ego. The neurotic's ego is committed to a policy of peace-through-repression; surely this is not a campaign to which the therapist wishes to be a party. Instead he "aligns" himself with the parts of the personality that have been excluded from consciousness and which could thereafter manifest themselves only in the form of "symptoms." Patiently but persistently, by means of interpretations—one might equally well say, by means of "translations"—the therapist works to get these denied energies readmitted to consciousness, on the assumption that then, and only then, can the ego grow, mature, gain the "strength" it has previously lacked. Of course, the fact that the therapist is "there" and shows no fear of the consequences of allowing a "return of the repressed" may provide a form of ego support for the patient. But it is difficult to see how anything could be achieved if the therapist, from the outset, aligned himself exclusively with the ego and never

That Freud was not altogether oblivious to the inconsistencies in his own thinking on this score is borne out by the following excerpts. He says:

It is certainly possible to make all kinds of objections to the proposition that neurotic symptoms are substitutes for sexual gratifications. I will discuss two of them today. If any one of you has himself undertaken the analysis of a large number of neurotics, he will perhaps shake his head and say: "In certain cases this is not at all applicable, in them the symptoms seem rather to contain the opposite purpose, of excluding or of discontinuing sexual gratification." I shall not dispute your interpretation. In psychoanalysis things are often a good deal more complicated than we could wish: if they had been simpler, psychoanalysis would perhaps not have been required to bring them to light. Certain features of the ritual of our second patient are distinctly recognizable as being of this ascetic character, inimical to sexual satisfaction; e.g., her removing the clocks for the magic purpose of preventing erections at night, or her trying to prevent the falling and breaking of vessels, which amounts to a protection of her virginity. In other cases of ceremonials on going to bed which I have analysed this negative character was far more marked; the whole ritual could consist of defensive regulations against sexual recollections and temptations. But we have long ago learnt from psychoanalysis that opposites do not constitute a contradiction. We might extend our proposition and say that the purpose of the symptom is either a sexual gratification or a defense against it; in hysteria the positive, wish-fulfilling character predominates on the whole, and in the obsessional neurosis the negative ascetic character. . . .

It will not be easy to dispose of a second difficulty. When you consider a whole series of symptom-interpretations, your first opinion would probably be that the conception of a sexual substitute-gratification has to be stretched to its widest limits in order to include them. You will not neglect to point out that these symptoms offer nothing real in the way of gratification, that often enough they are confined to reanimating a sensation, or to enacting a fantasy arising from some sexual complex. Further, that the ostensible sexual gratification is very often of an infantile and unworthy character, perhaps approximating to a masturbatory act, or is reminiscent of dirty habits which long ago in childhood had been forbidden and abandoned. And further still, you will express your astonishment that anyone should reckon among sexual gratifications those which can only be described as gratifications of cruel or horrible appetites, or which may be termed unnatural. Indeed, we shall come to no

took up the cause of the repressed forces. (For further analysis of this problem, see the ensuing discussion of the meaning and management of panic reactions in patients.)

3. This discussion reminds one of the semantic and conceptual nature of many of the problems which we currently face in this area. There are some therapists who maintain that the id-ego-superego conceptual scheme is entirely unsatisfactory and who refuse to employ it. Our feeling is that, despite real difficulties, this tripartite division of the personality proposed by Freud is basically sound and that the solution to present problems in this area lies in the direction of refining and explicating this scheme, not in discarding it.

agreement on these latter points until we have submitted human sexuality to a thorough investigation and have thus established what we are justified in calling sexuality (pp. 264-65).

Here the chapter ends, and we can hardly call successful the later efforts of Freud to clarify the nature of sexuality as he conceived it. In attempting to develop "libido theory" in such a way as to eliminate the many difficulties to which his stated position leads, Freud resorted to speculations—see, for example, his "repetition compulsion" and the "death instinct"—which are regarded, even by many of his most devoted followers, as fantastic. In our view, the only defensible resolution of this paradox is to abandon Freud's notion of sexual repression and adopt instead the assumption, which we believe is not only logically more compatible with other aspects of Freud's thinking but also clinically more supportable, that the part of the personality which, in neurosis, becomes the victim of repression is not sex or any other "instinctive" impulse but the socially implanted part of the personality, namely conscience.

If Freud had made this assumption, he would not, we believe, have found it necessary to resort to such a doubtful device as the psychological equivalence of logical opposites or to stress the matter of "complexity" in support of his argument. Therapeutic transcriptions which are now being prepared for publication, as well as theoretical considerations and empirical findings which are reported in other chapters of the present volume, give ever growing evidence that in most—without too great incaution one can even say *all*—neurotics it is repudiated conscience, not sexuality (or aggression), that returns to haunt and harry its owner in the form of "symptoms" (see especially Chapters 3 and 17).

Varying Conceptions of Therapeutic "Help."—The alternative point of view just described has many advantages over the orthodox Freudian one, among them one that deserves special notice. So long as one holds the position that neurosis arises from repressed sexuality and that the therapist's major function is to help these blocked impulses break through to fuller gratification, just so long do resistance and transference constitute an enigma, however obvious and palpable they are empirically. But when one takes the position that it is the introjected voice of parental and social authority that the neurotic has muffled by repression and thus forced to manifest itself symptomatically, resistance and transference follow as day follows night.

In the passages already quoted, Freud speaks repeatedly of the paradox of the neurotic sufferer opposing the efforts of the analyst or other type of therapist to help him. Let us look more closely at this word "help." We may discover that it does not always mean the same thing to patient and therapist or, indeed, even to all therapists. To a therapist with the revised orientation held by the authors, there is quite regularly a difference in what the patient means, at least in the early stages of therapy, by "help" and what the therapist, from the outset, means by this term. For the therapist, the helping or corrective process consists of little by little bringing back into consciousness the sense of self-criticism and the capacity for the prompt and vivid experience of guilt which the neurotic, in the throes of earlier conflicts, has forcibly excluded; and as this "return of the repressed" proceeds, the patient grows and changes. With the aid of the therapist, the patient is now able to resist the temptation to deal with these conflicts, as in the past, dissociatively and works instead toward new and more *integrative* (mature, characterful, adult) solutions to his problems. The "ego-syntonic" functions are strengthened, and repressive resolutions become less and less necessary. But the critical thing to emphasize here is that this kind of "help" spells *change*.

Patients, characteristically, come to therapy with a different program in mind. They, to be sure, admit that they need and want "help," but, we soon discover, it is help in making their neurosis *work* that they are really seeking. They are not looking for assistance in changing their personal values and general life style; instead are they intent upon symptom relief, upon, that is to say, obliterating the objectionable *consequences* of their deceptions and dissociative strategies. In short, they complain of and seek deliverance from, not their personal weaknesses, but from the results thereof. Usually, as this picture unfolds to them, patients, despite the frustration and resentment they feel when they find the therapist unwilling and indeed unable to "help" them in the originally hoped-for way, succeed, over time, in modifying their objectives and accepting the temporarily painful but, in the long run, more workable approach to their problems for which the therapist stands. However, it sometimes happens that when a patient thus clearly perceives the nature of therapy, he will decide, quite consciously and definitely, against going on with it; and when this happens we are likely to see with special clarity the mechanisms just described.

This course of developments is well illustrated in the following excerpt from the fourth interview with a very intelligent college student in whom neurotic tendencies were heavily alloyed with psychopathy. This patient had a history of erratic work habits and conduct at the various private schools he had attended; he complained of mildly obsessional thoughts, bad dreams, and a tendency to fatigue and excessive sleep; and at the time of the therapeutic contacts, he was doing none of his classwork, was pursuing a girl who obviously had no interest in him, and was drinking a good deal more than was good for him. He had previously undergone a Freudian psychoanalysis.

After the patient had talked in a desultory fashion for about thirty minutes, the therapist began as follows:

T.:   All right. Let's take a look at this now. I'm going to try to pull a little of this material together, but again in a very exploratory and tentative way. Let's see what we've been able to learn so far.

First of all, we've identified some conflict in values, social values perhaps, some difference and inconsistency between your parents in terms of what they've stood for with you. Apparently there is enough wealth in your family so that you are not, don't feel any great pressure about making a living.

P.: Well not, not until the last few years.

T.: Uh-huh.   The wealth is relatively recent.

P.: Well, in other words— No, the wealth— In other words, growing up, you see, I seemed to grow up with virtually everything I wanted.

T.: Yes, I see.

P.: In the last few years it kind of struck me as a hell of a poor way to be brought up.   Just as soon as I get out of school and start working, it'll be a nice anticlimax.

T.: Uh-huh.

P.: And the fact of not being successful just was enough to, whenever that thought went through my mind, to frustrate me—and in a sense *damn the folks* for it.   In other words, if I were a barber's son, I could go out and in two years be making what my dad was and duplicate my environment.   The way the story is with my folks, I'd have to work for *thirty years* in order to duplicate my environment.   And I'll be lucky if I can do it; in other words, I'll have to be *extremely* successful.   Instead of having anything to, let's say, where I can go *further* than my dad, in that sense of the word, why, hell!   I haven't got a chance.   [Pause.]

T.: All right.   Now, some of the assets certainly are good intelligence, courage, intellectual honesty, and a core of just plain human decency. But what's the shooting all about now?   Where's the trouble?

Now we don't know too surely yet, but, as I say, we can take a guess at it.   It looks to me as if, to put it very simply, as if there is a pretty terrific fight going on between you and, or a part of you, and another part of you.   Or to put it perhaps oversimply, between you and conscience, or something we might call conscience.   We've touched on this a little bit before.   Here we have to be exceedingly tentative, but I would suppose that you're, that one of the ways in which you're fighting or defying conscience is in terms of not working, not really being able to do your school work, perhaps lying down on what your conscience considers to be your job at the present time.

P.: You mean in the form of a partial or sort of self-punishment? Maybe running after this girl is a form of self-punishment.

T.: Well, let's, just for the moment we might call it self-indulgence, running after the girl, as you say, instead of doing your work.   Now I know there are complications about doing your work.   You tried to read the book [a textbook mentioned earlier] and you fell asleep We may get some enlightenment on that; but the drinking, it seems to me, is again an attempt to anesthetize or neutralize your conscience, your self-criticism.

P.: Or let's put it this way.   If my system would let me be an alcoholic, I would have been an alcoholic years ago.   There's just no two ways about it: I can take a whiff of bourbon, and it can absolutely make me sick to my stomach.   And yet I used to be able to guzzle it, until

I just got *so* sick one time that I just couldn't touch the stuff for about eight months.

T.: Now, if we can assume that there's a part of you that is fighting this other part that we can call conscience for the moment, I think we can assume equally that conscience is fighting right back. It's, it's really giving you quite a run for your money. It's giving you your symptoms, and I think it's probably also giving you your dreams. Although it can't make you obey it, although it can't make you listen to it, although it can't keep you from drinking as a means of neutralizing it, it can, in unguarded moments, call you, in effect, a pervert [referring back to some earlier material]. It can make you have these dreams. And so, just as you fight it with such means as you have at your disposal, it fights you with such means as it has at its disposal. And it sounds to me as if there's a pretty lively battle going on here—lots of strength on both sides. [Pause.] Put it a little bit differently. It's as if conscience is saying, "If you won't do what I want you to do, I'll see to it that I don't let you do what *you* want to do. If you won't listen to me, I'll certainly spoil things for you. I'll take all the joy out of living; I'll cancel, I'll neutralize every pleasure you try to have. I'll harry you and harass you." [4] And thus suicide [of which the patient occasionally spoke] would be both an escape from this thing and a way, as I indicated the other day, of bumping it off as well. It would be suicide, but also a kind of murder, perhaps a murder of this fellow [mentioned in connection with a dream] with the ghastly face.

P.: Well [laughs!] Is there, is there a way of [laughs again] of subduing the conscience?

T.: A way of *subduing?*

P.: Well, let's say, in other words— Well now, uh, the reason I think that— I, I would say ordinarily it, as far as the sex angle— Under normal circumstances— In other words, if I hadn't read a book on or thumbed through a book on psychiatry or on a case of psychoanalysis, I don't know if I'd *ever* tell that! [The reference here is obscure.] Yet it seemed to me that in virtually every case, there's always that, that sex angle tied up with it. In other words, in the end it would always boil down to it. [Pause.] And, and it seems to me I could save a hell of a lot of waste and effort and time and so on and so forth, to go ahead and grapple with it, fight it. *Make* myself reveal it. [T. Ummm, uh-uh.] In other words, in the therapy angle, if it was going to do me any good. On the other hand, I don't know if it does me any good or not.

---

[4] If this interpretation seems improbable we have only to remind ourselves that one of the common strategies used by parents in disciplining children is to withhold privileges and pleasures. If we are to take seriously the proposition that conscience assumes many of the parental functions, it is by no means far-fetched to conceive of conscience as a "joy-killer" when the ego has acted in such a way as to bring down upon itself the displeasure of the internalized representative of parental authority.

T.: I think your question of a moment ago is a very significant one. You say, "Is there, is there any way of *subduing* this thing, this conscience, this leering, watchful, critical face?"

P.: What does it have to do? Does it have to be a relearning process or—? In other words, in a sense I would think that— Well, I don't know. Well, *can* you subdue it or can you completely, let's say, *rid* yourself of it? [Pause.] I'll tell you this, though, I think that like, when getting undressed for a shower or something like that, uh, then's when, when I'm *not* asleep is when my conscience is liable to bother me.

T.: I wonder— You, you pretty much have the feeling that you would like to get rid of this force within you.

P.: [Laughs.] You, you [still laughing], you mean would I *like* to get *rid* of it? You damn right I'd like to get rid of it.

T.: So that you could go ahead and do any kind of, any kind of irresponsible or antisocial act without having guilt or any—

P.: No! No! Not necessarily! No, so that [laughs], so that I can go ahead and be guided by my conscious reasoning and, and— Well, in other words, I want to be able to con-, to be happy and to conform socially. I, I don't *want* to be guided by— In other words, these dreams— I don't want to be a homosexual, 'cause I really don't believe that is my desire.

T.: Uh-huh. My way of thinking about these things is a little different from that of the usual analyst. I think that it may go something like this: that you've been trying very hard, at least on occasion you've tried pretty hard to get rid of conscience; and you somehow recognize that conscience is responsible for your symptoms. And you come to me as a therapist in order, in the hope of getting help in getting rid of your symptoms and perhaps, incidentally, in trying to get rid of this thing that's causing the symptoms, or conscience. Now, I don't know how to help you do that. I'm not sure that's what you would really like help in if I knew *how* to do it. I *don't* know how to banish conscience, and therefore I don't know how to banish symptoms by means of banishing conscience.[5]

But there is the alternative possibility—and a less attractive one from many points of view—of coming to terms with conscience, of learning to communicate with it, of listening to what it's trying to tell you *directly* instead of forcing it to tell you things indirectly, in the form of these, as you probably perceive them, very frightening, kind

[5] The orthodox analyst to whom this man had previously gone had apparently taken the conventional position that in neurosis the superego is "too severe" and needs to be softened, "subdued," made more "reasonable," in order to allow freer, less obstructed, libidinal expression. We cannot be sure, therefore, to what extent the expectations which the patient brought with him to the second therapist were those which are native to neurotics or had been learned from his Freudian analyst. However, we shall presently see from a second case, in which there had been no previous analytic contact, almost exactly the same outlook.

of crazy dreams, and perhaps your "narcolepsy" [the patient's term for his sleep-proneness] and so on. In other words, if we know anything about this field today, it is that symptoms are the voice of conscience speaking out of context, in disguise, in a bizarre language, because we refuse to listen to it more directly. So that the only path I know out of this woods involves, not subduing conscience, not getting rid of it, but turning and saying: "Well, this is a part of me; apparently it's a permanent part of me, and it's a powerful part of me. Now instead of fighting it, let's see if I can come to terms with it and have it on my side, have it *with* me instead of against me." [Pause.] As I say, that's not so attractive a possibility as being able just, just to blow it out.

By the end of the interview it was evident to the patient that if *this* was what therapy meant, he wanted no more of it. The next day he petitioned out of school, came for a terminal interview, and left town—ostensibly to return home, although there was some uncertainty on this score.

By taking the point of view that this man's difficulties stemmed back to repressed sexuality and an overly severe superego, it might have been possible to keep him in "therapy"—but to what end? The therapist who aligns himself with the patient in opposing the superego is, from the standpoint of the present argument, aligning himself, not with the healthy forces within the patient, but instead with the "neurosis." Alexander and French (1946) have commented upon the fact that orthodox analysis commonly leads, not to recovery, but to a "deep narcissistic regression." Without attempting to determine what precisely they mean by this phrase, we can substitute the expression, "a morass of confusion and despair." When a therapist gives or implies a promise to "help" the patient on his own terms, there is often a kind of honeymoon period (sometimes called, ambiguously, the *"positive* transference"); but as the patient comes to perceive that this promise is bearing no very tangible results, discouragement, resentment, and bitterness develop.[6] These reactions are commonly termed the "negative transference." They are, to be sure, *negative,* but one wonders whether they are so much "transference" as reactions which are justified by the situation. Such a state of "negative transference" may persist indefinitely, the therapist being powerless to bring it to an end because he has compromised himself by initially taking a position in opposition to the superego instead of with it. In other words, he has placed himself in a role which opposes the development of a genuine and therapeutically valuable form of transference; it is not surprising that the clinical phenomena which ensue are "complicated"!

[6] In this respect there is perhaps more than a passing parallelism between the ultimate reactions of a patient to a too permissive and inconsistent therapist and those of a person who has had too permissive and inconsistent parents; cf. the indulgence and inconsistencies of the parents of the patient just described and his condemnation of them and his feeling that this was "a hell of a poor way to be brought up." And to this experience had been added that of an orthodox psychoanalysis. It is not surprising that the patient at this point took a dim view of what either parents or therapists can do for one.

If one follows the dictates of the alternative point of view described above, there is little or no initial "positive" transference; transference in the true sense of the word develops very quickly (often in the second or third interview), and the stage is soon set for therapeutic developments which are dramatic and swift. There are, to be sure, cases in which we "fail"—witness the case just discussed; but is it not preferable to reach this result promptly than to take hundreds of hours, over a period of two or three years, to arrive at no better outcome?

That patients, when confronted by the unrealistic nature of their expectations regarding therapy, tend to react in much the same way but do not always abandon the therapeutic enterprise is indicated by the following passages from the second interview with a young man, in his middle twenties, who came into therapy complaining of phobias and obsessions. He had spoken fairly volubly during the first session, but by the second session it was evident that he felt he had told the therapist enough and that it was now the therapist's responsibility to start producing results. Toward the end of the hour, after many silences, the therapist spoke of the evident resistance which the patient was feeling and conjectured that this might be a "re-creation of some of the conflicts [previously mentioned] that you had with your father." The following exchange then took place:

P.: Mmmm. I don't know about that. I, uh, in terms of, let's say— When you said that I want you to help me, but that I want you to help me on my terms or on my preconceived ideas of how it should be done, in that respect I have the preconceived idea that, uh, I have been bothered with this a long time and every day it is extremely bothersome, very upsetting. I want to get rid of it as soon as I possibly can, and so let's, let's not dilly-dally around or talk about things that are unnecessary. Let's get right down to it and get it over with as quickly as possible. Now if we sit here and don't say anything, that's not getting anything done; or if we just talk about everyday things, that's not getting anything done either. We, I mean in that respect, maybe —But I, I don't know about any, any re-creation of a conflict I might have had with my father; had a lot of them—they're just petty little things.

T.: I recall something a psychiatrist friend once said to me. He said people come to you with their symptoms and want you to eliminate the symptoms, but they don't want you to change their fundamental life style. Now it seems to me that what you're saying is that if I'm any good I'll wave a wand and banish your symptoms. But be careful that I don't try to teach you anything; be careful that you don't have to learn anything. "Get rid of my symptoms, but don't ask me to change."

P.: Aaaaah, not consciously. I mean, I'm willing to learn anything, I'm willing to change if I'm doing something wrong, or something that isn't beneficial; but my primary interest is getting rid of the

symptoms as quickly as possible. Now as I understand it, often you
have to go through a long process of, of learning and changing, as you
say, the pattern of life before you get rid of some of these symptoms.
Uh, I would consider that extremely unfortunate because, uh,—
It would be fortunate in the respect that I have eventually started
on the process of learning these things and eventually getting rid of
the symptoms, but unfortunate from the standpoint that I can't get
rid of them quickly, which is what I would like. [Long pause.]

T.: So that you're pretty well satisfied with yourself as you are, and
if you can just eliminate these bothersome symptoms then life would
be pretty much ideal.

P.: Uh-huh— Well, no, no, of course not. Uh, I don't know, I don't
know.

T.: For a little while you're going to have trouble staying in therapy
because you're—

P.: Staying in?

T.: Staying in therapy, because you're not at all convinced that this
is the way out yet; you're not at all sure you're ready to pay the price.

Although there were many other occasions on which this man's resistances were exceedingly vigorous, he stayed in therapy, worked hard,
and, at the end of forty-three interviews, had achieved what appears to
be a radical "cure of his neurosis," which is to say he had become a
changed, a more integrated person.

Thus, by revising the Freudian system as logic and clinical experience
both indicate, we get a technique by means of which we drastically reduce the time required, not only for our "failures," but also for our
successes. Moreover, therapy based upon the assumption that it is
conscience rather than libido which the neurotic is struggling to repudiate seems *safer*. When the superego senses in the therapist an
ally, a person who with the "third ear" will hear its voice and interpret
its claims at the court of consciousness, the superego is less likely to
precipitate those catastrophic attacks of panic and "unconscious guilt"
which sometimes lead to suicide or psychosis than it is when the therapist aligns himself, explicitly or more subtly, with the id and *against*
the superego. In the latter instance, the superego, now even more
disadvantaged and hard-pressed, must redouble its efforts to make
itself felt and effective in modifying the behavior of the individual: panic
may be the result. While we believe that no form of therapy should
be practiced without sound training and a full sense of professional responsibility, more good and less harm can, in any case, be done by a
therapist who sees in symptoms the muted voice of self-reproach and
admonition than by the therapist who pushes persons already weighed
down with sexual guilt toward still greater indulgence and "freedom"
on this score.

The Freudian Fallacy in Retrospect.—Anyone who has studied
the writings of Freud and watched his brilliant mind bring lucidity and

light into one of the most obscure and tragic areas of all human experience will understandably ask, when confronted by considerations of the kind here advanced, how it is possible for these formulations to have any validity and yet to have been overlooked by Freud and so many of his followers.

Sometimes an attempt is made to reconcile this paradox by suggesting that perhaps the neurotics whom Freud saw *did* suffer from repressed sexuality, whereas those one sees today suffer more from repressed moral sense. Perhaps in the Victorian era people *did* get into neurotic difficulties because of moral scruples that were unrealistically strong; and perhaps today, the pendulum having swung to the opposite extreme, we are seeing more and more persons in whom it is not the ascendency of the moral forces over the "instinctual" ones, but the reverse, that is responsible for personality disorders. This is certainly not an unreasonable proposal, but neither can we convince ourselves that it is a valid one.

Let us first of all recall Freud's own doubts with respect to his assumption that symptoms are a means of achieving an indirect and disguised form of sexual gratification. Only by interpreting "sexual" in a very special way could even Freud escape the suspicion that "the symptoms seem rather to contain the opposite purpose." Moreover, *most* of the observations that Freud reported sound too much like the ones we make with our patients today for one easily to assume that neurotics then and now differ in the way which this attempted resolution would require. As already indicated, much of Freud's thinking with respect to resistance, repression, and transference meshes well with contemporary clinical experience. And the folk literature of Freud's day further suggests that his presuppositions regarding the direction of repression were as wide of the mark in Vienna in 1900 as they are in New York or Podunk today.[7]

Let us press the paradox involved in Freud's thinking a step further. It is reasonable to suppose, if a conflict arises within a human being, that that one of the contending forces will be most likely to be rejected and possibly repressed which is the latest arrival upon the scene and hence least well consolidated within the personality. Freud repeatedly observed that in the beginning the human personality is "all id," utterly dominated by instinctual impulses and devoid of those sentiments which we commonly associate with morality, ethics, and social responsibility. Against the earlier view that the "sense of right and wrong," i.e., conscience, in fully developed form, is divinely given to everyone at birth, Freud contended, with great persuasiveness and to good effect, that the moral sentiments are instead the product of social experience, first with the

---

[7] For discussion of another major schism in Freud's thinking, namely that having to do with his formulations regarding identification, on the one hand, and sexual fixations, on the other, as the determinants of character traits and trends, see Mowrer (1950, ch. xxi). The resolution which has been proposed for this other inconsistency is compatible with the position taken in the present chapter. See also Mowrer (1952c, 1953a, and 1953b).

parents and later with other persons who significantly influence the child's development. For example, Freud has remarked:

Conscience is no doubt something within us, but it has not been there from the beginning. In this sense it is the opposite of sexuality, which is certainly present from the very beginning of life, and is not a thing that only comes in later. But small children are notoriously amoral (Freud, 1933c, p. 89).

Now according to Freud the whole of human culture is a burden which the human animal never accepts willingly and, at best, bears grudgingly (Freud, 1930). And yet the same writer would have us believe that neurosis arises because conscience is accepted *so* fully, culture is assimilated *so* completely that, in the face of conflict with the primal instinctive functions, it is the latter that are rejected and denied access to consciousness. How much more reasonable, on the basis of the same premises, to infer that those elements in the personality which develop *last* are the most likely to be repudiated when otherwise irreconcilable conflict arises! [8]

Or let us examine Freud's position from still another perspective. Because of his particular emphasis upon the place of sexuality in neurosis, Freud appears to have misevaluated one important transference strategy. In one of the passages first quoted in this chapter, Freud speaks of a "tender erotically tinged transference to the analyst" which women commonly develop in therapy and which "is bound to injure the personal relationship with the physician, and so to put out of action one of the most powerful propelling forces in the analysis." This need not be the case at all. If one operates, as did Freud, upon the assumption that all neurotics suffer from impeded sexual expression, then, to be sure, when a patient starts releasing some of his or her erotic affect upon the person of the therapist, the position of the therapist becomes an awkward one: he recognizes that such impulses must meet "unavoidable rejection" by the therapist, yet it is also his stated objective to promote the freer expression of frustrated sexual needs on the part of the patient.

The solution of this dilemma is exceedingly straightforward, once one sees the neurotic's problem as stemming from a struggle to hold back and inactivate the forces of conscience rather than from too austere an attitude toward sexual needs. Female as well as male neurotics often present a full spectrum of both normal and perverse sexual activities when the truth is fully known, very commonly including the use of such activities for nonsexual purposes. Just as the "anxious eater" is a clinical commonplace, so also are there persons who use sexual activities not so much to gratify sexual needs as to comfort themselves with respect to and

[8] Both neurological and psychological observations have shown that when an organism is under morbid stress new habits are more quickly lost than old ones. By analogy, if nothing more, one would expect, in the face of conflict, the biologically given (phylogenetically older) elements of personality to be more durable and persistent than the socially instilled (phylogenetically more recent) ones. We are indebted to Vertus E. Bixenstine for this notion.

to counteract depression, anxiety, inferiority feeling and other neurotic affects.

The "tender erotically tinged transference" which Freud regarded as so great a stumbling block in the treatment of women patients is closely related. Women who "fall in love" with a male therapist are not, save possibly in the rarest instances, revealing any great, unsatisfied sexual need. Instead they are using, in the sense of ab-using, a very old device for grappling with moral authority as they perceive it in the person of the therapist. If a woman can provoke sexual appetite in a therapist, she has therewith neutralized him as a father figure and as a person who might otherwise have advanced her development toward greater personal maturity. Just as little girls sometimes succeed in controlling their fathers by giving or withholding their favors, so does it happen in therapy that the same little girls, now grown large, will attempt to bring the therapist to terms by the same strategy. Such behavior on their part—"seduction of authority" is a convenient term for it—is far closer to hostility than it is to love; and a well-timed interpretation to this effect will usually end the strategy, with a decidedly beneficial effect upon the therapeutic relationship, rather than with the reverse effect which Freud feared.[9]

All things considered, we must again return to the question of why Freud was so resistant to a conclusion that follows so naturally from his other observations and assumptions Why, in short, did he reject the view that the neurotic suffers from repressed conscience rather than repressed sexuality? Perhaps closer to the mark than any of the proposals which have thus far been advanced is an explanation which goes as follows. It is easy to overlook the fact that from the beginning one of Freud's most tenaciously held objectives was to develop a naturalistic conception of human personality, i.e., a conception of both normal and abnormal psychic functioning which would be completely divorced from theological and metaphysical presuppositions. For this much there is ample historical proof: see Freud's autobiography (1935b) and his book *The future of an illusion* (1928). Moreover, we need to remind ourselves that Freud was waging this campaign in a country and in an era in which any tendency toward concession, compromise, or qualification would have been turned to quick advantage by the opposition. If, for example, Freud had said that people fall ill of neurosis because they have barricaded their consciences, this would have perhaps seemed to be a confirmation rather than a refutation of the traditional religious views in such matters. But by seeing in neurosis an *excess* of conscientiousness, an expression of *moral interference* with natural biological forces, he was able to strike not only at the method (metaphysics) but also at the conclusions of his religious opponents.

If this is the price which Freud had to pay, perhaps all unwittingly, for the herculean accomplishment of founding a truly objective and

---

[9] Cf. the further discussion of this problem in the latter sections of this chapter.

naturalistic approach to the study of human personality and its vagaries, who can say it was a greater price than the accomplishment justified? Even if Freud failed to give us a completely valid system of theory and technique, he has demonstrated the feasibility of the naturalistic approach in this area; and, with his advances as our operating bases, it would poorly become us, of another generation, if we could not in some measure improve upon and extend his magnificent beginnings.

Actually there are indications which have been noted elsewhere (Mowrer, 1950, chap. xviii) that in his last years Freud himself was starting to question and re-examine some of his basic suppositions; and granted another few decades of productive life, it is by no means certain that he himself would not have been the leader in rectifying his own early errors and building an ever stronger system of explanatory concepts and therapeutic technique.

The Rogerian View of Resistance and Transference

Having reviewed and in certain respects revised Freud's formulations regarding the role of resistance and transference in neurosis and its treatment, it may now be useful, in our quest for a generally consistent and comprehensive theory, to examine the distinctive approach to psychotherapy advocated by Carl Rogers. In his first book, Rogers (1942) does not discuss "transference" but refers to "resistance" a number of times. In one of the most concise passages he says:

Although much has been written on the subject of resistance in therapy, the present writer is inclined to disagree with most of the opinions which have been expressed, and offers another hypothesis, which may be tested, it is hoped, as our knowledge of therapy increases. This hypothesis is that resistance to counseling and to the counselor is not an inevitable part of psychotherapy, nor a desirable part, but that it grows primarily out of poor techniques of handling the client's expression of his problems and feelings. More specifically, it grows out of the unwise attempts on the part of the counselor to short-cut the therapeutic process by bringing into the discussion emotionalized attitudes which the client is not yet ready to face (p. 151).

Although Rogers' evaluation of interpretation, i.e., the use of inferences which go beyond the data immediately given by the client, was not entirely disparaging, it was certainly one of caution and reservation. As the following quotation will show, Rogers felt that the procedure of preference was "reflection" and that when this technique is strictly adhered to resistance does not develop or, if it does develop, is easily managed. He says:

It should also be emphasized that only those feelings should be verbally recognized which have been expressed. Often the client has attitudes which are implied in what he says, or which the counselor through shrewd observation judges him to have. Recognition of such attitudes which have not yet appeared in the client's conversation may, if the attitudes are not too deeply repressed, hasten the progress of therapy. If, however, they are repressed attitudes, their recognition by the counselor may seem to be very much of a threat to the client, may create resentment and resistance, and in some instances may break off the counseling contacts (p. 52).

Even more explicit is the following excerpt with respect to the connection Rogers saw between interpretation and resistance:

As the client reveals himself more and more fully in the counseling interviews, the counselor begins to develop insight into the client's problems. Not infrequently the major patterns of reaction are relatively clear to the counselor at the end of the first or second interview. There is the greatest temptation to most counselors, whether they are psychiatrists, psychologists, guidance counselors, or social workers, to inform the client as to his patterns, to interpret his actions and his personality to him. We have already seen the type of reception this is likely to receive. The more accurate the interpretation, the more likely it is to encounter defensive resistance. The counselor and his interpretations become something to be feared. To resist this temptation to interpret too quickly, to recognize that insight is an experience which is achieved, not an experience which can be imposed, is an important step in progress for the counselor (pp. 195-96).

It is hazardous to try to reconstruct an author's motives, but one can conjecture that Rogers' misgivings with respect to interpretation arose from his awareness of and wish to avoid the deep and almost interminable "negative transference" into which patients commonly sink in orthodox Freudian analysis. But we have already seen, in the foregoing sections, that it is not interpretation per se but rather *mis*interpretation, i.e., interpretation based upon mistaken premises regarding the fundamental nature of neurosis, that is responsible for this undesirable feature of Freudian analysis. There are many indications, some of which will be cited in the following pages, that by restricting his technique to *reflection,* Rogers has placed a quite unnecessary limitation upon its range of effectiveness. Reflection is often a highly useful device, especially in the early stages of therapy, as a means of establishing rapport and communication, and it may be useful on occasion throughout the course of therapy; but if one operates within a theoretical frame of reference which avoids the misconceptions of classical psychoanalysis and if the therapist puts forward his surmises with an appropriate degree of tentativeness, interpretation can be used as frequently and as radically as otherwise seems indicated.

In some respects the position taken by Rogers in his new (1951b) book with regard to these matters is very similar to the earlier one, but in other ways there is definite movement in the direction of what may eventually become well-authenticated common ground between therapists. Although in his recent volume, Rogers refers hardly at all to the phenomenon of "resistance," he speaks at length about "transference." He begins with this summary of the Freudian position:

It is not easy for me to put myself into the frame of reference of the analyst, and to understand fully the meaning these concepts have for him. But in so far as I can understand, I would gather that transference is a term which is applied to attitudes transferred to the therapist which were originally directed, with more justification, toward a parent or other person. These attitudes of love, hate, dependence, and so on, are utilized by the analyst as an immediate expression of the client's basic attitudes and conflicts, and it is through the analysis of these attitudes that the most significant part of the psychoanalysis takes place. For this reason, the method of dealing with the transference attitudes is the most important part of the analyst's work (p. 198).

For reasons previously given we can understand why Rogers, along with a good many others, might confess to some uncertainty regarding the exact nature of the Freudian conception of transference. But we believe that Rogers may tacitly share with Freud one major assumption of doubtful validity. We refer to the assumption that transference is characterized by the occurrence of behavior on the part of the patient in relation to the therapist which is "unjustified" (see above quotation), "inappropriate" (Rogers, 1951*b*, p. 218). Just as Freudians, when faced by transference behavior, commonly try to show patients that their expectations regarding the therapist (especially in the area of morality and social authority) are not warranted, so do Rogers and his followers commonly attempt to provide their clients with an interpersonal atmosphere that is "warm, permissive, understanding, nonjudgmental." In both cases the assumption seems to be that the neurotic is a person who in his earlier contacts with authoritative figures has been overwhelmed, crippled, distorted, and that the main responsibility of the therapist is to provide a psychological environment which will permit a natural but heretofore inhibited kind of blossoming or unfolding on the part of the patient. In the one case (Freudian analysis), this is presumably accomplished by "lessening the severity of the superego," whereas in the other (Rogerian therapy) the assumption is that "the client can restore himself to healthier patterns of behavior if he is placed in an approving therapeutic climate" (Beier, 1951).

The alternative view expressed earlier by the present authors holds that neurosis represents real personal immaturity, real deficiency in meeting the necessary standards of society, and that "transference" in therapy represents the defiance, resistance, and opposition which the individual has previously shown in his relationship with those who have already tried to "bring him up." To say that such reactions to the therapist are "unjustified" or "inappropriate" is thus tantamount to saying that the negativism of children in relations to their parents, teachers, and other authoritative adults is unjustified and inappropriate. If the therapist perceives his task as that of trying to carry through to successful completion a complex process in which natural parents have, in certain important respects, failed, then he welcomes in his relationship with the patient the revival of unresolved conflicts and oppositional strategies. He does not take the position with the patient or client that these reactions toward him are unjustified or inappropriate; he does not insist that he is "different," that he, unlike parents and others, does not stand for anything in terms of personal conduct and integrity. Rather does the therapist help the patient see what he is trying to accomplish by means of his "transference" behavior—which is now just as real and just as meaningful as it originally was—and to understand the circumstance in which this type of behavior originated and why it was not earlier resolved. While the therapist may, indeed *must,* deal with the attacks and other oppositional strategies of the patient in ways which are different from those employed by parents (i.e., the therapist must avoid "countertransference"), this is not to say that the therapist regards these phenomena as "unjustified" *or* that his objectives with respect to the influence he brings to bear upon the patient are, in principle, different from those of parents and of adult society in general. The difference is definitely one of means, not ends. The therapist is very literally a parent substitute, one to whom socially immature adults can go and have a "second chance" at growing up; and the therapist who sees his major role as that of undoing and reversing what natural parents have presumably done or overdone seems likely to succeed less well than does the therapist who, with special insights and skills and full consciousness of the nature of his role, is willing to try to help patients complete developmental tasks which other relationships have left unfinished.

Rogers has pointed to the nonfunctional—one can almost say pathological—nature of the so-called transference which develops in many Freudian analyses and has stressed the success of "client-centered" techniques in avoiding this undesirable development. He says, for example:

In client-centered therapy . . . this *involved and persistent dependent transference relationship* does not tend to develop. Thousands of clients have been dealt with by counselors with whom the writer has had personal contact. In only a small minority of cases handled in a client-centered fashion has the client developed a relationship which could in any way be matched to Freud's terms. In most instances the description of the relationship would be quite different. . . .

It is this possibility of therapy without a *deep transference relationship* which deserves close attention. The possibility of effective brief psychotherapy seems to hinge on the possibility of therapy without the transference relationship, since the resolution of the transference situation appears to be *uniformly slow and time-consuming* (Rogers, 1951b, p. 201, italics added)

We are entirely in accord with Rogers' misgivings regarding the necessity and the helpfulness of the type of "transference" which Alexander and French have spoken of as a deep and relatively intractable "narcissistic regression." But in our experience the choice is not between this undesirable extreme, on the one hand, and, on the other, the equally questionable position of professional self-delimitation imposed by strict and exclusive adherence to the technique of reflection. Following the passages just quoted, Rogers gives three examples of behavior on the part of patients which *might* have developed into a "transference" impasse had not the technique of reflection, combined with "understanding and acceptance," circumvented such a development. And these examples neatly pose the question as to whether one prefers to insist upon "depth" at the price of a Freudian-type transference *or* to insist upon avoiding this phenomenon at the risk of superficiality in the sense of leaving the patient's neurosis, if deep-seated, essentially untouched. The last of the three examples is so instructive on this score that it should be examined in some detail. Rogers describes the patient involved in these words:

The excerpts which follow are from interviews with a single woman in her thirties, Miss Tir, a person so deeply disturbed that she would probably have been diagnosed as psychotic in terms of an external evaluation. It should be stressed that attitudes like this would be found very infrequently in a community counseling center. On the other hand, in a psychiatric ward or state hospital they might be more frequent. In the course of the interviews, this woman has wrestled with deep guilt feelings, many of which center around possible incest with her father. She cannot be entirely sure whether the events really occurred or whether they exist only in her own mind. Some brief excerpts may give an inkling of the depth of the transference attitudes, and of the counselor's method of handling (Rogers, 1951*b*, p. 210).

The following excerpts are given from the ninth interview:

S. [Client]: This morning I hung my coat out there instead of here in your office. I've told you I like you, and I was afraid if you helped me on with the coat, I might turn around and kiss you.

C. [Counselor]: You thought those feelings of affection might *make* you kiss me unless you protected yourself from them.

— — — — — —

S. [later in interview]: I've never told anyone they were the most wonderful person I've ever known, but I've told you that. It's not just sex. It's more than that.

C.: You really feel very deeply attracted to me (p. 211).

If an orthodox analyst were to respond to productions of this kind, he would probably do so in terms of an interpretation that stressed the Oedipus complex and libidinal fixation upon the patient's father; and the stage would be set for the kind of interminable "negative transference" previously discussed. Although the nondirective therapist in the present case avoided such an interpretation, he appears to have made the equally serious error of "accepting" the patient's intimation that she was sexually attracted to him. On the basis of the very considerable information which the therapist probably had at this point—including the patient's fantasies, and possible experiences, with respect to *incest*—we believe it was incumbent upon him to make, not a reflection, but an interpretation, one which would have stressed the essentially *nonsexual* nature and objectives of what the patient had done and said. In many similar situations, we have found that if the patient's attention is drawn to the possibility that she is trying to get the therapist sexually interested in her, not because of her own sexual needs, but in order to neutralize and discredit him as a proper father figure and therefore as an effective therapist, this kind of behavior can be quickly liquidated, new material released, and a great positive step taken toward the patient's self-understanding and recovery.

The developments, dictated by a philosophy of therapy which depreciates interpretation, were as follows. In the next (tenth) interview this interchange occurred:

S.: I think emotionally I'm dying for sexual intercourse but I don't do anything about it. . . . The thing I want is to have sexual intercourse with you. I don't dare ask you, 'cause I'm afraid you'd be nondirective.

C.: You have this awful tension, and want so much to have relations with me.

S.: [*Goes on in this vein. Finally:*] Can't we do something about it? This tension is awful! Will you relieve the tension. . . . Can you give me a direct answer? I think it might help both of us.

C.: [*gently*] The answer would be no. I can understand how *desperately* you feel, but I would not be willing to do that.

S.: [Pause. Sigh of relief.] I think that helps me. It's only when I'm upset that I'm like this. You have strength, and it gives me strength (Rogers, 1951*b*, p. 211).

That the patient perceived the therapist's reactions as a rebuff and condemnation is indicated by her immediate self-justification and quasi-apology: "It's only when I'm upset that I'm like this." Although she professes to have been helped by the therapist's nonacceptance of her sexual offer, other material quoted from later interviews shows that this rejection, this reversal of professed permissiveness and unreserved approval and respect, plunged the patient into a series of violent attacks upon the therapist.[10] Rogers' summarizing statement follows:

Here again, in very deep material, the client again comes to realize that the attitudes she holds toward others, and the qualities she attributes to them, reside in her own perceptions, not in the object of her attitudes. This would seem to be the essence of the resolution of transference attitudes (p. 213).

It would be our feeling that in this case the "transference attitudes" were *not* resolved. Lacking the powerful resource of a correctly conceived and properly timed interpretation, the therapist, in the face of this transference, or "acting out," on the part of the patient, was help-

---

[10] Cf. Freud's remark, previously quoted (p. 3): "The inevitable jealousy and the embitterment consequent upon the unavoidable rejection, however considerately it is handled, is bound to injure the personal relationship with the physician, and so to put out of action one of the most powerful propelling forces of the analysis."

less, when asked for a "direct answer," to do anything except "set a limit" on the patient's behavior. In a footnote, Rogers makes this comment:

As in setting any limit in the therapeutic experience, this is purely the responsibility of the therapist, and he takes that responsibility. He does not attempt to evaluate the client's experience by some such statement as "That really wouldn't help you." He simply takes responsibility for his own behavior, at the same time indicating understanding and acceptance of the client's experience of the situation (p. 211).

Our feeling is that the therapist did not really "understand" this patient any more than he "accepted" her, and the follow-up on the case seems to bear out such an inference. With admirable candor and respect for data, Rogers reports:

For ten months she [Miss Tir] held these gains, and then was troubled once more by her conflicts. She tried in a peculiar way to get in touch with the counselor, who was out of the city for some months, for more help. Because of the channel she had chosen, the counselor knew nothing of her request and she received no reply. Within a month she had a frankly psychotic episode, from which she gradually made a partial recovery. What the outcome would have been had the counselor been available, it is impossible to state (p. 213).

Nor can we say with certainty what the outcome would have been if the patient's behavior had been interpreted as a transferred seduction-of-authority strategy, but experience with similar cases has shown us that correct perception and interpretation of these *attacks* upon the therapist in the guise of "love" can be a profoundly therapeutic experience for women patients and may mark the turning point on the road to recovery.

There is, we believe, in the Rogerian approach a basic inconsistency. In attempting to avert transference, the client-centered therapist eschews interpretation and employs reflection only. This, Rogers believes, gives the client a great feeling of security and provides the requisite setting for self-healing and recovery. He says:

This, very obviously, does not come from approval by the counselor, but from something far deeper—a thoroughly consistent acceptance. It is this absolute assurance that there will be no evaluation, no interpretation, no probing, no *personal* reaction by the counselor, that gradually permits the client to experience the relationship as one in which all defenses can be dispensed with —a relationship in which the client feels, "I can be the real me, no pretenses." . . .

The client does not feel that someone is behind him, that someone approves of him. He does experience the fact that there is someone who respects him *as he is,* and who is willing for him to take any direction which he chooses. . . . But that this is a secure experience in which there need be no fear of threat or attack—not even of the subtlest sort—of this the client gradually becomes sure. And this basic security is not something the client believes because he is told, not something about which he convinces himself logically, it is something he *experiences,* with his own sensory and visceral equipment (Rogers, 1951*b*, pp. 208-9).

The inconsistency to which we have referred seems to us to lie between such statements as the ones just quoted and the fact that full-fledged client-centered therapists are really implacable on two scores. (*a*) They *insist* that patients take full responsibility for the content and direction of their productions, the therapist merely going along *with* them but never leading or directing their progress; and (*b*) they *persistently* focus attention upon the client's feelings and perceptions.

Rogers quotes a client who, in referring to client-centered therapy, says, "But in a way it's disciplinary. I mean it's—it acts as a discipline so far as I'm concerned, so that I don't confront everybody with approval or disapproval." Is it not, therefore, revealing that despite the counselor's repeated insistence that he "accepts and respects" the patient just *as he is,* the patient nevertheless perceives the relationship as "disciplinary"? And what can such a term mean if it does not imply on the part of the counselor pressures toward and expectations of *change*? There seems to be an inherent contradiction here, and one which we do not believe can be resolved without major modifications in the theoretical framework of the client-centered approach.

Although we believe, as already indicated, that reflection is often a highly useful device, we do not believe that it alone is sufficient for a radical and versatile psychotherapy. That some members of the client-centered school are moving in the direction of admitting interpretation as a companion technique is indicated in a recent paper by Beier (1951). This author puts the issue in these words:

The question arises whether or not the client-centered therapist can reflect "unaware needs" [make interpretations concerning unconscious mechanisms] without destroying the basic tenets under which he operates. The basic tenets are: (1) growth occurs in freedom from threat, (2) in this freedom the primary responsibility for growth should be the client's. Do we violate these tenets if we reflect needs and anxiety that we observe but that have not been expressed by the client?

In order to grasp the full import of Beier's compact argument, the reader must consult his paper in the original, but the gist of his conclusion follows:

These criticisms are well taken with a majority of cases, but in consideration of failures in client-centered therapy a varying emphasis on the two basic tenets may be necessary. Some clients do not seem to be ready to feel understood by a therapist who conveys to them acceptance of what they are.[11]   They

---

[11] This would seem especially true since the neurotic is a person who does not "accept himself" (Chapter 13), and a therapist who "accepts" him, completely and unreservedly, might constitute something of an enigma for the patient, to say the least.

feel that they are more than they can *voice* at this moment, and they desire the support of the therapist for this unexpressed part of themselves. Not to get this support may be threatening to them. The support afforded these clients may make the difference. It may lead individuals otherwise not reached by client-centered therapy, to the point where they can accept responsibility for their own psychological growth.[12] In this manner many clients who do not stay with the therapist because of the therapist's too strict application of the two basic tenets will be able to enter the therapeutic situation, and client-centered therapy may serve more diversities of maladjustment (Beier, 1951, pp. 361-62).

We conjecture that, as theory regarding the nature of neurosis becomes clarified, the distrust of interpretation will disappear and that both it and reflection will be used by psychotherapists, flexibly and confidently, with a resulting over-all technique better suited to a wide range of patients and more conducive to positive outcomes. But as interpretation is readmitted to the therapeutic setting, transference phenomena and resistance take on the importance that Freud attributed to them; and their proper understanding and practical management become centrally important. For reasons already indicated, it seems that the Freudians have partially misconceived and have, in practice, often mismanaged transference phenomena. The Rogerians, aware of these shortcomings, have sought to develop a form of therapy which avoids transference altogether or which at least avoids the development of the deep, interminable forms of transference. To the Freudian thesis, the Rogerian approach can be thought of as a kind of antithesis; certainly it has many of the marks of a protest movement. Somewhere along the lines suggested in the preceding pages may lie a kind of Hegelian synthesis.

Quantitative Measures of Tension

From the two preceding parts of this chapter, it is clear that resistance and its proper management are centrally important in psychotherapy. Further clarification of the issues here involved will rest not only upon clinical impressions and logical analysis but also upon quantitative measurements of the relevant parameters of the therapeutic process. One such parameter would seem to be the phenomenon of psychological and physiological *tension*. That resistance, in the sense of the negative transference strategies which the patient directs toward the therapist, will prove to have a one-to-one relation with tension indicators is perhaps unlikely. Nevertheless, it is probable that the interpersonal phenomena

---

[12] Many therapists would hold that while dissociation can be instigated by the patient alone, the patient very commonly has to have specialized help from another in order to get the process reversed. The question which Beier thus seems to be raising is whether patients in whom dissociation is well established *can* take the responsibility for undoing the process so long as the person in the role of therapist is unwilling or untrained to render expert interpretative assistance.

which we call resistance will to some extent be reflected by tension changes within the patient and, possibly also, within the therapist.

With these surmises in mind, we have obtained the cooperation of a small group of persons undergoing psychotherapy and have collected data with respect to three variables:

1. "Tension" and "happiness" as subjectively rated by the patients.
2. Palmar sweating as measured by a new technique shortly to be described.
3. Discomfort-relief quotients, derived from an analysis of transcribed interview recordings.

Subjective Ratings on Tension and Happiness Scales.—It ought to be a maxim of all scientific inquiry first to get information by simple means before employing indirect and complicated approaches. With this thought in mind, we decided, in our attempt to quantify the tension or stress which patients feel while undergoing psychotherapy, simply to "ask them." In order to standardize the replies, we prepared two forms, one a five-point tension scale, ranging from "no tension" to "extreme tension" and the other a seven-point happiness scale, ranging from "extremely happy" through "neutral" to "extremely unhappy." Before each therapeutic session, the subjects were required to indicate where they stood on each of these two scales; and the same request was made of them after each session. In all, twenty persons participated in this part of the study.

The two most obvious ways in which data of this kind can be treated are as follows: we can use them (a) as a means of indicating whether, during the course of therapy, there is a change in absolute level of "tension" and/or "happiness" felt by patients and (b) as a means of showing whether patients tend, in general, to feel better, no different, or worse following therapeutic sessions than they do immediately prior thereto.

One reason for being interested in measures which are related to resistance is that they may distinguish patients who remain in therapy from those who do not and those patients who remain in therapy but "fail" from those who "succeed." The twenty persons who participated in this part of the study have therefore been divided, first of all, into those who stayed in therapy and those who, because of extreme resistance or poor motivation, left. There were fifteen of the former and five of the latter. This division of patients enables us to make an analysis of their tension and happiness ratings and thus to see if these measures reliably differentiate the two groups.

In order to give maximal meaning to the data which will shortly be given in tabular form, two cases, one a person who "stayed" in therapy and one who "left," will be briefly described and their individual ratings graphically presented. The first of these, Patient No. 1, was described by her therapist, post-therapy, as follows:

Patient No. 1: Female, married; approximate age, twenty-four. High average intelligence; tall, attractive woman.

Presenting symptoms: Anxiety, claustrophobia, depression. Inability to hold a position because of a feeling of paralysis in arms (hysteric type of reaction) when typing. Fear of going out alone.

Neurosis seems to have been precipitated by marriage. Real masculine striving present. Sexuality: No premarital intercourse. Liked husband best when he was without erection. Husband a rather passive male.

Extremely close attachment to father. Experienced sexual excitement with him during childhood. Weak mother, hypochondriacal, nagging person. Father had affair with another woman.

Shy as a child. Found illness very good escape during childhood. Frightened in school.

Response to therapy: Very resistive to therapy at first. Quite a hostile, castrating woman. Vacillated between extreme femininity in dress, to compensate for masculinity, and slacks, loafers, and casualness. In general, responded well to therapy. Never gave up her resistive mechanisms completely. Made good strides in therapy, developed insights, but "complete" resolution of neurosis could only result in divorce. She was not prepared to make this step. (B. H. L.)

Figure 78 gives a graphic presentation of this patient's tension ratings before and after each of the fifty-one interviews which she had with the therapist. The over-all picture is a rise from "mild" or "medium" tension to strong tension and then a terminal decline to "mild" tension or "no" tension. The before-interview ratings are represented by the curve with open circles and the after-interview ratings by the curve with the filled circles.

Figure 79 shows comparable data for the happiness ratings. Since "happiness" involves more of a long-term evaluation of oneself than does "tension," it is not surprising that the curves shown in Figure 79 are more stable than those shown in Figure 78. This difference was found to hold generally, for most patients. However, it was not uncommon for the patients who made good responses to therapy to show over-all changes in their happiness ratings as well as in their tension ratings. In this respect Patient No. 1 is not wholly typical.

On the basis of the data presented in Figures 78 and 79, it is possible to make cumulative curves for the changes occurring in the tension and happiness ratings before and after each therapeutic session. Such cumulative curves are shown in Figure 80. The cumulative curve for tension change (open circles) shows that for roughly the first seventeen sessions, Patient No. 1 had an *increment* in tension during the therapeutic sessions; for the next ten sessions, however, she experienced very marked decrements during the therapeutic hour; and after Session 27 there was no very marked change in this respect. The patient, during this final period, thus tended to feel about the same amount of tension after the

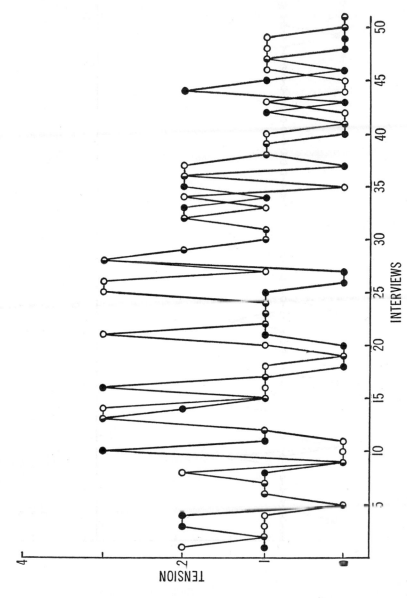

Fig. 78.—Graphic record of the self-ratings of Patient No. 1 with respect to felt "tension" before (open circles) and after (filled circles) each of fifty-one therapeutic sessions. The initial rise in the ratings is followed, as therapy progresses, by a terminal decline which brings the ratings very low.

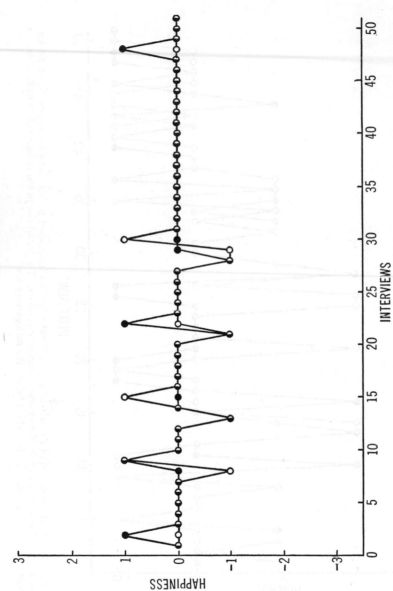

FIG. 79.—"Happiness" self-ratings for Patient No. 1, comparable to the "tension" ratings shown in Figure 78. Note that "happiness" is a more stable, long-term phenomenon than is "tension." In successful therapy, patients commonly report an increase in happiness, as well as a decline in tension. In this respect Patient No. 1 is not entirely typical. Tension is obviously the more "sensitive" measure.

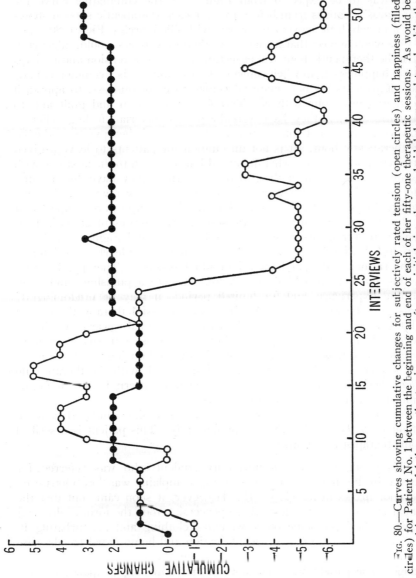

FIG. 80.—Curves showing cumulative changes for subjectively rated tension (open circles) and happiness (filled circles) for Patient No. 1 between the beginning and end of each of her fifty-one therapeutic sessions. As would be expected in successful therapy, the tension curve, after an initial rise, shows a decided downward trend, while the happiness curve rises somewhat. Curves of this kind are constructed by progressive algebraic summation of the changes (positive or negative) which occur from the beginning to the end of each session.

hour as she had felt before and may be said to have reached in therapy a point of "diminishing returns."

As was to be expected from Figure 79, the cumulative curve for "happiness" changes from before to after each therapeutic session shows comparatively little movement (curve with filled circles, Figure 80).

One would expect that in successful therapy patients would, in general, leave the therapeutic hour feeling better, in terms of tension and perhaps also in happiness, than when entering it. Certainly it is a common experience of patients, as new material comes to consciousness, to approach the therapeutic hour with considerable apprehension and guilt and to leave the hour, if they have verbalized this material, feeling relieved. However, it does not follow that all the gains of therapy occur *during* the therapeutic hour. It is not uncommon for patients to leave a given therapeutic session somewhat disturbed but to return to the next one with a statement to the effect that, in the meantime, they have "been doing a lot of thinking" and have arrived at new and very rewarding insights and are "feeling better." [13] Therefore we do not necessarily expect that all the changes *during* therapeutic sessions will represent gains in happiness and decrements in tension. As Figure 78 and Figure 80 indicate, there may be, for a time, increments both in absolute level of tension and in the ratings before and after individual sessions. Therapy, in other words—and here is a kind of paradox—is both a punishing and a rewarding experience, and for limited periods it may be predominantly punishing. However, we assume that in successful therapy the patient will from the beginning experience at least occasional rewards within the therapeutic hour, that as progress quickens these experiences will be increased, and that there will be a terminal period during which the gains will become so small as to make continued work with the therapist no longer rewarding or necessary. This general pattern is shown in the cumulative tension curve in Figure 80.

For purposes of comparison, let us now examine similar data for a patient (No. 9) who left therapy prematurely. This patient is described by his therapist as follows:

This young man was a university student who was referred for therapy by his mother. The presenting complaint was low motivation and poor marks in his classwork. However, it soon came out that the patient was a sexual fetishist whose perversion took the form of dressing in his mother's or some other woman's clothing and masturbating in a peculiar manner. Feminine identification and homosexual trends were much in evidence, with little incentive on the part of the patient to change. The patient was casual, vain, and unwilling to make any real sacrifice to eliminate the minor inconveniences which his life style caused

---

[13] By the same token, we assume that therapy does not stop when the patient ceases to see the therapist. In successful therapy, what has been learned is perceived, not as a transitory "treatment," but as a *way of life* (cf. Cameron and Magaret, 1951).

him. Appointments were sporadic, and when it became evident that therapy consists of deep personal change rather than merely getting "help" in making one's present personality pattern work more satisfactorily, the patient discontinued therapy.

This patient had previously seen the University psychiatrist for a few sessions. At last report he had transferred to another university. (O. H. M.)

Figure 81 gives a picture of this patient's self-ratings on the Tension scale, before (open circles) and after (filled circles) each of the fifteen interviews which he had with the therapist. The over-all trend is slightly upward. Figure 82 shows the patient's self-ratings on the happiness scale; here a slight downward trend is in evidence.

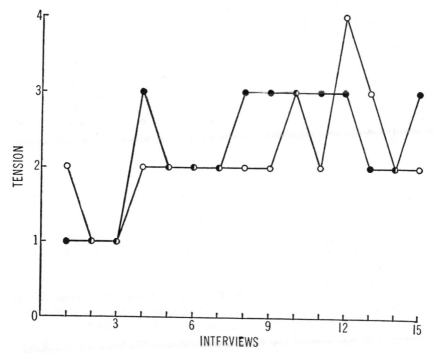

FIG. 81.—Self-ratings of Patient No. 9 with respect to "tension" before (open circles) and after (filled circles) each of fifteen interviews. This patient "left" therapy. The over-all trend is clearly in the direction of greater tension.

When a cumulative analysis is made of the changes in "tension" from beginning to end of each of the fifteen interviews, the curve with the open circles shown in Figure 83 is obtained. The generally upward trend of this curve shows that whenever the patient's rated tension changed during an interview, the change was usually in the nature of an increment. The curve with the filled circles in Figure 83 represents the cumulative happiness data. The only "movement" in this curve is the slight downward dip at the end.

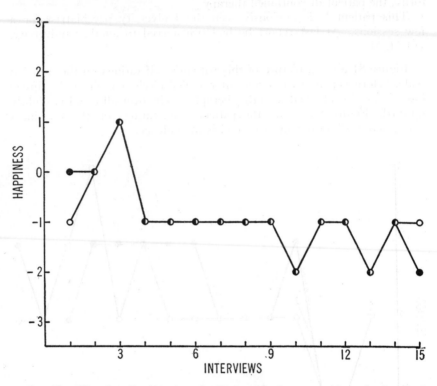

Fig. 82.—"Happiness" self-ratings for Patient No. 9, comparable to the "tension" ratings shown in Figure 81. A slight downward trend is apparent. Patient No. 9 is presented here as more or less typical of persons who leave therapy prematurely.

The results for Patient No. 9 show, as do those for Patient No. 1, that the tension scale is more "sensitive" than the happiness scale. They show—and this is confirmed by the results for the other eighteen patients included in this part of the study—that, in general, these two measures are reciprocal, i.e., that when one goes up the other goes down and vice versa. However, the reciprocity is not symmetrical; it usually takes a good deal of movement on the tension scale to produce change on the happiness scale.

Table 19 gives an over-all statistical picture, for all twenty subjects, of the changes in "tension" and in "happiness" as these occurred during each therapeutic session. The 15 patients who did not leave therapy until both they and the therapist saw some gain in respect to the resolution of their problems had a total of 390 sessions. In 60 of these tension increments were reported; in 132, tension decrements; and in 198, no change. This means that 15 per cent of the total number of sessions, with the fifteen patients who stayed in therapy long enough to accomplish something, were marked by increased tension, 34 per cent by decreased tension, and 51 per cent by no change. These results are to be contrasted with those for the five patients who were judged to have left therapy

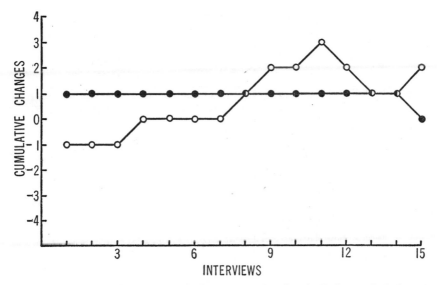

INTERVIEWS

Fig. 83.—Curves showing cumulative changes for "tension" (open circles) and "happiness" (filled circles) for Patient No. 9 between the beginning and end of each of his fifteen therapeutic interviews. The tension curve shows that, in general, this patient emerged from these interviews feeling more tense than when entering; the happiness curve shows only a slight change, and this is the downward direction. These two curves for Patient No. 9, who left therapy prematurely, should be contrasted with those shown in Figure 80, for Patient No. 1.

prematurely. Of their 72 total sessions, 32 sessions were characterized by an increase in tension, 10 by a diminution, and 30 by no change. In terms of percentages, these figures mean that 44 per cent of the total sessions with the persons leaving therapy were marked by increased tension, 14 per cent by reduced tension, and 42 per cent by no change.

Both numerically and percentage-wise, one thus sees the patients who "stayed" and those who "left" moving in opposite directions in terms of intrainterview changes in rated tension. As a check upon the significance of the obtained differences, the data were subjected to the chi-square test. The trichotomous division was used, and with two degrees of freedom, a chi-square of 34.79 was obtained—a value which is significant at the .001 level of confidence. The difference between the patterns of response for the two groups is thus one that would have occurred by chance only once in 1,000 repetitions of the same set of observations.

TABLE 19

NUMBER AND PERCENTAGE OF THERAPEUTIC SESSIONS IN WHICH PATIENTS REPORTED TENSION INCREMENTS, TENSION DECREMENTS, AND "NO CHANGE" AND HAPPINESS INCREMENTS, HAPPINESS DECREMENTS, AND "NO CHANGE"

Fifteen of the twenty patients included in this study are said to have "remained" in therapy and five are said to have "left" therapy. This table shows that those patients who "remained" in therapy tended to experience decrements in tension and increments in happiness, whereas the reverse is true of those patients who broke the therapeutic contact prematurely.

Patients Remaining in Therapy	Total Number of Sessions	Sessions of Tension Increment		Sessions of Tension Decrement		Sessions Involving No Change		Sessions of Happiness Increment		Sessions of Happiness Decrement		Sessions Involving No Change	
		No.	%	No.	%	No.	%	No.	%	No.	%	No.	%
No. 1	51	10	19	15	30	26	51	5	10	2	4	44	86
2	10	2	20	6	60	2	20	4	40	1	10	5	50
3	45	12	27	2	4	31	69	1	2	20	45	24	53
4	43	4	9	16	37	23	54	14	32	6	14	23	54
5	50	7	14	16	32	27	54	21	42	2	4	27	54
6	57	8	14	23	40	26	45	24	42	5	9	28	49
7	15	6	40	5	33	4	27	6	40	4	27	5	33
8	26	4	15	5	19	17	65	5	19	2	8	19	73
14	14	0	0	5	36	9	64	5	36	1	7	8	57
15	12	1	8	9	75	2	17	5	42	0	0	7	58
16	23	4	17	7	30	12	53	7	30	0	0	16	70
17	12	1	8	6	50	5	42	3	25	1	8	8	67
18	14	1	7	5	36	8	57	2	14	2	14	10	72
19	9	0	0	6	67	3	33	2	22	1	11	6	67
20	9	0	0	6	67	3	33	6	67	1	11	2	22
Total	390	60		132		198		110		48		232	
% of Total			15		34		51		28		12		60

TABLE 19 (Continued)

Patients Leaving Therapy	Total Number of Sessions	Sessions of Tension Increment		Sessions of Tension Decrement		Sessions Involving No Change		Sessions of Happiness Increment		Sessions of Happiness Decrement		Sessions Involving No Change	
		No.	%	No.	%	No.	%	No.	%	No.	%	No.	%
No. 9	15	5	33	3	20	7	47	1	7	1	7	13	86
10	14	7	50	3	22	4	28	1	7	1	7	12	86
11	9	4	44	0	0	5	55	1	11	3	33	5	56
12	15	4	27	2	13	9	60	2	13	4	27	9	60
13	19	12	63	2	10	5	27	3	16	8	42	8	42
Total	72	32		10		30		8		17		47	
% of Total			44		14		42		11		24		65
Grand Total	462	92		142		228		118		65		279	

Reference to the right-hand portion of Table 19 will show that in the case of the 15 persons who continued in therapy, in 110 of the 390 total sessions happiness increments were reported, in 48 sessions happiness decrements, and in 60 sessions no change. Rated happiness thus increased in 28 per cent, decreased in 12 per cent, and remained unchanged in 60 per cent of all sessions. For the patients who left therapy, however, only 8 of the total 72 sessions were marked by happiness increments, 17 by decreased happiness, and 47 per cent by no change. This means that 11 per cent of the total sessions for patients leaving therapy resulted in increased happiness ratings, 24 per cent in decreased ratings, and 65 per cent in no change. Here again, as in the case of the ratings on the tension scale, the results for the two groups move in opposite directions. A chi-square of 12.87 was obtained, which value, with two degrees of freedom, is significant at the .01 level of confidence.

One rather complicated question of interpretation arises in connection with the data which are here under review. Reference to the curves appearing in Figures 81, 82, and 83 will show that they are actually not much different from the curves given in Figures 78, 79, and 80 *up to* a comparable number of interviews, namely fifteen. That is to say, during the first fifteen interviews with Patient No. 1, there was an increase in reported tension, both absolutely (Figure 78) and cumulatively (Figure 80), and little or no change in reported happiness, either absolutely (Figure 79) or cumulatively (Figure 80). And this is very much the picture we find for Patient No. 9. The difference consists mainly in the fact that Patient No. 1 *continued* in therapy and soon achieved very considerable tension reduction, whereas Patient No. 9 did not; but up to Interview 15, the self-rating data look about the same for these two cases. The data would not, in other words, have enabled one to *predict* that one patient was going to continue and the other was not.

In order to broaden our basis of comparison here, let us look at a patient who, like Patient No. 9, was in therapy for a comparatively small number of sessions but who, unlike Patient No. 9, left therapy because of a feeling, on the part of both therapist and patient, that she had probably achieved the limited objectives with which she entered therapy. For purposes of such a comparison, Patient No. 2 will serve admirably. Her therapist described her thus:

Patient No. 2: Female, about thirty-three years old, married, three children; husband learning to be a printer under G. I. Bill of Rights.

Description: Rather plump, tried to dress in a sexy manner, with high heels and black dresses; smoked a great deal; fairly intelligent but very suggestible, apathetic, and flat.

Problem: Rejection of oldest son. Son was carried by J. S. in play therapy. In third interview, patient brought in lengthy autobiographical story of her infidelity. In written form, sounded much like a "True Romance" theme. Didn't seem to be too unhappy about this extramarital affair. Blamed a lot of her shortcomings on her husband.

Finally discovered that her difficulties were due to her own immaturities and not entirely those of her husband.

Progress: Patient seemed to improve considerably during later interviews. At first found it hard to talk, but "opened up" after telling about her affair. In general, the problem did not seem too complex. She was a woman of lower socioeconomic status who felt some guilt about extramarital activities, and she projected and rejected her own immaturities by personifying them in her older son. He was also constantly reminding her of her inadequacy by his ability to control her by his misbehavior.

Was unable to determine real adequacy of husband (B. H. L.)

Figure 84 shows this patient's self-ratings on the tension scale, and Figure 85 shows her ratings on the happiness scale; there is a distinct

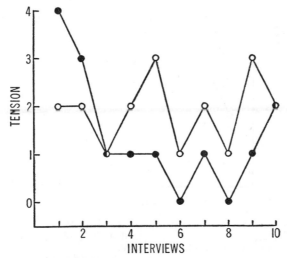

FIG. 84.—Curves for self-ratings on "tension" for a patient (No. 2) who was in therapy for only a few interviews and who, unlike Patient No. 9, left therapy because of a sense of having accomplished what she had set out to do.

downward trend in the first and an upward trend in the second. Moreover, when the same data are analyzed and plotted in terms of cumulative intrainterview changes, the results shown in Figure 86 are obtained. Here, again, is a picture of progressive gain, with respect to both "tension" and happiness. Of course, in such a case it can always be said that the patient's "real problems" were never touched and that the gains reported represent a "flight into health" (see Chapter 13). Fortunately, the palmar-sweating data which will be discussed shortly provide something of a check on this possibility; they suggest that the ratings were honestly made and accurately represent the patient's true emotional state.

Space permitting, it would be instructive to reproduce here the curves, comparable to those just discussed, for all twenty of the subjects who took part in this study. Each patient shows interesting and more or less unique characteristics, and the interest becomes particularly great when the self-rating data are collated with the content of the corresponding

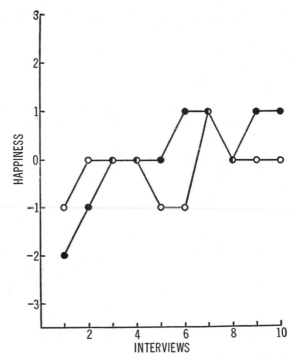

Fig. 85.—Curves showing the self-ratings of Patient No. 2 on the happiness scale. Such a rapid rise as is seen here suggests that the problems involved were more "situational" than psychologically deep-seated.

interviews. However, certain purely statistical trends are also evident. These may be listed as follows:

1. Certainly our patient group—and they are probably no different from human beings generally in this respect—regard "tension" as *negatively* related to "happiness."

2. Our data also show, with considerable consistency, that "tension" is regarded as a relatively temporary, changeable state, whereas "happiness" is a more over-all, protracted, stable state. If, during a series of interviews, tension goes "down," happiness is likely to come "up," and vice versa; but the movement of the latter is nearly always less than the movement of the former.

3. The numerical data given in Table 19 show, at a high level of confidence, that persons who "complete" therapy are distinguishably different in respect to the measures here under discussion from persons

who "break off" the relationship. As already indicated, however, we cannot necessarily *predict* from these measures, during the early phase of therapy, those patients who are going to leave therapy prematurely and those who are going to continue to a satisfactory, or indeed even an unsatisfactory, ending.

In this study no attempt has been made to differentiate systematically between those patients who stayed in therapy with a "successful" outcome from those who stayed but achieved relatively poor results. However, it is of special interest to call attention in this connection to Patient No. 3.

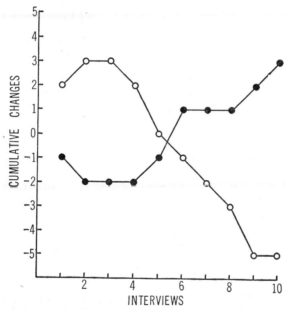

FIG. 86.—Curves showing cumulative changes for "tension" (open circles) and for "happiness" (filled circles) for Patient No. 2. The first two interviews involve tension increments; in the third interview the patient discusses guilt connected with marital infidelity; thereafter there are fairly consistent tension decrements. As noted before, the happiness curve is a kind of "restricted" mirror-image of the tension curve, indicating that tension may change rapidly whereas happiness tends to change more slowly.

In Table 19 this patient is included among those who "stayed" in therapy, but his therapist reports that after the present study was completed this patient returned for a number of further interviews and that during these he was exceedingly negativistic, hostile, and rebellious. The therapy had clearly not brought about much change in his basic personality structure, and he was determined still to persevere in a life style which was in certain respects very immature and close to homosexuality. Reference to Table 19 shows that this patient was the only one of the fifteen persons staying in therapy who rated himself as more often experiencing tension increments (12) during interviews than tension decre-

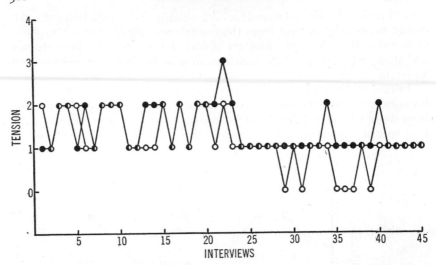

Fig. 87.—Curves for self-ratings of Patient No. 3 on the tension scale. These results are somewhat paradoxical in that they show a slight over-all decrement in tension level but indicate that individual therapeutic sessions were more commonly accompanied by tension increment than by tension decrement (see Figure 89).

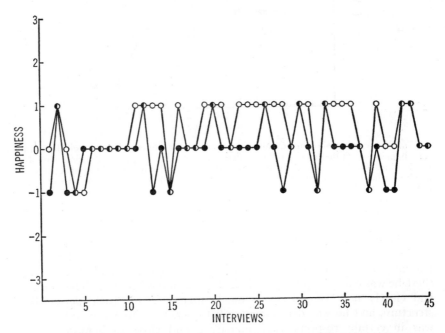

Fig. 88.—Curves for self-ratings of Patient No. 3 on the happiness scale. Here, again, is a paradox: although there is a discernible over-all increment in happiness, the patient reports an increment in happiness following only one interview and a decrement following twenty interviews (cf. Figure 89).

ments (2); and he also shows the highest incidence of "no change" ratings of any of this group of patients, both in absolute terms (31 out of 45 interviews) and also relatively (69 per cent).

Figure 87 shows that there was a slight over-all reduction in the level of tension as rated by this patient throughout the course of therapy; and Figure 88 contains just a suggestion of a rise in rated happiness. However, close inspection of these two graphs indicates, in keeping with the

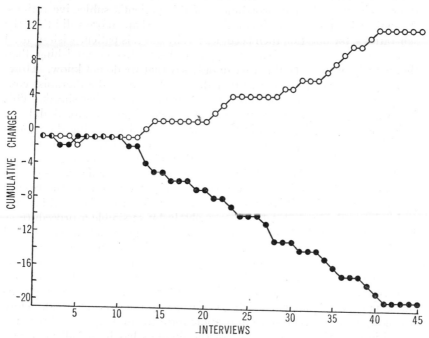

FIG. 89.—Curves showing cumulative change for self-ratings of "tension" (open circles) and "happiness" (filled circles) for Patient No. 3. According to these findings, this patient found therapy a pretty consistently punishing experience. However, there is some reason to believe that there was a systematic distortion in these ratings (see text).

numerical data given above, that very commonly the patient rated himself at the end of an hour as higher on tension and lower on happiness than he had at the beginning of the hour. This tendency to perceive, or at least report, the therapeutic hour as disturbing becomes particularly evident in Figure 89. Here we see that although this patient, like the others, shows a negative or reciprocal relationship between his tension ratings and his happiness ratings, he is aberrant in two other respects: (a) whereas most of the other patients in the same group showed greater movement on the tension scale than on the happiness scale, the reverse was true for this man; and (b) whereas all of the other patients in the group who remained in therapy showed an over-all increment in happiness and a decrement in tension when their results were plotted cumulatively, the reverse was true for Patient No. 3.

In light of these findings one is prompted to ask: Why, then, if therapy was such a consistently punishing experience did this patient continue with it for forty-five sessions (and subsequently return for further sessions)? As we shall see in a later section of this chapter, objective measures of palmar perspiration indicate that therapy was *not* a predominantly punishing experience, a fact which immediately raises questions concerning the trustworthiness of this patient's subjective ratings. Assuming that the perspiration measures are perhaps more valid than the self-ratings, the question then becomes: Why did this patient wish or need to report that the interviews were more distressing or punishing than they actually were? To this we can only say that we do not know. However, it is relevant to add here that during this study the therapist concerned made a point of not looking at their patients' rating sheets. This fact was explained to all patients, but perhaps Patient No. 3 did not believe what was said to him in this connection and was using the ratings as an indirect form of communication with the therapist, as a way of trying to "tell" him something which the therapist never "heard."

As indicated earlier and just exemplified by specific reference to Patient No. 3, the self-rating results for almost every one of the twenty patients included in this study had one or more features of special interest and indicate the kind of data one can obtain by so simple a procedure as just "asking them." As could have been anticipated in advance, personal idiosyncrasies are almost certain to enter the picture and complicate the results from the standpoint of a strictly statistical treatment—witness the fact that Patient No. 3 was included, quite properly, among those persons who continued in therapy but that he gave results, at least on the self-rating part of the inquiry, which go contrary to the over-all trend. Here it is not possible to reproduce in graphic form the findings for all patients (see Light, 1951), but the tenor of the findings has been indicated, and the picture will be further clarified in the following sections.

The reader will note that no statistical analysis is made here of the *absolute* changes in tension and happiness reported by our two groups of subjects. As indicated in Table 19 and the attendant discussion, the same data when analyzed in terms of *cumulative* changes show a highly reliable difference between these groups—and had it not been for the behavior of Patient No. 3 this difference would have been even more striking. A comparable statistical analysis of the same data, in absolute terms, would have been desirable, but there was no very feasible way of handling these data in a statistically meaningful manner.

As indicated above, the curves based upon cumulative changes in tension and happiness are, in general, more "sensitive" than the curves which show the absolute levels for these variables, i.e., the cumulative curves more often show marked differences between patients and in the same patient from time to time. However, it should be remembered that both types of analysis have value, since they show different things. While a person who usually experiences a decrement in tension from beginning to end of the therapeutic hour would be expected to show also a decline, gradual or ultimate, in absolute tension level, it is entirely possible, as some of our records indicate and logic independently suggests, for these two measures to move independently, even in opposition to one another, as in the case of Patient No. 3. While such a reversal is exceptional, the fact that it occurs raises some interesting problems, which will be further considered in later sections.

The Measurement of Palmar Perspiration: History and Technique.—For reasons which have already been adumbrated, it is desirable to have one or more purely objective measures of tension and tension change during therapy to compare with the self-ratings on the tension and happiness scales discussed in the preceding section. However, as is well known, objective techniques for measuring emotionality have usually been plagued by unreliability and/or great instrumental complexity.

The response which, in many ways, seems to have greatest promise in this connection is that of palmar perspiration. The fact that perspiration is associated with emotional stress is a common feature of folk wisdom—witness such expressions as "sweating it out"—and has often been commented on in scientific and medical literature. For several decades it has also been known that if electrodes are put on the volar and palmar surfaces of the hand (or foot) and if a startling or otherwise disturbing event is made to occur for the subject, the electrical resistance between the electrodes will dramatically drop and then, presently, recover. This reaction has been called the galvanic skin response (GSR) or psychogalvanic reaction (PGR).

But it remained for Kuno (1934) to provide a plausible and well-documented rationale for the use of palmar sweating as an indicator of emotion. His book, *The physiology of perspiration,* is beautifully concise, excellently organized, and well worth reading in its entirety; but for present purposes the paragraphs which follow are of greatest importance:

The factors causing sweating, such as exposure to heat and muscular exercise, are processes which result in an increase of body temperature. On the other hand, emotion, mental stress and sensory stimulations, which are also known as causal agents of sweating, have little bearing on the body temperature. Some factors of the latter group seem to be quite opposite in nature to those of the former. For instance, the phenomena accompanying emotion, such as constriction of the skin vessels, goose skin and glycemia, are identical with those appearing on cooling of the body, but contrary to those induced by heating. It seemed to me very strange that both these contradictory agents act in the same sense in the provocation of sweating, and I have long doubted whether the sweating caused by one group is identical with that caused by the other (p. 129).

Researches of the most varied nature consistently showed that what Kuno calls "emotional" sweating occurs on the palms of the hands, the soles of the feet, and, in the sexually mature human being, in the armpits; whereas perspiration which is concerned with heat regulation "always appears universally over the general body surface." So-called "thermal" sweating does not occur on the palms or soles.

The palms, the soles and the axillae are therefore the parts of the skin which are to be distinguished from all the other body surfaces in regard to the function of the sweat glands. The sweating on the former differs from that on the latter not only in its causation, but also in its features and its physiological significance (p. 131).

Kuno believes that there are two distinct neurological centers for the control of these two forms of sweating.

In conclusion he says:

The theory that heat elimination is the object of sweating no longer holds good for the sweating on the palm and the sole, since this sweating never appears on exposure of the subject to high temperature. If this sweating has any physiological significance, it may conceivably be in some relation to mental stress or emotion which is its most adequate cause. We have a peculiar habit of moistening the palms of the hands with saliva when muscular exercise is undertaken. This seems to be a habit common to the human race, physiological and not ethnological in origin, because the expression for "spitting on the hands" is found in many different languages. Moistening the surface of the palm would increase the friction between it and the objects with which it comes into contact. Consequently every sort of muscular work would be facilitated, not only for this physical reason but also for the physiological reason that the sense of touch becomes acute when friction increases. In human beings, mental stress is not necessarily accompanied by muscular work, but it is almost inevitably so in animals, because they become excited only from such reasons as self-defense against enemies and battle for the acquisition of food or for the other sex, when more or less muscular exercise is required. It is, therefore, a great advantage for animals that the pads of their feet should become wet through sweating as soon as they are excited. The sweating on the human palms and soles on emotion or mental stress may be regarded as a phenomenon transmitted from animal life. Even in human beings, it is not always useless, e.g., during strenuous exercise, sweat always appears on the palms, and it actually facilitates the performance of work. It is interesting to note that in some languages—e.g., Japanese and Chinese, and in English too—the expression "spitting on the hands" conveys an implication of general physical and mental stress.

The regional difference of sweating on the palms and soles strongly supports the view above mentioned, since the amount of sweat on any parts of these regions varies in proportion to the likelihood of touching objects on grasping or walking. Quite independently of us, Minor came to the same conclusion from his experiments. From all the accounts described above, it seems highly probable that the object of sweating on the palms and soles is to facilitate physical work (pp. 228-29).

Kuno and colleagues (at the Manchuria Medical College) observed that palmar sweating could be produced by a variety of sensory stimuli, among them: the touch of a hot knife blade or electric lamp to the skin, sight of blood from a cut, congestion produced by circulation restriction, forced inspiration, grasping a dynamometer, and "a strong desire to urinate." All these are in some sense danger signals and might appropriately be thought of as justifying the physiological "emergency reaction" of Cannon. One of the most interesting occasions for palmar or "emotional" sweating mentioned by Kuno is the following. He found that, in general, palmar sweating does not occur in response to an elevated temperature of the surroundings. "If, however, the increase of surrounding temperature is of extreme degree so that heat stroke may gradually develop, sweating appears on the palms and soles" (p. 139). In other words, if surrounding temperature, which is normally not a stimulus for palmar sweating, becomes excessively high and taxes the thermoregulatting mechanism of the organism, then this may be perceived as a danger situation, one which may properly justify *action,* with accompanying palmar sweating (see p. 630 ff.).

The sensitivity of the palmar sweating response to stress is particularly well indicated by experiments in which Kuno and coworkers asked subjects questions "in simple addition for five to twenty minutes. This may be regarded as moderate mental stress . . ." (p. 131). During such periods palmar perspiration was sharply elevated, whereas general bodily perspiration remained unchanged.

Although Kuno cannot be said to have used palmar perspiration as a "diagnostic" device in the psychological sense, he nevertheless noted marked individual differences. He says:

The activity of the sweat glands of the palms and soles varies considerably in different individuals. In some individuals, these parts are usually dry, and when sweat is produced by adequate stimuli, its amount is small. In others, these parts are always wet to a greater or lesser extent, and considerable sweating sometimes breaks out. Again there are individuals who suffer from an abnormally intense secretion of sweat on these parts so that sweat may drop from the palms on occasion. In this college, there is a student who cannot write examination-papers without making them wet by dripping sweat (pp. 139-40).

The laboratory as well as naturalistic material which Kuno cites is extremely rich in meaningfulness and interest, and we shall touch upon it again later. However, our immediate purposes are best served if we now turn to a series of papers by Silverman and Powell which may be regarded as the next milestone in the investigation of the topic under consideration. Their first two papers (1944a, 1944b) are mainly methodological in character and need not be reviewed at length here. These investigators, in an attempt to develop a technique for measuring palmar perspiration which would involve a minimum of instrumentation (Kuno's techniques, while precise, were often very cumbersome) seized upon the fact that earlier investigators had shown that "colorimetric" methods could be used in this connection. Kuno and Kosaka, following Minor, were able to demonstrate sweating visibly by applying to the area of the body under examination a compound which, when put into solution by means of perspiration, resulted in a dark stain (Figure 90). And other methods had been devised whereby "prints" could be transferred from the perspiring surface to paper. These, however, were in many respects imperfect, and Silverman and Powell introduced important improvements.

The details of a modified version of the method of Silverman and Powell will be given presently; but it consists, essentially, of coating the area to be studied, let us say the fingertips, with a solution of ferric chloride, drying it, and then placing the fingers, with a "light but firm pressure" on paper which has been impregnated with a solution of tannic acid and dried. When and to the extent that perspiration flows, it carries the ferric chloride into solution with the tannic acid. Of the resulting reaction, Silverman and Powell say:

The arrangement of the active sweat glands is portrayed upon the chemically treated paper. Sweat is approximately 99% water, and will carry with it in solution the readily soluble ferric chloride. The size and intensity of the pattern is directly proportional to the amount of sweat excreted. In the tannic acid technique the tannic acid reacts with iron to form a stain on the paper ranging between grey-blue and blue-black. The combination of tannic acid and iron salts is used commercially in the preparation of writing inks. When potassium ferrocyanide [an alternative to the tannic acid] is used, the interaction with ferric chloride leaves a blue stain. This is the familiar Prussian blue reaction (1944a, p. 298).

In respect to the meaning and function of palmar sweating, these authors, in the second of their studies (1944b), have the following to say:

Normally emotional sweating is commonly seen in states of anticipation and has sometimes been referred to as anticipatory sweating. A student before an examination, an expectant father before the delivery of his child, or a draftee waiting for his number will show sweating, particularly of the palms. The relationship of emotions to sweating was noted by Sanctorius in 1614. . . . The relationship of palmar sweating to emotional stress or strain has expression in many fields of human endeavor (p. 300).

The clinical observation of excessive palmar sweating is not new. Da Costa in 1871 in his classical paper on the "irritable heart" stated: "But there was also evidence of disorder of the skin and excessive perspiration from which many suffered. Inordinate sweating of the hand was several times complained of (as in case 159)." It is interesting to note that Da Costa advised the use of atropine which has later been shown to be a powerfully anti-parasympathetic drug. . . . Palmar sweating is such a constant and

The distribution of sweat on the palm.
(Kosaka.)

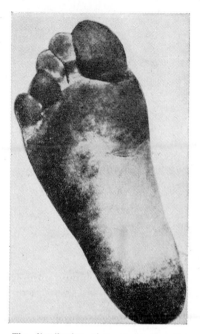

The distribution of sweat on the sole.
(Kosaka.)

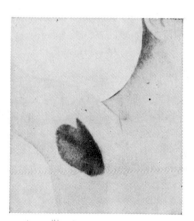

Sweating on the axilla due to mental arithmetic. (Kosaka.)

FIG. 90.—Photographs reproduced from Kuno (1934) which illustrate an early "colorimetric" method of demonstrating perspiration on the palm of the hand, the sole of the foot, and in the armpit. This method is unsatisfactory in that it does not leave a permanent record and is not easily quantified.

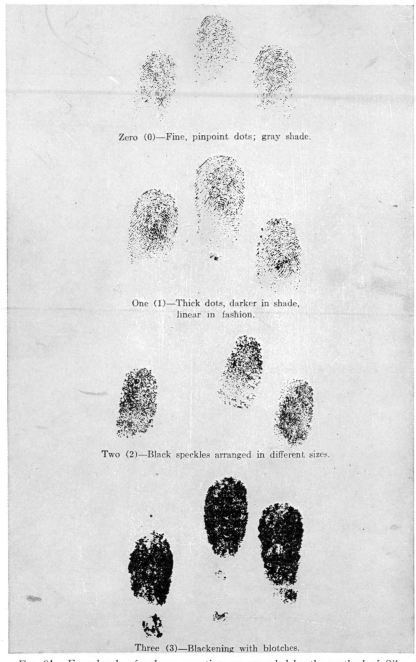

Zero (0)—Fine, pinpoint dots; gray shade.

One (1)—Thick dots, darker in shade,
linear in fashion.

Two (2)—Black speckles arranged in different sizes.

Three (3)—Blackening with blotches.

Fɪɢ. 91.—Four levels of palmar sweating, as recorded by the method of Silverman and Powell (1944c). Stains somewhat similar to those shown in Figure 90 are here transferred to paper, thus providing a permanent record of a subject's reaction. Silverman and Powell did not, however, solve the problem of precise quantification, relying instead upon the ranking of each subject's "prints" by comparison with the standards shown.

striking feature of neurocirculatory asthenia that its presence should always be looked for as a point in diagnosis (p. 304).

As already indicated, Kuno had been struck by the paradoxical nature of palmar sweating, i.e., the fact that it is often accompanied by phenomena "such as constriction of the skin vessels, goose skin and glycemia [which] are identical with those appearing on cooling of the body, but contrary to those induced by heating." Silverman and Powell explore the neurology of palmar sweating along the following lines:

The relationship between sweating and parasympathetic centers in the diencephalon was noted by Cushing. . . . Although sweating on anatomic grounds travels along a sympathetic pathway, pharmacologically it behaves as a parasympathetic mechanism. . . .

That sweating, a parasympathetic response, occurs in states of increased sympathetic activity may at first seem confusing. "Breaking out in cold sweat" is a common expression. This confusion may result from the arbitrary separation of the autonomic system into the parasympathetic and sympathetic divisions. This separation implies a reciprocity of action.

. . . Gellhorn has recently shown that emotional excitement evokes a stimulation of *both* branches of the autonomic nervous system, although under normal conditions the sympathetic system predominates. The principle of reciprocal innervation of both divisions of the autonomic nervous system is also not borne out on clinical grounds (1944b, p. 131).

Against the background of this reasoning, it is understandable that Silverman and Powell should have wished to validate their method of measuring palmar perspiration—and their assumption that this reaction is an indicator of emotional disturbance—with a group of neuropsychiatric patients and a group of normal persons. For the former they used 1,160 patients in an Army general hospital, a majority of whom "were originally admitted to the hospital with a diagnosis of psychoneurosis." For purposes of control, they used 71 members of the hospital staff, "which included enlisted ward attendants, nurses and duty medical officers." But before their subjects could be accurately compared, Silverman and Powell needed some way of quantifying their results. They accordingly selected specimen responses to indicate four levels of palmar perspiration (Figure 91) and had the responses of all their subjects put into one of four categories according to whether they most closely resembled one or another of the four models. The results are shown in Figure 92. Here it will be seen that the two groups distributed themselves quite differently in respect to their palmar sweating. Heavy responses (levels 2 and 3) predominate in the patient group, whereas the lighter responses (0 and 1) predominate in the normal control group. Assuming that these two groups differed significantly in emotionality, the results (without statistical treatment) appear to support the view that emotionality produces heightened palmar sweating and that this response can be reliably, and certainly conveniently, measured by the colorimetric method which Silverman and Powell describe.[14]

In his doctoral thesis, Gladstone (1949) has made some interesting extensions of and refinements in the method of Silverman and Powell. The method had a special appeal to Gladstone in that it is basically so

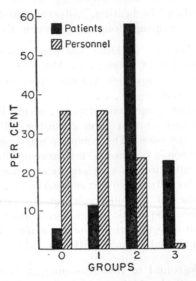

Fig. 92.—Distribution of the palmar perspiration response of neuropsychiatric patients and normal persons on the four-point scale of Silverman and Powell (1944c). The patient group perspires more heavily, according to these findings, than do the normal controls.

simple that it can be used as a "group test," i.e., the testing materials can be distributed to the members of as large a group as desired and instructions given for the self-administration of the test. Among other purposes to which Gladstone put the test was, for example, its use as a means of measuring the general level of palmar perspiration in classrooms of school children under varying circumstances. Whereas Silverman and Powell had used the method primarily for diagnostic purpose (i.e., for the study of individual differences), Gladstone used it more in the sense of Kuno,

[14] In a personal communication, Erick Wright of the University of Kansas has recently informed us of a study carried out in 1945 by him and Leon Witzell at the Santa Cruz U. S. Naval Convalescence Hospital in which the method of Silverman and Powell was used with a group of psychoneurotic patients and a group of "psychopaths." Wright reports that there was a marked difference between these two groups with respect to the palmar perspiration index, the neurotics showing much more perspiration than the psychopaths. Since one of the differentiating criteria of neurotics is that they experience more anxiety than do psychopaths, the finding of Wright and Wetzell provides further confirmation of the assumption that palmar perspiration, as measured by the Silverman and Powell method, is a correlate of anxiety.

to study the effects of certain types of situational stimulation, but with groups rather than with individuals.

Gladstone made three notable improvements in the method:

1. Whereas Silverman and Powell had used "ordinary mimeograph paper" for their prints, Gladstone substituted "Dietzgen No. 198M."

2. Whereas Silverman and Powell used a solution of ferric chloride which, when applied to the fingertips, was slow-drying, Gladstone substituted "anhydrous ferric chloride and reagent grade or chemically pure acetone . . . in the proportion of 13g. $FeCl_3$ to 400 cc. acetone. This gives the same concentration of $FeCl_3$ to liquid as in a 25 per cent tincture of ferric chloride solution. The difference lies in the fact that the liquid evaporates much more rapidly. This solution may be stored for several weeks in a dark brown bottle, but deteriorates in several months" (p. 37).

3. Gladstone introduced a photometric method of measuring the perspiration prints, in place of the method of visual comparison used by Silverman and Powell: ". . . the measuring process consists of shining a light through the paper, catching the [transmitted] light on a light cell, and measuring the resulting current with a microammeter" (p. 41).

On the basis of his findings, Gladstone concludes:

The writer is reluctant at this time to take a position in favor of any particular psychological label or labels which pretend to describe the psychological atmosphere of the various affective situations used. They have something in common, however—they cause an increase in palmar sweat, and, therefore, presumably have affected the sympathetic [sic] nervous system (p. 104).[15]

In another doctoral thesis, Light (1951) has still further refined the method under discussion and has applied it, apparently for the first time, to the measurement of the changes in palmar sweating which occur during the course of psychotherapy. His methodological innovations were as follows:

1. He found that Gladstone's ferric chloride and acetone solution was somewhat unstable, but that, by adding three drops of hydrochloric acid, this solution (13 g. of anhydrous ferric chloride in 400 cc. of chemically pure acetone) can be considerably stabilized. It is still desirable to keep it in a brown, well-stoppered bottle to protect it from light and from evaporation; but the solution can be used for several weeks without change in effectiveness.

2. Instead of using the transmittance measure employed by Gladstone, Light used the Baumgartner reflectometer. Here light is shown upon a print and the amount of light reflected from a circumscribed surface of the paper is then measured photoelectrically.

3. Since the darkness of a print varies somewhat as a function of the pressure with which the fingers are held on the paper, Light standardized this aspect of the test by placing the paper on the top of a small postage

[15] Gladstone, incidentally, gives a good survey of the literature on "the validity of palmar sweating as an index of emotion."

scale and having the subject hold his fingers on the paper with a standard amount of pressure, namely one pound. "The top was covered with chamois skin and the impregnated paper was securely fastened to the top by means of a small clamp. . . . In this way, all patients exerted the same amount of pressure, and the scale itself was a type of self-correcting regulator" (p. 30).

Light required his subjects to allow their fingers to dry for thirty seconds after application (by means of a cotton swab on the end of an applicator stick) of the ferric chloride in acetone, before placing them in contact with the impregnated paper. The period of contact, with a pressure of one pound, was three minutes.

No essential improvement has been made in the method described by Silverman and Powell (1944a) for impregnating the paper. They say:

A 5 per cent solution of tannic acid is prepared in distilled water, filtered, and poured into a flat-bottom glass dish. Ordinary mimeograph paper [Dietzgen No. 198M is better] is used and is allowed to soak in this solution for approximately three minutes. Metal containers are avoided. The paper is then dried and cut to desired dimensions. Where tannic acid is not available, a 5 per cent solution of potassium ferrocyanide is used. The latter solution has the disadvantage of being less stable (p. 298).

The impregnated paper darkens slightly with age, but its chemical efficiency does not seem to be much impaired thereby. However, it is important that the impregnation be carried out while the tannic acid solution is fresh. If the solution is allowed to stand for more than a day or two, a mold is likely to collect on the surface of the solution, making it less usable.

We have been at some pains in this section to give both the history of and some of the most recent developments with respect to the so-called colorimetric method of measuring palmar sweat for the reason that we believe this method has special promise for measuring "emotional sweating" under a variety of circumstances, including psychotherapy. The method, as already indicated, can be applied in five minutes or less, it is simple and inexpensive, it can be used repetitively, and patients do not object to it. From the standpoint of practicality, it is therefore nearly ideal. In the following section, certain additional technical improvements are described, and the question of the method's meaning and validity will also be given attention. However, enough has now been said to provide a background adequate for discussing the results obtained thus far from the method as a means of providing an objective and precisely quantifiable measure of palmar perspiration at various stages during psychotherapy.

Measurement of Palmar Perspiration during Psychotherapy.—
In this section we shall be concerned, first of all, with the palmar sweating responses of ten of the twenty patients whose self-ratings re-

garding tension and happiness have been discussed above. Circumstances were such that we were not able to secure perspiration data on the other ten.

We shall begin by considering the results for the same cases that were used as reference examples in the previous discussion. Patient No. 1, it will be recalled, was a young married woman with masculine strivings who suffered from anxiety, claustrophobia, and depression. The curves showing the absolute levels of her self-ratings on the tension and happiness scales are reproduced in Figures 78 and 79, and the curves for the cumulative changes derived from the same data are reproduced in Figure 80. Figure 93 shows curves based upon the reflectometer readings for the finger prints of this patient before and after forty-nine of the fifty-one interviews comprising her therapy. There is a decided over-all drop in these readings between the beginning and end of the period of treatment, and we see that most of this drop occurred, for some reason, between Sessions 30 and 32. It would be interesting to go to the recordings for this patient and analyze the content of these interviews, but this would carry us beyond the scope of this chapter.

The curves shown in Figure 93 correspond moderately well to the self-ratings for tension shown in Figure 78. Although there is an initial rise in rated tension which is not shown in the fingerprint data, the curves for the self-ratings drop markedly at about the same point as do the perspiration curves, namely in the neighborhood of the thirtieth interview.

When the data shown in Figure 93 are converted into a curve of cumulative change, the result shown in Figure 94 (filled circles) is obtained. With this curve is shown also the cumulative tension curve already reproduced in Figure 80. As will be seen, the parallelism is quite good. Although this patient did not rate herself on the tension scale in such a way that her ratings correspond very closely, in absolute terms, to the perspiration scores, her ratings of *tension change* during each interview do, however, correspond reasonably well with the *changes* in perspiration output, as shown in Figure 94.

The parallelism between the tension self-ratings and the perspiration measures are even more striking for Patient No. 2. This married woman, it will be recalled, presented a relatively superficial type of problem and was apparently much relieved merely as a result of telling the therapist about her marital infidelity. The absolute "tension" curves for this patient have been reproduced in Figure 84. Comparable data for the perspiration measure are reproduced in Figure 95. Here it is interesting to note that whereas the after-interview perspiration level drops markedly during the brief course of therapy, the before-interview level drops less markedly. The same relative picture is seen in Figure 84 with respect to the before- and after-interview ratings on the tension scale.[16] But most striking of all is the parallelism between the curves showing cumulative

[16] The *DRQ* data of Rollins and Twaite reproduced in Chapter 11 also give this same picture (see Figure 34).

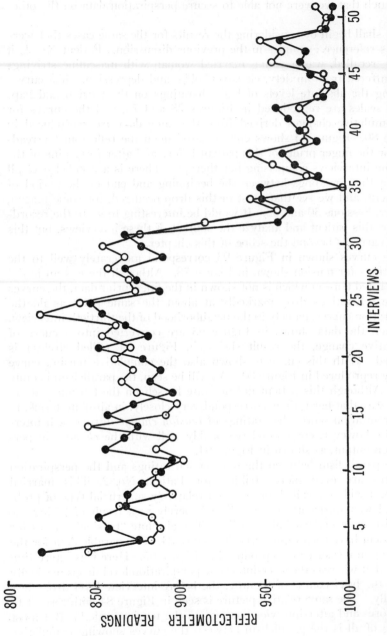

FIG. 93.—Absolute measures of palmar sweating during the treatment of Patient No. 1, obtained by a "colorimetric" method described in the text. Numerically high reflectometer readings (toward 1,000) indicate *less* perspiration than do low readings. (Data not available for first and second interviews.)

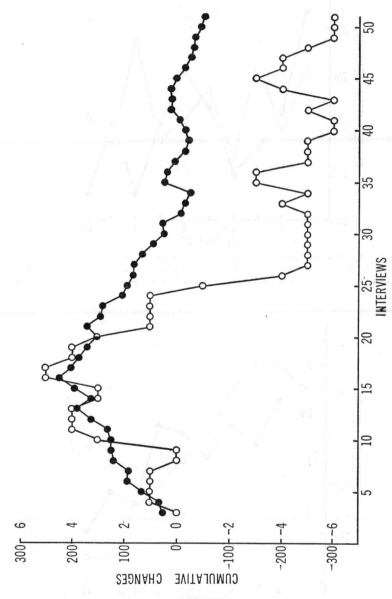

Fig. 94.—Cumulative curves for tension self-ratings (open circles) and for palmar sweating (filled circles), in the case of Patient No. 1. Whatever it is that one of these curves measures is obviously related to what the other one measures The assumption is that they both are indicators of psychological tension or stress. The "outside" scale on the ordinate is for reflectometer units, the "inside" scale for subjective-tension units.

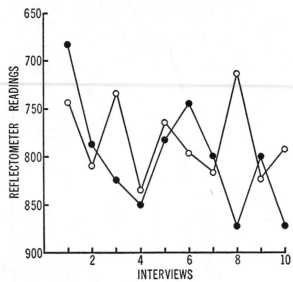

FIG. 95.—Absolute measures of palmar sweating on the part of Patient No. 2 during a brief but "successful" therapy. A downward trend appears in both the before- and the after-interview curve, although it is more pronounced in the latter.

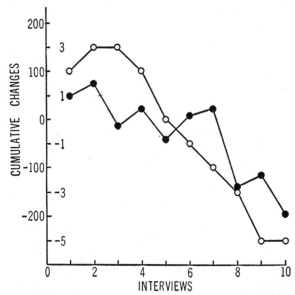

FIG. 96.—Cumulative curves for tension self-ratings (open circles) and for palmar perspiration (filled circles), Patient No. 2. The parallelism suggests that both measures are, at least in this case, valid.

changes in tension and in perspiration. These are juxtaposed in Figure 96.[17]

Both of the cases just considered were "success" cases. Let us now look at a case which was terminated before anything very substantial was accomplished, therapeutically. The data derived from self-ratings by Patient No. 9 on the tension and happiness scales have already been reproduced graphically in Figures 81-83. Both in terms of absolute level and cumulative change, the results for this male college student with fetish perversions indicate an increase in tension. Figure 97 shows the

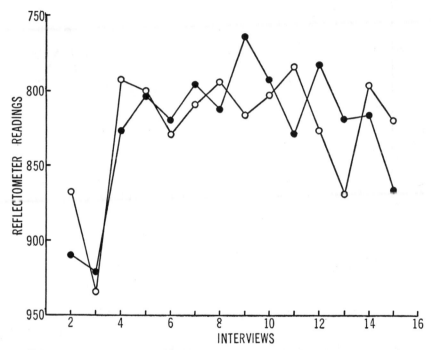

FIG. 97.—Absolute perspiration levels for Patient No. 9, who left therapy prematurely. Therapy appears to have been a decidedly upsetting experience for him, and he did not have the necessary motivation to see it through.

palmar-perspiration data for the same person. After the first two interviews, there is a sharp increase in palmar perspiration; evidently therapy served to activate his tensions, which in the beginning were relatively low. Toward the end of the period this man was in treatment, there is a suggestion that his tensions were again starting to decline, but this may

[17] The possibility that one of these measures might have artificially influenced the other is much reduced by the fact that the tension rating was always made before the perspiration test was taken. If the reverse procedure had been followed, there would have been the possibility for the patient to try to make his tension rating correspond to the heaviness of his fingerprints.

be only because he had privately "decided" to leave therapy and thus felt an anticipatory relief.

Figure 98 shows the cumulative changes in self-rated tension and in perspiration. Here the upward trend for the self-ratings is substantiated by the even more pronounced upward trend in the cumulative perspiration changes. In this case, then, as in the more successful ones, the evidence points clearly in the direction of a parallelism between the subjective ratings and the objective measures of palmar perspiration.

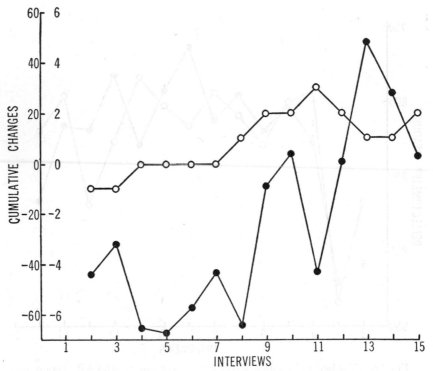

Fig. 98.—Cumulative curves for Patient No. 9, showing again a parallelism between self-rated tension (open circles) and objectively measured perspiration (filled circles).

As will be recalled, Patient No. 3 remained in therapy for forty-five interviews (and later returned for further contacts) and thus could not be classified as having "left prematurely," yet there was some question as to how "successful" this case was. Figures 87 and 88 show, respectively, a very slight downward trend in the tension ratings and a very slight upward trend in the happiness ratings, but Figure 89 shows that the curves based upon cumulative change went in the reverse directions. In other words, this patient pretty regularly reported "feeling worse," both in terms of tension and happiness, following the therapeutic hour than before. When we examine Figure 99, which shows the absolute level of perspiration throughout therapy, we see ever so slight an upward trend to the forty-first interview, then a decided drop. This drop might have meant a sudden resolution of the patient's difficulties, but it might, equally well, have come from an unannounced resolution to leave therapy. To the extent that the absolute perspiration level rises in this case and the rated tension declines, there may be said to be a *reverse* parallelism between the subjective and objective data. However, the reverse trends, in any case, are very slight.

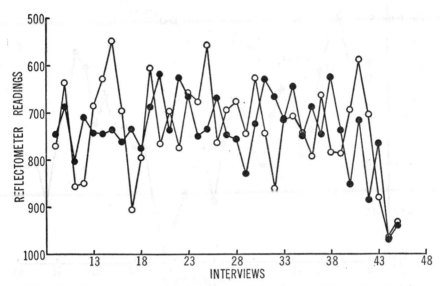

Fig. 99.—Absolute measures of palmar perspiration in Patient No. 3 before (open circles) and after (filled circles) the therapeutic hour. Although this patient stayed in therapy for a relatively long while, the case was not regarded as very "successful." It is conjectured that the drop in perspiration level toward the end of therapy may reflect the relief the patient felt at having decided to leave therapy, rather than from a resolution of his problems.

But when cumulative changes for rated tension and perspiration are plotted, as in Figure 100, the inconsistency between these two measures becomes conspicuous. Here it will be seen that during the first thirty interviews, the patient experienced, in terms of the perspiration index, marked relief from the therapeutic sessions, even though he rated these sessions as accompanied by tension increase. Presumably the perspiration measures are the more trustworthy, and if they are they might explain why the patient remained in therapy for a rather protracted period despite the fact that he was experiencing no reduction in absolute tension. If a patient finds the therapeutic hour relieving he may well continue in therapy, even though no over-all gain is occurring. Therapy would thus become a kind of "addiction habit," without real therapeutic significance.[18]

A further glance at Figure 100 shows that whatever it was that therapy meant for this patient during the first thirty interviews, the pattern altered and we see a marked rise in the cumulative curve for perspira-

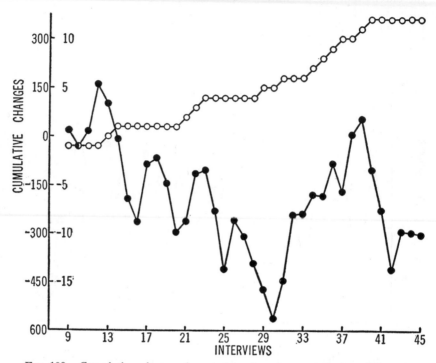

Fig. 100.—Cumulative changes in rated tension (open circles) and in palmar perspiration (filled circles) for Patient No. 3. From the 9th (earlier data not available) to the 30th interview, this patient often indicated that he felt more tense after the therapeutic hour than before, whereas the palmar perspiration data during the same period suggest that the patient found the hours relaxing. From the 30th to the 39th interviews, both indices show an upward trend, while for the remaining interviews the perspiration index drops and the tension index remains about the same.

tion change. In other words, between interviews No. 30 and No. 39, this patient found therapy a distinctly punishing experience, which, we may conjecture, produced the decision to leave therapy—and the terminal decline in tension. In a case which shows such a number of seemingly paradoxical results as does Patient No. 3, it would be particularly instructive to study the protocols in the light of these results. However, as already indicated, this would carry us beyond our immediate objectives.

[18] One might conjecture that in such a case the patient is using the fact that he is in therapy to assuage self-criticism—"After all, I *am* in therapy"—rather than to effect a basic change and cure.

Although it is obvious that, in this case, the parallelism between the subjective and objective data is far from perfect—and thus raises the question of validity—the two measures taken in conjunction give a more complete picture of the case than would either alone, thus usefully supplementing one another.

It is not feasible to reproduce here curves showing the palmar perspiration of all ten of the patients for whom such data were collected. However, there are two remaining patients whose reactions in this connection are particularly interesting and warrant special comment. Patient No. 8, a "G.I." college student who had had a neuropsychiatric discharge from the Army, reported, during the course of twenty-six interviews, no change in absolute level of happiness and a very slight rise in absolute tension. In terms of cumulative changes, there was a very slight rise in happiness and a very slight lowering of tension. In light of this pattern of self-ratings, let us examine this man's palmar sweating. Figure 101 shows

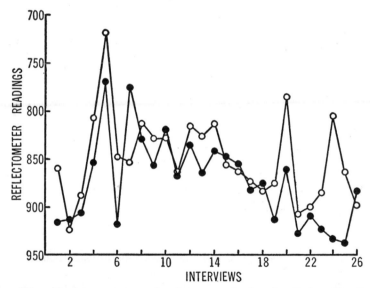

Fig. 101.—Absolute measures of palmar perspiration for Patient No. 8. The rather marked changes to be noted here are in contrast to the negligible changes in self-ratings for "tension" and "happiness" during the same series of interviews.

the absolute perspiration readings for this patient before and after each therapeutic session. Following an initial sharp rise, there is a gradual but fairly continuous decline. The objective measures thus give a picture very different from that of the subjective ratings.

As already stated, the cumulative changes in rated tension for Patient No. 8 drop only insignificantly during the course of therapy. This is shown graphically in Figure 102. In the same figure appear the cumulative changes in perspiration. Whereas the curve for the former remains almost flat, the curve for the latter drops dramatically. Here, then, we see an instance in which the subjective data show little or no change during the course of therapy either absolutely or in terms of cumulative changes, whereas the objective data, based upon the colorimetric measurement of perspiration, show marked changes in both respects.

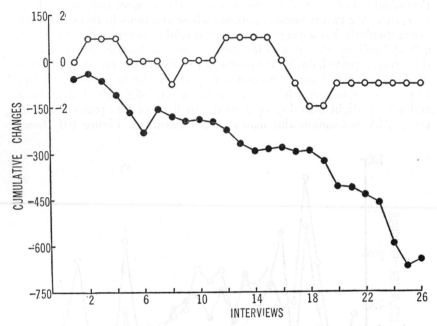

Fig. 102.—Curves showing the cumulative changes in self-rated tension (open circles) and in palmar perspiration (filled circles) for Patient No. 8. Here the discrepancy between the self-ratings and the more objective data is striking and perhaps related to a tendency toward general verbal unreliability in the patient.

The findings for Patient No. 7 also have some unusual features. The absolute-tension curves for this patient, during the course of the fifteen interviews that she had, dropped rather decidedly, and there was also a rise in the absolute level of rated happiness. Cumulatively there was, for the first five or six interviews, a rise in tension, then a gradual but continuous decline, while the cumulative happiness curve was a flattened reciprocal of the cumulative tension curve. Figure 103 shows the absolute perspiration readings, before and after each hour, for this patient; and here a definitely downward trend is revealed, in keeping with the curves (not shown) for absolute tension ratings. However, the curves for cumulative changes in rated tension and in perspiration, shown in Figure 104, are somewhat enigmatic. At first glance they seem to be almost mirror-images of each other; certainly the parallelism between these two measures, previously noted, is not immediately evident here. But further study of these two curves will show that from the ninth interview on, both curves follow much the same downward curve and that it is only during the first eight interviews that there is such a discrepancy between the patient's rating of changes in tension level between the beginning and end of the therapeutic hour and the course of the palmar sweating index.

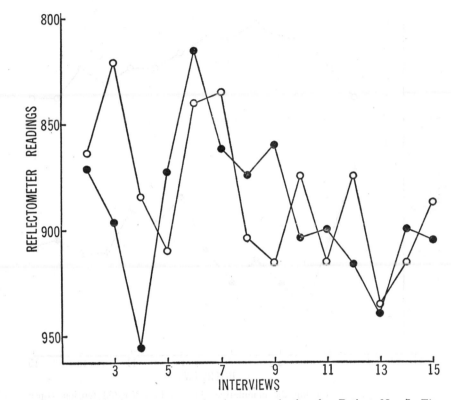

Fig. 103.—Absolute measures of palmar perspiration for Patient No. 7. The general decline noted here is in keeping with a decline in tension and an increase in happiness reported, on the basis of self-ratings, by the patient.

Perhaps, near the middle of this therapy, there was some change in set or self-instructions on the part of the patient which brought the two measures into line; or the explanation of this lack of early congruence may be attributable to other causes.

Because of the small number of patients for whom palmar perspiration data are available, it hardly seems worth while to reproduce these data here in tabular form or to report in detail upon the statistical evaluation thereof (see Light, 1951). However, it may be said that the chi-square test, applied in a manner similar to that illustrated in connection with Table 19, differentiates between the group of eight patients who "stayed" in therapy and the patients who left prematurely at the .05 level of confidence. Similar data on a larger sample of subjects might thus well lead to more highly reliable differences.

In summarizing this section, we may note that in most of the ten cases for which both subjective ratings and objective perspiration measurements are available, there is good congruence between these two indices.

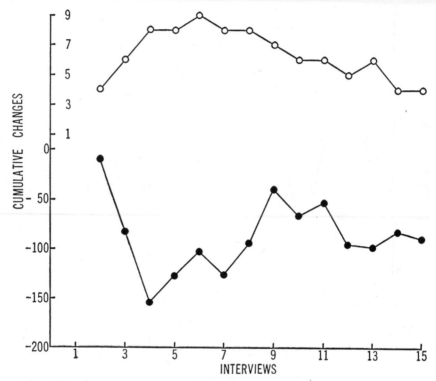

Fig. 104.—Curves showing the cumulative changes in self-rated tension (open circles) and in palmar perspiration (filled circles) for Patient No. 7. Whereas in most cases there is considerable parallelism between these two measures, in the present instance there is a roughly inverse relationship.

The "face validity" of both methods thus seems relatively high. However, in some instances there are striking discrepancies between them. Here it is assumed, tentatively, that the palmar perspiration measure is the more trustworthy one and that the self-ratings have, in these instances, been influenced by negativism or some other form of more or less conscious distortion of the patient's true feelings. In such instances, the lack of correspondence between the subjective and the objective measures, instead of "invalidating" one or both of the measures, may instead constitute a useful new dimension of information. In a future study it might be instructive to examine the recorded interviews of all ten of these patients and see to what extent common trends as well as peculiarities in the relationship between the self-ratings and the palmar perspiration data can be accounted for in terms of the "dynamics" of each case.

Concomitant Measures of Palmar Perspiration in Patient and Therapist.—The results which have been presented and discussed in the preceding section suggest that the colorimetric method of measuring palmar sweating is a sensitive and relatively valid means of indicating the

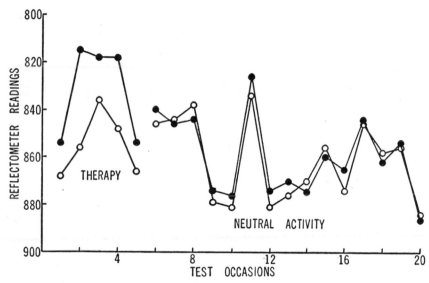

FIG. 105.—Palmar sweating on the part of a psychological intern (*a*) before and after five therapeutic sessions and (*b*) before and after fifteen "neutral" hours. Following the therapeutic hours, this individual's perspiration output is regularly higher, but there is little difference before and after the "neutral" hours. Day-to-day variations are, however, much in evidence.

changes in psychological tension that occur in the course of therapy, i.e., both *during* and *between* successive interviews. However, a very natural question to raise in this connection is the following: May not normal persons, in the course of everyday life, show comparable changes and trends?

One approach to this problem has been made by Light (1951) as follows.[19] He asked six interns in a psychological clinic to allow him to take perspiration measures on them before and after diagnostic or therapeutic interviews which they might be conducting and before and after like periods of time in which they might be reading, talking to friends, or engaging in similar activities. More or less typical of the results obtained are those for Intern No. 1, shown in Figure 105. Here

[19] Another approach to this problem is currently being made by Mr. and Mrs. Vertus E. Bixenstine. They are applying this measure to themselves on a daily and, every eighth day, on an hourly basis and correlating the results with both the ordinary and the extraordinary events in their daily lives.

it will be seen that on the five occasions when the colorimetric method was applied before and after interviews, this intern uniformly showed a perspiration increment (suggesting, perhaps, that the professional role was still a somewhat trying one for him); but when the same test was given to this individual before and after hours of "neutral" activity, there was remarkably little variation. Although the results shown in Figure 105 reveal considerable variation in the level of perspiration output from occasion to occasion, no clear trend is discernible.

Light summarizes his findings, for all six of his "control" subjects, as follows:

> The results seem to add up to the fact that (a) under conditions of neutrality, differences between "before" and "after" measurements are negligible; (b) although great individual differences exist in the amount of palmar sweat exuded, and in the uniformity of the sweating reaction, there are no gross fluctuations of palmar sweat within a particular hour for any of the controls; (c) therapy produces greater fluctuations in tension than does reading, talking or relaxing . . . ; (d) the mean differences between measurements taken immediately prior to and immediately after therapy and those taken before and after an hour of neutral activity are statistically significant.
>
> The evidence thus seems to indicate that under situations which are capable of arousing tension, palmar sweat changes are likely to occur, while under conditions of neutrality, tension remains very stable from one hour to the next. The latter finding is suggestive of a high degree of reliability for the colorimetric procedure employed (p. 133).

But perhaps the best type of "control" with respect to the meaning of a patient's changes in palmar perspiration during psychotherapy is that afforded by concomitant measures taken on the therapist. Light (1951) reports one set of such measurements taken on a patient and her therapist before and after each of the last 23 sessions of a 30-session therapy. These are shown in Figure 106. Here it will be seen that although there is no downward trend in the patient's perspiration index during this therapy, the patient, subsequent to the fifteenth interview, rather consistently registers less perspiration after the interview than before. Evidently these therapeutic sessions were "relieving," in and of themselves, even though no over-all reduction in absolute tension level seems to occur.

The corresponding perspiration measures for the therapist show, during sessions eight to fifteen, a fairly consistent increment from before to after the hour, but thereafter there is little difference. In other words, it appears that when a relationship was established in which the patient began to find the therapeutic hour relaxing, the hour ceased to be tension-arousing for the therapist.

In Figure 106 there is a slight downward trend in the therapist's perspiration level, from beginning to end of the therapy, whereas the patient shows no change or perhaps a slight increment in this respect. It is to be noted here that the usual level of the therapist's perspiration response is slightly *higher,* in absolute terms, than that of the patient. Does this mean that the therapist was really more tense than the patient, or is it perhaps a reflection of individual differences in the "normal" level of palmar perspiration in these two persons (see topic 4 in the next section)?

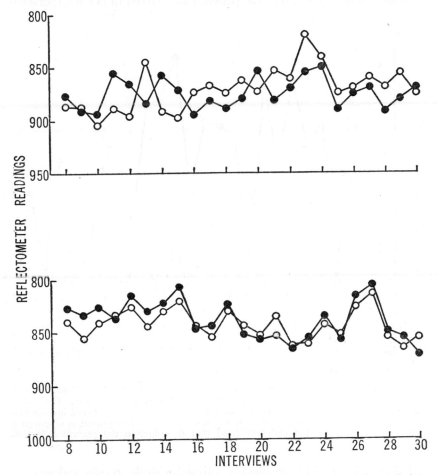

FIG. 106.—Curves showing the palmar perspiration of a patient (above) before and after each of twenty-three therapeutic sessions and the palmar perspiration of the patient's therapist (below) before and after the same sessions. A number of interesting trends will be seen here; these are discussed in the text.

Following the work of Light, the present writers have made a more extended study of the relationship between therapist's and patient's perspiration changes during therapy. The first results to be obtained in this connection are shown in Figure 107. The patient in this instance, No. 20M, was a single woman in her early thirties who came into therapy because of tension states and obsessive preoccupation to the effect that there was "something wrong" with her sexually. Therapy revealed an array of childhood and adolescent sexual episodes about which the patient had been very secretive and in respect to which she was extremely guilty. Therapy brought a ventilation of these episodes and a correction of certain false impressions which the patient had fostered in her interpersonal

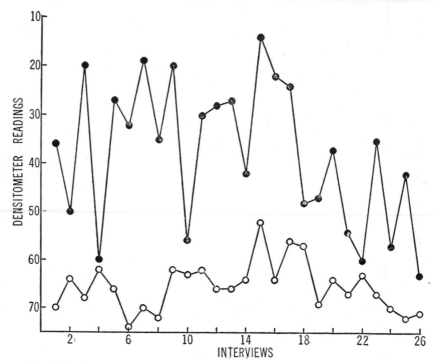

FIG. 107.—Curves showing the course of palmar perspiration in Patient No. 20M (filled circles) and her therapist (open circles) during psychotherapy. The values shown in the two curves are derived from colorimetric tests administered immediately before each interview. As explained in the text, the method employed in quantifying these results is somewhat different from that described in the preceding section.

relations. The patient left therapy satisfied with the results and was not subsequently seen. The therapist in this case was one of the present writers.

Although there are marked fluctuations in the perspiration index for this patient from interview to interview, two general trends are clear. From the first to the fifteenth interview there is a generally upward movement in this index, and from the fifteenth interview to the twenty-sixth or last interview, there is a rapid and decided decrement. The patient ends therapy with a perspiration index considerably lower than the initial one, although, in order to reach this point, she had to pass through a period of heightened perspiration—and, presumably, heightened tension. As we shall see presently, this is a pattern with considerable typicality.

The perspiration curve for the therapist in this case is shown at the bottom of Figure 107. It will be noted, first of all, that the palmar perspiration output for the therapist is, throughout, lower than that of the patient; however, as therapy draws to a close, the patient's perspiration level approximates that of the therapist. It is also noteworthy that there

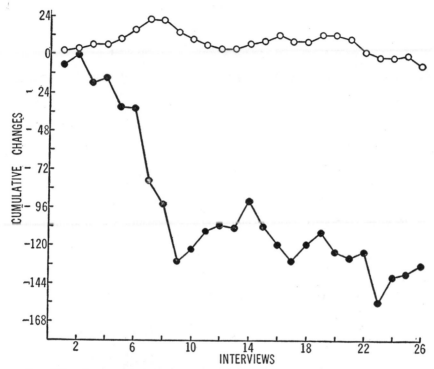

Fig. 108.—Curves showing cumulative changes (from beginning to end of each therapeutic hour) in palmar perspiration for Patient No. 20M (below) and her therapist (above). In terms of this index, it appears that the patient "profited" more from the therapeutic experience than did the therapist.

seems to be a kind of "resonance" effect between the general course of the patient's tensions and those of the therapist. Thus, as the patient's tension level rose from the first to the fifteenth interview, so did that of the therapist, and there is a similar downward parallelism during the latter part of therapy.

The two curves shown in Figure 107 are based solely upon perspiration measurements taken *before* each therapeutic session. However, like measurements were also taken after each session, thus making possible the type of analysis of cumulative change described in the preceding section. Figure 108 shows the cumulative curves thus derived for the patient and the therapist. The cumulative curve for the patient shows that the interviews were, in general, quite rewarding to her, whereas the therapist reacted much more neutrally to them, his perspiration neither increasing nor decreasing much during the individual sessions. During the first nine

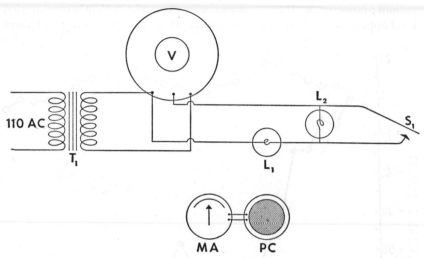

Fɪɢ. 109.—Schematic wiring diagram for the densitometer shown in Figure 110. Attention should be called to Switch 1 (S_1). When this is open, Light 2 (L_2, see top of apparatus, Figure 110) is in series with Light 1 (L_1 immediately above the test aperture), causing Light 1 to glow at such a low intensity that its rays, shining unobstructed through the test aperture, do not overload the photoelectric cell (PS) or the microammeter MA, scale 0-25). When, however, a specimen has been placed over this aperture, thus protecting the photoelectric cell and micro-ammeter, Switch 1 can be closed (foot-pedal operation is most convenient), cutting out Light 2 (as a source of resistance) and increasing the intensity of Light 1. The latter is then adjusted by means of the "Variac" (V, controlled by knob visible in Figure 110) in keeping with instructions given in the text. Another feature of the above diagram which should be noted is the "Sola" (No. 30806) automatic voltage-stabilizing transformer (T_1). This transformer compensates for voltage surges in the power line and thus keeps the intensity of Light 1 essentially constant for any given setting of the "Variac." Light 1 has a rating of 60 watts; Light 2, 40.

interviews the patient seemed to derive especially great relief from the sessions; then for the next five interviews, there was a reverse trend, the patient leaving the hour with a higher perspiration index than at the beginning. This period, from the ninth to the fourteenth interview, corresponds to a period of rapid absolute tension rise, as seen in Figure 107. During the fifteenth interview a crisis seems to have been reached, which was followed by a rapid descent in the absolute curve (Figure 107) and a gradual but fairly steady drop in the cumulative curve (Figure 108). Again it would be interesting to study these events in the light of a content analysis of the case, but such a venture is not feasible at this time.

Fig. 110.—A simple but highly efficient densitometer which is specifically adapted to the reading of colorimetric records of palmar perspiration. The knob shown in the upper right-hand side of the apparatus varies the intensity of the electric lamp which is located directly above the horizontal platform with the small hole in it. Beneath this hole is a photoelectric cell which, when activated by light falling upon it, causes current to pass through the microammeter. The wiring diagram for this instrument is given in Figure 109, and its operation is discussed in the text.

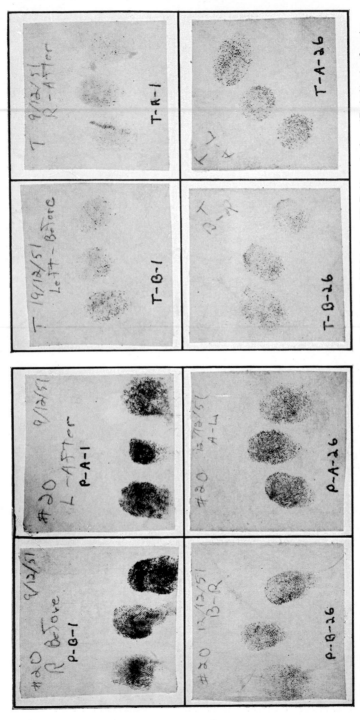

Fig. 111.—Colorimetric fingerprint records of palmar perspiration for Patient No. 20M before (P-B-1) and after (P-A-1) the first interview and before (P-B-26) and after (P-A-26) the twenty-sixth, or last, interview and for her therapist before (T-B-1) and after (T-A-1) the first interview and before (T-B-26) and after (T-A-26) the last interview. Notice that by the end of therapy, the patient's perspiration level had approximated that of the therapist. The intervening course of palmar sweating for this patient and the therapist is shown in the two curves appearing in Figure 106. The method by which densitometer readings are obtained from specimens such as those shown above is described in the text.

The observant reader will have noted that the ordinates for Figures 107-8 are different from the ordinates of the other figures for palmar perspiration shown in the preceding section. This difference is due to a change in the method of reading the intensity of the perspiration prints. The palmar perspiration data described heretofore have all been quantified by means of the Baumgartner reflectometer, whereas the data just referred to have been quantified by means of a specially constructed, but extremely simple, densitometer. This instrument is shown in Figure 110, and the wiring diagram for it is shown in Figure 109. One of the advantages of this instrument over the Baumgartner reflectometer is its greater convenience in use and the fact that with it one gets readings for each individual fingerprint, rather than for an area large enough to include the prints for all three fingers (see page 591). As shown in Figure 110 there is a small, oblong aperture in the flat white surface upon which the colorimetric specimen is placed, and this aperture is such as to have about the same area and shape as the smallest fingerprint one is likely to obtain. Larger prints are moved about until the position is found at which the maximal reading occurs. This procedure makes for great objectivity in the measuring process, as indicated by an obtained coefficient of reliability of .99.

As background for explaining the operation of the instrument shown in Figure 110, it is desirable to reproduce here an example of the type of raw data obtained by the colorimetric method. In Figure 111 will be seen the fingerprints obtained for Patient No. 20M and for her therapist before and after the first interview and before and after the last (twenty-sixth) interview. To convert such data into densitometer units, a specimen such as those shown in Figure 111 is placed over the test aperture, the luminosity of the electric lamp directly above is increased by closing Switch 1 (see Figure 109 and legend), the specimen is moved until a "clear" area is over the aperture, and the "Variac" control knob is adjusted until the illumination falling upon the specimen and passing through it is just sufficient to give a full-scale (25-microampere) reading on the microammeter (see also topic 5 in the next section). Then each of the three fingerprints comprising any one specimen is placed in turn over the test aperture, each print being moved about until its darkest portion is over the aperture, thus giving the lowest possible reading on the microammeter. A very, very light print may read as high as 24 or 24.5 on the microammeter, whereas a very heavy one may read as low as 3 or 4. The readings for each of the three prints on any given specimen are added, and the resulting value (which, theoretically, might range from 0 to 75) is taken as the combined densitometer value for that specimen. It is this summated type of value that is used in Figure 107. Since a high densitometer reading means a very small amount of perspiration, the densitometer readings along the ordinate in this figure are inverted, in order to make profuse sweating appear high on the graph and light sweating low.

Densitometer readings (which are based upon the amount of light transmitted by a specimen) and reflectometer readings (based upon the amount of light reflected by a specimen) are probably about equally satisfactory for most purposes. However, a densitometer of the type here described can be constructed very inexpensively, whereas a reflectometer, to be equally efficient, must be considerably more elaborate and correspondingly expensive. Moreover, the impregnation with tannic acid of the paper used in the colorimetric method tends to be somewhat discolored with the passage of time (see Figure 111) and it is possible that the resulting loss of contrast between a print and the surrounds is a less serious matter for densitometry than for reflectometry (see topic 5 in the next section).

With this description of the method whereby the results shown in Figure 107 were quantified, we may report certain further findings ob-

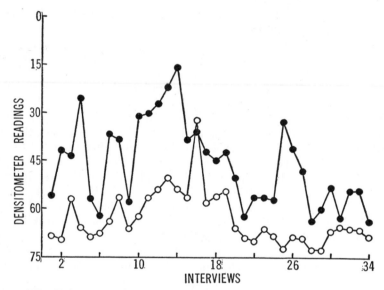

Fig. 112.—Palmar sweating curves for Patient No. 19M (filled circles) and his therapist (open circles), showing an over-all picture very similar to that of Figure 107. The two high points in the curve for the therapist, at Interview 13 and Interview 16, represent days on which public addresses were given, thus suggesting that the general elevation of the therapist curve between Interviews 11 and 19 may be reflections of pressures in the daily life of the therapist rather than a reaction to the high tension which the patient was experiencing during this period.

tained by the use of this method. Figure 112 shows for Patient No. 19M (neither 19M nor 20M were subjects in the researches reported in the preceding section) results comparable to those already given for Patient No. 20M. Figure 112 shows the same initial rise in palmar perspiration, for the first fifteen interviews, followed by a decided downward trend. (This patient, a male university student, continued in therapy beyond the thirty-four interviews indicated, but data can be reproduced here only to the thirty-fourth interview.) And we note, once again, the apparent "resonance" effect in the therapist, i.e., that his palmar sweating tends to follow a course roughly similar to that of the patient, except that it is more attenuated. However, in Figure 112 we get an intimation of a different sort of explanation for the elevation of the central portion of the perspiration curve for the therapist. As will be seen, the therapist's perspiration was almost twice as high on the densitometer scale on the six-

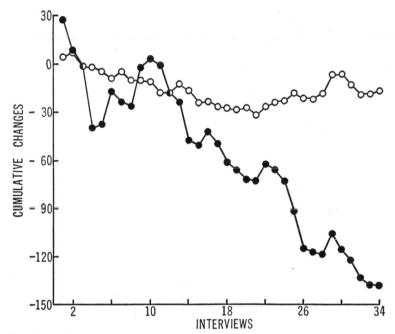

F ig. 113.—Curves showing cumulative changes in palmar perspiration before and after thirty-four interviews for Patient No. 19M (filled circles) and his therapist (open circles). The general pattern is much the same as shown in Figure 107, for Patient No. 20M and her therapist.

teenth interview as it was at any other time; and it so happens that this particular measurement was taken about thirty minutes after the therapist had addressed an audience of some three hundred persons. The notable effect of this "outside" situation upon the therapist's perspiration level suggests the possibility that the generally elevated character of his palmar perspiration between the eleventh and the nineteenth interview might be due to experiences connected with his regular daily life, rather than with the therapeutic situation.

It will be recalled that in Figure 107 there is a similar elevation in the therapist's perspiration curve, but Cases No. 20M and 19M were in treatment at the same time, so the fact that an elevation occurs at about the same time in both cases is ambiguous: it leaves open the question of whether these elevations were responses to the crises through which the patients were passing or were rather due to stresses which the therapist was experiencing in the course of his ordinary daily life. Fortunately, similar records were being kept during the same period in connection with the treatment of another patient, No. 18M, and it therefore seemed useful to plot on one and the same graph the palmar sweating level for the therapist, as obtained in connection with all three of these cases, with a calendar base line rather than an interview base line. The result is shown in Figure 114. Here it will be seen that the period from October 20 to November 15 was one of generally heightened palmar perspiration for the therapist; and examination of his appointment book shows that on October 26 was another address to a large audience, similar to that addressed on November 2. There may have been other reasons for some tension on the part of the therapist during the period under discussion, but it seems probable that these two public appearances contributed importantly in this connection.

The therapist under discussion usually carries six or eight patients simultaneously, and ordinarily their crises are "out of phase," so that circumstances connected with his therapeutic case load would almost never conspire to produce a very marked over-all effect upon him. When one patient is having hard going, another is likely to be getting along unusually well, and so on. Moreover, the experienced therapist is likely to handle each interview in such a way as to leave little residual tension on his part. Sometimes a particular interview will have been unusually trying or interesting, producing a slight elevation of the therapist's perspiration level immediately after the hour; but these effects ordinarily pass quickly and are not at all summative. On the other hand, "outside" pressures may be much more substantial and persistent. These inferences, obviously, are based upon very limited data and need to be supplemented by studies involving a number of therapists.

Granting, then, that there is probably not ordinarily much "resonance" on the part of an experienced therapist with respect to the tensions, as measured by the perspiration index, which his patients show, we may now appropriately ask: To what extent is the inverted V shape of the perspiration curves shown in Figures 107 and 112 typical for patients undergoing therapy? As we already know from curves for patients who have been discussed in the preceding section, the inverted V pattern is by no means universal. However, it is probably the most nearly typical pattern, and it makes good sense theoretically since the first phase of therapy may be thought of as a period in which the neurotic organization of the patient's old "self-system" undergoes dissolution and the second phase is one in which a new and more workable personality pattern is being developed, one which, in the end, enables the patient to achieve a higher degree of integration and a lower degree of tension than was possible with the old pattern.

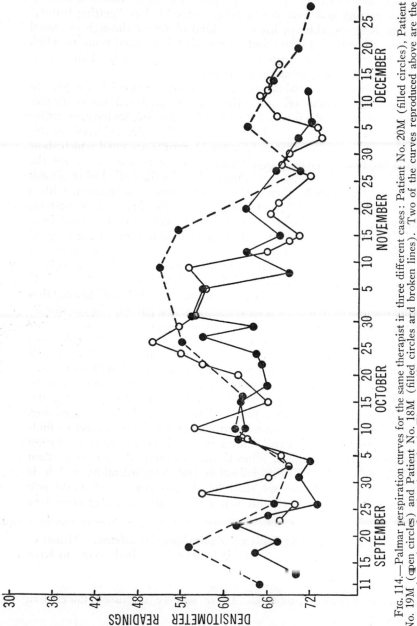

Fig. 114.—Palmar perspiration curves for the same therapist in three different cases: Patient No. 20M (filled circles), Patient No. 19M (open circles) and Patient No. 18M (filled circles and broken lines). Two of the curves reproduced above are the same as those shown for the therapist in Figures 107 and 112, except that the curves above have a calendar base line instead of an interview base line. These three curves, placed in juxaposition, seem to indicate that the elevated portion of the curves, between October 20 and November 15, is related to events in the therapist's "outside" life rather than being a kind of "resonance" response to vicissitudes in therapeutic relationships.

To the extent that the above interpretation is valid, we can see a reason why neurosis tends to be self-perpetuating rather than self-correcting: since getting well involves "getting worse" before "getting better," since, that is to say, therapy involves a kind of *detour* through increased suffering, rather than a direct and progressive downward route to relief, it is understandable that many patients persist indefinitely in their neurotic life style and self-defeating strategies.

Although neither the palmar perspiration data reported in the present section nor the results on subjective ratings analyzed above (pages 572-91) indicate that the inverted V pattern is universal, we have, in earlier chapters of this volume, some interesting corroborative evidence on this score. It will be recalled that in Chapter 11 results are cited which show that in analytically oriented psychotherapy there is a tendency for the *DRQ* index of tension to rise and then to drop as the period of treatment draws to a close. Here, then, is an independent confirmation, with a different method and different subjects, of the inverted V pattern. Furthermore, and even more interestingly, it will be remembered from Chapter 16 that results are cited there which show that on the Osgood "semantic differential" test the first two patients to whom this test was applied gave results which show a rather remarkable parallelism. At the beginning of therapy both of these patients had well "polarized" personality structures but ones in which there existed closer identification with the opposite-sexed than with the same-sexed parent. In the middle of therapy, the Osgood-test results show that the polarization had broken down and that some kind of personality reorganization was going on. And, finally, at the end of therapy the polarization had re-established itself but with the patient now much more closely identified with the same-sexed parent than with the opposite-sexed one. Here, again, we seem to get a picture of therapy which emphasizes the disorganizing, destructuring nature of the first phase of therapy and the reorganizing, restructuring nature of the second, terminal phase. These objective findings correspond well with the clinical impressions one receives during the course of many therapies. Sometimes, of course, there is more than one of these "cycles" of disorganization and reorganization, and it is possible that in the future we shall be able to study such multicycle therapies both from the standpoint of test results and from that of content analysis.

The Palmar Sweating Index: Technique Problems.—Measurement of palmar perspiration by the colorimetric method seems to have sufficient promise as an index of tension and tension change during the course of psychotherapy to justify a few additional comments regarding some special technical problems. These will be discussed under five headings.

1. LOW VALIDITY OF MOST PHYSIOLOGICAL MEASURES OF EMOTION. A wide variety of measures of physiological processes have been heralded as objective indicators of emotion, only to be discredited by

further investigation. One of the principal difficulties, it seems, is this. While there is little doubt that emotions and physiology are connected, any physiological response which occurs on a purely "emotional" basis, i.e., which occurs anticipatorily, in response to signals, rather than in response to a "physiologically adequate" stimulus, is likely to produce a homeostatic imbalance and to be counteracted by some compensatory process. This circumstance has led many investigators to be pessimistic regarding the possibility of finding any one physiological index which will correlate highly with any given emotional state or states. Instead, by many it is held that the only possibility of thus obtaining a really trustworthy index of emotion is to use *multiple* physiological measurements simultaneously (see Lacey, 1950).

While the above argument is, in general, probably sound, it places severe practical limitations upon the uses which can be made of this type of measurement. It is therefore highly desirable, as Silverman and Powell (1944a) and others have pointed out, to keep looking for some simple, single measure which will perform the needed service of objective quantification. Whether the colorimetric measurement of palmar perspiration answers this need must, for the present, remain uncertain; but there is one purely a priori basis for supposing that this index may be uniquely useful. As already pointed out, most physiological responses which occur other than to specific metabolic needs tend to upset the nice balance ordinarily maintained in the internal environment of an organism and thus to put into action antagonistic, compensatory processes. However, palmar perspiration is exceptional in this respect, that is, it is a response which can occur, perhaps quite profusely, without necessarily disturbing the organism's homeostatic equilibrium. Excessive sweating on the general surface of the body would undoubtedly have the effect of dissipating more heat than compatible with physiological well-being; but in the case of the sweating response—the so-called emotional or mental sweating—which is restricted to the palms of the hands and the soles of the feet (and to some extent the axillae), the situation is different. These areas are so small, relatively speaking, that the lowering of general bodily temperature produced by this "cold sweat" is probably negligible under most circumstances. Nor can one readily see any reason why profuse palmar sweating would otherwise be biologically injurious and thus likely to be counteracted by "safety" mechanisms. On the contrary, so long as danger is in some way perceived to be present, the kind of preparation which sweaty palms and soles provide (see pages 590-600) may be a distinct advantage.

If this reasoning be sound, we have some grounds for believing that palmar perspiration may be an unusually valuable indicator of emotion and for pursuing with special vigor techniques for precisely measuring it.

2. THE PGR AND THE COLORIMETRIC INDEX. The psychogalvanic reflex has probably been more widely used than any other of the so-called physiological indicators of emotion, but the literature on this phenomenon

presents an admixture of claims and counterclaims concerning its validity and meaning (McCurdy, 1950). However, in one respect there seems to be general agreement: no one holds that the *PGR* is a "pure" measure of palmar sweating. Wenger and Gilchrist (1948) put the matter well when they say:

Anyone who makes measurements of palmar conductance on many individuals . . . cannot escape being impressed by the instances in which a relatively high conductance is found for an apparently dry skin, and in which a relatively low conductance is coupled with an apparently moist skin. He will be forced to conclude, as we have, that palmar conductance is not an entirely satisfactory measure of individual differences in palmar sweating (p. 757).

These writers then go on to say:

In 1944 Silverman and Powell reported a simple colorimetric technique for the measurement of sweat secretion which is relatively objective and which provides a permanent record. . . .

According to Silverman and Powell the intensity of the stain is directly proportional to the amount of sweat secreted, *but they present no data to support this statement.* . . .

At the time of their report one of us was engaged in a research involving measurements of individual differences in a number of physiological functions, which included determinations of palmar conductance as an indirect index of palmar sweating. The opportunity was taken to obtain concurrent determinations by the tannic acid-ferric chloride technique. This report provides a comparative study of the two sets of data with respect to (*a*) test-retest reliability, and (*b*) validity for measurement of autonomic function (pp. 757-58).

Wenger and Gilchrist end with the somewhat negative conclusion that:

Palmar conductance was shown to be a more reliable measure than the stain index, and to bear a closer relationship to the other autonomic variables. The coefficient of correlation between the two indices themselves was .31 (p. 761).

However, there are a number of reasons why the findings of this investigation may not be entirely reliable. The first source of possible error is the fact that Wenger and Gilchrist did not control the pressure with which their subjects held their fingers on the tannic-acid impregnated paper. They say, ". . . all pressure of contact was controlled by the E" (p. 758). For reasons which are not entirely clear their subjects were, moreover, seated, "during the determinations by the stain method" and were required to stand during the *PGR* determinations.

These investigators tested and retested eighty-four of their subjects by the stain method within the space of half an hour and obtained a correlation of .67. Tested and retested after intervals ranging from seventeen to sixty-four days, forty-seven subjects showed a correlation of .33. On the basis of these results the authors observe:

It will be seen . . . that a given stain index of sweating is a fairly reliable indication of response one-half hour later on the same day, but that individual prediction for periods of 17-64 days (mean = 39 days) could hardly be considered satisfactory for a study of individual differences (p. 759).

Perhaps the variability obtained in this measure over protracted periods is an index, not of "unreliability," but of *sensitivity*. What are the reasons for supposing that the subjects, in the relatively long intervals between tests, had not themselves changed with respect to their levels of tension and palmar sweating?

Later Wenger and Gilchrist remark:

The results in Table II show that, without exception, palmar conductance bears closer relationship to the other autonomic variables than does the ferric chloride-tannic acid stain index. It may be concluded that for the measurement of autonomic functions in terms of these variables, palmar conductance is the more significant of the two indices (p. 760).

However, inspection of the Wenger-Gilchrist Table II shows that all of the correlations on which the above inferences are based are low and several of them statistically nonsignificant. The highest correlation in the table cited is of the order of .31 and is for the relationship between the palmar conductance (PGR) measurements and the colorimetric measurements. That this correlation is as low as it is elicits the following comment from the investigators:

The correlation of .31 between the two indices themselves is of particular interest. In view of the known inadequacies of palmar conductance as a measure of individual differences in sweating, it was not anticipated that it would demonstrate a close relationship to the stain index, but neither was such a lack of correspondence to be expected, since both are purported to measure the same function. Although the same area of sweating was not studied by these two techniques, it is to be doubted that the explanation for their lack of relationship lies in this fact. Sweating from the palmar aspect of the fingers is generally believed to parallel hand-palm sweating. This assumption, however, is a point which may deserve further investigation. A more reasonable conclusion concerning the low degree of relationship between the two indices would seem to be that both are influenced by factors other than sweating (p. 760).

On the basis of the evidence reviewed on pages 600-26 of this chapter, it would appear that palmar sweating as recorded by the colorimetric method and quantified either by the reflectometer or the densitometer technique has relatively high "face validity." Moreover, under topic 1 immediately preceding, we have advanced an argument for supposing that this may be a freer and less complicated measure of emotion than any of the other common physiological measures, including those employed by Wenger and Gilchrist. It is therefore not inconceivable, and perhaps even likely, that these investigators found a correlation of only .31 between the stain method and the PGR because the stain method is dependent solely upon palmar perspiration, whereas the PGR is more complexly determined, more likely to be influenced by the homeostatic dynamics alluded to above, and thus more ambiguous in its implications.

Wenger and Gilchrist, to the best of our knowledge, are the only investigators who have thus far undertaken a study of the kind they report. Lindsley (1951) cites the work of Silverman and Powell and that of Wenger and Gilchrist. He conservatively concludes:

Since it reveals areas of differential sweating, the [colorimetric] method is probably mainly useful for diagnosing clinical cases where lesions affecting the sympathetic system are suspected. It seems possible that it might also be applied to problems involving differential autonomic activity in certain emotional states (p. 479).

On a later page of this chapter we will show that there are characteristic differences in the extent to which different individuals show their tension states through palmar sweating. However, the evidence which has already been cited and which is currently being collected (cf. the study of Bixenstine, page 613) would seem to warrant a more hopeful outlook for the colorimetric method than the passages quoted above imply.

3. PALMAR SWEATING AND ATMOSPHERIC TEMPERATURE. Amidst many uncertainties, this much seems definite: within a comparatively broad range, palmar sweating is not influenced by the temperature of the environment surrounding the subject. Figure 115 shows a graph, reproduced from Kuno (1934), which indicates how differently related to atmospheric temperature are the two types of perspiration, "thermal" sweating and "emotional" sweating. Figure 116 gives further confirmation of this independence of function. Although all the colorimetric specimens cited in the preceding section were collected in a room thermostatically held at 72°F., the outside temperature varied considerably. In Figure 116 are reproduced the same two curves, for Patient No. 19M and his therapist, as appear in Figure 112; but superimposed on the same coordinates is a curve for the daily mean temperature as locally recorded. It is at once evident that there is no relationship between this latter curve and the two palmar perspiration curves.

4. THE COLORIMETRIC METHOD AND INDIVIDUAL DIFFERENCES. Reference has already been made to the fact that different persons do not perspire on the fingertips to the same degree under approximately equal amounts of inner tension. In making such a statement, one immediately invites the question: But how can one tell if the "inner tension" of one person is equal to, or greater or less than, that of another person. The answer is that, of course, one cannot, at least not in any precise way. Yet the fact is that of two persons who *appear*, clinically, to be

under about the same amount of psychological pressure, one may characteristically show a good deal more palmar perspiration than the other.

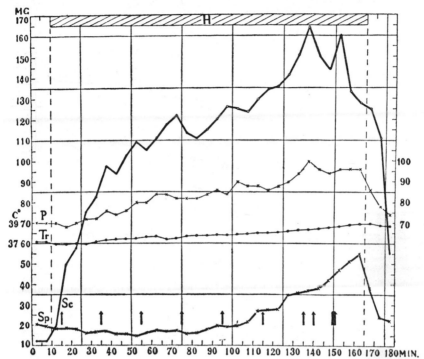

FIG. 115.—Graph from Kuno (1934, p. 138) showing independence of palmar and general body sweating, under conditions of protracted high temperature. For a period of 155 minutes (H), Ito and Kosuge kept human subjects lying in a hot chamber at constant temperature (46°C, dry bulb), with drinking water available. During this period, general bodily perspiration (as measured on the chest) increased as shown by curve Sc, while palmar perspiration varied as shown in curve Sp. (P and Tr show pulse and rectal temperature, respectively.) As Kuno observes concerning these and similar experimental findings, "Our personal experiences agree with these results, because we know that, on hot summer days, sweat may run down from the forehead or from many other parts of the skin, but never from the palms or soles" (p. 139)—witness the stability of the palmar sweating during the first 100 minutes in the heat chamber. "If, however, the increase [or duration] of surrounding temperature is of extreme degree so that heat stroke may gradually develop, sweating appears also on the palms and soles" (p. 139)—witness the rise in palmar sweating during the latter part of the experimental period, when the organism may be said to be in crisis, threatened.

Patient No. 9, in the series of numbered cases discussed above, entered therapy with complaints of tension, "jumpiness," and a variety of minor psychosomatic symptoms. However, as Figure 117 reveals, this man's perspiration was minimal. He described himself as such a "light sweater" that in the chemical laboratory where he was employed he could handle polished surfaces without leaving finger marks on them, surfaces which most persons would not dare to touch. Something happened between the

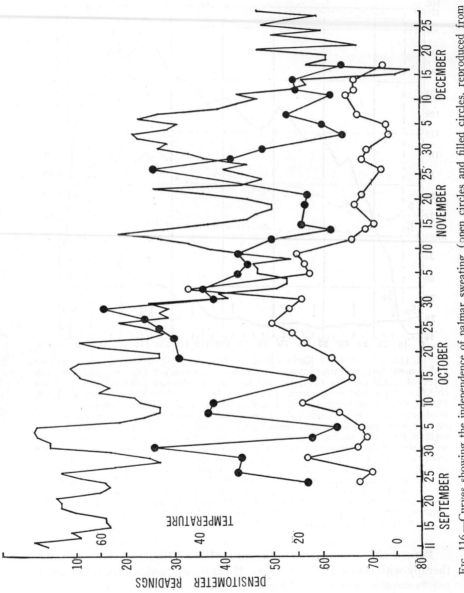

Fig. 116.—Curves showing the independence of palmar sweating (open circles and filled circles, reproduced from Figure 112) and atmospheric temperature (continuous line, no circles). There is no discernible relationship between these two variables.

sixteenth and seventeenth interviews which caused this patient's perspiration to rise and to remain, for him, relatively high for some weeks, at the end of which it dropped equally abruptly. But the over-all level was phenomenally low throughout, and yet it could hardly be said that this man's "tension" was correspondingly low.

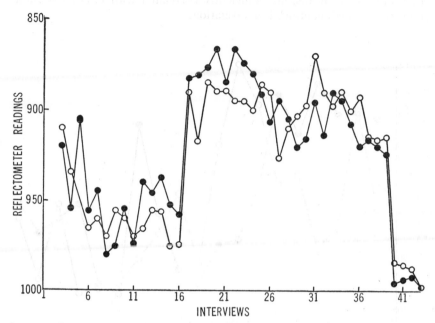

Fig. 117.—Curves showing the amount of perspiration before (open circles) and after (filled circles) therapeutic interviews with a patient (No. 9) whose reactivity in this respect was unusually slight. A reading of "1,000" on the reflectometer scale means no detectable stain whatever. This patient often approximated such a null response.

Reference has already been made (see Figure 114) to the perspiration record of the therapist of Patient No. 18M, but the patient's own record was not reproduced. This appears in Figure 118, along with that of the therapist. Here it will be seen that the palmar sweating of these two persons is statistically indistinguishable. For both, the level of sweating is relatively light; but one of these persons, a recently married woman in her early thirties, was in sufficient trouble to bring her into and to keep her in therapy. She would not, to be sure, have been described clinically as extremely tense or anxious, yet she had real neurotic problems and made good progress with respect to them during the course of treatment.

The conclusion with which we are left after reviewing the above and related data is that human beings differ conspicuously, perhaps at the constitutional level, in the degree to which, when under pressure, they "sweat it out." This finding is hardly surprising, although from the standpoint of our immediate research objectives, it might be more convenient if this were not the case. However, granting the existence of such individual differences, we may still assume that, for any given individual, fluctuations in palmar perspiration output, whether large or small in absolute terms, are sufficiently correlated with internal tension states to be worth continued investigation.

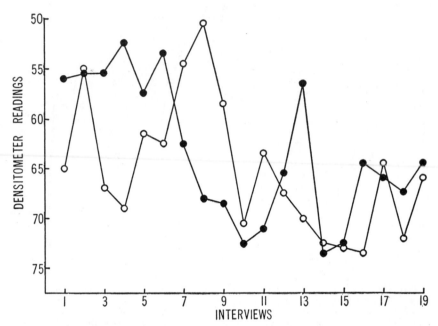

Fig. 118.—Curves showing the virtual equivalence of the perspiration level of a woman patient (No. 18M) and her therapist. In absolute terms, the sweating of both of these persons may be described as light, since a densitometer reading of 75, like 1,000 on the reflectometer scale, means no detectable colorimetric stain.

5. Reflectometry and Densitometry Compared. Unhappily, it has not been possible for us to obtain both reflectometer and densitometer readings for one and the same series of colorimetric fingerprints. We are not, therefore, in a position to state the exact extent to which these two methods of measurement agree with or deviate from one another. Our general impression, however, is that they are almost equally satisfactory for present purposes. (Subsequently we have correlated reflectometer and densitometer readings for 45 samples and obtained an r of $+.68$. Most of the disparity we believe is accounted for by considerations discussed below. The densitometer method now seems to us the more precise, at least for present purposes.)

Attention has already been called to the fact that a densitometer of the kind described can be easily and cheaply constructed, whereas an equally efficient reflectometer is a more complicated and expensive piece of equipment. And another consideration which slightly favors the densitometer method is this. A reflectometer reading will necessarily be influenced, not only by the intensity of the prints within the test area, but also by their *size*. Said otherwise, a person with large fingers will make fingerprints which will cover a larger proportion of a standard test area of paper than will the fingerprints of a person with small fingers, and the greater the proportionate area of the paper which is stained, the lower will be the reflectance index. Absolutely, intensity and size of prints are thus confounded, so that persons with fingers of different size cannot be readily compared (without a correction formula of some sort) with respect to perspiration intensity. With the densitometer, on the other hand, a test area can be selected which is small enough that even the smallest fingerprint will cover it, so that all fingers are made more or less equivalent in terms of size, and intensity becomes the sole variable.[20]

The issue of reflectometry vs. densitometry is also of some importance in connection with certain problems connected with the acid-impregnated paper. In the first place, this paper, like paper in general, tends to vary sufficiently in thickness and transparency to produce variations in densitometer readings which, on occasion, may be as much as 1 or 2 units on a 25-unit scale. Usually the variation from place to place on this paper is much less, but in any event it is sufficiently great so that the transparency of the paper needs to be checked for each colorimetric record. Whether there are comparable variations in the *reflectance* of this paper we cannot at present say, although one would certainly assume some variation on this score as well as on that of transparency.

In future work, it is planned that colorimetric prints will be obtainable from only one finger rather than from three. This modification of procedure has the advantage of somewhat simplifying computations, and we believe it also makes possible a better control of the variations, just discussed, in the paper's natural transparency.

Finally, we may note, as have both Gladstone (1949) and Light (1951), that paper which has been impregnated with tannic acid tends to become slightly discolored (grayish-yellow) with the passage of time (see Figure 111). Such a change will, of necessity, tend to decrease the contrast between areas where there are colorimetric stains and where there are no such stains. It is probable that this diminished contrast can be corrected for about equally well with both the reflectometer and the densitometer methods. However, we lack empirical data on this score and have no proven basis for suggesting that the methods do not differ significantly in this respect.

[20] A reflectometer can probably be modified to meet this difficulty, but it would involve complications.

Palmar Sweating and the DRQ Compared.—In Chapters 10 and 11 evidence has been advanced for believing that the psychological stress or tension experienced by a person undergoing psychotherapy or other forms of professional interviewing is reflected, in some degree, by the relative number of "discomfort" and "relief" words used by such a person in discussing and describing himself and his problems. This relationship has been formalized in the discomfort-relief quotient or DRQ.

In concluding the present discussion of palmar sweating as an indicator of psychological tension, it is pertinent to ask: To what extent do these two measures—the DRQ and palmar perspiration—agree when applied to the same person during the course of psychotherapy?

The procedure adopted for the purpose of obtaining at least a preliminary answer to this question was as follows. Five of the therapy cases included by Light in the investigation previously described in this chapter (see pages 572-90) had been fully recorded. Four or five equally spaced interviews were selected from each of these and were transcribed and scored in the manner described by Dollard and Mowrer (Chapter 10), with certain modifications designed to make the method more specifically applicable to psychotherapeutic records. The social-agency records employed in the Dollard-Mowrer study were dictated by the worker in the case, and the DRQ was, so to say, all-inclusive: it included all discomfort and relief words in the record, regardless of whether they had been uttered by the client(s) or others, or whether they represented the worker's own interpretations and evaluations. Since it is an easy matter, in verbatim transcriptions of individual psychotherapy, to restrict DRQ scoring to what the patient alone has said, this was the procedure here followed. Independent clauses were selected (as opposed to words or sentences) as the scoring unit; and each clause was scored, as nearly as possible, without reference to context and with a minimum of interpretation, i.e., inference, imputation, or "reading in."

Within the framework just described, two different scoring procedures were used for all interviews. The "regular" DRQ involved scoring all positively or negatively toned clauses, i.e., all relief and all discomfort clauses, uttered by the patient. By contrast, the "self" DRQ involved scoring only clauses, or statements, referring to the patient's *own feelings*.

As has been generally reported, the two investigators (Z. L. and M. P. Z.) who scored this material found that they did so with considerable agreement. Table 20 gives the per cent of agreement for this performance.

Later, another fully recorded case, but one not included in Light's study, was transcribed and all twenty-six interviews scored by the method described above.

When the DRQ values of all interviews, obtained by both the "regular" and the "self" method, were correlated with before-interview and after-interview palmar perspiration data, the results shown in Table 21

TABLE 20

PERCENTAGE OF AGREEMENT BETWEEN TWO *DRQ* SCORERS

All clauses were scored as indicating "discomfort," "relief," or "neutrality." On the basis of chance alone, the agreement between the two scorers would therefore be 33⅓ per cent. The reliability of the difference between chance expectation and the obtained results is, of course, a function of the number of clauses involved in each case; but the results are clearly indicative of the fact that both scorers identified these three types of clauses with a high degree of consistency. This test of reliability was based upon the "regular" method of *DRQ* scoring (see text), but the results would have been virtually the same if the "self" method had been employed.

Patient	% of Agreement	Number of Clauses
No. 6	.93	947
" 4	.93	1462
" 9	.84	2369
" 10	.93	993
" 1	.88	3375

were obtained. As hypothesized, the correlations between *DRQ* and the amount of palmar sweating were positive and apparently substantial.

In each of the first five cases (Nos. 6, 4, 9, 10, and 1), only five (in some instances only four) interviews were transcribed and scored, whereas in the sixth case (20M) all twenty-six interviews were so treated. That the correlations obtained in the latter case were among the lowest, despite the greater number of interviews involved, is probably due to a speech mannerism of this patient which involved the use of certain phrases that had to be scored negatively despite their rather obviously stylized nature. Both scorers felt that these mannerisms gave this patient an uncommonly stable (invariant) *DRQ,* despite rather obvious differences in the emotional loadings of interviews. For this reason, we

TABLE 21

PEARSONIAN CORRELATION COEFFICIENTS OF "SELF" AND "REGULAR" *DRQ*'S WITH PALMAR SWEATING BEFORE AND AFTER THERAPEUTIC SESSIONS

These correlations, for each of the first five cases, are based upon data from only four or five evenly spaced interviews. These correlations, while predominantly positive and, in several instances, relatively high, cannot therefore have very great reliability. The correlations for the sixth case are based upon all (twenty-six) interviews. Here the correlations are fairly reliable, but—probably because of a speech peculiarity described in the text—they are of small magnitude.

Patient	Self DRQ P.S. Before	Self DRQ P.S. After	Regular DRQ P.S. Before	Regular DRQ P.S. After
No. 6	+.32	+.92	−.26	+1.00
" 4	+.53	+.51	+.64	+ .63
" 9	+.31	−.41	+.69	+ .04
" 10	+.82	+.68	−.22	+ .71
" 1	+.43	+.36	+.35	+ .26
" 20M	+.27	+.22	+.24	+ .30

have felt justified in excluding case 20M in estimating the over-all correlation. The "self" DRQ's for the other five cases correlate .54 with after-interview palmar perspiration, and their "regular" DRQ's correlate .57 with this same measure. With thirteen degrees of freedom, both of these correlations are significant at better than the .05 level. When case 20M is included, the over-all correlations are, of course, still positive, but not so significantly so.[21]

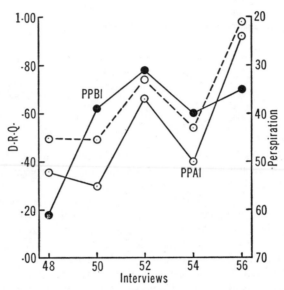

Fig. 119.—Curves showing agreement between palmar perspiration and the Discomfort-Relief Quotient. Palmar perspiration before interviews is shown by the curve labeled PPBI, while palmar perspiration after interviews is shown by the curve labeled PPAI. The third curve (broken lines and open circles) shows the course of the DRQ. During the segment of therapy here sampled (Patient No, 6), palmar perspiration and the DRQ show a good deal of agreement. The sample happens to be drawn from a period of the therapy wherein the patient's tensions, as measured by these indices, were rising.

We have already noted that patient 20M had certain linguistic peculiarities that tended to mask the normal fluctuations in DRQ as a correlate of emotion tension. There are also persons who, when under stress, "sweat it out," while others do not, showing their emotion instead in other ways (see page 630). Such individual differences necessarily lower cor-

---

[21] In saying that the correlation between the DRQ and palmar sweating was "positive," we mean that as the incidence of "discomfort" words increased there was a tendency toward greater perspiration. However, in order to obtain coefficients of correlation which were numerically positive, it was necessary to make a systematic transformation in our data. As will be recalled, a high incidence of "discomfort" words is represented by a high DRQ, but increased palmar sweating results in *low* densitometer readings. Therefore, in order to avoid obtaining a *negative* correlation between our DRQ data and the densitometer readings, it was necessary to change the sign of one of these—we chose the latter—so that the resulting correlations would be in the direction demanded by the logic of the situation.

relations when a group of subjects is involved. There are, of course, some persons in whom both the DRQ and the palmar sweat index work as they are "supposed" to, i.e., both of these measures fluctuate together, as indicated by the findings for patient No. 6, which are reproduced graphically in Figure 119. On the other hand, if one of these indices fails, as occurred in patient 20M, then a picture such as shown in Figure 120 is

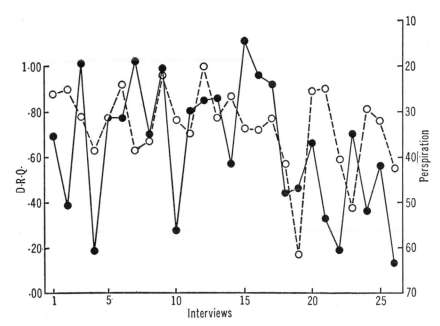

Fig. 120.—Curves showing rather poor agreement between palmar perspiration and the DRQ. The curve for palmar perspiration (solid lines and circles) is the same as that appearing in Figure 107 (Patient 20M). The accompanying curve (broken lines and open circles) shows the DRQ for the same patient. For reasons suggested in the text, the DRQ does not correlate very highly with the palmar sweating. There is, however, a general, over-all correspondence.

obtained. Here the perspiration index behaves more nearly as expected than does the DRQ. The moral of these observations is, of course, that there is probably no one measure which gives, in all persons, a reliable indication of emotional tension. As many investigators (see, for example, Freeman, 1948) have suggested, a more trustworthy procedure is to employ multiple measures, although, as already noted, the palmar-sweat index is probably as satisfactory as any other *single* index.

In the foregoing discussion we have spoken of the reliability (consistency) of measures and of their interrelatedness, but we have not ventured to use the term "validity." The reason is obvious: no very definitive validity criterion for the outcomes of psychotherapy has to date been devised (see, for example, Kelly and Fiske, 1951, pp. 99-113). As far as the cases just discussed are concerned, we do not even have systematic ratings by their respective therapists as to the degree of "success" which each of them represents.

In conclusion, therefore, all that can be said very confidently at this time is that the palmar sweat index and the *DRQ* are two measures which, in general, show changes in the expected direction during the course of psychotherapy. These measures should be further employed in conjunction with as many other measures as are practicable. Really definitive data would call for a highly organized investigation of considerable magnitude.

CHAPTER 19

PHYSIOLOGICAL CHANGES DURING PSYCHOTHERAPY

Lawrence I. O'Kelly, Ph.D.

At the present time the possible contributions of the physiological psychologist to research in psychotherapy center around the somatic components of emotion. There are at least two good reasons why this is so. In the first place, recording techniques have largely been developed for measurement of vegetative phenomena, and by far the largest amount of methodological research has been done in the detection and transcription of vascular and respiratory functions. Secondly, the apparently intimate connection between such autonomically controlled bodily activities and emotion gives us some reason for expecting the former to be a useful index of variations in the latter.

One of the central reference constructs in psychopathology is the notion of "anxiety." However anxiety may be described from the psychological level, it is reasonably safe to classify it as an emotional experience having a great deal in common with "fear" when viewed from a physiological standpoint. Insofar as the goal of psychotherapy is the reduction of anxiety, therefore, valuable information concerning the success of therapy may be secured from studies of the physiological differences between the *anxious* and the *nonanxious* (or less anxious) subject. Also, periodic measurement of the physiological status of the individual as he proceeds with a course of psychotherapy should show some parallelism between the session-to-session changes in anxiety and the corresponding status of relevant physiological variables. Further, detailed analysis of such parallel records should yield information on the effect of various therapeutic techniques on the emotional status of the patient, leading, possibly, to clearer understanding of the interplay of influences in the therapist-patient relationship.

While for our purposes it is unnecessary to indulge in extended discussion of the "mind-body" problem, it is essential to state clearly the extent to which explanatory concepts at the physiological level may be applied to our efforts to understand psychotherapy. In the recent history of psychology there is a conviction, now almost universally accepted, that a distinction can be made between two levels of description of behavior. These were aptly labeled by Tolman as *molar* and *molecular;* the former type of description is concerned with activities which have meaning or relevance as goal-directed activity,[1] the latter is a reduction of such activities to their component anatomical and physiological correlates. In systematic psychology there has been much argument over the most appropriate level of description, with the early behaviorists, for example, championing the molecular approach. The more recent adoption of the molar point of view by almost every psychological theorist has thrown the molecular approach into considerable disrepute, and has been one of the circumstances leading to the creation of such programmatic slogans as "the empty organism."

While there may still be room for debate on this basic issue, it would certainly seem obvious that, for effective description of the therapeutic process, the molar level of description is more appropriate. Where, then, is there a place for the physiological analysis of behavior? The answer to this question may perhaps best be presented by first noting that much of the "molar-molecular" controversy has been of an "either-or" variety, the choice being rightly regarded as basic to the whole *modus operandi* of a psychological system. It is equally true, however, *that the two approaches are not separate entities in fact, and that all molar behaviors are accomplished by particular patternings of molecular function* (cf. Hebb,* 1949). Thus, although no amount of knowledge of the anatomical and physiological facts of arm movement can give the proper emphasis to a particular "molar arm movement," such as "throwing-a-forward-pass-on-fourth-down" or "throwing-a-shoe-at-the-neighbors'-cat," nevertheless all such molar activities are accomplished by the sensory-neuromuscular mechanisms of some particular organism. Because behavioral acts are also always somatic acts, it is possible in many instances to use the measures of somatic processes as indicators of the types of molar behavior which do not lend themselves readily to direct observation.

In the examples of arm movement given above such refinement of observation would be of little help to the student of molar behavior because of the easily observable nature of the entire act-sequence. Unfortunately, in psychotherapy much of the psychological activity is not accompanied by an abundance or excess of such easily observed overt behavior.[2] Usually the patient sits or lies quietly, and the most energetic activity is a vocal production of verbal symbols whose translation by the observer involves far more than a dictionary knowledge of the language. The therapist, through training, acquires great proficiency

---

[1] Strictly speaking, these terms can only be defined relative to some given universe of discourse—descriptions couched in the terms or frame of reference of the phenomena themselves being *molar,* reductionistic explanations within another frame of reference, or in terms of some more "basic" level of description, being *molecular.* The definition above is specific to the concerns of the present discussion.

* References are to the bibliography at the back of the book.

[2] When the therapy is so arranged as to provide for free bodily movement, there is of course relatively little need for the use of subtle physiological techniques as aids to observation; in play therapy, psychodrama, and finger-painting the molar and molecular activities speak vividly to the unaided sense organs of the trained observer.

in translating these symbols into a meaningful pattern of molar activity, and in this task he is aided by a keenness in the observation of other minimal molecular movements: he detects increased postural tonus, tremor, fugitive eye-movements, parched oral mucosa, restless persevera-tive movements of small amplitude in the extremities, sweating, blushing, pallor, and so on. These surface manifestations of the activities of the physiological systems he then quite properly uses to extend his under-standing of the psychological (molar) significance of the verbal behavior which he is also observing. Now, none of these small bits of physiological data he is collecting is, *in itself,* of the slightest direct significance to the therapist in his efforts to understand the patient's problems. Sweating and blushing, for example, are not even exclusively symptoms of emotion, since they have also a part to play in the prosaic duty of body-temperature regulation. Yet, when viewed in conjunction with specific behavioral circumstances they may become highly suggestive and valid indicators of aspects of psychological situations which are not otherwise observable.

The most widespread and extensive use of this sort of procedure is to be found in the "lie detector." Here a person is, if we may be allowed a certain leniency, in a therapeutic interview situation (albeit shockingly non-nondirective), in which the interrogator asks questions bearing on a past happening which the subject, wittingly or otherwise, is attempting to conceal. Attached to the subject are instruments which make continu-ous measurement of rate and amplitude of breathing, pulse rate, pressure of arterial blood, and changes in the electrical resistance of some part of the body liberally provided with sweat glands. After suitable pre-liminary questions on matters of little affective concern, the subject may be asked, "Did you do such-and-such?" It will be assumed that the subject answers in the negative. The physiological indices, however, will more often than not indicate an autonomic disturbance at variance with the verbal response. This finding will be true of the "innocent" and "guilty" alike if the crime involved is of sufficient seriousness and if the subject knows why he is being questioned. The examiner proceeds and, by asking questions about circumstances which could have specific meaning only to a guilty person, is able to differentiate, on the basis of fluctuations in the physiological indices, the "guilty" person. Observa-tions of overt behavior are aided by measurement of the correlated physiological functions.

In lie detection a "voluntary" concealment or distortion by the sub-ject is usually assumed, and it might be supposed that the autonomic changes are in some way generated by the obvious strain and vigilance involved in knowing something and being obliged to act as if one did not. Fortunately, this assumption does not necessarily express the whole truth of the matter. If a subject is given a Jung word-association test, similar fluctuations in physiological indices of tension may be noted and correlated with difficult or emotion-producing associations of which the subject may be otherwise quite unaware. W. W. Smith (1922), for example, found that ranking the six words with the slowest reaction time (out of a list of 100) yielded the following: "name," "friend," "despise," "make," "sad," "proud," whereas the six words which produced the greatest change in skin resistance were: "kiss," "love," "marry," "divorce," "name," "woman." As Symonds (1931) remarks, in discussing this finding, "it is not difficult to estimate that the affective quality of the second group of words is greater" (p. 431). The amount of dependence we can place on the assumption that reaction time is more dependent upon volitional factors than is the PGR may be debatable, but it is worth noting that the two indices do not, in Smith's instance, point toward the same set of words as emotionally disturbing. It is probably more a task for the clinical than for the physiological psychologist to decide which of the two lists is more relevant to the patient's problems.

Continuing our examination of the lie-detector experiment as a possible example of physiological techniques applicable to research in psychotherapy, we may note other significant circumstances. Most important is the type of sampling procedure that is followed, and the assumptions which the operator follows, in carrying out his study. In the first place, *the population is an individual subject* or, more strictly, the response or behavior repertoire of the subject. The unit for sampling is the "response." This differs from one of the most commonly used of conventional designs ordinarily followed in the laboratory investigations of the "physiological correlates of emotion" whose population is "adult human beings" and whose unit for sampling is the individual subject who, selected at random, is then given a standardized or constant series of test stimuli. The results that have been gained from this type of procedure, as we all know, are ambiguous and are unreliably related to other criteria of emotional change. In the lie-detector experiment a degree of practical success is achieved because a long series of successive samples of physiological response are recorded from the individual while he is being subjected to *a representative sampling of stimulus situations that are relevant to the investigator's (and the guilty person's) purposes.* Control measurements are made a part of the process, are drawn from the same subject, and are interpolated in some fashion into the same series of observations and recordings. The parallels to psychological studies of personality from the clinical point of view is striking. As Mowrer points out elsewhere in this volume (Chapter 13), a series of recorded interviews with a patient reveal more about his personality and about the fundamental interplay of etiological variables than the best cross-sectional testing of a group of people, even when the latter are presumably drawn from a population homogeneous with respect to the personality difficulty being investigated. The strength of the clinical method lies partly in the greater representativeness of its sampling procedure, which, paradoxically, requires no assumptions of the homogeneity of the parent population, neither with respect to the usual variables of human personality nor with respect to clinical diagnostic "type." *As a unique case, the patient is the population to be sampled.* This is not to say, however, that clinical procedures are safe from all forms of bias; indeed, they are overly susceptible to just the types of bias which experimental designs minimize—those which arise from the experimenter or observer in the course of his observations.

A further improvement in design found in the lie-detector situation is the relatively greater freedom from artifice. A major problem in the experimental study of emotion in the laboratory has always been the matter of contriving stimuli which are generally and dependably productive of emotional response. Aside from the very excellent utilization of the sudden startling kind of stimulus (Landis and Hunt, 1939), most laboratory workers have succeeded in creating only the most pallid sorts of situations for their subjects. But in the interrogation of suspected criminals or in the psychotherapy of an emotionally troubled patient, the emotional situation is, for the subject, genuine and realistic. This very possibly has a great deal to do with the differences between the inconclusive correlations of emotions with autonomic disturbance in the laboratory and the relatively great practical success of the lie-detector technique in the life situation.

Another important aspect of the "lie-detection" procedure is the possibility of continuous correlation and coordination of physiological recording with psychological variables of a flexibly controlled interview. Questions are asked and objects are shown to the subject, and in all of the interchange the polygraph goes on recording pulse, respiration, blood pressure, skin temperature, PGR, or whatever combination of indices may be selected. The experimenter codes the questions and answers onto the polygraph tape, observes the changes in physiological variables with various types of stimulation, varies his questions in accordance with such indications, and, generally speaking, produces (if he has the requisite skill) a combined verbal and physiological recording which gives him the desired insight into the subject's life-situation. In most instances neither the physiological measures alone nor the language responses alone are sufficient to yield valid conclusions. The two types of response, the volitional and the vegetative, must be put side by side. Interpretation grows out of the interrelationships observable between the two.

The lie-detector operator proceeds under a basic assumption that the physiological concomitants of fear and anxiety may be aroused differentially by neutral situations and stimuli as compared with situations or stimuli having specific meaningful connotations with respect to the subject's anxieties. Experimental research of half a century, for all its lack of precision (see Ruckmick, 1936; Young, 1943), gives the operator confidence that the subjective experience of genuine emotion will be accompanied by alterations in the peripherally observable vegetative functions. For his practical purpose, it makes little difference to the operator what the exact correlation between autonomic symptoms and any systematic classification of emotions might turn out to be, or, as a matter of fact, whether any dependable correlation does or does not exist. All that is necessary for his purpose is that the autonomic behavior fluctuate in a fairly sensitive manner with serial presentation of stimuli which are graded in intensity with respect to the stimulus variables which the operator wishes to explore. It is not necessary that the correlation be perfect, or that the changes be uniformly in a given direction —the interview situation provides abundant opportunity to repeat, with profuse variation, doubtful stimuli. In the end, the integration of the evidence is made by the operator, clearly exercising what we may term *clinical judgment.*

The process of judgment in this situation is dependent upon many factors, a host of which are probably derivable from aspects of the situation other than the polygraphically recorded physiological variables. However, without the contribution of the tracings of autonomic function, in the case of lie-detection, successful judgment is considerably lower than when physiological variables are available (Burtt, 1948). A guess might be hazarded that the judgments of therapists about the specific nature of patients' reactions during therapeutic interviews might likewise be improved if similar physiological data could be made available. Several difficulties, however, stand in the way. Some of them can be handled with little trouble, and others may prove insuperable. It is hard to make definite statements about this, of course, for the requisite experiments have not been done. Existing knowledge of psychotherapy and of the physiology of emotion may help us to make a provisional estimate of the situation and sketch some of the considerations preliminary to designing research in this area.

Physiological research in psychotherapy is justifiably comparable to lie-detection in most of the features we have already discussed. There are also some equally important differences between them, and it is the differences that may be the source of the majority of our technical problems. In lie-detection the operator is concerned with a very restricted part of the life history of his subject, and he has (usually) abundant knowledge of the facts of deed and motive; his major problem is fitting these known facts to one of a number of suspects. As the various chapters of this book demonstrate, the process of psychotherapy is a good deal more complex. We do not have a single "crime" and a number of subjects potentially responsible. We have, rather, a complex social situation in which a distressed person, aided, in ways that are still obscure, by a therapist, goes through a lengthy learning or relearning process, terminated (ideally) only when the patient has become free of his complaints. We have every reason to believe that the patient's progress toward this goal is not a steady climb to the summit of health; but rather, like a fever chart, the curve of mental health shows the irregularities and fluctuations we have come to expect in any form of complex learning. Sometimes, indeed, as every therapist knows, the learning takes untoward courses, and rather than indicating improvement in adjustment, shows increasing deterioration. The dynamics or laws of learning in psychotherapy become the essential goal of our research efforts; until they are understood, we do not have a sure basis for the psychotherapeutic art. The dynamics of psychotherapy, it almost goes without saying, are infinitely more complex than those met with in the relatively simple lie-detection procedure. Instead of simply registering the emotional changes accompanying bluntly direct references to life situations whose relevant aspects are in the forefront of the guilty person's awareness, and in a situation so structured as to put maximal emotional pressure on the concealment by the subject of overt indications of his knowledge, in psychotherapy we have the spectacle of a patient talking about a variety of remembered life situations in an atmosphere of permissive acceptance. The emotional manifestations of these revived memories occur in ways that often appear unrelated or incongruous both to the patient and to the therapist. We have, too, the gradually increasing complexity, over a number of interviews, of the active causal factors for emotional behavior. As old memories are revived, as contemporary conflicts are linked to old and chronic problems, it often seems to the psychotherapist that the skein of cause and effect for emotional behavior assumes a complexity defying any attempt at analysis.

When we add to this the almost certainly important part that the therapist assumes in the process, the immensity of the problem is indeed great; each response of the therapist plays its part in determining the future emotional reactions of the patient. Exactly how great or little a part each act of the therapist plays is difficult to analyze. Time relationships in this connection are not simple. A chance remark of the therapist often bears its emotional fruit only in the next or an even more remote therapeutic session. The uncertainty in time relationships is an outstanding difficulty of therapy research. Even the most faithfully recorded typescript of successive therapy sessions often fails to reveal the significant interactions between therapist and patient. The extent to which more delicate measures of the physiological symptoms of emotion would contribute to this analysis remains to be seen. One thing appears certain. If a verbal statement by the therapist or patient is emotionally critical *at the time of its occurrence,* there is more likelihood of one's recognizing that fact if records are being taken of concurrent physiological reactions. If the material assumes critical importance only in the interval between therapy sessions (and this is often the case), then we have still before us the interesting research question of whether or not the relatively autonomous vegetative response may not antedate the coherent verbal expression of the significant material. We simply do not know the answer to this. One cannot help voicing here a clinical hunch, however. Often, when emotionally significant material is near the surface, the therapeutic hour may be singularly dull and commonplace. Or, the patient will be following a course of recollections and quite gradually shift his conversation to safe and conventional topics. In such a sequence there appears no definite indication of disturbed emotionality. One often gets the impression, however, that the patient has dimly glimpsed the threatening nature of the memories ahead and, like an aviator avoiding a thunderhead on the horizon, has changed his course before reaching the emotional storm. The forces of repression and dissociation, with accompanying feelings of ambivalence, are eloquently expressed in the following excerpt from an electrically recorded interview:

I had this sort of feeling . . . like crying . . . of being unhappy and miserable. This feeling comes over me. It scares me. I feel that I should tell you about it.

I've been wondering all along how this therapy is going to help me. I mean I can see how I come up here and talk and talk and talk. . . . I feel like I really don't get anywhere sometimes. And I doubt it at times because I haven't as yet seen it clearly. Yet, I had a glimpse of it last night, of how it was really getting somewhere—getting awfully deep, and I always thought of myself as an amateur psychologist. . . . And I often try to figure myself out. And when I first came up here I told you the important things, that I could remember and often thought of, which I thought influence me and made me the way I am. But now I see that there are things so much deeper than that. Things that I can't see myself really. They come out maybe once in a while, and then when they come out I don't know whether that's what makes me get to thinking about them, and I get this funny feeling in my mind—or what. And I tried so last night to remember what it was I was thinking of so I could tell you the next day. But save my soul, I can't remember it. I try to put it out of my mind. Also before I went to bed I knew I wouldn't be able to sleep all night if that kept on. And I've been trying so hard to remember what these little teeny things were that I wanted to bring up.

And it seems as if there is something in our talk yesterday that sort of helped bring this on. I mean, I kept going over some of the things we talked about and they led to other things. But what they were I can't remember. I wanted to tell you, if I could, how this feeling is with me. I mean, I—its the only time I ever experienced it, anything like it. A fear of it and all. . . . I had that fear then of being too close and as if you just open your eyes you could really see it. You know what I mean? . . . Yet, I had this fear that I didn't want to get that close to it. I backed away from it. . . . I tried to put it out of my mind right away. . . . I'm getting too close for comfort, whatever it is; and even though it's some little things that are coming out, they are aggravating to my mind or something. And I can't remember them for you, and I don't know what to do. I wanted so much to try to get it off my mind by talking to you about it, and I felt that I was getting this closeness to therapy . . . and I felt it . . . as it's what you wanted maybe, yet, I didn't know if I wanted it.

The question for the physiological psychologist here is whether or not his techniques are sufficiently delicate or appropriate to detect these changes in heading, or, even, whether or not such a discrimination is accompanied by emotion. The clinical hunch is that there *are* small but detectable physiological changes in such circumstances; the poorly comprehended threat of what lies ahead produces anxiety of sufficient intensity to call for verbal avoidance behavior, and anxiety of such intensity is probably measurable. In this early stage of research, it is impossible to do more than guess at the outcome of the appropriate experiments, or, indeed, to guarantee that present types of design are adequate for such purposes.

In our discussion thus far we have not specifically considered the types of physiological measures that might best lend themselves to our work. A number of factors must be considered in selecting measures: (*a*) degree of relationship between the physiological activity and the molar behavior under investigation, (*b*) validity of available recording techniques, (*c*) practicality of securing physiological measures in the treatment situation, and (*d*) susceptibility of the measure to quantitative description.

We must first decide what aspect of psychological function we are interested in studying when we do research in psychotherapy, and then select the measures which have been shown to vary in some concomitant way with these functions. In psychotherapy, it seems, we are most interested in those aspects of behavior which can be designated as "emotional," or more specifically, as "anxiety." This means, as we have said before, that the physiological activities which, at their level, constitute emotionality are the ones most appropriately studied. There is a vast literature on physiological measures of emotionality (Ruckmick, 1936; Young, 1943; Darrow, 1943); and merely to list the physiological variables whose correlation with emotionality has been studied would take a great amount of space. Most of the attempts to correlate peripherally measurable physiological variables, as Darrow has noted, have produced very scanty results: " . . . peripheral autonomic events which now may bear one relation and now another to initiating processes in the nervous system need have no constant relation to those manifestations of nervous system function known as 'behavior'" (Darrow, 1943, p. 1). There is good reason for believing that there are few, if any, physiological measures to which this statement does not apply. But, if perfect correlations cannot be accomplished, what are the best possibilities? If we assume that increases in emotionality can be thought of in terms of sympathetic nervous system dominance and decreases in emotionality in terms of parasympathetic dominance, then it might be assumed that what we should do is secure a "pure" measure of activity in the sympathetic nervous system. This is difficult, however, since most organ systems are innervated by both divisions of the autonomic nervous system. In the human subject the physiological mechanism most accessible to study which meets this criterion is the sweat glands; changes in palmar skin resistance which we call the psychogalvanic skin reflex are dependent upon sweat-gland excitation from the sympathetic nervous system. The

PGR has, accordingly, been used extensively in instrumental investigations of emotional behavior, but with disappointing results. Although extremely sensitive to emotional changes, it is also, unfortunately, very sensitive to almost any other type of alteration in the responses of the subject. This has the effect of producing many seemingly random and uncorrelated deviations in skin resistance, making the *PGR* record difficult to interpret. .

Also widely used are the various superficially recordable aspects of the activities of the vascular system. Blood pressure, pulse rate, and vasomotor activities have all been studied from the early days of emotion research. None of these functions is a pure indicator of sympathetic activity; they always reflect a dynamic balance between excitation in the sympathetic and parasympathetic systems. However, within the half-hour to one-hour period of continuous recording which would ordinarily be used during psychotherapy sessions, changes in blood pressure or pulse rate would, judging from the evidence in the literature (Young, 1943), cumulatively lend themselves to interpretation as indicators of changes in emotional tension patterns. The vascular measures are less sensitive and labile than the *PGR,* and hence involve a somewhat different time scale in their coordination with behavioral observations.

The third most commonly used measure is respiration. Changes in respiratory rate and depth are also controlled by influences from both parts of the autonomic nervous system and, like the vascular functions, record the resultant of the two influences. One rather bothersome handicap of respiratory measures for psychotherapy research is the dependence of the inspiration-expiration ratio on explicit speech. As Fossler (1930) has shown, the quiet resting subject devotes about 40 per cent of the inspiration-expiration cycle to inspiration, but the same subject, when conversing, uses only about 15 per cent of the cycle for inspiration. This type of influence on respiration has always proved a problem to those who sought quantitative indices of emotional response. In spite of this, the summary of findings with respect to the inspiration fraction under various conditions lends some justification to its use:

In speech	0.16
In laughter	0.23
In attentive mental work	0.30
In the resting condition	0.43
In excitement	0.60
In posed wonder	0.71
In sudden fright	0.75 [3]

There are many other measures of autonomic function which have some claim to validly representing emotional changes in the subject. But most of them are poorly suited to continuous recording, since they involve operative procedures which preclude their use with human subjects, or which require periodic samples of blood or other tissue products for chemical analysis.

[3] Data from Woodworth (1938, p. 264).

As a very promising technique, let us consider recording the state of tension in the peripheral skeletal musculature. As the researches of Jacobson (1938), Max (1937), Stetson (1933), Davis (1938), and others have shown, the electrical recording of muscle potentials is correlated with many behavioral phenomena in a meaningful manner. Recently, with the widespread development and use of electroencephalographic techniques, powerful and reliable amplification systems have been devised and are available for use in recording the electrical activity of muscle. The relatively rapid nature of skeletal-muscle response following disturbing stimulation would be advantageous if correlations are to be made between the verbal productions of therapy and tension indices.

Turning to the application of these techniques in psychotherapy research, there are two types of experimental design which should be considered. The type of design in which we are interested has as its primary purpose the use of physiological variables as indicators of changes in the emotional reactions of subjects as they undergo psychotherapy; in this connection, we are not fundamentally interested in research on the physiological variables in maladjustment and recovery as such. Thus our discussion of possible designs will be limited in a way that would not be the case were we investigating the complex physiology of the emotional processes themselves. Inherent in the designs to be discussed are the assumptions that (a) clinical and "subclinical" anxiety are accompanied by greater or lesser fluctuations in the effector systems served or influenced by the autonomic nervous system; (b) successful psychotherapy ultimately serves as a means of reducing the manifestations of anxiety, even though, at some stages of therapy, anxiety may actually be increased; and (c) psychotherapy represents a complex type of learning which takes place over a measurable span of time, and accordingly appropriate periodic measurement of the patient with respect to this learning would yield some type of function not dissimilar from learning in general.

Concerning the justifiability of these assumptions, it seems that the first is fairly well established on the basis of clinical observations. Subjective complaints of the type we subsume under "anxiety" are quite regularly accompanied by such autonomic manifestations as hyperhydrosis; vascular instability as in blushing, faintness, tachycardia; cold extremities, etc.; respiratory alterations such as hyperventilation and breathlessness; muscular tremor and tonus alterations; pupillary hippus; and a host of other more or less obvious disturbances. Whether or not the more minimal or converted anxieties of the "subclinical" type give similar alterations of autonomic function is not as well established. However, if we may use the evidence from psychosomatic medicine, it would seem that quite frequently a person may have rather serious alterations of vegetative function in the absence of subjective complaints of anxiety and that psychotherapy may furnish a proof that connections exist between the buried anxiety and the somatic complaint. A good deal of careful methodological research is needed here.

The second assumption, concerning the ultimate reduction of anxiety by psychotherapy, seems obvious and axiomatic, whether or not, in any given case, the goal of anxiety reduction is obtained. We know that many forms of compromise must be accepted in clinical practice, and in many instances the therapist must be content with the hope that he has helped his patient to learn "to live with his neurosis" or endure his anxiety in a more insightful or resourceful manner. Nevertheless, the ultimate goal of psychotherapy is a transformation of the anxiety-ridden patient into the anxiety-free, well-adjusted, "healthy" person. Since therapy often involves some form of increasing awareness on the patient's part of his conflicts, the therapeutic course cannot be thought of as a steadily progressing decrease of anxiety, but rather as a succession of advances and regressions whose trend is, in the broad view, in the direction of recovery.

The third assumption is also well-nigh universally accepted, and has been elaborated in a number of ways by Mowrer (1950) and by Alexander and French (1946). We still do not know precisely what course the temporal progress of such learning takes. Clinical observation suggests that the plot of recovery against time would resemble more the curves seen in eliminating errors in problem-solving than the slow and steady improvement seen in the acquisition of a list of nonsense syllables. The great difficulty here, of course, is finding a measure of learning or improvement. Suggestions for measurement, growing out of the psychodynamics of therapy, are discussed elsewhere in this volume (Chapters 10-14). The use of recordings of physiological processes as a measure of learning is based, obviously, on the assumption that what is learned in therapy is accompanied by anxiety reduction.

The first type of experimental design that grows out of these assumptions is characterized by periodic assessment of the patient's status with respect to physiologic stability. Here the observations are made apart from the therapy sessions, and would have the same function in the course of therapy that periodic physical examinations would have in the radiological treatment of a tumor, or the therapeutic course of a cardiac patient whose schedule is punctuated with electrocardiographic tests. The periodic measures, plotted against time, furnish the index of therapeutic progress. Unfortunately there are major difficulties to be overcome. It is not enough simply to record physiological activity for a given period of time while the patient remains passive. There must obviously be standardized test situations, comparable on a psychological level to the familiar "hop twenty times on one foot, and then twenty times on the other" of the physical examination of the cardiovascular system. But what should these test situations be? They should be capable of imposing a somewhat known amount of stress upon the patient, of a kind which is representative, in one way or another, of the life situations toward which he has failed to adjust before therapy, and where gains in therapy would be reflected by calmer or more adequate reactions. This presentation of genuine situations, however, is just the difficulty which has steadfastly confronted the laboratory worker in the field of emotion, and there is not a great deal of help to be found from his researches. Additionally, there is the difficulty of standardizing test situations when the emotional or stress material would have to be varied with the circumstances of each patient's life history.

There is a possibility that the work of Osgood (1952) on a "meaning-structured" word-association technique may provide a way to measure changes in the patient's status, particularly if such measurements are taken in conjunction with the autonomic indices already discussed (see Chapter 17). The essentials of Osgood's procedure include tachisto-scopic presentation of words, pictures, or other meaningful material to subjects who are instructed to assign the item a scale position on a number of "semantic continua" whose polar extremes are "good-bad," "strong-weak," "hard-soft," and the like. Intercorrelations of the scale values of a large number of words on the various continua seem to indicate that a relatively small number of semantic dimensions will account for the pattern of meanings operant in perception. As in the original Jung word-association experiment, individually deviant scaling is accompanied by longer response latencies and presumably by variations in the motor accompaniments of the judgmental act. Experimentation now in progress in our laboratory is directed at the study of this issue. R. C. Davis (1950) has reported the results of recording muscle potentials during judgments of tonal intensity while varying the time interval between presentation of the standard and comparison tones. He finds that derived measures of spike-potential amplitude faithfully reflect the well-known "'time error" in judgment. This lends additional hope that the even more difficult influences which are produced by emotional blocking will be accompanied by physiological changes of sufficient magnitude to be recorded and meaningfully interpreted.

A start at the utilization of this type of design for the evaluation of psychotherapy has been made by Thetford (1949). PGR, blood pressure, and respiration of patients before and after nondirective counseling were taken during a frustrating situation. As compared with a control group of uncounseled subjects, a reduction in autonomic evidence of emotionality during frustration was noted in the counseled subjects. An extension of Thetford's approach to cover several stages between the start and termination of therapy would be desirable. Here the greatest difficulty lies in contriving a series of frustrations which will avoid the twin difficulties of (a) interfering with the progress of therapy and (b) producing rapid habituation toward the test procedures by the patient.

An early study of methodological interest, although with generally negative results, was reported by Ebaugh and Barnacle (1935). Using the Luria technique of measuring alterations in involuntary tension of a nonpreferred hand which maintained supposedly constant pressure on a rubber bulb, while the preferred hand signaled the time of verbal reaction to stimulus words from a word-association test, patients with various neurotic and psychotic disturbances were tested before and after therapy. Although a number of subjects showed rather dramatic decreases in motor disturbance, a statistical analysis of the measurable results failed to reveal differences in which any high degree of confidence could be placed.

Alexander (1939) recorded the daily fluctuations in blood pressure of a hypertensive patient who was working through pyschoanalysis. He found a distinct correlation between emotional tensions as revealed in the analysis and height of blood pressure. As the patient improved, the average blood-pressure level decreased. Furthermore, throughout the time the patient was under observation, the correlation between day-to-day mood fluctuations and blood pressure was unmistakable.

A promising method for the physiological assessment of anxiety has been introduced by Malmo, Shagass, and Davis (1950). Following the evidence adduced by Jacobson that skeletal-muscle tone is augmented during emotional disturbances, Malmo and his associates recorded action potentials from the right forearms of ten psychiatric patients with severe anxiety neurosis and from ten control subjects matched for age and sex. With the subject in a prone position and maintaining slight pressure with his right hand on a rubber bulb, a click of moderate intensity was presented through binaural earphones. Measurement of the magnitude and latency of spike potentials from the arm for the two groups showed that the initial muscular tension response was approximately equal, but that the controls returned rapidly (0.4 sec.) to a resting state, whereas the patients remained at a high state of excitation for a significantly longer time. Furthermore, the peak response for the controls occurred much sooner than that of the patients, a difference which was highly reliable. This method, applied to periodic assessment of anxiety in patients during therapy, should yield valuable results. Measurements of this type avoid rather nicely the difficulty of contriving periodic frustrations appropriate to the individual patient. Another advantage of using the skeletal rather than the autonomic responses of a subject is the much shorter latency of the former. Autonomic responses develop slowly, and if correlations are being made between stimulus situations and physiological response mechanisms, the possibility of clean-cut resolution of the stimulus-response relationship is considerably greater when the response latency is small.

The second type of design for physiological evaluation of psychotherapy is characterized chiefly by its emphasis on studying the patient *during* the time that he is actually undergoing treatment. Whatever physiological measures are found to be appropriate would be recorded throughout the entire treatment hour, together with voice-recording of patient and therapist, and whatever observations the therapist wishes to note. The entire sequence of measurements can then be analyzed in terms of the actual incidents and flow of therapy.

This design represents a more direct attack on the therapeutic situation itself. Physiological index functions become measures, not of a generally existing tension status which differentiates patients as a group from some control standard, but rather of moment-to-moment alterations in the tension level as a function of therapeutic procedures. If adequate techniques can be devised for correlating the recorded content of interviews with the physiological data, we will have a powerful investigative tool for the assessment of therapeutic techniques. We can observe the effect of the therapist's give and take with the patient, the effect of directive versus nondirective responses by the therapist, the effect of ventilation and catharsis by the patient, the "quotidian" variability of tension, the differential tension associated with recollection of various aspects of past history, and many other equally pertinent aspects of therapy. By this technique of correlating the voice records and the independent physiological tracings, we have a means of making the physiological components of behavior appear in their true relevance to the content of behavior as habitually observed by the therapist.

While this approach has much promise, it also has practical difficulties whose extent can only be determined by experimental trial. Adequate placement on the subject of the recording paraphernalia sufficient to detect respiration, *PGR,* blood pressure, skin temperature, muscle potentials, and *EEG* might prove somewhat overpowering to an insecure person. Mowrer and others have shown, however, that patients soon become accustomed to wearing rather cumbersome microphone holders and are able to accept, with little reluctance, the knowledge that a transcription is being made of their verbal productions. It is possible that patients would also accept the physiological apparatus as a part of the therapy situation. Another difficulty lies in the rather constant attention which must be given to the adjustment and servicing of the recording devices; if the therapist were to attempt this in addition to his therapeutic duties, one or the other would most certainly suffer. Because of this it would be necessary for an assistant to manage the apparatus and, unavoidably, become a part of the therapeutic situation. The recent experiences of the Rogers group with the use of more than one therapist indicate that it is possible for a patient to accept the notion that professional confidence can be extended by two as well as by one.

Speaking of the application of physiological recording techniques in general, there are a host of problems worthy of research. Technical difficulties do not appear, in any instance, to be insuperable. We have not discussed in any detail the possible contributions to the theory of psychopathology or psychotherapy which might come from the type of research here presented, but here again the possibilities should not be ignored. To take but one example, a thorough search of the literature convinces one that only the merest beginning has been made on an understanding of the influences of emotion on learning and retention. Recent work on one-trial learning (see Hudson, 1950) does much to recall the prediction made by Kempf (1918) that learning which involves the autonomic nervous system may well proceed in unusual and novel ways. The report by Brady and Hunt (1950) that electroconvulsive shock differentially effects emotional avoidance responses and nonemotional bar-pressing behavior is also suggestive. But before we can prosecute research on these aspects of psychotherapy we must do the preliminary work of exploration; we must know much more than we do today about the bodily accompaniments of actual psychotherapy on human subjects. This chapter has attempted simply to indicate the directions which physiological research in psychotherapy may take.

BIBLIOGRAPHY

ABT, L. E. & BELLAK, L. 1950. *Projective psychology*. New York: Alfred A. Knopf, Inc.

ACKERMAN, N. H. 1945. Some theoretical aspects of group psychotherapy. In *Group psychotherapy: a symposium*. New York: Beacon House.

ADLER, A. 1929. *The practice and theory of individual psychology*. Trans. P. Radin. London: Kegan Paul, Trench, Trubner & Co.

AIDMAN, T. 1951. An objective study of the changing relationship between the present self and the ideal self pictures as expressed by the client in nondirective psychotherapy. Unpublished Ph.D. dissertation, University of Chicago.

ALDRICH, C. A. & ALDRICH, M. M. 1947. *Babies are human beings*. New York: The Macmillan Co.

ALEXANDER, F. 1931. Schizophrenic psychoses: Critical considerations of the psychoanalytic treatment. *Arch. Neurol. Psychiat.*, **26**, 815-28.

——. 1935. The problem of psychoanalytic technique. *Psychoanal. Quart.*, **4**, 606.

——. 1939. Psychoanalytic study of a case of essential hypertension. *Psychosom. Med.*, **1**, 139-52.

——. 1941. The voice of the intellect is soft. *Psychoanal. Rev.*, **28**, 12-29.

——. 1948. *Fundamentals of psychoanalysis*. New York: W. W. Norton & Co., Inc.

—— 1950. *Psychosomatic medicine*. New York: W. W. Norton & Co., Inc.

ALEXANDER, F. & FRENCH, T. M. 1946. *Psychoanalytic therapy*. New York: The Ronald Press Co.

ALLPORT, G. W. 1937. *Personality: a psychological interpretation*. New York: Henry Holt & Co., Inc.

——. 1943. The ego in contemporary psychology. *Psychol. Rev.*, **50**, 451-78.

ANASTASI, A. 1932. Further studies on the memory factor. *Arch. Psychol.*, **142**, 60.

ANGYAL, A. 1941. *Foundations for a science of personality*. New York: Commonwealth Fund.

APPEL, K. E. 1944. Psychiatric therapy. In J. McV. HUNT (ed.), *Personality and the behavior disorders*. New York: The Ronald Press Co.

ASHLEY-MONTAGU, M. F. 1950. On being human. New York: H. Schuman.

ASSUM, A. L. & LEVY, S. J. 1948. Analysis of a nondirective case with followup interview. *J. Abnorm. Soc. Psychol.*, **43**, 78-89

BAILEY, P. 1935. *Theory and therapy: an introduction to the psychology of Dr. Otto Rank*. Paris: Jouve et Cie., Editeurs.

BAKER, S. J. 1951. Ontogenetic evidence of a correlation between the form and frequency of use of words. *J. Gen. Psychol.*, **44**, 235-51

BALDWIN, A. L. 1942. Personal structure analysis: A statistical method for investigating the single personality. *J. Abnorm. Soc. Psychol.*, **37**, 163-83.

——. 1946. The study of individual personality by means of the intra-individual correlation. *J. Personality.*, **14**, 151-69.

——. 1950. Statistical problems in the treatment of case histories. *J. Clin. Psychol.*, **6**, 6-12.

BALES, R. F. 1950. *Interaction process analysis*. Cambridge: Addison-Wesley Press.

BALINSKY, B. 1941. An analysis of the mental factors of various age groups from nine to sixty. *Genetic Psychol. Monogr.*, 23, 191-234.

BARTLETT, M. R. and STAFF. 1949. Data on the personal adjustment counseling program for veterans. Personal Adjustment Counseling Division, Advisement and Guidance Service, Office of Vocational Rehabilitation and Education, Washington, D. C.

BARZUN, J. 1946. *Teacher in America.* Boston: Little, Brown & Co.

BEEBE-CENTER, J. G. 1932. *The psychology of pleasantness and unpleasantness.* New York: D. Van Nostrand Co., Inc.

BEIER, E. G. 1949. The effect of induced anxiety on some aspects of intellectual functioning: a study of the relationship between anxiety and rigidity. *Amer. Psychol., 4,* 273-74 (abstract).

——. 1951. The problem of anxiety in client-centered therapy. *J. Consult Psychol., 15,* 359-62.

BENEDEK, T. 1946. Control of the transference relationship. In F. Alexander and T. M. French, *Psychoanalytic therapy.* New York: The Ronald Press Co.

BENEDEK, T. & RUBENSTEIN, B. 1939. The correlation between ovarian activity and psychodynamic processes: I. The ovulative phase. *Psychosom. Med., 1,* 245-70. II. The menstrual phase. *Psychosom. Med., 1,* 461-85.

BENEDICT, R. 1934. *Patterns of culture.* Boston: Houghton Mifflin Co.

BERGMAN, D. V. 1950. The relationship between counseling method and client self-exploration. Unpublished M.A. thesis, University of Chicago.

BERGMAN, P. 1949. The germinal cell of Freud's psychoanalytic psychology and therapy. *Psychiatry, 12,* 265-78.

BERNREUTER, R. G. 1933. The theory and construction of the personality inventory. *J. Soc. Psychol., 4,* 387-405.

BETZ, B. 1950. Strategic conditions in the psychotherapy of persons with schizophrenia. *Amer. J. Psychiat., 107,* No. 3, 203-15.

BILLINGS, E. G. 1949. The dynamics of psychotherapy: an eclectic point of view. *Amer. J. Psychiat., 106,* 346-57.

BINNS, H. & BURT, C. 1922. A comparison of judgments in the evaluation of cloths. *J. Nat. Inst. Industr. Psychol., 1,* 93-98.

BIXLER, R. H. 1948. Counseling: eclectic or systematic? *Educ. & Psychol. Meas., 8,* 211-14.

BLEULER, E. 1950. *Dementia praecox or the group of schizophrenias.* New York: International Universities Press.

BLOCKSMA, D. D. 1951. An experiment in counselor learning. Unpublished Ph.D. dissertation, University of Chicago.

BLOS, P. 1946. Psychological counseling of college students. *Amer. J. Orthopsychiat., 15,* 571-80.

BODER, D. P. 1940. The adjective-verb quotient; a contribution to the psychology of language. *Psychol. Rec., 3,* 309-44.

——. 1949. *I did not interview the dead.* Urbana: University of Illinois Press.

——. 1951. The DRQ as a measure of tension in personal documents. Unpublished paper, Illinois Institute of Technology.

BORDIN, E. S. 1943. Factor analysis in experimental designs in clinical and social psychology. *Psychol. Rev., 50,* 415-29.

——. 1948. Dimensions in the counseling process. *J. Clin. Psychol., 4,* 240-44.

BORDIN, E. S. & BIXLER, R. H. 1946. Test selection: a process of counseling. *Educ. & Psychol. Meas., 6,* 361-73.

BOUSFIELD, W. A. & BARCLAY, W. D. 1951. The application of Zipf's analysis of language to sequences of restricted associative responses. *J. Gen. Psychol., 44,* 253-60.

BOWMAN, P. H. 1951. A measure of discrepancy between different areas of the self-concept. Unpublished Ph.D. dissertation, University of Chicago.

BOWN, O. H. 1951. An investigation of therapeutic relationship in client-centered psychotherapy. Unpublished Ph.D. dissertation, University of Chicago.

BRADY, J. V. & HUNT, H. F. 1950. An exploratory study of some effects of electroconvulsive shock on a conditioned emotional response. *Amer. Psychol., 5,* 256.

BRENMAN, M., GILL, M., & KNIGHT, R. P. 1952. Spontaneous fluctuations in depth of hypnosis and their implications for ego-functions. *Int. J. Psychoanal.,* **33,** 22-33.

BRILL, A. A 1929. Unconscious insight. *Int. J. Psychoanal.,* **10,** 145-61.

BRODY, E. B., NEWMAN, R., & REDLICH, F. C. 1951. Sound recording: the problem of evidence in psychiatry. *Science,* **113,** 379-80.

BRONNER, A. F. 1949. The objective evaluation of psychotherapy. *Amer. J. Orthopsychiat.,* **19,** 463-91.

BUGENTHAL, J. F. T. 1952. A method for assessing self and not-self attitudes during the therapeutic series. *J. Consult. Psychol.,* **16,** 435-39.

BURNHAM, W. H. 1924. *The normal mind.* New York: Appleton-Century-Crofts, Inc.

BURT, C. 1937. Correlations between persons. *Brit. J. Psychol.,* **28,** 59-96.

———. 1940. *The factors of the mind.* London: University of London Press, Ltd.

BURT, C. & MOORE, R. C. 1912. The mental differences between the sexes. *J. Exp. Pedagogy,* **1,** 237-84.

BURT, C. & STEPHENSON, W. 1939. Alternative views on correlations between persons. *Psychometrika,* **4,** 269-81.

BURTON, W. H. 1944. *The guidance of learning activities.* New York: Appleton-Century-Crofts, Inc.

BURTT, H. E. 1948. *Applied psychology.* New York: Prentice-Hall, Inc.

BUTLER, J. M. 1948. On the role of directive and non-directive techniques in the counseling process. *Educ. & Psychol. Meas.,* **8,** 201-7.

———. 1952. Assessing psychotherapeutic protocols with context coefficients. *J. Clin. Psychol.,* **8,** 199-202.

BUTLER, J. M. and OTHERS. 1952. A quantitative study of aspects of the self-concept in psychotherapy. Unpublished research, University of Chicago.

CAMERON, N. 1938. Reasoning, regression, and communication in schizophrenics. *Psychol. Monogr.,* 50, No. 1.

———. 1939. Deterioration and regression in schizophrenic thinking. *J. Abnorm. Soc. Psychol.,* **34,** 265-70.

———. 1947. *The psychology of the behavior disorders.* Boston: Houghton Mifflin Co.

CAMERON, N. & MAGARET, A. 1951. *Behavior pathology.* Boston: Houghton Mifflin Co.

CANTRIL, H. 1950. Psychology. Article in the series The Age of Science: 1900-1950. *Scientific American,* **183**(3), 79-84.

CARLSON, H. B. & HARRELL, W. 1942. Voting groups among leading congressmen obtained by means of the inverted factor technique. *J. Soc. Psychol.,* **16,** 51-61.

CARR, A. C. 1949. An evaluation of nine nondirective psychotherapy cases by means of the Rorschach. *J. Consult. Psychol.,* **13,** 196-205.

CARROLL, J. B. 1938. Diversity of vocabulary and the harmonic series law of word-frequency distribution. *Psychol. Rec.,* **2,** 379-86.

CASSIRER, E. 1944. *An essay on man.* New Haven, Conn.: Yale University Press.

CATTELL, R. B. 1943. The description of personality: I. Foundations of trait measurement. *Psychol. Rev.,* 50, 559-93.

———. 1946. *Description and measurement of personality.* Yonkers: World Book Co.

———. 1947. Primary personality factors in the realm of objective tests. *J. Personality,* **16,** 459-87.

———. 1949. r_p and other coefficients of pattern similarity. *Psychometrika,* **14,** 279-98.

———. 1950a. *Personality: a systematic theoretical and factual study.* New York: McGraw-Hill Book Co., Inc.

———. 1950b. The main personality factors in questionnaire, self-estimate material. *J. Soc. Psychol.,* **31,** 3-38.

CATTELL, R. B. 1951. On the disuse and misuse of P. Q. Q$_s$, and O-techniques in clinical psychology. *J. Clin. Psychol., 7*, 203-14.

——. 1952a. *Factor analysis for the social sciences.* New York: Harper & Bros.

——. 1952b. The three basic factor-analytic designs—their interrelations and derivations. *Psychol. Bull., 49*, 499-520.

CATTELL, R. B., CATTELL, A. K. S., & RHYMER, R. M. 1947. P-technique demonstrated in determining psychophysiological source traits in a normal individual. *Psychometrika, 12*, 267-88.

CATTELL, R. B. & LUBORSKY, L. B. 1950. P-technique demonstrated as a new clinical method for determining personality and symptom structure. *J. Gen. Psychol., 42*, 3-24.

CHOTLOS, J. W. 1944. Studies in language behavior: IV. A statistical and comparative analysis of individual written language samples. *Psychol. Monogr., 56*, 77-111.

CLARK, R. 1948. The relationship of schizophrenia to occupational income and occupational prestige. *Amer. J. Sociol., 13*, 325-30.

COFER, C. N. & CHANCE, J. 1950. The discomfort-relief quotient in published cases of counseling and psychotherapy. *J. Psychol., 29*, 219-24.

COFFEY, H. S., FREEDMAN, M. B., LEARY, T. F. & OSSORIO, A. G. 1950. Community service and social research—group psychotherapy in a church program. *J. Soc. Issues, 6*, 1-65.

COLLIER, R. M. 1950. A basis for integration rather than fragmentation in psychotherapy. *J. Consult. Psychol., 14*, 199-205.

COMENIUS, J. A. 1668. *Via Lucis.* Trans. E. T. Champagnac (1938). London: Hodder & Stoughton.

COUNSELING CENTER RESEARCH PROGRAM, University of Chicago, 1952. A study of the relationship of therapy to emotionally mature behavior.

COUTU, W. 1949. *Emergent human nature.* New York: Alfred A. Knopf, Inc.

COVNER, B. J. 1942. Studies in phonographic recordings of verbal material: I. The use of phonographic recordings in counseling practice and research. *J. Consult. Psychol., 6*, 105-13.

CRONBACH, L. J. 1948. A validation design for qualitative studies of personality. *J. Consult. Psychol., 12*, 365-74.

——. 1950. Further evidence on response sets and test design. *Educ. & Psychol. Meas., 10*, 3-31.

——. 1952. A generalized psychometric theory based on information measure. Unpublished, University of Illinois.

CRONBACH, L. J. & GLESER, G. C. 1952. Similarity between persons and related problems of profile analysis. Technical Report No. 2, Project No. N6ori-07135. Mimeographed, University of Illinois.

CURETON, E. E. 1951. Validity. In E. F. Lindquist (ed.), *Educational Measurement.* Washington, D. C.: American Council on Education.

CURRAN, C. A. 1945. *Personality factors in counseling.* New York: Grune & Stratton.

DARLEY, J. 1943. Review of *Counseling and psychotherapy. J. Abnorm. Soc. Psychol., 38*, 199-201.

DARROW, C. W. 1943. Physiological and clinical tests of autonomic function and autonomic balance. *Physiol. Rev., 23*, 1-36.

DAVIES, M. 1939. The general factor in correlations between persons. *Brit. J. Psychol., 29*, 404-21.

DAVIS, R. C. 1938. The relation of muscle action potentials to difficulty and frustration. *J. Exp. Psychol., 23*, 141-58.

——. 1950. Electromyographic study of stimulus traces as response determiners. *Amer. Psychol., 5*, 256.

DE LAGUNA, G. 1927. *Speech: Its function and development.* New Haven: Yale University Press.

DEMAREE, R. G. 1950. An investigation of homogeneity in the interpretation and scaling of test results. Unpublished Ph.D. thesis, University of Illinois.

DEUTSCH, F. 1949. *Applied psychoanalysis.* New York: Grune & Stratton.

DEWEY, J. 1920. *Democracy and education.* New York: The Macmillan Co.

——. 1926. *Experience and nature.* La Salle: Open Court Publishing Co.

DI CARLO, L. 1948. Hearing aids for hearing handicapped children. *Hearing News,* Reprint No. 194.

DI CARLO, L. & KATAJA, R. 1951. An analysis of the Utley lipreading test. *J. Speech & Hearing Disorders,* **16,** 226-40.

DOLLARD, J., DOOB, L., MILLER, N. E., MOWRER, O. H., & SEARS, R. R. 1939. *Frustration and aggression.* New Haven: Yale University Press.

DOLLARD, J. & MILLER, N. E. 1950. *Personality and psychotherapy.* New York: McGraw-Hill Book Co., Inc.

DOLLARD, J. & MOWRER, O. H. 1947. A method of measuring tension in written documents. *J. Abnorm. Soc. Psychol.,* **42,** 3-32.

DORFMAN, E. 1951. Play therapy. In C. R. Rogers (ed.), *Client-centered therapy.* Boston: Houghton Mifflin Co.

DRATWA, E. J. 1951. An investigation into the attitudes toward emotional maturity in a twenty-year interval by the Willoughby E-M scale. Unpublished M.A. thesis, in progress, University of Chicago.

DUNCKER, K. 1945. On problem solving. *Psychol. Monogr.,* 58, No. 5.

DUNLAP, J. W. 1938. Recent advances in statistical theory and applications. *Amer. J. Psychol.,* **51,** 558-71.

EBAUGH, F. G. 1935. Assoziationsexperimente bei Psychosen und Neurosen. Paper presented at Second International Congress of Neurology and Psychiatry, London.

EDER, M. D. 1930. Dreams as resistance. *Int. J, Psychoanal.,* **11,** 40-47.

EDWARDS, A. L. 1947. *Statistical analysis for students in psychology and education.* New York: Rinehart & Co.

EISENBERG, P. 1941. Individual interpretation of psychoneurotic inventory items. *J. Gen. Psychol.,* **25,** 19-40.

EISSLER, K. 1943. Limitations to the psychotherapy of schizophrenia. *Psychiatry,* **6,** 381-91.

ELDRIDGE, R. C. 1911. *Six thousand common English words.* Buffalo: The Clement Press.

ELLIS, A. 1946. The validity of personality questionnaires. *Psychol. Bull.,* **43,** 385-440.

ELLSWORTH, R. B. 1951. The regression of schizophrenic language. *J. Consult. Psychol.,* **15,** 387-91.

ENGLISH, H. B. 1948*a.* The counseling situation as an obstacle to non-directive therapy. *J. Consult. Psychol.,* **12,** 217-20.

——. 1948*b.* Factor analysis explained (without mathematics!). *Egypt. J. Psychol.,* **3,** 475-84.

ERICKSON, M. H. & KUBIE, L. S. 1941. The successful treatment of a case of acute hysterical depression by a return under hypnosis to a critical phase of childhood. *Psychoanal. Quart.,* **10,** 583-609.

ESTES, S. G. 1948. Concerning the therapeutic relationship and the dynamics of cure. *J. Consult. Psychol.,* **12,** 76-81.

EWING, T. N. 1952. A study of changes in attitude toward self and parents during therapy. Unpublished research, University of Illinois.

EYSENCK, M. D. 1944. An experimental and statistical study of olfactory preference. *J. Exp. Psychol.,* **34,** 246-52.

FAIRBANKS, G. & JAEGER, R. 1951. A device for continuously variable time delay of headset monitoring during magnetic recording of speech. *J. Speech & Hearing Disorders,* **16,** 162-64.

FAIRBANKS, H. 1944. Studies in language behavior: II. The quantitative differentiation of samples of spoken language. *Psychol. Monogr.,* 56, 19-31.

FARBER, I. E. 1948. Response fixation under anxiety and non-anxiety conditions. *J. Exp. Psychol.,* **38,** 111-31.

FARIS, R. E. L. & DUNHAM, H. W. 1939. *Mental disorders in urban areas.* Chicago: University of Chicago Press.

FARR, J. N., JENKINS, J. J., PATERSON, D. G., & ENGLAND, G. W. 1952. Reply to Klare and Flesch re "Simplification of Flesch reading ease formula." *J. Appl. Psychol.,* **36,** 55-57.

FEDERN, P. 1943*a.* Psychoanalysis of psychoses, I. Errors and how to avoid them. *Psychiat. Quart.,* **17,** 1-19.

———. 1943*b.* Psychoanalysis of psychoses, III. The psychoanalytic process. *Psychiat. Quart.,* **17,** 470-87.

———. 1947. Principles of psychotherapy in latent schizophrenia. *Amer. J. Psychotherapy,* **1,** 129-44.

FENICHEL, O. 1941. *Problems of psychoanalytic technique.* New York: Psychoanalytic Quarterly, Inc.

———. 1945. *The psychoanalytic theory of neurosis.* New York: W. W. Norton & Co., Inc.

FIEDLER, F. E. 1949. A comparative investigation of early therapeutic relationships created by experts and non-experts of the psychoanalytic, non-directive, and Adlerian schools. Unpublished Ph.D. dissertation, University of Chicago.

———. 1950*a.* The concept of the ideal therapeutic relationship. *J. Consult. Psychol.,* **14,** 239-45.

———. 1950*b.* A comparison of therapeutic relationships in psychoanalytic, non-directive, and Adlerian therapy. *J. Consult. Psychol.,* **14,** 436-45.

———. 1950*c.* Unpublished research.

———. 1951*a.* Factor analyses of psychoanalytic, nondirective, and Adlerian therapeutic relationships. *J. Consult. Psychol.,* **15,** 32-38.

———. 1951*b.* A method of objective quantification of certain countertransference attitudes. *J. Clin. Psychol.,* **7,** 101-7.

FIEDLER, F. E. & SIEGEL, S. M. 1949. The free-drawing test as a predictor of non-improvement in psychotherapy. *J. Clin. Psychol.,* **5,** 386-89.

FIEDLER, F. E. & SENIOR, K. 1952. An exploratory study of unconscious feeling reactions in 15 patient-therapist pairs. *J. Abnorm. Soc. Psychol.,* **47,** 446-53.

FISHER, R. A. 1948. *Statistical methods for research workers* (10th Ed.). New York: Hafner Publishing Co.

FISHER, V. E. 1944. Psychic shock treatment for early schizophrenia. *Amer. J. Orthopsychiat.,* **14,** 352.

———. 1950. *The meaning and practice of psychotherapy.* New York: The Macmillan Co.

FISKE, D. W., FIEDLER, F. E., & ISAACS, K. S. 1950. Rigidity in clinical judgments. Paper read at meeting of Midwestern Psychological Association, May, 1950.

FLESCH, R. F. 1948. A new readability yardstick. *J. Appl. Psychol.,* **32,** 221-23.

———. 1951. *How to test readability.* New York: Harper & Bros.

———. 1952. Reply to "Simplification of Flesch Reading Ease Formula." *J. Appl. Psychol.,* **36,** 54-55.

FOSSLER, H. R. 1930. Disturbances in breathing during stuttering. *Psychol. Monogr.,* **40,** 1-32.

FRASER, R. 1947. *The incidence of neurosis among factory workers.* London: His Majesty's Stationery Office.

FREEMAN, G. L. 1948. *The energetics of human behavior.* Ithaca: Cornell University Press.

FRENCH, T. M. 1933. Interrelations between psychoanalysis and the experimental work of Pavlov. *Amer. J. Psychiat.,* **12,** 1165-1203.

FREUD, A. 1949. Reported in L. Jekels and E. Bergler, Transference and love. *Psychoanal. Quart.,* **18,** 325-50.

FREUD, S. 1921. *Group psychology and the analysis of the ego.* New York: Boni and Liveright.

FREUD, S. 1922. *Vorlesungen zur Einfuehrung in die Psychoanalyse.* Vienna: Psychoan. Verlag.
——. 1927. *The problem of lay-analyses.* New York: Brentano.
——. 1928. *The future of an illusion.* London: Hogarth Press.
——. 1930. *Civilization and its discontents.* London: Hogarth Press.
——. 1933a. Psycho-analytic notes upon an autobiographical account of a case of paranoia (1911). Reprinted in *Collected papers,* Vol. III. London: Hogarth Press.
——. 1933b. Neurosis and psychosis. (1924) *Collected papers,* Vol. II. London: Hogarth Press.
——. 1933c. *New introductory lectures on psycho-analysis.* New York: W. W. Norton & Co., Inc.
——. 1934a. The unconscious. (1915) *Collected papers,* Vol. IV. London: Hogarth Press.
——. 1934b. Repression (1915). Reprinted in *Collected papers,* Vol. IV. London: Hogarth Press.
——. 1935a. *A general introduction to psycho-analysis.* New York: Liveright Publishing Corp.
——. 1935b. *Autobiography.* New York: W. W. Norton & Co., Inc.
——. 1949. *An outline of psychoanalysis.* New York: W. W. Norton & Co., Inc.
——. 1950. Splitting of the ego in the defensive process. (1938) *Collected papers,* Vol. V. London: Hogarth Press.
FROMM, E. 1941. *Escape from freedom.* New York: Rinehart & Co.
——. 1947. *Man for himself, an inquiry into the psychology of ethics.* New York: Rinehart & Co.
——. 1950. *Psychoanalysis and religion.* New Haven: Yale University Press.
FROMM-REICHMANN, F., 1939. Transference problems in schizophrenics. *Psychoanal. Quart.,* **8,** 412-26.
——. 1948. Notes on the development of treatment of schizophrenics by psychoanalytic psychotherapy. *Psychiatry,* II, 263-73.
——. 1950. *Principles of intensive psychotherapy.* Chicago: University of Chicago Press.
GARRETT, H. E. 1946. A developmental theory of intelligence. *Amer. Psychol.,* **1,** 372-78.
GESELL, A. & ILG, F. L. 1943. *Infant and child in the culture of today.* New York: Harper & Bros.
GILLILAND, A. R. & COLGIN, R. 1951. Norms, reliability, and forms of the MMPI. *J. Consult. Psychol.,* **15,** 435-38.
GINSBURG, E. L. 1950. *Public health is people.* New York: The Commonwealth Fund, Division of Publications.
GITELSON, M. 1948. Character synthesis: the psychotherapeutic problem of adolescents. *Amer. J. Orthopsychiat.,* **18,** 422-31.
GLADSTONE, R. 1949. An investigation of the relationship between palmar sweating and emotion as measured by a group test of palmar sweating. Unpublished Ph.D. thesis, University of Illinois.
GOLDSTEIN, K. 1939. *The organism a holistic approach to biology.* New York: American Book Co.
GOODSTEIN, L. D. 1951. The language of schizophrenia. *J. Gen. Psychol.,* **45,** 95-104.
GORDON, A. T. 1952. A study of the effects of client-centered therapy upon attitudes toward others. Unpublished research, University of Chicago.
GOSS, A. E. 1952. Stuttering behavior and anxiety as a function of the duration of stimulus words. *J. Abnorm. Soc. Psychol.,* **47,** 38-50.
GOUGH, H. G. 1947. Simulated patterns on the Minnesota Multiphasic Personality Inventory. *J. Abnorm. Soc. Psychol.,* **42,** 215-25.
——. 1952. Some common misconceptions about neuroticism. Unpublished research.

GRUMMON, D. L. 1950. An investigation into the use of grammatical and psychogrammatical categories of language for the study of personality and psychotherapy. Unpublished Ph.D. dissertation, University of Chicago.

GRZEDA, S. C. 1948. Investigation of pattern responses in personality. Unpublished Ph.D. thesis, University of Illinois.

GUETZKOW, H. & BROZEK, J. 1947. Intellective tests for longitudinal experiments on adults. *Amer. J. Psychol.,* **60,** 350-66.

GUILFORD, J. P. 1936. *Psychometric methods.* New York: McGraw-Hill Book Co., Inc.

———. 1952. When not to factor analyze. *Psychol. Bull.,* **49,** 26-37.

GUMP, P. V. 1944. A statistical investigation of one psychoanalytic approach and a comparison of it with nondirective therapy. Unpublished M. A. thesis, Ohio State University.

HAIGH, G. 1949. Defensive behavior in client-centered therapy. *J. Consult. Psychol.,* **13,** 181-89.

HAIMOWITZ, M. L. 1950. Ethnic hostility-displacement and psychotherapy. Unpublished Ph.D. dissertation, University of Chicago.

HAIMOWITZ, N. R. 1948. An investigation into some personality changes occurring in individuals undergoing client-centered therapy. Unpublished Ph.D. thesis, University of Chicago.

HAMMOND, P. 1951. The psychological impact of unprecedented social catastrophe: An analysis of three topical autobiographies of young displaced persons. Unpublished M.A. thesis, Illinois Institute of Technology.

HANLEY, M. L. 1937. *Word index to James Joyce's Ulysses.* Madison, Wis.

HARLOW, H. F. 1949. The formation of learning sets. *Psychol. Rev.,* **56,** 51-65.

HART, B. 1925. *The psychology of insanity.* London: Cambridge University Press.

HARTLEY, M. 1950. Q-technique: its methodology and application. Mimeographed, University of Chicago.

———. 1951. An investigation of the nature of the change in concept of self as a result of client-centered therapy. Unpublished Ph.D. dissertation, University of Chicago.

HATHAWAY, S. R. 1948. Some considerations relative to nondirective counseling as therapy. *J. Clin. Psychol.,* **4,** 226-31.

HATHAWAY, S. R. & McKINLEY, J. C. 1940. A multiphasic personality schedule (Minnesota): I. Construction of the schedule. *J. Psychol.,* **10,** 249-54.

HAUSER, G. 1951. Measuring tension in electrically recorded initial social casework interviews: the content-analysis approach *versus* the over-all judgment approach. M.A. thesis, New York School of Social Work.

HAYAKAWA, S. I. 1947. Meaning, symbols and levels of abstraction. In NEWCOMB, HARTLEY and OTHERS, *Readings in social psychology.* New York: Henry Holt & Co.

HAYWARD, M. L. 1949. Direct interpretation in the treatment of a case of schizophrenia. *Psychiat. Quart.,* **23,** 720-37.

HEBB, D. O. 1949. *The organization of behavior.* New York: John Wiley & Sons.

HEIDER, F. 1949. Social perception and phenomenal causality. *Psychol. Rev.,* **51,** 358-74.

HEINE, R. W. 1950. An investigation of the relationship between change in personality from psychotherapy as reported by patients and the factors seen by patients as producing change. Unpublished Ph.D. dissertation, University of Chicago.

HELPER, M. M. 1951. Some relationships of personality integration to number and diversity of occupational interests. Unpublished M.A. thesis, University of Illinois.

HENRY, J. 1951. The inner experience of culture. *Psychiatry,* **14,** 87-103.

———. 1952. Toward a system of socio-psychiatric invariants: a work paper. *J. Soc. Psychol.* (in press.)

HERZBERG, A. 1946. *Active psychotherapy.* New York: Grune & Stratton.

HILGARD, E. R. 1949. Human motives and the concept of the self. *Amer. Psychol.,* **4,** 374-82.

HOBBS, N. 1951. Group-centered therapy. In C. R. ROGERS, *Client-centered therapy.* Boston: Houghton Mifflin Co.

HOCH, P. H. 1947. Discussion of John M. Rosen's "The treatment of schizophrenic psychosis by direct analytic therapy." Unpublished.

HOCH, P. H. & ZUBIN, J. (eds.) 1950. *Anxiety.* New York: Grune & Stratton.

HOFFMAN, A. E. 1948. An investigation of the relationship between attitudinal change and reported overt behavior changes. M.A. thesis, University of Chicago.

——. 1949. A study of reported behavior changes in counseling. *J. Consult. Psychol.,* **13,** 190-95.

HOFSTAETTER, P. R. 1941. Ueber Typenanalyse. *Arch. Ges. Psychol.,* **105,** 305-403. *Psychol. Abstr.,* No. 3891.

——. 1951. A factorial study of cultural patterns in the U.S. *J. Psychol.,* **32,** 99-113.

HOGAN, R. 1948. The development of a measure of client defensiveness in a counseling relationship. Ph.D. dissertation, University of Chicago.

HOGBEN, L. 1940. *Mathematics for the million.* New York: W. W. Norton & Co., Inc.

HOLMES, T. H., GOODELL, H., WOLF, S. & WOLFF, H. G. 1947. Changes in the nasal function associated with variations in emotional state and life situation. *Trans. Amer. Acad. Opthol. Otolaryngol.,* May-June, 3-14.

HOLT, R. R. 1950. An approach to the validation of the Szondi Test through a systematic study of unreliability. *J. Project. Techniques,* **14,** 435-44.

HORN, D. 1950. Intra-individual variability in the study of personality. *J. Clin. Psychol.,* **6,** 43-47.

HORN, E. 1926. *A basic writing vocabulary.* Iowa City: University of Iowa.

HORNEY, K. 1937. *The neurotic personality of our time.* New York: W. W. Norton & Co., Inc.

——. 1945. *Are you considering psychoanalysis?* New York: W. W. Norton & Co., Inc.

——. 1950. *Neurosis and human growth.* New York: W. W. Norton & Co., Inc.

HOROWITZ, F. 1951. The relation between the client's expression of tension and his self-concept in initial social casework interviews. M.A. thesis, Boston University School of Social Work.

HORVITZ, V. S. 1950. An attempt to measure psycho-therapeutic progress by means of a frequency analysis of the patient's speech. Unpublished, University of Illinois.

HOWIE, D. 1950. Some theoretical implications of Rogers' nondirective therapy. *J. Gen. Psychol.,* **42,** 225-41.

HSU, E. H. 1946. On the correlation between a variable and its super-factor. *J. Psychol.,* **22,** 89-92.

——. 1949. The intrapersonal factor and its clinical applicability. *J. Personality,* **17,** 273-86.

HUDSON, B. B. 1950. One-trial learning in the domestic rat. *Genetic Psychol. Monogr.,* **41,** 99-145.

HUIZINGA, J. 1924. *The waning of the middle ages.* London: Edward Arnold & Co.

HULL, C. L. 1934. The concept of the habit-family hierarchy and maze learning. *Psychol. Rev.,* **41,** 33-54, 134-52.

——. 1943. *Principles of behavior.* New York: Appleton-Century-Crofts, Inc.

——. 1949. Stimulus intensity dynamism (V) and stimulus generalization. *Psychol. Rev.,* **56,** 67-76.

HUNT, J. McV. 1947. Measuring the effects of social casework. Trans. N. Y. Acad. Sci., Ser. II, **9,** 78-88.

——. 1948. Measuring movement in casework. *J. Soc. Casework,* **29,** 343-51.

HUNT, J. McV. 1949a. A social agency as a setting for research—the Institute of Welfare Research. *J. Consult. Psychol.*, **13**, 69-81.

——. 1949b. The problem of measuring the results of psychotherapy. *The Psychological Service Center Journal*, **1**, 122-35.

——. 1952. Toward an integrated program of research on psychotherapy. *J. Consult. Psychol.*, **16**, 237-46.

HUTT, M. L. 1949. Projective techniques in guidance. In W. T. DONAHUE, C. H. COOMBS, and R. M. W. TRAVERS (eds.), *The measurement of student adjustment and achievement*. Ann Arbor: University of Michigan Press.

ISAACS, K. S., FIEDLER, F. E. & FISKE, D. W. 1950. Some factors involved in the understanding of patients by clinicians. Paper read at meeting of Midwestern Psychological Association, May.

JACOBSON, E. 1938. *Progressive relaxation.* Chicago: University of Chicago Press.

JOHNSON, D. M. 1950. Problem solving and symbolic processes. In *Annual Review of Psychology*. Stanford, Calif.: Annual Reviews, Inc.

JOHNSON, D. M., JOHNSON, R. C., & MARK, A. L. 1951. A mathematical analysis of verbal fluency. *J. Gen. Psychol.*, **44**, 121-28.

JOHNSON, W. 1944. Studies in language behavior. I. A program of research. *Psychol. Monogr.*, 56, 1-15.

——. 1946. *People in quandaries.* New York: Harper & Bros.

——. 1948a. The semantics of maladjustment. In L. A. PENNINGTON & I. A. BERG (eds.), *An introduction to clinical psychology.* New York: The Ronald Press Co.

——. 1948b. Speech and personality. In L. BRYSON (ed.), *The communication of ideas.* New York: Harper & Bros.

JONES, M. C. 1924. A laboratory study of fear: the case of Peter. *Ped. Sem.*, **31**, 308-15.

JONIETZ, A. K. 1950. A study of changes in perception in relation to psychotherapy. Unpublished Ph.D. dissertation, University of Chicago.

KAFKA, F. 1930. *The castle.* Trans. from German by Edwin and Willa Muir. New York: Alfred A. Knopf, Inc.

——. 1937. *The trial.* Trans. from German by Edwin and Willa Muir. New York: Alfred A. Knopf, Inc.

——. 1946. *Metamorphosis.* Trans. from German by A. L. Lloyd. New York: Vanguard Press.

KARDINER, A. 1945. *The individual and his society—the psychodynamics of primitive social organization.* Foreword and two ethnological reports by Ralph Linton. New York: Columbia University Press.

KASANIN, J. S. (ed.). 1946. *Language and thought in schizophrenia: collected papers.* Los Angeles: University of California Press.

KATZ, D. & BRALY, K. W. 1947. Verbal stereotypes and racial prejudice. In NEWCOMB, HARTLEY and OTHERS, *Readings in social psychology.* New York: Henry Holt & Co.

KAUFFMAN, P. E. & RAIMY, V. C. 1949. Two methods of assessing therapeutic progress. *J. Abnorm. Soc. Psychol.*, **44**, 379-85.

KAUFMANN, P. 1950. Changes in the Minnesota Multiphasic Personality Inventory as a function of psychiatric therapy. *J. Consult Psychol.*, **14**, 458-64.

KELLY, E. L. & FISKE, D. W. 1951. *The prediction of performance in clinical psychology.* Ann Arbor: University of Michigan Press.

KEMPF, E. 1918. *The autonomic functions and the personality.* Washington, D. C.: Nervous and Mental Disease Publishing Co.

KESSLER, C. 1947. Semantics and non-directive counseling. Unpublished M.A. paper, University of Chicago.

KIERKEGAARD, S. 1946. *Philosophical fragments, or a fragment of philosophy* (1844). Trans. by David F. Swenson. Princeton: Princeton University Press.

KILBY, R. W. 1949. Vocational counseling methods. *Educ. & Psychol. Meas.*, **9**, 173-92.

KILPATRICK, W. H. 1925. *Foundations of method.* New York: The Macmillan Co.

KLARE, G. R. 1952. A note on "Simplification of Flesch Reading Ease Formula." *J. Appl. Psychol.,* **36,** 53.

KLEIN, D. B. 1944. *Mental hygiene.* New York: Henry Holt & Co.

KLUCKHOHN, C. & MOWRER, O. H. 1944. "Culture and personality": a conceptual scheme. *Amer. Anthropol.,* **46,** 1-29.

KNIGHT, R. P. 1941. Evaluation of the results of psychoanalytic therapy. *Amer. J. Psychiat.,* **18,** 434-46.

———. 1946. Psychotherapy of an adolescent catatonic schizophrenic. *Psychiatry,* **9,** 323-39.

KOGAN, L. S. 1951. The distress-relief quotient (DRQ) in dictated and verbatim social casework interviews. *J. Abnorm. Soc. Psychol.,* **46,** 236-39.

KOGAN, L. S., HUNT, J. McV., & BARTELME, PHYLLIS F. 1953. *A follow-up study of the results of social casework.* New York: Family Service Association of America.

KROUT, M. H. & ROSS, A. E. 1935. Clinical material in the study of human behavior. *J. Gen. Psychol.,* **13,** 402-12.

KUBIE, L. S. 1934. Relation of the conditioned reflex to psychoanalytic technique. *Arch. Neurol. Psychiat.,* **32,** 1137-42.

———. 1950. *Practical and theoretical aspects of psychoanalysis.* New York: International Universities Press.

KUNO, Y. 1934. *The physiology of human perspiration.* London: J. & A. Churchill.

LACEY, J. I. 1950. Individual differences in somatic response patterns. *J. Comp. Physiol. Psychol.,* **43,** 338-50.

LANDIS, C. & HUNT, W. A. 1939. *The startle pattern.* New York: Rinehart & Co.

LANGER, S. K. 1948. *Philosophy in a new key.* New York: Penguin Books. (First issued by Harvard University Press, 1942.)

LASSWELL, H. D. 1935. Verbal references and physiological changes during psychoanalytic interview: a preliminary communication. *Psychoanal. Rev.,* **22,** 10-24.

———. 1936. Certain prognostic changes during trial (psychoanalytic) interviews. *Psychoanal. Rev.,* **23,** 241-47.

LAZOWICK, L. M. & YOUNG, N. 1950. A preliminary analysis of a specific patient's personal references to discern movement in psychotherapy. Unpublished, University of Illinois.

LECKY, P. 1945. *Self-consistency: a theory of personality.* New York: Island Press.

LEE, D. D. 1947. A linguistic approach to a system of values. In NEWCOMB, HARTLEY and OTHERS, *Readings in social psychology.* New York: Henry Holt & Co.

LEMKAU, P., TIETZE, C., & COOPER, M. 1941-43. Mental hygiene problems in an urban community. *Ment. Hyg.,* **25,** 624-46; **26,** 100-19; 275-88; **27,** 279-95.

LEMKAU, P. &. COOPER, M. 1947. Mental hygiene problems in a well-baby clinic. *Ment. Hyg.,* **31,** 440 56.

LEPLEY, W. M. 1950. An hypothesis concerning the generation and use of synonyms. *J. Exp. Psychol.,* **40,** 527-30.

LEUBA, J. 1949. "Les Trébucheuses," (Stumbling Women), *Bull. Amer. Psychoanal. Ass'n.,* **5,** 14-15. See also, Women who fall. *Int. J. Psychoanat.,* **31,** 6-7.

LEWIN, K. 1947. Group decision and social change. In NEWCOMB, HARTLEY and OTHERS, *Readings in social psychology.* New York: Henry Holt & Co.

LEWIS, V. 1943. Changing the behavior of adolescent girls. *Arch. Psychol.,* No. 279, 87.

LIDDELL, H. S. 1950. The role of vigilance in the development of animal neurosis. In HOCH and ZUBIN, *Anxiety.* New York: Grune & Stratton.

LIEBER, H. G. & LIEBER, L. R. 1944. *The education of T. C. Mits.* New York: W. W. Norton & Co., Inc.

LIGHT, B. H. 1951. Tension changes in patients undergoing psychotherapy. Unpublished Ph.D. thesis, University of Illinois.

LINDNER, R. M. 1944. *Rebel without a cause.* New York: Grune & Stratton.

LINDSLEY, D. B. 1951. Emotion. In S. S. Stevens (ed.), *Handbook of experimental psychology.* New York: John Wiley & Sons., Inc.

LINTON, R. (ed.) 1945. *The science of man in the world crisis.* New York: Columbia University Press.

LOEVINGER, J. 1947. A systematic approach to the construction and evaluation of tests of ability. *Psychol. Monogr.,* 61, 1-49.

LORENZ, K. Z. 1950. The comparative method in studying innate behavior patterns. In *Symposia of the Society for Experimental Biology.* New York: Academic Press.

LOUTTIT, C. M. 1936. *Clinical psychology.* New York: Harper & Bros.

LUFT, J. 1950. Implicit hypotheses and clinical predictions. *J. Abnorm. Soc. Psychol.,* 45, 756-59.

LUNDY, B. W. 1950. An investigation of the process of psychotherapy. Unpublished M.A. thesis, University of Chicago.

LURIA, Z., OSGOOD, C. E., & MOWRER, O. H. 1953. Case studies of meaning changes during therapy. Unpublished research, University of Illinois.

MACHOVER, K. 1949. *Personality projection in the drawing of the human figure.* Springfield, Ill.: Charles C Thomas.

MACKINNON, D. W. 1944. The structure of personality. In J. McV. HUNT (ed.), *Personality and the behavior disorders.* New York: The Ronald Press Co.

MACLEOD, R. B. 1949. Perceptual constancy in the problem of motivation. *Can. J. Psychol.,* 3, 57-66.

MACPHERSON, D. J. 1949. Introduction. In HOCH & ZUBIN, *Psychosexual Development.* New York: Grune & Stratton.

MAGARET, A. 1950. Generalization in successful psychotherapy. *J. Consult. Psychol.,* 14, 64-70.

MALMO, R. B., SHAGASS, C., & DAVIS, J. F. 1950. A method for the investigation of somatic response mechanisms in psychoneurosis. *Science,* 112, 325-28.

MANN, M. B. 1944. Studies in language behavior III. The quantitative differentiation of samples of written language. *Psychol. Monogr.,* 56, 41-74.

MARGOLIN, S. F., ORRINGER, D., KAUFMAN, M. R., WINKELSTEIN, A., HOLLANDER, F., JANOWITZ, H., STEIN, A., & LEVY, M. H. 1950. Variations of gastric functions during conscious and unconscious conflict states. *A.R.N.M.D.,* 29, 656-64.

MARQUIS, D. G. 1948. Research planning at the frontiers of science. *Amer. Psychol.,* 3, 430-38.

MASLOW, A. H. 1949. Our maligned animal nature. *J. Psychol.,* 28, 273-78.

MAX, L. W. 1937. An experimental study of the motor theory of consciousness. IV. Action current responses during waking kinaesthetic imagery and abstract thinking. *J. Comp. Psychol.,* 24, 301-44.

MAY, M. A. 1948. Experimentally acquired drives. *J. Exp. Psychol.,* 38, 66-77.

MAY, R. 1950a. The work and training of the psychological therapist. *The Psychological Service Center Journal,* 2:1.

——. 1950b. *The meaning of anxiety.* New York: The Ronald Press Co.

——. 1950c. Historical roots of modern anxiety theories. In HOCH & ZUBIN, *Anxiety.* New York: Grune & Stratton.

MAYO, E. 1945. *The social problems of an industrial civilization.* Boston: Harvard Graduate School of Business Administration.

McCURDY, H. G. 1950. Consciousness and the galvanometer. *Psychol. Rev.,* 57, 322-27.

McGEOCH, J. A. 1942. *The psychology of human learning.* New York: Longmans, Green & Co., Inc.

McKINLEY, J. C., HATHAWAY, S. R., & MEEHL, P. E. 1948. The Minnesota Multiphasic Personality Inventory: VI. The K Scale. *J. Consult. Psychol.*, **12**, 20-31.

McNEMAR, Q. 1949. *Psychological statistics.* New York: John Wiley & Sons, Inc.

McQUITTY, L. L. 1938. An approach to the measurement of individual differences in personality. *Char. and Pers.*, **7**, 81-95.

———. 1941. An approach to the nature and measurement of personality integration. *J. Soc. Psychol.*, **13**, 3-14.

———. 1942. Conditions affecting the validity of personality inventories: II. *J. Soc. Psychol.*, **15**, 41-47.

———. 1949. Diversity of self endorsements as a measure of individual differences in personality. *Educ. & Psychol. Meas.*, **9**, 3-14.

———. 1950a. A measure of personality integration in relation to the concept of self. *J. Personality*, **18**, 461-82.

———. 1950b. A measure of individual differences in personality integration. *Can. J. Psychol.*, **4**, 171-78.

———. 1951. Clinical implications for a measure of mental health. *J. Abnorm. Soc. Psychol.*, **46**, 73-78.

———. 1952a. Effective items in the measurement of personality integration: I. *Educ. & Psychol. Meas.*, **12**, 117-25.

———. 1952b. Another method of measuring personality integration. *Educ. & Psychol. Meas.*, **12**, 720-29.

———. 1953. Implications of certain measures of personality integration for theories of social psychology. (in press.) *J. Abnorm. Soc. Psychol.*

MEAD, G. H. 1947. Language and the development of the self. In NEWCOMB, HARTLEY and OTHERS, *Readings in social psychology.* New York. Henry Holt & Co.

MEADOW, A., GREENBLATT, M., LEVINE, J., & SOLOMON, H. C. 1952. The discomfort-relief quotient as a measure of tension and adjustment. *J. Abnorm. Soc. Psychol.*, **47**, 658-66.

MEEHL, P. E. 1945. The dynamics of "structured" personality tests. *J. Clin. Psychol.*, **1**, 296-303.

———. 1950a. Using the Minnesota Multiphasic Personality Inventory in counseling—A summary of selected new research results. Mimeographed and privately distributed by the Guidance Center, VRED, Veterans Administration Center, Fort Snelling, St. Paul, Minn.

———. 1950b. Bibliography on the Minnesota Multiphasic Personality Inventory. (Mimeographed.)

MEEHL, P. E. & HATHAWAY, S. R. 1946. The K factor as a suppressor variable in the Minnesota Multiphasic Personality Inventory. *J. Appl. Psychol.*, **30**, 525-64.

MENNINGER, K. A. 1940. Psychoanalytic psychiatry: theory and practice. *Bull. Menninger Clin.*, **4**, 105-23.

MERTON, R. K. 1949. The role of applied social science in the formation of policy. *Phil. Sci.*, **16**, 161-81.

MERTON, R. K. & KENDALL, P. L. 1946. The focused interview. *Amer. J. Sociol.*, **51**, 541-57.

MEYER, A., BOLLMEIER, L. N., & ALEXANDER, F. 1945. Correlation between emotions and carbohydrate metabolism in 2 cases of diabetes mellitus. *Psychosom. Med.*, **7**, 335-41.

MIDDLEWOOD, E. L. 1951. Mental health films in community education. *Amer. J. Orthopsychiat.*, **21**, 47-53.

MILLER, G. A. 1951. *Language and communication.* New York: McGraw-Hill Book Co., Inc.

MILLER, G. A. & SELFRIDGE, J. A. 1950. Verbal context and the recall of meaningful material. *Amer. J. Psychol.*, **63**, 176-85.

MILLER, N. E. 1948. Studies of fear as an acquirable drive: I. Fear as motivation and fear-reduction as reinforcement in the learning of new responses. *J. Exp. Psychol.*, **38**, 89-101.

MIRSKY, I. A., KAPLAN, S. & BROH-KAHN, R. H. 1950. Pepsinogen excretion (uropepsin) as an index of the influence of various life situations on gastric secretion, *A.R.N.M.D.*, **29**, 628-46.

MITTELMANN, B. 1942. Emotions and gastro-duodenal function; experimental studies on patients with gastritis, duodenitis and peptic ulcer. *Psychosom. Med.*, **4**, 5-61.

——. 1943. Emotions and skin temperature: observations on patients during psychotherapeutic (psychoanalytic) interviews. *Psychosom. Med.*, **5**, 211-31.

MITTELMANN, B. & WOLFF, H. G. 1939. Affective states and skin temperature: experimental study of subjects with "cold hands" and Raynaud's Syndrome. *Psychosom. Med.*, **1**, 271-92.

MOORE, T. V. 1939. Psychoses and prepsychotic personality. *Amer. J. Orthopsychiat.*, **9**, 136-45.

——. 1941. The prepsychotic personality and the concept of mental disorder. *Char. & Pers.*, **9**, 169-87.

——. 1946. Factorial analysis of anthropological measurements in psychotic patients. *Human Biology*, **18**, 133-57.

MOORE, T. V., STAFFORD, J. W., & HSU, E. H. 1947. Obverse analysis of personality. *J. Personality*, **16**, 11-48.

MORENO, J. L. 1945. *Group therapy.* New York: Beacon House.

MOSAK, H. 1950. Evaluation in psychotherapy: a study of some current measures. Unpublished Ph.D. dissertation, University of Chicago.

MOSIER, C. I. 1937. A factor analysis of certain neurotic symptoms. *Psychometrika*, **2**, 263-87.

MOSSMAN, L. C. 1938. *The activity concept.* New York: The Macmillan Co.

MOWRER, O. H. 1947. On the dual nature of learning—A reinterpretation of "conditioning" and "problem-solving." *Harv. Educ. Rev.*, **17**, 102-48.

——. 1948. Learning theory and the neurotic paradox. *Amer. J. Orthopsychiat.*, **18**, 571-610.

——. 1950. *Learning theory and personality dynamics.* New York: The Ronald Press Co.

——. 1951a. Anxiety theory as a basis for distinguishing between counseling and psychotherapy. In R. F. BERDIE (ed.), *Concepts and programs of counseling.* Minneapolis: University of Minnesota Press.

——. 1951b. Two-factor learning theory: Summary and Comment. *Psychol. Rev.*, **58**, 350-54.

——. 1952a. Motivation. *Annual review of psychology*, **3**, 419-38.

——. 1952b. Neurosis and its treatment as learning phenomena. In D. Brower and L. E. Abt (eds.), *Progress in clinical psychology*, Vol. I. New York: Grune & Stratton.

——. 1952c. The therapeutic process: III. Learning theory and the neurotic fallacy. *Amer. J. Orthopsychiat.*, **22**, 679-89.

——. 1952d. Learning theory. *Rev. of Educ. Research*, **22**, 475-95.

——. 1952e. Speech development in the young child: I. The autism theory of speech development and some clinical applications. *J. Speech and Hearing Disorders*, **17**, 263-68.

——. 1953a. Neurosis: A disorder of conditioning or problem solving? In E. J. Kempf (ed.), *Comparative conditioned neuroses.* New York: New York Academy of Sciences.

——. 1953b. Learning theory, language, and the problem of personality disorder. (In press.)

MOWRER, O. H. & AIKEN, E. G. 1953. Contiguity vs. drive reduction in fear conditioning: Temporal variations in conditioned and unconditioned stimulus. *Amer. J. Psychol.* (in press.)

Mowrer, O. H., Aiken, E. G., & Solomon, L. N. 1953. Two-factor learning theory: A proposed modification and articulation with field theory and cybernetics. (In press.)

Mowrer, O. H. & Kluckhohn, C. 1944. Dynamic theory of personality. In J. McV. Hunt (ed.), *Personality and the behavior disorders.* New York: The Ronald Press Co.

Mowrer, O. H. & Solomon, L. N. 1953. Contiguity vs. drive reduction in fear conditioning: The proximity and abruptness of drive reduction. *Amer. J. Psychol.* (in press.)

Mowrer, O. H. & Ullman, A. D. 1945. Time as a determinant in integrative learning. *Psychol. Rev.,* **52,** 61-90.

Muench, G. A. 1947. An evaluation of nondirective psychotherapy by means of the Rorschach and other tests. *Applied Psychol. Monogr.,* No. 13, Stanford University Press.

Murray, H. A. 1938. *Explorations in personality.* New York: Oxford Press.

Nietzsche, F. 1937. *Beyond good and evil.* New York: Modern Library.

Nunberg, H. 1931. The synthetic function of the ego. *Int. J. Psychoanal.,* **12,** 123-40.

——. 1948. Practice and theory of psychoanalysis. *Nerv. and Ment. Dis. Monogr.,* No. 74, 218 pages.

Ogden, C. K. 1938. *Basic English, a general introduction with rules and grammar.* London: Kegan Paul, Trench, Trubner & Co.

Osgood, C. E. 1952. The nature and measurement of meaning. *Psychol. Bull.,* **49,** 197-237.

Osgood, C. E. & Suci, G. J. 1950. Objective studies in meaning, I, A graphic method for representing interrelationships among meaningful concepts. *Amer. J. Psychol.,* **5,** 297.

——. 1952. A measure of relation determined by both mean difference and profile information. *Psychol. Bull.,* **49,** 251-62.

Pavlov, I. P. 1927. *Conditioned reflexes.* London: Oxford University Press.

Pennington, L. A. & Berg, I. A. 1948. *An introduction to clinical psychology.* New York: The Ronald Press Co.

Pepinsky, H. B. 1947. Therapeutic counseling. In C. E. Erickson (ed.), *A basic text for guidance workers.* New York: Prentice-Hall, Inc.

Pepinsky, H. B., Clyde, R. J., Olesen, B. A., & Pielstick, N. L. 1950. Individual personality and behavior in a social group. Paper read to Div. 17, APA., Sept., 1950.

Perls, F. S. 1948. Theory and technique of personality integration. *Amer. J. Psychotherapy,* **2,** 565-86.

Perry, W. G., Jr. 1948. Of counselors and college. *Harv. Educ. Rev.,* **18,** 8-34.

——. 1950. Conflict in the learning process: the students' response to teaching. In B. B. Cronkite (ed.), *Handbook for college teachers* Cambridge: Harvard University Press.

Pickford, R. W. 1950. Aspects of the psychology of meaning. *J. Gen. Psychol.,* **77,** 231-55.

Pious, W. L. 1949. The pathogenic process in schizophrenia. *Bull. Menninger Clinic,* **13,** 152-59.

——. 1950. Obsessive-compulsive symptoms in an incipient schizophrenic. *Psychoanal. Quart.,* **19,** 327-51.

Porter, E. H. 1943. The development and evaluation of a measure of counseling interview procedures. *Educ. & Psychol. Meas.,* **3,** 105-26; 215-38.

Postman, L., Bruner, J. S., & McGinnies, E. 1948. Personal values as selective factors in perception. *J. Abnorm. Soc. Psychol.,* **43,** 142-54.

Prados, M. 1951. The use of films in psychotherapy. *Amer. J. Orthopsychiat.,* **21,** 36-46.

Preston, G. H. 1940. *Psychiatry for the curious.* New York: Rinehart & Co.

PRONKO, N. H. 1946. Language and psycho-linguistics: a review. *Psychol. Bull.,* **43**, 189-239.

QUINN, R. D. 1950. Psychotherapists' expressions as an index to the quality of early therapeutic relationships established by representatives of the non-directive, Adlerian, and psychoanalytic schools. Unpublished Ph.D. dissertation, University of Chicago.

RADO, S. 1925. The economic principle in psycho-analytic technique. *Int. J. Psychoanal.,* **6**, 35-44.

RAIMY, V. C. 1943. The self concept as a factor in counseling and personality organization. Unpublished Ph.D. dissertation, Ohio State University.

———. 1948. Self reference in counseling interviews. *J. Consult. Psychol.,* **12**, 153-63.

RANK, O. 1945. *Will therapy and truth and reality.* New York: Alfred A. Knopf, Inc.

RASKIN, N. J. 1949. An objective study of the locus of evaluation factor in psychotherapy. Unpublished Ph.D. dissertation, University of Chicago.

RAZRAN, G. H. S. 1938. Conditioning away social bias by the luncheon technique. *Psychol. Bull.,* **35**, 693 (abstr.).

REICH, W. 1945. *Character analysis: principles and technique for psychoanalysts in practice and training.* Trans. by T. P. Wolfe. New York: Orgone Press.

REIK, T. 1948. *Listening with the third ear.* New York: Farrar, Straus & Co.

REYMERT, M. L. (ed.). 1950. *Feelings and emotions, the Mooseheart Symposium.* New York: McGraw-Hill Book Co., Inc.

RICHARDS, I. A. 1943. *Basic English and its uses.* New York: W. W. Norton & Co., Inc.

RIOCH, J. M. 1949. Analytic therapy. In P. MULLAHY (ed.), *A study of interpersonal relations.* New York: Hermitage Press.

ROBINSON, F. P. 1950. Are "non-directive" techniques sometimes too directive? In A. H. BRAYFIELD (ed.), *Readings in modern methods of counseling.* New York: Appleton-Century-Crofts, Inc.

ROETHLISBERGER, F. J. 1943. *Management and morale.* Cambridge: Harvard University Press.

ROGERS, C. R. 1942. *Counseling and psychotherapy.* Boston: Houghton Mifflin Co.

———. 1947. Some observations on the organization of personality. *Amer. Psychol.,* **2**, 358-68.

———. 1948. Divergent trends in methods of improving adjustment. *Harv. Educ. Rev.,* **18**, 209-19.

———. 1949. The attitude and orientation of the counselor in client centered therapy. *J. Consult. Psychol.,* **13**, 82-94.

———. 1951a. Perceptual reorganization in client-centered therapy. In R. E. BLAKE and G. V. RAMSEY, *Perception: an approach to personality.* New York: The Ronald Press. Co.

———. 1951b. *Client-centered therapy.* Boston: Houghton Mifflin Co.

———. 1952. The case of Mrs. Oak—a research analysis. In C. R. ROGERS, *et al.,* *Studies in client-centered psychotherapy.* Washington, D. C.: Psychological Service Center Press.

ROGERS, C. R. and ASSOCIATES. 1949, 1950. *A study of the process and outcomes of client-centered therapy.* Mimeographed first and second interim reports, Counseling Center, University of Chicago.

ROGERS, N. 1948. Measuring psychological tension in non-directive counseling. In E. H. PORTER (ed.), *The personal counselor.* Hectographed, University of Chicago.

ROHRER, J. H. 1949. An evaluation of college personnel work in terms of current research on interpersonal relationships. *Educ. & Psychol. Meas.,* **9**, 429-44.

ROLLINS, E. M. & TWAITE, B. 1950. An experimental investigation of progress in psychotherapy as measured by the DRQ technique. Unpublished paper, University of Illinois.

ROSEN, J. N. 1946. A method of resolving acute catatonic excitement. *Psychiat. Quart.*, **20**, 183.

———. 1947. The treatment of schizophrenic psychosis by direct analytic therapy. *Psychiat. Quart.*, **21**, 30-37; 117-19.

ROSENZWEIG, S. 1936. Some implicit common factors in diverse methods of psychotherapy. *Amer. J. Orthopsychiat.*, **6**, 412-15.

———. 1950. Norms and the individual in the psychologist's perspective. In M. L. REYMERT (ed.), *Feelings and emotions.* New York: McGraw-Hill Book Co., Inc.

ROSHAL, J. M. 1952. Changes in behavior variability with psychotherapy as measured in language behavior. Ph.D. dissertation, Pennsylvania State College.

ROTH, W. F. & LUTON, F. H. 1943. The mental health program in Tennessee. *Amer. J. Psychiat.*, **99**, 662-75.

ROYCE, J. R. 1950. A synthesis of experimental designs in program research. *J. Gen. Psychol.*, **43**, 295-303.

RUCKMICK, C. A. 1936. *The psychology of feeling and emotion.* New York: McGraw-Hill Book Co., Inc.

RUESCH, J. 1948. Experiments in psychotherapy: I. Theoretical considerations. *J. Psychol.*, **25**, 137-69.

———. 1949. Experiments in psychotherapy: II. Individual social techniques. *J. Soc. Psychol.*, **29**, 3-28.

RUESCH, J. & BATESON, G. 1951. *Communication, the social matrix of psychiatry.* New York: W. W. Norton & Co., Inc.

SANFORD, F. H. 1942a. Speech and personality. *Psychol. Bull.*, **39**, 811-45.

———. 1942b. Speech and personality: a comparative case study. *Char. and Pers.*, **10**, 169-98.

SARBIN, T. R. 1941. Clinical psychology—art or science? *Psychometrika*, **6**, 391-400.

SAUNDERS, D. R. 1951. On P-technique. Unpublished, University of Illinois.

SCHAEFFER-SIMMERN, H. 1948. *The unfolding of artistic activity.* Berkeley, Calif.: University of California Press.

SCHILDER, P. 1939. The psychology of schizophrenia. *Psychoanal. Rev.*, **26**, 380-98.

———. 1951. *Psychoanalysis, man, and society.* New York: W. W. Norton & Co., Inc.

SCHOFIELD, W. 1950. Changes in responses to the Minnesota Multiphasic Inventory following certain therapies. *Psychol. Monogr.*, 64, 33.

SCHWEITZER, A. 1911. *J. S. Bach.* Leipzig and New York: Breitkopf and Härtel.

SCHWING, G. 1940. *Ein Weg Zur Seele des Geisteskranken.* Zurich: Rascher Verlag.

SEARS, R. R. 1944. Experimental analysis of psychoanalytic phenomena. In J. McV. HUNT (ed.), *Personality and the behavior disorders*, Vol. I. New York: The Ronald Press Co.

SEEMAN, J. 1948. A study of client self-selection of tests in vocational counseling. *Educ. & Psychol. Meas.*, **8**, 327-47.

———. 1949a. A study of the process of nondirective therapy. *J. Consult. Psychol.*, 13, 157-68.

———. 1949b. An investigation of client reactions to vocational counseling. *J. Consult. Psychol.*, **13**, 95-104.

SEEMAN, J. et al. 1948. A study of the process of non-directive therapy. Paper presented at APA, 1948.

SEYMOUR, F. E. & SMITH, P. J. 1941. *Plane geometry.* New York: The Macmillan Co.

SHAFFER, L. F. 1947. The problem of psychotherapy. *Amer. Psychol.*, **2**, 459-67.

SHANNON, C. E. & WEAVER, W. 1949. *The mathematical theory of communication.* Urbana: University of Illinois Press.

SHAW, F. J. 1946. A stimulus-response analysis of repression and insight in psychotherapy. *Psychol. Rev., 53,* 36-42.

——. 1949. Some postulates concerning psychotherapy. *J. Consult. Psychol., 12,* 426-31.

SHEERER, E. T. 1949. An analysis of the relationship between acceptance of and respect for self and acceptance of and respect for others in ten counseling cases. *J. Consult. Psychol., 13,* 169-75.

SHERIF, M. & CANTRIL, H. 1947. *The psychology of ego-involvements.* New York: John Wiley & Sons, Inc.

SHOBEN, E. J. 1948. A learning-theory interpretation of psychotherapy. *Harv. Educ. Rev., 18,* 129-45.

——. 1949. Psychotherapy as a problem in learning theory. *Psychol. Bull., 46,* 366-92.

SILVERMAN, J. J. & POWELL, V. E. 1944a. Studies on palmar sweating; I. A technique for the study of palmar sweating. *Amer. J. Med. Sci., 208,* 297-99.

——. 1944b. Studies on palmar sweating; II. The significance of palmar sweating. *Amer. J. Med. Sci., 208,* 299-305.

——. 1944c. Studies on palmar sweating. *Psychosom. Med., 6,* 243-49.

SINGH, J. A. L. & ZINGG, R. M. 1942. *Wolf-children and feral man.* New York: Harper & Bros.

SKINNER, B. H. 1951. *Walden Two.* New York: The Macmillan Co.

SLAVSON, S. R. 1950. *Analytic group psychotherapy.* New York: Columbia University Press.

SMITH, G. 1949. *Human relationships in public health.* New York: The Commonwealth Fund, Division of Publications.

SMITH, M. 1950. The communicative act. *J. Soc. Psychol., 31,* 271-81.

SMITH, W. W. 1922. *The measurement of emotion.* New York: Harcourt, Brace & Co.

SNYDER, W. U. 1945. An investigation of the nature of nondirective psychotherapy. *J. Gen. Psychol., 33,* 193-223.

——. 1946. Warmth in non-directive counseling. *J. Abnorm. Soc. Psychol., 41,* 491-95.

——. 1947a. The present status of psychotherapeutic counseling. *Psychol. Bull., 44,* 297-386.

—— (ed.). 1947b. *Casebook of non-directive counseling.* Boston: Houghton Mifflin Co.

SNYGG, D. & COMBS, A. W. 1949. *Individual behavior.* New York: Harper & Bros.

SPEARMAN, C. 1927. *The abilities of man.* New York: The Macmillan Co.

SPOCK, B. 1945. *The common sense book of baby and child care.* New York: Duell, Sloan & Pearce.

STAFFORD, J. W. 1950. Psychology and moral problems. *Homiletic and Pastoral Rev., 51,* 118-24.

STAFFORD, J. W. & HSU, E. H. 1947. The super-factor of persons. *J. Psychol., 24,* 63-70.

STEPHENSON, W. 1935a. Technique of factor analysis. *Nature, 136,* 297.

——. 1935b. Correlating persons instead of tests. *Char. and Pers., 4,* 17-24.

——. 1936a. The inverted factor technique. *Brit. J. Psychol.* (Gen. Sec.), **26,** 344-61.

——. 1936b. Introduction to inverted factor analysis, with some applications to studies in orexis. *J. Educ. Psychol., 27,* 353-67.

——. 1936c. Some recent contributions to the theory of psychometry. *Char. and Pers., 4,* 294-304.

——. 1936d. The foundations of psychometry: four factor systems. *Psychometrika, 1,* 195-209.

——. 1939. Methodological consideration of Jung's typology. *J. Ment. Sci., 85,* 185-205.

STEPHENSON, W. 1950a. A statistical approach to typology: the study of trait-universes. *J. Clin. Psychol.*, **4**, 26-38. (Also available in Monograph Supplement No. 7.)

——. 1950b. The significance of Q-technique for the study of personality. In M. L. REYMERT (ed.), *Feelings and emotions.* New York: McGraw-Hill Book Co., Inc.

——. 1951. Some methodological implications of Q-technique. Paper read at the Midwestern Psychological Association, April, 1951.

——. 1952. Some observations on *Q* technique. *Psychol. Bull.*, **49**, 483-98.

STERN, W. 1911. *Differentielle psychologie.* Leipzig: J. A. Barth.

STETSON, R. H. & BOUMAN, H. D. 1933. The action current as a measure of muscle contraction. *Science,* **77**, 219-21.

STEVENS, S. S. & STONE, G. 1947. Psychological writing, easy and hard. *Amer. Psychol.,* **2**, 230-35.

STEWART, R. G. 1951. Patterns of self endorsements in community persons and mental patients. Unpublished Ph.D. thesis, University of Illinois.

STOCK, D. 1949. An investigation into the inter-relations between the self-concept and feelings directed toward other persons and groups. *J. Consult. Psychol.,* **13**, 176-80.

STODDARD, G. D. 1949. *The meaning of intelligence.* New York: The Macmillan Co.

STONE, D. R. 1950. Logical analysis of the directive, non-directive counseling continuum. *Occupations,* **28**, 295-98.

STRACHEY, J. 1934. The nature of the therapeutic action of psychoanalysis. *Int. J. Psychoanal.,* **15**, 127-59.

SULLIVAN, H. S. 1925. Peculiarity of thought in schizophrenia. *Amer. J. Psychiat.,* **82**, 21-86.

——. 1947. *Conceptions of modern psychiatry.* Washington, D. C.: William Alanson White Psychiatric Foundation.

SWEET, L. 1929. *The measurement of personal attitudes in younger boys.* New York: Association Press.

SYMONDS, P. M. 1931. *Diagnosing personality and conduct.* New York: Appleton-Century-Crofts, Inc.

——. 1946. *The dynamics of human adjustment.* New York: Appleton-Century-Crofts, Inc.

——. 1949. Education in psychotherapy. *J. Educ. Psychol.,* **40**, 1-32.

SZASZ, T. S. 1950a. A psychosomatic aspect of salivary activity. I. Hyper-salivation in patients with peptic ulcer. *A.R.N.M.D.,* **29**, 647-55.

——. 1950b. Psychosomatic aspects of salivary activity. II. Psychosomatic observations concerning hypersalivation. *Psychosom. Med.,* **12**, 320-30.

TABA, H. & ELKINS, D. 1950. *With focus on human relations.* Washington, D. C.: American Council on Education.

TAFT, R. 1950. Some correlates of the ability to make accurate social judgments. Unpublished Ph.D. dissertation, University of California (Berkeley).

THETFORD, W. N. 1949. The measurement of physiological responses to frustration before and after nondirective psychotherapy. Unpublished Ph.D. dissertation, University of Chicago.

THOMPSON, C. 1950. *Psychoanalysis: evolution and development.* New York: Hermitage House.

THOMSON, G. H. 1935. On complete families of correlation coefficients, and their tendency to zero tetrad-differences: including a statement of the sampling theory of abilities. *Brit. J. Psychol.,* (Gen. Sec.), **26**, 63-92.

——. 1939. *The factorial analysis of human ability.* Boston: Houghton Mifflin Co.

——. 1950. *The factorial analysis of human ability.* Boston: Houghton Mifflin Co.

THOMSON, G. H. & BAILES, S. 1926. The reliability of essay marks. *Forum of Educ.,* **4**, 85-91.

THORNDIKE, E. L. 1921. *The teacher's word book.* New York: Columbia University Press.

THORNE, F. C. 1948. Principles of directive counseling and therapy. *Amer. Psychol.,* **3**, 160-65.

——. 1950. *Principles of personality counseling; an eclectic viewpoint.* Brandon, Vt.: *J. Clin. Psychol.*

TRAVERS, R. M. W. 1951. A critical review of the validity and rationale of the forced-choice technique. *Psychol. Bull.,* **48**, 62-70.

THURSTONE, L. L. 1931. Multiple-factor analysis. *Psychol. Rev.,* **38**, 406-27.

——. 1935. *The vectors of mind.* Chicago: University of Chicago Press.

——. 1938. *Primary mental abilities.* Chicago: University of Chicago Press.

——. 1947. *Multiple-factor analysis.* Chicago: University of Chicago Press.

——. 1948. Psychological implications of factor analysis. *Amer. Psychol.,* **3**, 402-8.

THURSTONE, L. L. & THURSTONE, T. G. 1930. A neurotic inventory. *J. Soc. Psychol.,* **1**, 3-30.

UHER, A. 1952. An analysis of four topical autobiographies of mature displaced persons. Unpublished M. A. thesis, Illinois Institute of Technology.

ULICH, R. 1940. *Fundamentals of democratic education.* New York: American Book Co.

——. 1945. *History of educational thought.* New York: American Book Co.

VERNON, P. E. 1935. Can the "total personality" be studied objectively? *Char. and Pers.,* **4**, 1-10.

——. 1938. *The assessment of psychological qualities by verbal methods.* London: His Majesty's Stationery Office.

WALSH, J. L. 1949. (Review) Zipf, G. K., Human behavior and the principle of least effort: an introduction to human ecology. *Sci. Amer.,* **180-181**, 56-58.

WARRINGTON, W. G. 1952. The efficiency of the Q-sort and other test designs for measuring the similarity between persons. Unpublished Ph.D. dissertation, University of Illinois.

WATSON, R. I. 1952*a*. Research design and methodology in evaluating the results of psychotherapy. *J. Clin. Psychol.,* **8**, 29-33.

——. 1952*b*. Measuring the effectiveness of psychotherapy: problems for investigation. *J. Clin. Psychol.,* **8**, 60-64.

WATSON, R. I. & MENSH, I. N. 1951*a*. The evaluation of the effects of psychotherapy: I. Sources of material. *J. Psychol.,* **32**, 259-73.

——. 1951*b*. The evaluation of the effects of psychotherapy: II. A case study. *J. Psychol.,* **32**, 275-91.

WATSON, R. I., MENSH, I. N. & GILDEA, E. F. 1951. The evaluation of the effects of psychotherapy: III. Research design. *J. Psychol.,* **32**, 293-308.

WEISSKOPF, E. A. & DIEPPA, J. J. 1951. Experimentally induced faking of TAT responses. *J. Consult. Psychol.,* **15**, 469-74.

WENGER, M. A. & GILCHRIST, J. C. 1948. A comparison of two indices of palmar sweating. *J. Exp. Psychol.,* **38**, 757-61.

WERTHEIMER, M. 1945. *Productive thinking.* New York: Harper & Bros.

WESMAN, A. G. 1952. Faking personality test scores in a simulated employment situation. *J. Appl. Psychol.,* **36**, 112-13.

WESTBURGH, E. M. 1937. *Introduction to clinical psychology.* Philadelphia: The Blakiston Co.

WEXLER, M. 1952. The structural problem in schizophrenia: the role of the internal object. In *Psychotherapy of Schizophrenia.* New York: International Universities Press.

WHITE, R. K. 1951. *Value-analysis, the nature and use of the method.* New York: Society for the Psychological Study of Social Issues.

WHITEHORN, J. C. & ZIPF, G. K. 1943. Schizophrenic language. *Arch. Neurol. & Psychiat.,* **49**, 831-51.

WHORF, B. L. 1947. Science and linguistics. In NEWCOMB, HARTLEY and OTHERS, *Readings in social psychology.* New York: Henry Holt & Co.

WICKMAN, E. K. 1928. *Children's behavior and teachers' attitudes*. New York: The Commonwealth Fund. Division of Publications.

WIENER, D. N. 1950. Supplement on subtle and obvious keys. In P. E. Meehl, Using the Minnesota Multiphasic Personality Inventory in Counseling. VRED, VA Center, Ft. Snelling, St. Paul, Minn.

WILDER, J. 1945. Facts and figures on psychotherapy. *J. Clin. Psychopath. Psychotherapy*, **7**, 311-47.

WILLIAMS, H. R. V. M. 1949. A P-technique study of personality factors in the psychosomatic areas. Unpublished Ph.D. thesis, University of Illinois.

WILLIAMS, J. R. 1950. A study of change in vocabulary balance and verbal time perspective during psychotherapy. Unpublished, University of Illinois.

WINCH, R. F. 1947. Heuristic and empirical typologies: a job for factor analysis. *Amer. Soc. Rev.*, **12**, 68-75.

WINNICOTT, D. W. 1949. Hate in the counter-transference. *Int. J. Psychoanal.*, **30**, 69-74.

WINTHROP, H. 1946. Semantic factors in the measurement of personality integration. *J. Soc. Psychol.*, **24**, 149-75.

——. 1949. Two concepts of personality disintegration: I. Attitude-inconsistency as failure to order values; and II. Schizophrenic disturbances of thinking as failure to order meanings. *J. Gen. Psychol.*, **40**, 177-218.

WISCHNER, G. J. 1948. An experimental approach to stuttering as learned behavior. *Amer. Psychol.*, **3**, 278-79 (abstr.).

——. 1950. Stuttering behavior and learning: a preliminary theoretical formulation. *J. Speech & Hearing Disorders,* **15**, 324-35.

——. 1951. Anxiety-reduction as reinforcement in maladaptive behavior: evidence in stutterers' representations of the moment of difficulty *Amer. Psychol.*, **6**, 336 (abstr.).

——. 1952. An experimental approach to expectancy and anxiety in stuttering behavior. *J. Speech and Hearing Disorders,* **17**, 139-54.

WOLFLE, D. 1940. Factor analysis to 1940. *Psychometric Monogr.* (University of Chicago Press), No. 3.

WOODWORTH, R. S. 1938. *Experimental psychology*. New York: Henry Holt & Co.

YOUNG, P. T. 1943. *Emotion in man and animal*. New York: John Wiley & Sons, Inc.

ZIMMERMAN, J. 1950. Modification of the discomfort relief quotient as a measure of progress in counseling. Unpublished M.A. thesis, University of Chicago.

ZIMMERMAN, W. & LANGDON, J. 1949. A preliminary attempt to establish criteria for measuring progress in psychotherapy. Unpublished, University of Illinois.

ZIPF, G. K. 1949. *Human behavior and the principle of least effort*. Cambridge: Addison-Wesley Press.

ZUBIN, J. 1938. A technique for measuring like-mindedness. *J. Abnorm. Soc. Psychol.*, **33**, 508-16.

INDEX OF NAMES

INDEX OF SUBJECTS

685

Repressed, The, 543
  fear of, 648
Repression
  of conscience, 147
  devitalizing, 76
  direction of, 82, 146, 156
  extension of, 148
  lifting of, 137, 138
  precondition for neurosis, 548
  reduces anxiety, 131
  reversal of, 648
  and self-awareness, 24
  of superego, 145
  and transference, 82
  and verbalization, 130
Repudiated conscience, 553
Research, 206 ff.
  multivariate, 351
  needs for, 197 ff.
  process of, 228
  univariate, 350, 351
Resistance, 288
  earned, 81
  enigma of, 546
  Freudian view of, 546
  and interpretation, 79
  and negative transference, 80
  in neurosis and psychosis, 291
  paradoxical, 547
  and perception, 100
  and repression, 79, 549
  a technical error, 564
  in therapy, 399
  and transference, 547, 564
Respect
  for client, 44
  of client, 44
Respiration, and emotion, 650
Response, harmony of, 418
Responsibility
  of client, 105, 106
  in counseling, 104
  for evaluation, 105
Role, concept of, 385
Role-taking, 225
Rorschach Test, 233
  changes, 234

S sort
  analogous to wirephoto, 340
  compared with MMPI, 370 ff.
  eliminates absolute means, 370
  for ideal, 319
  issues raised by, 354
  and item selection, 359, 370
  items used, 370
  limitation of, 372
  and progress in therapy, 371
  for self, 319
Sampling, problem of, 234, 358
SAQ (self-approval quotient), 266
Scaling, subjective, 333
Schizophrenia
  adjustment in, 290

Schizophrenia (Cont.)
  catatonic, 158
  confusion regarding, 163
  diagnosis of, 163
  and education, 163
  and intelligence, 505
  language in, 486, 507
  morality of, 159
  paranoid, 486, 494
  and parts of speech, 505
  pathogenic process in, 168
  and regression, 505
  self-reference in language, 512
  social disarticulation in, 507
  and social withdrawal, 90
  successful treatment, 154
  superego in, 161
  theories of treatment, 164
  therapeutic implications, 150 ff.
  understanding of, 163
  use of negatives, 506
Schizothymia, 394, 395
Science, faith in, 20
Score matrix, 326
Scores
  heterogeneity of, 335
  noncompatability of, 332
Scoring, configurational, 250
Screening, psychological, 448
Scrupulosity, 93
Seduction, of authority, 563, 569
Selective inattention, 92
Selective learning, 100, 141
Self
  aspects of, 212
  attitudes toward, 53
  experiencing of, 24, 46 ff.
  perception of, 526
  preoccupation with, 529
  references to, 522
Self-acceptance, 53, 66
  and DRQ, 275
Self-approval quotient (SAQ), 266
Self attitudes, and DRQ, 275 ff.
Self concept, 134, 209
Self-condemnation, 91
Self-consciousness, capacity for, 22
Self-consistency, and mental health, 446
Self-criticism
  admission of, 533
  capacity for, 554
  release of, 554
Self-defeating strategies, 626
Self-description
  emotionally toned, 424
  harmony of, 424 ff., 431
  sample of, 424
Self-direction, and consultative assistance, 118
Self-esteem, satisfaction of, 102
Self-instruction, 611
Self-knowledge, 11
Self-liking, 53 ff.
Self-mutilation, 159